Praise for *Programming the Windows Runt*

"This is a great from-the-ground-up, very complete b... on building Windows Store Apps. You'll find it on your desk a year from now all dog-eared and marked up from use."

Dave Campbell, MVP, WindowsDevNews.com

"*Programming with Windows Runtime by Example* is a must-have book for any professional developer building apps for WinRT/Win8.1, especially in the LOB space for modern apps on Windows 8.1. For me it is the reference I provide my team building LOB applications for WinRT. Jeremy and John have done a great job putting together a great reference and educational book on professional development for the WinRT platform."

David J. Kelley, CTO, Microsoft MVP

"Jeremy and John are both very much IT masters from the old guard of software development. With countless years of bending, shaping, and influencing the world of software development behind them both, they continue to do so as they push forward into new and emerging technologies.

"As with everything they do, this book also reflects their ongoing dedication and passion for their quest to bring the reader not only the information he or she requires, but far more beyond that, they build knowledge step-by–step, then deliver it to the reader with cutting-edge, ninja-like precision to deliver exactly what knowledge is needed, when it's needed, and where it's needed.

"If you want to learn the Windows Runtime, then I can think of no finer book, and no finer guides to the WinRT landscape. By the end of this book, you'll have the knowledge, the power, and a hefty dose of passion to go out into the new millennium and create some of the best WinRT apps available."

Peter "Shawty" Shaw, LinkedIn .NET User Group manager

"This book is an invaluable resource for budding WinRT developers. It covers the basics to more advanced topics like MVVM. Readers will find the chapter entitled 'Connecting to the Cloud' especially useful in getting up to speed with Azure and creating cloud connected apps."

Daniel Vaughan, President of Outcoder, Microsoft MVP,
Author of *Windows Phone 8 Unleashed*

"There are books that provide reference for a development topic, and others that you will read from cover to end. *Programming the Windows Runtime by Example* by Jeremy Likness and John Garland should be your go-to guide for getting up to speed on WinRT. Jeremy and John wrote this book with the intention of being easy to follow and hard to forget, and they succeeded in both areas. I recommend this book for all developers, whether new to WinRT development, or those like me who just want to fill in the gaps on advanced topics."

Chris Woodruff, DeepFriedBytes.com, Microsoft MVP

Microsoft Windows Development Series

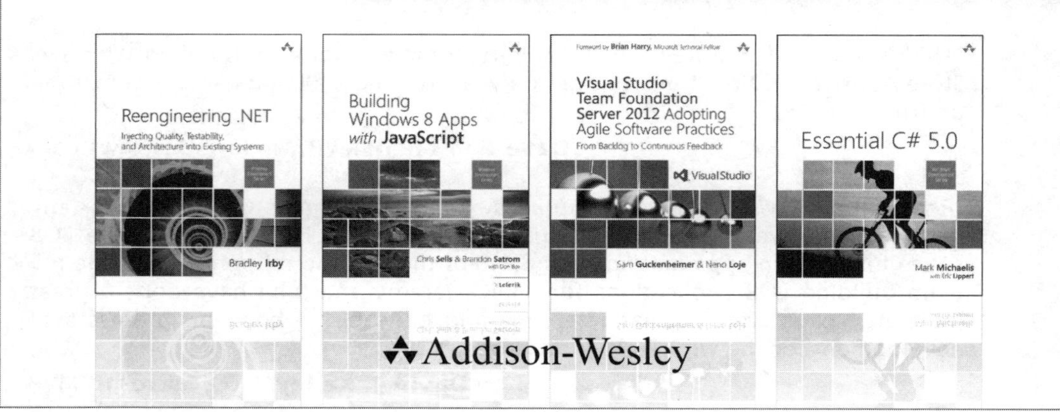

Visit informit.com/mswinseries for a complete list of available publications.

The Windows Development Series grew out of the award-winning Microsoft .NET Development Series established in 2002 to provide professional developers with the most comprehensive and practical coverage of the latest Windows developer technologies. The original series has been expanded to include not just .NET, but all major Windows platform technologies and tools. It is supported and developed by the leaders and experts of Microsoft development technologies, including Microsoft architects, MVPs and RDs, and leading industry luminaries. Titles and resources in this series provide a core resource of information and understanding every developer needs to write effective applications for Windows and related Microsoft developer technologies.

"This is a great resource for developers targeting Microsoft platforms. It covers all bases, from expert perspective to reference and how-to. Books in this series are essential reading for those who want to judiciously expand their knowledge and expertise."

– JOHN MONTGOMERY, Principal Director of Program Management, Microsoft

"This series is always where I go first for the best way to get up to speed on new technologies. With its expanded charter to go beyond .NET into the entire Windows platform, this series just keeps getting better and more relevant to the modern Windows developer."

– CHRIS SELLS, Independent Consultant specializing in Windows, devices, and the cloud

Make sure to connect with us!
informit.com/socialconnect

Safari Books Online

ALWAYS LEARNING PEARSON

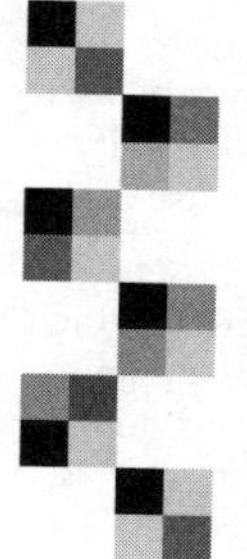

Programming the Windows Runtime by Example

A Comprehensive Guide to WinRT with Examples in C# and XAML

- Jeremy Likness
- John Garland

Addison-Wesley

Upper Saddle River, NJ • Boston • Indianapolis • San Francisco
New York • Toronto • Montreal • London • Munich • Paris • Madrid
Capetown • Sydney • Tokyo • Singapore • Mexico City

For information about buying this title in bulk quantities, or for special sales opportunities (which may include electronic versions; custom cover designs; and content particular to your business, training goals, marketing focus, or branding interests), please contact our corporate sales department at corpsales@pearsoned.com or (800) 382-3419.

For government sales inquiries, please contact governmentsales@pearsoned.com.

For questions about sales outside the U.S., please contact international@pearsoned.com.

Visit us on the Web: informit.com/aw

Library of Congress Control Number: 2013954295

ISBN-13: 978-0-321-92797-2
ISBN-10: 0-321-92797-4

Text printed in the United States on recycled paper at Edwards Brothers Malloy, Lillington, North Carolina

First printing, June 2014

For Doreen and all her arrows, Lizzie and all her travels,
and Gordon and all his paint.
—Jeremy Likness

To Karen, Callie, Winnie, and Dude,
for the new adventure that is soon to begin.
—John Garland

Contents at a Glance

Contents

Foreword

The concept of an app has changed dramatically over time, and more increasingly so in the past eight years. The approachability for the masses to have super computers in their pockets has led to the rapid adoption of mobile apps at the fingertips of every user—not just those in cubicles all day long. You can't sit in public transit, walk down a street, or even enjoy a nice meal without looking around and seeing the glow from a screen of some sort on someone's face. Everyone is a part of the app ecosystem now. Whether it is a mobile phone, music device, e-reader, watch, or even glasses, apps are a part of our lives. People desire them to make their lives and jobs more productive or just to have fun. As a software developer, it is hard to ignore this surge in opportunity and the desire to capitalize on this ecosystem.

Microsoft technologies present a large opportunity to software developers to reach a vast ecosystem of traditional users who have used Windows technologies in their personal, educational, and professional lives. These users seek out new ways to accomplish tasks and have fun on their technology devices. Microsoft has computing devices across the various screens presented in our lives in our hands, on our desks, and in our living rooms. All these represent opportunities for you, the developer, to extend your reach and ideas into the world.

As this evolution of mobility, multiple screens, and wearables has increased, so has technology. Microsoft technologies have evolved as well on the client app areas. Over time Microsoft has delivered various ways to write client applications through standard C++, MFC, Windows Forms, Windows Presentation Foundation (WPF), Silverlight, and HTML. Putting developers on a better path for development, Microsoft introduced the Windows Runtime (WinRT). This technology and principles enable developers to have a single platform to target that extends their potential across the personal, professional, and entertainment endpoints we have in our lives. WinRT enables developers to choose how they can be most productive using their skills in C++, C#, Visual Basic, or JavaScript. Alongside the language of choice, developers have a native UI framework in XAML they can use for the best client app experience on Windows. XAML is everywhere now in Windows, from system shell UI to system apps to key experiences delivered from Microsoft, such as Microsoft Office. When developing an app in C# and XAML, you'll be joining other successful developers in the world and can tap into that ecosystem of knowledge, experience, and examples.

Software is an art. Just like any art project, approaching software development requires thought into the necessary tools, philosophies, and principles you will use to create your app. I still remember one of my earliest "professional" software development jobs, sitting in a meeting listening to the customer describe all these (what was at the time) high-tech requirements of their app, all needing to be done in Internet Explorer 3. I scribbled notes as fast as I could while my dev lead at the time, all too quickly I thought, was busy nodding his head in acceptance of the requirements. As we walked out of the meeting, I expressed my concern about the requirements and available technology at the time. He smiled and shrugged like it was no problem stating, "No worries Tim, we just need the right tools."

One of the key tools is a good guide and mentor. In my early days, for me that was books just like this one you have now. To this day I still prefer books on my shelf when learning new technology concepts. I've had the pleasure of working with Jeremy Likeness over the years in the XAML ecosystem, and I can attest to his expertise in building real-world apps using these technologies. In *Programming the Windows Runtime by Example*, Jeremy and John provide these key tools for any software developer to understand the fundamentals of the Windows Runtime and XAML, and be successful quickly. This book doesn't try to only focus on singular concepts but also provides an end-to-end perspective on building an app in WinRT. Jeremy and John know that your scenarios are connected ones and deal with web services, data, security, and integration. The book will walk you through understanding how the pieces fit together in WinRT while still providing you the knowledge and tools to be productive at the core concepts of working with C# and XAML in the Windows Runtime. John and Jeremy describe philosophies and different approaches to using WinRT, empowering you with knowledge to make the best decisions for your app. This knowledge will enable you to write the best apps for Windows, Windows Phone, Xbox, and whatever future Microsoft has in store for WinRT areas.

Like any artist, tools are essential. This book is one of those essential tools for Windows developers and will help you complete your software goals sooner than without it! To this day, my bookshelf is filled with books just like this one that I refer to often. Even as your experience grows, you'll find yourself referring back to this book for knowledge when developing, just like I did.

—**Tim Heuer**, Principal Program Manager Lead, XAML Platform, Microsoft Corporation

Preface

In 2011 I heard the first rumors about Windows 8 and knew immediately what my next book would be about. Unlike *Designing Silverlight Business Applications* that captured years of experience writing Line of Business (LOB) apps in Silverlight, this book would be an introduction to an entirely new platform. My goal was to take what I knew and loved about Silverlight, find its similarities in the new platform, and then highlight what I felt were some amazing developer experiences. It was important to get to market fast, so through several iterations of the Windows 8 releases (including changes to terminology) that required substantial rewrites of content and a rapid release cycle, I managed to release *Building Windows 8 Apps with C# and XAML* as Windows 8 was revealed to the world.

By necessity, this book introduced developers to the new platform but didn't dig into best practices (there were none yet) or get very deep (there simply wasn't time). I vowed to release another book that would fill in the missing pieces and provide a comprehensive overview of the entire Windows Runtime. Because anyone can read the documentation and reference the API, my intent with this book was to make it example-driven and provide thousands of lines of code for you to integrate and use to kick-start your own Windows Store apps.

I was relieved at the thought of not rewriting most of the book three times, as I had to do with the first one, but Microsoft once again proved too fast for me. What sounded at first like a relatively minor release (Windows

8.1) managed to integrate enough changes to warrant revisiting every one of the ten chapters I had completed to date. With an eye on //BUILD in 2014, I reached out to Windows Store expert and Wintellect colleague John Garland to help me finish the remaining chapters. John and I have worked on several projects together (and incidentally two of them won awards for their groundbreaking use of XAML for touch and mobile), and he helped write pilot code for several of our customers who were early Windows 8 adopters, so I knew he was the right person to bring a fresh set of example projects and content-rich chapters. As a bonus, he is also well-versed in cloud technology and brought this firsthand knowledge to bear in the chapters that deal with connecting to Azure.

In Windows 8.1 and the Windows Runtime, Microsoft has successfully demonstrated their commitment to the development ecosystem by providing us with a rich, vast array of APIs, SDKs, and tools for building incredible apps that run on a variety of devices. I was absolutely amazed when I discovered how easy it was to connect to a web cam, open a web socket, download files in the background, or profile my app to find "hot spots" that I could target to improve performance using WinRT. I was delighted to find that Portable Class Libraries (PCL), something I evangelized heavy as a solution to target multiple platforms in the Silverlight and WPF days, was evolving to embrace Windows Store apps. The first-class support for mature design patterns like MVVM makes it easier than ever to write stable, reusable code that runs on a variety of target devices.

In *Building Windows 8 Apps with C# and XAML*, I shared my intent to guide you through the process of learning the new territory quickly to begin building amazing new applications using skills you already had with C# and XAML. In this book, it is our goal to take you beyond that initial exposure and help you dive deep into all the various APIs WinRT makes available. Our goal was to hit virtually any scenario possible using the Windows Runtime—not just provide code snippets, but full projects you can use to experiment, learn, and use as a starting point for your own apps. The most rewarding feedback I received from my first book was hearing from authors sharing with me their excitement having their first Windows 8 apps approved for the Store. I hope this book not only helps take those apps to the next level, nor simply inspires your imagination, but empowers you to implement solutions you only dreamed possible using this incredible new platform. I know I speak for both John and myself when I say we look forward to hearing back from you about what you were able to achieve with Visual Studio, Windows 8.1, and this reference on your desk.

What This Book Is About

The purpose of this book is to explain how to write applications—mainly Windows Store apps—that are based on the Windows Runtime. The intent is to explore every available API, exposing you to possibilities across all areas and diving deep into major areas that are likely common to most apps that will be built. Instead of a traditional reference guide that shares API details and code snippets, this book includes more than 80 sample projects. These projects provide a "by example" approach to learning the various APIs; and the text either walks through how they were built, or breaks apart the code step-by-step to make it easy to understand and use as a template for your own projects.

This book is not an introduction to Windows 8.1. We assume you have some experience working with C# and XAML and are familiar with Windows Store apps. We also assume that you are at least familiar with the concept of design patterns and the notion of decoupled code. Both of these ideas have been core to the success of the applications we've helped build and will be used as foundations for the concepts presented in this book.

Whether you're a Windows 8.1 developer looking to improve an existing app, or an experienced client technologies developer transitioning to the Windows Runtime for the first time, this book will give you the guidance, proven patterns and practices, and example projects you'll need to build functional apps that run well across the myriad Windows 8.1 devices.

This version of the book specifically addresses Windows 8.1 using Visual Studio 2013. At this writing, the Windows 8.1 Update was announced at //BUILD, but fortunately the changes did not impact development as much as use of the OS and deployment options. During the course of this book, several changes have occurred that may not be reflected throughout: Visual Studio 2013 Update 2 was released, the name SkyDrive was changed to OneDrive, Windows Azure became Microsoft Azure, and Azure Mobile Services are constantly being revised.

Where to Access the Source Code

The source code for this book is open source and will be maintained and updated as needed to match any future revisions that may come out. You can download the code samples from the companion website: winrtexamples.codeplex.com.

How to Use This Book

The aim of this book is to enable you to discover the appropriate APIs to build your Windows Store apps. Each chapter is designed to help you discover what features are available in that area of the framework and how they are applied through example projects. Code examples are provided that demonstrate the features for programming them using C# and XAML. Although different chapters may relate to various parts of a comprehensive project, the individual samples are designed to stand on their own.

Each chapter is similarly structured. The chapters begin with an introduction to a topic and an inventory of the capabilities that topic provides. This is followed by explanations of areas of the framework and runtime and a walkthrough of the target APIs. The code samples are explained in detail, either as a walkthrough "lab" or by analyzing the existing sample, and the topic is summarized to highlight the specific information that is most important for you to consider.

I suggest you start by reading the book from start to finish, regardless of your existing situation. Inexperienced developers will find their understanding grows as they read each chapter and concepts are introduced, reinforced, and tied together. Experienced developers will gain insights into areas they might not have considered or had to deal with in the past, or simply didn't factor into their software lifecycles. Once you've read the book in its entirety, you will then be able to keep it as a reference guide and refer to specific chapters any time you require clarification about a particular topic.

Acknowledgments

Jeremy Likness: Although this is my third book through Pearson and fourth full book I've authored, writing a good book still depends on a solid team. I continue to be grateful for my superhuman Editor, Joan Murray, who has been patient and understanding, encouraging, and continuously provided her support and guidance throughout the process. Once again, Eleanor Bru braved working with me on this very ambitious project and, like Joan, was very patient and understanding while keeping me honest and on target. I can't thank Lori Lyons and the production team (including Krista Hansing and Debbie Williams) enough for taking my rambling and helping turn it into coherent prose.

The content of this book was amazingly enriched by our thorough and passionate technical editors. Thank you, Harry Pierson and Christophe Nasarre, for your incredible attention to detail. If anything was missed, I'll take the blame because Harry and Christophe ran every example, pored over every word, and provided me with volumes of suggestions and feedback that helped shape the book to its present form. It is always a pleasure to work with technical editors who bring strong technical insights to the table and help keep me honest when I want to take a shortcut and leave a thread spinning where it shouldn't.

Many thanks to my boss and friend, Steve Porter, for letting me devote a large chunk of my time to a project that made me disappear for a few hours every day. Thanks to Barbara Keihm for her support and encouragement, to Todd Fine for always recognizing our hard work and being one of the first to pre-order copies whenever they are available, and Bethany Vananda and Sara Faatz for working tirelessly to help spread the word and share what we're doing.

A special note goes to Dave Baskin, Dave Black, Josh Carroll, Aaron Carta, Phil Denoncourt, Dave Frommer, James Katic, Edward Kim, Wes McCammon, and Dan Sloan. This team worked with me on a major project that has lasted longer than the writing of this book and always understood when I had to turn down dinner or other outings so I could get back to my hotel and write. OK, who am I kidding—sometimes I managed to break away.

My wife and daughter have waited patiently through several books now, so they know the routine. Doreen is always quick to remind me when I need to push away from the dinner table and get back to writing, but Lizzie always noticed when I'd been writing too much and was always ready to have a movie date so I could unwind.

Finally, last but certainly not least, thank you! I appreciate my readers—and of course it is for you this was written—so it is my sincere hope you receive tremendous value from these pages.

John Garland: Like Jeremy, I'd very much like to thank Joan Murray, Eleanor Bru, and Lori Lyons, as well as everyone else at Pearson for their unwavering help and guidance throughout this project. Many thanks go to Harry Pierson and Christophe Nasarre for their invaluable help and insight throughout the technical review process—especially for helping to me find the right mix of code and prose, which invariably was along the lines of less prose and more code.

I'd like to very much thank my friends and colleagues at Wintellect. It is truly a privilege for me to count myself in your company and your passion for your craft is absolutely contagious. Many thanks to Steve Porter and Todd Fine for the continued opportunity, and to Bethany Vananda for all the help in putting my work in the best possible light. Much gratitude is owed to Jeff Richter, Jeff Prosise, and John Robbins for their insights into the writing process and for providing the Wintellect stage that I am fortunate to be able to stand on.

Families often have to take a back seat when these projects are in high gear, and mine was no exception. My wife Karen has been more than understanding and forgiving of many late nights, lost weekends, and grumpy mornings. My daughter Callie continues to be a walking smile that forces me to keep things in perspective, despite our having had to skip a few of our priceless Daddy-Callie days. Now that the book is done and the snow has melted, we can get back to bike rides, games of tag, and swing-pushes in the backyard.

I owe many thanks to the folks on and involved with the Zumo (Azure Mobile Services) team, including Kirill Gavrylyuk, Yavor Georgiev, Merwan Hade, and Heinrich Nielsen, among several others. Your insights into the Mobile Services inner workings, and prompt and helpful replies to my inquiries, have been invaluable both for the content included in this book as well as in my professional endeavors.

Finally, I'd like to thank Jeremy for asking me to come along not only on this ride as his co-author, but also as a technical editor on two of his previous books. The experiences, insights, and most importantly, the friendship, have been both personally and professionally invaluable.

About the Authors

Jeremy Likness is a multi-year Microsoft MVP for XAML technologies. A Principal Consultant for Wintellect with 20 years of experience developing enterprise applications, he has worked with software in multiple verticals ranging from insurance, health and wellness, supply chain management, and mobility. His primary focus for the past decade has been building highly scalable web-based solutions using the Microsoft technology stack with client stacks ranging from WPF, Silverlight, and Windows 8.1 to HTML5 and JavaScript. Jeremy has been building enterprise line of business applications with Silverlight since version 2.0, and he started writing Windows 8 apps when the Consumer Preview was released in 2011.

Prior to Wintellect, Jeremy was Director of Information Technology and served as development manager and architect for AirWatch, where he helped the company grow and solidify its position as one of the leading wireless technology solution providers in the United States prior to their acquisition by VMware. A fluent Spanish speaker, Jeremy served as Director of Information Technology for HolaDoctor (formerly Dr. Tango), where he architected a multilingual content management system for the company's Hispanic-focused online diet program. Jeremy accepted his role there after serving as Development Manager for Manhattan Associates, an Atlanta-based software company that provides supply chain management solutions.

John Garland is a Principal Consultant for Wintellect with more than 15 years of experience developing software solutions. Prior to consulting, he spent much of his career working on high-performance video and statistical analysis tools for premier sports teams, with an emphasis on the NFL, the NBA, and Division 1 NCAA football and basketball. His consulting clients range from small businesses to Fortune-500 companies, and his work has been featured at Microsoft conference keynotes and sessions.

John is a Microsoft Client Development MVP, as well as a member of the Windows Azure Insiders and Windows Azure Mobile Services Advisory Board. He lives in New Hampshire with his wife and daughter, where he is an active speaker and participant in the New England software development community. He is a graduate of the University of Florida with a Bachelor's degree in Computer Engineering and holds Microsoft Certifications spanning Windows, Silverlight, Windows Phone, and Windows Azure. John is the author of the ebook *Windows Store Apps Succinctly* (Syncfusion, 2013).

1

The New Windows Runtime

The Windows Runtime (WinRT) provides developers with an object-oriented, language-independent application programming interface (API) for creating applications that run on the Windows 8.1, Windows RT, and Windows Server 2012 and later operating systems. It is based on existing technologies such as the .NET Framework and the decades-old Common Object Model (COM) specification. Microsoft used the best parts of these existing technologies to create something better. Instead of using the .NET Framework to execute code, WinRT is an unmanaged object-oriented runtime that supports multiple development languages. Managed developers can use WinRT from the .NET Framework, thanks to an updated version of the Common Language Runtime (CLR) that interoperates seamlessly with the WinRT APIs.

Windows Runtime Specifics

The Windows Runtime runs on three fundamental architectures: the Intel-based x86 (32-bit) and x64 (64-bit), and the 32-bit ARM. The Intel-based architecture is the most common, and the majority of modern Windows laptops and desktops are based on it. These devices are capable of running Windows 8.1, the latest version of the Windows operating system. Windows 8.1 can run programs from previous versions of Windows (including Windows 7, Windows Vista, and Windows XP).

The ARM-based chip is designed to allow fewer transistors in the microprocessor, resulting in lower power usage and longer battery life on smaller devices that generate less heat. This has made it popular for use in smaller devices such as tablets and smartphones. To address the growing popularity of this chip, Microsoft created the Windows RT operating system. This is a version of Windows 8.1 that targets the ARM architecture but will not run programs built for previous versions of Windows (although Microsoft has ported some popular software, including Microsoft Office, to the platform). It is available only preinstalled on new PCs or tablets. Although the ARM architecture allows for incredibly thin form factors that produce little to no heat, Intel has begun manufacturing a low-power version of its x86 chips, codenamed Atom, that can run Windows 8.1 and retain backward compatibility.

TIP

The Windows Runtime terminology is often a source of confusion. The Windows Runtime is abbreviated as WinRT and refers to the underlying runtime that powers Windows Store apps and desktop applications. Windows RT is the name of the Windows 8.1 operating system version designed specifically for ARM chipsets. Windows RT is a target platform, whereas Windows Runtime (WinRT) is the framework this book discusses that runs on all the target platforms.

Why should you care about WinRT? Unlike the .NET Framework, which runs on top of an underlying operating system, WinRT is part of the native operating system itself. It exposes a set of native APIs that not only provides direct access to components of the operating system, but also evolves and is built as part of the operating system. This gives you access to native APIs that developers working on both native and managed platforms can immediately consume.

WinRT is available only to programs written for Windows 8.1, Windows RT, and Windows Server 2012. You must have a Windows 8.1 or later machine to develop applications that use WinRT, and those applications must target Windows 8.1 or Windows RT machines. You can develop two types of applications that use WinRT: desktop applications and Windows Store apps. Desktop applications can target only Windows 8.1 machines and are not supported by Windows RT devices. Windows Store apps are supported by both Windows 8.1 and Windows RT. Table 1.1 summarizes these restrictions.

TABLE 1.1 Windows Runtime Support

Application Type	Windows 8.1 Targets	Windows RT Targets
Windows Store app	x86 (32-bit), x64 (64-bit)	ARM (32-bit)
Desktop application	x86 (32-bit), x64 (64-bit)	None

A powerful benefit of developing WinRT applications is that they can be written in a variety of languages because of the object-oriented and language-independent nature of WinRT. The same APIs are exposed to every supported language and are supported as native constructs of those languages. In addition to C# (the focus of this book), the runtime currently supports VB.Net, C++ (a special version of C++ that includes component extensions to simplify writing applications that interact with the WinRT), and JavaScript. JavaScript relies on HTML markup and a browser host to render content, but the other language options all rely on Extensible Application Markup Language (XAML) for the user interface (UI). It is also possible to use DirectX (including Direct2D and Direct3D) in addition to XAML. Table 1.2 provides a brief overview of the various language options and their implementation. You also can create custom WinRT components to add APIs beyond what the operating system exposes. You cannot create custom WinRT components using the JavaScript language option, and custom components are not available to desktop applications.

TABLE 1.2 WinRT Language Options

Language	Runtime	Rendering Engine	WinRT Components
C++	N/A (native code)–requires specific builds for x86, x64, and ARM	XAML, DirectX	Yes
C#	CLR	XAML, DirectX	Yes
JavaScript	Chakra (JavaScript runtime)	Trident (HTML browser)	No
VB.NET	CLR	XAML, DirectX	Yes

Custom WinRT components can be used only from Windows Store apps. Every Windows Store app is actually a WinRT component itself.

Windows Store Apps

Windows Store apps are unique to Windows 8.1, Windows RT, and Windows Server 2012. They run in a single full-screen window without Chrome or in a smaller snapped view side by side with another Windows Store app. They are specifically designed to support different layouts and views (such as portrait and landscape orientations) out of the box and provide first-class support for various forms of input, including stylus and touch. Windows Store apps enable you to engage your users through unique features such as tiles, contracts, and cloud services.

Creating a Windows Store app is simple. Visual Studio 2013 provides several templates for the task. The templates address various forms of navigation, including hierarchical and flat navigation, as well as a blank template to start your app from scratch. The templates also have built-in features such as commonly used value converters and classes that facilitate use of the Model-View-ViewModel (MVVM) pattern.

The MVVM pattern appears throughout the examples in this book. It is a special pattern that takes advantage of the data-binding features of Windows Store apps. The *model* refers to the data and functionality of the app, and the *view* references the user interface as commonly described by XAML in Windows Store apps. The *viewmodel* is a special class that maintains state and encapsulates presentation logic. You learn more about the parts of the MVVM pattern as the book breaks down the sample app.

Example: Create a Windows Store App

To supplement this book, you can download dozens of example projects that illustrate the Windows Runtime. The solution is available online at http://winrtexamples.codeplex.com/, organized by chapter. The first chapter contains a simple "Hello, World" application (the project is called **HelloWorldGridApp**) that demonstrates one of the default templates for creating a Windows Store app. Figure 1.1 illustrates the **Add New Project** dialog box for a Windows Store app. The template is under the **Visual C#** menu when you select **Windows Store**. This example uses the **Grid App** template.

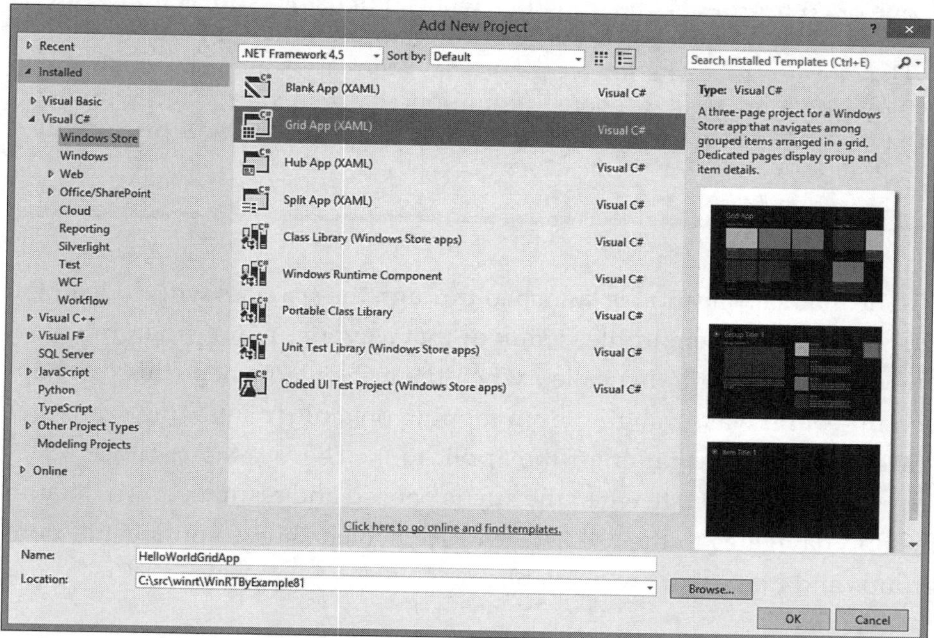

FIGURE 1.1 The Grid App template for a new Windows Store app

The resulting application is fully functional and contains groups of data with subsets of items. The navigation provides the capability to inspect data at the group level, drill into a specific group, and view the details of a specific item. A navigation engine that can persist state is built into the template, along with a base Model-View-ViewModel (MVVM) implementation. The rest of this book makes extensive use of this pattern (Chapter 9, "Model-View-ViewModel [MVVM]," covers it in more detail). The template itself provides several parts you can use to build your own app. You learn more about how to use these parts in Chapter 2, "Windows Store Apps and WinRT Components," which covers the templates in more detail. This is a high-level overview of the key components the template provides.

> **TIP**
>
> If you are creating your own projects, you might notice that they do not exactly match the sample code provided with the book. This is because the sample projects use a technique to share common code and assets. The Common solution folder contains assembly settings that all projects share. To use the `CommonAssemblyInfo.cs` attributes in one of your projects, the file should be added using **Add as Link** from the **Add Item** dialog box (instead of using the default **Add** option). This applies to assets for the Windows Store apps as well. This technique enables you to change common items in one place without having to update each individual project, and it is a good practice to follow for your own applications.

The main application is launched through the `App` class with code in the `App.xaml.cs` code-behind file. Think of that as your "main program" loop. The `OnLaunched` method is called when the app is launched (this can happen in several ways, ranging from tapping on a tile to invoking search). A `Frame` hosts the navigation of the application. The `SuspensionManager` class saves and restores state when the app is paused and resumed. As a default, the app navigates to the `GroupedItemsPage`, which shows you a list of both groups and items that are available.

```
rootFrame.Navigate(typeof(GroupedItemsPage))
```

The pages of the app include the `GroupItemsPage` (all groups and items), the `GroupDetailPage` (all items for a single group), and the `ItemDetailPage` (individual item). All are designed to help the user navigate through the "model" that is exposed through the `SampleDataSource` class in the `DataModel` folder. This class generates several groups that contain items with images (the default shades of gray provided in the `Assets` folder).

Open `GroupDetailPage.xaml.cs` and look at the code-behind. The control is based on the `Page` class, which a `Frame` can use for navigation. The page uses the `DefaultViewModel` viewmodel to synchronize state (notice how it hosts the current group and the items for the group), handle presentation logic, and act as an arbiter between the rest of the application and the XAML view.

The `NavigationHelper` class provides a `LoadState` method. This method takes either a parameter passed through navigation or a parameter that was saved when the app was suspended and then uses that to construct the view. This provides consistent behavior, whether navigating to the page or returning it when you resume the app. The parameter references the group passed (or saved) for the page; then the group and its corresponding list of items are assigned to the viewmodel. You learn more about this helper in Chapter 2.

```
var group = await SampleDataSource
    .GetGroup((String)navigationParameter);
this.DefaultViewModel["Group"] = group;
this.DefaultViewModel["Items"] = group.Items;
```

When an individual item is selected, the identifier is passed to the `Frame` to navigate to the detail page.

```
var itemId = ((SampleDataItem)e.ClickedItem).UniqueId;
this.Frame.Navigate(typeof(ItemDetailPage), itemId);
```

The bulk of the presentation logic is encapsulated in the underlying viewmodel. For example, the `OnNavigatedTo` method of the page is overridden to preserve the navigation request in a "back stack" that can be used to allow backward and forward navigation in the app (this is referred to as the journal). It preserves the navigation parameter and then calls the method on the derived class to `LoadState`, as shown earlier. It also uses the

`SuspensionManager` to save the state to disk when the user navigates away from the page. This preserves the history and restores it when the user returns to the app after it has been suspended.

The XAML view itself also handles layout changes (such as changing the orientation of the page or snapping it). Figure 1.2 shows a general overview of how the template works and its relation to the MVVM pattern.

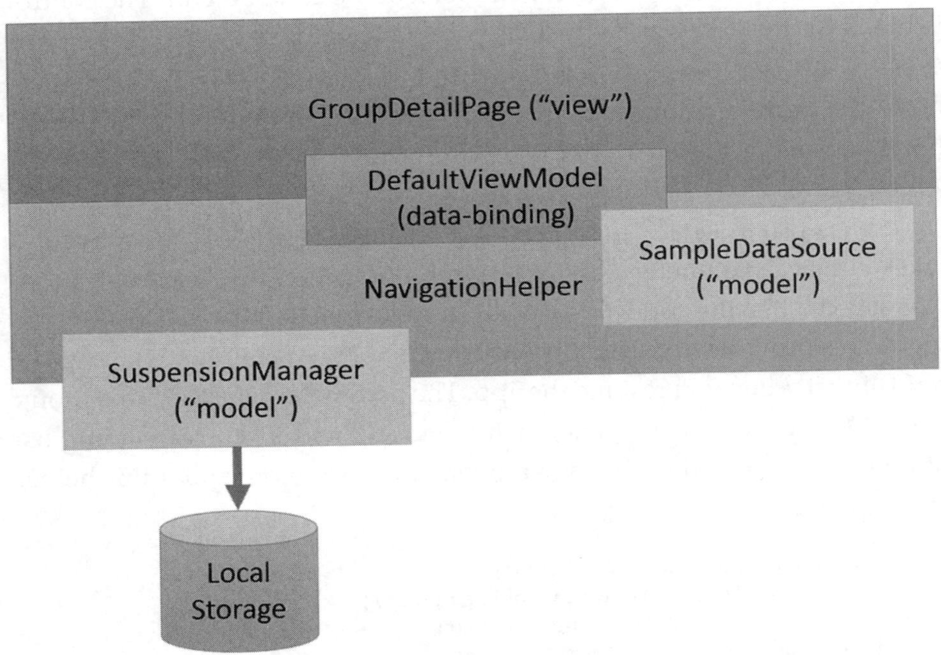

FIGURE 1.2 The sample template and the MVVM pattern

The built-in templates have many parts that you won't always use. The next several chapters provide more details about how the view, viewmodel, and application model work together to provide you with the tools you need to build apps using WinRT. Although WinRT provides its own set of APIs, understanding how WinRT interoperates with the .NET Framework is important.

.NET and WinRT

You might have noticed that the sample app uses C# and references .NET types. When you program Windows Store apps using C#, you interact with both the Windows Runtime and a special .NET Framework 4.5 profile. The profile enables you to create both Windows Runtime components with managed code (only Windows Store apps can consume these components) and Windows Store apps. This profile provides a set of reference assemblies that expose only the relevant types and members allowed to be consumed by Windows Store apps. It removes features from the .NET Framework API that exist in the Windows Runtime and provides direct references to the full set of WinRT APIs available to Windows Store apps.

The .NET Framework 4.5 for Windows Store apps is selected for you when you indicate that you want to build a Windows Runtime component or a Windows Store app using C#. It is important to understand how it is implemented because it uses a combination of type mapping, language projection, compiler-specific features, and CLR enhancements to create the interoperability between the .NET Framework and the Windows Runtime. Although most of the functionality is handled "behind the scenes," you should understand some nuances to avoid side effects or unwanted errors in your applications. For example, although you might reference .NET types in your code, some magic is happening behind the scenes.

Fundamental Types

Fundamental types from the Windows Runtime appear in Visual Studio and source code as their .NET equivalents. For example, the metadata information for a 4-byte integer in WinRT is coded as `ELEMENT_TYPE_I4`. When you are developing in the .NET Framework, it appears as the familiar `System.Int32`. This is done automatically, and you have no way to reference an underlying type directly from your source code. When you use an alias for a common type such as `int`, Visual Studio automatically maps that as `System.Int32`, and the compiler automatically emits the `ELEMENT_TYPE_I4` metadata.

Note that no support for null strings exists in the Windows Runtime. If you attempt to pass a null string to a WinRT component, you receive an `ArgumentNullException`. An empty string should be represented using `String.Empty`.

Mapped Types

A number of types appear as one type in the Visual Studio but are generated as another type by the compiler. Table 1.3 lists these types and their maps.

TABLE 1.3 Mapped Types Between the .NET Framework and WinRT

.NET Type	WinRT Type	Notes
`System:` `AttributeUsage`	`Windows.Foundation.Metadata:` `AttributeUsage`	
`System:` `AttributeTargets`	`Windows.Foundation.Metadata:` `AttributeTargets`	
`System:` `DateTimeOffset`	`Windows.Foundation:` `DateTime`	1
`System:` `EventHandler<T>`	`Windows.Foundation:` `EventHandler<T>`	2

`System.Runtime.`
`InteropServices.`
`WindowsRuntime:`
`EventRegistrationToken`
	`Windows.Foundation:`
	`EventRegistrationToken`
		2

`System:` `Exception`	`Windows.Foundation:` `HResult`	3
`System:` `Nullable<T>`	`Windows.Foundation:` `IReference<T>`	4
`System:` `TimeSpan`	`Windows.Foundation:` `TimeSpan`	
`System:` `Uri`	`Windows.Foundation:` `Uri`	5
`System:` `IDisposable`	`Windows.Foundation:` `IClosable`	6

.NET Type	WinRT Type	Notes
System.Collections. Generic: IEnumerable<T>	Windows.Foundation.Collections: IIterable<T>	
System.Collections. Generic: IList<T>	Windows.Foundation.Collections: IVector<T>	
System.Collections. Generic: IReadOnlyList<T>	Windows.Foundation.Collections: IVectorView<T>	
System.Collections. Generic: IDictionary<K,V>	Windows.Foundation.Collections: IMap<K,V>	
System.Collections. Generic: IReadOnlyDictionary<K,V>	Windows.Foundation.Collections: IMapView<K,V>	
System.Collections. Generic: KeyValuePair<K,V>	Windows.Foundation.Collections: IKeyValuePair<K,V>	
System.Collections: IEnumerable	Windows.UI.Xaml.Interop: IBindableIterable	
System.Collections: IList	Windows.UI.Xaml.Interop: IBindableVector	
System.Collections. Specialized: INotifyCollectionChanged	Windows.UI.Xaml.Interop: INotifyCollectionChanged	
System.Collections. Specialized: NotifyCollectionChanged EventHandler	Windows.UI.Xaml.Interop: NotifyCollectionChangedEvent Handler	
System.Collections. Specialized: NotifyCollectionChanged EventArgs	Windows.UI.Xaml.Interop: NotifyCollectionChangedEvent Args	

.NET Type	WinRT Type	Notes
System.Collections. Specialized: NotifyCollectionChanged Action	Windows.UI.Xaml.Interop: NotifyCollectionChanged Action	
System.ComponentModel: INotifyPropertyChanged	Windows.UI.Xaml.Interop: INotifyPropertyChanged	
System.ComponentModel: PropertyChangedEvent Handler	Windows.UI.Xaml.Interop: PropertyChangedEventHandler	
System.ComponentModel: PropertyChangedEventArgs	Windows.UI.Xaml.Interop: PropertyChangedEventArgs	
System: Type	Windows.UI.Xaml.Interop: TypeName	7

The following list summarizes the notes from Table 1.3:

1. Dates are always converted to Coordinated Universal Time (UTC). The time zone is not stored in WinRT, so when the dates are converted back to the .NET Framework equivalent, the local time zone is assumed. If you are using time zones other than the local time zone, you need to apply further conversions when the date is passed back.
2. WinRT event handlers generate a unique token when a subscriber is added. The subscriber uses this token to unsubscribe. In the .NET Framework, you do not have to use these tokens; you can simply add or remove delegates in the standard way using the += and -= operator overloads. The compiler generates the necessary code to call a helper function to maintain a map between the delegates you register and their corresponding tokens.
3. WinRT exceptions are really just a 32-bit integer that, in COM, is known as an HRESULT.[1] The CLR maps well-known exceptions to

[1]HRESULT, http://bit.ly/W8WBxF

the COM equivalent; conversely, an exception returned from WinRT can be converted to a well-known .NET `Exception` type. When there is no well-known mapping, the HRESULT is converted to a generic `Exception` object, with the value of the HRESULT stored in the `HResult` property.

4. WinRT uses `IReference<T>` for two scenarios: boxing values and providing support for `Nullable<T>`. You can read more about how this is implemented in the previous section.
5. The Windows Runtime does not support relative URIs. If you try to pass a relative URI to a WinRT component, an `ArgumentException` is thrown. If you must use a relative URI, the workaround is to provide a base URI to create an absolute URI and then ignore the base portion when the URI is returned.
6. The Windows Runtime requires all I/O operations to be asynchronous. The mapped `Close` method on the WinRT `IClose` interface maps to the `Dispose` method on the .NET Framework `IDisposable` interface. This interface is not marked as asynchronous. Therefore, you should not perform any I/O in your `Dispose` method. You must implement your components so that they flush or close streams before they are disposed.
7. Types in WinRT are far more simplified than in the .NET implementation. A WinRT type is simply the fully qualified name for the type, and the metadata system is used to parse any relevant information about that type.

Note that the restrictions for mapping apply only to calls between the CLR and WinRT. You can still build C# class libraries to use within your projects without any restrictions. In fact, it is recommended that you use C# class libraries instead of WinRT components for reusable code in your applications if you are not planning to consume those components using any other languages. Create a managed WinRT component only when you want to access it from nonmanaged language options such as C++ and JavaScript.

Streams and Buffers

The Windows Runtime contains several interfaces for streams that existing classes in the .NET Framework do not directly support. To close this gap, you can use one of several extension methods provided by the `System.IO.WindowsRuntimeStorageExtensions` class and defined in `System.Runtime.WindowsRuntime.dll`. They effectively convert streams between WinRT and the CLR by performing quite a bit of work, such as ensuring that each stream has its own unique adapter and buffer to provide the best performance possible and ensuring that the stream behaves as expected within your .NET code.

WinRT provides the `IStorageFile` interface to work with local and roaming storage. You can use the two extension methods `OpenStreamForReadAsync` and `OpenStreamForWriteAsync` to generate, from an `IStorageFile` instance, a `Stream` object to pass to your .NET components. Several overloads exist to work with directories and relative paths and specify various options when creating a new file. You learn more about storage in Chapter 4, "Data and Content."

WinRT stream interfaces include `IRandomAccessStream`, `IInputStream`, and `IOutputStream`. The `System.Runtime.WindowsRuntime` namespace provides several extension methods to convert between these stream types and .NET streams: `AsStream`, `AsStreamForRead`, `AsStreamForWrite` to convert from WinRT to .NET Framework streams; and `AsInputStream` and `AsOutputStream` to pass .NET Framework streams to WinRT APIs.

Sometimes you need to pass blocks of data to WinRT APIs. You cannot pass a byte array or memory stream directly to the Windows Runtime, so WinRT provides the `IBuffer` interface. The interface declares only two properties: the total capacity for the buffer and the number of bytes in use. You cannot access, read from, or write to the actual underlying buffer. This makes the interface a safe way to pass buffers among various language implementations. Internally, WinRT can access the buffer with a COM interface that can access its actual contents.

Several extension methods exist in the `System.Runtime.InteropServices.WindowsRuntime.WindowsRuntimeBufferExtensions`[2] class. You can convert a byte array into an `IBuffer` instance by using the `AsBuffer` extension methods. You can also convert a `MemoryStream` instance into an `IBuffer` instance by using the `GetWindowsRuntimeBuffer` extension methods.

Conversely, you can convert an `IBuffer` instance to either a byte array or a `Stream` instance. The same helper class provides the `AsStream` and `ToArray` extension methods to perform this conversion for you. The class contains other methods to parse, compare, and copy data to and from buffers.

Desktop Applications

The Windows Runtime is also available from the desktop-style applications you are likely familiar with, although this is fairly rare. Most of this book focuses on Windows Store apps, but it is important to know that various APIs in WinRT are available to traditional desktop applications.

You can write desktop applications that use the Windows Runtime in C++, C++/CX,[3] or C#. To use C#, you must target the .NET Framework 4.5. The capability to reference WinRT APIs is not provided out of the box. Instead, you must modify your project to change the references manually.

Example: Reference WinRT from a Desktop Application

The sample project **DesktopWinRT** in the **Chapter 1** solution folder demonstrates a desktop application that calls WinRT APIs. To create a similar project yourself, choose the option to add a new project from within Visual Studio 2013. Navigate to **Visual C#** and **Windows**, and then choose the template for a **WPF Application** as in Figure 1.3.

---

[2]WindowsRuntimeBufferExtensions, http://bit.ly/XOBVtL

[3]C++/CX Reference, http://bit.ly/XLP5Yd

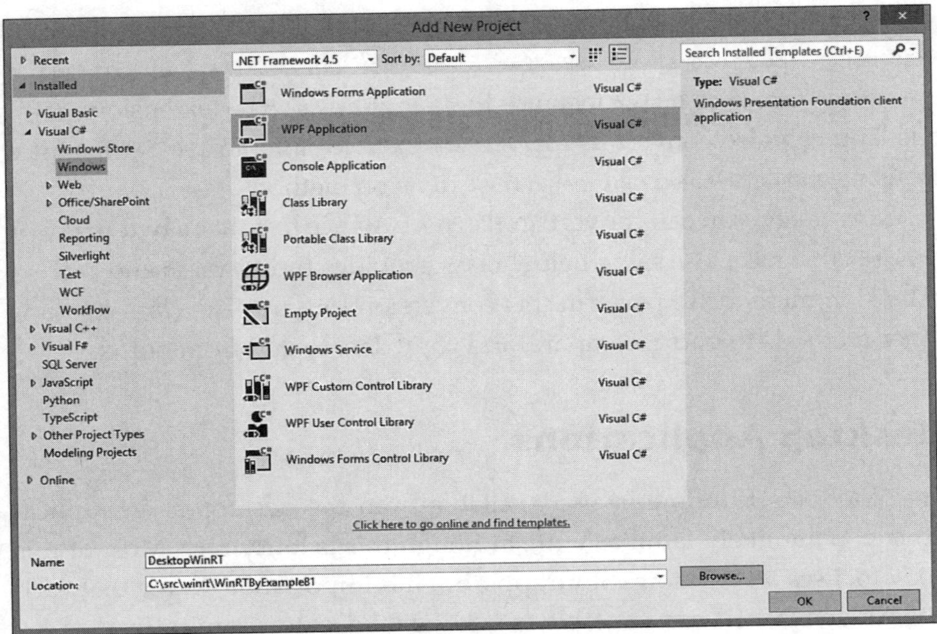

FIGURE 1.3 Creating a desktop application

Make sure that the project targets the .NET Framework 4.5 or later. Although a number of default assembly references are added, accessing WinRT APIs is not yet possible. Doing this involves a few steps. The first step is required because it is not possible to update a project to access WinRT from the IDE. Instead, you must edit the project file directly. First, right-click the project in the **Solution Explorer** and choose the option **Unload Project**. This project should show as "unavailable" in the Solution Explorer (see Figure 1.4).

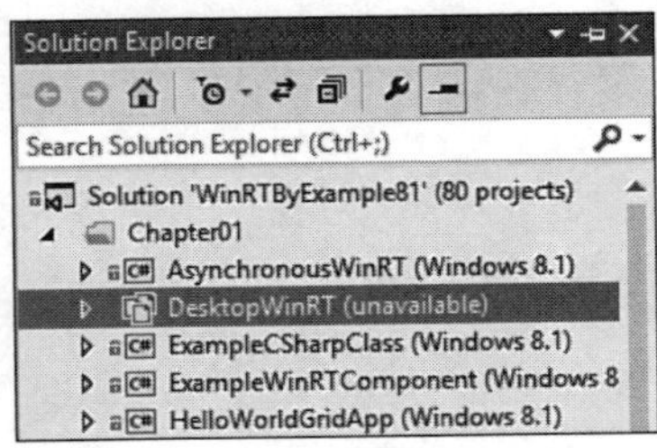

FIGURE 1.4 Unloaded project

When the project is unloaded, you can edit the XML contained in the project file by right-clicking the project node and selecting **Edit**. If you receive a message about inconsistent line endings, feel free to accept the dialog box to clean the document. To allow you to reference WinRT, the project must target Windows version 8.1 or later. This is done by adding the following snippet inside the first `PropertyGroup` element:

```
<TargetPlatformVersion>8.1</TargetPlatformVersion>
```

Note that IntelliSense might suggest `TargetFrameworkVersion`, but that is not the correct tag to update. After you've made the change, save the file, right-click the project node, and select **Reload Project**. If you receive a prompt about the project file already being open, select the option to close it. After the project has reloaded, you are ready to add a WinRT reference.

Right-click the **References** node in the **Solution Explorer** and select **Add Reference**. You should notice a new tab with the text **Windows** and a child tab named **Core**. Select this tab and check the box next to the **Windows** assembly, as in Figure 1.5.

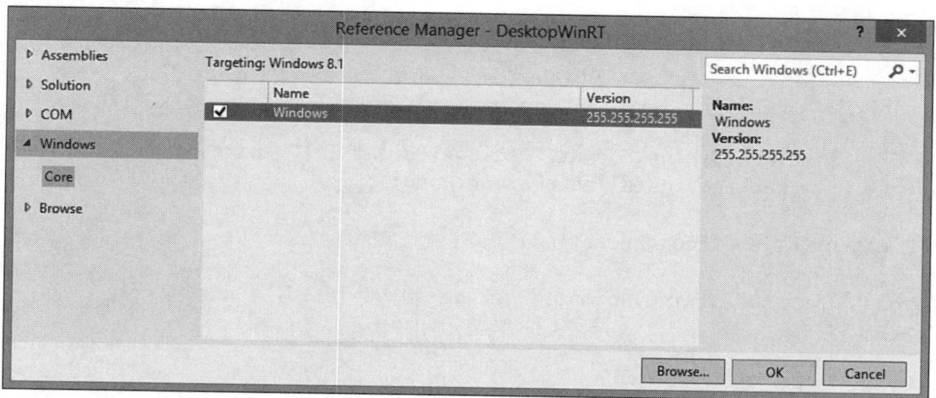

FIGURE 1.5 Adding the WinRT reference

After you click **OK**, you're ready to reference the interfaces. For the example program, the following `using` statement was added to **MainWindow.xaml.cs**:

```
using Windows.Management.Deployment;
```

This statement provides access to a set of WinRT APIs for enumerating packages (installed apps) in the system. The following line inside the event handler for the main window load event references a WinRT component:

```
var packageManager = new PackageManager();
```

A query on the Package Manager returns a list of packages for the user that are added to a list in the WPF control. Listing 1.1 shows the full code for this.

LISTING 1.1 Package Manager List

```
var list = new List<string>();
var packageManager = new PackageManager();
var identity = WindowsIdentity.GetCurrent();
if (identity == null || identity.User == null)
{
    MessageBox.Show(
        "Unable to determine the current user's identity.");
    return;
}
var query = packageManager.FindPackagesForUser(identity.User.Value);
foreach (var package in query)
{
    var name = package.Id.Name;

    try
    {
        list.Add(string.Format("Package {0} at {1}", name,
            package.InstalledLocation.Path));
    }
    catch (FileNotFoundException)
    {
        list.Add(string.Format("Package {0} deleted.", name));
    }
}

Packages.ItemsSource = list;
```

Unfortunately, adding the references and compiling the program isn't enough, and the compiler generates several errors (see Figure 1.6). This is because additional assemblies are needed for the WPF example.

Error List

2 Errors | 0 Warnings | 0 Messages | Search Error List

	Description	File	Line	Column	Project
1	The type 'System.Collections.Generic.IEnumerable`1<T0>' is defined in an assembly that is not referenced. You must add a reference to assembly 'System.Runtime, Version=4.0.0.0, Culture=neutral, PublicKeyToken=b03f5f7f11d50a3a'.	MainWindow.xaml.cs	55	13	DesktopWinRT
2	foreach statement cannot operate on variables of type 'System.Collections.Generic.IEnumerable`1<Windows.ApplicationMo	MainWindow.xaml.cs	56	13	DesktopWinRT

Error List | Output | Undo Close | Package Manager Console

FIGURE 1.6 Compiler errors when attempting to reference WinRT

The dependent assemblies exist in a special path on the system, and references to them are required to successfully call WinRT APIs from the WPF desktop application. To fix this, you add another reference to the project and browse to the following folder:

```
C:\Program Files (x86)\Reference Assemblies\Microsoft\Framework\
➥.NETFramework\v4.5\Facades
```

Select `System.Runtime.dll` and click **Add** to include it within your project references. You should then be able to compile your program. In the reference example, you should see a window with a list of packages on the system, similar to Figure 1.7.

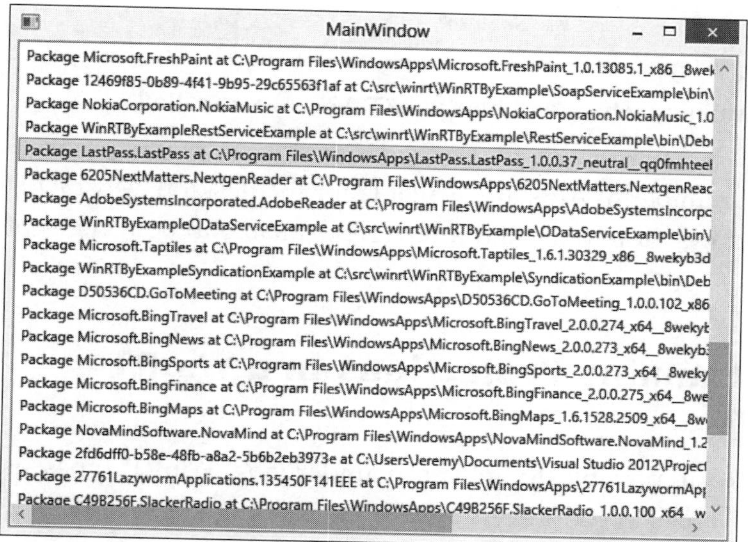

FIGURE 1.7 Package listing from a WinRT API called from a WPF application

Referencing WinRT from a desktop application is not straightforward, but it is possible. Remember, three steps are required:

1. Modify the project file to target the platform version 8.1.
2. Add the Windows Core reference.
3. Browse and add the `System.Runtime.dll` reference.

The MSDN library provides a list of WinRT APIs that you can call from Windows 8.1 desktop applications.[4] The MSDN documentation for each WinRT component includes a section that provides information about the requirements to use a particular API. Figure 1.8 shows an example for the `PackageManager` class.

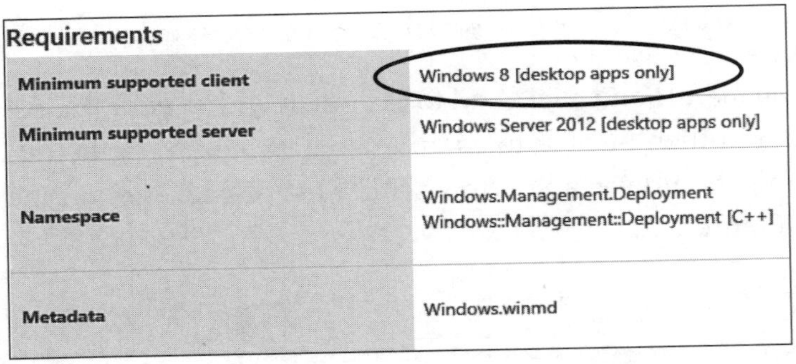

Requirements

Minimum supported client	Windows 8 [desktop apps only]
Minimum supported server	Windows Server 2012 [desktop apps only]
Namespace	Windows.Management.Deployment Windows::Management::Deployment [C++]
Metadata	Windows.winmd

FIGURE 1.8 Determining where and how WinRT APIs can be called

Only a small number of APIs are available for the desktop. Most APIs are for the Windows Store only, and a few are available to both types of apps.

Example: Examine Projections in a WinRT Component

Projections make it possible to reference underlying WinRT types as equivalent .NET types in code, even though the running app will use the

[4]Windows 8.1 API list, http://bit.ly/Slcq53

unmanaged component. The example solution contains a project named **ExampleCSharpClass** that illustrates the differences between C# class libraries and WinRT components and demonstrates how projections work. Figure 1.9 shows the code map for the simple API this class exposes. A method takes in a URI and fires an event that encapsulates the string representation of the URI. This shows the specific differences between how events are handled in the Windows Runtime vs. the .NET Framework and how types are mapped. Keep in mind that you will most likely create simple C# class libraries unless you specifically need to reference your libraries from C++ or JavaScript code.

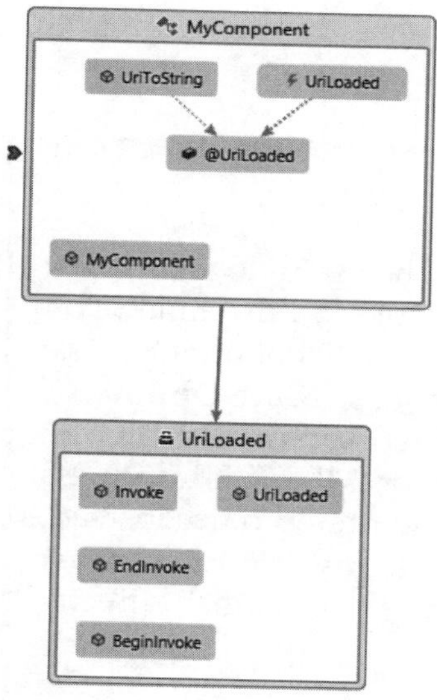

FIGURE 1.9 The code map for the example project

The event arguments simply reference the URI.

```
public sealed class UriLoadedArgs
{
    public string Uri { get; set; }
}
```

The component exposes the signature of the event:

```
public delegate void UriLoaded(object sender,
    UriLoadedArgs args);
```

It also defines the event itself:

```
public event UriLoaded UriLoaded;
```

Compile the C# class library and navigate to the output directory using the Developer Command Prompt link. (If you're not sure how to find the output directory, right-click the project name in the **Solution Explorer** menu and choose **Open Folder in File Explorer** to dig into its **bin\debug** subfolders.) Use the `ildasm.exe` tool to inspect the DLL by typing the following on the command line in the folder that contains the DLL:

```
ildasm ExampleCSharpClass.dll
```

> **TIP**
>
> If you use the `ildasm.exe` tool quite often, it can be useful to associate it with the DLL files you are inspecting. On Windows 8.1 machines, you can right-click a DLL and choose **Open With** for a list of options. The tool will not likely show by default. Instead, choose **More Options** (if that is available), followed by **Look for Another App on This PC**. Be sure to check the box labeled **Use This App for All .dll Files** unless you have another application installed that you prefer to use instead. Simply browse to the folder `C:\Program Files\Microsoft SDKs\Windows\v8.1A\bin\NETFX 4.5.1 Tools` and select `ildasm.exe` to launch directly into the tool from **File Explorer**.

When the component is loaded, you should see three top-level entities defined:

- `MyComponent` is the main class definition.
- `UriLoaded` is the definition of a delegate.
- `UriLoadedArgs` is the class definition for the event arguments.

The signature of the `UriToString` method of `MyComponent` is:

```
UriToString: void(class [System.Runtime]System.Uri)
```

The signature of the event handler methods to subscribe and unsubscribe by passing a delegate is:

```
add_UriLoaded: void(class ExampleCSharpClass.UriLoaded)
remove_UriLoaded: void(class ExampleCSharpClass.UriLoaded)
```

Notice that the methods for the event handlers are empty and take in a single parameter that is the delegate for the event. Now compile the WinRT version of the component by building the **ExampleWinRTComponent** project. The code is identical to the class library but resides in a different namespace. If you browse to the output location, the first thing you'll likely notice is that there is no DLL. Instead, the compiler has produced a WinRT metadata file named **ExampleWinRTComponent.winmd**.

Open this file using `ildasm.exe`. The first thing you'll notice is that the public classes have been renamed with a `<CLR>` prefix and made private. This is how the .NET Framework and WinRT interoperate together. The internal classes are marked private so they are not visible to WinRT, and the projected implementations are made public. In addition, both classes had an interface automatically generated. The main component class implements the `IMyComponentClass` interface. In COM, clients must interoperate with services through interfaces, but the compiler has made this transparent for you by generating the interface if you did not provide one yourself.

Also notice that no "special" class was created for the delegate. The metadata for the base delegate type in WinRT is marked the same way as the CLR type, so no conversion is needed. When you look at the interface `IMyComponentClass`, you'll see that the signature of the `UriToString` method is different:

```
UriToString: void(class [Windows]Windows.Foundation.Uri)
```

The methods to add and remove event handlers have also changed:

```
add_UriLoaded: valuetype [Windows]Windows.Foundation.
   EventRegistrationToken(class ExampleWinRTComponent.UriLoaded)
remove_UriLoaded: void(valuetype [Windows]Windows.Foundation.
   EventRegistrationToken)
```

The URI has been converted to the WinRT type, and the event code has changed to implement the WinRT method of managing registrations with a token. If you want to see how the component is projected back to the CLR, go to the command line and open the file again, but this time add the **/project** command line switch:

```
ildasm /project ExampleWinRTComponent.winmd
```

The same metadata will be parsed, but this time projections are applied so you can see the types as they appear in managed code. For example, the `UriToString` signature on the interface is now this:

```
UriToString: void(class [System.Runtime]System.Uri)
```

You can use `ildasm.exe` to inspect metadata for WinRT types. Using the **/project** switch parses the same metadata but displays the projections and mappings for consumption by managed code.

Asynchronous Functions

In C#, you can expose and consume asynchronous methods using the `async` and `await` keywords. In the .NET Framework, you typically write the implementation of an asynchronous interface using the Task Parallel Library (TPL).[5] The **AsynchronousWinRT** example provides an example of this in the `AddNumbersInternal` method (see Listing 1.2). This is how you typically wrap and return a long-running task.

Listing 1.2 Using Task for Asynchronous Operations in the .NET Framework

```
private static Task<long> AddNumbersInternal(
    ICollection<int> array)
{
    return Task.Run(
        () =>
            {
```

[5]Task Parallel Library (TPL), http://bit.ly/UcpUhS

```
                long result = 0;
                for (var index = 0; index < array.Count;
                    index++)
                {
                    result += index;
                }

                return result;
            });
}
```

If you try to make the method public, you will receive an error. This is because WinRT doesn't contain a `Task` type. Instead, it supports four distinct asynchronous operation interfaces. All asynchronous interfaces inherit the `IAsyncInfo` interface, which provides a unique identifier for the operation, a status of the operation, an error code in case the operation aborts, and methods to cancel and close the operation:

- `IAsyncAction` is an asynchronous operation that does not report progress and does not return a result.
- `IAsyncActionWithProgress<TProgress>` is an asynchronous operation that reports progress but does not return a result.
- `IAsyncOperation<TResult>` is an asynchronous operation that does not report progress but returns a specific result when complete.
- `IAsyncOperationWithProgress<TResult, TProgress>` is an asynchronous operation that reports progress and returns a result when complete.

The .NET Framework provides extension methods that enable you to convert `Task` objects to WinRT equivalents or launch asynchronous tasks directly. For example, the following code converts the task-based asynchronous operation from Listing 1.2 into a WinRT asynchronous operation:

```
public IAsyncOperation<long> AddNumbers(
    [ReadOnlyArray] int[] array)
{
    return AddNumbersInternal(array).AsAsyncOperation();
}
```

Notice the use of the `ReadOnlyArray` attribute to flag the array as input-only. This marks the array so that WinRT understands which of the three allowed array-passing methods is being used (passed, filled, or received). The extension method that the framework provides converts the `Task` to an `IAsyncOperation`. To return a task that supports progress, you can use the `AsyncInfo` static class to launch the instance, as in Listing 1.3. This listing uses the TPL to create a long-running task but wraps that in a WinRT asynchronous operation that supports progress reporting.

LISTING 1.3 Creating a WinRT Asynchronous Operation That Reports Progress

```
public IAsyncOperationWithProgress<long, double>
    AddNumbersWithProgress([ReadOnlyArray] int[] array)
{
    return AsyncInfo.Run(
        async (
            CancellationToken cancellationToken,
            IProgress<double> progress) =>
            {
                progress.Report(0);
                return await Task.Run(
                    () =>
                        {
                            long result = 0;
                            for (var index = 0;
                                index < array.Length;
                                index++)
                            {
                                progress.Report(
                                    (double)index /
                                    array.Length);
                                result += index;
                            }

                            return result;
                        });
            });
}
```

Writing asynchronous operations that the Windows Runtime can consume is easy using the extension methods that the framework provides.

Summary

This chapter introduced you to the concept of two types of programs that can interoperate with the Windows Runtime: desktop applications and Windows Store apps. You learned how WinRT uses the best parts of COM and the .NET Framework to allow multiple languages to seamlessly consume components. This projection is coupled with features of the CLR and the compiler that maps WinRT types and classes to their CLR equivalents. Various extension methods make it easy to interoperate with WinRT components and expose managed code to the Windows Runtime by converting between types and generating boilerplate code that handles events, streams, buffers, and asynchronous operations.

In the next chapter, you learn more about Windows Store apps. The Windows Runtime provides a host environment with services for suspending and resuming Windows Store apps, as well as creating interfaces between Windows Store apps, other applications, and the operating system itself. You will also create a Windows Runtime component and learn how to consume it from unmanaged code and JavaScript-based Windows Store apps.

2

Windows Store Apps and WinRT Components

WINDOWS STORE APPS IS A LABEL WITH A BIT OF HISTORY behind it. The story began in 2010 when Microsoft announced the Windows Phone 7 Series. Microsoft later dropped the *Series* part of the name, but new developers to the platform quickly learned that Windows Phone 7 featured the design philosophy referred to as Metro. Earlier Microsoft projects, including Zune and Windows Media Center, heavily influenced it. Many developers were excited to see the Metro design language appear in the earliest versions of Windows 8.

If you created a Windows Store app in early 2011 when the Developer Preview version of Windows 8 was released, you fired up a copy of the Visual Studio 11 Preview and chose your language and the option for the Windows Metro Style application. By the Consumer Preview, the menu item changed to Metro App for the Metro style framework. Sometime after this, potential trademark infringements led Microsoft to drop the term *Metro* altogether. Documentation began referring to either the "Modern UI" or the "Microsoft design language," and after Visual Studio 11 was renamed to Visual Studio 2012, it provided an option to build a Windows Store app for Windows 8. Eventually, Visual Studio 2013 was released with the capability to build the same apps to target Windows 8.1.

This history might help explain why you can visit the Windows Store to purchase desktop applications (that are not Windows Store apps) or why you can install Windows Store apps without ever visiting the Windows Store. When I refer to a "Windows Store app," think of it as a Windows 8.1 application that is built and deployed as a WinRT component. That should help separate these apps from desktop applications in your mind.

The Windows Runtime provides a special set of services for Windows Store apps. The runtime hosts Windows Store apps as needed, loads the CLR for managed apps, and invokes a web host to render HTML and interpret client script for apps written with JavaScript. Windows Store apps are deployed in special packages that contain unique assets and resources. They have access to local and temporary storage that is sandboxed from the rest of the system and can manipulate roaming settings that automatically synchronize across multiple Windows 8.1 devices. Windows Store apps operate in a special lifecycle designed to maximize battery life and end-user productivity by suspending and resuming applications as they are brought in and out of focus.

In addition to creating special WinRT components that are published as Windows Store apps, you can create standalone WinRT components in C# that other apps written in native C++ or interpreted JavaScript can invoke. Managed components might appear as native WinRT components to their clients but impose special dependencies. An instance of the CLR must exist to host managed code for native code to call it. The fact that managed WinRT components generate Common Intermediate Language (CIL) code means they can be compiled once and run on x86, x64, and ARM systems. Native code must be compiled to target each system it will run on.

Fundamentals of a Windows Store App

Windows Store apps have a unique look and feel, can target multiple devices, and are most often distributed through the Windows Store. The Windows Store is Microsoft's platform for software distribution and supports a variety of targets, including Windows 8.1 and Windows RT. Note that Windows Store apps can be developed only on Windows 8.1 machines; no SDK is available for Windows 7 or other versions (for example, you can target Windows 8 only on a Windows 8 machine, so it is recommended that you upgrade your environment to 8.1).

Windows Store apps are designed to run either in a single window with no chrome, or arranged horizontally side by side, with other apps taking up the full vertical space available in the display. The intention is to provide maximum focus, avoid distractions, and make the best use of available real estate. A common technique is hiding common commands until they are needed. Temporary panels appear as either modal dialogs or panels that fly out to overlay content until they are dismissed (hence the term *flyout*). The apps are also designed to scale to different form factors, such as portrait and landscape, high resolution and low resolution, and a narrow mode when several apps are run side by side.

Windows Store apps provide first-class support for touch and pen input. All the built-in controls you will learn about have built-in capabilities to recognize touch, taps, and gestures. Although touch is important, apps can also be launched on traditional hardware that uses mouse and keyboard input. You should design your apps to accommodate these modalities and all the built-in controls come out of the box with keyboard and mouse support, in addition to the support for pen and touch.

Windows 8 introduced contracts and extensions. Contracts were considered an agreement between apps that enabled rich content sharing and other features. They allow your app to communicate with other apps you don't know about because the interface is a common contract. Extensions were defined as agreements between Windows Store apps and the operating system that allow apps to participate in file picking operations, camera functions, file associations, and more. These features have evolved in Windows 8.1 and are referred to generically as *declarations*. The capability for an app to use these features is declared in the application's manifest, which you learn more about in this chapter. Chapter 11, "Windows Charms Integration," and Chapter 12, "Additional Windows Integration," cover declarations in more detail.

A variety of Windows Store app templates are available to help you start a new project. In fact, most of the templates generate fully functional and interactive reference applications you can modify to create your own Windows Store apps. Understanding the differences between templates is important to choose the right starting point for your application.

Windows Store App Templates

The Windows Store app templates are accessible from Visual Studio 2013 via the **New Project** menu. Eight templates (plus the "bonus" Portable Class Library template you will learn about) are available for developing Windows Store apps using C#. Figure 2.1 shows the templates.

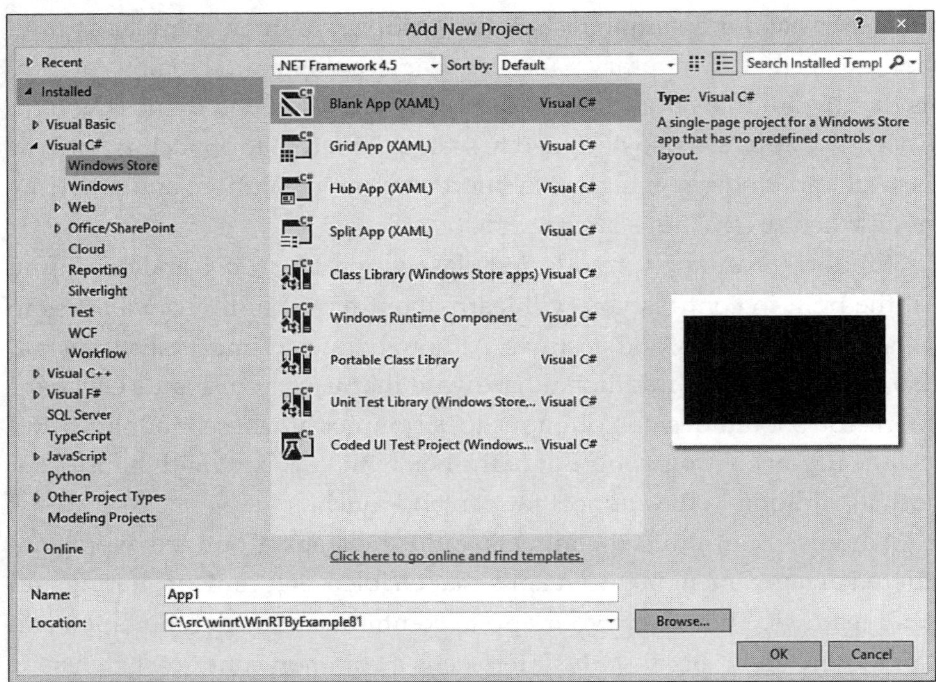

FIGURE 2.1 Available project templates for Windows Store apps

Blank App

This template provides the bare minimum you need to get up and running with a Windows Store app. It provides an application object, a basic set of styles, and an empty main page. Use this template when your application doesn't follow the hierarchical navigation patterns of the grid and split application templates.

Grid App

The **HelloWorldGridApp** project from Chapter 1, "The New Windows Runtime," provides an example for this template. The template is designed for data that can be logically grouped. Use this template if your application provides data in logical groups or categories. Examples include news applications that group items by topic and cooking applications that group recipes by meal or major ingredient. The main page shows a summary of items by group. You can then drill down into the group or category level and/or the item level. Figure 2.2 shows an example.

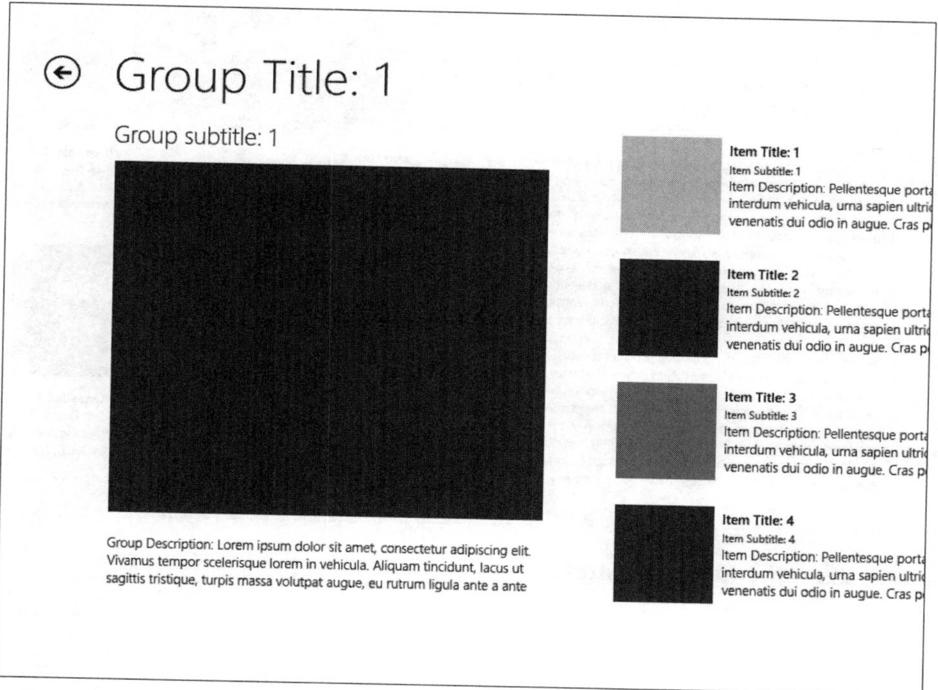

FIGURE 2.2 Grid-style template

Hub App

The hub app template, introduced with Windows 8.1, demonstrates how to use the new Hub control. This control is ideal for apps that present a view the user can pan through. The user can then pan through different sections that present different pieces of information. An example of a hub-style app is the free Bing news app included with the Windows 8.1 installation. You can run the included **ReferenceHubApp** project in the `Chapter2` solution folder (available online at http://winrtexamples.codeplex.com/) to see how the default template works (see Figure 2.3).

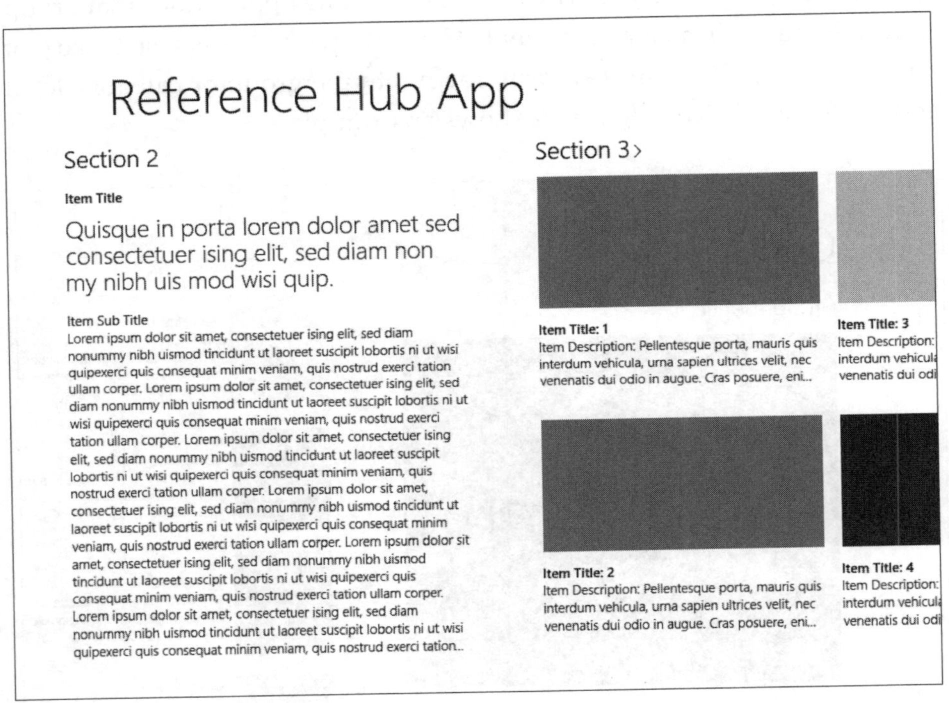

FIGURE 2.3 The hub template

Split App

The split app is similar to the grid app, but it does not provide a single-item view. Instead, it provides a list of groups that enables you to drill down to individual items. The "split page" is a page that lists the items for the group, with details for the item in a side pane. The project **ReferenceSplitApp** demonstrates this template. Figure 2.4 shows the split view.

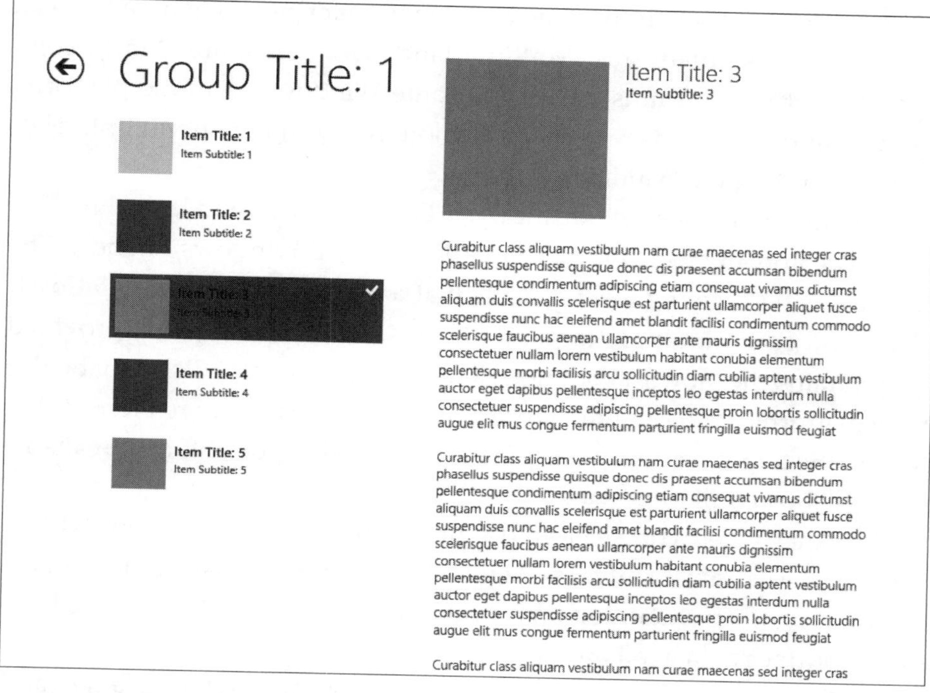

FIGURE 2.4 The split view

Class Library (Windows Store Apps)

The class library template enables you to create a managed library that other managed Windows Store apps or WinRT components can share. This assembly is not compiled as a WinRT component, so it is available only to other managed code projects (you cannot call a C# class library from C++ or JavaScript Windows Store apps).

Portable Class Library

The Portable Class Library (PCL) provides support for multiple target platforms, including Windows Store apps, .NET Framework desktop applications, Silverlight 5 apps, and even Windows Phone 8 applications. If you don't develop for those platforms, you can skip this section.

The PCL enables you to create a common managed code base that can be shared across platforms. Multiple languages can share WinRT components, but they all must target the same Windows Runtime platform. Portable libraries can be referenced without recompiling on multiple platforms, including the Windows Runtime.

Available platforms include the .NET Framework 4.0 and later, .NET For Windows Store apps (8 and 8.1), Silverlight 5, and Windows Phone 8. The PCL works by defining a list of APIs that are available for each platform. When you select multiple target platforms, a special profile is provided that contains the "lowest common denominator" set of APIs available for those platforms. You can then write a library that uses only references that exist on the target platform. The library is flagged as portable and available to projects you build that target those platforms.

Note that when you select more platforms, the list of supported features narrows dramatically. The key to developing a Portable Library is to pick only platforms that you know you will be targeting, to have the largest API surface area available.

MSDN documentation helps you easily discover which classes and methods the PCL supports. Figure 2.5 shows the documentation for the `WebRequest` object. The icons in the first column indicate whether the given method or constructor is available to the PCL or whether it is accessible from Windows Store apps. You can also scroll to the bottom of the documentation and view the **Versions** section to see whether the given class is available (and for which versions) to the .NET Framework, PCL, and Windows Store apps.

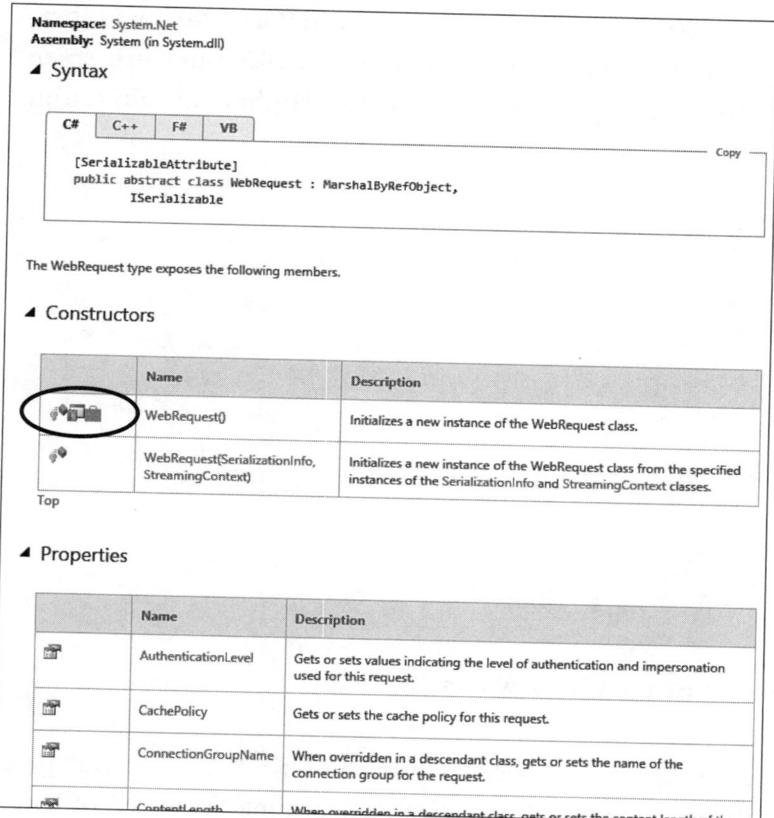

Namespace: System.Net
Assembly: System (in System.dll)

◢ Syntax

C# | C++ | F# | VB

Copy

```
[SerializableAttribute]
public abstract class WebRequest : MarshalByRefObject,
        ISerializable
```

The WebRequest type exposes the following members.

◢ Constructors

	Name	Description
	WebRequest()	Initializes a new instance of the WebRequest class.
	WebRequest(SerializationInfo, StreamingContext)	Initializes a new instance of the WebRequest class from the specified instances of the SerializationInfo and StreamingContext classes.

Top

◢ Properties

	Name	Description
	AuthenticationLevel	Gets or sets values indicating the level of authentication and impersonation used for this request.
	CachePolicy	Gets or sets the cache policy for this request.
	ConnectionGroupName	When overridden in a descendant class, gets or sets the name of the connection group for the request.
	ContentLength	When overridden in a descendant class, gets or sets the content length of the

FIGURE 2.5 Documentation for the `WebRequest` object

The PCL helps avoid duplication of code. Instead of copying code for different platforms or using linked files, you can create a single library that is referenced directly. All changes can be consolidated to a single location, and you need to write only one suite of tests against the library. The support for MVVM means you can even include presentation logic in your shared code.

The example solution at http://winrtexamples.codeplex.com/ contains a project called **PortableMvvm** in the `Chapter02` solution folder. To create a Portable Class Library, you add a new project and choose the template for

Portable Class Library. After you click **OK**, the **Add Portable Class Library** dialog appears. For this example, you can choose **.NET Framework 4.5 and Higher, Windows Store Apps (Windows 8) and Higher**, and **Silverlight 5**. Uncheck the other options, as in Figure 2.6.

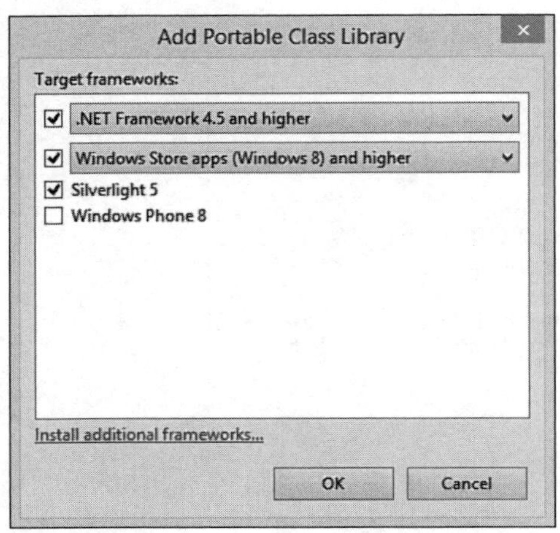

FIGURE 2.6 Selecting target frameworks for a PCL

The PCL template uses a special Platform SDK[1] to create your project. Based on the profile you choose, a reference is made to a set of DLLs that are specially created to expose only the set of functionality that exists across all your target platforms. This enables you to reference components without accidentally including an API that is not compatible.

Listing 2.1 shows the first of two classes the library provides. This demonstrates some presentation logic by exposing a command that can be run only once. It takes in a delegate to perform an action and then sets a flag to indicate that it was run when that action is triggered. It implements the `ICommand` interface that is commonly used with implementations of the MVVM pattern (you learn more about the MVVM pattern in Chapter 3, "Layouts and Controls," and later in Chapter 9, "Model-View-ViewModel [MVVM]").

---

[1]How to: Create a Software Development Kit, http://bit.ly/SRpH4m

LISTING 2.1 A Portable Class That Implements ICommand

```
public class RunOnceCommand : ICommand
{
    private readonly Action thingToDo
        = delegate { };

    private bool alreadyRan;

    public RunOnceCommand(Action thingToDo)
    {
        this.thingToDo = thingToDo;
    }

    public event EventHandler CanExecuteChanged;

    public bool CanExecute(object parameter)
    {
        return !this.alreadyRan;
    }

    public void Execute(object parameter)
    {
        this.thingToDo();
        this.alreadyRan = true;

        var handler = this.CanExecuteChanged;
        if (handler != null)
        {
            handler(this, EventArgs.Empty);
        }
    }
}
```

This command is perfectly valid to use in multiple platforms. It is also testable without having to invoke a user interface. The second class defined in the portable library uses the command to expose a text property that changes after the command is executed. Listing 2.2 shows that code.

LISTING 2.2 A Portable Class That Implements `INotifyPropertyChanged`

```
public class PortableViewModel : INotifyPropertyChanged
{
    private string tapText;

    public PortableViewModel()
    {
        this.TapCommand = new RunOnceCommand(this.OnTapped);
        this.TapText = "Tap or Click Me.";
    }

    public event PropertyChangedEventHandler PropertyChanged;

    public ICommand TapCommand { get; private set; }

    public string TapText
    {
        get
        {
            return this.tapText;
        }

        set
        {
            if (value == this.tapText)
            {
                return;
            }

            this.tapText = value;
            this.OnPropertyChanged("TapText");
        }
    }

    protected virtual void OnPropertyChanged(string propertyName)
    {
        var handler = this.PropertyChanged;

        if (handler != null)
        {
            handler(this, new PropertyChangedEventArgs(propertyName));
        }
    }

    private void OnTapped()
    {
        this.TapText = "Disabled.";
    }
}
```

The viewmodel simply exposes some text with a call to action. The command is configured so that after it executes, the text changes. This uses data-binding (see Chapter 3) to display the text and invoke the command.

The project includes three sample applications that reference the PCL: **PortableSilverlight** (a Silverlight 5 application), **PortableDesktop** (a WPF application), and **PortableStore** (a Windows Store app). Each project was created by choosing the target platform and template, and then referencing the Portable Library (in the solution it is referenced by project, but you can also generate the PCL assembly and reference that directly). Listing 2.3 shows the XAML used to reference the viewmodel from the Silverlight project. This XAML is almost identical across all three platforms. The only exceptions are how the references are declared and the styles used for the main grid.

LISTING 2.3 Data-Binding Using the Portable viewmodel

```
<Grid x:Name="LayoutRoot" Background="White">
    <Grid.DataContext>
        <portableMvvm:PortableViewModel/>
    </Grid.DataContext>
    <Button
        HorizontalAlignment="Center"
        VerticalAlignment="Center"
        Margin="10"
        Content="{Binding TapText}"
        Command="{Binding TapCommand}"/>
</Grid>
```

Even more incredible is that the logic is all contained within the PCL, so no code-behind exists. I did not have to change a single line of code within the various applications to build the application; all the work was done in XAML by referencing the portable viewmodel and binding to it.

Each program displays a button that asks you to tap or click it. After you complete the requested action (on a touch screen or touch pad if you're tapping, of course), the button is disabled and displays the text Disabled.

Windows Runtime Component

This template enables you to create a managed WinRT component that any Windows Store app or other custom WinRT component can use. The power of this option is that applications written in any language the Windows Runtime supports can then reference your component. The disadvantage is that you can use your component only in Windows Store apps and cannot target multiple platforms the same way you can with PCL.

Unit Test Library

The unit test library enables you to stand up tests that the Windows Runtime runs. The applications are created as a special type of WinRT component that can be called from Visual Studio. Unit tests are written in the same way you do using Microsoft Test System. Consider an example unit test for the `RunOnceCommand` class defined in the **PortableMvvm** project (the test itself is located in the **PortableTests** project).

```
[TestMethod]
public void GivenNeverExecutedWhenCanExecuteCalledThenShouldBeTrue()
{
    var target = new RunOnceCommand(() => { });
    Assert.IsTrue(
        target.CanExecute(null),
        "Test failed: can execute should return true when command
➥ has not been executed.");
}
```

If you expand the **Test** menu and choose **Windows, Test Explorer** a dialog opens that lists the available tests (if tests aren't showing and you are in a test project, try rebuilding the project). Figure 2.7 shows the results of running the tests from Visual Studio.

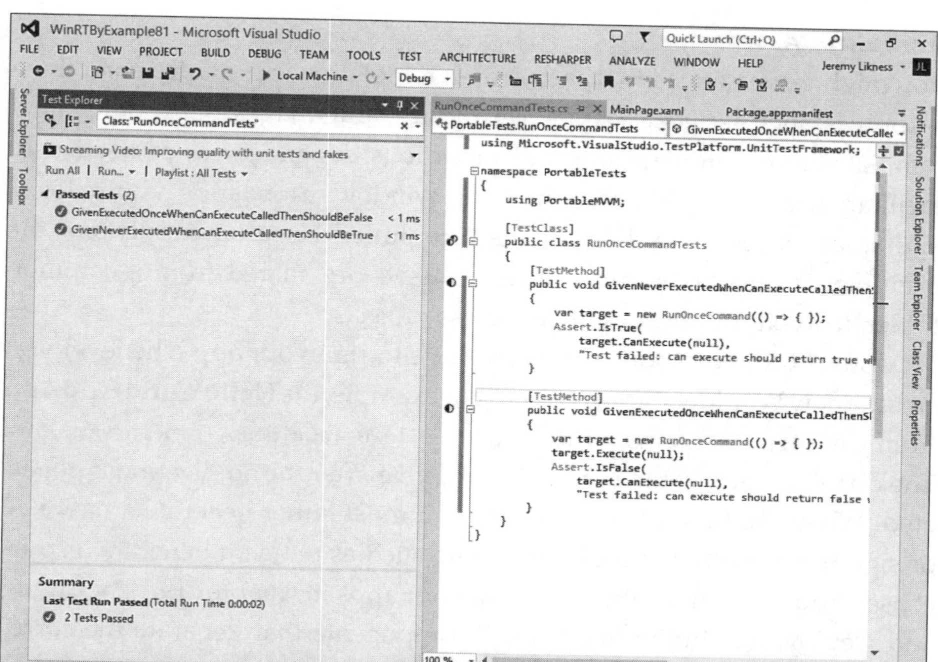

FIGURE 2.7 Running the unit test project

The example project uses the Portable Class Library, but you can reference any valid Windows Store or WinRT component to write your tests against.

Coded UI Test Project

Coded UI tests are automated tests based on the concept of recording a set of actions and playing them back. They are often useful for regression testing an application because you can save a known path through the app and run the test after making changes to ensure that the user interaction is still valid. The MVVM pattern this book advocates enables you to unit-test your logic without having to interface with the UI, so coded UI tests are not covered.

Template Assets

You might have noticed that each project template also provides predefined resources, such as classes, styles, certificates, and images. Some of the item templates also automatically pull in various dependencies as needed to facilitate the functionality required. All Windows Store apps require logos and splash screens, so those images are pulled in automatically. For the examples in this book, most of those assets are shared from a common folder, to avoid duplicating them across projects.

Visual Studio provides a test certificate to sign your app whenever you create a new Windows Store project.[2] For example, the **HelloWorldGridApp** from Chapter 1 contains a file named `HelloWorldGridApp_TemporaryKey.pfx`. The certificate generated is good for one year after the application is generated. When the time period expires, you must either generate a new key or sign the project with a different key (such as one you generate or purchase). You learn more about signing your apps in Chapter 19, "Packaging and Deploying." Individual WinRT components that generate the corresponding metadata files cannot be strong-named and signed.

The more advanced templates include classes to support data-binding and the MVVM pattern. The following list summarizes these classes.

- `NavigationHelper`—Class that aids in navigation between pages and works in conjunction with the `SuspensionManager` to handle process lifetime management.
- `ObservableDictionary`—Class that enables you to keep track of state for views by holding a dictionary of observable objects (that is, objects that implement property and collection change notification).
- `RelayCommand`—Implementation of the command pattern that enables you to specify delegates for execution logic.
- `SuspensionManager`—Helper class for saving values. It is especially useful for restoring state (you learn more about application state later in this same chapter).

[2]Signing an app package, http://bit.ly/XKaJdF

TIP

The **Blank App** template provides only the basic main page and does not include any of the classes that help you implement the MVVM pattern and manage navigation and state. Sometimes you simply don't need the additional pages and code that the more complex **Grid App** and **Split App** templates provide. If you decide to use the **Blank App** template and need the supporting classes as well, adding them to your project is easy. In the project context, go to **Add** and choose **New Item**; then select the template for **Basic Page** instead of **Blank Page**. A dialog appears, prompting you to add dependent files. Click **OK** to add all the supporting files to the project.

Regardless of the template you choose, the end result is a fully functional Windows Store app. One file included with every Windows Store app that this book hasn't yet discussed is the package manifest. The next section covers the contents of the `Package.appxmanifest` file.

Understanding the App Manifest

Listing 2.4 shows the contents of the app manifest for the **HelloWorldGridApp** project. As you can see, the manifest is a simple XML document that helps describe the application. A package is another name for the content of a Windows Store app. The package contains all the code and resources necessary for the application to run. The app manifest describes the content and capabilities of the package.

LISTING 2.4 Contents of `Package.appxmanifest` for HelloWorldGridApp

```
<?xml version="1.0" encoding="utf-8"?>
<Package xmlns="http://schemas.microsoft.com/appx/2010/manifest"
    xmlns:m2="http://schemas.microsoft.com/appx/2013/manifest">
  <Identity Name="WinRTByExampleHelloWorldGridApp"
    Publisher="CN=Jeremy" Version="1.0.0.0" />
  <Properties>
    <DisplayName>Hello World Grid App</DisplayName>
    <PublisherDisplayName>Jeremy</PublisherDisplayName>
    <Logo>Assets\StoreLogo.png</Logo>
  </Properties>
  <Prerequisites>
    <OSMinVersion>6.3.0</OSMinVersion>
    <OSMaxVersionTested>6.3.0</OSMaxVersionTested>
```

```
  </Prerequisites>
  <Resources>
    <Resource Language="x-generate" />
  </Resources>
  <Applications>
    <Application Id="App" Executable="$targetnametoken$.exe"
    EntryPoint="HelloWorldGridApp.App">
      <m2:VisualElements DisplayName="Hello World Grid App"
    Square150x150Logo="Assets\Logo.png"
    Square30x30Logo="Assets\SmallLogo.png"
    Description="An example. . ."
    ForegroundText="light"
    BackgroundColor="#464646">
        <m2:DefaultTile>
          <m2:ShowNameOnTiles>
            <m2:ShowOn Tile="square150x150Logo" />
          </m2:ShowNameOnTiles>
        </m2:DefaultTile>
        <m2:SplashScreen Image="Assets\SplashScreen.png" />
      </m2:VisualElements>
    </Application>
  </Applications>
  <Capabilities>
    <Capability Name="internetClient" />
  </Capabilities>
</Package>
```

You don't have to know the app manifest schema to edit it. Visual Studio 2013 provides a rich user interface for modifying the contents. Double-click the app manifest file in the Solution Explorer to show the **Manifest Designer**.

Application UI

Figure 2.8 shows the Application tab. This tab contains properties that identify and describe the application. The display name is how your app appears in the various dialogs that handle package installation and deployment. The entry point is the class that is called when the app is launched. This is provided by the template and is the class defined in the `App.xaml` and `App.cs` files. The default language[3] is self-explanatory (you learn more about languages in Chapter 18, "Globalization"); it is followed by a description of the application.

---

[3]Choosing your languages, http://bit.ly/X29FBg

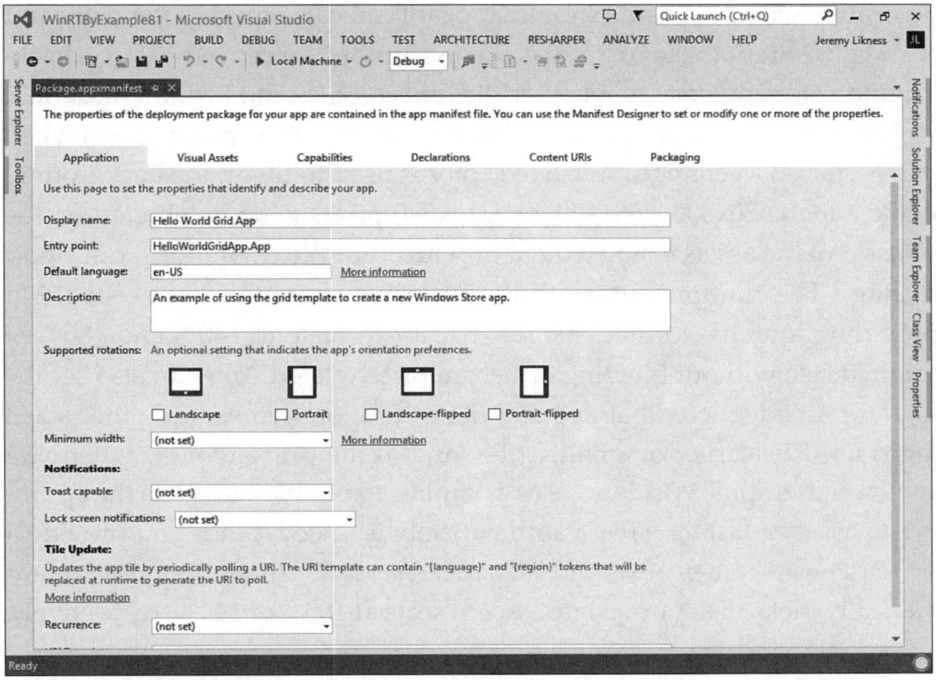

FIGURE 2.8 The Application tab of the manifest

You can use supported rotations to influence the behavior of your app in different orientations. By default, all orientations are supported, and the app resizes to fit the device's orientation when it is rotated. If your app makes sense only in portrait orientation, check the **Portrait** and **Portrait-flipped** options so that the app will not rotate or resize if the user orients the device in landscape mode. (Also note that you can test this feature only on an actual device; the simulator does not support orientation restrictions.)

You can set up **Notifications** for your app to update the live tile (more on this in Chapter 6, "Tiles and Toasts"). You can also specify a URL that dynamically supplies a template for your tile with localization support. In Windows 8.1, the URL is called automatically when the app gets installed, enabling live tiles even before the user starts the app.

The Visual Assets (the next tab) are important because they describe how your app appears to Windows 8.1. For example, the Tile section enables you to enter a Short name that appears on the Start menu and determine when the name should appear (you can suppress the name if it is already part of the logo graphic, for example). You can indicate the background color and specify whether the font color should be light or dark.

Windows Store apps require Windows to display a splash screen when it gets started. A configurable fixed color is used to fill up the background, while a logo 620x300, 868x420, or 1116x540 pixels wide is centered on the screen. All the assets enable you to provide multiple resolutions to support scaling.[4] The runtime automatically scales your graphics as needed, but providing a native format ensures that it can scale to 140% and 180% of original size without blurring or becoming pixelated. You can also set the logo for a badge icon that appears in notification flyouts and other sized logos used for larger or smaller tiles, and in the preview view when you switch active apps. Windows uses a naming convention to select the appropriate asset. `SplashScreen.png` automatically is scaled, but if you provide a `SplashScreen.scale-100.png` and `SplashScreen.scale-140.png`, Windows automatically picks the appropriate asset to scale at 100% or 140%, respectively.

Capabilities

The Capabilities tab enables you to specific the features and sensors your app will use. Capabilities help inform the Windows Store about what features to test, and having many capabilities can increase the level of testing of your app when submitted.[5] Some capabilities, such as Document Library access, require a Corporate developer account, and Internet access might require your app to include a privacy policy. The manifest also informs users of the capabilities your app needs when listed in the Windows Store. At execution time, the Windows Runtime checks the capabilities you set when the corresponding APIs are called. Table 2.1 lists the available capabilities, along with a brief description.

---

[4] Guidelines for scaling to pixel density, http://bit.ly/111GtSc

[5] App capability declarations, http://bit.ly/Uvcein

TABLE 2.1 Windows Store App Capabilities

Capability	Description
Enterprise Authentication	Connects to intranet resources that require domain credentials.
Internet (Client)	Turned on by default; enables access to the Internet and other networks in public places (when the user has designated the active network as public).
Internet (Client & Server)	Provides both inbound and outbound access to the Internet and other networks when the active network is designated as public.
Location	Accesses the current location (aggregated from various sources, including the network address and GPS sensor, when available).
Microphone	Accesses the audio feed for the attached microphone devices.
Music Library	Adds, changes, and deletes files in the Music Library (applies to both local PC and HomeGroup libraries).
Pictures Library	Adds, changes, and deletes files in the Pictures Library (applies to both local PC and HomeGroup libraries).
Private Networks (Client & Server)	Provides both inbound and outbound access to networks that have been designated as home or work networks, or ones that require domain authentication.
Proximity	Allows Near Field Communications (NFC).
Removable Storage	Adds, changes, and deletes files on removable storage devices. As with the Documents Library, access is restricted by the File Type Associations, and access to HomeGroup is excluded.
Shared User Certificates	Accesses certificates (smart cards, x.509, and so on) used to validate the user's identity.
Videos Library	Adds, changes, and deletes files in the Videos Library (applies to both local PC and HomeGroup libraries).
Webcam	Accesses the video feed from connected webcams.

All capabilities are associated with WinRT APIs and components. For example, use of the `MediaCapture` component implies the webcam capability. You must declare the proximity capability if you will use the `ProximityDevice` class. You learn more about various WinRT APIs in later chapters.

Declarations

Declarations provide extensibility points for your app by allowing it to either connect with other apps through contracts or enhance the OS through extensions.[6] You learn more about declarations in Chapters 11 and 12. Table 2.2 summarizes the available declarations.

TABLE 2.2 Windows Store App Declarations

Declaration	Description
Account Picture Provider	Enables your app to appear as an option and be invoked to provide an account picture when the user is changing settings.
AutoPlay Content	Registers the app to handle events such as the user inserting a DVD.
AutoPlay Device	Registers the app to handle device change events, such as the user connecting a webcam.
Background Tasks	Enables the app to specify the name of a class that can run code in response to triggered events, including audio, notifications, timer, and more.
Cached File Updater	Enables the app to provide files to other Windows 8 apps and provides the triggers to synchronize the files based on local or remote updates.
Camera Settings	Indicates that your app can provide a custom user interface for selecting camera options when the user is taking a picture or recording video.
Certificates	Used to install certificates with the Windows Store app to enable secure communications channels, signing of digital content, and encryption of data.

[6] App contracts and extensions, http://bit.ly/WhFJVa

Declaration	Description
Contact Picker	Enables your app to provide contact information when users access their contacts from any other app.
File Open Picker	Makes your app an option when the user invokes the file picker to browse for files. For example, a cloud storage app such as OneDrive (formerly SkyDrive) can provide a UI that enables users to pick content from their OneDrive account.
File Save Picker	Enables your app to appear as an option when the user is saving content.
File Type Associations	Indicates file types that your app can manage. The Documents Library and Removable Storage capabilities use this declaration.
Print Task Settings	Indicates that your app will supply custom UI for printer settings.
Protocol	Enables your app to manage an existing communications protocol (for example, register the **mailto** protocol to handle email messages) or define a custom protocol.
Search	Registers to participate as a search provider, enabling the user to search your app from the Search Charm while it is active on the screen. Note that using the SearchBox in Windows 8.1 instead of implementing this contract is recommended. If a SearchBox is used in an app that implements the Search contract, an exception is thrown.
Share Target	Indicates that your app is capable of receiving shareable content. Includes the data formats and file types your app can receive.

Another way to think about declarations is as alternative entry points to start your application. For example, when the user invokes the Share Charm or opens a file picker, your app might be activated to handle that specific interaction.

Content URIs

In Chapter 3, you learn about the `WebView` control, which is used to render and interact with websites. Web pages can even be written to send information to your Windows Store app using JavaScript. These pages must be hosted on a secure site that is accessed using the `HTTPS` protocol and must be listed on the Content URIs tab for your app to recognize them.

Packaging

The final tab defines how your Windows Store app is packaged to be deployed (both locally and on other systems). The package name is a unique identifier for your package. The system generates a GUID by default, but you can change the name to something more readable. The name cannot contain spaces or special characters other than the dash. The name should be unique on a user's system, so you want to include your company name and other information that distinguishes the name from similar packages other programmers have developed.

The package display name appears to users and can be localized based on the languages your package supports. The version follows the common major, minor, build, and revision approach. The publisher is based on the publisher name in the certificate used to sign the project. After you generate a new certificate or choose one you've created or purchased from a third party, this field updates with the publisher indicated on the certificate. The publisher display name defaults from the certificate but can be overwritten and localized. The package family name is used to uniquely identify your package in the Windows Store. After you link to your Windows Store developer account[7] and reserve the app name, a family name is generated that you can use to link to your app in the store.

Finding Your Package on Disk

As you learned in Chapter 1, packages are copied once for all users to a physical location on disk, and a per-user storage area is created. On the command line, type the following:

```
cd %userprofile%\AppData\Local\Packages
```

[7]Registering for a Windows Store developer account, http://bit.ly/WhHCRL

This drops you to the folder where the settings for the packages are created. You can list the directory to see available packages and then navigate to the folder with the package name for your app (either the GUID generated by default or the package name you set). In the target folder, three key subfolders that end with the State suffix contain local, roaming, and temporary data. You learn more about package storage in Chapter 4, "Data and Content."

The folder described contains the internal state content the app created, but what about the actual binaries and assets for the app itself? Those are deployed to this location:

```
%programfiles%\WindowsApps (c:\Program Files\WindowsApps)
```

However, by default, you do not have access. Although browsing these folders to build and deploy apps is not necessary, if you want to gain access, several steps are involved. First, right-click the folder from **File Explorer**, choose **Properties**, and then navigate to the **Security** tab. See Figure 2.9.

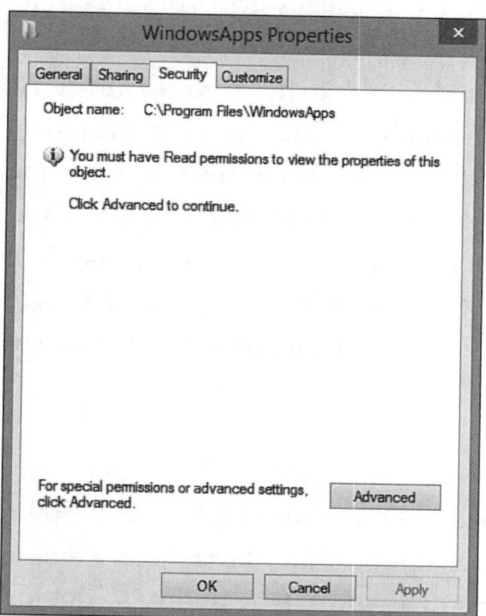

FIGURE 2.9 **The Security tab for the `WindowsApps` folder**

Click **Advanced** to see the dialog in Figure 2.10. Click **Change** to the right of the **Owner** label and the administration icon.

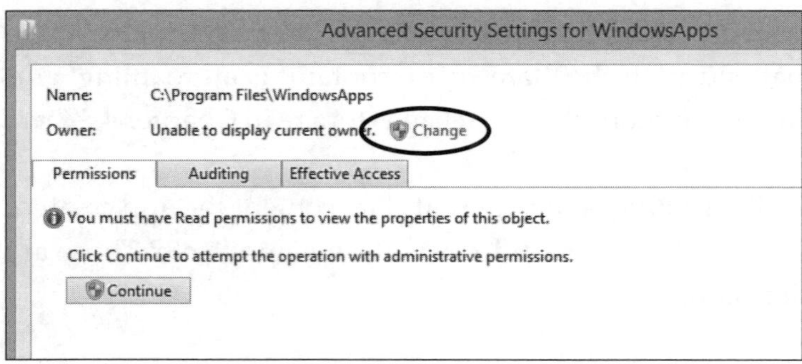

FIGURE 2.10 The security dialog

Enter the username you use to log in (for example, your Windows Account ID, if you use that) and click **OK**. Click **OK** again to close the security dialog, and click **OK** a third time to close the properties dialog. Try to access the folder again. You might receive a security error, but this time, you can click **Continue** to obtain access.

The contents of the folder are organized similar to the `Packages` directory, with the package monikers used for the folder names for each Windows Store app that is deployed. The folders contain all the resources for the app, including XAML, HTML, and JavaScript, along with the manifest and metadata files for the components. The package must be deployed before the folders appear. Visual Studio 2013 automatically deploys the package for you when you run it from the IDE. You can run and debug your app in several ways.

Running Your App

You might have noticed that the Play icon to run your app is a drop-down for Windows Store apps. You have three options: Local Machine, Remote Machine, and Simulator. These options give you the flexibility to deploy and run the application locally, on a remote device, and even locally through a simulator that enables you to test with virtual resolutions, orientations, touch inputs and even mock locations.

Local Deployment

Local deployment is the default option and does not require any configuration. Using this option deploys the app to your local machine and launches it directly. By default, the app launches as if you tapped the tile from the Start Screen. If you want to activate the app yourself for debugging (for example, you want to test activating the app from the File Picker or by invoking a secondary tile), you can change the default settings. Access the **Properties** panel for the project and choose the **Debug** tab. There, simply check the option **Do Not Launch, but Debug My Code When It Starts** (see Figure 2.11).

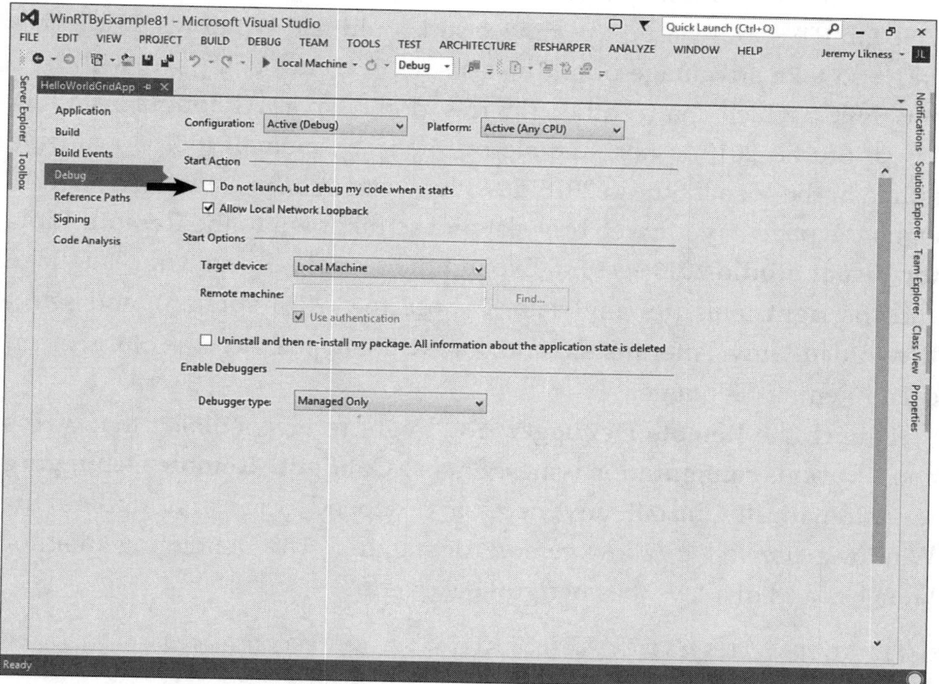

FIGURE 2.11 The debug properties for the Windows Store app project

After you check the box, launching the app in the debugger (for example, by pressing **F5**) only spins up the debug session; it does not activate the app. After you activate it either through the Start Screen or through one of the various contracts or extensions, the debugger immediately launches into the first line of code. This gives you the flexible option of troubleshooting your app regardless of how it is activated.

Remote Deployment

Visual Studio 2013 provides the powerful capability to deploy and debug your package remotely. Even if your laptop, tablet, or other remote device doesn't have Visual Studio installed, it's possible to download a small program that enables deployment and debugging. Windows RT machines don't support the installation of Visual Studio 2013, so this is the only way to debug your application on a Windows RT device.

To start, prepare the target device. For this example, I used my ASUS VivoTab RT.[8] I purchased this device so I could test Windows RT devices and also take advantage of all the sensors: It comes equipped with GPS and NFC, which many other devices don't have. Although installing Visual Studio 2013 is not possible on the slate, a small tool is available online in the Visual Studio 2013 download site at http://bit.ly/WxSSGO. Open the page in your web browser and scroll down to the **Remote Tools for Visual Studio 2013** section. Expand the section, choose your language and the right tools (for my slate, I chose the ARM version), and select **Download Now**. After installation, a new tile appears on the Start Screen called Remote Debugger.

Launch the **Remote Debugger**. You might receive a dialog that warns about various configuration issues. Choose **Configure Remote Debugging** to automatically install any necessary dependencies and update the Windows firewall to allow remote debugging. The debugging monitor launches and displays the configured server:

```
12/31/2013 11:59:53 PM Msvsmon started a new server named
'JRLVIVOTAB:4016'. Waiting for new connections.
```

[8]ASUS VivoTab RT, http://bit.ly/VsxIPm

Now that the server is launched, you can configure remote debugging from Visual Studio. Open the **HelloWorldGridApp** project. Open the debugger options drop-down and choose the **Remote Machine** option (see Figure 2.12).

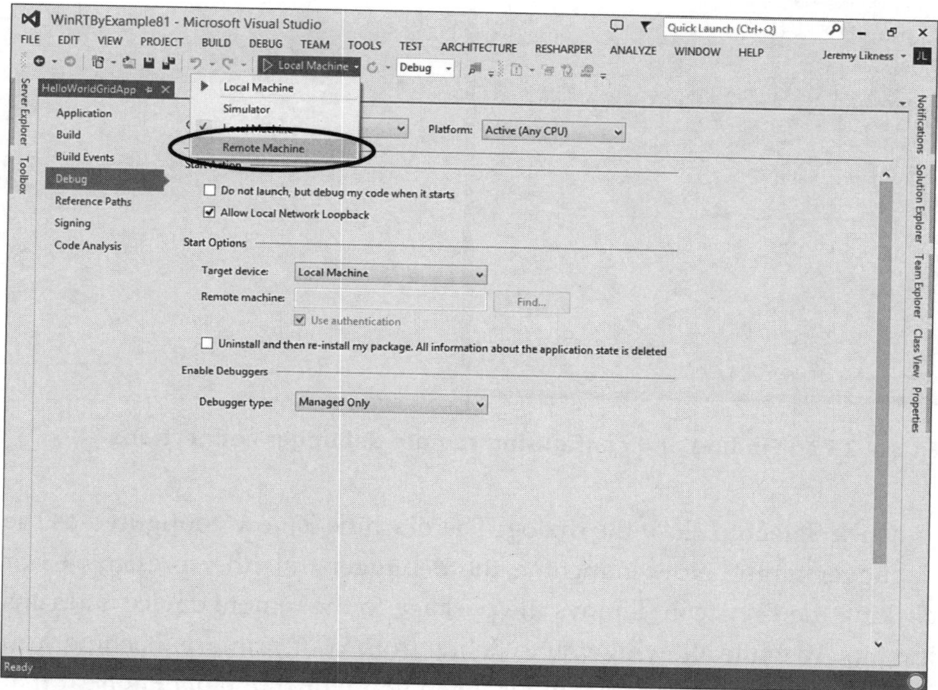

FIGURE 2.12 Choosing the Remote Machine debugging option

Choosing the option invokes the Remote Debugger Connections dialog. You can use this dialog to either enter the IP address or domain name and port of a known server, or select an existing server from the subnet. In Figure 2.13, you can see that the dialog has discovered the ASUS VivoTab RT device and lists it as an option.

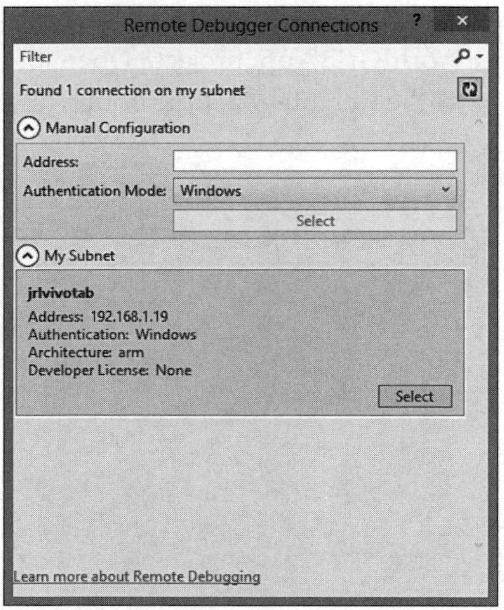

FIGURE 2.13 Finding and configuring remote debugger connections

Click **Select** to close the dialog. The machine is now configured as the debugger target. Now launching the debugger by either pressing **F5** or clicking the **Play** icon deploys the package to the remote device and runs it remotely while allowing you to debug from your primary machine. You might be prompted for credentials when you launch the debugger. If that happens, simply enter the username and password you use to log into the machine (for example, your Windows Account information, if you use that).

Microsoft requires a developer license for every device you test on. The first time you debug remotely, a dialog appears on the target device prompting you to obtain a developer license. When you agree to the terms and conditions by clicking **Agree**, the license is downloaded and installed. The app is deployed and launched, and the debugger starts immediately. You will not be prompted for the license again until it expires. It's a pretty slick experience to debug from my main machine and watch the application run on my 10.1-inch slate.

Simulator

Not all developers have a touch-enabled device or one with a built-in GPS sensor. Visual Studio 2013 provides a simulator that enables you to test these features on your primary machine, even if it does not support them. It also provides a virtualized display so you can test your app under various resolutions, even ones your display does not natively support. Under the covers, the simulator deploys the package locally and then opens the equivalent of a remote desktop session to your device. This is run from a special window with chrome that simulates a tablet device.

When the simulator is running, you control your actions through a set of icons on the right side of the simulator. The arrow enables you to test using a mouse, and the small hand enables touch mode. In touch mode, your mouse acts like a fingertip; you press the mouse button to emulate a tap. The two arrows with a circle in the middle are for simulating pinch and zoom, by holding down the mouse button and rotating the mouse wheel. The circle with a curved arrow enables emulation of rotation.

> **TIP**
>
> Rotations typically work best when your fingertips are more than a centimeter or so apart. Making this work in the simulator requires two steps. First, choose the pinch and zoom emulation. You should see two circles on the simulator that indicate where your virtual fingertips are located. Scroll the mouse wheel so the circles move apart until they appear to be about the same distance you would use to perform a rotate gesture. Next, choose the rotation emulation. The fingertips remain the same distance you set up in the previous step, so it should be simple to hold down the left mouse button and spin the mouse wheel to rotate the target when rotations are supported.

The next two icons are in a section by themselves and control orientation. You can use them to rotate the simulator clockwise or counter clockwise. Use this to test how your app appears in portrait mode or when the display is flipped. The monitor provides you with access to emulated resolutions. You can choose a diagonal screen size and resolution to see how your app scales. Figure 2.14 shows an emulated 27-inch display at a 2560x1440 resolution displayed on a monitor with an actual resolution of 1024x768.

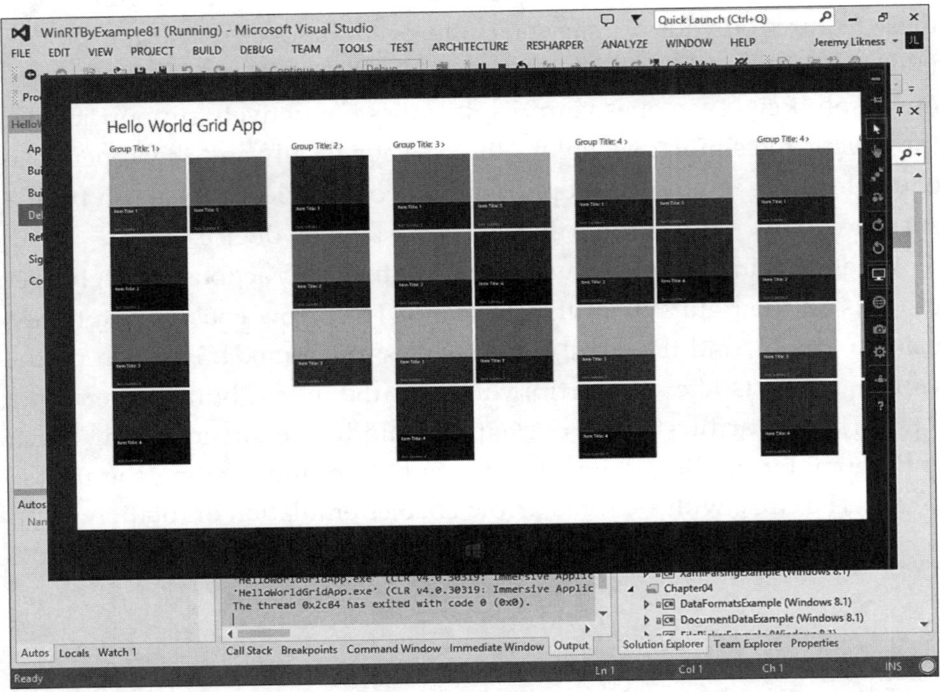

FIGURE 2.14 A large, high-resolution monitor emulated by the simulator

The globe icon is for testing location-aware apps. Select the dialog to enter a latitude, longitude, altitude, and error radius for the GPS sensor to report to the simulator. To test it, simply enter the settings and make sure you have **Use Simulated Location** checked. In the simulator, click the **Home** button (the Windows logo at the bottom center of the tablet) to open the Start Screen; then click or tap the **Maps** tile. It should zoom to your emulated location.

The camera icon takes a screenshot. This is a powerful feature because it generates the screenshot using the resolution you selected. Even when you have a low-resolution display, the screenshot results in a high-resolution graphic if you are emulating a high-resolution display. The simulator creates a subfolder in your **Pictures** library named `Windows Simulator` and saves your screenshots there. You can override the location by clicking the gear icon. Not surprisingly, the question mark icon invokes help for the simulator.

Use the networking icon to configure your network connection. You can update the network properties to simulate a metered network, for example, or change the roaming state for your application. For performance reasons, the simulator remains running even when you stop your debug session; this enables it to quickly resume when you start a new session. When you are done, you can right-click the simulator in the taskbar and choose **Close Window** to terminate the simulator application.

Application Lifecycle

In the traditional Windows environment, users manage the lifetime of their applications. They are in control of finding and launching the application, as well as choosing when the application should terminate. Multiple applications can run at the same time, taking system resources such as CPU and memory even when they are not visible. This impacts overall performance and increases power use, which drains your laptop batteries faster.

Windows Store apps follow a different paradigm. The user still chooses what apps to run, but because apps are typically run in a full-screen window without chrome or snapped side by side (no overlapping) with another app, the user is also in charge of which apps are in the foreground. Instead of the user controlling the apps that are no longer visible, the system decides. It can suspend and even terminate background apps to preserve resources and ensure the best possible experience for the active app that is visible. This management of Windows Store apps is referred to as Process Lifetime Management (PLM).

Four key events affect the lifecycle of a Windows Store app:

- **Activating**—Your app is first activated by a contract or extension, such as the user tapping a tile or sharing content and choosing your app as the share target.
- **Suspending**—Approximately 5 seconds after your app is sent to the background because the user requests another app to be in the foreground, your app is suspended and the threads are frozen in place.

- **Terminating**—Your app can be terminated under various circumstances, such as an unexpected exception or when it has been suspended and system resources are scarce.
- **Resuming**—Your app can be resumed from a suspended state when the user chooses to swap your app back to the foreground.

To see the lifecycle in action, launch the **Weather** app and then tap the **Windows key** to return to the Start Screen and either launch a different app or jump to the desktop. Now you have two apps running. Launch the **Task Manager** by holding down **Ctrl+Shift+Esc**. Configure Windows Store apps status in the Processes tab by choosing **View**, **Status Values**, and then select the option **Show Suspended Status**. After a few seconds, you should see the **Weather** app suspend as in Figure 2.15.

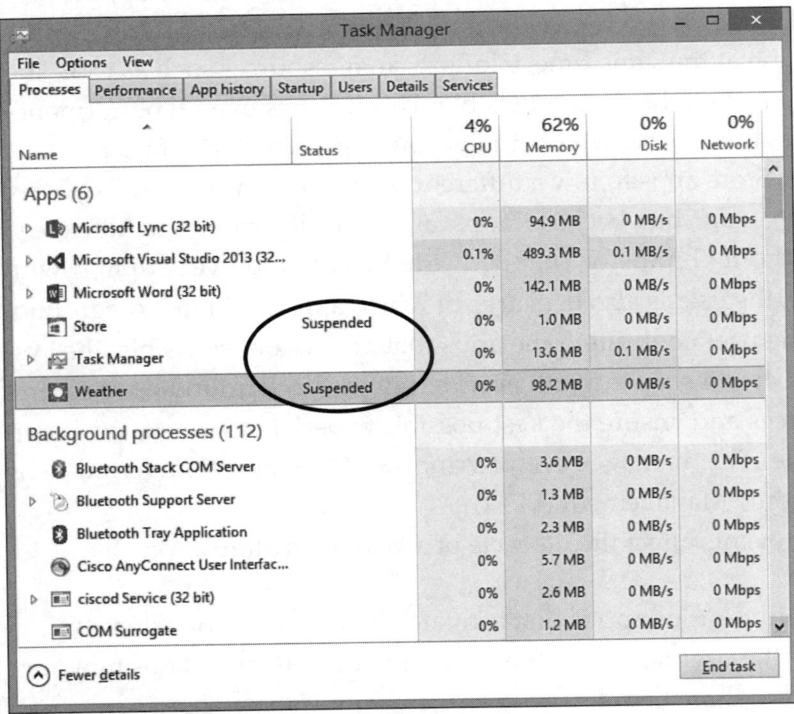

FIGURE 2.15 Suspended Weather app

If you then swipe or press **Windows key+Tab** through your apps until the **Weather** app appears again, it will leave the suspended state and other apps will eventually suspend. Figure 2.16 shows the general application lifecycle for a Windows Store app.

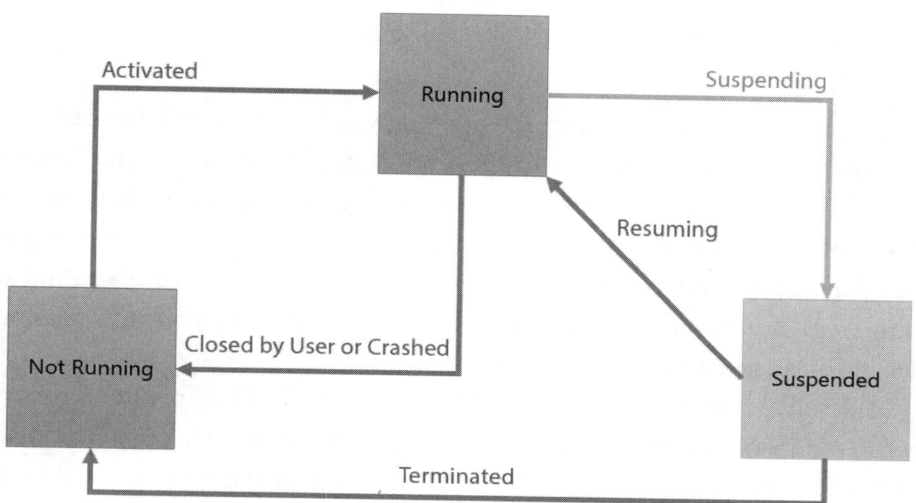

FIGURE 2.16 The application lifecycle of a Windows Store app

The app is frozen in place when it is suspended, and the kernel no longer schedules the threads associated with that app. Any critical sections are allowed to exit first. When the app is resumed, the threads are simply unfrozen and the app continues as if nothing happened. Note that no event signals when an app will be terminated. Because this happens without warning, you must take action during or before the suspension event, to preserve app state.

Fortunately, the built-in project templates provide a framework for maintaining state during the app lifecycle. Open the **HelloWorldGridApp** project from Chapter 1 and then open `App.xaml.cs`. Note that the constructor registers a handler for the suspension event:

```
public App()
{
    this.InitializeComponent();
    this.Suspending += OnSuspending;
}
```

The handler requests a deferral and then saves the state using the `SuspensionManager` helper class.

```
private async void OnSuspending(object sender, SuspendingEventArgs e)
{
    var deferral = e.SuspendingOperation.GetDeferral();
    await SuspensionManager.SaveAsync();
    deferral.Complete();
}
```

When an app is suspended, the app is given just 5 seconds[9] to perform any actions that are necessary to preserve state, flush buffers, and release resources. If your operations are all synchronous, you do not have to tag the method with the `async` operator; you can simply make your changes and exit the handler. In this example, an asynchronous save operation is launched. If you have any asynchronous operations in your suspension handler, you must request a deferral.

A deferral is simply a notification to the Windows Runtime that you are performing an asynchronous operation. Without the deferral, the Windows Runtime assumes that you're done when you exit the handler and continues with the suspension of your app. With the deferral, you indicate that the handler may finish, but an asynchronous task is being performed and you will inform the runtime that your task is finished by calling the `Complete` method on the deferral. Requesting a deferral is sort of like having someone show up to inspect your room, and saying, "I'm not ready yet, but please give me your number and I'll call when I am."

Two possibilities arise after your app has been suspended. The first is that the app will resume. When the app resumes, the kernel simply reschedules the threads, and they continue running. The `Resuming` event on the `App` class is also raised. Most of the time, you do not need to perform any special action when the app is resumed. If your app provides time-sensitive data, such as weather information or news, you can use the event to refresh your data so it is not stale to the end user. You need to keep track of time elapsed yourself.

---

9 How to suspend an app, http://bit.ly/WPG2F8 (this is the C++ reference because the C# reference does not document the 5-second limit)

The second possibility is that the app is terminated. When the app is terminated, it must be launched again to restart. The `OnLaunched` handler is called anytime the app is explicitely launched via a tile or the task list, whether for the first time or after it was previously terminated.

TIP

Most out-of-the-box examples show state being handled in the suspension event. This is not the best design because you have only a small window of opportunity (5 seconds) to save all the data necessary. A better strategy is to save state as it changes. For example, if a user navigates to a new page or enters data into a form, don't wait until the app is suspended to save the data. Instead, save it right away. This way, you don't have to worry about the 5-second limit and you are always ready to restore state as needed. You can then simply optimize the suspension code to ensure that any save operations complete before the app is suspended.

You can use `LaunchActivatedEventArgs` to determine the previous state of the app before being launched. In the `OnLaunched` method of the `App` class, you can see that when the app was previously terminated, the code restores the previous state.

```
if (args.PreviousExecutionState == ApplicationExecutionState
    .Terminated)
{
    try
    {
        await SuspensionManager.RestoreAsync();
    }
    catch (SuspensionManagerException)
    {
        //Something went wrong - just continue
    }
}
```

To see how this works, run **HelloWorldGridApp** from the debugger by setting it as the startup project and pressing **F5**. Choose the **Group Title 3** heading to drill down to the items for that group. Then press **Alt+F4** to terminate the app. Launch the app again from the debugger, and you'll see that you return to the main screen. This is expected because you explicitely closed the app.

Choose **Group Title 3** again to drill down to the items for that group. This time, choose the **Suspend and Shutdown** option in Visual Studio 2013 (see Figure 2.17). These special controls enable you to debug a suspension, resume operation, and simulate a termination by Windows. Use **Suspend** and **Resume** to test your code in the `Resuming` event, and use **Suspend and Shutdown** to test any `OnLaunched` code that should run after a suspension.

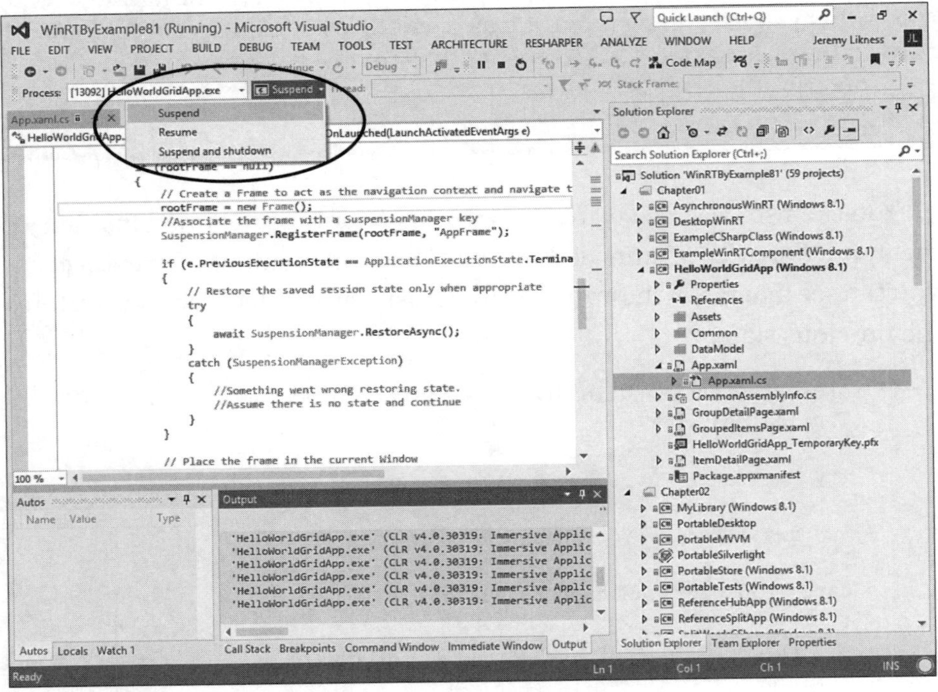

FIGURE 2.17 Suspend, Resume, and Suspend and Shutdown options

After you choose the option, the app terminates and the debugging session stops. Launch the app again by pressing **F5**; this time, you go directly into the **Group Title 3** items detail. This is because the app saved the navigation state and "remembered" where you were, to provide a seamless transition from the termination (remember, terminations can happen simply due to system resources, so the user should have a consistent experience when navigating back to the app). In fact, the entire navigation state was saved, so you can use the **Back** icon in the upper left to return to the main page.

The Navigation Helper and Suspension Manager

The **Grid App**, **Hub App**, and **Split App** project templates provide a `SuspensionManager` class that, when used in conjunction with `NaviationHelper`, automatically preserves navigation state and provides a simple means for maintaining application state. For many apps, this is the only mechanism you need to easily persist information when your app is suspended, terminated, and re-activated. The full source for the classes is included in your project so you can tweak and modify this as needed. If you want to add the class to a project created with the **Blank App** template, simply add a new **Basic Page** to the project.

The default Windows 8.1 navigation is based on the `Frame` control. This control supports navigation and operates on a set of controls that derive from the `Page` control. The control surfaces several events that fire when navigation is requested and after a new `Page` has been navigated to. Figure 2.18 illustrates how these events fire as the user navigates between two pages.

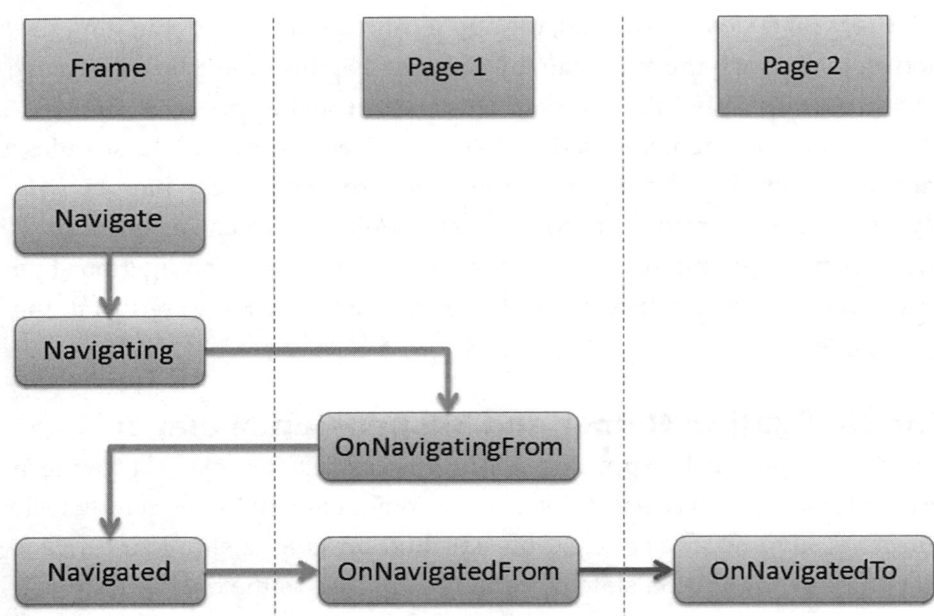

FIGURE 2.18 Navigation using the Frame control

The control offers several services that make it easy to build rich navigation in your applications. Navigating to a page is as simple as sending the type of the target page to the `Navigate` method of the `Frame`. You can pass an optional parameter to the page, making it easy for the page to process specific data (for example, your page might accept the identifier for a detail record that it then displays to the end user). The `Frame` control automatically keeps a navigation journal so the user can easily navigate forward and backward as needed. It can also cache existing pages to improve efficiency when the user navigates to the same page multiple times.

The `NavigationHelper` class taps into the navigation events to automatically manage state for navigation. You can see in the constructor that the `NavigationHelper` field is initialized with the instance of the page (take a look at the code-behind for any of the pages in **HelloWorldGridApp**). The navigation events for the page also pass the arguments through to the class. After a page is navigated to, the frame for the page is passed into the `SuspensionManager` class. A dictionary is created for that frame that is keyed by the combination of the page and its depth in the stack (this is because you may access the page multiple times to view different sets of data). Each page instance is also provided with a dictionary to store any state necessary for the page.

The `NavigationHelper` provides a `LoadState` and corresponding `SaveState` events you can listen to if you need to manage your view state. If your state is driven by parameters, you have to process only the `LoadState` event because the parameters are automatically saved when the page is navigated to.

Example: Navigation and State Management

The **HelloWorldGridApp** from Chapter 1 is a reference for handling navigation and state management in a way that provides a consistent user experience. The **StateManagementExample** project is designed specifically to illustrate how navigation and state management works. To see this in action, build and run the app. You're presented with a simple list of items with an Add button and a `SearchBox` control (see Figure 2.19).

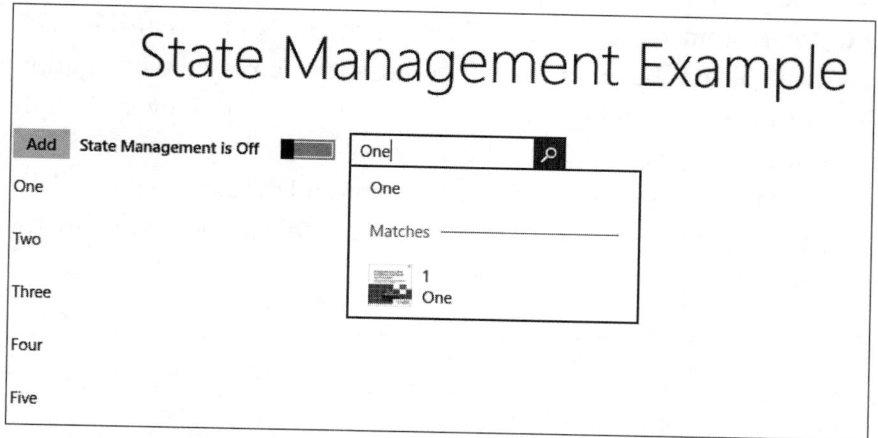

FIGURE 2.19 The session state management example app

The default mode is to turn off state management. Although navigation works in this scenario, the lack of state management is evident when you return to the main page. Select an item from the list, and you are taken to a page to edit that item. Change it to anything—for example, update the text *two* to the Spanish equivalent *dos*. Tap **Save** to return to the main page.

The update is reflected in the list, and the Back button appears. Notice that whenever you return to the main page, no item is selected. You can also search for a term, navigate, and then click **Cancel** for the same result—the list has no selected items.

Build a navigation stack by selecting, saving, and canceling various items in the list. After you have done this a few times, use the debugger to choose the option entitled **Suspend and shutdown**, as you learned earlier in this section. Restart the app, and you are presented with a fresh page and no Back button.

Now use the toggle switch to turn on state management. Select an item and then navigate to a new page. Tap **Save** (you can edit the item, if you like, or just save it right away). Notice that you return to the main page, this time with the item you just edited selected. Now tap **Add**. Type some new text and tap **Save**. You return to the main page, where you can see the newly added item selected. Tap **Add** and then tap **Cancel**. You return to the main page, and the previously selected item is still highlighted.

When you have a few navigation events stored up, choose **Suspend and Shutdown** from the debugger. Then restart it. Notice that the Back button is available on the main page; if you use it, you play the navigation in reverse. It continues to highlight the items you selected, even though you are returning from a complete shutdown.

The main page always restores the list of items and the current item when it is navigated to. In `MainPage.xaml.cs`, you can see this in the `OnNavigatedTo` method. Notice the call to `navigationHelper`.

```
ItemListControl.ItemsSource = App.ItemList;
ToggleControl.IsOn = App.StateManagement;
App.CurrentItem = ItemListControl.SelectedItem as Item;
navigationHelper.OnNavigatedTo(e);
```

When you tap an item or select it from the search box, the app navigates to the detail page. The detail page has the same logic as the main page. If you cancel, the app essentially cancels the navigation by using the `GoBack` method on the frame.

```
this.Frame.GoBack();
```

If you save your edits, the app navigates back to the main page and passes it the ID of the item you are editing.

```
this.Frame.Navigate(typeof(MainPage), this.item.Id);
```

The navigation helper always raises the `LoadState` event when a page is navigated to. In the main page, this is ignored when state management is turned off. When it is turned on, the method `NavigationHelperLoadState` uses the parameter to set the selected item. This behavior illustrates only how the app checks for the state management flag for navigation. You always get navigation for "free" with the navigation helper, meaning it always remembers the parameters you passed even if you suspend and return to the app (I explain where it saves the navigation stack shortly).

The item detail page is a different story. Turn off state management and tap **Add** to add an item. Type some text and then choose the option for **Suspend and shutdown**. Now restart the app. All state is lost. Even if the app were able to "remember" you were on the add page, it would not be capable of restoring the text you were typing because the built-in helper remembers only pages and navigation parameters.

Take a look at `NavigationHelperSaveState` in `ItemDetail.xaml.cs`. When the app is managing state, it saves text into a special `PageState` dictionary.

```
if (App.StateManagement)
{
    e.PageState[ItemTextKey] = ItemEditControl.Text;
}
```

The converse is true in the `NavigationHelperLoadState` method. The following code restores the text:

```
if (e.PageState != null && e.PageState.ContainsKey(ItemTextKey))
{
    this.ItemEditControl.Text = e.PageState[ItemTextKey].ToString();
}
```

With state management turned on, tap **Add** and again type some text. Choose **Suspend and shutdown**. Restart the app. You are back on the item detail page, and the text you typed is restored. This is the user experience you want to provide—users should be able to pick up right where they left off. If you have more items on your page that you need to save, it's as simple as adding them to the dictionary. If the app is shut down, the navigation helper automatically calls the method to save state and uses your code to save what's on the page.

Now I can share how the navigation state is actually persisted and restored when your app is terminated. The save is triggered in `App.xaml.cs` in the `OnSuspending` event handler that fires just before the app gets suspended. You can see the asynchronous save operation:

```
await SuspensionManager.SaveAsync();
```

The navigation helper always passes the page state to the suspension manager when the user navigates to a page. The suspension manager itself maintains a list of the page state as well as the navigation. It does this by interacting with the `Frame` control and listening for navigation events. In the case of a shutdown, it flushes the history of navigation and, when you relaunch the app, restores it so users feel like they are still in the middle of using the app the first time.

In the `SuspensionManager` class, the state is first serialized into a buffer using the `DataContractSerializer`.

```
MemoryStream sessionData = new MemoryStream();
DataContractSerializer serializer =
    new DataContractSerializer(typeof(Dictionary<string, object>),
        _knownTypes);
serializer.WriteObject(sessionData, _sessionState);
```

It is then flushed to disk. The only caveat for the example is that if you add items, the app does not restore those items. This is because the state being managed is navigation state and page state, not the state of the underlying data source. You still can navigate through the screens you used to add, but the added items just won't be there. You learn more about local storage and how to manage the underlying data in your app in Chapter 4.

You can see how the navigation and page state is serialized by inspecting the file that is saved to local storage. Launch the app from the debugger; then select several items, type in some text, and use the **Go Home** option to return to the main list. Choose **Suspend and shutdown** in Visual Studio 2013. Navigate to the app's package folder (as discussed earlier in this chapter) and open the `LocalState` folder. You can see a file named `_sessionState.xml` that contains the serialized dictionaries the `SuspensionManager` class keeps track of. The restore operation simply loads the navigation state to the `Frame` control directly.

Knowing that the `DataContractSerializer` is being used to save state is helpful because you might encounter a situation in which a custom class is not properly serialized because the serialization process doesn't know the type. The `SuspensionManager` class exposes a dictionary called `KnownTypes` to address this scenario.[10] To register custom types for serialization, pass them to the dictionary when the app is activated.

```
SuspensionManager.KnownTypes.Add(typeof(MyCustomType));
```

Understanding navigation is also useful so you can properly manage page state within your app. For example, **HelloWorldGridApp** maintains a global list of items referenced by various pages. State is preserved at the global item level, not the page level. That enables users to consistently see the same text when they view a specific item, unlike the behavior in the example app that saves the text at the page navigation level.

The SearchBox Control

One new feature the sample app introduces is the example of the `SearchBox` control. You learn more about controls in the next chapter (Chapter 3). The `SearchBox` control is a special text box control with a search icon. The most straightforward use of the control is to handle the `OnQuerySubmitted` event that is triggered when the user presses Enter or taps the search icon. Typically, you use this event to navigate to a new page that displays a view of items in your app that correspond to the search results. In this simple example, the text is used to filter the list to the entries that start with the text, and the list is modified based on those matches (see the `SearchBoxControlOnQuerySubmitted` method in the code-behind for `MainPage.xaml.cs`).

---

[10] Data Contract Known Types, http://bit.ly/UFKMyr

As the user types, the `OnQueryChanged` event is fired. Use that to respond to the selections. If you have a large data source, you can take advantage of this event to begin loading and caching records in anticipation of the user submitting the search. At the same time, the search control fires the `SuggestionsRequested` event. This event gives you the opportunity to provide suggestions and results. A suggestion is a term that corresponds to the text the user entered and is likely to provide relevant results. If your app reads blog entries, you might use the text the user entered to scan the titles of your entries and provide matching words as a suggestion. Windows automatically remembers searches the user conducted and shares them with the user on future searches. Adding a suggestion is as simple as appending it to the collection that is passed with the argument to the event handler, as shown in the `SearchBoxControlOnSuggestionsRequested` method.

```
var collection = args.Request.SearchSuggestionCollection;
...
foreach (var item in results)
{
    separator = true;
    collection.AppendQuerySuggestion(item.Text);
}
```

A result is an actual match. The user input might identify specific elements in your app that make sense to present as navigation targets. These results provide a thumbnail, title, and description for the element. The simple example uses them to navigate to the edit page for the text item, but you might show a recipe, an article, an exercise, or any other item your app is designed to handle. The result includes a thumbnail, a title, and a description, as well as a unique tag you can use to identify the item.

```
var image = RandomAccessStreamReference.CreateFromUri(uri);
collection.AppendResultSuggestion(
    item.Id.ToString(), // text
    item.Text,          // detail
    item.Id.ToString(), // tag (identifier)
    image,              // image thumbnail
    item.Text);         // image alt tag
```

If the user selects one of your results, the `ResultSuggestionChosen` event is raised. Use the tag passed into the event to identify the item the user suggested and navigate. In the `SearchBoxControlOnResultSuggestionChosen` method, the tag is checked to verify that it is an integer identifier for a text item:

```
int id;
if (string.IsNullOrWhiteSpace(args.Tag) ||
    !int.TryParse(args.Tag, out id))
{
    return;
}
```

If the tag is an identifier, the item associated with the tag is pulled from the list and the app navigates to that item.

```
App.CurrentItem = App.ItemById(id);
if (App.CurrentItem != null)
{
    this.Frame.Navigate(typeof(ItemDetail), App.CurrentItem.Id);
}
```

The advantage of using the `SearchBox` control is that all the UI aspects are handled for you. The end user sees the suggestion list along with the result list, and the events are raised for you to navigate. The search control integrates with Windows and remembers suggestions between app sessions, to provide a powerful interface for the user to learn. This is just one example of how controls can improve your users' experiences with the app. The next chapter has more examples.

Managed WinRT Components

You can create your own WinRT components in managed code. Compiling a managed WinRT component creates the metadata necessary for other languages to access the component. Language projection enables your component to appear as a native object in the target language. The Windows Runtime automatically spins up an instance of the CLR as needed to host your managed component.

In Chapter 1, you learned about interoperability between COM and the CLR. When the CLR calls a COM object, it automatically generates a Runtime Callable Wrapper (RCW).[11] This is essentially a managed component that provides access to the interfaces on the COM objects and keeps track of references so the COM object can be released when it is no longer needed. The CLR can automatically generate an RCW from the Windows Runtime because of the metadata provided for the components.

A managed component, on the other hand, is wrapped in a COM Callable Wrapper (CCW).[12] This is a proxy for COM objects. Similar to the RCW, its purpose is to provide a set of interfaces for COM to call into the managed instance. It is also responsible for maintaining the reference to the managed object until COM no longer needs it. The managed object the CCW wraps becomes available for garbage collection when the client COM objects no longer reference it.

Creating a Managed WinRT Component

To create a managed WinRT component, add a new Windows Store project and choose the **Windows Runtime Component** template. In the `Chapter2` solution folder is an example WinRT project named **MyLibrary** with a single component exposed by the `WorldSplitter` class. Note that the class is sealed. It takes a string as a parameter and returns an array.

```
public sealed class WordSplitter
{
    public string[] Split(string source)
    {
        return (from word in source.Split(' ')
                where !string.IsNullOrEmpty(word)
                orderby word
                select word).ToArray();
    }
}
```

[11] Runtime Callable Wrapper, http://bit.ly/VEjmrW

[12] COM Callable Wrapper, http://bit.ly/11yxZ0n

Internally, you may use any managed code and libraries necessary to implement your WinRT Component. This example uses LINQ to parse the words out of a string. LINQ is not part of the Windows Runtime; it exists as a Base Class Library (BCL) in the .NET for Windows Store apps profile.[13] This is perfectly fine because the only rule is that all public-facing components and APIs follow the rules for the WinRT type system. The full set of rules is available in the MSDN library under the topic "Creating Windows Runtime Components in C# and Visual Basic," at http://bit.ly/OWDe2A.

The rules for creating WinRT types in C# relate to any publicly visible types and members your component provides. The restrictions exist because the Windows Runtime Component must be bound by the WinRT type system. The fields, parameters, and return values you expose must all be WinRT types (it's fine to expose .NET types that are automatically mapped to WinRT types). You can create your own WinRT types to expose those types, which, in turn, follow the same set of rules.

Any public classes or interfaces you expose can't be generic and can't implement any non-WinRT interface. They must not derive from non-WinRT types. The root namespace for Windows Runtime Components must match the assembly name, which, in turn, can't start with *Windows*. Public structures are also restricted to have only public fields that are value types. Polymorphism isn't available to WinRT types, and the closest you can come is implementing WinRT interfaces; you must declare as sealed any classes that are publicly exposed by your Windows Runtime Component except for XAML-based controls.

After you compile your WinRT component, a metadata file is generated. You can navigate to the output directory for the **MyLibrary** project to see the file on disk. Feel free to inspect it using the `ildasm.exe` tool. Now that it has been built as a WinRT component, you can reference it from any Windows Store app, regardless of the language it is written in.

---

[13]System.Linq namespaces, http://bit.ly/11fBWwx

Calling Managed WinRT Components from Any Language

The `Chapter2` solution folder contains two projects that reference the **MyLibrary** WinRT component. The **SplitWordsCSharp** project references the component from a managed Windows Store app. The project reference is added like any other reference. Accessing the component is no different than referencing classes defined in a standard C# class library. The `MainPage.xaml.cs` code-behind declares a reference to the component.

```
private readonly WordSplitter splitter;
public MainPage()
{
    this.InitializeComponent();
    this.splitter = new WordSplitter();
}
```

When the component is called, it splits the text based on spaces and then returns an array with the results sorted alphabetically. For the C# example, this array is set as the source for a list box:

```
SplitText.ItemsSource = this.splitter.Split(TextToSplit.Text);
```

The **SplitWordsJavaScript** project is an HTML5/JavaScript–based Windows Store app that uses the managed component. Adding the reference to the project is the same as adding references to a managed project: You right-click the **References** item in the **Solution Explorer**, choose **Add Reference**, and then check the box next to the project reference for **MyLibrary**. The IDE can inspect the metadata for the component and project it to the JavaScript app. Under the `js` folder, open `default.js`.

An instance of the component is created using the JavaScript convention (it looks identical to how you create a new instance in C#). The instance is assigned to an object that is put in the `WordSplitter` namespace. This creates a global reference for other JavaScript to reference the component.

```
WinJS.Namespace.define("WordSplitter", {
    splitter: new MyLibrary.WordSplitter()
});
```

After a button is clicked in the HTML page, a function is called that passes the text to the component. The component is being referenced in JavaScript, so the method name is changed to follow the camel case convention (the first character is set to lower case). The path is defined by the namespace that was declared earlier, the property name that was used to hold the instance, and the actual method on the component.

```
var words = WordSplitter.splitter.split(text);
```

The value of `words` is a native JavaScript array that contains the values the component created. The JavaScript parser marshals the values from the component across the managed boundary into the JavaScript space. The resulting array is not a reference to the managed array you returned, but an actual local array that the values were copied into. Chapter 1 covers this behavior in the "Streams and Buffers" section that discusses WinRT arrays.

You can run the project to see that the component performs fine when called from JavaScript (in this example, a bulleted list is populated dynamically with the results). The same component can also be called from C++. The capability to create managed WinRT components is a powerful feature that enables you to leverage .NET libraries, existing code you have authored, and your knowledge of C# to create components that Windows Store apps can reuse regardless of the language they are written in.

Summary

This chapter introduced Windows Store apps and explored the various templates that are available to build them. You learned about the supporting classes that are provided with these templates and how they help you build apps. You investigated the Portable Class Library (PCL) as a special library that can target multiple platforms. You also explored the various parts of the manifest, including UI, capabilities, declarations, and packaging.

In addition, the chapter looked at the various ways to run a Windows Store app, including local deployment, remote deployment, and with the simulator. After a Windows Store app is deployed, it follows a very specific lifecycle referred to as Process Lifetime Management (PLM). This chapter covered the built-in navigation and services used to manage state, to create a consistent user experience even when the app is terminated. The chapter concluded with coverage of managed WinRT components and how other languages can consume them, including an example in JavaScript.

In Chapter 3, you learn about how WinRT leverages XAML for the UI of Windows Store apps. XAML controls are special WinRT components that support inheritance and can be accessed only from managed and native (C++) Windows Store apps. You learn how to use these controls to assemble a UI using special layouts and data-binding.

3

Layouts and Controls

LAYOUTS AND CONTROLS ARE THE BUILDING BLOCKS OF THE USER interface for Windows Store apps. You declare these building blocks using Extensible Application Markup Language (XAML, pronounced "zammel"). XAML is an open specification[1] that provides a declarative syntax for instantiating objects and setting their properties. XAML was originally used to declare the UI for WPF applications and was later included with Silverlight. The Windows Runtime extends XAML with the capability to create and set properties on WinRT components.

Elements in XAML documents represent objects. The following XAML snippet defines a `Rectangle` instance.

```
<Rectangle/>
```

It is the equivalent of instantiating the same object in code.

```
var rectangle = new Rectangle();
```

Attributes in XAML map to properties. The following XAML snippet sets the width and height properties of a `Rectangle` object.

```
<Rectangle Width="100" Height="20"/>
```

---

[1]XAML Object Mapping Specification, http://bit.ly/XRX03O

It is the equivalent of using an object initializer:

```
var rectangle = new Rectangle
                    {
                        Width = 100, Height = 20
                    };
```

XAML supports the declaration of rich object graphs. The `Rectangle` control has a `Fill` property that you can set to a brush. Different types of brushes exist, including solid brushes and gradient brushes. Using XAML syntax, for example, you can declare a nested `SolidColorBrush` object to be assigned to the `Fill` property.

```
<Rectangle Width="100" Height="20">
    <Rectangle.Fill>
        <SolidColorBrush Color="Red"/>
    </Rectangle.Fill>
</Rectangle>
```

The equivalent object graph looks like this in code:

```
var solidbrush = new SolidColorBrush(Colors.Red);
var rectangle = new Rectangle
                    {
                        Width = 100,
                        Height = 20,
                        Fill = solidbrush
                    };
```

To simplify the declaration of properties, XAML supports the concept of a `TypeConverter`.[2] The `TypeConverter` class is capable of converting one type to another. The XAML parser passes a string to the converter and receives an object that the string maps to. An easier way to declare the `Rectangle` is to declare the color directly. The `TypeConverter` automatically parses the text into a `Color` object and passes it to a `SolidColorBrush`.

```
<Rectangle Width="100" Height="20" Fill="Red"/>
```

In the .NET Framework, XAML is used to instantiate managed objects. The Windows Runtime extends this functionality to WinRT components.

---

[2]`TypeConverter` class http://bit.ly/Y53Nbj

This enables you to access controls from both the managed languages (C# and VB.NET) and the native C++ language option. The JavaScript language has its own set of HTML-based controls for building Windows Store apps.

The Visual Tree

XAML is hierarchical in nature. A single parent element (the *root*) declares its properties and children. The topmost element rendered defines the overall layout for the control and is referred to as the *layout root*. The visible hierarchy is referred to as the *visual tree*. Understanding the visual tree is important because some operations might involve referencing parent and child nodes within the tree. The tree also impacts how data-binding works.

Listing 3.1 is the full XAML markup from `MainPage.xaml` in the Chapter 3 sample project **DataBindingExample**.

LISTING 3.1 XAML for `MainPage.xaml`

```
<Page
    x:Class="DataBindingExample.MainPage"
    xmlns="http://schemas.microsoft.com/winfx/2006
➥/xaml/presentation"
    xmlns:x="http://schemas.microsoft.com/winfx
➥/2006/xaml"
    xmlns:local="using:DataBindingExample"
    xmlns:d="http://schemas.microsoft.com/expression
➥/blend/2008"
    xmlns:mc="http://schemas.openxmlformats.org
➥/markup-compatibility/2006"
    mc:Ignorable="d">
    <Grid Background="{StaticResource
➥ ApplicationPageBackgroundThemeBrush}"
          d:DataContext="{local:ViewModel}">
        <Grid.RowDefinitions>
            <RowDefinition Height="1*"></RowDefinition>
            <RowDefinition Height="1*"></RowDefinition>
        </Grid.RowDefinitions>
        <local:CustomControl>
            <local:CustomControl.DataContext>
                <local:ViewModel/>
            </local:CustomControl.DataContext>
        </local:CustomControl>
        <local:CustomControl Grid.Row="1">
            <local:CustomControl.DataContext>
                <local:DependencyModel/>
```

```
            </local:CustomControl.DataContext>
        </local:CustomControl>
    </Grid>
</Page>
```

The root control is the `Page`. The `Page` hosts parts of the UI that participate in navigation, but it does not render any content itself. The layout root for the example is actually the topmost `Grid` control. Figure 3.1 illustrates the visual tree for this app. Notice that the elements contained within the `CustomControl` class are expanded as well.

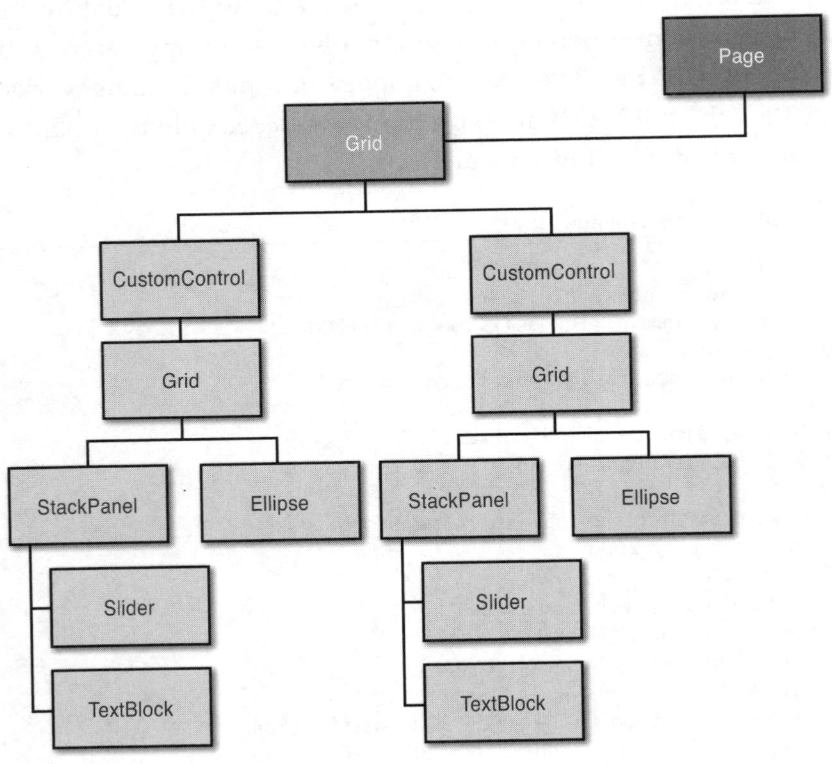

FIGURE 3.1 The visual tree

An *event* enables classes to provide notifications that contain information when something interesting happens. When an interesting event occurs, the class delivers the notification by publishing or raising the event.

Other interested classes register for or subscribe to events. This means they provide a delegate to call when the event is raised so that the interested class can inspect and react to the event. The most common events in XAML are UI-related events.

Events can be related to the lifecycle of a control. For example, most controls fire a `Loaded` event when they are constructed and added to the visual tree. Controls can fire events in response to user input, such as firing the `Tapped` event when the user taps the control. Events can also be raised in response to state changes, such as when the control is enabled or disabled.

Some events aren't isolated to the control where the event originated. For example, a tap in the `TextBlock` control can technically be considered a tap in the parent `StackPanel`, the grandparent `Grid`, or even the great-grandparent `Grid` controls. These events, referred to as routed events,[3] are said to "bubble" because they float up the visual tree until they are handled or ultimately ignored. The handlers for routed events all share the same event data and objects so that any modifications to arguments are passed along to the next control the event is routed to.

The next section covers data-binding. An important concept with data-binding is inheritance. An object that participates in data-binding automatically passes the context to its children. If you bind data to the parent `StackPanel` control, that data automatically is available to the child `Slider` and `TextBlock` controls unless they are explicitly bound to something else.

Data-Binding

One of the major advantages of XAML is that it provides for a separation of concerns between design and development. It enables designers to work on themes, layout, and look and feel of the app while developers work on the code. The concept of data-binding enables this separation. The easiest way to think of data-binding is as a proxy that sits between your application and your application's UI. The proxy exposes data but, more important, monitors changes and notifies the UI when the data needs to be refreshed.

---

[3]Events and routed events overview, http://bit.ly/Y9Uerm

Figure 3.2 illustrates the concept.

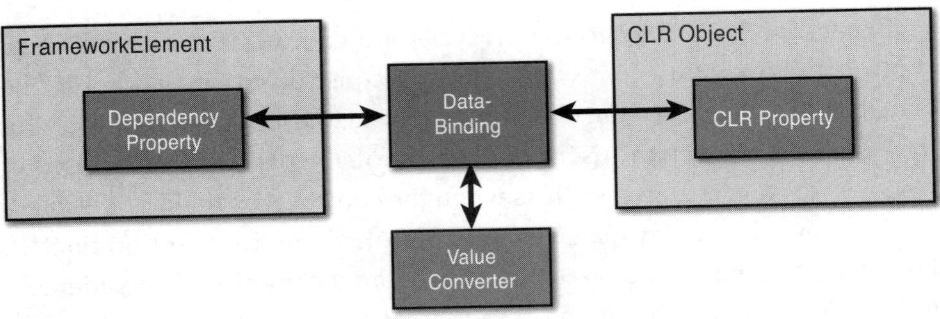

FIGURE 3.2 Data-binding

The data-binding proxy glues two sides together. On one side is a Plain Old CLR Object (POCO) that exposes properties. On the other side is a UI control (referred to as an *element*) that derives from the special `DependencyObject` class. The data-binding proxy exposes the values of the property to the UI control, allowing the control to render the data for the user to see. A `TextBlock` renders readable text, and a `Slider` displays numeric input using the position of a thumb on the slider. You can also use a class that implements `IValueConverter`[4] to manipulate the data before it is passed to the target element.

The element in the UI is derived from special classes that support data-binding. Table 3.1 lists some of the key classes the Windows Runtime provides that facilitate data-binding operations.

TABLE 3.1 Key Classes from the `Windows.UI.Xaml` Namespace

Class	Description
`Application`	Encapsulates all the app functionality, including services and key events.

[4]`IValueConverter` interface, http://bit.ly/X5ZL5k

Class	Description
`DataTemplate`	Provides a template for the visual representation of a data object.
`DependencyObject`	Provides support for the dependency property system.
`DependencyProperty`	Provides support for data-binding, property change notification, and inheritance.
`FrameworkElement`	Adds further support for visuals and programmatic layout, and exposes properties and methods for data-binding support. Derives from `UIElement`.
`ResourceDictionary`	Allows definition of XAML resources that can be referenced and reused within the app.
`Style`	Defines property values ("setters") that are reused for a given type.
`UIElement`	Enables objects that have a visual appearance and will be rendered and/or process input. Derives from `DependencyObject`.

Interestingly, the XAML base classes are all Windows Runtime components. They are special because they expose themselves only to managed and native language projections (you cannot reference XAML controls from JavaScript apps). They are different from other WinRT classes because they allow inheritance, which WinRT supports but the JavaScript language option does not. If you inspect the classes in the framework, you'll find they are marked with the `WebHostHidden` attribute. This specifically prevents them from being visible when you choose the JavaScript language option.

The data-binding operation starts with a *binding source* object that you surface through your app. This is bound to a *binding target* that exists as a `DependencyProperty` on the element that will render the data (the target must exist on a class that derives from `FrameworkElement`). In the center sits the `Binding` object that moves the data (optionally passing it through the value converter). You can set several properties to influence how the data-binding works (see Table 3.2).

TABLE 3.2 Data-Binding Attributes

Attribute	Description
`Converter`	Specifies an instance of a class that implements `IValueConverter` to transform data as it is passed from the source to the target, or vice versa.
`ConverterLanguage`	Enables you to pass a language to the converter in the case of conversions that require awareness of locale.
`ConverterParameter`	Enables you to pass a user-defined parameter to the converter.
`ElementName`	Specifies the name of a XAML element to use as the binding source.
`Mode`	Sets the direction of the data-binding operation. Options are: `OneWay` (the target is updated from the source, and changes to the source are updated to the target) `OneTime` (the target is updated when the binding is created, but further changes to the source are ignored) `TwoWay` (the target is updated from the source—any changes to the source update the target, and any changes to the target update the source)
`Path`	Provides a path to the source property. You can set the `Path` property to any property on the object, including nested classes with their own properties. The `Path` property supports referencing indexers and attached properties.
`RelativeSource`	Specifies that the binding is relative to the position of the target. Options are: `TemplatedParent` (useful within a `ControlTemplate` to reference the template itself) `Self` (useful to bind to another property on the source)
`Source`	Sets the source for the binding. By default, the source is the object that the `Binding` proxy is applied to; this enables the binding to reference a resource instead.

The **DataBindingExample** project in Chapter 3 of the example project available from http://winrtexamples.codeplex.com/ demonstrates how data-binding works. Open `CustomControl.xaml` and scroll down to the definition of the `Slider` control. The binding is specified like this:

```
Value="{Binding Percentage, Mode=TwoWay}"
```

This binds the `Value` property on the `Slider` (the target) to the `Percentage` property of whatever data object is being used (the source). The mode is two-directional, so changes to the `Slider` are updated to the source, and vice versa. A `TextBlock` control is set to show the value of the current percentage:

```
<TextBlock Text="{Binding Percentage}"/>
```

Finally, an ellipse is rendered and scaled based on the value. The raw percentage doesn't work for scaling because it could go from invisible to 100 times its size; instead, a value converter modifies the percentage value. The definition of the converter simply takes the input value and divides by 100.0:

```
public class PercentageConverter : IValueConverter
{
    public object Convert(object value, Type targetType,
      object parameter, string language)
    {
        if (value is double)
        {
            return ((double)value) / 100.0;
        }
        return value;
    }
}
```

The conversion is only one-way. The `Ellipse` doesn't update the value back (as a `TextBox` might), so the backward conversion is not implemented:

```
public object ConvertBack(object value, Type targetType,
      object parameter, string language)
{
    throw new NotImplementedException();
}
```

The `IValueConverter` interface is a special interface you can implement in your classes that provides a way to transform data that is presented through data-binding. The main methods are used to convert from data to the UI (`Convert`) and convert from the UI back to the underlying data (`ConvertBack`). The method takes four parameters:

- The first parameter is the value to be converted.
- The target type is often ignored because you usually know the types you are dealing with (for example, a converter that expects a Boolean can convert to and from a Boolean), but it is useful if you're not aware of the type of the underlying data.
- An optional parameter can be passed that enables you to modify the conversion, such as a format string for converting a date to text.
- The language is passed so that you can perform any appropriate globalization and localization in your method.

Although the example returns the same type and simply modifies it, you can do much more with converters. For example, if you want a number to fall within a certain range, you can return a color with a converter to indicate a safe range (green) or a dangerous range (red) and show that color on the UI. Using a converter enables you to make this transformation without having to put any presentation logic in your code. The underlying code can simply work with the actual data type and let the converters do the work of transforming the data into something more visual.

The `Application` class is the parent to the entire app, so the resource for the converter is defined in `App.xaml`:

```
<Application.Resources>
    <ResourceDictionary>
        <local:PercentageConverter x:Key="ToPercentage"/>
    ...
    </ResourceDictionary>
</Application.Resources>
```

The dictionary is simply a set of reusable resources. The reference to the converter literally instantiates an instance and then places it into a dictionary with the key `ToPercentage`. Any item in a resource dictionary can be referenced multiple times, so you should not instantiate any classes that are UI elements. This is because an element can have only one parent in the visual tree, so referencing it more than once doesn't make sense. Resource dictionaries are hierarchically scoped. A resource dictionary defined at the `App.xaml` is available to the entire application, whereas in XAML, only children of the grid can reference a dictionary defined in a `Grid` control. To define UI structures for reuse, you use templates instead. Templates are explained later in this chapter in the "Templates" section.

Back to `CustomControl.xaml`, the `Ellipse` control contains a transformation to scale the size of the ellipse. Both the horizontal and vertical scales are bound to the percentage and passed through the converter:

```
<Ellipse.RenderTransform>
    <ScaleTransform ScaleX="{Binding Percentage,
➥Converter={StaticResource ToPercentage}}"
                            ScaleY="{Binding Percentage,
➥Converter={StaticResource ToPercentage}}"></ScaleTransform>
</Ellipse.RenderTransform>
```

Compile, deploy, and debug the application (although that sounds like a lot of work, it really just involves setting **DataBindingExample** as the startup project and then pressing **F5**). Drag the slider back and forth, and watch the percentage update in the text as well as the ellipse. With the debug window open on another screen, you'll also notice messages for each change in value. You might wonder why two instances of the control exist. This is to illustrate the various ways you can use a source to update the target binding. The first example uses a dependency object. Dependency objects are the root of all UI elements.

Dependency Properties

The dependency property system is the key to understanding how the XAML engine and certain built-in controls and elements work in WinRT. Dependency properties extend ordinary CLR and Windows Runtime properties. They are designed to appear as normal properties to your classes and code. Dependency properties allow multiple inputs to determine their actual value. A normal property is often set directly, but a dependency property can be influenced by data-bindings, storyboards, styles, and parent–child relationships.

The host object for the dependency property system is the `DependencyObject`. It is the immediate base class for many common elements in the framework. Dependency objects provide the `GetValue` and `SetValue` methods to interact directly with dependency properties, and they contain an internal backing store of values. Although ordinary properties exist in the context of the type they are defined for, dependency properties are stored in a dictionary on the `DependencyObject`.

Two types of dependency properties exist. *Dependency properties* themselves are owned by a specific type. Dependency properties can participate in data-binding and can be influenced by styles and animations. These properties also can inherit values from the parent. In the **DataBindingExample** project, the text block could bind to the percentage value because it inherited the data context from the parent control that it was a child of—in other words, the dependency object was scoped to the parent control but became available to all its children, including the `TextBlock`:

```
<local:CustomControl Grid.Row="1">
    <local:CustomControl.DataContext>
        <local:DependencyModel/>
    </local:CustomControl.DataContext>
</local:CustomControl>
```

Attached properties are a special type of dependency property that are owned by a specific type but can be applied to another type. An example of an attached property is the `Grid.Row` property defined by the `Grid` type. Although the `Grid` owns the property, `Grid.Row` can be applied to other types. For example, the `CustomControl` class does not have a `Row` property, but it can set the `Grid.Row` property to `1`, to indicate that it belongs in the first row. This flexibility in both inheriting and extending properties to other objects makes the dependency property system much more powerful than ordinary properties.

A dependency property is exposed internally as a static field that is registered with the dependency property system. By convention, the name of the field should end with `Property`. To register the property, you call the `Register` method on the `DependencyProperty` object. Take a look at the definition of the `DependencyModel` class:

```
public class DependencyModel : DependencyObject
```

The dependency property for `Percentage` is defined with a `double` type. It is declared using a static, read-only dependency property:

```
public static DependencyProperty PercentageProperty =
   DependencyProperty.Register("Percentage",
   typeof(double), typeof(DependencyModel),
   new PropertyMetadata(0.0, OnPropertyChanged));
```

The first parameter is the name of the property itself (without the suffix). The next parameter is the type of the property—for this example, it is `double`. The third parameter is the type that owns the property, the class that derives from the `DependencyObject` on which the dependency property lives. The last parameter is optional and can provide a default value for the property, as well as a method to call whenever the property changes. In this case, a method is used to write the change in values to the debugger output:

```
private static void OnPropertyChanged(DependencyObject d,
   DependencyPropertyChangedEventArgs e)
{
   Debug.WriteLine(
   "Dependency property changed from {0} to {1}",
   e.OldValue, e.NewValue);
}
```

Finally, you can create a wrapper so that the dependency property appears as a regular property. This is known as "backing" the property. It simply passes through to the corresponding methods on the `DependencyObject` to retrieve and set the values:

```
public double Percentage
{
    get
    {
        return (double)this.GetValue(PercentageProperty);
    }

    set
    {
        this.SetValue(PercentageProperty, value);
    }
}
```

That's all it takes to create a dependency object with its own dependency properties. The dependency property system automatically handles change tracking. The dependency object is set as the data context; when you move the slider, the data-binding updates the value. Because it is a dependency object, it fires the callback for the property change (this writes the debug messages) and notifies the other data-bindings so that the text for the current percentage is shown and the ellipse changes size accordingly.

Attached Properties

The second type of dependency property is called an attached property. Attached properties can be defined in one type but applied to other types. The definition of an attached property is similar to that of a regular dependency property. Instead of calling `Register`, you use the `RegisterAttached` method. The attached property also is not backed the same way dependency properties are because they can exist on other types. Therefore, a static getter and setter are defined to hold the dictionary of values on the host object.

If you had to build your own `Grid` element, the attached property for the row would look like this:

```
public static readonly DependencyProperty RowProperty =
   DependencyProperty.RegisterAttached(
        "Row", typeof(int), typeof(Grid), null);
public static void SetRow(DependencyObject obj, int row)
{
   obj.SetValue(RowProperty, row);
}
public static int GetRow(DependencyObject obj)
{
   return (int)obj.GetValue(RowProperty);
}
```

Notice that the backing method doesn't assume that the call is being made on the owning object. Instead, a dependency object is passed in. In XAML, this is the element that hosts the attached property (for example, in the case of a `TextBlock` using the `Row` property, the `TextBlock` would be passed in as the `DependencyObject` instance). This is the dependency object that the value is attached to, and the attached property is housed in a dictionary on that object. In the case of the custom control, the control itself is passed to the method, and then the row property is set. When the grid is arranging the layout of its children, it can inspect the attached property to determine what row and column they belong in. The values are important to the grid but live on the objects they are attached to.

Value Precedence

You can impact the value of a dependency property in several ways, so how does WinRT decide what value to ultimately use? This is done through *value precedence,* which determines what values are considered more important when calculating the final value of the property.

The following order determines the actual value of a dependency property. The lowest-numbered items are highest in precedence, so the remaining values in the list are ignored if others are already met.

1. The value determined by an actively running storyboard (you learn about storyboards in the "Animations" section of this chapter)
2. A local value set either in XAML or directly through code
3. A value set in a data or control template (the "Templates" section of this chapter covers templates)
4. A value set in a style (see the "Styles" section later in this chapter)
5. The default value set in the property definition

Styles and animations are fundamental building blocks for a XAML-based UI. You've already been using styles in your Windows Store apps, even if you weren't aware of it. Styles are defined as a core resource; you learn more about them later in the "Styles" section. First, it's important to explore another feature made possible with the `Storyboard` control: animations.

Property Change Notification

The dependency property system is useful for creating controls and extending XAML functionality. The `DependencyObject` base class exists in the `Windows.Xaml.UI` namespace. This makes it available to your presentation layer. You do not want to have to take a dependency on the UI to expose data from other layers of your application. This creates unnecessary coupling and limits your capability to test the code. However, you can still bind data in a way that does not depend upon the `DependencyObject` class. For one-time binding, you can use any type of CLR object as the data-binding source. For other bindings, you can implement property change notification.

In the **DataBindingExample** project, open the `ViewModel` class. This is a simple CLR class with one distinction: It implements the `INotifyPropertyChanged` interface. The interface, part of the `System.ComponentModel` namespace (mapped from the underlying `Windows.UI.Xaml.Data` namespace), defines a `PropertyChanged` event that should be raised any time one of the properties on the instance is updated. The data-binding proxy can access your types with this interface and update the UI anytime the underlying data changes.

The implementation is in the `Percentage` property setter. When the value is set, if the value has changed from the previous value, the `OnPropertyChanged` method is called. This method uses the .NET Framework 4.5 `CallerMemberName` attribute to obtain the name of the property it was called from and then passes the name of the property to the `PropertyChangedEventHandler`.

The example project explicitly implements the event handler so that it can generate a message for the debugger whenever the event is subscribed to. Run the application and watch the debug window. You should see the subscription message appear four times.

Open `CustomControl.xaml` and inspect the bindings. Note the four bindings: `Slider`, `TextBlock`, and both `ScaleX` and `ScaleY` for the `ScaleTransform` defined in the `Ellipse`. The data-binding proxy in each case inspected the data object (in this case, an instance of `ViewModel`), determined that it implemented `INotifyPropertyChanged`, and registered its own event handler for the property change notification. When you move the slider, the property on the class is updated and it fires the property change notification, which causes each data-binding to inspect the property and update the other controls on the page.

TIP

The .NET Framework provides several base classes that support property change notification. Another interface besides `INotifiyPropertyChanged` is `INotifyCollectionChanged`. This interface informs the data-binding system that the items in a list have changed because of either adding new items or removing items from the list. Several base classes implement the interface, including `ObservableCollection<T>`, which you can use when data-binding to collections. Windows Runtime supports observable collections, and the CLR classes that implement this functionality are automatically mapped to the corresponding WinRT types for you.

You can see from the example that the property change notification ultimately operates the same way the dependency property system does without taking a dependency on the UI. You can easily test your viewmodel independent of any UI in this scenario. This is why using property change notification for your data and relying on the dependency property system for controls and other UI-specific types is recommended. Although much discussion centers on various frameworks that support the Model-View-ViewModel (MVVM) pattern, the basic essence of MVVM is the class that implements property change notification to facilitate data-binding. In fact, the key purpose of the viewmodel is to expose data-binding as a way to synchronize the UI with the rest of the application.

Animations

The `Storyboard` class provides a way to update the value of dependency properties over time. You can create discrete updates or animate values over a period of time. The class provides plenty of flexibility. You can set discrete values, automatically reverse the animation, and even apply special functions that modify the velocity over time.

Example: Dynamically Apply Animations to a Control

Open the **AnimationsExample** project. It demonstrates several types of animations that are all applied to a ball. The first example plays continuously.

In `MainPage.xaml`, an `EventTrigger` kicks off the animation when the grid loads:

```
<Grid.Triggers><EventTrigger RoutedEvent= "Grid.Loaded">
```

The animation itself is defined using the `Storyboard` class. The target is set to the `MainEllipse` that is defined later in the XAML. A `DoubleAnimation` defines a range of values that iterates from 10 to –10.0 over a period of 1 second. The advantage of using this approach is that the interim values are computed based on the speed at which the UI renders on the host device. This provides a consistent experience, regardless of the performance of the device (so the animation will be the same on a slower CPU as on one with a faster processor and more memory).

```
<DoubleAnimation From="10"
            To="-10"
            Duration="0:0:1"
            AutoReverse="True"
            RepeatBehavior="Forever"
            Storyboard.TargetProperty="(FrameworkElement
➥.RenderTransform).(TranslateTransform.Y)">
```

The animation is set to autoreverse and repeat forever. This means that the values will cycle back and forth between the ranges. In addition, an easing function is added. Notice that the animation targets the y-axis of a transformation that is applied to the `Ellipse`. The notation is referred to as a path property. You can specify the path in several ways. The easiest is to specify the name of the property, or the path to the property name using dot notation. For more complex scenarios, you can use the convention of placing a property name in parenthesis. The first part indicates you are targeting the `RenderTransform` property of a `FrameworkElement`:

```
(FrameworkElement.RenderTransform)
```

The next part indicates you are then targeting the `Y` property of a `TranslateTransform` that is the child of the `RenderTransform` property:

```
(TranslateTransform.Y)
```

You can use this notation to specify the generic path on a control based on the types of classes and properties you expect to find. In this case, the animation cycles through values that result in the ball being translated from its natural position to an offset. This produces the effect of a bouncing ball.

Without the easing function, the change in offset would be linear and the ball would move stiffly between its upper and lower bounds. The easing function applies a more organic effect—in this case, the ball appears to "bounce," with appropriate acceleration between the upper and lower bounds.

```
<DoubleAnimation.EasingFunction>
    <BounceEase Bounces="3" EasingMode="EaseIn"></BounceEase>
</DoubleAnimation.EasingFunction>
```

The vertical bounce demonstrates how to set up an animation with XAML. The example also shows how to programmatically create animations. For example, open the `FadeOutThemeType` class. This class shows a built-in animation that is part of the Windows 8.1 animation library.[5] The animation library provides a set of standard animations to provide a consistent Windows 8.1 experience across apps. The animation is fast and subtle but is easy to wire up in code:

```
var fadeOutTheme = new FadeOutThemeAnimation();
Storyboard.SetTarget(fadeOutTheme, target);
var storyboard = new Storyboard();
storyboard.Children.Add(fadeOutTheme);
return storyboard;
```

In this case, only the target of the effect needed to be specified. Animations can also be composed. Notice when you try the various animations that the originally triggered animation is still in effect: The ball continues to bounce vertically, despite applying the other animations to it. The `MultipleAnimationType` class aggregates the color animation and the bounce animation and applies a fade that manipulates the `Opacity` property of the target. All these animations are simply set as children of the parent `Storyboard`:

[5]Animating your UI, http://bit.ly/XsNsjP

```
var storyboard = new Storyboard();
storyboard.Children.Add(colorAnimation.GenerateAnimation(target));
storyboard.Children.Add(bounceEase.GenerateAnimation(target));
storyboard.Children.Add(doubleAnimation);
return storyboard;
```

Clearly, the `Storyboard` class can host animations as well as aggregate other `Storyboard` instances. You might have noticed that selecting the option in the drop-down does not kick off the animation. After you select an option, press **Begin**. The animation then starts. After it plays, you might notice that the ball ends up in a new location. This illustrates an important point about animations: An animation that has *completed* is not the same as a *stopped* animation. To see why, press **End**. Notice that the ball ends up back in its original position (with the original animation playing).

This is the key to understanding animations. The duration specifies how the values iterate through time, but the last value is always applied and remains in effect until the animation stops. The animation has the highest priority of anything that can influence the value of a dependency property and, therefore, continues to affect the target even after it has run for its specified duration. Only when the animation stops does the property fall back to other values, based on the value precedence.

The Visual State Manager

Understanding animations leads to the next powerful feature in XAML: the Visual State Manager (VSM). The VSM makes it possible to build apps that can respond to various device resolutions and orientations; it facilitates a clean separation of concerns between the UI/UX experience and the back-end business logic in Windows 8.1 apps.

The VSM handles all logic and transitions for controls. Controls are not limited to custom controls (such as widgets you create to display) or control templates (a way you can customize the look and feel of existing widgets). The VSM works equally well for managing the state of pages and user controls. User controls provide a simple way to aggregate several existing controls in a reusable manner. The VSM always targets a UI element that derives from `Control`, and the VSM should be defined in the parent visual of the control.

Example: Visual State Manager

The included **VisualStateExample** project for Chapter 3 demonstrates different ways you can use the VSM. If you inspect `MainPage.xaml.cs`, you will find no code-behind for the page. However, compiling and running the program reveals some interesting behaviors, especially when you switch the orientation of the device (use the simulator if you don't have a device that can sense orientation changes) or when you narrow the width of the window your app is running in to the default minimum size of 500 pixels (you can optionally specify down to 320 pixels in the manifest if you want to support smaller widths or for backward compatibility with Windows 8 apps that used the snapped view).

These behaviors are all driven through a *behavior* that is applied using an attached dependency property. A behavior is a special type of attached property that, when applied to an element, changes the way that element behaves. In this example, the `OrientationHandler` class defines the behavior. The class defines two attached properties. One, called `HandleOrientation`, is set to `true` when you want to apply the behavior to a control. The other, called `LastOrientation`, tracks the previous orientation to determine whether it should update to a new orientation.

After the property is attached to the page and activated by setting it to `true`, the behavior hooks into three events in the `OnHandleOrientationChanged` method.

```
control.Loaded += (sender, args) => SetLayout(control);
control.LayoutUpdated += (sender, args) => SetLayout(control);
control.SizeChanged += (sender, args) => SetLayout(control);
```

The code uses a method on the `ApplicationView` to get the current orientation, as well as to determine whether the app is running in full screen. Typically, your app is designed to handle the orientation, so whether it is running in full screen doesn't matter. This example uses these properties to map modes that are backward compatible with Windows 8. In the previous Windows version, four modes were available: a full-screen landscape, a partial-screen landscape (called filled mode), a full-screen portrait, and a special minimized portrait view (called snapped mode). Snapped mode was removed in Windows 8.1, but you can still emulate it by inspecting the width of your app.

After the mode is determined, it is compared to the previous mode. If the mode has changed, it is stored on the attached property. The VSM then is instructed to transition to the new visual state.

```
VisualStateManager.GoToState(control, newMode, true);
SetLastOrientation(control, newMode);
```

The state itself is defined in XAML. In the example, open `MainPage.xaml` and navigate to the bottom. You'll find some XAML that looks like this:

```
<VisualStateManager.VisualStateGroups>
    <VisualStateGroup x:Name="ApplicationViewStates">
        <VisualState x:Name="FullScreenLandscape"/>
        <VisualState x:Name="Filled">...</VisualState>
        <VisualState x:Name="FullScreenPortrait">...</VisualState>
        <VisualState x:Name="Snapped">...</VisualState>
    </VisualStateGroup>
</VisualStateManager.VisualStateGroups>
```

These states define how the app should appear in the various orientations and screen real estate available. They mirror the states from Windows 8. If you are building Windows 8.1 apps from scratch and you want to support these views, you might consider renaming `Filled` to `Partial` and `Snapped` to `Minimum`, to reflect those modes. This achieves a true separation of concerns between the logic (transition to a state) and the implementation of the logic in the presentation layer (how a state is presented to the end user). In the example, the color of the rectangle and some text is changed. You can easily update these visuals without changing the underlying logic.

A more practical example of using the VSM is the `Button` control. The template for the control uses the VSM to manage states for the control. You learn more about templates in the "Templates" section later in this chapter. In `MainPage.xaml`, the built-in template for the button has been expanded for you to review as the resource `CustomButtonStyle`. Notice that the root layout for the button (defined inside of the `ControlTemplate`) is a `Grid` control, and within that grid is the definition for the visual groups and states for the control. Groups are the first step to understanding the VSM.

Groups

A group is a set of mutually exclusive states. As the name implies, groups create an association between related states. For example, the built-in `Button` control has several "common" states defined by the button's template:

- `Disabled`—When disabled, everything else about the button is ignored.
- `Normal`—Nothing interesting is happening, but the button is ready to be pressed.
- `PointerOver`—The mouse or stylus is over the button, but the button is not pressed.
- `Pressed`—The mouse or stylus is over the button *and* the button is pressed. (Note that you cannot press the button with the mouse pointer unless the mouse is also over the button.)

The states are mutually exclusive; the VSM allows only one state within a group at a given time. The button also has a second group called `FocusStates` that includes `PointerFocused` and `Unfocused`. This is a separate group because these states are not mutually exclusive to the common states. A button might have focus when the pointer goes over it, or it might not have focus. The introduction of the second group provides a matrix of possible states, as Table 3.3 shows.

TABLE 3.3 Button Groups and States

Common State/ Focus State	`PointerFocused`	`Unfocused`
`Disabled`	Disabled and in focus	Disabled and not in focus
`Normal`	Enabled and in focus	Enabled and not in focus
`PointerOver`	Enabled and in focus, with the pointer over the button	Enabled with the pointer over the button, but the button does not yet have focus

Common State/ Focus State	PointerFocused	Unfocused
Pressed	Enabled, in focus, and pressed	Not in focus, but enabled and pressed (will gain focus after the tap is processed)

The parts in the ControlTemplate represent a contract for drawing the button on the screen. A button as defined by WinRT must have a Border, two Rectangle elements to help visualize focus, and a content area defined by the ContentPresenter for rendering the surface of the button. The groups represent a contract for the behavior of the button. You are given a set of states that the button will honor, and you must manage the button within the context of those states. The Windows Runtime manages the states through its internal mechanisms (for example, going into the Pressed state when the user taps the control or the PointerFocused state when the user tabs to the button). The VSM then enables you to customize what happens to the visual appearance of the button in a given state.

An important rule for groups is that they must be orthogonal to each other. A control can have multiple states (one state for each group), but the groups should not overlap which visual aspects they impact. The control contract cannot enforce this rule because you can create whatever storyboards you like within a given state. Failure to follow this rule, however, can lead to unexpected results.

To understand why this rule is important, consider for a moment the case of groups overlapping. What if the PointerOver state set the button to red, and the PointerFocused state set the color of the button to blue? When the button is focused and the pointer is over it, what color should it be? No concept of "precedence" exists for states, so one state cannot win over the other.

The scenario of multiple states at the same time does not cause an error. When a storyboard tries to act on a duplicate property, the runtime throws an exception that the VSM silently swallows. The offending state isn't applied, which leads to unexpected results. Ensure that different groups affect different parts of the templates, and do not attempt to change overlapping properties, to avoid any potential conflicts or inconsistent behavior.

States

As you learned in the previous section, groups are containers for related, mutually exclusive states. What is a state? A state has both a logical and a physical definition. Logically, it indicates a mutually exclusive status for the control. States enable you to decouple the details of how the control appears in a given state from the state itself. In code, you can simply set the control to a given state and let the VSM take care of how that state appears. This makes it easier to test and implement the control, as well as to extend and/or customize the control.

Take a look at the states defined in `CustomButtonStyle` for the `CommonStates` group. The `Normal` state contains no additional definition. This makes it a baseline state that simply reflects the appearance of the control as it is initially rendered. The `PointerOver` state contains an animation, as Listing 3.2 shows. The animation changes the background of the button to use a predefined brush for the hover state, although it also updates the foreground of the button to use another brush. This causes the button to change slightly when the pointer moves over it.

LISTING 3.2 Visual State for the `Button` Control

```
<VisualState x:Name="PointerOver">
    <Storyboard>
        <ObjectAnimationUsingKeyFrames Storyboard.TargetProperty=
        "Background" Storyboard.TargetName="Border">
               <DiscreteObjectKeyFrame KeyTime="0" Value=
               "{StaticResource
➥ ButtonPointerOverBackgroundThemeBrush}"/>
        </ObjectAnimationUsingKeyFrames>
        <ObjectAnimationUsingKeyFrames Storyboard.TargetProperty=
        "Foreground" Storyboard.TargetName="ContentPresenter">
               <DiscreteObjectKeyFrame KeyTime="0" Value=
               "{StaticResource
➥ ButtonPointerOverForegroundThemeBrush}"/>
        </ObjectAnimationUsingKeyFrames>
    </Storyboard>
</VisualState>
```

The VSM uses animations to manage states. Animations have the highest precedence for setting the value of a dependency property. In this example, the animation overrides the brush used for the `Background` of the `Border` control and the `Foreground` of the `ContentPresenter` control. This provides the subtle highlight you see when you move the pointer over a button.

TIP

Although focusing too heavily on the design aspects of XAML is beyond the scope of this book, it is important to note that Visual Studio 2013 ships with a companion application called Blend. Both use the same underlying engine, but the Visual Studio 2013 designer is more developer focused, whereas Blend is more designer focused. Blend makes it possible to "record" visual states. You can add states and transitions and choose the properties in the designer, as well as animate actual transitions to see how they will appear without compiling or running the application. If you are working heavily on UI, be sure to learn more about Blend and its features.

Understanding how to manage states requires understanding animations. When a control goes to a specific state, the VSM stops any animations for other states within the same group (remember, states in a group are mutually exclusive) and then begins animations for the target state. Now that you have the states worked out, it's time to transition.

Transitions

Transitions add flexibility to the Visual State Manager by providing control over how a UI element moves (or transitions) between states. You can specify a transition anytime the control moves to a specific state, or you can restrict the transition to only when moving to a state from another specific state. This is a powerful feature.

The included example uses a custom control with transitions. Open `VisualStateControl.xaml` and navigate to the section enclosed within the `VisualStateGroup.Transitions` tag. The length of the transition is set using the `GeneratedDuration` property of the transition. You can animate whatever properties you like. In the example, the `Ellipse` is animated to spring upward when it switches to the `Stretched` state (see Listing 3.3).

LISTING 3.3 Animation for the Transition to the `Stretched` State

```
<VisualTransition GeneratedDuration="0:0:2" To="Stretched">
    <Storyboard Duration="0:0:2">
        <DoubleAnimation From="0" To="-100"
           Storyboard.TargetName="MainEllipse"
           Storyboard.TargetProperty="(Ellipse.RenderTransform)
➥.(TranslateTransform.Y)">
            <DoubleAnimation.EasingFunction>
                <ElasticEase Oscillations="3"
                 Springiness="3"></ElasticEase>
            </DoubleAnimation.EasingFunction>
        </DoubleAnimation>
    </Storyboard>
</VisualTransition>
```

Compile, deploy, and run the application; then tap on the circle at the bottom. Note how the circle stretches, springs up, and then reverts to its original location (but stays stretched) when the transition is complete. This is because the VSM stops any transition animations after the control has transitioned to the new state. It does not stop the state animations until the state changes.

The Visual State Manager Workflow

Figure 3.3 is an overview of the workflow the VSM uses. Use this as a reference when you are defining control states and transitions or when you need to troubleshoot what is going on (for example, when you find that an animation doesn't run the way you expect or a transition doesn't seem to fire).

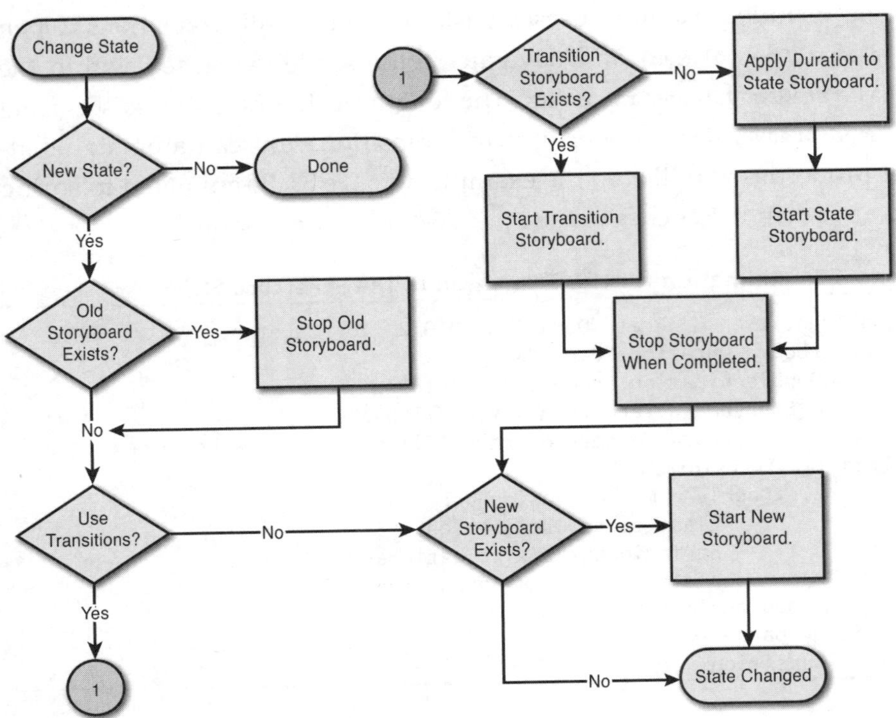

FIGURE 3.3 The Visual State Manager workflow

Note that the diagram is simplified somewhat because of the nature of storyboards. Nested storyboards are possible. In the case of transitions, both a generated duration and an explicit storyboard might exist. Regardless of the case, all transitions stop when the transition is complete, and all storyboards for other states stop when a new state is transitioned to.

Sometimes the VSM doesn't behave the way you expect: Either transitions aren't happening or they don't happen over the duration you set. In most cases, this happens when conflicting storyboards exist (for example, a common mistake is to have state and transition storyboards that act on the same property). Fortunately, you can hook into the VSM to troubleshoot what is happening.

Programmatic Access to Visual States

The Visual State Manager enables you to iterate the collection of groups, states, and transitions available for a given control and hook into events that fire when the states change. When you debug the **VisualStateExample** project, you see a list of groups, states, and transitions in the debugger window. The VSM provides the list of groups for a given `FrameworkElement` in the `SetupTroubleshooting` method of the code-behind file `VisualStateControl.xaml.cs`:

```
var groups = VisualStateManager.GetVisualStateGroups(
    this.Content as Grid);
```

Each instance of a group provides a list of available states. It also exposes two events, one that fires when the change in state is requested and another that fires after the state has fully transitioned. After you tap the circle, notice that the first event fires immediately, but the state doesn't fully transition until after the generated duration of 2 seconds has passed. When tapping the second time to revert back, both events fire at the same time because no transition is defined.

When a state has an animation defined, you can access the supplied `Storyboard` class. This makes it possible to parse the animations, if needed. You also can programmatically update animations by manipulating the underlying class. The main purpose of the VSM is to separate the UI from the underlying programming logic, so programmatic manipulation of the underlying animations should not be common.

Custom Visual State Managers

Usually the built-in Visual State Manager provides all the functionality you need. Sometimes you might need to either track changes or override the behavior and take control yourself. The main motivation for doing this is likely to create custom animations and transitions, or to trigger some logic on your own when states change (although you can also accomplish this by wiring into the exposed events). For those circumstances, you can create a custom VSM. Creating your own VSM is a two-step process.

The first step is to create a class and derive it from the core Visual State Manager. Listing 3.4 is an example implementation that simply passes functionality along to the base and prints some additional debug information, such as the type and name of the root element that the VSM is attached to.

LISTING 3.4 A Custom Visual State Manager

```
public class CustomVisualStateManager : VisualStateManager
{
    protected override bool GoToStateCore(
        Windows.UI.Xaml.Controls.Control control,
        FrameworkElement templateRoot,
        string stateName,
        VisualStateGroup group,
        VisualState state,
        bool useTransitions)
    {
        Debug.WriteLine(
            "Custom: {0} with template root {1} going to state {2}",
            control.GetType().FullName,
            templateRoot.GetType().FullName,
            stateName);
        return base.GoToStateCore(control, templateRoot,
           stateName, group, state, useTransitions);
    }
}
```

The next step is to create an instance of the custom class and let the VSM know that it should pass control over to the instance. This is done by setting the `CustomVisualStateManager` property on the VSM itself. You do this in the `VisualStateControl.xaml`:

```
<VisualStateManager.CustomVisualStateManager>
    <local:CustomVisualStateManager/>
</VisualStateManager.CustomVisualStateManager>
```

The custom implementation traces information to the debugger window as you run the application. Of course, you can do much more with the custom VSM, if you like. You have full access to the host control and the template to modify and apply changes as needed.

Styles

In `VisualStateControl.xaml`, you might have noticed a `Style` tag with the key `DefaultEllipse`. The `Style` class is a special WinRT type that can set the values of properties on dependency objects. A `Style` instance always targets a specific type. It contains a collection of `Setter` objects that specify a property and its value. The `Setter` instances can target complex types such as transformations and brushes. Listing 3.5 shows the `Style` defined for the ellipse. It sets the width and height to 100 pixels, fills it with the coral color, and places a 2-pixel-wide border using the chocolate color.

LISTING 3.5 Example `Style`

```
<Style x:Key="DefaultEllipse" TargetType="Ellipse">
    <Setter Property="Height" Value="100"></Setter>
    <Setter Property="Width" Value="100"></Setter>
    <Setter Property="RenderTransform">
        <Setter.Value>
            <TranslateTransform/>
        </Setter.Value>
    </Setter>
    <Setter Property="Fill" Value="Coral"></Setter>
    <Setter Property="Stroke" Value="Chocolate"></Setter>
    <Setter Property="StrokeThickness" Value="2"></Setter>
</Style>
```

Setting the `Style` a control uses requires specifying the resource key:

```
Style="{StaticResource DefaultEllipse}"
```

The resource key has two parts. The part in braces is a custom binding (known as a *markup extension*) that refers to an item in a resource dictionary. The parameter is the key that was set. This literally references the dictionary by the key and then obtains the instance of the `Style` class you defined in XAML. You can update the `Style` setting for a control programmatically or by using animations. It is common to use `Style` instances to define visual states, and indeed this is how the built-in templates change the look and feel of controls such as the Back button in response to orientation changes. Styles can be based on other styles and inherit all properties except ones that are explicitly defined. For some examples of this, open the `StandardStyles`.

xaml resource file in the Common folder. Search for BaselineTextStyle, which defines the default, basic style for text rendered in a TextBlock control. Other styles, such as HeaderTextStyle and SubheaderTextStyle, are defined based on the BaselineTextStyle.

Although programmatically creating and modifying Style instances is possible, the class becomes immutable after it is referenced by a control that is rendered. Any attempt to modify a Style after it has been used results in an exception. For this reason, creating multiple Style definitions and simply changing what a control uses instead of attempting to update the Style itself is best.

Templates

Templates provide a way to describe the look and feel of controls as a reusable resource that you can apply as needed. Two types of templates exist. A ControlTemplate describes the elements that make up the visual tree for a control. Although a control has built-in behaviors, you can modify part of the look and feel using the ControlTemplate. This type of template can also define states using the VSM.

The second type of template is a DataTemplate. This template defines how data is displayed. It assumes a data object and provides the elements necessary to visualize that data object using data-binding. You can define both types of templates as resources and reuse them throughout your code.

Example: Using Templates

The included **TemplatesExample** project demonstrates how to use templates to customize the look and feel of a control, as well as represent data. The data is represented using the MessageInstance class. It contains the text of a message and an enumeration value for the type of message. The ViewModel class exposes a list of messages in an ObservableCollection so that data-binding is aware when items are added to the list. It exposes a command to add a random message to the list.

This approach provides several advantages. Using data-binding instead of manipulating controls directly enables you to test portions of your application independent of the UI. For example, you could write unit tests for both the `AddMessageCommand` implementation and the `ViewModel` implementation without any UI. The former would test that the command is enabled only when a delegate has been passed in and that the `Execute` method calls the delegate. The latter could then mock the command and validate that the `GenerateMessage` method successfully creates a new message and adds it to the list.

The second advantage is evident when you are in the Visual Studio designer. Figure 3.4 shows how `MainPage.xaml` looks. Notice that there are actual items populated in the `ListView` control. Instead of an empty control on the screen, the control contains formatted content. This enables you to tweak the look and feel and preview how the final app will look.

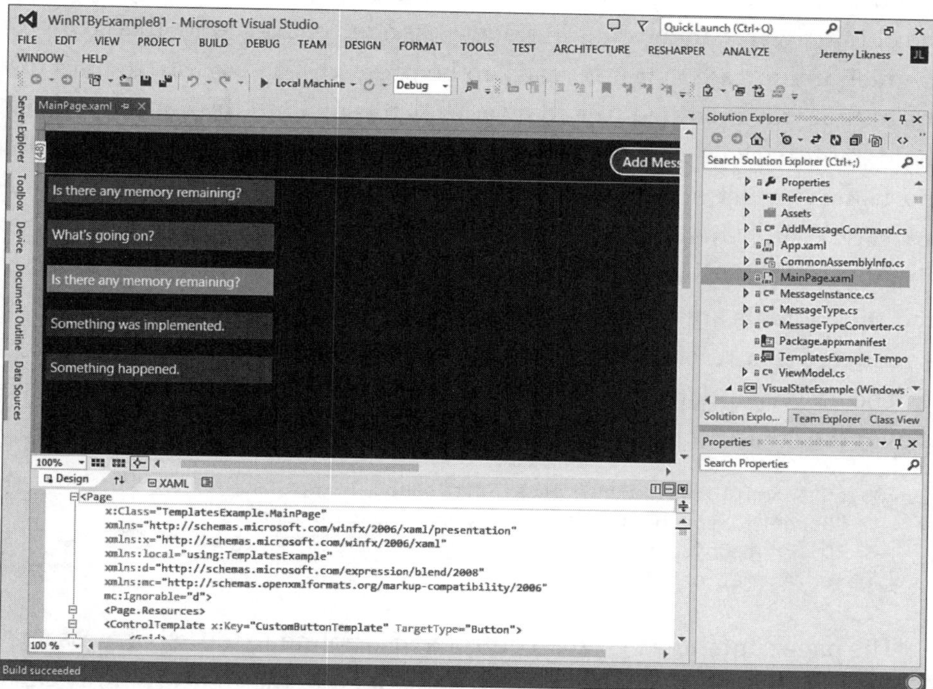

FIGURE 3.4 The design-time view

The `ViewModel` class adds the design data. The constructor checks to see whether the designer is creating the instance (in the Visual Studio designer, XAML classes and associated data-binding objects are instantiated to render the design surface). If the app is not in design mode, the constructor exits. Otherwise, it generates five sample messages that are then rendered to the display through data-binding.

```
if (!Windows.ApplicationModel.DesignMode.DesignModeEnabled)
{
    return;
}
for (var x = 0; x < 5; x++)
{
    this.AddMessage.Execute(null);
}
```

The example demonstrates both types of templates. You might notice that the Add button is rounded and that it changes colors when you move the pointer over it. In the default state, it has a red background; this changes to green to indicate that it is ready to be pressed. The `ControlTemplate` for the button was modified to add a `CornerRadius` of 15 to the border and set the default background to `DarkRed`. You can completely re-create the button using any set of elements. The only requirement is that you place a `ContentPresenter` that binds to the `Content` of the button somewhere in the visual tree. Everything you define becomes chrome for the `Button` control, and the contents are rendered within (by default, if `Content` is set to `text`, it is rendered in a `TextBlock` control).

The VSM is updated to set the background to `DarkGreen` when the pointer is over the control.

```
<ObjectAnimationUsingKeyFrames Storyboard.TargetName=
    "Border" Storyboard.TargetProperty="Background">
    <DiscreteObjectKeyFrame KeyTime="0" Value="DarkGreen" />
</ObjectAnimationUsingKeyFrames>
```

The page contains a `ListView` control that is bound to the list of messages (the `Messages` property on the `ViewModel`). By default, the control simply calls the `ToString` method on the data objects in the list and renders them using a `TextBlock` control. In the example, a `DataTemplate` is specified using the `ItemTemplate` property that describes how to render the `MessageInstance` elements.

```
<ListView Grid.Row="1"
          ItemsSource="{Binding Messages}"
          ItemTemplate="{StaticResource MessageTemplate}">
```

The `DataTemplate` defines a `Grid` with a background that is set using a value converter and a `TextBlock` that displays the text. Note that the templates can specify data-binding directives and also reference styles. The `TextBlock` uses the `MessageStyle` to define the properties of the text. The `ListView` control reuses the template itself for every element that it renders.

So far, you've seen the use of the `Grid` control to define layout and the `ListView` control to render a list of items. WinRT provides several built-in controls that help define the layout of your apps. Each control handles layouts in a different way; understanding the differences can help you choose the appropriate layouts your app needs.

Layouts

Many apps must display data, either as a raw list of content or grouped into logical categories. You learn more about how to retrieve and store data in Chapter 4, "Data and Content." For displaying data, WinRT provides several controls that help you specify how you want to show the information in your app. These controls can display data in a horizontal, vertical, or grid format and have varying levels of support for logical groups or categories of data. All layouts derive from a special base control called the `Panel`.

Panel

This is the base class for all elements that have children. It provides various properties and methods for positioning and arranging child UI elements. It is most often used as a base class for more specialized controls that arrange children.

Border

The `Border` control is a special control that takes only a single child element. The purpose of the border is to provide a border, background, or both around the child object. You can provide an outline, fill the background, and even specify rounding to style how the child element is framed.

Canvas

The `Canvas` best accommodates a fixed surface. It is used when you need specific precision over the layout of your containers and when you are not building a fluid layout. The `Canvas` hosts other controls on a simple matrix; you position children by specifying the offset from the top-left corner of the `Canvas` to the top-left corner of the element. The `Canvas` enables you to specify a `ZIndex` to control how elements are rendered relative to each other. Higher values cause the controls to render closer to the viewer, or the top of the stack of controls.

The `Canvas` always provides a fixed layout. It does not respond to resize events and, therefore, does not flow children to fit smaller or larger screen sizes. It is the least flexible of all the built-in panel types.

Grid

The `Grid` is by far the most common—and the most powerful—layout control. The `Grid` is often compared to an HTML table because it enables you to specify rows and columns. The layout system in XAML is flexible. You can specify the size of cells based on pixels, points, a ratio relative to other cells, or automatic sizing based on the cell contents. You also can nest controls inside other controls. A common layout practice is to define an automatic or fixed height or width for the navigation or ribbon bar and then allow the remaining cells to expand to fit the available width.

One important feature of the `Grid` is that it participates well in fluid layouts. It is capable of stretching to fill the available space within the parent container, and it can accommodate the varying size requirements of its contents. You can specify the `GridLength` property that determines the width of a column or the height of a row in three ways:

- Using points
- Using `Auto` to determine the size based on the dimensions of the child elements contained within the cell
- Using star notation, which represents a fraction of the remaining available space

The star notation is probably the trickiest to understand. The star modifier simply indicates the remaining space. The star modifier by itself represents 1 unit of the remaining available space. When you specify a different value, the proportion changes by that value. Table 3.4 illustrates how the star values are computed, given a grid that is exactly 400 pixels wide.

TABLE 3.4 Grid Sizes Using the Star Notation for a 400-Pixel-Wide Grid

Column 1	Column 2	Column 3	Formula
`*133.33`	`*133.33`	`*133.34`	1 + 1 + 1 = 3. Each column is 1/3 of 400.
`*200`	`0.5*100`	`0.5*100`	1 + 0.5 + 0.5 = 2. The first column is 1/2 of 400. The remaining columns are 1/4 of 400 (0.5/2).
`1*66.666`	`2*133.334`	`3*200`	1 + 2 + 3 = 6. The first column is 1/6 of 400, the second is 1/3, and the third is 1/2.
100100	`0.5*60`	`2*240`	0.5 + 2 = 2.5. The first column takes 100, so the remaining columns have 300. 0.5/2.5 = 1/5 of 300, 2/2.5 = 4/5 of 300.

The way the grid handles arranging and measuring is important because it can impact how you design custom controls.

`StackPanel`

The `StackPanel` is a special panel that stacks children either horizontally or vertically, depending on its orientation. It is a good choice when you don't have the requirement to align columns or rows, or when you have a dynamic list of items that you want to add without having to compute rows and columns beforehand. Based on its orientation, the `StackPanel` automatically computes the height or width of the element and places it either to the right or at the bottom of the previous control.

The caveat to using the `StackPanel` is that it always assumes infinite space in the orientation direction for its children. To view all items within a `StackPanel`, you must use a `ScrollViewer` to scroll the virtual pane. If you require a control to size based on available space, you need to use a `WrapGrid`, described in the "WrapGrid" section. The stack panel is best suited to smaller lists of data that you know can size and fit within the available space.

`VirtualizingPanel` and `VirtualizingStackPanel`

A specialized panel, referred to as a *virtualizing panel,* helps you deal with large amounts of data. The `ListBox` control uses the virtualizing stack panel for the default container to lay out content. It can be overridden, but there is a good reason for using it.

The ordinary stack panel takes on an infinite number of items because it provides an infinite length for the orientation. If you provide 5,000 items, the stack panel will generate 5,000 items even if the display will fit only 10 of them. This can obviously lead to tremendous overhead when dealing with large datasets.

The virtualizing stack panel, on the other hand, computes the required size for only the subset of data that is available to render on the display. If only ten items can fit, the virtualizing stack panel instantiates only ten controls. When the user scrolls through the list, it keeps the same fixed number of controls but swaps the content of the data.

The drawback to using a virtualizing stack panel is that the scrolling is not smooth. In the **LayoutsExample** project, two list boxes are rendered; one is overridden to use the base stack panel. You'll find that the base stack panel allows for smooth scrolling—you can slide the thumb a few pixels and reveal only part of the control that is off the top or bottom of the scroll window. In the virtualized stack panel, you can scroll only one item at a time—you cannot use a partial scroll because the entire item is swapped into or out of view. This is the tradeoff between handling large amounts of data without degrading performance and providing a smooth UI. You can also build a custom control that provides the benefits of both; many third-party control vendors have done this and provide it as part of their control suite.

`WrapGrid`

This control is a special type of grid that automatically handles rows and columns based on the data passed to it. Unlike a `Grid` control, which requires you to specify a specific row or column, the `WrapGrid` does this for you. It positions the child elements sequentially from left to right or top to bottom, based on an orientation, and then wraps to the next row or column.

This is a powerful control because it allows the data to flow and fill the available screen size by taking up as many rows and columns as are available. The user can still swipe to view more items as needed. This keeps you from having to compute how much available space exists because the grid resizes based on the current resolution.

`VariableSizedWrapGrid`

The Windows 8.1 Start screen is a great example of what the `VariableSizedWrapGrid` can do. Notice that some tiles are longer than others, so elements in the grid take up different amounts of space. This is common when you want to display different types of elements in the grid and some have different orientations or dimensions.

You can specify how many cells an item takes up in this grid in two ways. The first is to use the `VariableSizedWrapGrid.ColumnSpan` and `VariableSizedWrapGrid.RowSpan` attached properties on a child element. This technique instructs the host grid to span the required cells for that item. Figure 3.5 shows an example of the `VariableSizedWrapGrid` as it is used for the layout of a `GridView` control.

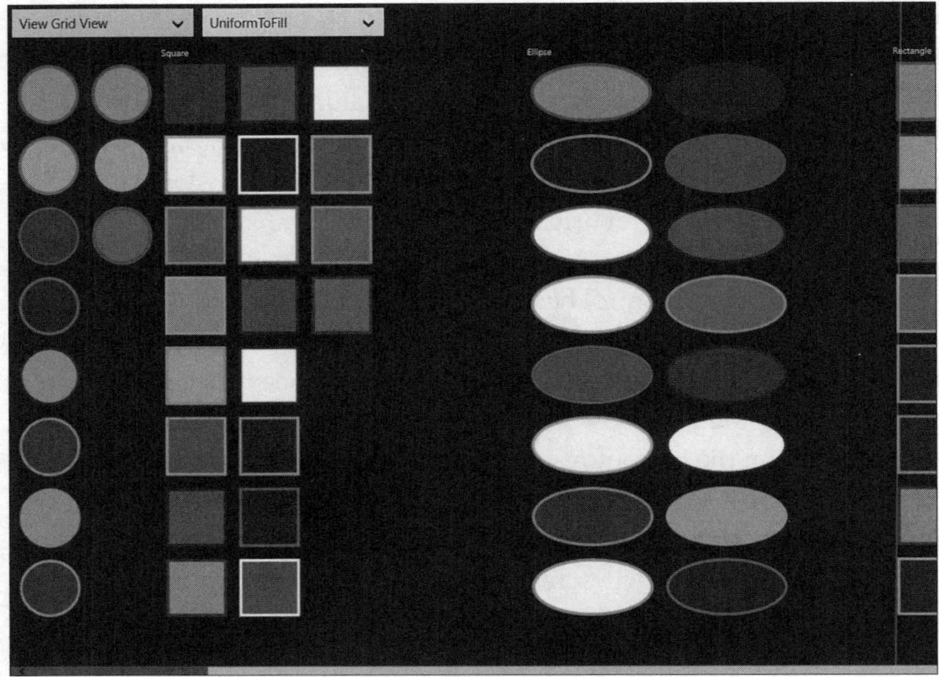

FIGURE 3.5 The `VariableSizedWrapGrid` control

Notice how the ellipses organize into neat columns, despite being twice as wide as the circles or squares. You'll learn more about how this is accomplished when you read about the **LayoutsExample** in the section "Example: Using the Viewbox and Various Layouts."

ContentControl

The `ContentControl` is the most basic container. It is simply a control with a single child element. It does not, by itself, specify any form of layout. The `ContentControl` is often used to mark a spot where a control (or controls) might render later, or for controls that can have one content item to inherit from. Note that the default behavior of the `ContentControl` is to provide a best fit for the child control.

Because of the behavior of the `ContentControl`, even when the container has stretched to fill the available space, it does not provide that space to the child. Unless the child has a fixed height and width, the child is not given any size to expand into, so `Stretch` ends up sizing the control to `0`. When a `HorizontalAlignment` and/or `VerticalAlignment` is specified, the child can position itself relative to the parent container; if the specification is `Stretch`, it gets the entire space to expand into.

`ItemsControl`

The `ItemsControl` is a special container designed for a collection of children. It is most often used with controls that require lists of data, such as list boxes and combo boxes. Figure 3.6 shows an example of this control. Notice that no scrolling or selection is available with the control.

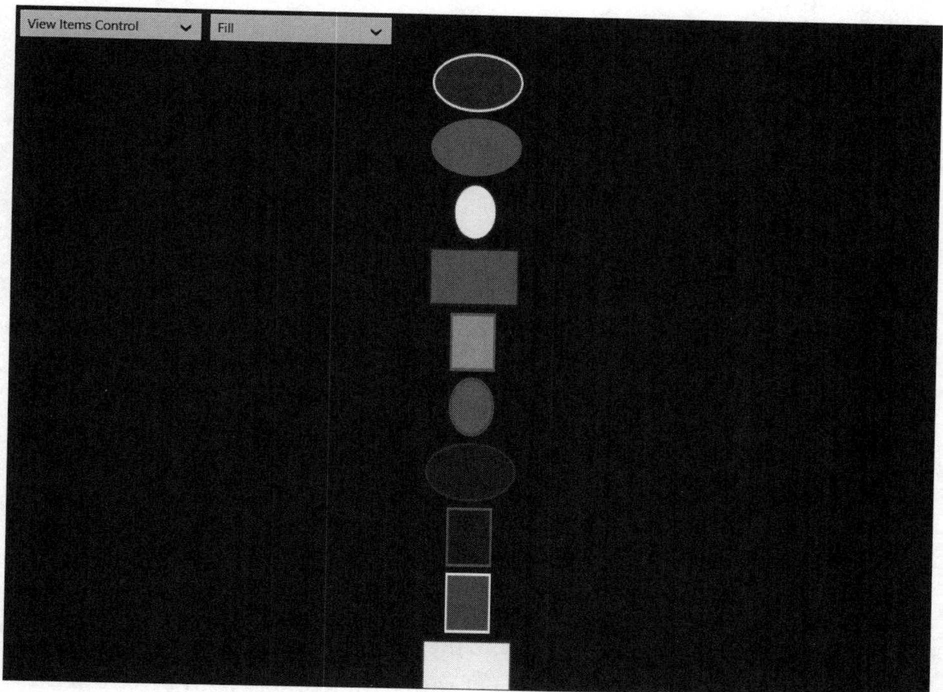

FIGURE 3.6 The `ItemsControl` control

In addition to a panel that determines how to arrange the content, the control exposes the `ItemsSource` property. You can assign this property any enumerable sequence (one that supports `IEnumerable`) that is used to generate the content for the control.

ScrollViewer

The `ScrollViewer` wraps a scrollable list of other UI elements. The `ScrollViewer` contains a virtual surface that is as large as is needed to render all the content. It contains only a single element that, in turn, can be anything from a control to a panel that has its own children. If the child item is a list that contains 1,000 items and each is 20 units high, the virtual surface of the `ScrollViewer` will be 20,000 units high. The "view port" is the visible portion of the `ScrollViewer` and represents the subset of the extent that is scrolled into view. `ScrollViewers` can scroll horizontally, vertically, or both. The `ScrollViewer` is built into most of the WinRT controls that support lists and views.

ViewBox

The `ViewBox` is a unique container. The sole purpose of the `ViewBox` is to resize content. You can create content that is a virtual size and then shape it to fit the visible screen. The `ViewBox` enables you to determine the method it uses to stretch the content to fill the available space. The different modes are as follows:

- `None`—The content is not resized and is simply clipped to fill the view box.
- `Fill`—The content is distorted to fill the space, and the aspect ratio is changed as needed.
- `Uniform`—The content is sized to fill the space as best as possible without changing the aspect ratio ("banding" might occur, with additional whitespace to the top and bottom or sides of the content).
- `UniformToFill`—The content is sized to fill the maximum space possible while preserving the aspect ratio (the content will be clipped if the aspect ratios don't match).

The various settings are easier to visualize with an example. You learn more about the **LayoutsExample** later in this chapter in an example that includes a visualization of the `Viewbox` control.

`GridView`

The `GridView` control is a powerful control that enables you to display a list of data in a format that is easy for the user to navigate. An important feature of the control is that it can handle grouped data. This means you can categorize long lists and provide subheaders to logically organize the data. Figure 3.5 showed an example of the `GridView`. Note how the shapes are grouped together with subheadings.

`ListBox`

The `ListBox` control is included to provide a comparison with the newer controls. It is capable of listing items but lacks the more advanced features of the `ListView` control (see Figure 3.7).

FIGURE 3.7 The `ListBox` control

The `ListBox` does not provide enhanced selection capabilities and does not support grouped data. However, it does facilitate simple selection and automatically wraps content in a `ScrollViewer`.

`ListView`

The `ListView` control is similar to the `GridView` control. The main difference is that the default orientation is vertical instead of horizontal. It is designed for more narrow views, such as when the application is snapped. It also has full support for grouping text with custom headings, as Figure 3.8 shows.

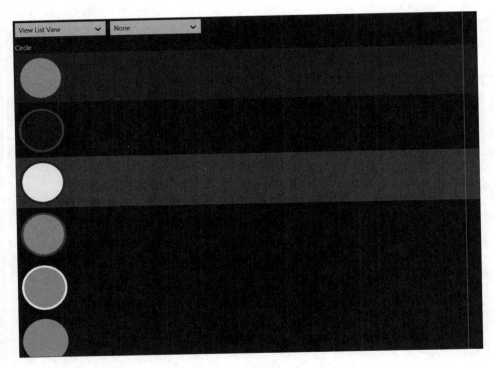

FIGURE 3.8 A `ListView` with a custom header showing

`FlipView`

The `FlipView` is a unique new control for iterating through elements in a list. It displays one item at a time and enables you to swipe left or right to navigate the list. It comes with a built-in animation that automatically slides the current item off the screen while sliding the new item into the current display when you are using touch. It is useful for close-up navigation of individual items or for flipping through items rapidly to see detail. Figure 3.9 shows the `FlipView` control.

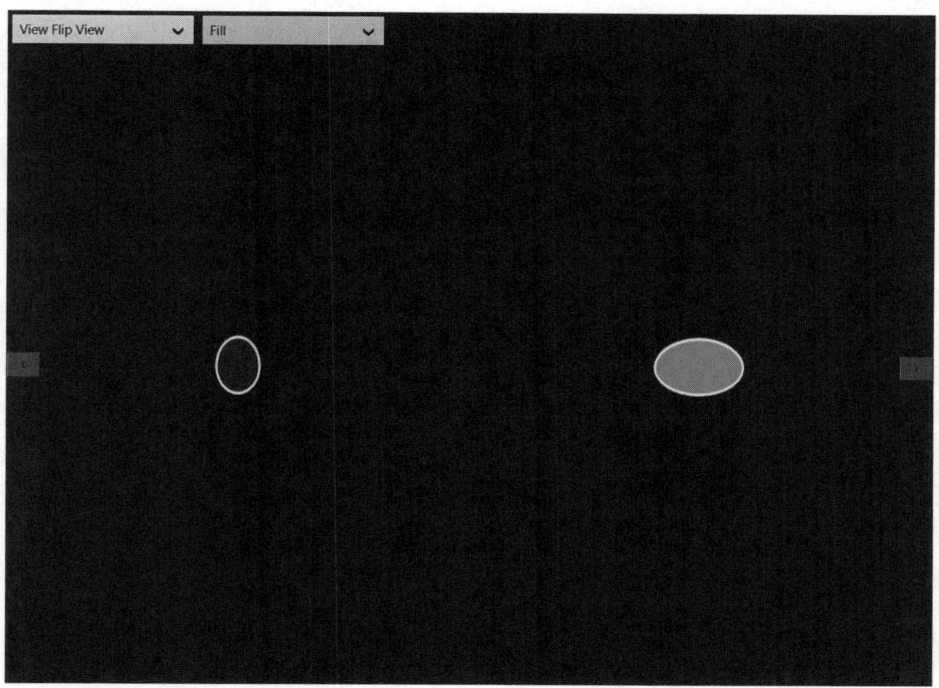

FIGURE 3.9 The `FlipView` control showing the navigation arrows when using the mouse

Most of the layouts in this section are included in the default templates for Windows Store apps. To better visualize and understand the layouts, consider the following example that demonstrates using various layout controls.

Example: Using the `Viewbox` and Various Layouts

The included **LayoutsExample** project provides a visual demonstration of the `Viewbox` in conjunction with various layout controls. The project defines a class called `ShapeInstance` that is assigned a shape from the `ShapeType` enumeration and exposes the description. A ShapeFactory generates random types, and the ShapeConverter renders the shapes with randomized colors.

One important aspect of the ShapeConverter class is the built-in support for the VariableSizedWrapGrid panel. If the shape is a wider shape (a rectangle or ellipse, as compared to a square or circle), the converter sets the ColumnSpanProperty to span two columns. This ensures that when the shape is rendered in a VariableSizedWrapGrid, it consumes adequate space to fully render. Other panels simply ignore the attached property.

```
uiElement.SetValue(VariableSizedWrapGrid.ColumnSpanProperty, 2.0);
```

The ViewModel class contains most of the logic for the app. It holds a list of 100 generated shapes that demonstrate various layouts. It also contains a list of possible layouts and another list of values that can be used for the StretchProperty of the Viewbox. A property is used to hold the current value for each. A Combobox control is bound to the list of options, and a two-way binding is created to the current selection (note the use of the StackPanel in MainPage.xaml to lay out the two Combobox controls next to each other).

```
<ComboBox Width="200"
          HorizontalAlignment="Left"
          Margin="5"
          ItemsSource="{Binding Source={StaticResource ViewModel},
➥Path=States}"
          SelectedItem="{Binding Source={StaticResource ViewModel},
➥Path=CurrentState, Mode=TwoWay}"></ComboBox>
```

This is how data-binding enables you to separate the logic of an item being selected from the actual selection process. The viewmodel has no awareness of what control is being used to control the selection of the current properties. After the user selects an item from the drop-down, the data-binding sets that selected item via the two-way binding. The ViewModel, in turn, intercepts this and takes action. In the case of the layout, it changes the visual state:

```
var visualState = string.Format("{0}State",
   value.Replace(" ", string.Empty));
this.GoToVisualState(visualState);
```

The first line of code removes spaces and adds a suffix to the selected text, so `View Items Control` becomes `ViewItemsControlState`. This corresponds directly to a visual state defined in `MainPage.xaml`. The state ensures that the default `ListBox` control is `Collapsed` and that the target control (an `ItemsControl`) is set to `Visible` so it displays.

The `GoToVisualState` method is actually a delegate defined with the `Action` class on the `ViewModel`.

```
public Action<string> GoToVisualState { get; set; }
```

This makes it easy to test. For unit tests, you can simply mock a delegate that checks that the correct value was passed without having to wire anything to the UI. In the implementation, the `MainPage.xaml.cs` code-behind wires in the call after the control is loaded.

```
viewModel.GoToVisualState = state =>
   VisualStateManager.GoToState(this, state, true);
```

A similar approach sets how the `Viewbox` renders. The string is based on the list of possible enumerations for the `Stretch` property. Therefore, the implementation simply parses the string to the actual enumeration instance and sets that to the `StretchProperty` on the control.

```
viewModel.GoToStretch =
    stretch =>
        {
            var newStretch = (Stretch)Enum.Parse(
               typeof(Stretch), stretch);
            ViewBoxInstance.SetValue(Viewbox.StretchProperty,
               newStretch);
        };
```

The various layouts are rendered on a virtual 2048x1080 pixel `Grid`. By default, the `Viewbox` shows only a corner of the virtual display when `Stretch` is set to `None`. You can set it to `Fill` to force it to shrink to fit the display, or `Uniform` to fit the display with banding (adjusted for the aspect ratio of your actual view). `UniformToFill` adjusts to the nearest dimension and crops the other, so you might find that you lost a scrollbar or the edge of the display.

> **TIP**
>
> The example for layouts uses a static list, so you do not have to implement any type of property or collection change notification. In some apps, you might have to manipulate large lists of data, apply complex queries, and expose those lists for grouping and sorting in the UI. This is not possible using an observable list such as the `ObservableCollection`. A common technique to handle this is to expose the list through a property or set of properties in the viewmodel the way shapes are in the included example. After the underlying data changes or the query is updated, you can simply raise a property change notification for the exposed list or query to ensure that the updated data is refreshed in the UI.

The example uses several `DataTemplate` instances. It also introduces a few new concepts. In previous examples, the viewmodel was set using the `DataContext` of the root control. In this example, an instance of the viewmodel is generated as part of the `Grid.Resources` so that it can be referenced using a key, as you saw in the previous code snippet for the `Combobox`.

```
<local:ViewModel x:Key="ViewModel"/>
```

The viewmodel exposes the list of shapes in two ways. The first is a simple enumerable list.

```
public IEnumerable<ShapeInstance> ShapesNotGrouped
{
    get
    {
        return this.shapes;
    }
}
```

The second uses LINQ to group the list by type and returns it as an orderable, grouped list.

```
public IOrderedEnumerable<IGrouping<ShapeType,
    ShapeInstance>> ShapesGrouped
{
    get
```

```
    {
        return this.shapes
            .GroupBy(shape => shape.Type)
            .OrderBy(g => g.Key);
    }
}
```

This exposes the necessary elements for the controls that support grouping to understand how to organize items. Both views are set to a special `CollectionViewSource`.[6] This is a helper class that provides services for grouping, sorting, and paging through underlying lists. Controls are bound to this kind of source that understand how to marshal requests down to the underlying data store.

```
<CollectionViewSource x:Name="ShapesGrouped"
                      Source="{Binding Source={StaticResource
➥ ViewModel}, Path=ShapesGrouped}"
                      IsSourceGrouped="True"/>
<CollectionViewSource x:Name="ShapesNotGrouped"
                      Source="{Binding Source={StaticResource
➥ ViewModel}, Path=ShapesNotGrouped}"
                      IsSourceGrouped="False"/>
```

Each control specifies which source to use based on whether it supports grouping.

```
<ListBox x:Name="ViewListBox"
    Visibility="Visible"
    ItemsSource="{Binding Source={StaticResource ShapesNotGrouped}}"
    ItemTemplate="{StaticResource ShapeTemplate}">
</ListBox>
```

The complete example demonstrates multiple types of layouts, templates, and data-binding techniques, as well as the Visual State Manager to swap between views. Notice the difference in default templates as you choose different layouts. Also note the behavior of the `FlipView` control. Moving your mouse causes some navigation arrows to appear that enable you to tap or click to move between shapes. If you use touch to swipe, the arrows disappear and the controls animate in the direction of your swipe.

---

[6] `CollectionViewSource` class (Windows), http://bit.ly/yYGgTV

Controls

When you understand the layout capabilities of XAML, you can begin to build your UI using a variety of built-in controls. All the controls that are supplied for Windows Store apps exist in the `Windows.UI.Xaml.Controls` namespace. Although you can easily insert the element tags for these controls in your XAML as with any other object, note that the majority of controls are implemented as high-performance native WinRT components.

Table 3.5 provides an alphabetical list of common controls, with a brief description.

TABLE 3.5 Common Controls

Control	Description
`AppBar`	Toolbar for displaying application-specific commands.
`AppBarButton`	Template button that is used as part of the application bar.
`AppBarSeparator`	Logical separator in the application bar.
`AppBarToggleButton`	Button that switches states and is displayed in the application bar.
`BitmapIcon`	Icon that uses a bitmap as the source for its content.
`Button`	Place for the user to click or tap and raises an event. It can also be bound to a command.
`CheckBox`	Simple control that can be either selected or cleared, usually used to manipulate Boolean values.
`ComboBox`	List of items the user can select from.
`CommandBar`	Special region specifically for providing layout and controls for the application bar.
`DatePicker`	Control that enables the user to pick a date value.
`FontIcon`	Icon that is defined using a glyph from the specified font.

Control	Description
Hub	Special control that follows Microsoft's "hub design pattern," featuring a large image followed by other sections that each might have its own data source. This control is featured in the Hub Visual Studio template.
HyperLink	Hyperlink that appears in a run of text, useful for inserting in the body of text without creating the unnatural breaks and margins that exist around a button.
HyperlinkButton	Text that is highlighted and marked up, usually to indicate that it can be clicked to provide navigation.
Image	Host control for bitmap images.
MediaElement	Surface to play back audio and video content.
MediaPlayer	Comprehensive control that enables playback and control of media content.
PasswordBox	Special text input control that masks the input so the user can securely enter a password or code.
PathIcon	Control for an icon that uses a Path to define its appearance.
PopupMenu	Custom menu that presents commands you specify to the user.
ProgressBar	Visual bar that indicates progress.
ProgressRing	Animated ring that displays indeterminate progress.
RadioButton	List of options that allow mutually exclusive selection.
RepeatButton	Special button that continues to raise events for the duration it is pressed.
RichEditBox	Control for rich editing that supports formatted text and graphics.
RichTextBlock	Surface to display rich formatted text and graphics.

Control	Description
`RichTextBlockOverflow`	Overflow container that is linked to other containers and allows for advanced formatting into regions or columns.
`ScrollBar`	Scrollbar with a sliding thumb.
`SearchBox`	Specialized control for entering search query text for the app.
`SemanticZoom`	Zoom control allows the user to swap between two views of a collection.
`Slider`	Bar with a thumb that enables the user to select from a range of values by moving the thumb.
`SymbolIcon`	Icon that uses a symbol from the Segoe UI Symbol font as its source.
`TextBlock`	Static text.
`TextBox`	Input control that enables the user to enter one or multiple lines of text.
`TimePicker`	Control that enables the user to select a time.
`ToggleButton`	Button that can toggle between two states.
`ToggleSwitch`	Switch that can toggle between two states.
`ToolTip`	Context window that pops up to display information for an element.
`WebView`	Browser control for rendering HTML content.

Many of these controls have a special purpose for Windows Store apps, including the `CommandBar` control (providing commands from within the application) and the `SemanticZoom`[7] (enabling you to zoom to quickly browse large lists of data). You are introduced to various controls throughout this book.

[7]Guidelines for Semantic Zoom, http://bit.ly/HfbuZg

App bars in Windows Store apps exist on the top, bottom, or both areas of the display. They remain hidden until the user swipes up from the bottom or down from the top; then they reveal buttons for navigation, commands, and tools. XAML provides the `AppBar` and `CommandBar` controls that can be dropped into any page and that automatically respond to the appropriate user gestures to show and hide. The `CommandBar` has the advantage of automatically formatting the region based on Microsoft guidelines and hosts specialized controls to show buttons and create separators.

The **FlyoutsExample** project contains an instance of the `CommandBar` in `MainPage.xaml`. It is used to host a button that takes advantage of the new flyout controls. The **WebViewExamples** project contains another example of the `CommandBar` control. You can choose to position your app bar commands on the top, on the bottom, or both. The `CommandBar` then contains a collection of specialized controls for buttons, toggle buttons, and separators. The buttons enable you to specify an icon. The icon can be a named enumeration of symbols listed online in the MSDN documentation.[8] You can also use one of the built-in icon controls to map the visual representation to a glyph from a font, a character from Segoe UI Symbol font, or a bitmap, or you can even describe the shape of the icon through a path definition.

Flyouts

Flyout controls enable you to display temporary content that involves a quick interaction and is easily dismissed. These controls temporarily overlay the rest of your app and display important information and, optionally, solicit user input. The user can choose to either respond by using the provided controls or tap somewhere away from the flyout to dismiss it. Flyout controls are thus fast, easy, and lightweight to use.

The **FlyoutsExample** project demonstrates several types of flyout controls. Figure 3.10 shows a flyout attached to an app bar button. The button displays the menu, and the user can tap on one of the options.

---

[8]Symbol Enumeration, http://bit.ly/18RIm4B

FIGURE 3.10 The flyout controls

Notice how the specialized controls are used to display different types of commands (buttons, toggles), as well as logical separators. The app can respond to the buttons via the `Click` event, as in Listing 3.6.

LISTING 3.6 XAML for the Flyout Controls and Related Events

```
<AppBarButton Icon="Bullets">
    <AppBarButton.Flyout>
        <MenuFlyout>
            <MenuFlyoutItem Text="Red"
                            Click="MenuFlyoutItemRed_OnClick"/>
            <MenuFlyoutItem Text="Yellow"
                            Click="MenuFlyoutItemYellow_OnClick"/>
            <MenuFlyoutSeparator/>
            <ToggleMenuFlyoutItem
                IsChecked="True"
                Text="Blue Border"
                Click="MenuFlyoutItem_OnClick"/>
        </MenuFlyout>
    </AppBarButton.Flyout>
</AppBarButton>
```

The example shows other flyout controls as well. The normal button that exists in the first row contains a more complex flyout with labels and an input box. This works the same way the application bar commands do: If you tap the button, the flyout appears. You can either type in some information and then tap the button to display a dialog message, or tap anywhere else on the screen to dismiss the menu.

The final example is invoked from the **Settings** charm. This is a page control that you can add using the **Add** dialog, followed by clicking **New Item...** and then selecting the **Settings Flyout** option. You create a new page that you can use to configure settings for your app. You must wire into a special event to show the settings command and display these. This is covered in more detail in Chapter 11, "Windows Charms Integration."

Custom Controls

In many situations, you need to reuse a control or set of controls. There are a few approaches to creating custom controls that you can reference and reuse. Chapter 2, "Windows Store Apps and WinRT Components," introduced the first approach. The **DataBinding** example project contains the file `CustomControl.xaml`. The example shows two different methods of data-binding, so the control encapsulates the use of a `Slider`, `TextBlock`, and `Ellipse` to demonstrate the data-binding. This approach uses the *user control* template. A user control provides a XAML surface for organizing and grouping controls in the designer. You do not need to define a template for it. You can then reference and reuse it.

If you want to create a control to share across projects or even publish for use by other parties, or if you want to expose a control in a way that provides customization and extensibility for the control, you'll want to use a *custom control*. This type of control follows the "parts and states" methodology for XAML design. It is "lookless" because you need only define a code file for the control. Any UI is defined as a resource that defines the parts or the elements that can be displayed. You can further extend the UI through states defined using the Visual State Manager.

Example: Creating a Custom Control

You can create a custom control as a class library for use by other managed projects, or as a WinRT component for use in managed or C++ projects. Creating a control that JavaScript apps can consume is not possible because the base class `Control` is set with the `WebHostHidden` attribute, making it invisible to JavaScript apps.

```
[MarshalingBehavior(MarshalingType.Agile)]
[Threading(ThreadingModel.Both)]
[Version(100794368)]
[WebHostHidden]
public class Control : FrameworkElement
```

The **CustomControlsLibrary** in the Chapter 3 solution folder was created as a simple C# class library. The control shown for this example is the `TrafficControl`. To add a custom control, choose **Add** and then **New from template**, and select the **Templated Control** option (see Figure 3.11).

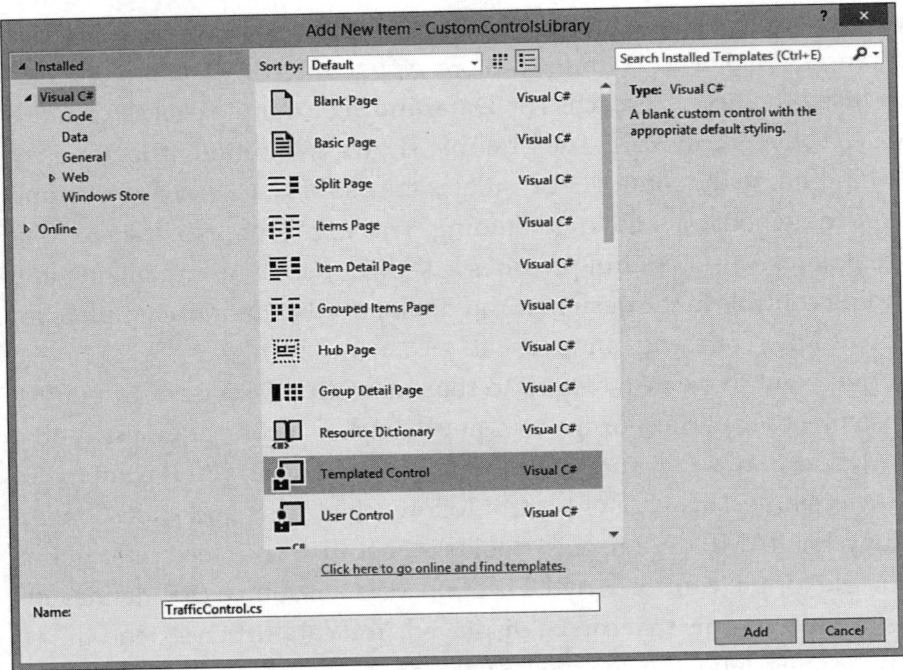

FIGURE 3.11 The template for custom controls

After the control is added, the template creates a special structure (see Figure 3.12). The structure includes a class file for the control, as well as a new `Themes` folder with a resource dictionary named `Generic.xaml`. This is the convention for creating custom controls that is compatible with the approach both WPF and Silverlight use.

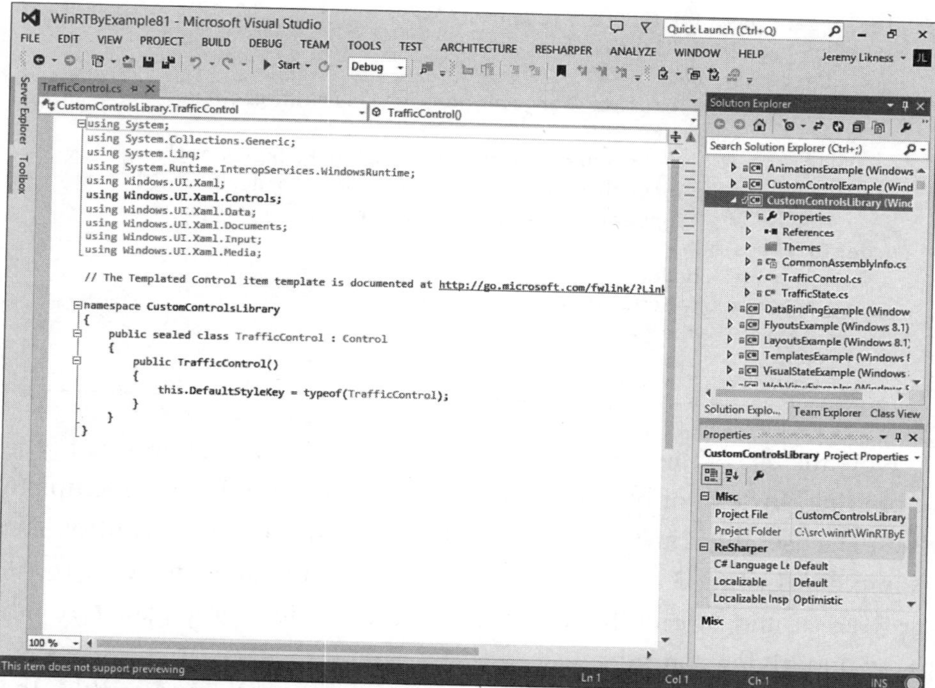

FIGURE 3.12 The default structure for a custom control

The code-behind simply specifies a `DefaultStyleKey` for the control. This is a key to the resource dictionary that provides the template for the parts and states of the control.

```
public sealed class TrafficControl : Control
{
    public TrafficControl()
    {
        this.DefaultStyleKey = typeof(TrafficControl);
    }
}
```

Listing 3.7 shows the default style added to the resource dictionary. By default, it simply contains a `Border` element. You can customize the contents of the `ControlTemplate` with anything you want, as the example has done for the `TrafficControl` class.

LISTING 3.7 The Default `ControlTemplate` for a Custom Control

```
<Style TargetType="local:TrafficControl">
    <Setter Property="Template">
        <Setter.Value>
            <ControlTemplate TargetType="local:TrafficControl">
                <Border
                    Background="{TemplateBinding Background}"
                    BorderBrush="{TemplateBinding BorderBrush}"
                    BorderThickness="{TemplateBinding
➥ BorderThickness}">
                </Border>
            </ControlTemplate>
        </Setter.Value>
    </Setter>
</Style>
```

Note the use of the `TemplateBinding` keyword. This is an important type of binding. Instead of binding to the `DataContext`, it binds to the template itself. The user then can specify those attributes when using the control. The example in Listing 3.7 makes it possible to specify values for `Background`, `BorderBrush`, and `BorderThickness` and have those values propagate through to the underlying control.

The included example uses a `Grid` instead of a `Border` and enables the user to set the `Width` and `Height` properties for the grid. It defaults to a `Gray` background. The `Grid` contains three rows, each with an `Ellipse` that is colored `Red`, `Yellow`, and `LightGreen`. This is a rough representation of a traffic light. The `Opacity` of each "light" is set low, to make it faded until it is turned on. The lights are handled through the VSM with a variety of states, including `Off` (all lights are powered off) and `Red`, `Yellow`, and `Green`.

The VSM transitions the lights to full opacity when a state is transitioned to. Notice that the transitions defined include a `GeneratedDuration`.

```
<VisualTransition To="Red" GeneratedDuration=
   "{TemplateBinding LightSpeed}"/>
```

This instructs the VSM to create the transition, resulting in a slow fade to the new value. The default transition time is defined by and exposed through a dependency property so that users can override it through bindings.

```
public static readonly DependencyProperty LightSpeedProperty =
    DependencyProperty.Register(
    "LightSpeed",
    typeof(TimeSpan),
    typeof(TrafficControl),
    new PropertyMetadata(TimeSpan.FromSeconds(0.5)));
```

The control itself waits until it is loaded and then sets itself to the `Off` state.

```
VisualStateManager.GoToState(this, "Off", false);
```

It then locates the main `Grid` in the template using the special `GetTemplateChild` method provided to custom controls.

```
var mainLight = this.GetTemplateChild("MainLight") as Grid;
```

Finally, it hooks into the `Tapped` and `DoubleTapped` methods. You can inspect the code to see how it uses the VSM to transition between states. A double-tap turns it off or sets it to the `Green` state, and a single tap moves between the various traffic light states.

After you create your control, you can share it with other projects in several ways. One way is to simply include it through a project reference. This is the approach the **CustomControlExample** project uses. The project references the `CustomControlsLibrary` with an instance of the `TrafficControl` on the XAML surface of `MainPage.xaml`. Note the override to the duration between transitions using the `LightSpeed` property. The property, a `TimeSpan`, can be specified using a string because `TimeSpan` contains an appropriate `TypeConverter` that instructs the XAML parser to transform the duration into an actual `TimeSpan` value.

```
<customControlsLibrary:TrafficControl Grid.Column="0"
    Grid.Row="1"
    Margin="5"
    LightSpeed="0:0:0.1"/>
```

This method works fine if you want to include the control in a project and have access to the source. If you want to distribute the control as a standalone library that can be installed and referenced without source, you must use an Extension SDK. You learn more about packaging your own Extension SDKs in Chapter 19, "Packaging and Deploying."

Parsing XAML

Sometimes you need to dynamically parse XAML to display in your app. In both WPF and Silverlight, XAML files were compiled into a binary format and packaged with the deployed application. The WinRT packages the original XAML files and parses these when your app is launched. Although this has raised some concerns about performance, they are mostly unwarranted because the parser is extremely fast and efficient.

To see how this is done behind the scenes, build the **XamlParsingExample** project. After it is compiled, ensure that the **Show All Files** icon in the Solution Explorer is selected (see Figure 3.13). Expand the `obj` folder, drill down to the `MainPage.g.i.cs` file, and open it.

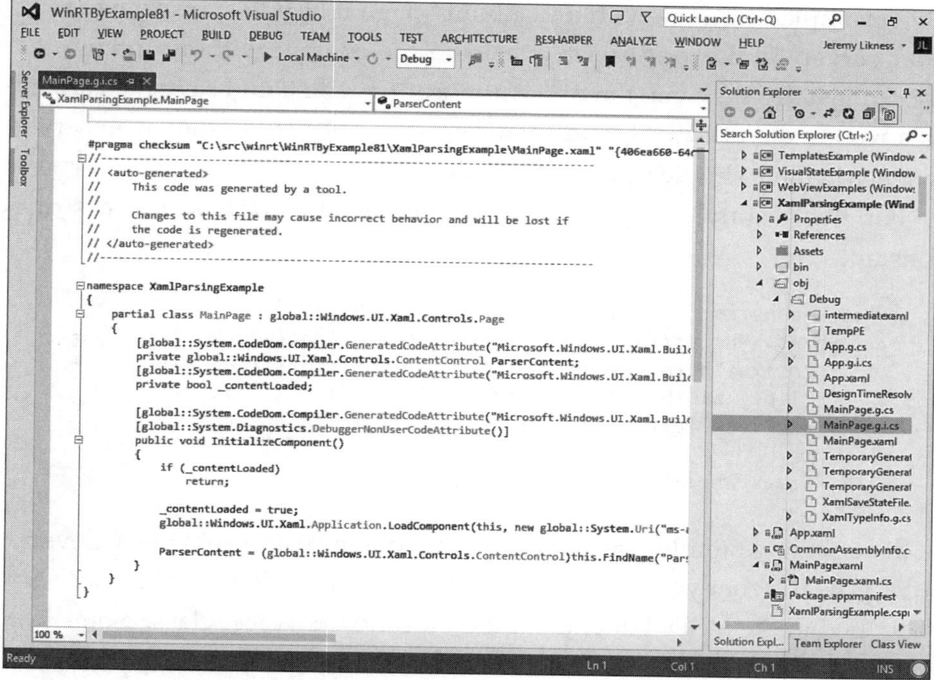

FIGURE 3.13 Showing the hidden files used to parse XAML

A simplified version of the code follows (without the long namespaces, to make it easier to read).

```
public void InitializeComponent()
{
   if (_contentLoaded)
      return;
   _contentLoaded = true;
   Application.LoadComponent(this, new Uri(
      "ms-appx:///MainPage.xaml"),
   ComponentResourceLocation.Application);
   ParserContent = (ContentControl)this.FindName("ParserContent");
}
```

The control loads the XAML content exactly once. It also parses the loaded content to locate named child controls and set their references so you can access them from the code-behind.

You can use the same parser to load your own XAML dynamically while the application is running. You might want to do this for several reasons.

One example might be with an "About" page that you synchronize with your server. To make it easier to refresh the content without forcing the user to install a new version of the application, you could save the content as a resource and load it, and then refresh a copy from your web server when you have simple updates to push out.

For this example, I've encoded a snippet of XAML inside a string constant.

```
private const string XamlToParse = "<StackPanel " +
    "xmlns=\"http://schemas.microsoft.com/winfx/2006/xaml...\" " +
    "xmlns:x=\"http://schemas.microsoft.com/winfx/2006/xaml\">" +
    "<Ellipse Width=\"200\" Height=\"200\" Fill=\"Red\"/>" +
    "<TextBlock Text=\"This was parsed from a XAML string
➥ constant.\"/>" +
    "</StackPanel>";
```

It contains a simple `StackPanel` with a red ellipse and some text. Several rules govern what you can do with dynamically loaded XAML; these are described in the MSDN documentation for the `XamlReader` class.[9] Some key points to remember are that you can have only one root element in the parsed XAML and you must include a namespace.

When you are ready, you simply call the `Load` method on the `XamlReader` class to parse the XAML. If all goes well, it returns the instantiated root element that you can then add to the visual tree.

```
var stackPanel = XamlReader.Load(XamlToParse);
ParserContent.Content = stackPanel;
```

The parser provides another method to validate templates within the parsed XAML. This is documented as a feature used mainly for handling the design time experience.[10] The XAML parser provides everything you need to create a custom and dynamic experience for your Windows Store apps, but many applications today rely heavily on HTML to generate and display content. What support does WinRT provide for HTML pages?

---

[9] `XamlReader` class (Windows), http://bit.ly/YQHlmG

[10] `XamlReader.LoadWithInitialTemplateValidation` method (Windows), http://bit.ly/VGfmZe

HTML Pages

You might want to show HTML content in your app for several reasons. You might have information that is updated frequently and makes the most sense to consume as HTML data. Your app might aggregate feeds that contain HTML content. You might be creating a native client that accesses an existing web-based application that you need to interoperate with. Fortunately, the WinRT has a control that addresses these needs: the `WebView` control.

Understanding the purpose of the control and how that might impact how you architect your app is important. The control itself is not intended to be a complete replacement for a browser. Indeed, Microsoft has made it clear that if you try to get an app approved in the Store that tries to solely interact with a web-based app or simply act as a web browser, it will be rejected.[11] Several limitations built into the control prevent many scenarios.

The control uses the Internet Explorer 11 engine. It does not support advanced features in HTML5, including caching, indexed databases, programmatic access to the clipboard, or geo location. It supports the same version of the Document Object Model (DOM) that Windows Store apps written in JavaScript use.[12] No support exists for any type of plug-in or ActiveX extension, including Flash, Silverlight, or embedded PDF documents; however, the control does support Scalable Vector Graphics (SVG) and Web Graphics Library (WebGL).

Full support for enhanced protocol handling is included.[13] This provides support for custom protocols that enable you to access resources embedded in your app, as well as links that automatically launch the program associated with them. You can generate a web page that, when viewed, not only provides content served from within your app, but also enables the user to open those resources using a preferred app (for example, a resource with a `.pdf` extension opens with the preferred reader app).

---

[11] Ten Things You Need to Know about `WebView`, http://bit.ly/13EKx7B

[12] Document Object Model (DOM) (Windows), http://bit.ly/YR9mdN

[13] Autolaunching with file and URI associations, http://bit.ly/Yryqva

The control participates in the XAML layout as any other control does. This means you can style it, transform it, and even overlay it with other elements. You can also use a special control called the `WebViewBrush` to render a surface with its contents. Another handy feature of the control is the capability to save a screenshot of the current display, to create thumbnails or static references to pages.

The final and perhaps most important feature of the `WebView` control is the capability to interoperate with your Windows Store app. Your app can communicate with the web page by invoking JavaScript functions and passing in parameters. The page can also interact with your app by calling a method on an object that WinRT creates in the DOM. You can create some truly interactive experiences between web content and your Windows Store app.

Example: Working with HTML and JavaScript

The **WebViewExamples** project contains several examples of working with HTML and JavaScript. `MainPage.xaml` defines a `WebView` control named `WebViewControl` and a brush named `WebBrush`. The `WebView` control can present either a URI or an HTML document. The `WebBrush` can project the rendered image to other surfaces.

When the page is loaded, a handler is registered to the `NavigationCompleted` event on the `WebView`. This fires anytime a new resource (whether it is a string literal or a web page) loads. It forces the brush to refresh and show a dialog indicating the content that was loaded.

```
WebBrush.Redraw();
var url = e.Uri != null ? e.Uri.ToString() : "Text Content";
var popup = new MessageDialog(url, "Content Loaded.");
await popup.ShowAsync();
```

The first button triggers a straightforward page load.

```
private void ButtonBase_OnClick(
    object sender,
    RoutedEventArgs e)
{
    this.WebViewControl.Navigate(new Uri(JeremyBlog));
}
```

The page is my main blog page. You'll find that it loads and renders fine. You can also click links and navigate just as if you pulled the page up in a web browser. No forward or backward buttons exist, and there is no place to enter a new address—you are stuck following the links the control provides. Notice that the dialog fires every time you navigate to a new page: You could easily use this feature to inspect where the user ended up and hide the control or reset it, if needed.

The second button invokes a specific page as a mobile client by writing a user agent that mimics an iPhone. My blog will detect that a mobile device is accessing the page and redirect to a mobile-friendly page. The code uses the `HtmlFormatHelper` class to "clean" the HTML. This class is most often used when sharing HTML and strips out dynamic content such as script tags. Cleaning up the content before presenting it in the application is perfectly valid. You might see that the top part of the page is cut off; this is simply an issue with the CSS formatting from the blog.

The only way to update the user agent that the `WebView` control uses is to employ some hacks to prevent your app from making it into the Windows Store. For those hackers in the audience, you'll need to invoke (using `p/Invoke`) `urlmon.dll` and call `UrlMkSetSessionOption` with option `0x10000001` and your user agent string before navigating with the control. A more direct approach is to download the page yourself and pass it to the control as text. Listing 3.8 shows the steps.

LISTING 3.8 Download a Page Using a Specific User Agent

```
private async void ViewMobile_OnClick(object sender,
   RoutedEventArgs e)
{
    var handler = new HttpClientHandler {
       AllowAutoRedirect = true };
    var client = new HttpClient(handler);
    client.DefaultRequestHeaders.Add("user-agent",
       MobileUserAgent);
    var response = await client.GetAsync(new
       Uri(JeremyYogaPost));
    response.EnsureSuccessStatusCode();
    var html = await response.Content.ReadAsStringAsync();
    var fragment = HtmlFormatHelper.GetStaticFragment(
        HtmlFormatHelper.CreateHtmlFormat(html));
    this.WebViewControl.NavigateToString(fragment);
}
```

You learn more about WinRT networking components in Chapter 10, "Networking." The example sets up a client that accepts redirects (in the case of the blog post reference, it redirects to a mobile version) and then creates a client and sets the user agent to mimic a mobile device. The page is requested, and the code ensures a successful response before loading the content of the response and sending it to the `WebView` control.

This technique is common for requesting content in a format that is suitable for viewing within your app (mobile content tends to have less chrome, so it is easier to process). You can also parse and analyze the content before presenting it to the end user. You can thus strip unwanted tags or even inject your own JavaScript and content as needed before the page is displayed.

In some apps, you might want to include embedded HTML resources for your apps to display. The third button demonstrates this technique. It also shows that the rendering engine has full support for Scalable Vector Graphics (SVG),[14] which can be useful if you need to integrate charts or vector-based graphics in your application and have existing implementations using SVG. The example app includes an embedded HTML file named `Ellipse.html` in the `Data` folder.

Referencing this resource is simple and straightforward. You learn more about special Windows Store app protocols in Chapter 4. The special `ms-appx-web` protocol provides a path to the `WebView` control that is embedded in the store app. Notice that it uses three forward slashes and then provides a path to the resource in the app from the package root.

```
private void ViewSvg_OnClick(
    object sender,
    RoutedEventArgs e)
{
    this.WebViewControl.Navigate(new
        Uri("ms-appx-web:///Data/Ellipse.html"));
}
```

You can also embed static text (or dynamic text that you build and generate before passing into the control). The fourth button triggers the load

[14]W3C SVG Working Group, http://bit.ly/XVgLuz

of a string literal. The literal contains the text for an HTML document and includes various header tags, an embedded image (the logo of the app itself), and a hyperlink that demonstrates you can navigate to embedded content or external content. If you follow the link to the external website, you'll see that the base URL is consistently reported as static text because that's how the original document was loaded.

```
private void ViewString_OnClick(
    object sender,
    RoutedEventArgs e)
{
    this.WebViewControl.NavigateToString(HtmlFragment);
}
```

The last button for WebGL shows a special page that includes the JavaScript source and working demo of a simple three-dimensional cube. It is intended to give you a brief introduction to the API that is used to render graphics with JavaScript and demonstrate how it runs inside the `WebView` control. This functionality was just introduced in Internet Explorer 11.

The second-to-last button demonstrates how your app can interoperate with the web. To show this, I included a JavaScript function in the template of my blog. The function is just a few lines of code. If you load any page from my blog and view the source, you can search for "supersecret" to locate the function:

```
function superSecretBiographyFunction(subPath) {
   window.location.href="http://csharperimage.jeremylikness.com/"
➥ + subPath;
}
```

The function is usually not called, but that changes if you load one of the blog pages using the example app and tap **Call JavaScript Function**. Listing 3.9 shows the implementation. The `InvokeScript` method calls the function. You can pass in `null` for a function that takes no parameters; otherwise, you can pass in an array of values. In this case, the path to my biography is passed in, and the page picks it up and navigates to the path. Note that you can call JavaScript on any type of page the control rendered, including embedded resources or literals you've passed in.

Listing 3.9 Code to Invoke a JavaScript Function Through the `WebView` Control

```
private async void CallJavaScript_OnClick(
    object sender,
    RoutedEventArgs e)
{
    MessageDialog popup = null;

    var parameters = new[]
                            {
                                "p/biography.html"
                            };

    try
    {
        this.WebViewControl.InvokeScript(
            "superSecretBiographyFunction",
            parameters);
    }
    catch (Exception ex)
    {
        popup = new MessageDialog(
            ex.Message,
            "Unable to Call JavaScript.");
    }
    if (popup != null)
    {
        await popup.ShowAsync();
    }
}
```

An attempt to invoke a function on a page that doesn't have that function results in a generic `Exception` instance. The code captures the very user-unfriendly exception and displays it for you. The pattern is important to note because using the `await` keyword from within a `catch` block is not possible. The workaround is to capture any necessary information needed in the `catch` and then wait for the dialog (using the `await` keyword) to display the information after the block is exited.

Although sending information to a page is nice, wouldn't it be great if you could receive information back? This scenario is possible—in fact, you can create apps that have two-way conversations with web pages. Choose the option to **View Source** on my blog page and search for "superSecretBiographyFunction" to find a code snippet.

```
if (document.title===
    'C#er : IMage: Synchronous to Asynchronous Explained') {
    if ((typeof (window.external) !== "undefined") &&
    (typeof (window.external.notify) !== "undefined"))
    {
       window.external.notify(new Date().toLocaleString());
    }
}
```

I would not normally do a string comparison against a topic title to trigger application logic, but I can get away with it here because I own the blog and am not planning to change the title. When the user navigates to a specific topic inside a `WebView` control, the web page itself sends a message to the Windows Store app with the browser's date and time. Figure 3.14 illustrates the communication between the web page and the Windows Store app.

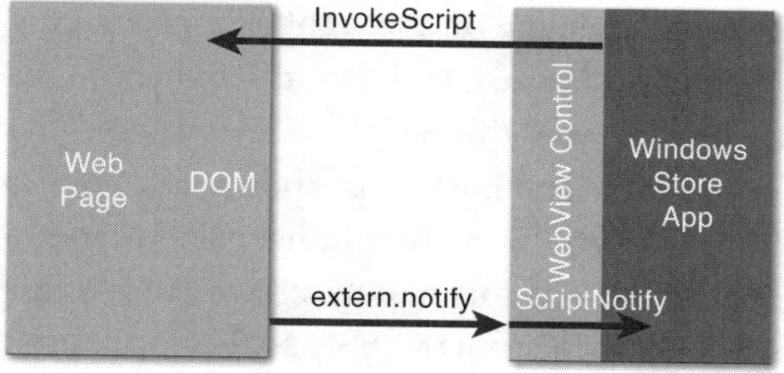

FIGURE 3.14 Communication between web page and a Windows Store app

The function first checks for the existence of the `window.external` object. Internet Explorer provides this to the JavaScript runtime to grant access to the object model of the host[15] (in this case, the host is the `WebView` control). The control exposes the `notify` method to the runtime. A call to this from the web page with a single string parameter raises the `ScriptNotify` event on the `WebView` control. These events are registered at the top of `MainPage.xaml.cs`.

```
this.WebViewControl.ScriptNotify += this.WebViewControlScriptNotify;
```

[15]External object (Internet Explorer), http://bit.ly/13c9v2H

The example app simply stores the value that is passed to a local variable.

```
private void WebViewControlScriptNotify(
    object sender,
    Windows.UI.Xaml.Controls.NotifyEventArgs e)
{
    this.message = e.Value;
}
```

After the entire web page is loaded, the `LoadCompleted` event checks for this value and displays it when present.

```
popup = new MessageDialog(
    this.message,
    "The Blog Has Spoken!");
this.message = string.Empty;
await popup.ShowAsync();
```

To see this in action, you use the timeline on the right side of my blog to navigate to the year 2012, the month August, and the title "Synchronous to Asynchronous Explained." In this case, the script doesn't trigger any action because the app doesn't trust it. The JavaScript shows you how to implement it, but to see it in action, you need two things. The first is a page that is served securely via HTTPS—unfortunately, no way to test this using unsecured pages exists (my blog does not use SSL, so the app cannot trust it). You must also declare the URI in the manifest. The manifest has a tab labeled **Content URIs** that enables you to enter a list of domains that are allowed to interact with your app. The example app lists a hypothetical domain for my blog to demonstrate how it would be configured. This closes the loop and demonstrates how Windows Store apps can load, display, and interact with HTML-based content.

Summary

This book is devoted to a deep dive of WinRT functionality. A significant surface area of WinRT components has been built specifically for the UI and XAML. This chapter covered the basics of XAML and the visual tree. You learned about data-binding and how the dependency property system, in conjunction with property change notification, enables apps to separate the data from the user interactions using the MVVM pattern.

Animations provide powerful interactivity with apps, and Windows Store apps have access to an existing library of canned animations to produce a consistent experience for the end user. Animations also drive a powerful XAML engine called the Visual State Manager that further enables a clean separation between development and design. Styles can impact the look and feel of controls by providing a reusable set of themes you can apply to your app. You can customize controls and reuse them through the powerful templates XAML supports.

The chapter provided an example app to explore the myriad layout options available and to summarize the various controls shipped out of the box. You also learned how to take advantage of the XAML parser to dynamically parse and integrate content to your app. Many apps are written using HTML, not XAML, and the `WebView` control provides a variety of options for interacting with HTML pages, rendering them in your application, and allowing bidirectional communication between your app and web pages.

Accessing data on the web is fine, but often you need to persist that data. The next chapter covers the WinRT APIs that enable you to manipulate data. You'll learn how to embed and reference data in your app, store data locally, and serialize settings that roam among all your Windows 8.1 and RT devices. You will also learn how to store data to the clipboard for retrieval by other applications and how to compress data to conserve disk space. Finally, I share with you an option for storing relational data that you can query and sort from your Windows Store app.

4 Data and Content

THE WINDOWS RUNTIME IS WELL EQUIPPED TO HANDLE ANY DATA you want to throw at it. It contains components to deal with text, binary data, HTML content, and just about anything else you can transfer or store. Using WinRT, you can save data locally or temporarily or persist it in a special roaming zone that synchronizes data across multiple Windows 8.1 devices. WinRT compresses the data for you, serializes and deserializes your objects, and parses XML documents with ease. You can even post data to the clipboard to share with desktop apps.

In this chapter, you explore all the data-related WinRT APIs. You learn how to send data to the clipboard and store information in local storage. You see how various helper classes make it easier to deal with files and interface with components that enable compression of data. This chapter covers the APIs to compress data, along with ways to create settings and store information that roams between Windows 8.1 devices so you can synchronize content between your tablet and laptop. This chapter also reviews system menus for interacting with file storage, along with various strategies for serializing and dealing with different data types.

Example: Data Manipulation with the Skrape App

The **Chapter 4** solution folder at http://winrtexamples.codeplex.com/ contains a reference application called Skrape that demonstrates the various data-related APIs. Skrape enables you to enter website addresses and pull down web pages for review. When you are connected to the Internet, the app opens a web browser for you to view. It also caches data so that you can browse and read content offline.

As with most examples in this book, this is not a Windows Store–ready app. I intentionally left out a lot of the plumbing and architecture required for actions such as maintaining navigation state and handling various display orientations, to instead focus on the core concepts in this chapter. Don't worry—later chapters refer to fully evolved apps that you can use as a template and checklist for full Windows Store submissions.

For now, feel free to pull down the app and start using it. A single website is included as an example. You can swipe from the top or bottom of the screen (or right-click) to pull up the app bar and add a new site or use the various other options. You can paste in a URL you have on the clipboard. Tap on a tile to pull down the page and store it. If you have another device, you can deploy the app and watch as data is synchronized between one app and the other. The app synchronizes the URLs you are storing but not the actual content—for that, you need to visit the individual page and allow it to pull down and cache.

The `Clipboard`

The `Clipboard` is a special object that has existed through several versions of Windows. It provides a set of functions and objects for exchanging data, ranging from simple text to complex embedded objects. The Windows Runtime includes two primary scenarios for sharing content between apps. When the focus is on the data and you need to share data between Windows Store apps and desktop applications, use the `Clipboard`. If the focus is sharing between Windows Store apps and providing an experience for the exchange that doesn't force the user to leave the primary app, use sharing. You learn more about sharing in Chapter 11, "Windows Charms Integration." A scenario also exists for *tap and send* that uses Near Field Communications (NFC) to share between devices; Chapter 10, "Networking," explores this.

The `Clipboard` is a static class that resides in the `Windows.ApplicationModel.DataTransfer` namespace. It provides methods to add and retrieve content, clear content, and expose an event to monitor when content changes. The content is prepared using a `DataPackage` and retrieved using a `DataPackageView`. Both classes provide methods to prepare, inspect, and format data appropriately based on the type of data being shared. You can provide multiple data formats in a single `Clipboard` operation so that different applications can access the type of data they are designed to receive.

Although the `Clipboard` is available to both Windows Store apps and desktop applications, some caveats apply. In a desktop application, you can hook into an event that monitors changes to the `Clipboard` and use that to determine whether content is available for your application.[1] The common pattern is to enable or disable a paste command based on the availability of content.

In Windows Store apps, access to the `Clipboard` is allowed only when you are responding to user input such as tapping a button. You can receive the change notifications, but any attempt to inspect the contents of `Clipboard` will fail if the app is not running in debug mode. This is an important behavior to understand because the app might appear to be working correctly in debug, but when you launch it without the debugger attached, it will crash by throwing an `UnauthorizedAccessException`.

The **Skrape** app handles the paste operation by making the command available and checking the `Clipboard` when the user invokes it. Figure 4.1 shows the result of invoking the paste command when no URL is available to process. The `AppBarControl` facilitates sharing application commands between pages and is inserted in the `AppBar` control.

---

[1]Clipboard.ContentChanged (Windows), http://bit.ly/WWdxEX

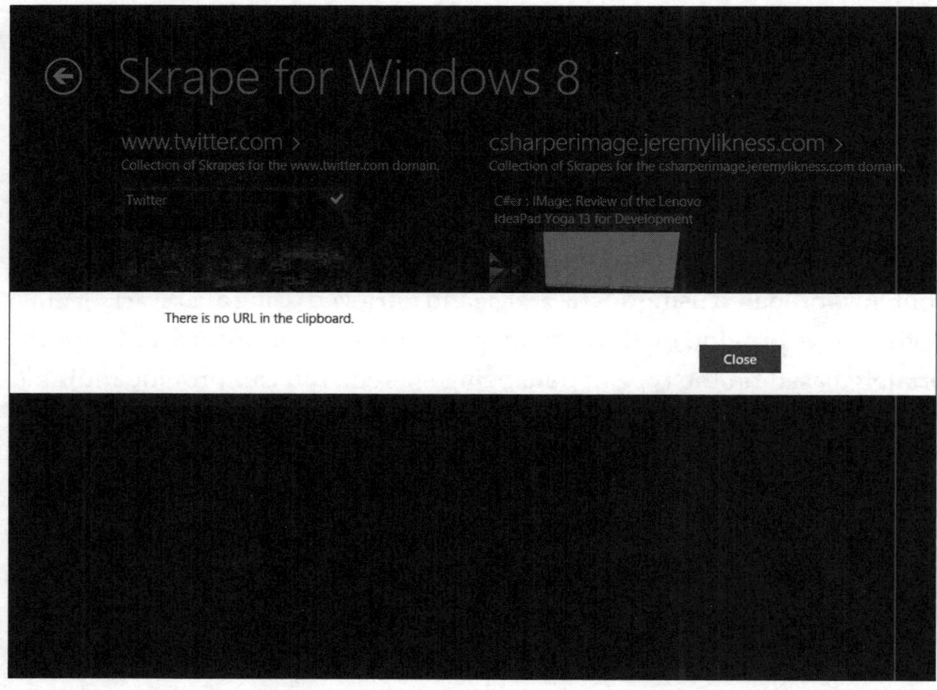

FIGURE 4.1 A failed paste operation

An instance of a `GlobalViewModel` is declared in the `App.xaml` as a resource:

```
<data:GlobalViewModel x:Key="GlobalResources"/>
```

A command on the viewmodel is referenced from the command bar at the top of `MainPage.xaml`:

```
<AppBarButton Icon="Paste"
   Label="Paste"
   Command="{Binding Source={StaticResource GlobalResources},
➥ Path=PasteCommand}"/>
```

A helper class called `ActionCommand` makes it easy to define commands that implement the `ICommand` interface by passing in a delegate for the action to execute and another delegate for the condition that determines whether the command can execute. The `GlobalViewModel` sets up the command as an asynchronous method call in its constructor.

```
this.PasteCommand = new ActionCommand(
    async () => await this.Paste(),
    () => true);
```

Listing 4.1 shows the implementation of the `Paste` method. The first step is to get the content of the `Clipboard` that is presented as an instance of `DataPackageView`. After the content is retrieved, the package is queried to see if it contains a web link or text that can be converted to a `Uri`. If the `Uri` exists, it is retrieved and used to add a new page to scrape to the application. If one does not exist, a message appears to indicate that no paste is available.

LISTING 4.1 Handling a Paste Operation from the Clipboard

```
private async Task Paste()
{
    MessageDialog dialog;
    try
    {
        var clipboardData = Clipboard.GetContent();

        var urlAdded = false;
        var uri = new Uri(
    "http://csharperimage.jeremylikness.com/", UriKind.Absolute);

        if (clipboardData.Contains(StandardDataFormats.WebLink))
        {
            uri = await clipboardData.GetWebLinkAsync();
            urlAdded = true;
        }
        else if (clipboardData.Contains(StandardDataFormats.Text))
        {
            var text = await clipboardData.GetTextAsync();
            if (Uri.TryCreate(text, UriKind.Absolute, out uri))
            {
                urlAdded = true;
            }
        }

        if (urlAdded)
        {
            await DataManager.AddUrl(uri);
            dialog = new MessageDialog("The URL was added.");
        }
        else
        {
            dialog = new MessageDialog("There is no URL in
```

```
➥ the clipboard.");
            }
        }
        catch (Exception ex)
        {
            dialog = new MessageDialog(ex.Message, "An Error Occurred");
        }

        await dialog.ShowAsync();
}
```

Table 4.1 lists the various formats that are available from the DataPackageView and shows how to both query for and retrieve them. Note that formats can range from simple text to rich text, HTML, and even bitmap images. These same formats are available for the share operations that you learn about in Chapter 11.

TABLE 4.1 Popular Data Formats

Format	Format Type	Method
Application link	ApplicationLink	GetApplicationLinkAsync
Bitmap	Bitmap	GetBitmapAsync
HTML	Html	GetHtmlAsync
Rich Text Format	Rtf	GetRtfAsync
Storage items	StorageItems	GetStorageItemsAsync
Plain text	Text	GetTextAsync
Universal Resource Identifier	Uri	GetUriAsync
Web link	WebLink	GetWebLinkAsync

You can query the DataPackageView using the Contains method and pass a property from StandardDataFormats, or you can iterate the AvailableFormats property to get a list of available formats. User-defined or custom formats that don't exist as part of the numeration also are available on the clipboard. These formats require advanced knowledge of the clipboard, and each application must understand the format to copy and paste it.

Sending content to the `Clipboard` is even easier. You simply create an instance of a `DataPackage`, call the appropriate method for the type of content you want to share, and then pass the `DataPackage` to the `SetContent` method on the `Clipboard`. The `Copy` method on the `GlobalViewModel` demonstrates this. It passes both text and HTML formats. To see how that works, navigate to a page and then invoke the copy command. First paste to Notepad to see the text format; then paste to Word to see the HTML format.

```
var package = new DataPackage();
package.SetText(this.DataManager.CurrentPage.Text);
package.SetHtmlFormat(HtmlFormatHelper.CreateHtmlFormat(
    this.DataManager.CurrentPage.Html));
Clipboard.SetContent(package);
```

For HTML content to appear correctly, it has to be formatted with special headers when it is passed into the `Clipboard`. Fortunately, you don't have to worry about that formatting because the static `HtmlFormatHelper` class does it for you. Two methods are used. The first, `CreateHtmlFormat`, prepares HTML for the `Clipboard`. The second, `CreateStaticFragment`, strips out any dynamic content, such as `script` tags, from the source string.

Application Storage

Application storage in WinRT follows a similar model to traditional isolated storage.[2] The storage provides isolation and safety because instead of providing access to the entire file system, you are given a sandbox specific to your package. You access the persisted data through a special class `ApplicationData` that represents files and settings for one of several containers that are scoped to your app.

Figure 4.2 shows a high-level representation of the storage hierarchy available for Windows Store apps. At the highest level, you have three containers available: roaming, local, and temporary. All containers provide a storage structure that enables you to group files within folders. The roaming and local containers also allow for special settings that can include

---

[2]Isolated Storage, http://bit.ly/YSeHnJ

their own nested containers, name/value pairs, and special composite values that aggregate name and value pairs.

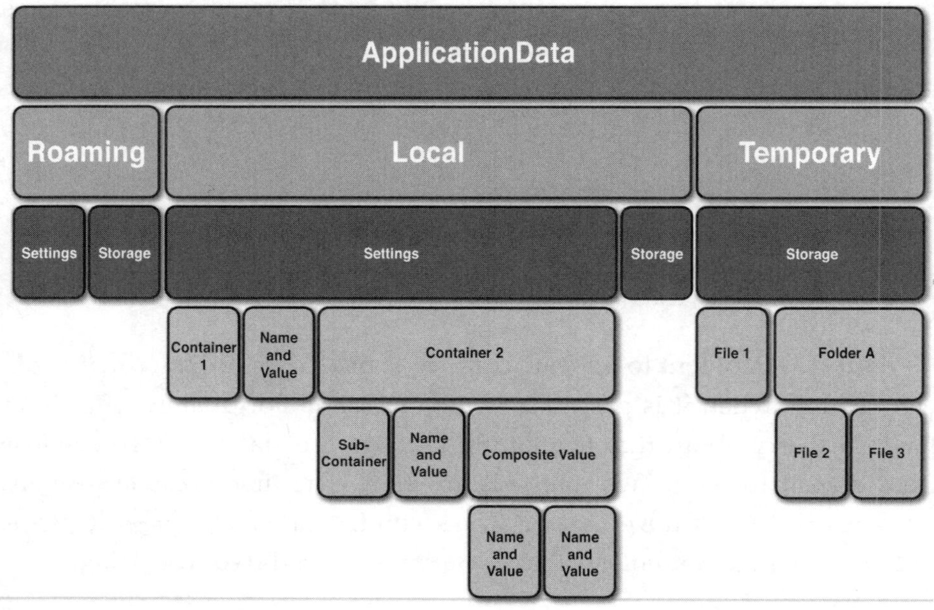

FIGURE 4.2 Windows Store app storage hierarchy

The temporary folder is like a scratch space where you can store transient information that does not need to persist between sessions. Use it for temporarily cached data or as a workspace when you need to write to the file system to perform certain operations (for example, if you are processing an image before allowing the user to export it). Local storage works the same way, but the information stored there persists for as long as the package remains installed on the system (or until you explicitly delete it). This is ideal for a persisted cache and for storing information that your app uses on a regular basis.

Roaming Data

Windows 8.1 enables you to sign in using your Microsoft Account and automatically synchronize information through the cloud. Roaming data enables you to use storage files and settings to create data that synchronizes across multiple devices. The API is no different than what you use to write to local storage, but it automatically uploads the data to the cloud and downloads it to other devices. The API also works if you are signed in with a local account; it simply falls through to local storage and doesn't synchronize. This enables you to program to the same API and not have to worry about checking the type of account the user used to sign in with.

Roaming does not happen instantly, but is based on various triggers. One trigger, for example, is the lock screen—roaming settings synchronize automatically when you lock your machine. This is important to know when testing roaming so you can force the synchronization to happen. If the user is not connected to the Internet, the settings cache locally and automatically upload when an Internet connection becomes available. The converse is also true: The app works fine offline on other devices and then synchronizes from the cloud when the Internet connection is available.

The infrastructure for roaming is all hosted through OneDrive.com (formerly SkyDrive). This service is free with your Windows Account. The roaming settings are not exposed through the OneDrive.com interface, but are hidden and do not impact your storage quota. Roaming is meant to be lightweight, so you should not use it to store large data files or exhaustive settings. The practical limit for roaming is 100K of data. The `Windows.Storage.ApplicationData.RoamingStorageQuota` property can be queried to determine the exact quota. The example Skrape app uses roaming to store titles and URIs but stores the actual web and text content locally.

Roaming is specific to apps, so it should not be used for user data. Data that multiple applications can use—such as documents, photos, and music—should be stored in common folders or roamed through the main SkyDrive APIs. The data that makes sense for roaming is data specific to the app, including settings that are not device dependent, preferences, state, and content that is specific to the application (such as the list of URIs the Skrape app uses).

Everything you learn about roaming data also applies to local data. The only difference is how you access the container. Folders and files are accessed under `Windows.Storage.ApplicationData.RoamingFolder`, and settings are accessed through `Windows.Storage.ApplicationData.RoamingSettings`. The settings property returns an `ApplicationDataContainer`.[3]

Containers

Containers are simply a logical way to group app settings. Access to settings is always through a container, starting with either `RoamingSettings` or `LocalSettings`. Containers can be nested within other containers. Nested containers are both created and accessed using the `CreateContainer` method on the parent container. The `PageAndGroupManager` class handles the containers for groups (domains) and pages. A private property encapsulates access to the `RoamingSettings`.

```
private static ApplicationDataContainer Roaming
{
    get
    {
        return ApplicationData.Current.RoamingSettings;
    }
}
```

Creating or accessing the container is as simple as calling `CreateContainer` with the name of the nested container and an enumeration indicating whether the container should already exist.

```
var container = Roaming.CreateContainer(
    PageKey,
    ApplicationDataCreateDisposition.Always);
```

The disposition can be `Always`, to either access an existing container or create a new one the first time, or `Existing`, which expects the container to already exist and fails if it does not. After the container is referenced, you can iterate the settings using the `Values` property.

[3]ApplicationDataContainer class (Windows), http://bit.ly/Y5PpDj

Settings

Settings are name/value pairs that can be stored in a container. Note that a container serializes all its settings when modified, so you should not use settings for large amounts of data. You'll learn more about handling larger data using storage files instead. The name for a setting can be up to 255 characters long, and the value can be as large as 8K. Every setting must be either a valid WinRT type or a `CompositeValue` that aggregates a group of settings.

The `RoamingSettings` container has a special setting named `HighPriority`. Assigning a value to this setting causes the roaming engine to roam the value more quickly than other data. This is useful when you want to provide a continuous experience across devices and need to roam a setting that frequently changes, such as the current item a user is looking at.

The Skrape app notifies other devices when a new URL is added in the `PageAndGroupManager` (note that `HighPriority` is a constant defined with the same value as a `string`).

```
public void AddUri(Uri uri)
{
    Roaming.Values[HighPriority] = uri == null ?
        string.Empty : uri.ToString();
}
```

The `ApplicationData` class provides an event that fires when roaming data changes.

```
ApplicationData.Current.DataChanged += this.CurrentDataChanged;
```

The arguments passed are null because you are responsible for querying the data to determine what changed. The sample application simply saves the most recent URI that was added and then rechecks it anytime the data changes. A property helps parse the string value in the setting to a URI.

```
if (Roaming.Values.ContainsKey(HighPriority))
{
    Uri uri;
    if (Uri.TryCreate(Roaming.Values[HighPriority]
    .ToString(), UriKind.Absolute, out uri))
    {
        return uri;
    }
}
return null;
```

If the URI is new, an event is raised and the URI is passed.

```
var uri = CurrentUri;
if (uri == this.currentUri)
{
    return;
}
this.currentUri = uri;
this.NewUriAdded(this, this.currentUri);
```

The `SkrapeDataManager` class listens for the event. If it fires, it dispatches a dialog that indicates the new URL and informs the user that the data has changed. This simple implementation asks the user to close the app and relaunch it. I purposefully left out the complexity of synchronizing the data on the fly. You can enhance the program by asking the users whether they want to synchronize. After they affirm, you can clear the list of groups and rebuild it from the roaming settings.

Unfortunately, the only way to test that your roaming settings are working is to set up multiple devices—I've tried doing it using the simulator, and it doesn't work. Deploy the app to more than one device and then add a new URL on the first device. Then press **Windows Key+L** to bring up the lock screen. This triggers the synchronization. After a few seconds, you should see a dialog pop up on the second device, like the one shown in Figure 4.3. The method is useful for keeping data in synch, but it does come with size and speed limitations.

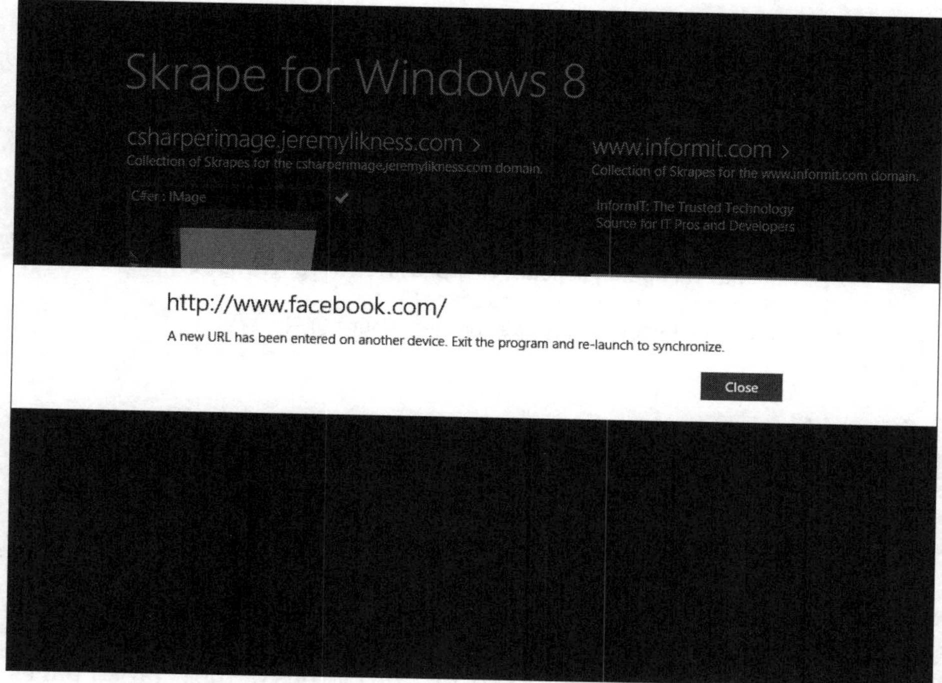

FIGURE 4.3 A roaming notification

Roaming is not a viable solution for constant communication between devices. You also can override the roaming subsystem to use your own cloud-based storage; you learn more about that in Chapter 7, "Connecting to the Cloud."

Composite Values

Some units of data make sense only when taken together as an aggregated unit. For example, if you are storing a location, it makes sense to have both the longitude and the latitude coordinates. Roaming might not roam all settings at the same time, so you need a way to keep related values together. This is the purpose of the `ApplicationDataCompositeValue` class: to store a group of settings that must be serialized and deserialized together.

The class works much like a container, in that it enables you to set name and value pairs. The same restrictions apply: Keys must be no more than 255 characters in length, and values must be WinRT types. The maximum size for a single composite value is 64K.

The PageAndGroupManager class uses composite values to store pages and groups. The class provides an initializer you can use to pass in the name/value pairs, as you can see in the SavePage method:

```
var compositeValue = new ApplicationDataCompositeValue
    {
        { IdProperty, page.Id },
        { TitleProperty, page.Title },
        { ThumbnailProperty, page.ThumbnailPath.ToString() },
        { UrlProperty, page.Url.ToString() },
        { ImageCountProperty, page.Images.Count() }
    };
```

When the composite value is prepared, you can apply it to a regular setting:

```
container.Values[page.Id.ToString()] = compositeValue;
```

Although settings are useful for storing small, discrete groups of values (mostly related to configuration and preferences), they are not well suited to larger chunks of data. The Html and Text properties of the scraped pages can be several hundred kilobytes (or even megabytes) in size, so they are not well suited for roaming or for storing in settings. For larger amounts of data, a storage file is more appropriate.

Storage Folders and Files

WinRT provides APIs to manipulate and interact with both folders and files in the storage system. In addition to the local storage and roaming storage you can access through the ApplicationData class, you can copy results of downloads via the DownloadsFolder class (the typical place to store content downloaded from the Internet) and a set of KnownFolders. Table 4.2 lists these folders and the requirements to access them.

TABLE 4.2 List of `KnownFolders`

Folder	Description	Access Notes
`DocumentsLibrary`	Documents	In addition to the Documents library capability, you must declare a File Type Association for each type of file you want to create or access from the folder.
`HomeGroup`	Home network	Accessing the Documents library within the HomeGroup folder is not possible. Any other access depends on the capabilities you set for Music, Pictures, and Videos.
`MediaServerDevices`	Digital Living Network Alliance (DLNA) devices	Accessing the Documents library is not possible for connected devices. You can access resources on DLNA-connected devices based on the capabilities you set for Music, Pictures, and Videos.
`MusicLibrary`	Music	You must declare the Music capability to access this folder.
`PicturesLibrary`	Photos and images	You must declare the Pictures capability to access this folder.
`Playlists`	Playlists for music	You must declare the Music capability to access this folder.
`RemovableDevices`	External, removable devices such as external hard drives and thumb drives	Accessing the Documents library is not possible for removable devices. You can access other resources based on the capabilities you set for Music, Pictures, and Videos.

Folder	Description	Access Notes
`SavedPictures`	Saved pictures	You must declare the Pictures capability to access this folder.
`VideosLibrary`	Videos	You must declare the Videos capability to access this folder.

Most of the time, to access the storage system, you get a reference to a `StorageFolder` and work with the APIs that it exposes. The top-level folders available to work with are provided as properties on the `Windows.Storage.ApplicationData` class. For example, you can access the root folder for local storage through the `ApplicationData.LocalFolder` property.

Storage Folders

You can see an example of using folders in the `GlobalViewModel` class of the **Skrape** sample project. When the user invokes the command to download the current page from the application bar, the `Download` method is called. The method generates a filename based on the URL for the page and then accesses the `Downloads` folder on the user's device to create a file.

```
var download = await DownloadsFolder.CreateFileAsync(
   filename, CreationCollisionOption.GenerateUniqueName);
```

The `DownloadsFolder` class is a static class that points to this special folder on the device. The default behavior is to create a subdirectory based on the name of the app and then place any files within that folder. The `CreateFileAsync` method creates a file inside the folder, using one of the available creation options. The options listed in Table 4.3 determine how WinRT handles situations when the requested filename already exists.

TABLE 4.3 `CreationCollisionOption` Values

Option	Description
`GenerateUniqueName`	Creates the file with the name requested. If a file already exists with the specified name, a number is appended to the end to make the name unique.
`ReplaceExisting`	Creates the file with the name requested. If a file already exists with the specified name, it is overwritten (replaced).
`FailIfExists`	Creates the file with the name requested. If a file already exists with the specified name, a generic exception is thrown.
`OpenIfExists`	Creates the file with the name requested. If a file already exists with the specified name, it opens the existing file instead of overwriting it.

The file operation returns a `StorageFile` object. Many of the methods on the `StorageFolder` class return instances of `StorageFile`. The operations available can be grouped into several broad categories: create, delete, get, query, and rename.

- Create operations include `CreateFileAsync`, to create a `StorageFile` instance, and `CreateFolderAsync`, to create a `StorageFolder` instance for a subfolder.
- Delete operations include overloads of `DeleteAsync` to delete the current folder, with options to perform a normal delete (and send the folder to the recycle bin) or a permanent delete (no recycle bin).
- Get operations include `GetFileAsync` and `GetFilesAsync`, to get files in the current folder; `GetFolderAsync`, `GetFolderFromPathAsync`, and `GetFoldersAsync`, to get subfolders in the current folder; `GetItemsAsync`, to get both files and subfolders in the current folder; and `GetThumbnailAsync`, to get a thumbnail image for the current folder.
- Query operations include `CreateFileQuery` and `CreateFileQueryWithOptions`, to specify filters and options to query the files and subfolders in the current folder.

Most of the operations return files, folders, or a combination of both for the current folder. Another set of operations is available through the `StorageFile` API.

Storage Files

The storage file APIs provide file-level operations, as well as methods for acquiring streams to read and write from the files. The **Skrape** project uses a stream to write the bytes for the text version of the page in the `Download` method of the `GlobalViewModel` class.

```
using (IRandomAccessStream stream = await download.OpenAsync(
   FileAccessMode.ReadWrite))
{
   await stream.WriteAsync(Encoding.UTF8.GetBytes(page.Text)
      .AsBuffer());
   await stream.FlushAsync();
}
```

The file-level APIs include operations to copy, create, delete, get, move, open, rename, and replace file-level content.

- The copy operations include `CopyAndReplaceAsync`, to replace the target file, and `CopyAsync`, to copy to a target folder with creation options.
- Creation options `CreateStreamedFileAsync` and `CreateStreamedFileFromUriAsync` are special operations that expose a stream or URI as a `StorageFile`, allowing the content to be sent on demand and appear as a file to the consumer.
- The delete operations are performed through the overloaded `DeleteAsync` method to either delete the file or delete with a specific option (such as deleting permanently so it does not end up in the recycle bin).
- Get operations include `GetBasicPropertiesAsync` (provides the basic properties of the current file); `GetFileFromApplicationUriAsync` and `GetFileFromPathAsync`, to get a `StorageFile` that represents a particular URI or file located at the specified path; and `GetThumbnailAsync`, to get a thumbnail image for the file.

- Move operations include `MoveAndReplaceAsync`, to move the file and replace an existing file, or `MoveAsync`, to move the file to the specified folder.
- The open operations create streams to access the file, including `OpenAsync`, to create a random-access stream; `OpenReadAsync`, for a read-only random-access stream; `OpenSequentialReadAsync`, for a read-only sequential-access stream; and `OpenTransactedWriteAsync`, for a random-access transacted stream.
- The rename operations include overloads of `RenameAsync` that enable you to change the current filename with collision options.
- The replace options include `ReplaceWithStreamFileAsync` and `ReplaceWithStreamedFileFromUriAsync`, to replace the contents of the current file with the contents of the specified stream or URI.

The key to successfully manipulating files is understanding streams and buffers. Streams are common in the .NET Framework, but buffers were introduced by the Windows Runtime.

Buffers and Streams

WinRT provides the `IBuffer` interface to work with arrays of bytes. The interface is simple and declares only two properties: `Capacity`, or how much the buffer can hold, and `Length`, or how many bytes are currently in use. This is a WinRT-specific type, so no corresponding .NET class can be mapped or projected. Instead, you can use the `AsBuffer` extension method from the `WindowsRuntimeBufferExtension`[4] class that exists in the `Windows.Runtime.InteropServices.WindowsRuntime` namespace to retrieve an instance that represents the underlying byte array. This class provides many more extension methods to manipulate `IBuffer` and .NET types.

Streams are an abstraction of byte sequences and can represent files, sockets, arrays, or input and output mechanisms. At a minimum, you can read or write to or from streams. Some streams enable you to write into the streams, and more advanced streams provide random access that enables

[4]WindowsRuntimeBufferExtensions methods, http://bit.ly/11p2WsK

you to seek to certain positions within the stream and access the bytes there.

The basic WinRT stream interfaces include:

- `IInputStream`—A sequential stream of bytes you can read using the `ReadAsync` method.
- `IOutputStream`—A sequential stream of bytes you can write using the `WriteAsync` method (and then flush with `FlushAsync`).
- `IRandomAccessStream`—A more advanced stream that allows reads, writes, and seeking positions in the stream. You can create a new instance of the underlying stream using `CloneStream`, seek to a position, and grab an instance of either an `IInputStream` (`GetInputStreamAt`) or an `IOutputStream` (`GetOutputStreamAt`). It also provides the `CanRead`, `CanWrite`, `Position`, and `Size` properties.

Another set of advanced stream interfaces includes `IDataReader` and `IDataWriter`. These interfaces provide enhanced methods for writing and reading primitive types to and from the underlying streams. Table 4.4 provides a list of classes that are implemented in the `Windows.Storage.Streams` namespace.

TABLE 4.4 Stream Implementations

Class	Description
`Buffer`	Represents the default implementation of `IBuffer`
`DataReader`	Supports reading multiple data types from an input stream
`DataReaderLoadOperation`	Returns from the `LoadAsync` operation of a `DataReader` to provide asynchronous management of the load operation
`DataWriter`	Supports writing multiple data types to an output stream
`DataWriterStoreOperation`	Returns from the `StoreAsync` operation of a `DataWriter` to provide asynchronous management of the storage operation

Class	Description
FileInputStream	Reads data from a file
FileOutputStream	Writes data to a file
FileRandomAccessStream	Provides read and write operations with the capability to seek position on a file
InMemoryRandomAccessStream	Provides read and write operations with the capability to seek position on a stream that is stored in memory
InputStreamOverStream	Wraps legacy COM types that implement the synchronous IStream interface in a Windows Runtime asynchronous instance
OutputStreamOverStream	Wraps legacy COM types that implement the synchronous IStream interface in a Windows Runtime asynchronous instance
RandomAccessStream	Provides read and write operations with the capability to seek position in underlying streams
RandomAccessStreamOverStream	Wraps legacy COM types that implement the synchronous IStream interface in a Windows Runtime asynchronous instance
RandomAccessStreamReference	Creates RandomAccessStream instances from files, other streams, and URIs

The **Skrape** project uses streams to save the downloaded text from a scraped page. In the `Download` method of the `GlobalViewModel`, you can see code that encodes the text as a UTF8 byte array, converts it to an `IBuffer` instance, and then writes the buffer asynchronously to an `IRandomAccessStream` that wraps the underlying file. Note the `FlushAsync` method called to flush the final bytes to disk.

```
using (IRandomAccessStream stream = await download.OpenAsync(
   FileAccessMode.ReadWrite))
{
    await stream.WriteAsync(Encoding.UTF8.GetBytes(page.Text)
       .AsBuffer());
    await stream.FlushAsync();
}
```

For the most part, streams and buffers are interoperable between the .NET Framework and the Windows Runtime. When you need to convert a buffer to a stream or vice versa, you can access the extension methods available on the `WindowsRuntimeBufferExtensions` class. Although the `StorageFile` class provides methods that make it easy to work with the underlying files, you can perform common operations in just a few lines of code using a few helper classes that WinRT provides.

Path and File Helper Classes

The two helper classes are `FileIO` and `PathIO`. Both classes make it easy to work with files, sometimes in as little as a single line of code. You can see an example of using the `FileIO` class in the `ProcessImage` method of the `SkrapeDataManager` class. After a `StorageFile` reference has been made to cache the image, the content of the image in a byte array is written to storage using a single line of code.

```
await FileIO.WriteBytesAsync(storageFile, buffer);
```

The `FileIO` class provides helper methods that operate against `StorageFile` instances. Table 4.5 lists the available file-based methods.

Table 4.5 Available Operations from the IO Helper Classes

`FileIO` Method	Description
`AppendLinesAsync`	Appends lines of text to the provided file (with an overload to specify encoding)
`AppendTextAsync`	Appends text to the provided file (with an overload to specify encoding)
`ReadBufferAsync`	Reads the contents of the provided file into a buffer
`ReadLinesAsync`	Reads the text from the file and returns it as a text array (one entry per line, with an overload to specify encoding)
`ReadTextAsync`	Reads text from the provided file (with an overload to specify encoding)
`WriteBufferAsync`	Writes data from a buffer to the provided file

FileIO Method	Description
WriteBytesAsync	Writes an array of bytes to the provided file
WriteLinesAsync	Writes lines of text to the provided file (with an overload to specify encoding)
WriteTextAsync	Writes text to the provided file (with an overload to specify encoding)

A previous example to explain streams showed several lines of code to write the text for a page to a file in the `Download` method of the `GlobalViewModel`. Using the helper class, that operation can be distilled to a single line of code (it is commented in the source of the example):

```
await FileIO.WriteTextAsync(download, page.Text,
   UnicodeEncoding.Utf8);
```

The `PathIO` class provides the same methods but takes a path instead of a file. Use this helper class when you have the path to a resource and don't need to take on the overhead of referencing the `StorageFile` instance first. The path notation can use special protocols such as `ms-appx:///` for resources embedded in the package (simply add the relative path from the root of the package) and `ms-appdata:///` for local, roaming, or temporary storage. The path helper is more often used to read resources than write because it does not give you the file creation options that are available in the storage APIs.

The `ms-appx:///` protocol is relative to the package root. If you have a top-level folder named `Assets` with an image called `MyImage.jpg`, you access it as `ms-appx:///Assets/MyImage.jpg`. Resources that the `ms-appdata:///` protocol references should start with the type of storage (local, temporary, or roaming), followed by the path relative to the root folder. If you have a top-level folder in your local storage named `Assets` that contains a bitmap image named `MyImage.jpg`, you reference it using `ms-appdata:///local/Assets/MyImage.jpg`.

Storage Query Operations

WinRT provides support for query operations against storage design to simplify your interactions with the file system. The **QueryPicturesLibrary** project demonstrates how to use the advanced APIs to query and navigate storage. The example parses all image files in the `Pictures Library` folder and displays the title along with a thumbnail on a grid. The application iterates through all subfolders to provide this list.

In a typical scenario, you can imagine the steps required: First, get an instance of the top-level folder. Next, grab all top-level items and recursively iterate. Filter the files by type and then call the operating system APIs to grab the thumbnail. Drill into subfolders and repeat this, eventually building a list of all the items. Perform any processing needed on the list for display and then bind to XAML.

Now take a look at `MainPage.xaml.cs` in **QueryPicturesLibrary**. After the main page is loaded, a query instance is created to search for images.

```
var queryOptions = new QueryOptions(
    CommonFileQuery.OrderByTitle,
    new List<string> { ".jpg", ".gif", ".tif", ".png" })
                     {
                         FolderDepth = FolderDepth.Deep,
                         IndexerOption = IndexerOption
                            .UseIndexerWhenAvailable
                     };
```

The `QueryOptions` instance takes two parameters in its constructor: a `CommonFileQuery` value and a list of file extensions (types) to filter by. Table 4.6 lists the available `CommonFileQuery` values.

TABLE 4.6 The `CommonFileQuery` Enumeration Values

Value	Description
`DefaultQuery`	A simple, default view of files in a folder.
`OrderByName`	A flattened recursive list of all items, sorted by the name display property.
`OrderByTitle`	A flattened recursive list of all items, sorted by the title property. Applies only to libraries and `HomeGroup`.

Value	Description
OrderByMusicProperties	A flattened recursive list of all items sorted by the music properties. Applies only to libraries and HomeGroup.
OrderBySearchRank	A flattened recursive list of all items, sorted by the search rank of the item. The search rank is evaluated at the time the query is executed, based on all other available filters and sorts (the type of the item and whether it is ordered by date or music properties, for example).
OrderByDate	A flattened recursive list of all items, sorted by the date of each item. The date depends on the item—for example, general files might use last modified, but photos use the date the photograph was taken. Applies only to libraries and HomeGroup.

In addition to the constructor, several other properties and methods are available from the query options. With an existing set of options, you can use SaveToString to serialize them to restore later with LoadFromString. You can force the query to load certain properties in advance with SetPropertyPrefetch. The method call takes a flag with options for the types of properties (such as basic, document, image, music, or video). The example project takes advantage of another method to generate the thumbnail.

```
queryOptions.SetThumbnailPrefetch(
ThumbnailMode.PicturesView, 150, ThumbnailOptions.ResizeThumbnail);
```

You can use different modes to generate the thumbnail, and each has a preferred size to render the thumbnail.[5] You can specify the size as well as the options for how the thumbnail is retrieved.[6] After setting your options, you can verify that the folder you want to query supports them and whether the CommonFileQuery enumeration you chose is applicable. For example, a query that sorts by music properties isn't applicable to PicturesLibrary.

[5]ThumbnailMode enumeration (Windows), http://bit.ly/Z6L4zk

[6]ThumbnailOptions enumeration (Windows), http://bit.ly/WZ1Qmm

```
var folder = KnownFolders.PicturesLibrary;
if (!folder.AreQueryOptionsSupported(queryOptions)
    || !folder.IsCommonFileQuerySupported(
          CommonFileQuery.OrderByTitle))
{
    return;
}
```

After you verify that the query options are applicable, you invoke the query.

```
var query = folder.CreateFileQueryWithOptions(queryOptions);
```

The query returns a `StorageFileQueryResult`.[7] You can use the result to iterate through the resulting list of `StorageFile` objects, query the options, and even apply new options as needed. If your goal is to display the results, however, another helper class makes it easy to get a list of results that is ready for data-binding. The `FileInformationFactory` class binds folder and files queries to XAML controls. Several constructor overloads enable you to specify how you want the thumbnails to be generated. The example program uses a simple option to format based on the `ThumbnailMode.PicturesView`.

```
var access = new FileInformationFactory(query,
    ThumbnailMode.PicturesView);
```

The factory exposes several methods to iterate the files, folders, and generic items (a combination of files and folders) that are contained within the query, but more important, it provides methods that expose a virtualized vector of objects that you can use in data-binding. *Virtualized* simply means that the vector will add more objects to the list as the user interacts with the UI, to optimize performance.

```
var fileList = access.GetVirtualizedFilesVector();
this.MainList.ItemsSource = fileList;
```

The example can sort all pictures in the Pictures Library by title and display them with thumbnails in about 20 lines of code. Figure 4.4 shows

[7] StorageFileQueryResult class (Windows), http://bit.ly/ZITf4V

the result. The query has picked up some pictures of previous book covers, running and archery events, a dinner I had in New York's Grand Central Terminal, and our family trip to Paris.

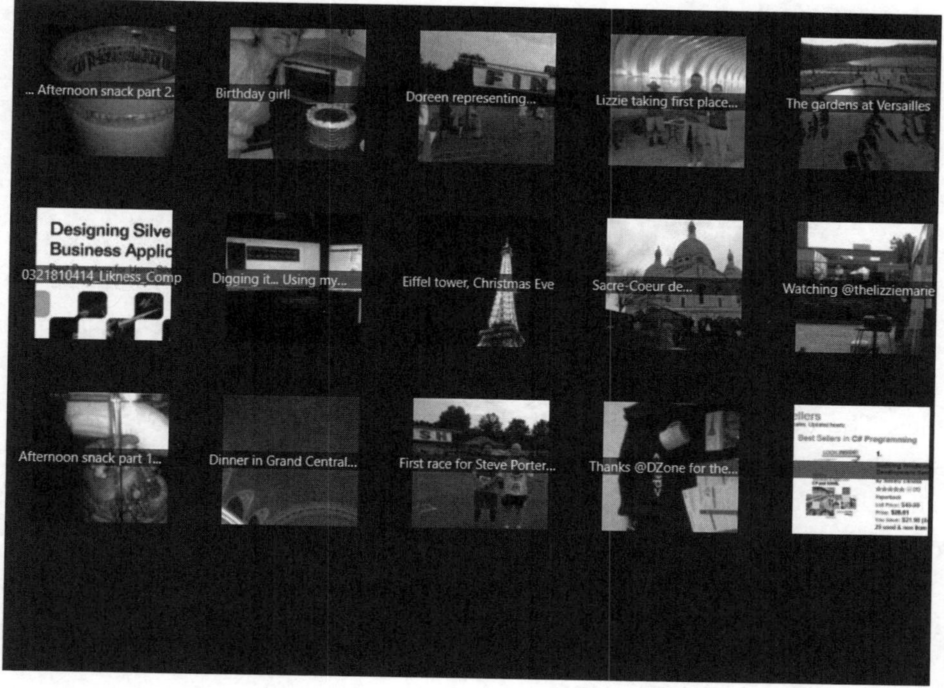

FIGURE 4.4 The result of querying the `Pictures Library`

This example builds a list of the files. You can also get a list of folders or a combined list of folders and files. These are delivered as virtual folders that can be grouped and organized according to the type of query you specify. The helper classes make it easy to provide a clean UI for the items you are interested in presenting to the user. You shouldn't attempt to re-create the experience of exploring the file system and selecting files using this technique, however. That is better handled through the pickers described later in the "Pickers and Cached Files" section.

You can apply the same queries to files stored in your application local storage. Windows provides the Windows Search Service (WSS) that continuously indexes files and folders to create an indexed catalog that facilitates faster searches. You can take advantage of this using the `QueryOptions.IndexerOption` to use the index instead of the file system for your queries. By default, files contained in your libraries (Documents, Pictures, and so on), email, and offline files such as your browser cache are indexed. You can use this same service to index files that you place in local storage. To take advantage of WSS, simply create a folder under the root local storage folder named `Indexed` (it is not case sensitive).

```
var indexed = await
    Windows.Storage.ApplicationData.Current.LocalFolder
   .CreateFileAsync(
                "indexed",
                CreationCollisionOption.OpenIfExists);
```

After the folder is created, you can create subfolders and place files within the folder structure, and WSS automatically begins indexing the files. The indexer supports created full-text indexes and enables full-text searches over text, HTML, PDF, XML, RTF, and Microsoft Office files. The folder can be created only when your app is running, so the recommended pattern is to create it when the app is first run and then store files as needed. WSS runs on its own schedule, so there is no guarantee that the indexes will be created immediately.

Pickers and Cached Files

Until now, you've mostly worked with either local storage or special "known folders" that your app can access. For security reasons, Windows Store apps cannot, through the WinRT APIs we have discussed so far, directly access the file system outside the special folders (such as the Documents, Music, and Pictures Libraries) and local, roaming, or temporary storage folders. Instead, WinRT provides a special set of UI components that enable the user to navigate to any area of the hard drive and select folders or files.

These pickers provide several features. First, they enable the user to opt in, to allow your app to access special locations on the hard drive. Instead of gaining direct access, you indirectly gain access by presenting end users with a dialog that they can use to select a file or folder and give your app explicit permission to interact with it. Second, the pickers provide a consistent (and extensible, as you learn in Chapter 11) user interface because the same dialog is shown regardless of the app it is invoked from.

The **Skrape** project includes an example of a file picker used to save files. This gives the user the option to save the file anywhere on the hard disk, even in a folder that is normally not accessible by a Windows Store app. To test the feature, open a scraped page and use the `FlipView` control in the left column to navigate to an image to save. After the image is selected, open the application bar and tap the save icon. Figure 4.5 shows an example of the resulting dialog.

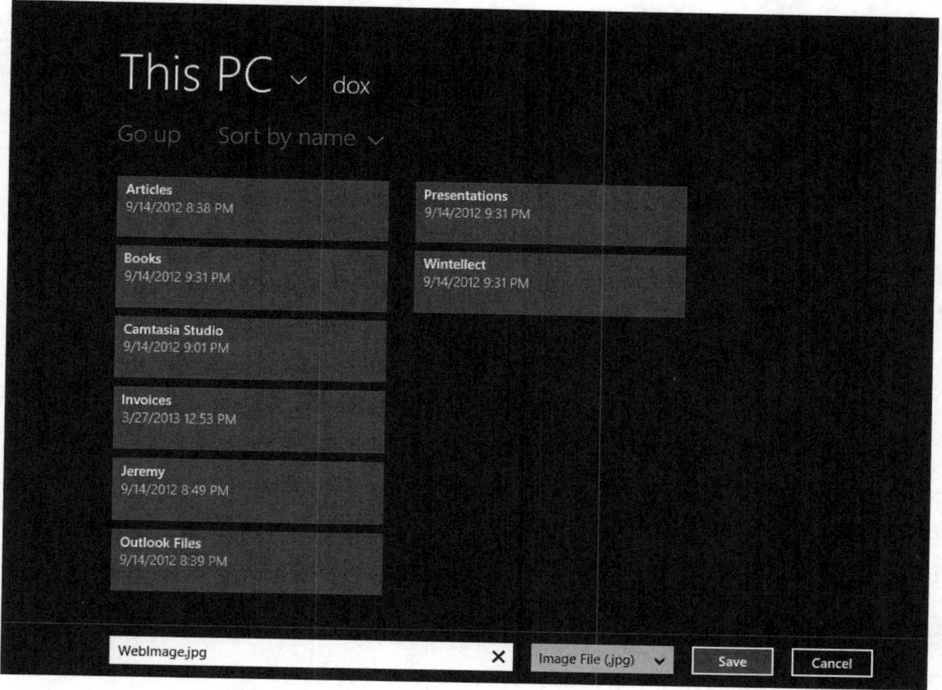

FIGURE 4.5 Example of the picker for saving files

The picker is invoked from the `SaveImage` method of `SkrapeDataManager`. After downloading the picture and determining the extension, an instance of `FileSavePicker` is created.

```
var saveFilePicker =
    new FileSavePicker
        {
            SuggestedFileName = "WebImage",
            SuggestedStartLocation =
               PickerLocationId.PicturesLibrary,
            DefaultFileExtension = extension
        };
saveFilePicker.FileTypeChoices.Add(
    "Image File", new List<string>(new[] { extension }));
```

You can pass several options to the picker, including a suggested filename, a suggested start location, and a default file extension. This gives the dialog enough information to open in a logical location but gives the users the flexibility to navigate to whatever folder they want to save the image to. In addition, you control the available extensions. If your file can be saved with different file types, you can specify a list and even process the file based on the extension provided. In this case, only the extension that matches the image type is provided, and it appears in the drop-down as Image File for the option.

The next line of code invokes the dialog so the user can choose the file to save the image to.

```
var storageFile = await saveFilePicker.PickSaveFileAsync();
```

The user can either navigate to a folder and enter a filename and extension or cancel the dialog. If the user chooses a file, you receive an instance of a `StorageFile` that represents the choice. If the user cancels, the result is `null`. After determining that a valid file was provided, the application makes a call to the `CachedFileManager`.

```
CachedFileManager.DeferUpdates(storageFile);
```

This is an important call because it informs the Windows Runtime that you are going to modify the file. This is especially helpful if the file is mapped to an online storage space such as OneDrive. The usual behavior is to synchronize any files when they change. It would be inefficient for OneDrive to synchronize a file that you are in the process of writing to because it could potentially require multiple synchronizations to happen until the file is done being written. The call to defer the updates allows the provider to wait until you are done updating the file before attempting to synchronize it. The next lines of code write the buffer to the file and then notify the `CachedFileManager` that you are done making updates.

```
await FileIO.WriteBytesAsync(storageFile, result.Buffer);
await CachedFileManager.CompleteUpdatesAsync(storageFile);
```

The picker enables you to save to a folder that the user chooses, but after your app closes, you no longer have access to that file without going via the picker again. Although the picker remembers the user's last location and automatically opens that location if you don't pass your own suggested location, sometimes you want users to simply open the last file they saved. It is not a great user experience to force them to navigate to the file every time they want to give access to your app. Fortunately, WinRT provides a way to transparently access those files outside the sandbox without user interaction by saving a special token that maps to the `StorageFile` or `StorageFolder` the user picked. You can then reference it again without violating security by knowing where it exists on the user's hard drive, network share, or even OneDrive.

Example: File Open Picker and Access Cache

The included **FilePickerExample** project demonstrates how to use the `FileOpenPicker` and how to save references to files so that you can access them without forcing the user to pick them a second time. The code-behind file `MainPage.xaml.cs` contains all the logic. The app prompts the user to select a text file and then displays the contents of the file. A list of recently opened files is provided, and the user can also opt to reopen the last file, even after closing and restarting the app.

The picker is invoked in the code-behind method `PickButton_OnClick` that is triggered by the button used to pick a file. You can choose to use a list view or show thumbnails. This example uses the list view and starts at the special computer folder that lists all the user's available storage options. The picker is limited to files with a `.txt` extension.

```
var picker = new FileOpenPicker
                    {
                        ViewMode = PickerViewMode.List,
                        SuggestedStartLocation =
                        PickerLocationId.ComputerFolder
                    };
picker.FileTypeFilter.Add(".txt");
```

When the picker is set up, the dialog displays to the user.

```
var file = await picker.PickSingleFileAsync();
```

Similar to the save picker, the load picker either returns the file if the user picked one or returns `null` if the user cancels. Figure 4.6 shows an example of the open picker.

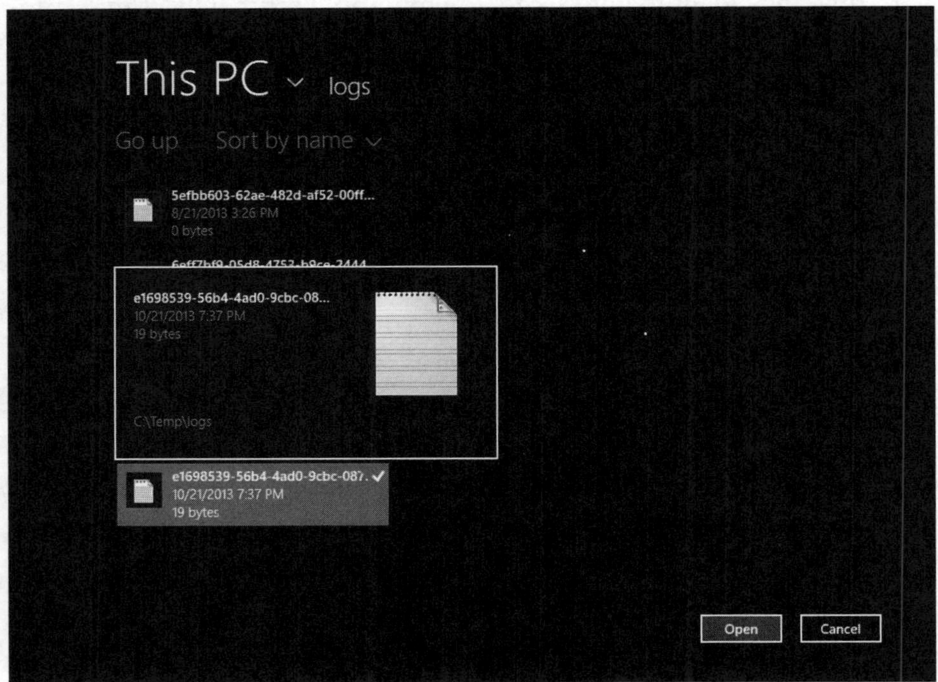

FIGURE 4.6 Dialog for picking a file to open

After the user picks a file, the app reads the content of the file and displays it using a `TextBlock` control.

```
var text = await FileIO.ReadTextAsync(file);
TextDisplay.Text = text;
```

You can save a reference to a file that the user picked in two ways so that you can open it later without prompting the user. One way is to add it to the "most recently used" list. This is a common list for apps that manipulate files. Visual Studio provides a way to open recent files, projects, and solutions, and Microsoft Office programs also show a list of recently opened files. You can add either the file or the file along with some metadata to reference later. In the example app, the name of the file is passed to the metadata.

```
StorageApplicationPermissions.MostRecentlyUsedList.Add(file,
   file.Name);
```

The call returns a unique token that you can save and use later to restore the file. The sample app doesn't save the token because it is available in the list of entries for the recently used files. The app parses this list anytime the main page is navigated to and subsequently when the list is changed. This is done in the `RebuildEntries` method.

```
var entries =
   StorageApplicationPermissions.MostRecentlyUsedList.Entries;
var recentList = entries.Select(item =>
    new RecentItem
    {
        Name = item.Metadata,
        Token = item.Token
    }).ToList();
RecentFiles.ItemsSource = recentList;
```

You can see that the entries are parsed into a special class that holds the name of the item and the unique token. The name is used to display a list. If the user selects a file from the list, the `Recentfiles_OnSelectionChanged` handler is invoked. The handler inspects the currently selected item and uses the token to load the file.

```
var file = await
   StorageApplicationPermissions.MostRecentlyUsedList
   .GetFileAsync(recentItem.Token);
```

The token keeps track of the actual file. The call to access the file succeeds even if the file has been renamed or moved. If the file has been deleted, the call throws a `FileNotFoundException`. The app captures the exception and removes the token from the list of recently used items.

```
catch (FileNotFoundException)
{
    TextDisplay.Text = "** The file no longer exists. **";
    StorageApplicationPermissions.MostRecentlyUsedList
       .Remove(recentItem.Token);
    this.RebuildEntries();
}
```

The `MostRecentlyUsedList` is a specific queue you can use to keep track of recently accessed items. The `FutureAccessList` is a more open-ended list that enables you to track any file you might need to access in the future, regardless of how recently it was accessed. You can either use the system-generated token or pass a token of your own. The `SetMostRecentlyUsedFile` method uses this list to always store the last file that was opened. This could be determined by querying the list of recently used items, but the example shows how you can track any type of file and use any token. The example uses a string token based on a defined constant.

```
private static void SetMostRecentlyUsedFile(IStorageItem file)
{
    StorageApplicationPermissions.FutureAccessList
       .AddOrReplace(LastUsedFile, file);
}
```

You access the file the same way by passing the token back. Listing 4.2 shows the handler for the button to load the last file. It first checks to see if the token exists in the cache; then it attempts to load the file. If the file has been deleted, the token is deleted from the cache.

LISTING 4.2 Using the `FutureAccessList`

```
private async void LastButton_OnClick(
    object sender,
    RoutedEventArgs e)
{
    if (!StorageApplicationPermissions.FutureAccessList
        .ContainsItem(LastUsedFile))
    {
        return;
    }

    try
    {
        var file = await StorageApplicationPermissions.FutureAccessList
            .GetFileAsync(LastUsedFile);
        var text = await FileIO.ReadTextAsync(file);
        this.TextDisplay.Text = text;
    }
    catch (FileNotFoundException)
    {
        StorageApplicationPermissions.FutureAccessList
            .Remove(LastUsedFile);
    }
}
```

The pickers give the user a consistent way to access the file system and provide explicit permissions to your app to manipulate files and folders. You can use the `StorageApplicationPermissions` caches to preserve access to resources through the use of tokens. In Chapter 11, you learn how you can extend the file picker to use your app as a source for the user to save and load files.

Compression

The resources in your app commonly take up quite a bit of space. For the **Skrape** project, the text and HTML for a page might take megabytes of data. This data is often repetitious and full of whitespace, and it takes up far less space when compressed. Compression and decompression are easy with WinRT. Two approaches to compression are useful.

The first approach is one you are likely familiar with. The zip archive is one of the most popular formats for sharing data because it allows compression of multiple folders and files into a single archive. The .NET Base Class

Library (BCL) provides an API in the `System.IO.Compression` namespace to deal with archives. First, create a stream for the archive to work with. In the `SavePageData` method of the `PageAndGroupManager` class, a file is created with the page ID and the zip extension.

```
var file = await folder.CreateFileAsync(string.Format(
ZipTemplate, page.Id), CreationCollisionOption.ReplaceExisting);
```

Next, the file is opened for writing and passed to a new instance of the `ZipArchive` class. The constructor enables you set the mode to create, read, or update the archive.

```
using (var zip = new ZipArchive(
await file.OpenStreamForWriteAsync(), ZipArchiveMode.Create))
```

When the archive is ready, you can create entries. Entries take relative paths and filenames so that you can construct a virtual folder structure within the archive. For this example, the archive is flat and contains the HTML and text for a page. The entry exposes a stream that you can use to write to the entry.

```
ZipArchiveEntry htmlEntry = zip.CreateEntry(HtmlEntry);
using (var htmlStream = new StreamWriter(htmlEntry.Open()))
{
    await htmlStream.WriteAsync(page.Html);
}
```

The same steps are repeated for the text file. After the archives are saved, you can navigate to the **Skrape** package local storage folder to view the archives. Windows 8.1 has built-in support for archives in the file system, so you can open the file by double-clicking. Inside, you see the archived HTML and text files, and you can extract and open them. Figure 4.7 shows an example of an archive.

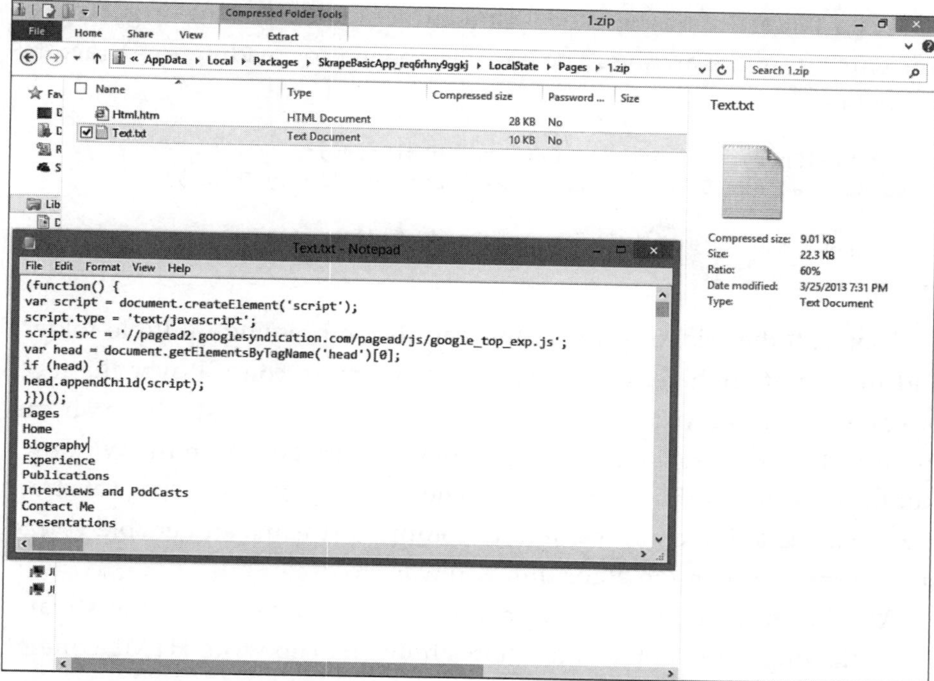

FIGURE 4.7 **Opening the contents of a zip archive using Explorer**

You can override the level of compression by entry. The `ZipFileExtensions` class from the `System.IO.Compression.FileSystem.dll` assembly also defines extensions methods that enable you to perform actions such as adding a file to the archive with a single line of code and extracting the archive to a given directory.

Opening the archive is as simple as creating a stream for reading from the file and passing it into the same archive class. This is done in the `RestorePageData` method.

```
using (var fileStream = await folder
.OpenStreamForReadAsync(string.Format(ZipTemplate, page.Id)))
{
   using (var zipArchive = new ZipArchive(fileStream,
      ZipArchiveMode.Read)) ...
```

When the archive is opened, you can iterate the entries or get a specific entry from the archive. The entry is opened for reading to extract the contents.

```
var htmlEntry = zipArchive.GetEntry(HtmlEntry);
using (var htmlStream = new StreamReader(htmlEntry.Open()))
{
    page.Html = await htmlStream.ReadToEndAsync();
}
```

That's all there is to compressing and decompressing multiple folders and files in an archive. If you want to have more control over the level of compression or you need to compress only a single stream, you can use the `Windows.Storage.Compression` namespace that exists in the Windows Runtime (WinRT APIs and not .NET). The classes in the namespace abstract the steps needed to compress and decompress streams and enable you to specify the compression algorithm you want to use.

As with the archive, the compression APIs overlay an existing stream. The following commented code shows how you can write HTML content to an output stream using the default compression algorithm.

```
using (var compressor = new Compressor(
   await file.OpenAsync(FileAccessMode.ReadWrite)))
{
    var htmlBytes = Encoding.UTF8.GetBytes(page.Html);
    await compressor.WriteAsync(
        BitConverter.GetBytes(htmlBytes.Length).AsBuffer());
    await compressor.WriteAsync(htmlBytes.AsBuffer());
    await compressor.FinishAsync();
}
```

You can pass a compression algorithm to the constructor. The available algorithms[8] include an invalid option to test error handling, a null algorithm that passes through the data unaltered for testing, MSZIP, XPRESS, XPRESS with Huffman encoding, and LZMS. You can also pass the block size for the compression algorithm to use. To decompress, simply wrap the stream you are reading with a `Decompressor` instance.

---

[8]CompressAlgorithm enumeration (Windows), http://bit.ly/YE9Zry

```
using (var decompressor = new Decompressor(fileStream
    .AsInputStream()))
{
    var decompressionStream = decompressor.AsStreamForRead();

    var sizeBytes = new byte[sizeof(int)];
    await decompressionStream.ReadAsync(sizeBytes, 0, sizeof(int));
    var totalSize = BitConverter.ToInt32(sizeBytes, 0);
    var byteBuffer = new byte[totalSize];
    await decompressionStream.ReadAsync(byteBuffer, 0, totalSize);
    page.Html = Encoding.UTF8.GetString(byteBuffer, 0,
        byteBuffer.Length);
}
```

The built-in APIs for compression make compressing and decompressing data relatively easy and straightforward. Consider using a zip archive if you need to store multiple files or you want to export your compressed data; otherwise, the `Compressor` and `Decompressor` classes should address your needs.

Data Formats

The Windows Runtime provides a few components for dealing with specific data types. These are WinRT components that you can use in place of existing .NET components. For example, the **HelloWorldGridApp** from Chapter 1, "The New Windows Runtime," uses the `SuspensionManager` class that is part of the template to serialize the state of the application to XML. The `SuspensionManager`, in turn, uses the `DataContractSerializer` that is part of the .NET Framework (available in the `System.Runtime.Serialization` namespace). Classes in namespaces that begin with `System` are typically .NET Framework classes; the WinRT components exist in namespaces that begin with `Windows` (the exceptions were noted in Chapter 1).

The two main data types you can work with directly are Extensible Markup Language (XML) and JavaScript Object Notation (JSON). Both are standards for storing structured data in a human-readable format. JSON has become more popular because the format uses a notation based on the JavaScript language that makes it easy for browsers to parse the information.

The classes to manipulate XML data exist in the `Windows.Data.Xml.Dom` namespace. The `Windows.Data.Xml.Xsl` namespace is also available to support applying Extensible Stylesheet Language Transformations (XSLT) to XML data. The `Windows.Data.Json` namespace supports parsing and creating JSON data. Although a `Windows.Data.Html` namespace also exists, it provides only a single static `HtmlUtilities` class with a method called `ConvertToText` that simply removes markup tags and turns an HTML document into its text content. The Skrape app did not use it because it does not distinguish between regular text and text in heading, title, and script blocks.

Example: Working with Data Formats

The **DataFormatsExample** project demonstrates how to use the WinRT components to parse and manipulate data. It contains a sample XML file[9] used by several MSDN examples. The file is a catalog containing books. Listing 4.3 shows an example entry for a single book.

Listing 4.3 A Book Entry in XML

```
<book id="bk102">
  <author>Ralls, Kim</author>
  <title>Midnight Rain</title>
  <genre>Fantasy</genre>
  <price>5.95</price>
  <publish_date>2000-12-16</publish_date>
  <description>
    A former architect battles corporate zombies,
    an evil sorceress, and her own childhood to become queen
    of the world.
  </description>
</book>
```

The `Parse_OnClick` method in `MainPage.xaml.cs` starts by getting a reference to the file that is part of the package.

```
var file = await StorageFile.GetFileFromApplicationUriAsync(
    this.booksUri);
```

[9]Sample XML File (books.xml), http://bit.ly/15VFIYu

Then it parses the contents of the file into an `XmlDocument` instance.

```
var xml = await XmlDocument.LoadFromFileAsync(file);
```

The resulting instance now exposes several methods and properties you can use to navigate and manipulate the XML document. For example, the catalog element is referenced as the root `XmlElement` for the document.

```
XmlElement catalog = xml.DocumentElement;
```

The `GetElementsByTagName` method gets a list of the child nodes that are instances of books, and each book is processed and parsed into a corresponding JSON reference. Getting the value of an attribute is as simple as calling `GetAttribute` with the attribute name, as shown in the `ParseBook` method.

```
book.GetAttribute("id")
```

Equally straightforward is the process of getting the name of an element and parsing the text contained inside the opening and closing tags.

```
obj.Add(element.NodeName,
   JsonValue.CreateStringValue(element.InnerText));
```

The classes also provide a set of methods you can use to create content (such as `CreateAttribute`), remove tags (`RemoveChild`), and save the resulting document (`SaveToFileAsync`). All the available methods are documented in the online MSDN library.[10] In the example, the XML is parsed to transform the data to JSON. At the highest level, JSON allows for objects or arrays of objects. JSON objects are specifically dictionaries of name/value pairs with support for numeric, Boolean, and string types. Other types must be stored as strings and translated as necessary (yes, surprisingly, no standardized way exists for dealing with dates in JSON).

The JSON helper classes provided by WinRT make it easier to parse and iterate through JSON data, as well as to construct it based on the various

[10]XmlDocument class (Windows), http://bit.ly/16if3Y7

components. For example, the catalog is an array of objects, so the name/value pair is `catalog` and an array type.

```
var json = new JsonObject();
var books = new JsonArray();
json.Add("catalog", books);
```

Of course, the array needs to be populated with data. This is achieved by supplying some name/value pairs. In the case of the book catalogs, the element name is paired with the text inside the element.

```
obj.Add(element.NodeName,
   JsonValue.CreateStringValue(element.InnerText));
```

After the JSON object has been constructed, you can convert it to its string representation by calling the `Stringify` method.

```
var jsonText = json.Stringify();
```

You can run the example to see the result. Listing 4.4 shows a book entry in JSON format.

LISTING 4.4 A Book Entry in JSON

```
{ id: "bk102",
  author: "Ralls, Kim",
  title: "Midnight Rain",
  genre: "Fantasy",
  price: 5.95,
  "publish_date": "2000-12-16",
  Description: "\nA former architect battles corporate zombies,
➥\nan evil sorceress, and her own childhood to become queen
➥\nof the world."
}
```

One of the advantages of using the built-in classes is that they automatically make values "JSON safe" by escaping special characters and adding new lines for you. To parse JSON from text into an object, use the `JsonObject.Parse` method. The MSDN library documents the full API online.[11]

[11]Windows.Data.Json namespace (Windows), http://bit.ly/16YNtR0

XSLT Transformations

A common way to display XML data is to transform the data into another format for easy viewing. You can accomplish this without having to translate the XML into an intermediary object. Extensible Stylesheet Language Transformations (XSLT)[12] translate XML into other text-based document formats. Using templates that translate XML into HTML to be displayed within a web page is popular.

Full coverage of what is possible through XSLT is outside the scope of this book, but it is a powerful format that uses templates to parse and translate XML documents. You can use templates to generate HTML that you send to a `WebView` control. The included **DataFormatsExample** project provides a simple transformation to format the XML in a text-based format that is displayed in a `TextBlock` control.

The XML file is loaded the same way it was in the previous example. The XSLT file is also loaded first as an XML file and then passed into an instance of `XsltProcessor` (this is in the `Windows.Data.Xml.Xsl` namespace). Finally, the `TransformToString` method is called on the processor with the root node of the XML document.

```
var xsltFile = await StorageFile
   .GetFileFromApplicationUriAsync(this.booksXslt);
var xslt = await XmlDocument.LoadFromFileAsync(xsltFile);
var processor = new XsltProcessor(xslt);
var xmlFile = await StorageFile
   .GetFileFromApplicationUriAsync(this.booksUri);
var xml = await XmlDocument.LoadFromFileAsync(xmlFile);
TransformedText.Text = processor.TransformToString(
   xml.DocumentElement);
```

This gives you many possibilities for formatting and displaying XML data. XML is still an incredibly popular data format. You can use many existing XSLT templates to transform the data into a usable format. One common application is to generate XSL Formatting Objects[13] that you can then use to create PDF documents and other file formats.

---

[12]XSLT Tutorial, http://bit.ly/XfiOgt

[13]XSL Formatting Objects, http://bit.ly/14zetXJ

Document Data

Many apps present data in a rich text format. The `Windows.UI.Xaml.Documents` namespace enables you to format text to display in a `RichTextBlock` control. You can format text elements as bold, italic, or underlined, and you can group them into runs (a discrete section of text that is either formatted or unformatted) or with other elements in spans. You can use line breaks to separate text and organize related blocks of text into paragraphs.

The **DocumentDataExample** project demonstrates formatting and displaying a document. You can use a similar technique to parse existing data such as an HTML page, to format it for presentation or to format data from the web or other data sources. The project contains two key assets: several Latin sentences in the `LoremIpsum.txt` file and a list of some of the fonts that come preinstalled with Windows 8.1 in the `Fonts.txt` file. The app starts by loading these assets and splitting the Latin into an array of sentences.

```
var text = await PathIO.ReadTextAsync("ms-appx:///LoremIpsum.txt");
var options = text.Split(new[] { "." },
   StringSplitOptions.RemoveEmptyEntries);
var fonts = await PathIO.ReadLinesAsync("ms-appx:///Fonts.txt");
```

The app then iterates through the sentences and loads them into multiple runs.

```
var regularRun = new Run { Text = options[idx++ %
   options.Length] };
var boldRun = new Run { Text = options[idx++ %
   options.Length] };
var italicRun = new Run { Text = options[idx++ %
   options.Length] };
var underlineRun = new Run { Text = options[idx++ %
   options.Length] };
```

A random font family and size are assigned to a paragraph instance.

```
var fontFamily = new FontFamily(fonts[random.Next(fonts.Count())]);
var p = new Paragraph
{
    FontSize = 9.0 + (random.NextDouble() * 10.0),
    FontFamily = fontFamily
};
```

Finally, the runs are combined with formatting options and added to the paragraph. The following snippet shows a regular run and a bold run being added.

```
p.Inlines.Add(regularRun);
var bold = new Bold();
bold.Inlines.Add(boldRun);
p.Inlines.Add(bold);
```

Each paragraph is then added to the `RichTextBlock` through the `Blocks` property. Figure 4.8 shows the result of running the app.

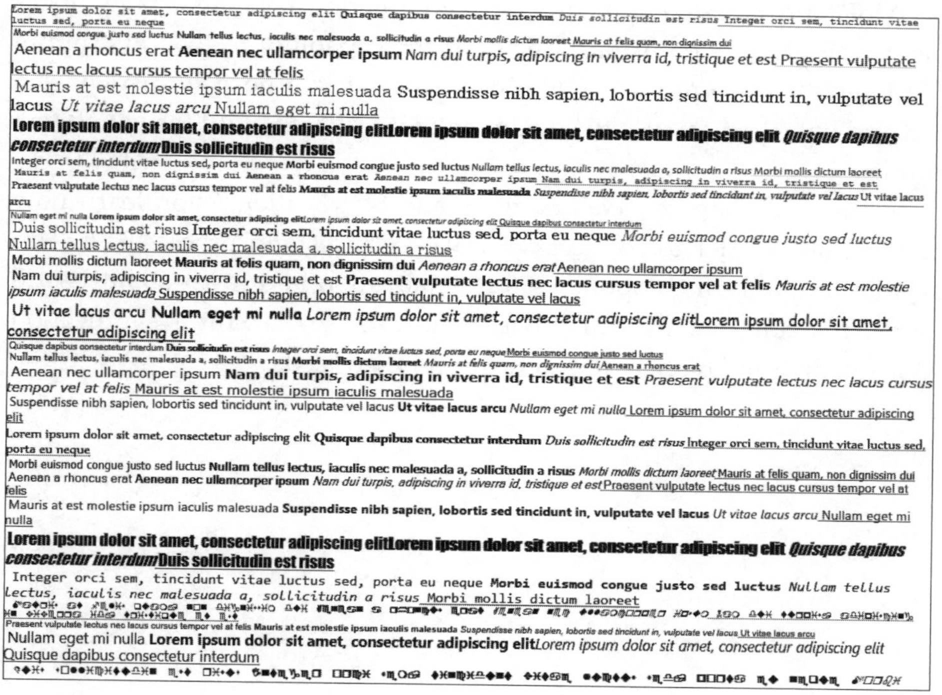

Lorem ipsum dolor sit amet, consectetur adipiscing elit Quisque dapibus consectetur interdum Duis sollicitudin est risus Integer orci sem, tincidunt vitae luctus sed, porta eu neque

Morbi euismod congue justo sed luctus Nullam tellus lectus, iaculis nec malesuada a, sollicitudin a risus Morbi mollis dictum laoreet Mauris at felis quam, non dignissim dui

Aenean a rhoncus erat Aenean nec ullamcorper ipsum Nam dui turpis, adipiscing in viverra id, tristique et est Praesent vulputate lectus nec lacus cursus tempor vel at felis

Mauris at est molestie ipsum iaculis malesuada Suspendisse nibh sapien, lobortis sed tincidunt in, vulputate vel lacus Ut vitae lacus arcu Nullam eget mi nulla

Lorem ipsum dolor sit amet, consectetur adipiscing elitLorem ipsum dolor sit amet, consectetur adipiscing elit Quisque dapibus consectetur interdum Duis sollicitudin est risus

Integer orci sem, tincidunt vitae luctus sed, porta eu neque Morbi euismod congue justo sed luctus Nullam tellus lectus, iaculis nec malesuada a, sollicitudin a risus Morbi mollis dictum laoreet

Mauris at felis quam, non dignissim dui Aenean a rhoncus erat Aenean nec ullamcorper ipsum Nam dui turpis, adipiscing in viverra id, tristique et est

Praesent vulputate lectus nec lacus cursus tempor vel at felis Mauris at est molestie ipsum iaculis malesuada Suspendisse nibh sapien, lobortis sed tincidunt in, vulputate vel lacus Ut vitae lacus arcu

Nullam eget mi nulla Lorem ipsum dolor sit amet, consectetur adipiscing elitLorem ipsum dolor sit amet, consectetur adipiscing elit Quisque dapibus consectetur interdum

Duis sollicitudin est risus Integer orci sem, tincidunt vitae luctus sed, porta eu neque Morbi euismod congue justo sed luctus Nullam tellus lectus, iaculis nec malesuada a, sollicitudin a risus

Morbi mollis dictum laoreet Mauris at felis quam, non dignissim dui Aenean a rhoncus erat Aenean nec ullamcorper ipsum

Nam dui turpis, adipiscing in viverra id, tristique et est Praesent vulputate lectus nec lacus cursus tempor vel at felis Mauris at est molestie ipsum iaculis malesuada Suspendisse nibh sapien, lobortis sed tincidunt in, vulputate vel lacus

Ut vitae lacus arcu Nullam eget mi nulla Lorem ipsum dolor sit amet, consectetur adipiscing elitLorem ipsum dolor sit amet, consectetur adipiscing elit

Quisque dapibus consectetur interdum Duis sollicitudin est risus Integer orci sem, tincidunt vitae luctus sed, porta eu neque Morbi euismod congue justo sed luctus

Nullam tellus lectus, iaculis nec malesuada a, sollicitudin a risus Morbi mollis dictum laoreet Mauris at felis quam, non dignissim dui Aenean a rhoncus erat

Aenean nec ullamcorper ipsum Nam dui turpis, adipiscing in viverra id, tristique et est Praesent vulputate lectus nec lacus cursus tempor vel at felis Mauris at est molestie ipsum iaculis malesuada

Suspendisse nibh sapien, lobortis sed tincidunt in, vulputate vel lacus Ut vitae lacus arcu Nullam eget mi nulla Lorem ipsum dolor sit amet, consectetur adipiscing elit

Lorem ipsum dolor sit amet, consectetur adipiscing elit Quisque dapibus consectetur interdum Duis sollicitudin est risus Integer orci sem, tincidunt vitae luctus sed, porta eu neque

Morbi euismod congue justo sed luctus Nullam tellus lectus, iaculis nec malesuada a, sollicitudin a risus Morbi mollis dictum laoreet Mauris at felis quam, non dignissim dui

Aenean a rhoncus erat Aenean nec ullamcorper ipsum Nam dui turpis, adipiscing in viverra id, tristique et est Praesent vulputate lectus nec lacus cursus tempor vel at felis

Mauris at est molestie ipsum iaculis malesuada Suspendisse nibh sapien, lobortis sed tincidunt in, vulputate vel lacus Ut vitae lacus arcu Nullam eget mi nulla

Lorem ipsum dolor sit amet, consectetur adipiscing elitLorem ipsum dolor sit amet, consectetur adipiscing elit Quisque dapibus consectetur interdum Duis sollicitudin est risus

Integer orci sem, tincidunt vitae luctus sed, porta eu neque Morbi euismod congue justo sed luctus Nullam tellus lectus, iaculis nec malesuada a, sollicitudin a risus Morbi mollis dictum laoreet

Praesent vulputate lectus nec lacus cursus tempor vel at felis Mauris at est molestie ipsum iaculis malesuada Suspendisse nibh sapien, lobortis sed tincidunt in, vulputate vel lacus Ut vitae lacus arcu

Nullam eget mi nulla Lorem ipsum dolor sit amet, consectetur adipiscing elitLorem ipsum dolor sit amet, consectetur adipiscing elit Quisque dapibus consectetur interdum

FIGURE 4.8 Example for formatting rich text

The formatting elements provide everything you need to format and present text. You can override the size of the font, specify various font families, and even add inline UI elements. The `RichTextBlock` also supports overflowing text to a `RichTextBlockOverflow` control. Using this feature, you can format multiple columns or even wrap text around other controls on the page.

Summary

In this chapter, you learned about Windows Runtime APIs for manipulating data and content. You can use the clipboard to share data between Windows Store apps and desktop applications. For Windows Store apps, application storage provides a way to persist settings and store files both locally and using built-in roaming features that automatically synchronize across devices. Pickers provide a consistent way for the user to authorize access to files and folders, and special components facilitate bulk search and storing file references for future use.

WinRT provides components for manipulating XML and JSON documents. The XML support also includes the capability to load and apply XSLT templates to process XML documents. If you need to display rich text and data, you can use the document data APIs to build formatted text entries.

In the next chapter, "Web Services and Syndication," you learn how you can use WinRT to connect with web services and process data. You explore the built-in components for serialization and learn about useful third-party components. You also learn how to use the built-in syndication APIs to parse and display RSS and Atom-based feeds.

5
Web Services and Syndication

Making two computers talk to each other 20 years ago was not an easy task. Literally hundreds of data formats existed, and exchanging even simple information often required complex software that could adapt and transform the data among various systems. Extensible Markup Language (XML) emerged as a human-readable standard for information in the late 1990s and was used to define the Simple Object Access Protocol (SOAP) developed for Microsoft. SOAP[1] is no longer an acronym, likely because there is nothing simple about dealing with it.

The popularity of JavaScript as the "assembly language of the web," combined with the lightweight footprint of mobile devices, helped promote Representational State Transfer (REST) as a way to ditch the overhead of using SOAP and share content using the ubiquitous Hypertext Transfer Protocol. XML is slowly giving way to JSON as a preferred data format. The latter is easy to read and build, and it takes up less space to transmit—plus, JavaScript automatically processes JSON.

Computers on the Internet connect in other ways as well. The web has seen a tremendous explosion in the number of content-based sites, ranging from news sources to personal blogs. These sites often share their content using the older Rich Site Summary (RSS,[2] renamed as Really Simple

[1]SOAP Version 1.2 Part 0: Primer, http://bit.ly/16BoC2A

[2]RSS 2.0 Specification, http://bit.ly/16BoSib

Syndication) format or the newer Atom[3] format. The sources of content are referred to as feeds and are available for you to aggregate and syndicate as needed.

Microsoft added a unique twist to the story by recognizing that although the most common web service operations in Internet applications are often CRUD (create, read, update, and delete) related, no common way existed to implement the services; one application's method for reading a list could be completely different than the next. The Open Data (OData[4]) protocol standardizes this using a combination of Atom and JSON to provide a protocol with full discovery and a consistent interface for filtering and manipulating entities.

Windows 8.1 represents the culmination of several decades of attempts by computers to strike up a casual conversation with each other to exchange useful information. The end result is a set of services that are equally easy to produce and consume. The Windows Runtime, in conjunction with the .NET Framework and several handy templates, provides all you need to connect to third-party services, syndicate content, and operate against remote data from your apps.

SOAP

For the sake of thoroughness, I included a SOAP project, although technically, SOAP has no direct support through WinRT. The Visual Studio IDE provides the capability to generate a set of proxies that enable you to connect with SOAP services. The command-line tool called `WSDL.exe` connects to a web service and interrogates the Web Service Discovery Language (WSDL[5]) for that service. It then generates the necessary C# classes to represent the data for the services and special clients that are capable of connecting to the service. Underneath the covers, it uses the `DataContractSerializer` to map the result of web services calls to their corresponding entities.

SOAP is a platform for exchanging messages between applications and machines over HTTP. It is most commonly implemented as a remote

[3]RFC 4287, The Atom Syndication Format, http://bit.ly/12s6VFK

[4]Open Data Protocol: OData, http://bit.ly/ZmKuRP

[5]Understanding WSDL, http://bit.ly/14VnNW7

procedure call (RPC)–based protocol. It provides a set of operations that typically take parameters and return results. No standard set of operations exists across all services. The author of the service can choose to provide a basic method syntax, such as the following:

```
IEnumerable<Widget> GetWidgets(Filter filter)
```

Or the author can opt for a set of fine-grained operations, such as this:

```
IEnumerable<Widget> GetWidgetsByStatus(Status status);
IEnumerable<Widget> GetWidgetsByName(string nameStartsWith);
```

The proxy that Visual Studio generates uses the WSDL to generate a proxy class that uses the data contracts to model parameters and results and the operational contracts to model method calls for the service. You can then program against the API using the proxy. Each call is a specific operation that flows through the SOAP channels created by the tool.

Take a look at the **SoapServiceExample** project. This example connects to a free, publicly available web service called CDYNE Weather.[6] As a general practice, I prefer to create domain-specific classes to represent the data I'm dealing with and map those from the proxies the service generates. You can see the design of the basic classes in Figure 5.1. A forecast for a city and state contains a collection of forecast entries for each date.

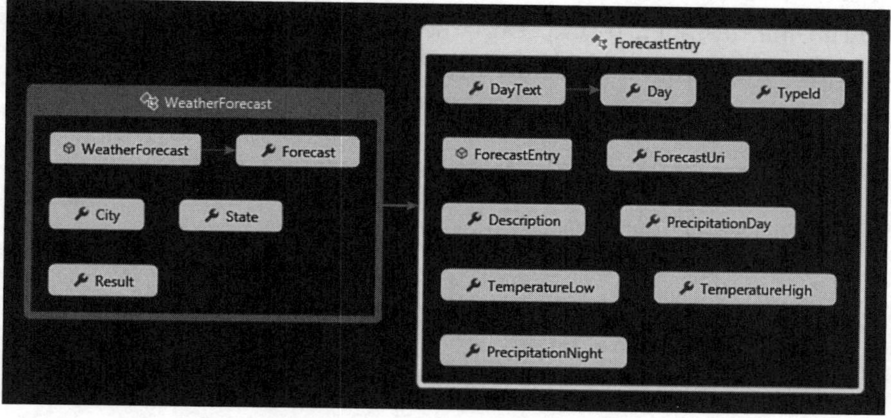

FIGURE 5.1 The forecast and forecast entries code map

[6]CDYNE Weather, CDYNE Wiki for Web Services, http://bit.ly/ZevXkc

This practice enables me to create design-time–friendly controls that I can populate with test data. Listing 5.1 demonstrates a design-time class called `DesignForecastEntry` that inherits from the base class and populates design-time data in the constructor.

LISTING 5.1 Design-Time Data for a Forecast Entry

```
public class DesignForecastEntry : ForecastEntry
{
    public DesignForecastEntry()
        {
            this.Day = DateTime.Now;
            this.ForecastUri = new
Uri("http://ws.cdyne.com/WeatherWS/Images/mostlycloudy.gif",
UriKind.Absolute);
            this.Description = "Sample day for weather";
            this.PrecipitationDay = "50";
            this.PrecipitationNight = "20";
            this.TemperatureLow = "25";
            this.TemperatureHigh = "49";
            this.TypeId = 1;
        }
}
```

I take this approach is it enables me to instantiate the design-time model directly in the XAML designer. You can see a similar approach taken with the overall forecast in the `DesignForecast` class. WinRT exposes a property called `DesignModeEnabled` that allows your code to determine whether it is running in the designer. In the `WeatherHelperService`, if the code is run in the designer, it returns design-time data instead of attempting to call the service directly in the `GetWeatherForZipCode` method.

```
if (Windows.ApplicationModel.DesignMode.DesignModeEnabled)
{
    return new DesignForecast();
}
```

> **TIP**
>
> Several approaches exist for creating design-time data. Native support for generating data is available through Blend that enables you to generate fairly complex objects and lists. I call this the "designer-first" approach because it helps designers create some data that they can then work with and build related domain classes. The approach in this example is what I call the "developer-first" approach because it makes it easy to use code to generate the design-time data and simply tag it in a view. If you are concerned about the design-time data appearing in production code, you can tag it with the `Conditional` attribute or use `#ifdef` blocks to condition inclusion of the code.

Before I even wire up the web service, I create a control to display the results. Listing 5.2 shows the XAML for the `ForecastEntry.xaml` control. Note the use of the `d:DataContext` attribute. This enables me to specify a data context that is used only in the designer. The designer is informed that the class is capable of being instantiated in design-time mode by setting the `IsDesignTimeCreatable` property to `true`. In the example, the instance of a class provides the design data. I provide the type and inform the designer that it is safe to instantiate.

LISTING 5.2 The XAML for a Forecast Entry

```
<Border Width="230" Height="200" Background="DarkBlue" CornerRadius="20">
<Grid d:DataContext="{Binding Source={d:DesignInstance
➥ Type=data:DesignForecastEntry, IsDesignTimeCreatable=True}}"
      Margin="10"
      Width="210">
   <Grid.RowDefinitions>
      <RowDefinition Height="40"/>
      <RowDefinition Height="60"/>
      <RowDefinition Height="Auto"/>
      <RowDefinition Height="Auto"/>
      <RowDefinition Height="Auto"/>
   </Grid.RowDefinitions>
   <TextBlock Text="{Binding DayText}"
              TextWrapping="Wrap"
              Style="{StaticResource BodyTextBlockStyle}"
              HorizontalAlignment="Center"/>
   <Image Width="50" Height="50" Grid.Row="1">
```

```
        <Image.Source>
            <BitmapImage UriSource="{Binding ForecastUri}"/>
        </Image.Source>
    </Image>
    <TextBlock Text="{Binding Description}"
               Grid.Row="2"
               Style="{StaticResource CaptionTextBlockStyle}"
               HorizontalAlignment="Center"
               Margin="5"/>
    <StackPanel Grid.Row="3"
               HorizontalAlignment="Center"
               Orientation="Horizontal">
        <TextBlock Text="Low:"/>
        <TextBlock Text="{Binding TemperatureLow}"
➥ Margin="10 0 0 0"/>
        <TextBlock Text=" / High:"/>
        <TextBlock Text="{Binding TemperatureHigh}"
➥ Margin="10 0 0 0"/>
    </StackPanel>
    <StackPanel Grid.Row="4"
               Orientation="Horizontal"
               HorizontalAlignment="Center">
        <TextBlock Text="Chance of Precipitation:"/>
        <TextBlock Text="{Binding PrecipitationDay}"
➥ Margin="10 0 0 0"/>
    </StackPanel>
</Grid>
</Border>
```

Figure 5.2 shows the result as seen in the designer. This example illustrates how you can design your XAML in a way that avoids dependencies on the implementation of other services. Although the service for this example already exists, I've worked on many projects in which a separate team was building the web services at the same time a client team was building the actual end user app. After both teams agree on the content of the data, it's a simple matter to stand up domain classes to represent the data and build the logic you need, even if the service is not available to connect to, because you can stub the necessary data.

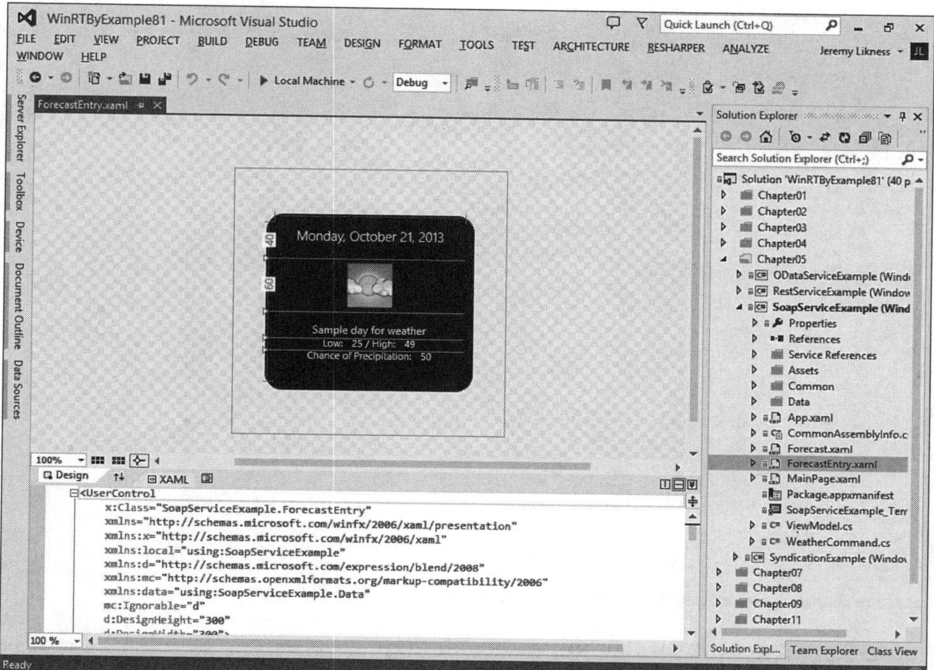

FIGURE 5.2 The design-time experience for a forecast entry

Visual Studio makes wiring in the service reference easy. Simply right-click the project node in the **Solution Explorer** and choose **Add Service Reference**. A dialog appears similar to the one in Figure 5.3. It enables you to enter the URL for the web service (in this case, the URL points to the WSDL that contains the definition of the service) and a namespace to use for the generated proxy. It also expands the service options for you and enables you to choose specific services and operations.

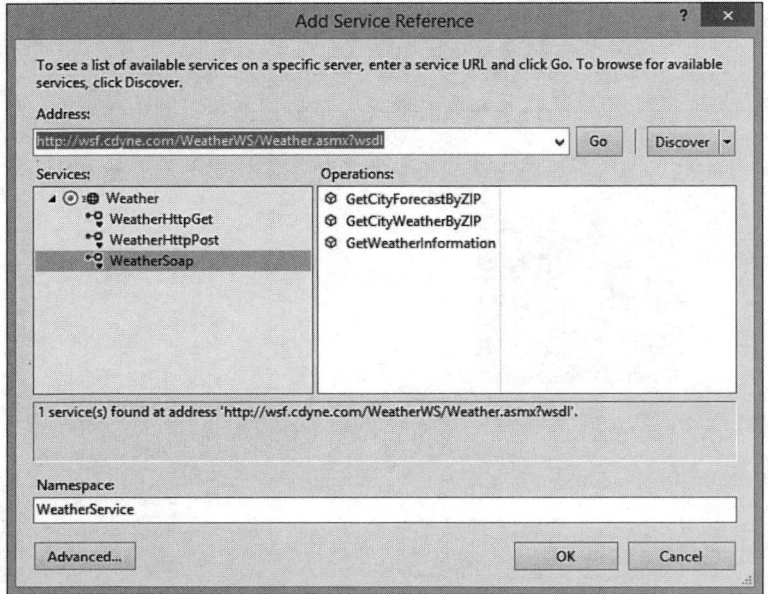

FIGURE 5.3 The Add Service Reference dialog

The dialog launches the `WSDL.exe` tool and both generates the proxies and integrates them into your project. The proxies are hidden from the project, but you can make them visible by selecting the option to Show All Files. The **Advanced** button enables you to specify how the proxies are generated (whether they are lists or arrays or implement property change notification). After you click or tap **OK** and the dialog closes, the proxies are available under `Reference.cs`, as Figure 5.4 shows.

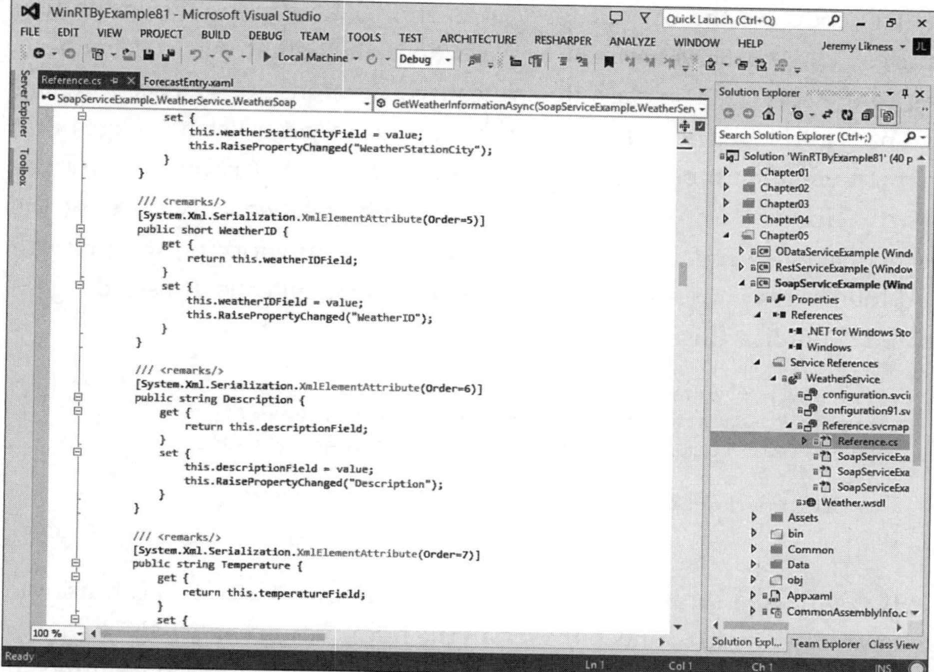

FIGURE 5.4 The generated proxies

The proxies make it easy to write some simple extension methods to map the service entities to their corresponding domain entities. The `Extensions` class contains a method called `AsForecastEntry` to map a forecast entry from the service to the local instance.

```
return new ForecastEntry
{
    Day = forecast.Date,
    Description = forecast.Desciption,
    PrecipitationDay = forecast.ProbabilityOfPrecipiation.Daytime,
    PrecipitationNight = forecast
       .ProbabilityOfPrecipiation.Nighttime,
    TemperatureLow = forecast.Temperatures.MorningLow,
    TemperatureHigh = forecast.Temperatures.DaytimeHigh,
    TypeId = forecast.WeatherID
};
```

The code for the overall forecast is similar and maps the individual entries. The `WeatherHelperService` class does the actual work of connecting to the service. The class illustrates two different approaches to using the proxy. The service provides an operation to get a list of images that map to weather types so you can display icons that show "sunny" or "partly cloudy," for example. This needs to be fetched only once, so the `GetImageUriForType` method caches the entries in memory on the first call and then maps entries from the cache on subsequent calls. It uses the generated client like this:

```
var proxy = new WeatherSoapClient();
var result = await proxy.GetWeatherInformationAsync();
foreach (var item in result.GetWeatherInformationResult)
{
    this.weather.Add(item);
}
```

If you have a service that exists at a well-known URL, you can use the generated proxy to connect. It uses all the information captured when you created the proxies to connect, and no other configuration is required. If you want more control, you can use the `ChannelFactory` to generate a proxy instead. The method enables you to specify a contract and then pass in endpoint information either directly or through named configurations stored in the `ClientConfig` file under the `Properties` folder (this is similar to the way configuration was generated in Silverlight applications).

The example in the `GetWeatherForZipCode` method creates a `BasicHttpBinding` and passes in the URL to the service. The code is wrapped in a `using` statement to properly dispose of the factory when done.

```
var factory = new ChannelFactory<WeatherSoapChannel>(
    new BasicHttpBinding(),
    new EndpointAddress(
      "http://wsf.cdyne.com/WeatherWS/Weather.asmx"));
```

After the factory is created, you can create a channel (the equivalent of the generated client, but configured with the information you provided) and call the service. In the example, the result is copied immediately to the domain class using the `AsWeatherForecast` extension method.

```
var channel = factory.CreateChannel();
var forecast = await channel.GetCityForecastByZIPAsync(zipCode);
var result = forecast.AsWeatherForecast();
```

The forecast is set as a property on the viewmodel and bound to the display so that the end result is a fully graphical display of the upcoming forecast for the city that the entered zip code maps to. If an `EndpointNotFoundException` is thrown, a result is created with a message indicating that the channel is unable to connect (because either the Internet connection is down or the service is down).

SOAP is an important protocol that has been around for a long time. In older versions of the .NET Framework, it was the default protocol exposed by services created by WCF; therefore, many systems rely on SOAP today. Mobile computing has pushed the landscape in a different direction. SOAP envelopes can be rather complex, even when you have toolkits available to generate proxies. REST services, on the other hand, use the readily available HTTP protocol that all mobile platforms must implement anyway. This combination has made REST a far more common and popular protocol, with direct support in Microsoft .NET through the `HttpClient`.

REST

SOAP is a messaging protocol most commonly implemented in an RPC manner. It can have a fairly complex implementation that is made easier by using tools to generate proxies. REST, on the other hand, is a resource-based protocol (commonly referenced as an architecture) that mainly uses features already built into the HTTP protocol to expose an API. The APIs generally follow a well-known format because the URL describes a resource while the HTTP headers provide the action to be performed. Building and consuming REST-based interfaces requires a shift in thinking from the traditional RPC-based approach to the resource-based model.

Table 5.1 illustrates some of the differences between the traditional RPC-based SOAP model and the resource-oriented REST model.

TABLE 5.1 SOAP vs. REST

SOAP Operation	REST HTTP Verb	REST URL	Description
`Person[] GetPersons()`	GET	http://rest/Persons	Gets the full list of `Person` entities
`Person GetPerson (int id)`	GET	http://rest/Persons(id)	Gets the single `Person` entity
`Person InsertPerson (Person newPerson)`	POST	http://rest/Persons	Creates a new `Person` entity
No SOAP equivalent	PUT	http://rest/Persons(id)	Creates a new `Person` entity with the ID specified or overwrites the existing one
`void UpdatePerson (Person person)`	POST	http://rest/Persons(id)	Updates the existing `Person` entity with the new values
`bool DeletePerson (int personId)`	DELETE	http://rest/Persons(id)	Deletes the `Person` entity with the specified ID
`Person[] SearchPersons (Filter filter)`	GET	http://rest/Persons?filter=1234	Returns a list of `Person` entities that match the specified filter
`void UpdateLastName (int personId, string newLastName)`	POST	http://rest/Persons(id)/lastName	Updates the last name of the `Person` entity

You can model most RPC methods as a resource. You can even model commands using REST. Commands that create or modify resources become the appropriate verb and URL combination, and commands that take a specified action can act against special URLs that represent a "resource" for an action that can be taken. The goal is to make the approach consistent, discoverable, and (because it uses the existing HTTP protocol) easy to implement.

The HTTP protocol is bidirectional. Table 5.1 listed a variety of ways to formulate an HTTP request, but the response can also contain data similar to what you expect to see in the return value of an RPC call. The standard way to implement the response is to provide the status of the operation using the HTTP status code and return any other information in the body of the response. For example, a successful call to get a specific `Person` results in the `200 OK` status, and the body contains the representation of the `Person` entity. A call to request a `Person` entity that doesn't exist receives a `404 Not Found` status and no body. Table 5.2 shows some common HTTP status codes.

TABLE 5.2 Common HTTP Status Codes and REST Correlation

Status Code	Description	Use
200	Successful	The operation completed normally.
201	Created	The operation resulted in the creation of a new resource. The body can contain the location of the newly created resource.
202	Accepted	The operation was successfully parsed by the server but is not done. Used for asynchronous operations—for example, you can return this code until the operation is complete and then return a success code.
301	Moved permanently	The operation has a new URL. The body should contain a reference to the new location, and the client should use the new location from now on.
400	Bad request	The server has no idea how to process the request—either it does not reference a resource or it contains malformed data or content.

Status Code	Description	Use
401	Unauthorized	The operation requires authorization, and the client either has not authenticated yet or has authenticated and is not allowed to perform the operation.
403	Forbidden	The client is not allowed to perform the operation, even if it has authenticated.
404	Not Found	The requested resource does not exist.
500	Server error	Something bad happened on the server.
501	Not implemented	The server understands the request but is unable to respond.

One final and important aspect of REST services is the notion of negotiation. A properly implemented REST service should try to provide data in a format that the client understands. Although you could specify this via the URL (that is, you provide an XML extension if you want the data in an XML format), the more practical approach is to use the built-in feature of HTTP 1.1 called content negotiation. Each request can specify a list of acceptable response formats, and the server should try its best to use one of those formats.

A great way to see content negotiation at work is to use a free tool called Fiddler,[7] a web-debugging proxy. The tool works as a proxy between your browser and the Internet and captures and logs requests. This enables you to inspect the headers, response codes, and content of the requests. Figure 5.5 shows the result of opening my blog in the browser. The left side contains all the individual web requests, and the right side shows the details of a specific request. In this example, the page was cached and had not changed, so the 304 status code ("not modified") indicated that the browser could use the cached version of the page.

[7]Fiddler Web Debugger, http://bit.ly/Z4s5qa

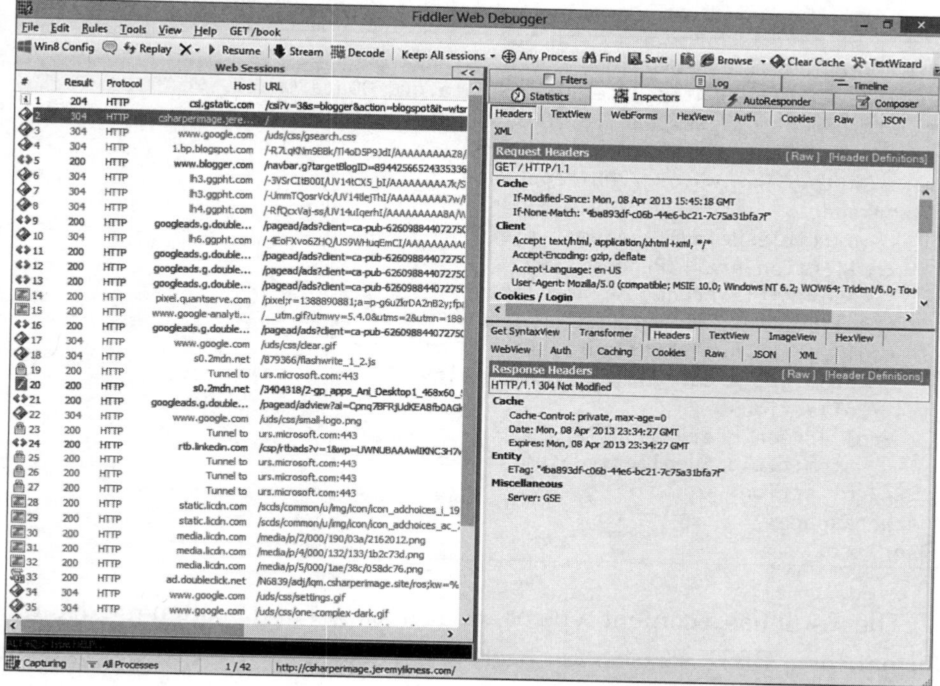

FIGURE 5.5 Using Fiddler to debug web traffic

The top of the right column shows the request that went to the server, sent by Internet Explorer 10. Notice that, by default, it indicated that it can accept HTML (`text/html`), XHTML (`application/xhtml+xml`), or anything the server is willing to throw at it (`*/*`). A neat aspect of Fiddler is that you can use it to create any type of request. Tap the **Composer** tab to create your own request. On the **Parsed** tab, set the action to GET and type the following URL before clicking **Execute**.

http://services.odata.org/OData/OData.svc

This is an example OData endpoint. OData is a REST-based service, so you can use it to explore REST. After the page is fetched, you should see two new sessions appear in the left column. The first is a 307 status code indicating a redirect to the same URL with a trailing slash. That request returns a 200 status code. Listing 5.3 shows the contents of the result. It is a list of available services. The `href` attribute specifies a relative path to the service that you can use to access resources.

LISTING 5.3 An Example Result from a REST Service Call

```
<?xml version="1.0" encoding="utf-8" standalone="yes"?>
<service xml:base="http://services.odata.org/OData/OData.svc/"
xmlns:atom="http://www.w3.org/2005/Atom"
xmlns:app="http://www.w3.org/2007/app"
xmlns="http://www.w3.org/2007/app">
  <workspace>
    <atom:title>Default</atom:title>
    <collection href="Products">
      <atom:title>Products</atom:title>
    </collection>
    <collection href="Categories">
      <atom:title>Categories</atom:title>
    </collection>
    <collection href="Suppliers">
      <atom:title>Suppliers</atom:title>
    </collection>
  </workspace>
</service>
```

The result has a content type of `application/xml` and is often the default format for a REST service. Go back to the **Composer** tab to the **Parsed** subtab and edit the **Request Headers**. Add a line to indicate that your request will accept the JSON format. The headers list should look like this:

```
User-Agent: Fiddler
Accept: application/json
Host: services.odata.org
```

Fix the URL (add a trailing slash at the end) and click **Execute**. Look at the session that is returned. This time, instead of XML, you should have received JSON, just as requested.

```
{"odata.metadata":
"http://services.odata.org/OData/OData.svc/$metadata",
"value":[{"name":"Products","url":"Products"},
{"name":"Advertisements","url":"Advertisements"},
{"name":"Categories","url":"Categories"},
{"name":"Suppliers","url":"Suppliers"}]}
```

You can now add the word `Categories` to the end of the URL. Click **Execute**, and you receive a list of categories. Listing 5.4 shows the JSON for a single category.

LISTING 5.4 JSON for a Category


```
{"odata.metadata":"http://services.odata.org/OData/OData.svc/
$metadata#Categories",
"value":[
   {"ID":0,"Name":"Food"},
   {"ID":1,"Name":"Beverages"},
   {"ID":2,"Name":"Electronics"}
]}
```


Now build and run the **RestServiceExample** project for Chapter 5. The app uses the API to display various categories and products. The `DataSource` class contains the code that connects with the service. The example expects JSON responses, so it creates an instance of `MediaTypeWithQualityHeaderValue` that you can use to set the accepted formats.

```
private static readonly MediaTypeWithQualityHeaderValue
   Json = new MediaTypeWithQualityHeaderValue("application/json");
```

The code to make a REST request is simple.

```
string jsonResponse;
using (var client = new HttpClient())
{
    client.DefaultRequestHeaders.Accept.Add(Json);
    jsonResponse = await client.GetStringAsync(productsUri);
}
```

That's all it takes to grab the string representation of the request response. From the previous chapter, you know that you can parse the string into a JSON object and then use the methods on that to grab the array of categories.

```
var json = JsonObject.Parse(jsonResponse);
var d = json["value"].GetArray();
```

Each entry in the array is used to create a category.

```
var category = new Category
    {
        Id = (int)categoryJson["ID"].GetNumber(),
        Name = categoryJson["Name"].GetString(),
        Location = categoryUri
    };
```

The categories can contain a list of products. In this case, the list is typically deferred, so the code parses the location of the products array and calls another method to iterate the products in a similar manner.

> **TIP**
>
> Although the built-in JSON parser provides everything you need to parse and manipulate JSON data, you might be interested in a third-party open source package called Json.NET. The Nuget entry for the package is online at http://nuget.org/packages/Newtonsoft.Json/. The package provides very high performance, but one of my favorite features is the capability to deserialize directly to strongly typed or dynamic objects. A favorite technique of mine is to create a template for the data using an anonymous type (for example, `var template = new { projectId: 1, projectName: "project" }`) and use the template to deserialize the data into a strongly typed instance that is easy to reference.

The example REST service doesn't support updates, but sending a `PUT`, `DELETE`, or other type of request is straightforward. The `HttpClient` class has methods to `DeleteAsync`, `PutAsync`, and `PostAsync`. To send JSON content, you simply create a `StringContent` instance, set the type in the header, and perform the appropriate action.

```
var content = new StringContent(json.Stringify());
content.Headers.ContentType = new
   MediaTypeHeaderValue("application/json");
var result = await client.PutAsync(uri, content);
```

The methods are consistent and straightforward. It's easy to mock the various operations using a contract and to implement the REST service for production code and stub a fake service for testing. The tradeoff of using pure REST services is that you cannot easily automatically generate a proxy from the service—when the API changes, so does your code (compared to other services, which sometimes make the process as easy as updating the service reference to regenerate the proxies). When the REST service also follows the OData protocol, using the service becomes far easier.

OData Client

The Open Data (OData) protocol is designed to address data APIs. It is based on the Atom format, with a special extension called OData-JSON that surfaces the API in a JSON format.[8] The format allows for representations of various basic data types that can be aggregated into entities, and it has rules for how content can be embedded or deferred. Available operations include reading, creating, updating, and deleting entities, as well as creating links between entities.

The previous examples of REST services used a sample service built on the OData protocol. In the example, you learned how to interact with the API directly and parse the structures to create content in a sample app. The **ODataServiceExample** project is the same app, with one difference: It uses the OData protocol directly through an add-on called WCF Data Services.[9] To install the add-on, make sure you do not have an instance of Visual Studio running. Visit the link and run the installer.

The installer adds the necessary packages to reference an OData feed from within Windows Store apps. To use the service, choose the **Add Service Reference** option the same way you would add a SOAP service. The tool automatically detects an OData source and generates a proxy. Unlike SOAP proxies that contain methods with parameters and return values, OData proxies contain data sources with collections of entities that you can manipulate.

To see how the proxy works, open the `DataSource` class and look at the `InitializeWithServiceData` method. The whole operation to load categories and products takes far fewer lines of code, compared to the raw REST service calls. The first step is to create an instance of what is called the "context" because it provides a context you can use to work with data.

```
var client = new ODataService.DemoService(ServiceBase);
```

The context exposes various collections. Although you can inspect the context, iterate values in the collection, and apply queries, these have no

---

[8]JSON Format of Open Data Protocol, http://bit.ly/12QvLf6

[9]Download WCF Data Services Tools for Windows Store Apps, http://bit.ly/1gq5Obu

meaning until the context is loaded. This is done asynchronously so that the context has time to access the service endpoints and retrieve data. By default, collections contained in other collections will not load. To force the categories to bring in product data, the query option to expand the `Products` entity is added. Several options are available.[10]

The next step is probably the most confusing. As of this writing, the proxy does not support the `Async` style methods you are used to seeing in WinRT apps. Instead, it exposes the old Asynchronous Programming Model (APM).[11] The older model involved initiating a request and getting an object that tracked the lifetime of the request, and then providing a callback to execute another method that ended the request and provided the final output. Fortunately, the model is common enough that Microsoft provided extension methods to convert the APM style to a `Task` you can await.

```
var categories = await Task<IEnumerable<ODataService.Category>>
    .Factory.FromAsync(
        categoryQuery.BeginExecute(result => { }, client),
        categoryQuery.EndExecute);
```

The API can potentially return extremely large data sets, so you have the option to receive a "continuation token" that enables you to page in data. The sample data set is small, so the example passes an empty delegate. This is why you provide two callbacks: One is for determining whether you want to continue populating the set, and the final returns the result set at the end (which is what the example waits for).

After the asynchronous call completes, the context is populated with the requested entities (as affected by any queries or filters you have provided). In the example, the collections are simply iterated and transferred to the domain instances to bind to the UI. If you use IntelliSense to expand the operations on the context, you'll find methods to add to existing collections, update objects, and delete objects. All these operations involve sending updates and refreshing the context to reflect the result of the change. You can also save updates without first querying the context by using the `AttachTo` method.

---

[10]OData by Example, http://bit.ly/19gSjKj

[11]Asynchronous Programming Model (APM), http://bit.ly/12O0AEP

When you are using the context to make updates, the context keeps track of all changes but queues them until you are ready to commit. You commit by calling the `SaveChanges` method on the context. This results in the appropriate operations sent to the server to update the entities. Provisions for handling concurrency are built in; you can read about them in the OData documentation.

Syndication

The OData protocol uses the Atom feed format as a template for managing transactions. RSS (Rich Site Summary or Really Simple Syndication) is an XML-based format that allows publication of dynamic data known as feeds. The Atom Syndication Format is a similar format. The Atom Publishing Protocol (AtomPub) describes how to create and update web-based resources through HTTP.

Feeds typically consist of special documents that contain text, images, videos, and other resources. Popular feed sources include blog entries and news articles, as well as syndicated video and image content. You might be familiar with one of the many feed reader applications. Most frequently updated websites provide a feed of some sort. You can provide the URL of a feed via the HTML `Link` tag with a type of `application/rss+xml` or `application/atom+xml`.

Feeds are so popular that most applications support both autodiscovering and subscribing to feeds. Internet Explorer 11, for example, provides a **Feed Discovery** option under the **Tools** menu that you can use to find feeds on the current page. Figure 5.6 shows the result of using the tool on my blog. You can see that it exposes feeds in both the Atom and RSS formats.

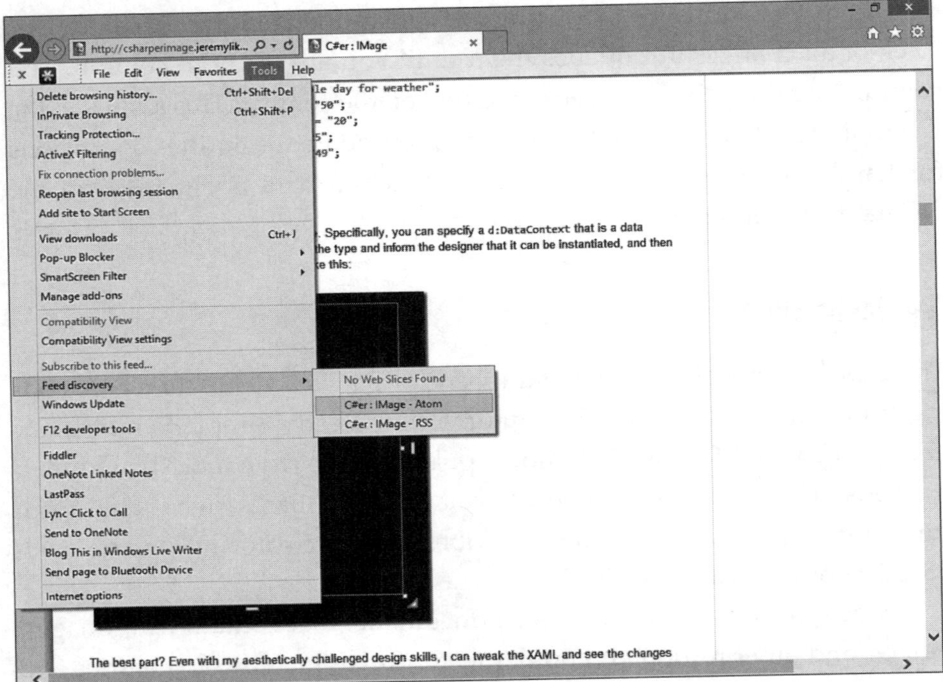

FIGURE 5.6 Feed discovery in Internet Explorer 11

The Windows Runtime provides a set of components to parse, manipulate, publish, and consume feeds in the `Windows.Web.Syndication` namespace that handles the various Atom and RSS formats. The **SyndicationExample** uses the APIs to syndicate the content from my blog called C#er : IMage. The project itself uses the built-in grid template. I modified the template so that a "group" represents a feed and an "item" represents a post. I removed the main page with multiple groups because only one feed exists here, but besides some code cleanup and light refactoring, I left most of the template as is (including the sample data).

All code specific to syndication is in the `LoadSyndicatedContent` method of the `DataSource` class. The first lines of code create an instance of the `SyndicationClient` that provides support to open a web connection, download a feed, parse it into XML, and map it into entities.

```
var client = new SyndicationClient();
var feed = await client.RetrieveFeedAsync(CSharperImageUri);
```

This loads the feed and all the items in the feed. A `DataFeed` instance is constructed, with the result of parsing the feed. This is added to the master groups list. If you want to extend the example to support more than one feed, you can construct another `DataFeed` instance and add it to the collection.

```
var group = new DataFeed(
    feed.Id, feed.Title.Text, AuthorSignature,
    feed.ImageUri.ToString(), feed.Subtitle.Text);
SingleDataSource.allGroups.Add(group);
```

Next, the individual items are parsed. To keep the example simple, I don't attempt to parse images from the pages; instead, I alternate the gray blocks that the template provides. I also use the `Windows.Data.Html.HtmlUtilities` class to strip the text out of the HTML contained within the feed. Figure 5.7 shows the running app.

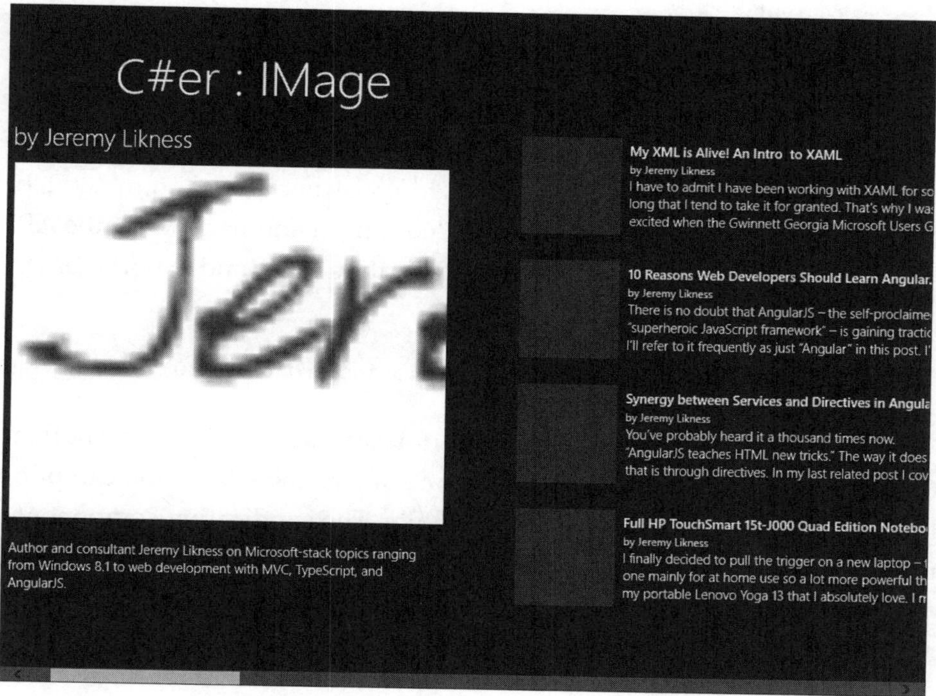

FIGURE 5.7 The syndication example

Listing 5.5 shows the code that populates the individual feed items. You can see that it is relatively straightforward because the class does all the parsing for you.

Listing 5.5 Code to Parse Individual Feed Items

```
foreach (var dataItem in
    from item in feed.Items
    let content = Windows.Data.Html.HtmlUtilities
        .ConvertToText(item.Content.Text)
    let summary = string.Format("{0} ...", content.Length > 255
        ? content.Substring(0, 255) : content)
    select
        new DataItem(
        item.Id,
        item.Title.Text,
        AuthorSignature,
        string.Format("ms-appx:///Assets/{0}",
            urls[idx++ % urls.Length]),
        summary,
        content,
        @group))
{
    @group.Items.Add(dataItem);
}
```

You can use the same components to construct a feed from scratch. Whether you've created the feed or loaded it from another source, the API also provides a method to format the syndication items and export them in Atom 1.0 or RSS 2.0 format.

```
var docXml = feed.GetXmlDocument(SyndicationFormat.Atom10);
```

You also can read the feed in one format and export it in another. Creating an XML document takes just one line of code; then you can publish it, send it to a stream, or save it to a file. The syndication components make it easy to both consume and produce content in the popular Atom and RSS feed formats.

Summary

In this chapter, you learned how Visual Studio, .NET, and the Windows Runtime work together to provide the tools you need to connect to data and services online. Clients and proxies enable you to connect to SOAP, REST, OData, and syndicated endpoints. Components exist to parse XML and JSON and process more robust Atom- and RSS-based data for consumption, manipulation, and publication to the web. In the next chapter, you learn how apps use tiles and toasts to remain alive and connected, even when they aren't running.

6

Tiles and Toasts

TILES AND TOASTS ARE FEATURES OF THE WINDOWS SHELL THAT enable your app to remain alive and connected even when it isn't running. Tiles represent your app on the Windows 8.1 Start Screen. The content of the tile can change regularly to reflect the latest information your app provides, including both text and images. You can enhance tiles by badges that provide timely notifications and at-a-glance information about important actions that can be taken by launching the app. Toast notifications can provide a pop-up message for users to decide whether to bring your app to the foreground or launch it to act on the information.

WinRT APIs also exist that send notifications from within applications that can display a toast to the user or update the tile and badge for your app. All notifications are formatted as a simple XML document that is sent through the appropriate channel. Tiles and toasts can use various templates to display information. In this chapter, you learn about these templates and see how to format and send the appropriate XML to enhance your app by updating the tile or badge or sending a toast.

You can generate notifications in several ways, including these methods:

- Locally from the app itself
- Polled from a web server
- Externally "on demand" from the cloud using the Windows Push Notification Service (WNS)

The style of notification you use varies based on the functionality of your app. Updating tile and badge information externally is important when your app provides services such as email, messaging, and social networking. Apps such as games, puzzles, and productivity software might send notifications internally to show the last document you opened or the high score. Apps that provide content might use the polling mechanism to surface new content as it becomes available from the host website.

Tiles

Tiles launch your app from the Start Screen. They enable you to provide dynamic information so the user can see what is available from your app at a glance. Your email app might cycle through the subjects of your latest emails, and a photo app might show the latest photographs added to an album. Tiles come in three square sizes (small, medium, and large) and one wide size (twice the width of the medium square). The small tile might only be static, whereas the other sizes might allow dynamic content. If your app allows more than one size, the user can customize the Start Screen and choose the desired size. All but the small size are capable of displaying text, images, or a combination of both. You can brand tiles with a small app logo or name, and you can overlay them with a badge. Microsoft's guidance is to choose the small or medium size for static content and to choose the larger tile sizes only if your app will update the tiles with dynamic contents.

Your app must support the medium tile size regardless of the other options you choose. The large and wide tile sizes are optional. If your app supports the large tile size, it must also support the wide tile size. This list provides the possible combinations of allowed tile sizes:

- Small and medium
- Medium only
- Medium and wide
- Small, medium, and wide
- Medium, wide, and large
- Small, medium, wide, and large

After your app is installed, the tile defaults to a static image that you define for the largest tile size supported. A live tile can then update the default tile to show new content. Live tiles support an expiration date for the dynamic content they present. The default tile is not shown again unless the live content expires.

Default Tiles

Your app has a default tile even if you never interact with the notification APIs. This is defined in the manifest under the **Visual Assets** section. Figure 6.1 shows the definition of the standard, 150-pixel-by-150-pixel-wide default tile. If you want to support wide tiles or large tiles, you must also provide a logo for those sizes. You do this by selecting **Wide 310x150 Logo** or **Square 310x310 Logo** and providing an image. The **Square30x30 Logo** is also called the **Store Logo** and is used to preview your app in the Store or when you are tabbing through applications. The **Square70x70 Logo** represents the small tile size. A default image suffices for any supported logo size, but it is recommended that you also provide assets scaled for the other pixel densities. These can be smaller (80%) or larger (180%) sizes to help maintain the clarity of the image at various pixel densities.

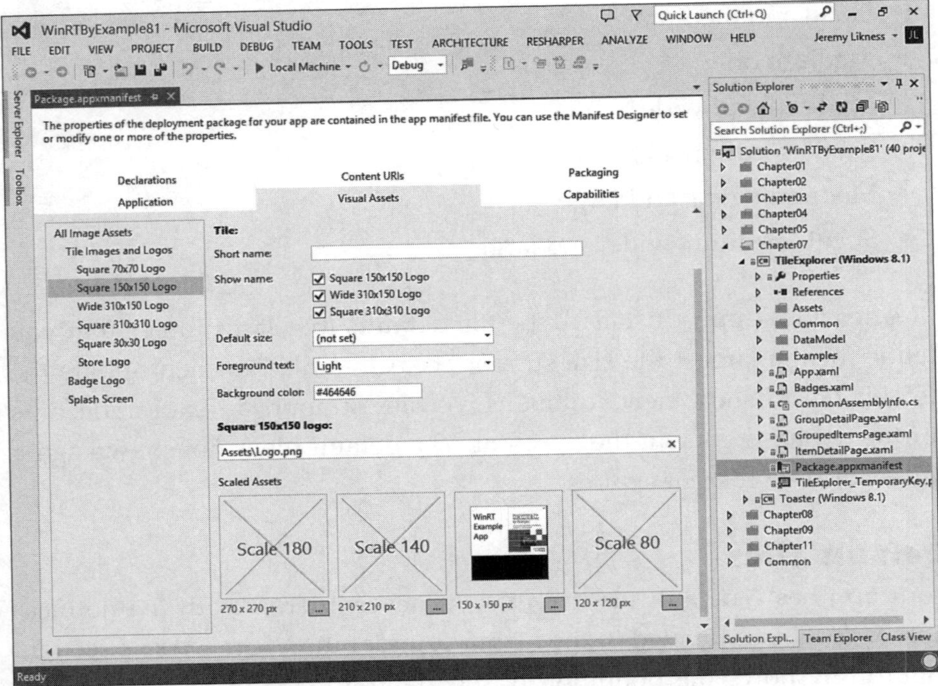

FIGURE 6.1 The setting for the default tile

Note that you can overlay the default tile with text and icons, depending on how you configure your tiles. If the **Show Name** option is set for the specific logo size, the name of the app appears overlaid on the tile. You can choose custom text by filling in the **Short Name** field. In the example apps, I keep the default foreground setting (light text) and provide a dark band at the bottom of the logo so the text is clearly visible. If your default tile is light in color, choose the darker foreground text. Figure 6.2 shows the result of lighter text with the example app tile.

Notice the wider tile with the gray background. This is a live tile. It was set up programmatically and animates through both images and text. Live tiles are the key to sharing relevant, timely information from your app with the Start Screen.

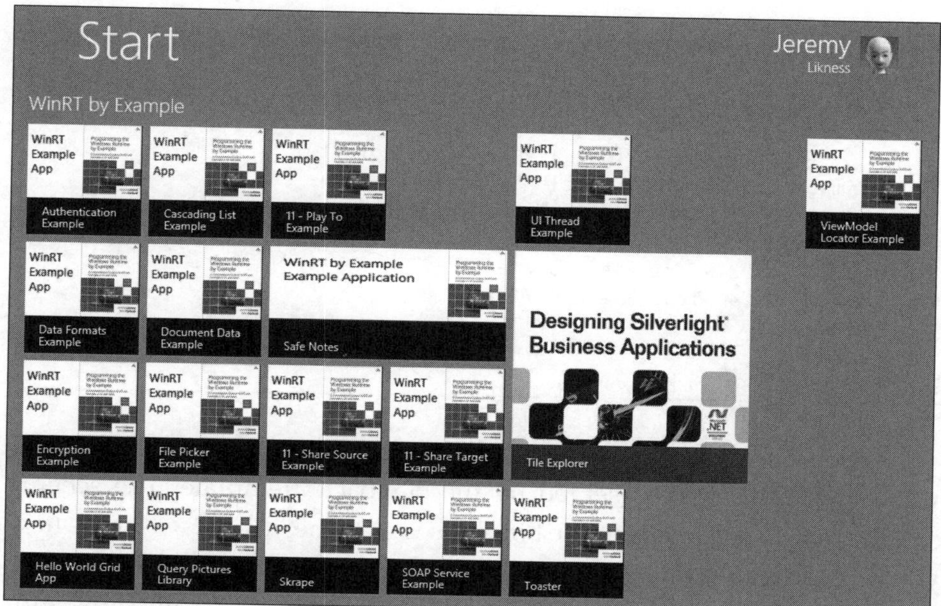

FIGURE 6.2 Example tiles

Live Tiles

Default tiles are fine to launch your app, but the real power of tiles shines when you provide dynamic information. This is the purpose of live tiles. Live tiles are capable of displaying up-to-date information about your app through images and text, and they can animate among multiple notifications. Updating your live tile is as easy as generating some XML and calling a WinRT API.

Windows 8.1 provides a set of templates for tiles. The information for the templates, such as images and text, is defined with XML. You can use the same XML to send a notification locally through a WinRT API or from an external service using a push notification channel. The schema for a tile includes one of several predefined templates combined with any text or images. Listing 6.1 shows the basic format for a tile.

Listing 6.1 The Schema for a Tile

```
<tile>
  <visual version="2" branding="none|logo|name">
    <binding template="TileSquare150x150PeekImageAndText01"
             fallback="TileSquarePeekImageAndText01">
      <image id="1" src="image1" alt="alt text"/>
      <text id="1">Text Header Field 1</text>
      <text id="2">Text Field 2</text>
      <text id="3">Text Field 3</text>
      <text id="4">Text Field 4</text>
    </binding>
  </visual>
</tile>
```

Version 2 refers to the Windows 8.1 tile format, as opposed to the older Windows 8 format represented by the "fallback" template. The schema enables you to specify multiple bindings within the `visual` tag. This is how you provide a tile update when your app supports square, wide, and large tiles. The XML contains a binding for the square format and any other supported formats. The template dictates the layout and animations that the tile supports, and the other elements specify the text and images for the tile.

The `Common` folder in the examples solution contains a project named **NotificationHelper**. This project is a C# class library for the Windows Store apps that wraps the underlying notification XML-based APIs for tiles, toasts, and badges, to make it easier for you to work with. For example, the `BaseTile` class contains everything you need to prepare and set a tile without dealing with XML. It is derived from the `BaseNotification` class for some common functionality that both tiles and toasts use.

The class is initialized with an enumeration. `TileTemplateType` lists all the available templates. The WinRT helper class `TileUpdateManager` provides several APIs you can use to manage tiles. The `GetTemplateContent` method returns an `XmlDocument` that represents the template you are interested in, complete with the elements to set text and images. The count of individual texts provides an indication of what the template can support.

```
this.xml = TileUpdateManager.GetTemplateContent(templateType);
this.TextLines = this.xml.GetElementsByTagName("text").Count;
this.Images = this.xml.GetElementsByTagName("image").Count;
```

The tile helper also makes it easy to add text or images. Listing 6.2 shows the basic code to add a new text line. Note that the method returns an instance of the class itself. This allows for the fluent API you will see shortly.

Listing 6.2 Adding Text to the Template

```
public T AddText(string text, uint id = 0)
{
    if (string.IsNullOrWhiteSpace(text))
    {
        throw new ArgumentException("text");
    }

    if (id == 0)
    {
        id = this.textIndex++;
    }

    if (id >= this.TextLines)
    {
        throw new ArgumentOutOfRangeException("id");
    }

    var elements = this.xml.GetElementsByTagName("text");

    var node = elements.Item(id);

    if (node != null)
    {
        node.AppendChild(this.xml.CreateTextNode(text));
    }
    return (T)this;
}
```

The code is structured to enable you to either add several lines of text or to overwrite an existing line by specifying the index. The image method works the same way and expects a string that represents the URL to an image. You can use images that are embedded in your package (`ms-appx`), images that are stored in the local storage for your app (`ms-appdata`), or images that exist on the web (`http`, `https`). If you specify a web-based image, the image appears when the user is connected to the Internet, or if the user has previously accessed the image, it lives in the browser cache. For this reason, you should use only images that are packaged with or stored with your app unless absolutely necessary (if you need to show fresh content, one technique is to download to local storage when you have Internet access and then reference the image by its local storage path).

If you will support both square and other tile sizes, you should always package all formats in your updates. This ensures that users will see the updates, regardless of what size they picked for their tile. The `WithTile` method handles merging one tile template into another.

```
public BaseTile WithTile(BaseTile otherTile)
{
    var otherBinding = this.xml.ImportNode(
        otherTile.xml.GetElementsByTagName("visual")[0]
            .LastChild, true);
    this.xml.GetElementsByTagName(
        "visual")[0].AppendChild(otherBinding);
    return this;
}
```

One more consideration is whether you want your live tiles to contain branding. The options for branding include the following:

- **None**—Your tile will display only the content you provide. This option enables you to use the full space the tile provides.
- **Logo**—Your tile will display a small logo in the lower-left corner. This obscures the last line of text in a template that supports multiple lines.
- **Name**—Your tile will display the short name of the app in the lower-left corner. As with the logo option, this obscures the last line of text.

After the XML is constructed, you can use the WinRT `TileUpdateManager` class to set the tile. Get an instance of a `TileUpdater` for your application, and then call `Update` with a `TileNotification` instance that contains your XML.

```
public void Set()
{
    TileUpdateManager.CreateTileUpdaterForApplication()
        .Update(new TileNotification(this.xml));
}
```

The **TileExplorer** project from Chapter 6 uses the helper classes to enumerate all tiles on the system. Everything in the app is pulled from the local APIs, with the exception of the preview images that were taken from the MSDN documentation.[1] You cannot automatically preview a tile using the built-in APIs, so the project maps the tile type to a sample image.

The first time you launch the app, it creates a default live tile for both the square and the wide tile sizes. Remember when I noted the helper API returns an instance of the class itself; this enables you to configure and set tiles fluently, as the `OnLaunched` method in `App.xaml.cs` demonstrates.

```
TileTemplateType.TileWide310x150Text03.GetTile()
    .AddText("Tile Explorer")
    .WithNoBranding()
    .WithTile(TileTemplateType.TileSquare150x150Text03
        .GetTile()
        .AddText("Tile Explorer")
        .AddText("A WinRT Example")
        .AddText("by Jeremy Likness"))
    .Set();
```

You can run the app and see the list of available tiles. If you tap on a tile, you can view a description and the XML for the template of the tile (see Figure 6.3). Open the application bar to copy the XML to your clipboard, set the current tile as the live tile for the app, or pin a shortcut to the Start Screen for the tile you are inspecting. You learn more about pinning secondary tiles in the "Secondary Tiles" section.

---

[1]The tile template catalog (Windows Store apps), http://bit.ly/10DOgpk

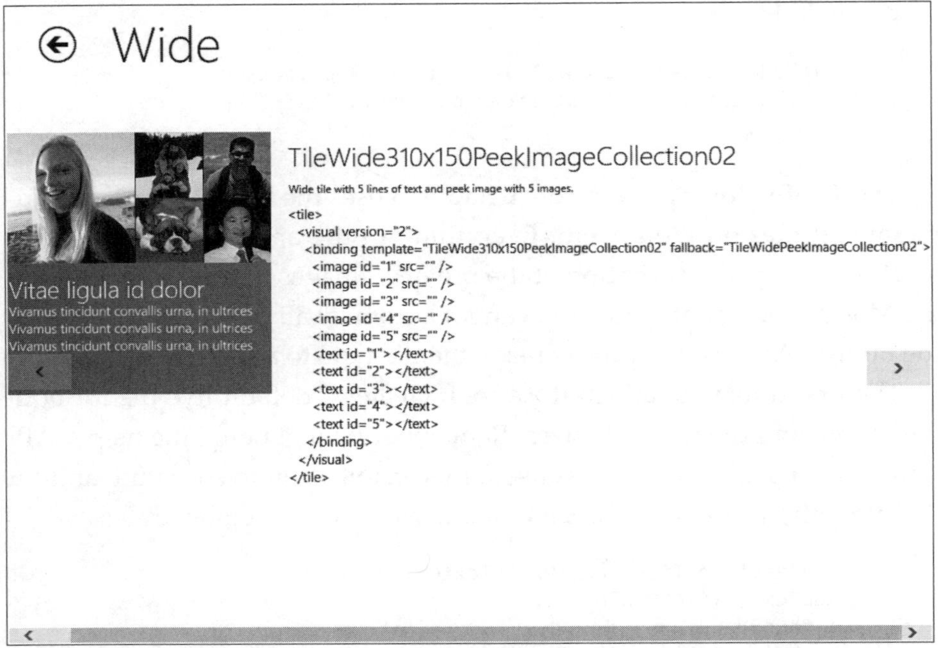

FIGURE 6.3 The details of a tile in the Tile Explorer app. *(Image courtesy of MSDN, used with permission from Microsoft.)*

You might have noticed that even the largest tiles have room for only a few lines of text. The templates allow you to change only the text, not the format of the template. You can't make text wrap, change the font or size of text, or otherwise impact the template, other than to provide the text or image it will show. This makes it difficult to manage cases such as email, when you might want to show text from several email messages as a preview. Fortunately, tiles have built-in support to cycle notifications so you can provide multiple updates for your app.

Cycling Tile Notifications

Cycling tile notifications is possible. You can use a single template or multiple templates in your notifications, although it is recommended that you use the same template, to provide a consistent user experience. When you are not cycling tiles, any tile update automatically overwrites any previous tile settings (unless the user turns off live tiles, in which case the default tile displays). With cycling turned on, you can queue up to five different tiles, and Windows then cycles them on the Start Screen, even when your application is not running. Note that although this provides useful updates to the end user, it is not possible to determine which content was displayed when the user taps on the tile—in other words, the user can launch your app with the tile, but you will not be able to determine which version of the tile was being displayed when he or she tapped it.

The `BaseTile` class contains a method `WithNotifications` to enable cycling and `WithoutNotifications` to disable cycling. The method uses the `TileUpdater` method `EnableNotificationQueue` and passes a `Boolean` that indicates whether the queuing should be enabled or disabled.

```
TileUpdateManager.CreateTileUpdaterForApplication()
    .EnableNotificationQueue(true);
```

When the queue is enabled, calls to update the tile queue tiles on a first-in-first-out (FIFO) basis. When the sixth tile is sent, the oldest tile is removed from the queue to keep the queue length at the maximum of five. The notification setting lasts the lifetime of your app, so you do not need to call it again whenever your app is launched (although there is also no harm in doing so). You can also choose which tile to update.

You can create tiles with a unique tag. After you create a tile from the XML template, you can set a tag property on the `TileNotification` instance, as shown in the `Set` method of the `BaseTile` class.

```
if (!string.IsNullOrWhiteSpace(this.Tag))
{
    tile.Tag = this.Tag;
}
TileUpdateManager.CreateTileUpdaterForApplication().Update(tile);
```

The tag enables you to send updates that target the tile's individual "slot." If you send several updates with the same tag, they only replace the existing tile with the same tag; they do not cycle other tiles through the queue. An example of this is a tile that shows world clocks. You can queue the notifications for five different regions and then update the times for each specific region using the tag.

Some tiles might have timely information that can go out-of-date. For this reason, tile updates can also specify an expiration time. The tile update shows only up to the expiration; then it reverts to other tiles in the notification queue or the default tile packaged with the app. The `WithExpiration` method on the helper class enables you to set expiration based on a fixed `DateTime` or a `TimeSpan` indicating time in the future from "now."

The **TileExplorer** project enables you to turn the notification queue on or off using the application bar when you are inspecting a specific tile. Try turning on the notifications and then setting several tiles in a row. Return to the Start Screen afterward; you should see the tile cycle through the various templates you set.

Secondary Tiles

Many apps provide "deep links," or shortcuts to features contained within the app. In the **TileExplorer** app, you can choose the **Pin** command to create a deep link to a specific template. The resulting tile, referred to as a secondary tile, enables you to jump straight into the information about the template you chose. Handling the secondary tile scenario involves two steps.

The first step is to provide the user with a means to pin the secondary tile. In the **TileExplorer** app, take a look at the `PinOnClick` method in `ItemDetailPage.xaml.cs`. The method first sets up some references to the default logo pictures that are packaged with the app, and then it creates an instance of a `SecondaryTile` (see Listing 6.3).

Listing 6.3 Creating a Secondary Tile

```
var logo150X150 = new Uri("ms-appx:///Assets/Logo.png");
var logo30X30 = new Uri("ms-appx:///Assets/SmallLogo.png");
var logo310X150 = new Uri("ms-appx:///Assets/WideLogo.png");

var tile = new SecondaryTile(
    selectedItem.Id,
    selectedItem.Id,
    string.Format("Id={0}", selectedItem.Id),
    logo150x150,
    TileSize.Square150x150);

tile.VisualElements.ForegroundText = ForegroundText.Light,
tile.VisualElements.Square30x30Logo = logo30X30;
tile.VisualElements.Wide310x150Logo = logo310X150;
tile.VisualElements.ShowNameOnSquare150x150Logo = true;
```

The tile is given a unique ID. This is useful because you can route tile updates to a specific secondary tile. This would be useful, for example, in a financial app that enables the user to pin favorite stocks. You could use the stock abbreviation as the ID for the stock, and you could route updates to the stock's price to the appropriate secondary tile so that it refreshes with the latest price. The short name is overlaid on the tile, and the description appears when the user hovers over the title.

The tile also takes a set of arguments. These are important for passing context into the app so that it can navigate appropriately. Finally, you can choose whether the name is shown on the logos and set the text color. The logos in the example share the default tile for the main app, but you can just as easily include a separate set of assets for secondary tiles, to make them stand out apart from the main app tile.

The code to handle a secondary tile activation exists in `App.xaml.cs` in the `OnLaunched` method. The argument is passed in as a name/value pair, as in `Id=TileWide310x150Text03`. If the argument passed in starts with `Id=`, the string is split to get the tile type. If the main page is currently active, the request to navigate to the specific tile is passed to it. This ensures that, if the app is being launched for the first time, the main page is navigated to first and ends up in the history stack even though the app immediately navigates to the tile. Otherwise, the app is assumed to be already running and the tile details are navigated to directly.

Only users can create secondary tiles. The `SecondaryTile` class is a helper class that provides some default information, but the user is ultimately in control. Instead of creating a secondary tile programmatically, you must request the tile and allow the user to "opt in." For this reason, the request must come from a method invoked by user input, such as a button click.

The rest of the code in the `PinOnClick` method finds the location of the button that was pressed in the app bar and creates a rectangle around it that can be used to position the dialog for the secondary tile. The call to request the tile is then made, and the user can name the tile and choose whether to pin it.

```
var transformation = appBarButton.TransformToVisual(null);
var point = transformation.TransformPoint(new Point());
var rect = new Rect(point, new Size(appBarButton.ActualWidth,
```

```
        appBarButton.ActualHeight));
    var success =
        await tile.RequestCreateForSelectionAsync(rect, Placement.Above);
```

Figure 6.4 shows the resulting dialog. Note the preview of the tile and the option to enter the preferred text. Also note that a flip-style dialog is presented, to enable you to navigate among various tile sizes.

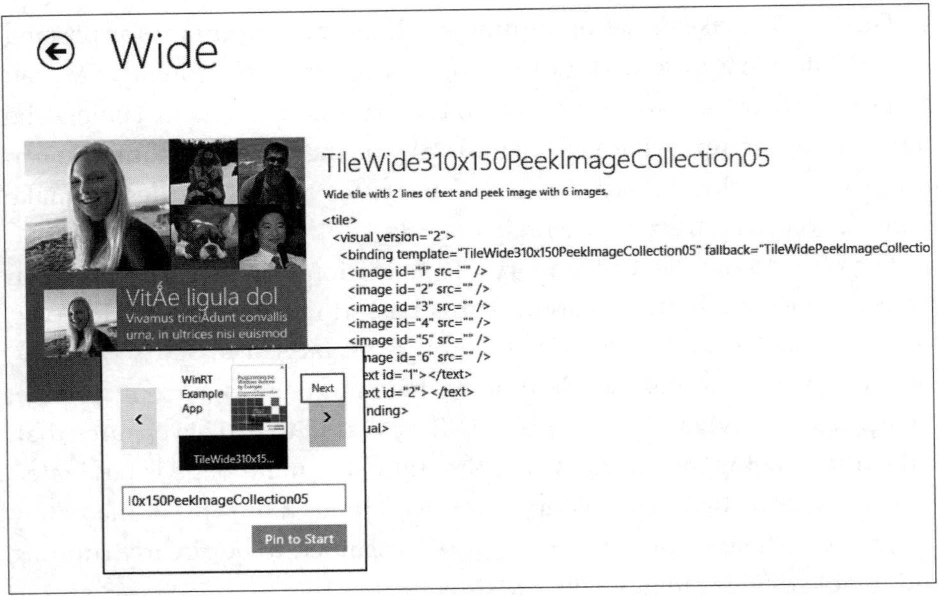

FIGURE 6.4 The request to pin a secondary tile. *(Image courtesy of MSDN, used with permission from Microsoft.)*

If the request was successful, you can save the identifier to interact with the tile later. The API to update and queue secondary tiles is nearly identical to the one for the primary tile. Instead of getting an instance of `TileUpdater` for the app, you get one for the secondary tile using the ID.

```
public BaseTile WithSecondaryNotifications(string secondaryId)
{
    TileUpdateManager.CreateTileUpdaterForSecondaryTile(secondaryId)
        .EnableNotificationQueue(true);
    return this;
}
```

The remaining APIs are identical to the ones for the app but are routed to the secondary tile instead.

Badges

Badges provide an easy way to overlay contextual information on your live tiles that will change frequently. You can use a numeric badge to provide a count of new items or use one of the included glyphs to show a status change. Do not use badges if they don't convey useful information. For example, if a badge is almost always going to be represented by the same glyph, it doesn't convey useful or new information and shouldn't be used. Badges also aren't useful for displaying large numbers such as a player's score (there is a limitation of 2 digits minimum and 99 maximum); that's better left to the content of the tile itself.

The **TileExplorer** app enables you to set the badge on the tile so you can see how it appears when overlaid on an existing tile. To access the badge, open the application bar on the main page (the grouped items page) of the app. You can access this by right-clicking or swiping from the top or bottom of the app. Notice a single icon with a star for accessing badges and the text "Update Badge." Tap this to navigate to a screen similar to the one in Figure 6.5.

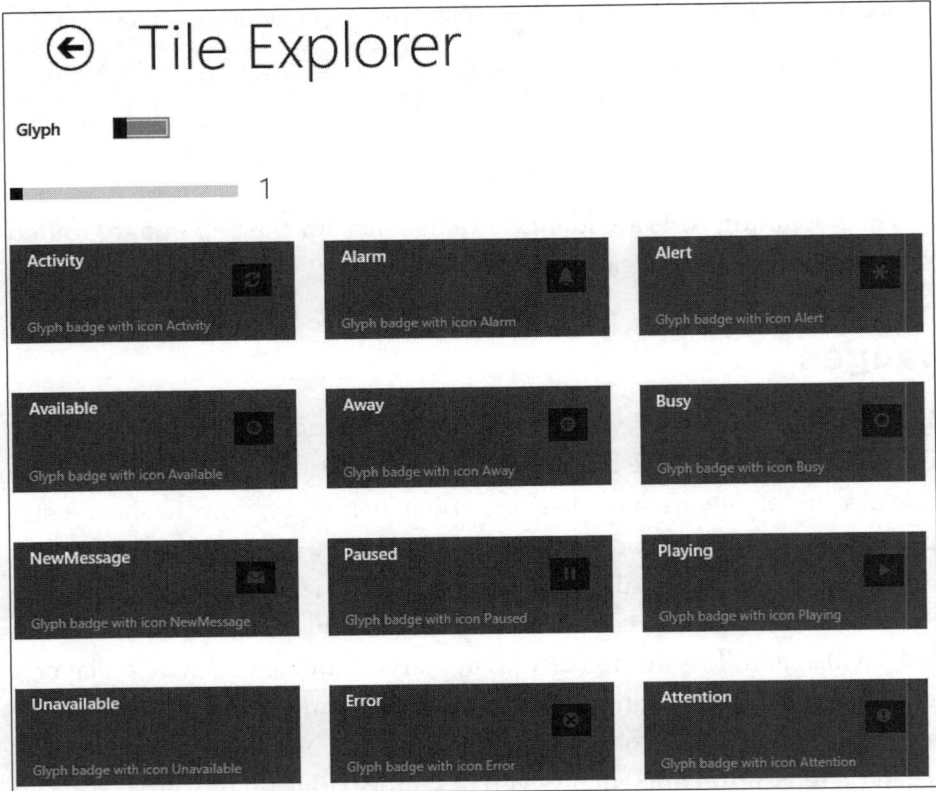

FIGURE 6.5 The badge explorer

From this page, you can select either a glyph (image) or a numeric badge. The slider enables you to choose the numeric value (any number in the range of 1 to 99), and you can pick which glyph to display from the list of available glyphs. At the bottom of the page are two buttons: one to set the badge and another to clear it. After you set the badge, you can return to the Start Screen and view the result; it should appear in the lower-right corner of your tile.

The `BadgeHelper` class in the **NotificationHelper** project contains the code you need to generate your badges. You can use extension methods to cast an integer or one of the glyph types (enumerated in `BadgeGlyphTypes`) to a tile, or call `ClearBadge` to get an empty badge. The `BaseBadge` class does the "heavy lifting" which is fairly straightforward. A similar call gets the template for the badge, but this time it uses the `BadgeUpdateManager` class instead of the `TileUpdateManager` class.

```
this.xml = BadgeUpdateManager.GetTemplateContent(this.Type);
```

The XML for badges is always the same:

```
<badge value="value"/>
```

The value can be either none, to clear the badge; a number, to set a numeric badge; or one of the preset glyph names, to set the appropriate glyph. The base class simply sets up the appropriate value and then enables you to apply the badge to either the main tile or a secondary tile. The API signature mirrors the tile API:

```
public void Set()
{
    var badge = new BadgeNotification(this.xml);
    BadgeUpdateManager.CreateBadgeUpdaterForApplication()
        .Update(badge);
}
```

The guidelines for badges are relatively straightforward. If the numeric value will be consistently high, consider using a glyph instead (that is, use a message icon to indicate new messages instead of the count). Code your app to show new information to the user. Instead of showing "Unread messages" for example, consider showing "Unread messages since the last time the app was launched." If you are indicating a state of the app, use one of the prebuilt glyphs.

Having the capability to show detailed text and images is useful with the badge feature. This gives users everything they need to get updates from your app without even leaving the Start Screen. This isn't helpful when the user is running another app or is in another window. How can your app convey real-time information, such as a scheduled appointment or a weather alert, if it's not running and the user is not looking at the Start Screen? For real-time notifications that can flash in front of users even when they are running other apps, you can use toast notifications.

Periodic Notifications

Tiles and badges both support the concept of periodic notifications. These are notifications you can schedule on a recurring basis to update the tile content automatically. Periodic notifications are useful for apps that require frequent updates, such as a weather app.

You must address two requirements when setting up periodic notifications. The first is that you must have a website that is capable of delivering the XML needed for a tile or a badge (typically as a web service instead of a static web page). This is the same XML generated using the helper classes. You can use the helper tool to construct a tile or badge and inspect the XML to determine what to configure on your website. The content might be dynamically generated, or the URL might point to a static XML document.

To set up the recurrence, simply give the URI for the content along with the recurrence (specified using `PeriodicUpdateRecurrence`) to the `StartPeriodicUpdate` method of the `TileUpdater` or `BadgeUpdater` class.

```
TileUpdateManager.CreateTileUpdaterForApplication().
    StartPeriodicUpdate(uri, PeriodicUpdateRecurrence.Hour);
```

You also can set up periodic notifications for secondary tiles. You can set a batch of up to five URLs for tile updates if you also enable the notification queue. This results in the tile cycling through the different templates you specify. To batch updates, send a list of URLs along with the recurrence to the `StartPeriodicUpdateBatch` method.

Toasts

Toast notifications are transient messages you send to the user. They appear in the upper-right corner of your screen (or upper-left corner, if you are displaying a right-to-left language) and enable you to communicate information regardless of whether the user is in your app, another app, the desktop, or the Start Screen. Toasts typically involve a "call to action" because, in addition to letting the toast fade out, the user can opt to either dismiss the toast or select the toast and navigate into your app.

The most common toast is called a standard toast. This toast appears for 7 seconds and plays a brief sound. During the time it is displayed, the user can either dismiss the toast by swiping to the right or tapping on the Close icon in the upper right, or activate the toast by tapping on it. Activating the toast calls the `OnLaunched` method of your `App` class and passes any related arguments. Your app can then respond appropriately. If the app is not running, it is activated. Another long-duration toast is explained later in this section.

To start using toasts, you must specify that your app is toast capable. You do this in the manifest by selecting **Yes** for **Toast Capable** on the **Application** tab. Figure 6.6 illustrates setting the app to be toast capable. If you don't set this property, your attempts to send toasts will silently fail.

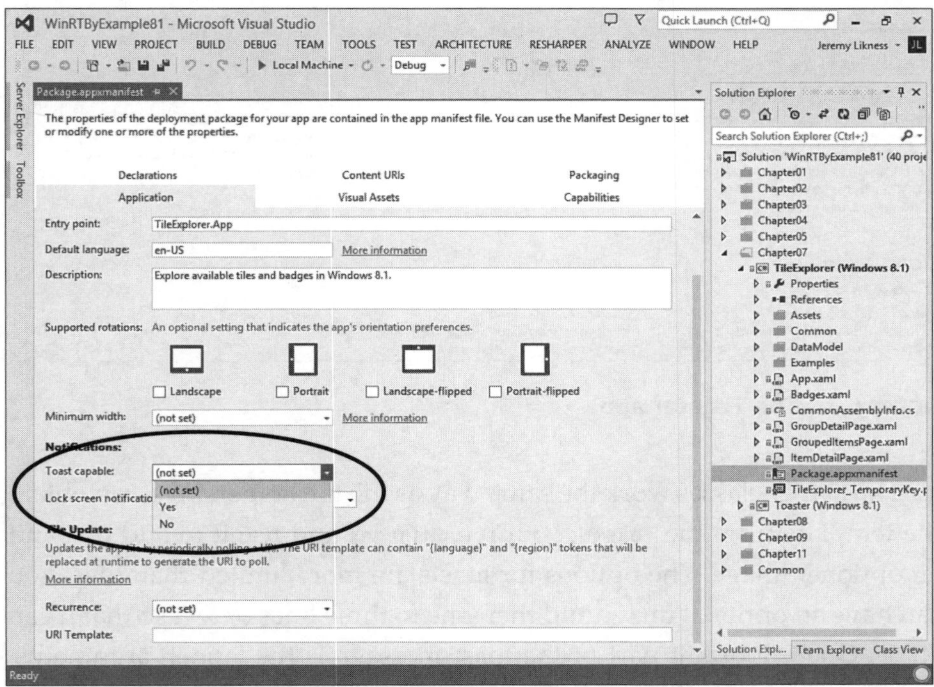

FIGURE 6.6 Setting the app to be toast capable

As with tiles, toasts use several pre-defined templates (see Figure 6.7). The screenshot shows the **Toaster** example project. This project enables you to configure a toast notification and send it based on a given delay. When the notification is received, you can use it to launch the app with the toast you used selected in the list of available options. It uses the **NotificationHelper** project to compose the toasts.

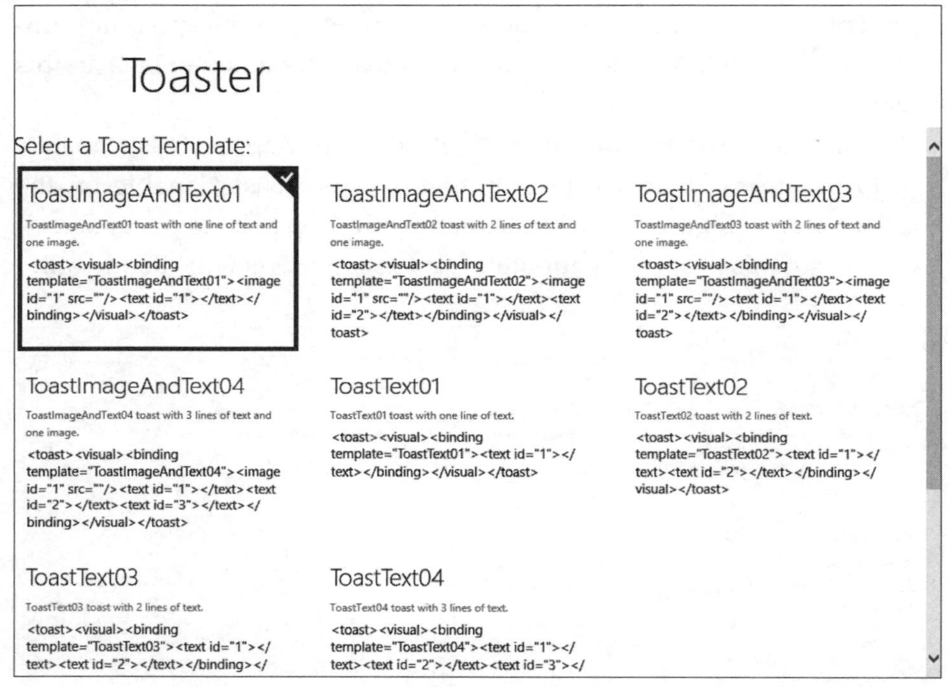

FIGURE 6.7 The Toaster app

The helper classes work the same way as the tile helpers. You can obtain the template from the `ToastNotificationManager` and use it to add text and an optional image. The options for toasts are more limited than tiles. You can have an optional image and then one to three lines of text so that it can wrap. One important part of the toast message is the launch arguments. These are passed via the `LaunchActivatedEventArgs` parameter `Arguments` property to the `OnLaunched` override in your app so you can respond to the notification. The arguments are a simple string that is set to the `launch` attribute of the `toast` XML document. In the **NotificationHelper** project, this is implemented in the `WithArguments` method.

```
public BaseToast WithArguments(string args)
{
    var visual = this.Xml.GetElementsByTagName("toast")[0];
    var launch = this.Xml.CreateAttribute("launch");
    launch.NodeValue = args;
    visual.Attributes.SetNamedItem(launch);
    return this;
}
```

As with tiles, toasts can have an expiration. If the toast notification system is unable to raise the toast in time, it discards the toast. The toast can be either sent immediately or scheduled for a future time. To send immediately, simply ask the `ToastNotifier` class to show the toast.

```
public ToastNotification Send()
{
    var toast = new ToastNotification(this.Xml);
    this.SetExpiration(toast);
    ToastNotificationManager.CreateToastNotifier().Show(toast);
    return toast;
}
```

If you send a toast immediately, because the `Show` method returns `void`, you need to listen to events on the toast itself to figure out how the user responds to the toast. These include `Activated` and `Dismissed`, as well as `Failed`. The last event is raised when the toast cannot be sent, such as when the user has disabled notifications from your app. The user is always in control and can go into the app settings at any time to enable or disable toasts (this is done through the built-in **Permissions** command in settings that display a switch to enable or disable notifications when your app is declared toast capable).

To schedule the toast, use the `AddToSchedule` method.

```
public void ScheduleAt(DateTime schedule)
{
    var toast = new ScheduledToastNotification(this.Xml, schedule);
    this.SetExpiration(toast);
    ToastNotificationManager.CreateToastNotifier()
        .AddToSchedule(toast);
}
```

The **Toaster** example app implements most of the business logic in the `ViewModel` class. The class itself implements `ICommand` for the action of actually sending the toast. In the `Execute` method, it creates a toast based on the selected template and adds the template type to the arguments.

```
var toast = this.SelectedItem.GetToast()
    .WithArguments(this.SelectedItem.Toast.TemplateType);
```

The arguments are passed in the same way as when a secondary tile is invoked. In `App.xaml.cs`, the arguments are passed to the main page of the app in the `OnLaunched` method.

```
rootFrame.Navigate(typeof(MainPage), args.Arguments)
```

In `MainPage.xaml.cs`, if the argument is not blank, it is used to parse the list of available toasts and set the selected toast to the option passed in.

```
var toastType = e.Parameter.ToString();
var toast = this.ViewModel.Toasts.FirstOrDefault(
    t => t.Toast.TemplateType == toastType);
if (toast != null)
{
    this.ViewModel.SelectedItem = toast;
}
```

The `ViewModel` also creates a live tile in the `Execute` method. If a toast is used with an image, an image template is also used for the tile; otherwise, a text-only template is used. The tile is set to expire when the toast notification should be received and shows the expected time. It also cycles if you send multiple notifications. One way to test the toasts is to schedule a few from the app, close the app, and then watch the tile. You should see your toasts appear. After the last toast is displayed, the tile reverts to the default tile for the app.

You also can override the audio for a toast. The **Toaster** project enables you to either silence the notification or select from one of the many audio options (see Figure 6.8).

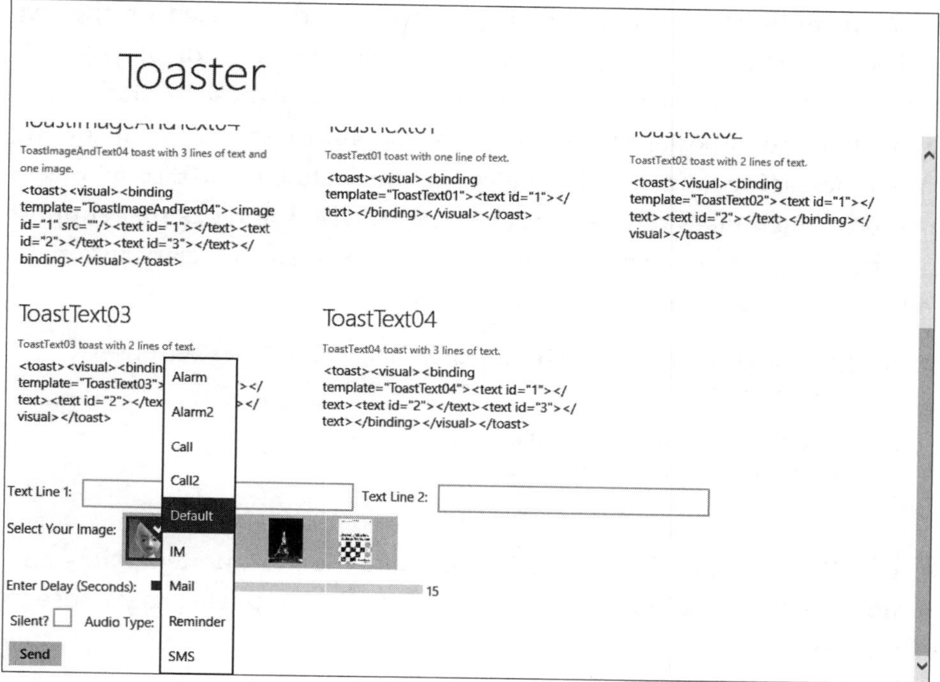

FIGURE 6.8 The toast audio types

To silence the toast, an audio element is added with the attribute `silent` set to `true`. Changing the audio involves adding an audio element with a `src` attribute that points to the audio type. The `BaseToast` class does this in the `WithAudio` method.

```
var audio = this.Xml.SelectSingleNode("toast/audio") as XmlElement ??
    this.Xml.CreateElement("audio");
audio.SetAttribute("src", string.Format("ms-winsoundevent:{0}",
    audioType.FullType));
audio.SetAttribute("loop", "false");
```

You can experiment with different audio options. The helper class makes it easy to set the audio based on an `AudioType` that is defined to expose the built-in types that are available.

```
toast.WithAudio(this.SelectedAudio);
```

Some audio is capable of looping. Looping audio is used for the second type of toast, called a long-duration toast. This toast displays for 25 seconds, unless the user activates or dismisses it. Use these toasts for situations that are important for the user to respond to, such as an incoming call in messaging software. The helper classes define the `WithLoopingAudio` method, which takes only a special `AudioLoopType` (the types that support looping). As part of setting up looped audio, the `BaseToast` class automatically sets the toast to have a long duration.

```
var toastNode = this.Xml.SelectSingleNode("/toast") as XmlElement;
if (toastNode != null)
{
    toastNode.SetAttribute("duration", "long");
    toastNode.AppendChild(audio);
}
```

Use the example **Toaster** app to try out the various templates and audio options so you can get a feel for how to design the toasts you use in your apps.

Toasts in Desktop Applications

You can send toasts from desktop applications, but this is a more involved process. In addition to configuring your desktop application to access the Windows Runtime, as shown in Chapter 1, "The New Windows Runtime," you must have a shortcut to the application configured in the Start menu with the special `AppUserModelID` set. Doing this involves calling COM objects with the help of the Windows API Code Pack.[2] The "Sending Toast Notifications from Desktop Apps" sample from Microsoft sends notifications and includes comments that explain how to configure the shortcut and set the appropriate values, to ensure that a desktop application is capable of sending toasts.[3]

---

[2]Windows API Code Pack for Microsoft .NET Framework, http://bit.ly/12Jy2b8

[3]"Sending Toast Notifications from Desktop Apps" sample, http://bit.ly/18nHYxq

Push Notifications

The Windows Push Notification Service (WNS) is a free service from Microsoft that enables you to send messages to your Windows 8 devices from the cloud. Messages can include updates for tiles, toasts, and badges, as well as raw updates. Although you can generate and update tiles, toasts, and badges from within your app, it is often more practical to have an external source trigger the updates. Your mail client is more helpful when it indicates how many unread messages are waiting for you, even if you haven't launched the app yet. A weather app might provide a toast to alert you to severe weather conditions even after you've exited the app.

Windows 8 devices commonly operate behind firewalls or other network security devices. The firewalls can block any incoming requests to a device. Devices on public networks are often assigned dynamic IP addresses that proxy through a single external-facing IP address, preventing other systems from addressing the device directly. One characteristic devices have in common, however, is the capability to initiate requests from inside the firewall—for example, when you send a request to navigate to www.bing.com, the firewall recognizes the outgoing request and allows the response to return to your client.

Push notifications take advantage of this feature through a component on the Windows 8 device called the Notification Client Platform (NCP). This platform is responsible for managing requests for the Windows 8 device. It works by establishing an outgoing connection to a server hosted by Microsoft that provides the Windows Push Notification Services. The NCP can poll this server periodically and receive updates that are directed to the device.

Working with WNS is a multistep process, as Figure 6.9 shows. Your Windows Store app must first request a unique channel (URI) from the NCP. The NCP then routes this request to WNS and obtains a unique channel that is specific to your app running on the specific device. The NCP returns the URI to your app so you can process it. Typically, you then send an outgoing request to your cloud service to register the URI. You can optionally send along other information associated with the device. After your server records the URI, it can then send XML updates to the URI. The

URI points to WNS, which then relays the payload back to the NCP and processes the notification. Most notifications are external to your app (as with toasts or tile updates), but you can also register for events to fire when the notifications are received.

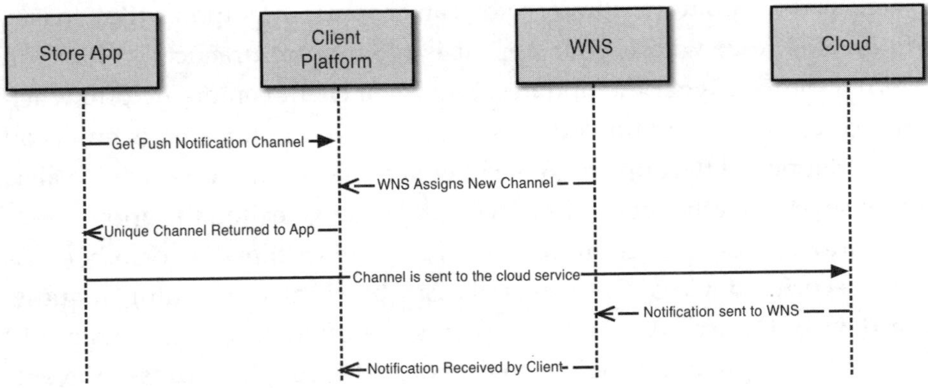

FIGURE 6.9 The steps required to use push notification services

The Chapter 6 project called **PushNotificationExamples** provides examples for all these steps. For convenience, the sample project simulates being both a notification client and a server that is sending notifications, although typically this functionality is split. The example shows how an app can go about registering for push notifications by requesting a notification channel, and then simulates how a server generates a toast notification using a simple XML template and the channel. In this example, the push notification code is separated into two helper classes. The `NotificationRegistrationHelper` class provides an example of how an app might obtain a push notification channel and publish that channel to a server (a fake server, in this example). The `SendNotificationHelper` class simulates that server and performs the activities that would likely be found in a server-side implementation where push notifications are being sent to client devices.

> **NOTE**
>
> To work with this example, your app must first be associated with a Windows Store entry. Chapter 19, "Packaging and Deploying," discusses working with the Windows Store in more detail, but the simplest way to associate your app with the Windows Store is to use the **Associate Your App with the Windows Store** wizard. You invoke this wizard by selecting the **Store** menu item either by using the **Project** menu in Visual Studio or by using the project file context menu in the Visual Studio Solution Explorer and then choosing the **Associate Your App with the Store** entry. From the wizard, you can sign into an existing Windows Store development account and then select an existing registered app name or reserve a new app name. If you do not have a Windows Store Developer Account, you can open one by selecting **Open Developer Account** from the **Store** entry in the Visual Studio **Project** menu, or by directly browsing to the Windows Dev Center at http://dev.windows.com, selecting **Get Started**, and following the links to register for a new account. Note that after you reserve a name and associate an app, the reservation lasts one year unless you publish the app to the store. You must publish the app to the store within that timeframe, or you lose the association.

Registering to Receive Push Notifications

From the client point of view, an app registers for push notifications by calling the `CreatePushNotificationChannelForApplicationAsync` static method that the `PushNotificationChannelManager` class provides. You also can register for notifications that can update secondary tiles by calling the `CreatePushNotificationChannelForSecondaryTileAsync` method and providing it with the desired secondary tile ID. These calls return a `PushNotificationChannel` instance that includes the URI that will be used to send a notification to this device. Note that this channel information expires over time, so you must periodically update it. The current normal expiration time is 30 days, although that could change in the future. In most cases, apps try to update this value every time they are launched.

As you can imagine, sending possibly updated channel information to a server every time an app is launched can result in a lot of unnecessary traffic being sent to the server. Therefore, common practice is to cache the most recently sent channel value in application storage and compare that value to the one that is obtained, updating the server only if the values have changed. You can see this behavior in the example, through the Initialize call in the `NotificationRegistrationHelper` class (see Listing 6.4). Note that if a problem occurs with the call to obtain the push notification channel, a general-purpose `System.Exception` is thrown. The only way to distinguish that this is an error specific to the push notifications is to inspect the exception's `HResult` value and compare it to the possible WNS COM error codes.[4]

LISTING 6.4 Obtaining, Caching, and Updating a Notification Channel

```
try
{
    Channel = await PushNotificationChannelManager.
➥CreatePushNotificationChannelForApplicationAsync();
}
catch (Exception ex)
{
    // Exception from request may be generic with just an HRESULT.
    // TODO - Have app react to exceptions in obtaining a channel
    return;
}

var originalChannel = String.Empty;

// Try to locate the locally cached channel value
var localSettings = ApplicationData.Current.LocalSettings;
if (localSettings.Values.ContainsKey("NotificationChannel"))
{
    originalChannel =
        localSettings.Values["NotificationChannel"].ToString();
}

// Check to see if the value has been updated
if (Channel.Uri != originalChannel)
{
    // Send the updated value to the "server"
    // and cache the new current value
    UpdateStoredChannelUri(Channel.Uri);
    localSettings.Values["NotificationChannel"] = Channel.Uri;
}
```

[4]WNS COM Error Codes, http://j.mp/WNS_COM_ErrorCodes

A running app also can receive an event when push notification is received by registering for the `PushNotificationReceived` event provided by the `PushNotificationChannel` class. The arguments provided to this event include the type of the notification being received, the content of the notification, and a `Cancel` parameter. This `Boolean` value can be set to `true` to suppress the default notification behavior, such as suppressing the display of a toast notification in favor of an in-app UI update when the app is already running.

Sending Push Notifications

Push notifications are sent to the WNS by composing an HTTP POST request directed to the address specified by the Channel URI. This request must specify the notification type in the message header and must include a properly formatted XML payload specifying the content of the notification. This is the same XML that you saw described in the earlier sections in this chapter. The request must also include authentication information, to validate that a legitimate source is sending the notifications at the behest of the client app and to prevent "notification spam."

The notification request is secured using two pieces of information: a security identifier for your app and a client secret. Both must be obtained from the Windows Store Dashboard,[5] through the settings for the Windows Store entry that your app has been associated with. From the Dashboard entry for your app, you can choose Services and locate the link to the **Live Services site**. This opens the **Push Notifications and Live Connect Services Info** page, where you can obtain the information you need. Use the **Authenticating Your Service** link to get the Package Security Identifier (SID) and client secret values for your app.

The SID and client secret ensure that only you can send notifications to your apps. You should not share either of these values, and you should take care to make sure they stay secret. Be sure to store both values in a secure way (behind the firewall) when you author your cloud applications that will send notifications; if other people are able to obtain the values, they will be able to compromise the security of the app by sending their

---

[5]Windows Store Dashboard, https://appdev.microsoft.com/storeportals/

own notifications. Although the SID value remains with your app as long as it is active, you can change the client secret value. If you feel that the secret has been compromised or you simply want to update it as a periodic security measure, you can choose **Create a New Client Secret** from your developer dashboard.

To send one or more push notifications, you need to get an access token based on these SID and client secret values. This is done by posting a secure request over SSL to https://login.live.com/accesstoken.srf. The post should contain the query parameters in Table 6.1.

TABLE 6.1 Query Parameters for Access Token Request

Query Parameter	Query Value
`grant_type`	`client_credentials`
`client_id`	The URL-encoded Package Security Identifier (SID)
`client_secret`	The URL-encoded client secret
Scope	`notify.windows.com`

In the part of the example app, this is handled in the `GetToken` method that is called through the `Initialize` method of the `SendNotificationHelper` class. To use this method, you need to include your app's SID and client secret values in the supplied `PackageSecurityIdentifier` and `ClientSecret` constants.

NOTE

Despite earlier warnings, the example app is actually using SID and client secret values from within a Windows Store app. This is *exclusively* for the purpose of the example; do not repeat it in production code. Although it has been stated before, it bears repeating: These values are important secrets for your app and should never be distributed inside client applications or transmitted over the network in an unencrypted or otherwise unsecure manner.

In the GetToken method, the .NET WebUtility helpers make it easy to encode the request.

```
var requestBody = string.Format(
    TokenRequest,
    WebUtility.UrlEncode(PackageSecurityIdentifier),
    WebUtility.UrlEncode(ClientSecret));
```

The text is then encoded into a StringContent instance.

```
var httpBody = new StringContent(
    requestBody,
    Encoding.UTF8,
    "application/x-www-form-urlencoded");
```

An instance of the HttpClient obtains a JSON-formatted response.

```
var response =
    await client.PostAsync(
    new Uri("https://login.live.com/accesstoken.srf",
       UriKind.Absolute),
    httpBody);
```

Finally, the response is parsed and the token is stored to use for subsequent notifications. A 200 - OK response indicates success; otherwise, a 400 - Bad Request indicates failure. You can inspect the parameters of the response to obtain more information about why the request failed. After obtaining the token, you can send push notifications through the channel using the token.

When an authentication token is available, the actual push notifications can be sent. The example app sends a toast notification using a basic template. The XML for a simple toast that contains only text is simple.

```
<toast>
    <visual>
        <binding template="ToastText01">
            <text id="1">Some text.</text>
        </binding>"
    </visual>
</toast>
```

The sample app formats the text you enter into the XML document and sends it to the channel. If the channel accepts the toast, it routes the toast to your client. This can take anywhere from a few seconds to several minutes—delivery time (and even actual delivery) is not guaranteed for push notifications. After the toast does arrive, you should see a small notification appear with the text of your message.

This process is handled in the `SendNotificationHelper` class through the `SendToastNotification` method. The text to send is first HTML encoded before being placed in the XML document.

```
var toast = string.Format(ToastTemplate,
    WebUtility.HtmlEncode(message));
```

Next, a request message is formatted using the XML that is directed to the channel that the Windows Store app obtained earlier in the process.

```
var requestMessage = new HttpRequestMessage(
    HttpMethod.Post,
    this.Channel.Uri)
{
    Content =
        new ByteArrayContent(Encoding.UTF8.GetBytes(toast))
};
```

Several headers are added, including the access token, to further clarify the request.

```
requestMessage.Content.Headers.ContentType =
    new MediaTypeHeaderValue("text/xml");
requestMessage.Headers.Add("X-WNS-TYPE", "wns/toast");
requestMessage.Headers.Authorization =
    new AuthenticationHeaderValue("Bearer", this.Token);
```

Table 6.2 lists the available headers you can use for a push notification request. The `Authorization`, `Content-Type`, `Content-Length`, and `X-WNS-Type` headers are required. All others are optional.

TABLE 6.2 Push Notification Request Parameters

Parameter (bold is required)	Description
Authorization	Standard header used to authenticate the request. The value should contain the OAuth token obtained from the login.live.com service.
Content-Type	Standard header used to indicate the type of the body of the request. Set this to `text/xml` for toasts, tiles, and badges, and to `application/octet-stream` for raw notifications.
Content-Length	Standard header used to indicate the size of the request payload.
X-WNS-Type	Specifies the type of the payload, either `wns/toast`, `wns/badge`, `wns/tile`, or `wns/raw`.
X-WNS-Cache-Policy	Indicates whether caching of notifications should be enabled or disabled. Possible values are `cache` and `no-cache`. Does not apply to toasts.
X-WNS-RequestForStatus	Indicates whether the response should give the status of the device and WNS. Can be `true` or `false`.
X-WNS-Tag	Contains a unique tag that may be used to uniquely identify a tile notification. If you resend a tile with the same tag, the notification is replaced. Can be an alphanumeric string no longer than 16 characters.
X-WNS-TTL	Specifies the lifespan of the notification in seconds. If WNS is delayed in sending the notification, it will not send it when the delay exceeds the amount of time specified here. This is useful when you are sending notifications that lose their meaning over time because there is no guaranteed delivery time from WNS.

The response contains a standard HTTP status code and various headers, depending on the type of message.

```
var response = await new HttpClient().SendAsync(requestMessage);
responseBuilder.AppendFormat("{0}: {1}", response.StatusCode,
    await response.Content.ReadAsStringAsync());
```

The reponse from the WNS can verify only receipt of the notification request. Because of the asynchronous nature of the process, the response does not include information about the status of notification delivery on the device where the app is installed. Table 6.3 lists the possible parameters that can be included in the response.

TABLE 6.3 Push Notification Response Parameters

Parameter	Description
`X-WNS-Debug-Trace`	Debugging information for the response that you can log to troubleshoot issues.
`X-WNS-DeviceConnectionStatus`	If requested, this returns the client device connection status as `connected`, `disconnected`, or `tempdisconnected`.
`X-WNS-Error-Description`	If an error occurred, this human-readable message is returned so that you can log for troubleshooting.
`X-WNS-Msg-ID`	A unique identifier for the notification. This is useful for troubleshooting and debugging issues with WNS.
`X-WNS-NotificationStatus`	The status of receipt for the notification. Possible values include `received`, `dropped` (either you did not flag your app as toast capable in the manifest or the user explicitly disabled notifications), and `channelthrottled` (the server exceeded the rate limit for the channel to avoid flooding the client).

The example application simply queries the response content and returns it to be displayed in the user interface.

This process can be slightly tedious and error prone, especially where the XML templates are involved. To mitigate some of these issues, the Microsoft DPE team has published the **WnsRecipe NuGet** package that provides an object model to build and send push notifications from .NET applications such as those that run on the ASP.NET platform. You can find detailed instructions for its use on the project GitHub repository.[6]

Summary

This chapter covered the various ways you can keep Windows Store apps alive and connected, even when they aren't running. Use live tiles to display at-a-glance information on the user's Start Screen to provide information and previews of content. Secondary tiles enable users to pin content inside your app. Badges inform the user when actions have occurred or provide information such as a count of new messages. Finally, toasts appear even when the user is in another app, on the Start Screen, or on the desktop. They can provide timely information, and they give the user the option to either dismiss the toast or activate it and launch your app. You saw that this information could not only be updated from within the app itself, but that the app could also be configured to work with the Windows Push Notification Service to allow external processes to send updates to these elements.

In the next chapter, you look at some other cloud services that you can take advantage of to enrich your application. You see how you can connect to Windows Azure Mobile Services, a service offering in Microsoft's Windows Azure cloud platform that is designed to address many of the common needs mobile apps have. You also see how you can take advantage of the Live Connect APIs to get access to information connected to a user's Microsoft Account, including profile information, contact and calendar access, and the capability to work with OneDrive cloud storage content.

[6]WnsRecipe GitHub repository, https://github.com/nickharris/WnsRecipe

7 Connecting to the Cloud

THE WINDOWS RUNTIME MAKES IT EASIER THAN EVER TO create applications that connect to cloud-based services. The Roaming Storage APIs work with integrated support for Microsoft Accounts and the OneDrive (previously SkyDrive) storage service to enable apps to share settings across machine boundaries. The Web Authentication Broker APIs facilitate the secure use of services that support authentication and authorization via the OAuth and OpenID protocols. As you saw in Chapter 6, "Tiles and Toasts," WinRT also works with the Windows Notification Service (WNS) to allow applications to support push notifications through APIs that enable Windows Store Apps to register to receive externally initiated Live Tile updates, pop-up Toast notifications, or raw data payloads.

Beyond these built-in features, it's possible to extend an application's functionality with other cloud-based services, making the application bigger than just the device it is running on. Many types of apps can take advantage of connectivity to the cloud. Your app might connect with third-party services such as Twitter or Facebook to send notifications when a status changes, or it might help the user tap into a database of information that is stored in the cloud.

Although many different kinds of cloud services and related APIs are available to fulfill a variety of application needs, this chapter focuses on a few Microsoft-provided cloud services and their accompanying client APIs that you can use to add functionality to apps built to run on Windows

8.1, among other platforms. These services include Windows Azure Mobile Services and the family of Windows Live Connect Services. Accessing the cloud is an important scenario to address in Windows Store apps, and these solutions are tightly integrated into the Windows ecosystem. Understanding and tapping into these services can greatly enhance the user experience of your Windows Store apps. The examples in this chapter illustrate how to consume these external services from applications built with WinRT.

> **NOTE**
>
> The services this chapter covers aren't a part of the Windows Runtime. Instead, they are provided through SDKs and .NET classes to enhance existing functionality. Some of these services might charge fees for usage. Certain APIs will not work unless you register your app to a Windows Store account (a typical account costs either $19 or $99, depending on the type). Cloud services also operate on a pay-per-use model. If you already have an existing MSDN developer license, you might be eligible for free access to certain services; you can verify this by logging into your account and navigating to the Benefits tab.

Windows Azure Mobile Services

Windows Azure Mobile Services (Mobile Services) is a part of Microsoft's Windows Azure cloud platform. Its purpose is to provide a set of cloud-hosted back-end capabilities that address the typical needs of developers of mobile apps, such as apps that are written using WinRT. Developers using Mobile Services can provision and consume these services without having to invest the typical amount of time and effort required in learning and implementation with larger cloud offerings. Key Mobile Services features include the following:

- Support for data storage
- Capability to define custom server-side business logic that executes as part of the data storage CRUD operations
- Cloud-based authentication and authorization with out-of-the-box support for Microsoft Accounts, Twitter, Facebook, and Google authentications
- Capability to issue push notifications through the platform-specific services offered for Windows Phone, Windows Store, Android, and iOS apps
- Custom API definitions
- Capability to schedule server-side logic to be run at preset time intervals

These features are complemented by support for logging, diagnostics, source control, and an infrastructure that is designed to scale as the service and apps that use it become more popular. It reduces the friction of common tasks and enables rapid development of your end-to-end solution.

To use Mobile Services, you first need an active Windows Azure subscription. You can acquire a subscription and associate it with either a Microsoft Account (formerly Live Id) or a Microsoft Organizational Account (such as those associated with Microsoft Office 365) in several ways. A variety of promotions and offers for free or discounted evaluation periods are usually available. Additionally, MSDN subscribers are currently eligible to receive a monthly allotment of credits to cover discounted Windows Azure fees. The specific amount depends on the MSDN subscription level; to access this offer, simply visit the Benefits section of your online account (note that this offer is restricted to development and test usage only and is not intended for production application use). Companies participating in Microsoft's BizSpark program currently also receive a similar monthly benefit. Finally, Windows Azure often offers free or credit-based trial periods for new subscribers. You can find online information about Windows Azure pricing and various promotions at www.windowsazure.com/pricing.

To provision a Mobile Services instance, log in to the Windows Azure Management Portal at https://manage.windowsazure.com with the credentials associated with a Windows Azure subscription. Then choose **New, Compute, Mobile Service**, as in Figure 7.1.

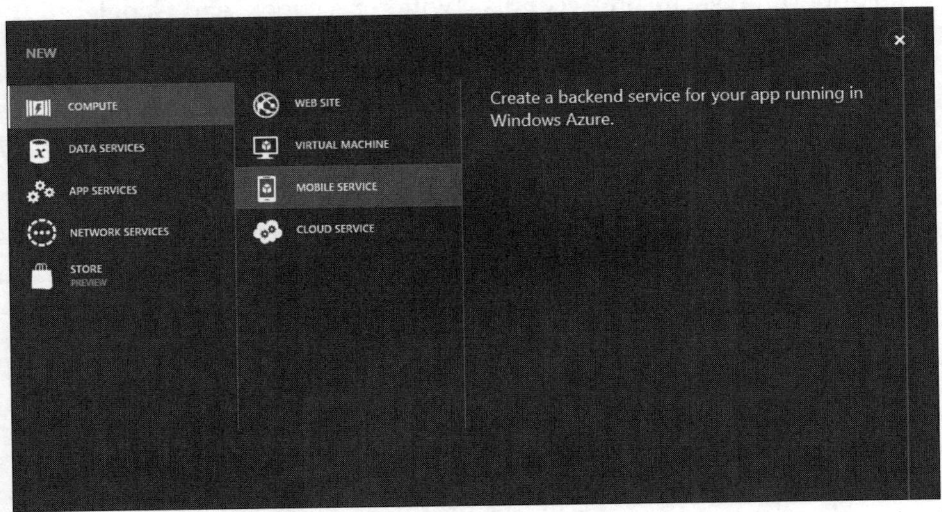

Figure 7.1 Adding a new Mobile Services instance

Choose the **Create** option. You are presented with a dialog to configure the new service (see Figure 7.2). The first step in configuring a Mobile Services instance is to name the new service. The name you provide must be unique because it will be used as part of the URL to access the service. If the current account used to log in to the portal has multiple subscriptions associated with it, an option is given to select the subscription to which the Mobile Services instance should be associated. You also need to specify whether the new Mobile Services instance should be backed by a pre-existing Windows Azure SQL Database or whether you'd like to create a new one. If it makes sense to create a new database for the service, there's also an option to create a free 20MB SQL database, if one has not already been created in the current subscription. This free but small database instance is especially useful during the development phase of an app, before it gets published and starts generating revenue to offset the cost of a larger database. At any point later in the app's lifecycle, you can choose to upgrade the database to a larger option.

The final option to select is the Region, which specifies the regional data center where the service will be provisioned. This selection can affect the performance of your application, depending on where in the world the users are when they access your service, relative to the service's geographic location. There's also a cost consideration related to the location of the service and its backing database, as well as any other Windows Azure services that the application might be consuming, such as a Windows Azure Storage instance for holding images in Azure Blob Storage. In Windows Azure, operations that cause data to traverse data centers incur additional per-transaction costs, whereas operations within the same data center do not. Therefore, it makes sense to co-locate related items, such as the Mobile Services instance and its backing database. Another consideration for selecting the data center location relates to regional laws that could impose restrictions on where personally identifiable information can be housed for citizens of certain countries. These laws can vary significantly over time and geographic boundaries, and determining their exact applicability to Mobile Services instances is outside the scope of this book. Currently, Windows Azure Mobile Services is offered in four data centers: East U.S., West U.S., North Europe, and East Asia.

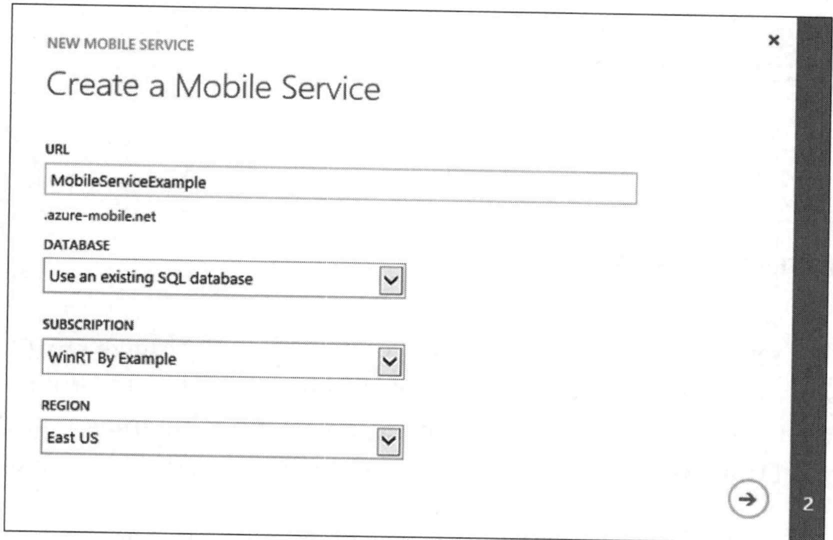

FIGURE 7.2 The dialog for configuring a new service

If you choose to create a database, you're presented with another dialog (see Figure 7.3). This dialog asks you to specify the name for the database instance and specify whether to include it in a pre-existing server or to create a new server to host it in. If you are creating a new server, be sure to remember your login name and keep your password in a secure location. You can also specify a region where your database should be hosted. Unless you have a specific reason not to do so, this should match the region that you previously specified for the Mobile Services instance (remember, if they are not co-located, you will incur additional costs related to moving data across data centers). Selecting the check mark button begins the process of provisioning the Mobile Services instance as it has been configured.

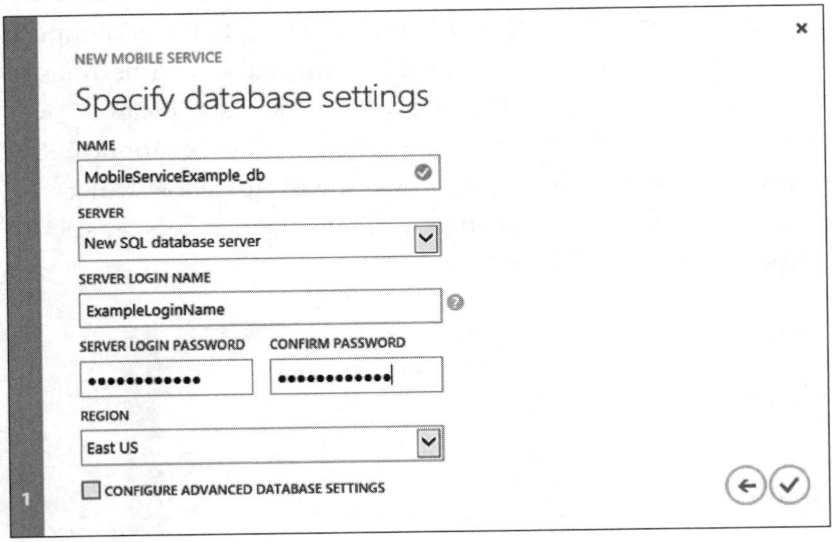

FIGURE 7.3 The Database Settings dialog

After the service is created, locating and opening it in the Management Panel displays the management tabs available for your service. These currently include Quick Start (symbolized by a cloud with a lightning bolt), Dashboard, Data, API, Scheduler, Push, Identity, Configure, Scale, and Logs.

The first page displayed by default is the Quick Start page. The Quick Start page offers the capability to choose a target platform, with choices that include Windows Store, Windows Phone 8, iOS, Android, and HTML/JavaScript. The selection here determines the specific content that is available in the rest of this page; it includes a step-by-step tutorial for quickly creating a new To-Do List sample app that is backed by Mobile Services, instructions for adding code to an existing application to connect it to the Mobile Services instance, as well as links to additional Mobile Services tutorials.

Example: Managing a Shared Group of Subscribers

The **MobileServicesExample** project contains the code for an app that demonstrates the Mobile Services concepts being discussed. The app allows for a collection of shared "subscriber" records to be managed in the cloud. When complete, the app will include the capability to send push notifications to a subscriber's creator when another user updates a contact he or she has created.

The solution contains a folder titled **Server Scripts** that contains the script content that will be entered into the Mobile Services web-based script editor. Mobile Services supports several mechanisms for developers to edit script files on their machines and then upload the files to the server. These include integration with the Visual Studio Server Explorer, script file management through the command-line interface (CLI), and integration via the Git distributed source control tool. For the purposes of this example, however, discussion is restricted to the web-based user interface for script management.

Because this example uses push notifications and also requires a connection to a specific Mobile Services instance, the source code will not work without some modifications for your specific application and Mobile Services identifiers. The code comments call out these modifications, and we discuss them throughout the chapter.

Connecting an App to a Mobile Services Instance

All the functionality Mobile Services instances offer is exposed through HTTP REST APIs that accept JSON data payloads. Although it is possible to interact with a Mobile Services instance from a client app exclusively through the use of these REST calls, client libraries for several platforms (including Windows Store apps) greatly simplify what would otherwise be a potentially tedious and error-prone process. Visual Studio 2013 includes integrated support for using Mobile Services in Windows Store apps. It simplifies the process of setting up the necessary client library references and connecting to a Mobile Services instance in code.

The simplest way to connect an app to your Mobile Services instance is to obtain references to the necessary client libraries through the Connected Services Manager in Visual Studio. From your app's project in the Visual Studio Solution Explorer, right-click and select **Add**; then select **Connected Service**. In the Services Manager dialog, select **Mobile Services** under the Windows Azure node. The dialog displays any Mobile Services instances registered to Windows Azure subscriptions, with an option to import additional Windows Azure subscription settings if needed. You can even create a new Mobile Services instance from this dialog if you haven't previously set one up. Selecting a Mobile Services instance and clicking OK makes two key changes to the project in Visual Studio. First, the latest Mobile Services client library and its dependencies are added as library references to the project. This is accomplished by installing the Windows Azure Mobile Services NuGet package. Second, a public, static instance of `Microsoft.WindowsAzure.MobileServices.MobileServiceClient` is defined in the App class. This client instance is used throughout the application to interact with the Mobile Service. The instance that is created is automatically configured to interact with the selected Mobile Services instance with the service instance's URL and its application key.

```
public static MobileServiceClient WinRTByExampleBookClient =
    new MobileServiceClient(
        "https://MOBILESERVICENAME.azure-mobile.net/",
        "APPLICATION KEY");
```

If you opt to set this up manually instead of using the Connected Services Manager, the URL and application key are available from the service's Dashboard page in the Windows Azure Management Portal. The URL is included in the page itself, and you can obtain the application key from the Manage Access Keys dialog that appears when you press the **Manage Keys** button in the command bar at the bottom of the page. Figure 7.4 shows these locations.

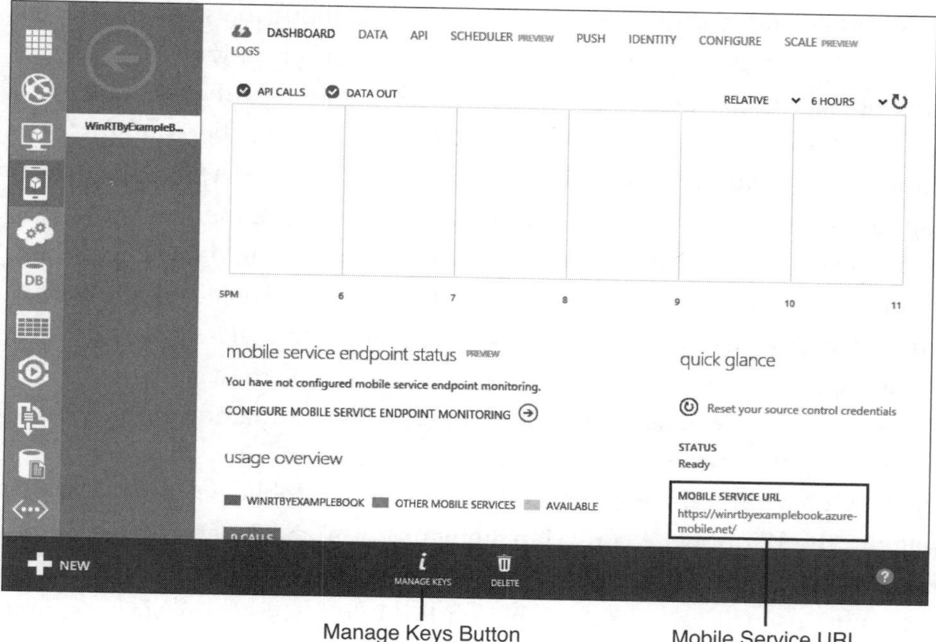

FIGURE 7.4 Obtaining the service URL and the application key values from the portal

Authentication

An identity provider is a service that you can rely upon with some degree of confidence to verify the identity of a user. Users interact with various identity providers throughout their daily activities. Some users enter credentials to log into their machines, which are authenticated against a company's Active Directory server; this login is used throughout their day to determine whether they are authorized to access company resources. Instead of forcing users to create new usernames and passwords for every service that they consume on the Internet, many sites enable users to use their credentials from some other well-known and reliable service to sign in, such as using their email or Facebook accounts. Not only is this easier for users because they do not have to remember yet another login and password, but the sites do not have to implement the authentication system themselves and do not have to be concerned about the intricate details involved in properly protecting the users' login information.

One service Mobile Services offers is integrated authentication with several commonly used identity providers. Apps can be configured to allow users to authenticate with any of several different accounts, including Microsoft Accounts (formerly LiveId), Facebook logins, Twitter logins, and Google logins. In the Mobile Services instance itself, data actions such as table data access and custom API calls can be restricted to allow only authenticated client access, and server-side code can make some use of the credentials provided when an authenticated user makes a call.

Before a client can use Mobile Services to handle authentication with one of these identity services, the Mobile Services instance needs to be configured by providing the appropriate values in the Mobile Services' Identity page in the Windows Azure Management Portal. Each service has different steps that must be performed to obtain these values, but fortunately, the context-sensitive help available on the Windows Azure Management Portal Identity page provides step-by-step instructions specific to each provider. You can access this help by clicking the question mark icon in the lower-right corner of the Identity page and selecting the corresponding application link. Take care with the various "secret" values that need to be entered into the Mobile Services' Identity page—the values are protected when they are stored in the Mobile Services' configuration, but they should not be shared carelessly or included within a client application that is being distributed. If the secret value is somehow compromised, the identity providers generally make available a set of steps to generate a new replacement value.

Registration and Configuration for Microsoft Account Logins

The example application is set up to use only Microsoft accounts for authentication, so this section focuses on the steps required to set this up. The first step is to enter the app's **Client ID** and **Client Secret** values in the **Microsoft Account Settings** section of the Identity page in the Windows Azure Management Portal. Figure 7.5 shows the boxes for entering these settings.

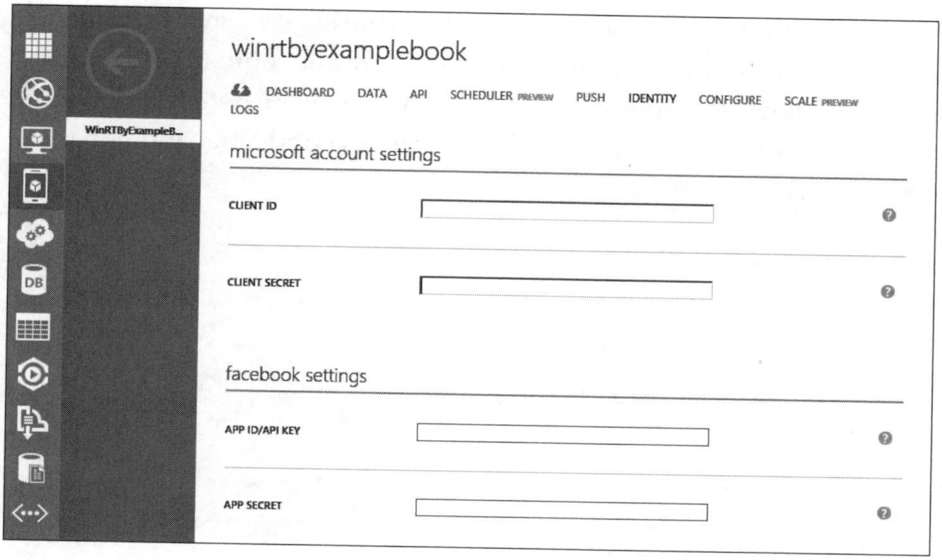

FIGURE 7.5 The Identity page in the Windows Azure Management Portal

To obtain the values for your app, you first need to access the **My Applications** section of the Live Connect Developer Center,[1] at https://account.live.com/developers/applications. From this site, you can manage any applications that are set up to use any of the Live services. You need to use a Microsoft Account to access this site, and it should be the same Microsoft Account you are using for your Windows Store developer account because the Client Secret setting is also used when setting up push notifications for a Windows Store app. (In fact, if you already have associated your app with a Windows Store app, as Chapter 6 detailed, your app should already appear in the application listing in the Live Connect site.) If the app is not yet listed in the application listing, follow the instructions on the page to create a new app entry—this mainly involves providing an application name. The API Settings section of the application's settings includes the Client ID and Client Secret values for the application that you need to enter into the Windows Azure Management Portal. However, you also need to enter the Mobile Services instance's URL into the **Redirect Domain** box in this configuration page, or the client apps

[1]Live Connect Developer Center, http://msdn.microsoft.com/live

will be unable to authenticate. Note that you do *not* have to configure the entry as a **Mobile Client App** (make sure this option is set to No). Figure 7.6 shows this configuration page. As Chapter 6 detailed, you must keep the Package SID and Client Secret values confidential and not available to the general public.

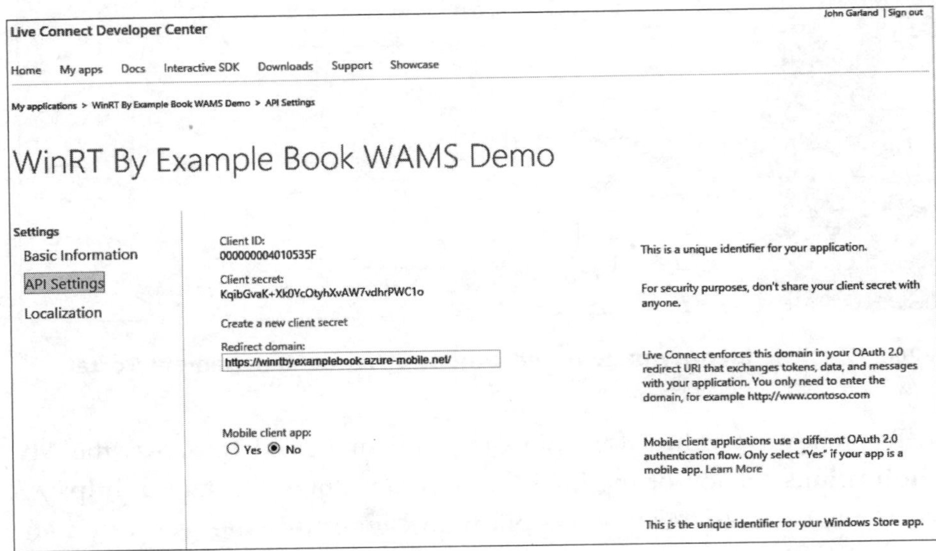

FIGURE 7.6 Configuration in the Live Connect Developer Center

Authenticating the User

After the server has been configured with the appropriate settings, allowing users to log in with client applications is trivial. It is merely a matter of indicating the authentication provider to use with a `MobileServiceClient` instance:

```
user = await App.WinRTByExampleBookClient
➥.LoginAsync(MobileServiceAuthenticationProvider.MicrosoftAccount);
```

Calling the `LoginAsync` method invokes the WinRT `WebAuthenticationBroker` to securely collect and validate the user's Microsoft Account credentials, as in Figure 7.7.

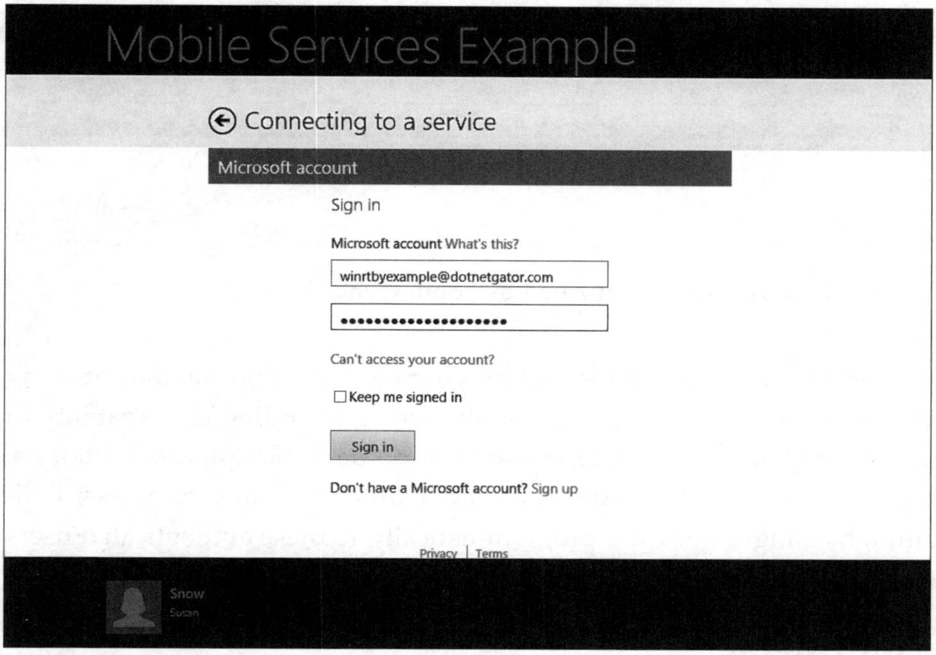

FIGURE 7.7 Logging in with a Microsoft Account

If the user cancels the login by using the Back button in the login dialog, or if an unexpected error occurs when processing the credentials, an `InvalidOperationException` is thrown. Otherwise, the method returns a `MobileServiceUser` object that also is used to set the `CurrentUser` property on the `MobileServiceClient` object that issued the call. The user object includes a `UserId` property, which is a string ID for the user in a format that is specific to each identity provider. The user object also includes a `MobileServiceAuthenticationToken` property that holds a JSON Web Token (JWT) string that contains a digitally signed value to identify the logged-in user on subsequent Mobile Services calls. Figure 7.8 shows an example for a returned user object. Most of the time, you don't need to worry about the details of the JWT contents, but in advanced scenarios, you can use custom authentication providers and generate corresponding JWT tokens.

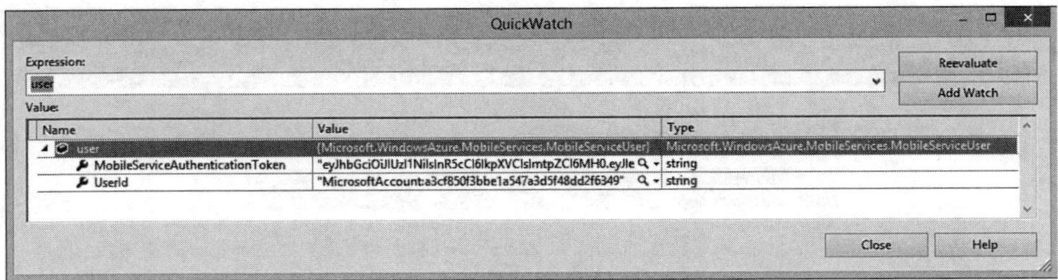

FIGURE 7.8 A user object returned by LoginAsync

Now that you have authenticated your end user, you can look at using Mobile Services to manage data on the server, including the capability to execute custom scripts in response to these data manipulation requests. You will then see how you can restrict different kinds of access, both through configuration and programmatically, to these authenticated users and use some information about authenticated users in your server scripts.

Data Storage

Another service Mobile Services offers is the capability to store and manage data in the cloud. Mobile Services manages data through named tables, which provides a structured repository of data for the client applications that use a Mobile Services instance. These tables are actually provisioned and stored in the Windows Azure SQL Database instance that was configured as part of the Mobile Services setup process.

Managing Data Tables

Tables are managed in the Mobile Service's Data page in the Windows Azure Management Portal. This page lists the existing tables that have been configured for the current Mobile Services instance. The page also provides the capability to add a new table with the Create button, remove the currently selected table with the Delete button, or view and manage the content of a table by clicking on its cell in the Table column. The table content management pages include Browse, Script, Columns, and Permissions. On the Browse page, you can view the data records stored in a table and delete individual records. The Script page enables you to manage the scripts executed as part of the various data access operations that can be performed. The Columns page lists the columns and data types in the selected table. Finally, the Permissions page enables you to manage the degree of access that each data access operation exposes.

When a table is created, you need to supply it with a name that is unique to the current Mobile Services instance. Each Mobile Services table is backed by a corresponding database table. When Mobile Services creates a new database table, that table is isolated from tables for different apps by using the service's instance name as the table's schema name.[2] This way, multiple Mobile Services instances can share the same database (usually for reasons related to cost savings) without worrying about collisions between identically named tables. The Create New Table dialog also includes a set of combo boxes for setting initial table access permissions. The upcoming "Authorization" section discusses these settings. As you can see in Figure 7.9, the example Mobile Services instance has two tables, Subscribers and Channels. The Subscribers table was created manually, whereas the Channels table was created as part of a wizard in Visual Studio 2013 (the upcoming section "Integrated Push Notification Support" discusses this more).

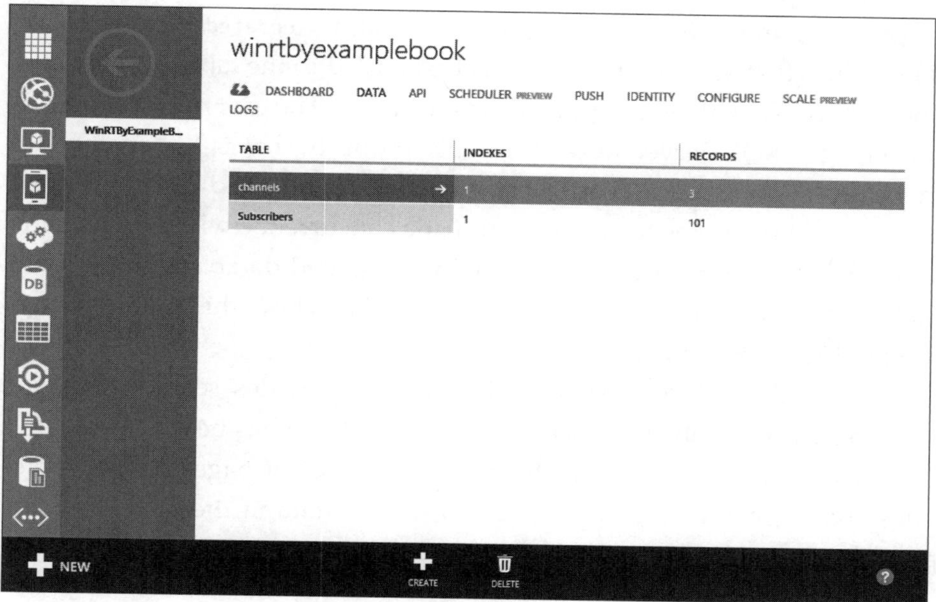

FIGURE 7.9 Two tables in the example Mobile Services instance

[2]SQL Server Best Practices—Implementation of Database Object Schemas, http://bit.ly/ZE3Egl

A newly created Mobile Services table includes four columns. The first column is named 'id' and is the unique identifier for each record stored in the table. The column is configured to use string values; any valid string can be used as a row identifier, as long as it is guaranteed to be unique within the table. In most cases, a GUID value is used. The default configuration for the table is to generate a new GUID whenever a row is inserted and the client application has not supplied a predefined ID value. Every Mobile Services table has this property. You can see the set of defined columns and their types by selecting the table and opening the Columns page.

In addition to the ID column, a set of System Columns is provisioned when the table is created. You can identify a System Column from the leading double underscore in its name. By default, these columns are maintained only on the server and are not exchanged with either the client application or the server-side data access scripts. The underlying SQL Server database is configured to automatically manage the values for these columns. If a client sends an insert or update request that contains a property that starts with a double underscore, Mobile Services rejects that request.

Currently, the predefined System Columns include `__createdAt`, `__updatedAt`, and `__version`. The `__createdAt` and `__updatedAt` columns are date values that are set when a row is first added to the table or whenever one of the row values is updated, respectively. The `__version` column is set with the SQL Server ROWVERSION property that SQL Server automatically updates whenever the row content is modified; it can be used in advanced scenarios to ensure optimistic concurrency when performing table updates and to prevent potentially unwanted database update conflicts. A detailed tutorial is available that explains how this can be configured in Mobile Services.[3]

The Windows Azure Management Portal provides several tools for working with a Mobile Services table. After a table has been defined, the Windows Azure Management Portal creates a set of pages for the table. These pages include a Browse page to see the data in the table, a Script page for managing server-side data access scripts (discussed shortly), a

---

[3]Handling Mobile Services Database Write Conflicts, http://j.mp/MobileServicesWriteConflicts

Columns page for working with the columns in a table, and a Permissions page for adjusting the permissions required for different kinds of access to the table (also discussed shortly).

You can use the Columns page for the Mobile Services table to add or remove table columns, as well as to set columns that should be indexed within SQL Server. In addition to using the portal to add or remove columns individually, Mobile Services includes a feature called Dynamic Schema that helps simplify the process. When Dynamic Schema is enabled from a Mobile Services instance, the data that is sent from a Mobile Services client app to be stored in a given table is analyzed, and table columns are dynamically added to accommodate the incoming data. The Dynamic Schema behavior can be enabled or disabled for the entire Mobile Services instance through the Configure page. Generally, this setting is enabled during development and testing. It should be disabled when the site and related apps are released—by that time, testing and sample data will have "shaped" the table storage columns.

Although Windows Azure SQL databases support a large number of T-SQL data types, Mobile Services works with only a subset of the available types. Table 7.1 lists the T-SQL data types Mobile Services tables support and their corresponding JSON data values.

Table 7.1 Supported T-SQL Data Types and Their Corresponding JSON Data Values

T-SQL Type	JSON Data
`float`	Numeric values
`bit`	Boolean values
`datetimeoffset(3)`	`DateTime` values
`nvarchar(max)`	Strings
`timestamp`	Used only for `system __version` column

NOTE

After you create the table through Mobile Services, you can manage the content of the SQL database tables using tools such as the Windows Azure SQL Management Portal or the SQL Server Management Studio. However, data management activities done this way bypass the normal operation of the Mobile Services framework. The main consequence is that any table-specific functionality that has been declared in Mobile Services (such as server scripting and per-table authentication) is skipped when changes are made using tools that connect directly to the database. Mobile Services still reflects changes made with these tools, such as column additions and removals and the addition, deletion, or modification of data.

Working with Data in Client Apps

After you have configured a table in a Mobile Services instance, a client app can access it through the same `MobileServicesClient` object you saw earlier. To use the strongly typed data access methods in the client library, a class needs to be defined for the data objects being stored in a Mobile Services table. The class's name identifies the Mobile Services table to use, and the class must define an `Id` property of type `String` that has a public getter and setter. Additional properties that return simple data types and have public getters and setters also are included by default; their property names are used as the corresponding table column names.

The `DataTable` attribute can be applied to the class declaration to explicitly specify the Mobile Services table name that should be used instead of the class name, by default. One of the class's property names also might not line up with the desired column name that it should use, or in some cases, properties in the data class should not be stored in a Mobile Services table (such as with complex data properties or other unsupported data types). Fortunately, the Mobile Services client library uses the Newtonsoft JSON.NET library (which is included in the Mobile Services NuGet package that was installed earlier) to handle the serialization and deserialization of the data for the Mobile Services calls. As a result, the mechanisms it provides for handling how a type is converted to and from JSON are available for use. These include the `JsonProperty` attribute, which enables you to set a `PropertyName` value to specify the table column name, and the `JsonIgnore` attribute, which you can use to tell the JSON serializer to skip the indicated property.

Listing 7.1 includes excerpts from the `Subscriber` class defined in the example app that illustrate these concepts. The class is named Subscriber, but the Mobile Services table that will store its data is titled Subscribers, as indicated by the `DataTable` annotation. The Subscriber class includes an `Id` column, as required. The Phone property includes a `JsonProperty` annotation to specify that its data should be stored in the table's PhoneNumber column. Finally, the Unused property includes a `JsonIgnore` attribute indicating that this data should not be exchanged with the Mobile Services instance.

LISTING 7.1 The Subscriber Class

```
[DataTable("Subscribers")]
public class Subscriber : INotifyPropertyChanged
{
    // omitted for brevity

    public String Id
    {
        get { return _id; }
        set
        {
            _id = value;
            OnPropertyChanged();
        }
    }

    public String FirstName
    {
        get { return _firstName; }
        set
        {
            _firstName = value;
            OnPropertyChanged();
        }
    }

    public String LastName
    {
        get { return _lastName; }
```

```
        set
        {
            _lastName = value;
            OnPropertyChanged();
        }
    }

    // omitted for brevity

    [JsonProperty(PropertyName = "PhoneNumber")]
    public String Phone
    {
        get { return _phone; }
        set
        {
            _phone = value;
            OnPropertyChanged();
        }
    }

    [JsonIgnore]
    public String Unused { get; set; }
```

To work with the table data from code, you first must obtain an `IMobileServiceTable<T>` reference from the Mobile Services client object, which acts as a proxy to the Mobile Services data table endpoint. The proxy exposes asynchronous methods for inserting, updating, deleting, and looking up individual records by their ID from table storage. An important side effect of the `InsertAsync` method is that the item provided to insert might be actually modified as part of the operation. If the item being inserted does not include a value for the `Id` property, the GUID `Id` value that is assigned by the Mobile Services instance when the item is inserted into its table is applied back to the provided object. If an `Id` value is supplied, Mobile Services attempts to use that ID for the record in the table, as long as it is truly unique; otherwise, the insert operation fails. This is particularly useful when records might be generated when the client application is offline and cannot wait for the server to generate an ID. Note also that the ID value does not have to be a GUID; any string is valid, as long as it is unique within the Mobile Services table. The following code shows the available operations for working with individual records in a Mobile Services table:

```
var table = App.WinRTByExampleBookClient.GetTable<Subscriber>();
await table.InsertAsync(subscriber); // Id updated if not provided
await table.UpdateAsync(subscriber);
await table.DeleteAsync(subscriber);
var item = await table.LookupAsync(subscriberId);
```

The table proxy also includes a `CreateQuery` method to obtain an `IMobileServiceTableQuery<T>` instance that can be used to build a query to retrieve data from the table. The query exposes two kinds of operations: fluent operations to define the query criteria and behavior, and execution operations that send the query to the Mobile Services instance for execution and return the results. Each fluent operation returns an `IMobileServiceTableQuery<T>` result, allowing the query operations to be "fluently" chained to each other to build up the complete query operation. The query operations that can be specified include a `Where` operation to define the query predicate expressions, `OrderBy`/`ThenBy`/`OrderByDescending`/`ThenByDescending` operations for indicating sorting behavior, and `Skip`/`Take` operations for specifying indexed blocks of data to retrieve as part of the results (most often used to provide paginated results). The execution operations include `ToEnumerableAsync` and `ToListAsync`, which request and return the entire query result set. `ToCollectionAsync` returns a collection that supports pagination by incrementally loading results in response to a `LoadMoreItemsAsync` call, setting its `HasMoreItems` property to false when all the matching results have been returned. Finally, `ToIncrementalLoadingCollection` returns a special collection that implements the `ISupportIncrementalLoading` interface. When paired with a control such as `ListView` that supports lists that implement this interface, the control works with the collection to initially request only a subset of the results. It requests additional records only as the user's scrolling in the control suggests that it should retrieve additional records; then it dynamically populates the list of elements in the control. Note that, unlike with the rest of the execution operations, the call to `ToIncrementalLoadingCollection` is not asynchronous. The actual asynchronous data requests and their responses are managed internally by the object that is returned. The following code shows an example of a query that returns only male subscribers, sorted first by their last names and then by their first names. The query is executed and returned as a collection with an initial page request size of 50 records.

```
var table = App.WinRTByExampleBookClient.GetTable<Subscriber>();
var query = table.CreateQuery()
    .Where(x => x.Gender == Gender.Male)
    .OrderBy(x => x.LastName)
    .ThenBy(x => x.FirstName);
var collection = await query.ToCollectionAsync(50);
```

Table access methods also provide "untyped" counterparts that directly exchange JSON payloads. Instead of inferring table names from the data classes, these methods require a string parameter for specifying the table name. Column names are retrieved directly from the JSON values.

Data Access Scripts

When a Mobile Services table is created, a set of table operation scripts is also created that corresponds to Insert, Update, Delete, and Read operations. Before data management requests to a Mobile Services instance actually reach the Windows Azure SQL Database tables, the Mobile Services infrastructure routes the request through the corresponding table operation script. You can modify these scripts to provide server-side logic that needs to execute as part of the desired data operation, including data validation, logging, or other custom behaviors that need to occur as part of the particular request. As Figure 7.10 shows, you can edit table operation scripts through a web-based script editor that is available in each table's Script page. To get to the Script page for a table, first select the table from the Mobile Services instance's Data page. Then select the Script page header and select the appropriate script operation from the combo box on the page. This is a feature-rich web-based text editor, with support for autocompletion and hot keys (for example, the Ctrl+S key combination saves your script changes when editing in a web browser running in a Windows environment).

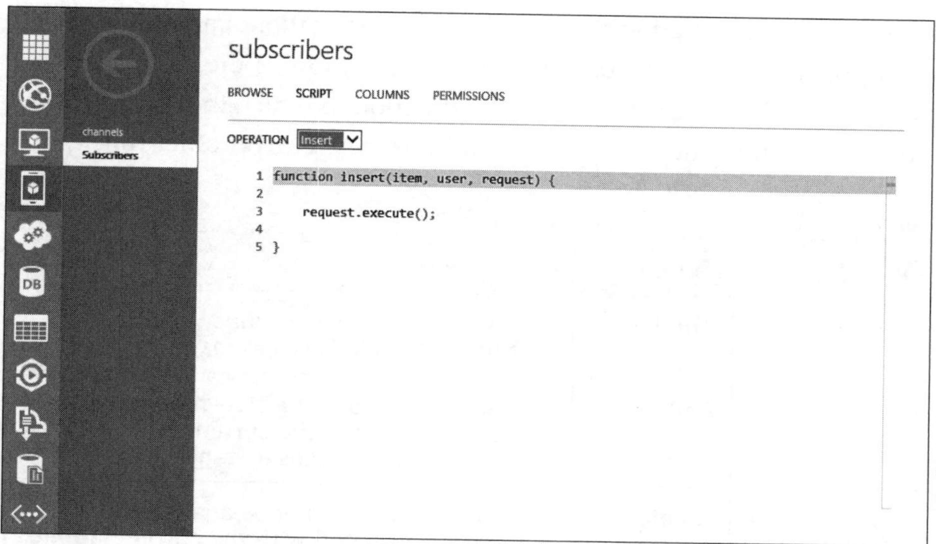

FIGURE 7.10 Accessing table operation scripts with the web-based script editor

Additional options for script editing also exist. For example, you can use Visual Studio 2013 and the integrated Mobile Services node in the Server Explorer. You can use the Azure command-line tools to download the script files locally and then upload the edited files with the same command-line tools. In addition, you can use the integrated support for the Git distributed source control management and edit the file on a local computer, and then synchronize the changes to the Mobile Services instance after they have been completed to your satisfaction. These editing methods are mentioned for completeness only, and further discussion is beyond the scope of this book.

Mobile Services table operation scripts are currently written in JavaScript and can include references to several built-in objects that define the available functionality that is exposed. Table 7.2 lists some of the helper objects that are available for use in your table operation scripts. For example, with the `console` object, you can write entries to the Mobile Services instance's logs, and the `push` object enables you to send push notifications to apps. The objects in Table 7.2 are categorized as either ambient objects or parameter objects. Ambient objects are available within the script function bodies and can simply be accessed without any prior initialization. Parameter objects are supplied as one of the parameters to one or more of the table operation methods. Their scope is limited to the function to which they were passed (unless, of course, they are provided as a parameter to another function).

TABLE 7.2 Table Operation Scripting Objects

Object	Type	Description
`console`	Ambient	Writes information, warnings, or error content to the Mobile Services instance's logs.
`tables`	Ambient	Interacts with table objects—requested by name or current for the current table—in the current Mobile Services instance.
`mssql`	Ambient	Runs ad-hoc T-SQL queries against the database associated with the current Mobile Services instance.
`push`	Ambient	Sends push notifications.
`statusCodes`	Ambient	Provides an enumeration of the supported HTTP status codes that can be returned by the `request.respond` method.
`query`	Parameter	Provided as the first argument to the `read` function; allows the script to access and potentially alter or extend the incoming data request.
`item`	Parameter	Provided as the first argument to the `insert` and `update` functions; allows the script to access and potentially alter or extend the item being stored in the database.
`id`	Parameter	Provided as the first argument to the `del` (delete) function; allows the script to access the ID of the item to be deleted. Changing this item in the script does not affect the default behavior.
`user`	Parameter	Provided as the second argument to all the table operation functions; allows access to the user currently issuing the request. If the request is authenticated, it includes a value in the `userId` property (along with additional values).

Object	Type	Description
`request`	Parameter	Provided as the third argument to all the table operation functions; every table operation script operation must result in a call to `request.execute` or `request.respond`.

All script operations must conclude with a call to one of the two methods available on the `request` object, or the operation will potentially become unresponsive or result in an error. The `request.execute` method informs Mobile Services to go ahead and run the requested operation using any changes that have been made thus far in the script to the `item` or `query` objects. The `request.respond` method provides options for returning a particular status code and some message text. It is possible to also specify success and error callbacks as parameters to the `execute` method. If these callbacks are provided, the callbacks must themselves conclude with calls to a `respond` method.

Listing 7.2 shows an example of a table operation script that supports the `insert` operation for the Subscribers table used in the example project. The script starts by performing a validation check to see if the item to insert includes non-empty values for the `LastName` and `FirstName` properties. If the data fails the check, an error is logged and a `BAD_REQUEST` (HTTP 400) response code is returned with a corresponding message. Otherwise, the script goes on to append a server-side data property to the incoming data object. Note that this property (ownerId) is not a property of the `Subscriber` class defined in the client and, as such, is not included in the JSON that is sent to the Mobile Services instance. Because of JavaScript's dynamic (as opposed to hard-coded or static) nature, grafting properties onto objects this way is perfectly acceptable. Because of the Dynamic Schema feature, the database table adjusts to accommodate the additional value the first time a record is inserted that includes this property. After the data has been properly shaped, the `execute` function is called to tell Mobile Services to actually insert the new record into the database. The listing also includes a success callback for the `execute` function, which uses the JavaScript `delete` keyword to strip the server-side data value off the object prior to returning to the client and then making the required call to the `respond` function.

This is not a required step because the JSON deserializer in the app simply ignores extra properties when converting the returned JSON payload to an instance of the `Subscriber` class. However, it is a useful technique if the server-side data that is being added is sensitive or should not be allowed to move off the server.

LISTING 7.2 Example Table Operation to Insert Script

```
function insert(item, user, request) {
    // Validate the input
    if (!item.LastName || !item.FirstName) {
        console.error("Invalid user data was provided");
        request.respond(statusCodes.BAD_REQUEST,
                "First and Last Names are required");
    } else {
        // Set the owner of the new item to be
        // the id of the logged-in user
        item.ownerId = user.userId;

        request.execute({
            success: function () {
                // Strip server-only properties off of the result
                if (item.ownerId) delete (item.ownerId);
                request.respond();
            }
        });
    }
}
```

NOTE

Mobile Services table operation scripts are supported by node.js and make use of its capability to extend functionality by including additional modules. In node.js, module content that is exported is consumed and scoped through the use of the `require` statement. Several common node modules are already available in Mobile Services and can be used in your scripts, including crypto (cryptography), querystring (to work with query strings), request (for making external HTTP calls), sendgrid (using the SendGrid email service), and azure (for accessing other services Windows Azure offers). Using the Mobile Services' Git source control integration provides access to a special "shared" folder for including additional custom or third-party node.js modules that you can import into your table

> operation scripts to share or further extend the available functionality. You can find additional information about the modules already exported and available to be imported via the require statement at www.windowsazure.com/en-us/develop/mobile/how-to-guides/work-with-server-scripts/#modules-helper-functions.

Authorization

You saw earlier in the "Authentication" section how to go about adding authentication support to a client app. Mobile Services provides the capability to configure permissions for individual data table operations to determine whether or not the operation should be limited to calls made by authenticated users, among other values. Available table permissions include **Everyone**, **Anybody with the Application Key**, **Only Authenticated Users**, and **Only Scripts and Admins**.

When the permission value is set to **Everyone**, any request to that particular table operation is allowed to pass into the corresponding data operation script function. When set to **Anybody with the Application Key**, requests are allowed to pass into the scripts only if the application key is included in the HTTP header, which the `MobileServiceClient` does if it was provided in the constructor when the object was first defined. This is the default setting that is provided in the permission boxes shown when you create a new table. As mentioned earlier, **Only Authenticated Users** filters out any requests made by an unauthenticated client. Finally, **Only Scripts and Admins** allows only calls either from other scripts in the same Mobile Services instance or from clients when the user has made the request as an administrator by including the service's master key in the X-ZUMO-MASTER custom header as part of the request. (Note that because this key is a sensitive piece of data, it should normally not be included in client applications.) These settings are set by selecting the desired values for the corresponding operations in each table's Permissions page (see Figure 7.11). In this case, the subscribers table is set to require authentication for the Insert, Update, and Delete operations, but any request that supplies a valid application key value can issue a Read request to obtain data from the table.

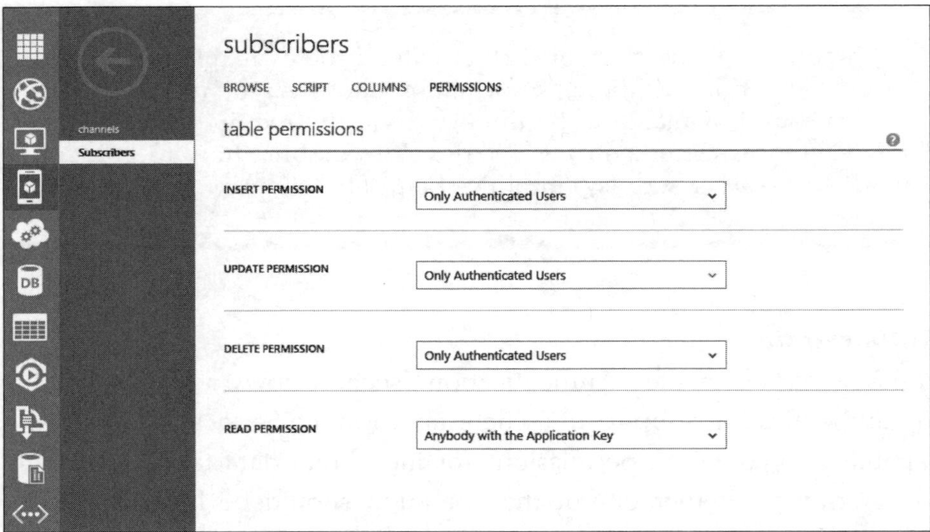

FIGURE 7.11 The Permissions page for table data operations

The previous section, "Data Access Scripts," mentioned that each table operation script's parameter includes a user object that contains certain values if an authenticated user calls the operation. This value can be used within the script's logic to allow additional functionality, such as isolating data so that only the user who published it can see it, or perhaps restricting data modification to the creating user, among other possibilities. Listing 7.3 provides a Delete script that follows the Insert script in Listing 7.2. In this case, logic is added to the Delete operation to restrict deletion to the user who initially created the record. The script first obtains a reference to the current table and then queries the table for a record with a matching id. If it finds no record, it returns an error. Otherwise, the record's `ownerId` property is compared to the current user's `userId` value. If the values do not match, an error is returned with a message indicating the restriction. Otherwise, `request.execute` is called to complete the deletion.

LISTING 7.3 Applying Business Logic to User Deletion

```
function del(id, user, request) {
    var subscriberTable = tables.current;
    subscriberTable.where({
        id: id
```

```
    }).read({
        success: function (items) {
            if (items.length === 0) {
                request.respond(
                    statusCodes.NOT_FOUND,
                    { error: 'No matching item found to
➥delete.' });
            } else {
                if (items[0].ownerId != user.userId) {
                    request.respond(
                        statusCodes.BAD_REQUEST,
                        { error: "Cannot delete someone else's
➥item." });
                } else {
                    request.execute();
                }
            }
        }
    });
}
```

Custom APIs

In some cases, you might want a client to trigger functionality in a Mobile Services instance without tying the request directly to a specific table operation. To support such calls, Mobile Services includes the capability to define custom API methods.

Custom API methods are managed in the Windows Azure Management Portal through the API page. To create an API, click the **Create** button and provide a name for the API in the dialog. Mobile Services creates an HTTP endpoint within your Mobile Services' API node that matches this name. Each API can include methods for each of the following HTTP verbs: GET, POST, PUT, PATCH, and DELETE. As with the table operation scripts, access to each of the custom API scripts is governed by a permission setting that can be set when the endpoint is defined or updated. The default value is again **Anybody with the Application Key**.

The script used in custom APIs is almost identical to the script used in table operations, except that different values are provided in the method parameters and, with the exception of the `console` and `statusCodes` objects, no ambient objects exist. All custom API methods are defined inside a single file, with each HTTP method defined using the following syntax:

```
exports.VERB = function(request, response){ }
```

Here, `VERB` denotes the specific HTTP VERB endpoint to expose. Instead of ambient objects, the utility objects are available as properties and sub-properties on the objects passed in as parameters to the methods. Table 7.3 shows the various objects available for use in a custom API script.

TABLE 7.3 Custom API Scripting Objects

Object	Description
`request.query`	Returns the parsed query string. (Names become parameters on the return object.)
`request.body`	Returns the parsed request body. (JSON keys become params on the returned object.)
`request.headers`	Provides access to a collection of the message headers included in the request.
`request.user`	Returns the user object that represents an authenticated user (same as the user param in the table operation scripts).
`request.service.tables`	Provides access to tables in the current Mobile Services instance (same as the ambient `tables` object in the table operation scripts, although the `current` property is not defined).
`request.service.push`	Provides access to push notification APIs in the current Mobile Services instance (same as the ambient `push` object in the table operation scripts).
`request.service.mssql`	Provides access to the current SQL database for issuing T-SQL queries (same as the ambient `mssql` object in the table operation scripts).
`response.send`	Returns a result to the caller. Can include a status code and optionally either some message text or a JSON object that contains data being exchanged.

Listing 7.4 shows a custom API declaration that includes both POST and GET endpoints. The POST method uses the `request.service.mssql` object to issue a T-SQL query against the Mobile Services instance's database to count the number of records in the Subscribers table. Upon

successful completion of the query, the API returns a status of OK and an object defined by a count property that includes the number of records in the table.

LISTING 7.4 A Custom API Declaration

```
exports.post = function(request, response) {
    var mssql = request.service.mssql;
    mssql.query('SELECT COUNT(*) as TotalSubscribers
➥FROM Subscribers',
    {
        success: function(results){
            response.send(
                statusCodes.OK,
                {
                    count: results[0].TotalSubscribers
                });
        },
        error: function(){
            console.error('An error has occurred.');
            response.send(statusCodes.INTERNAL_SERVER_ERROR);
        }
    });
};

exports.get = function(request, response) {
    // Omitted for brevity
};
```

Custom APIs can be called by the `MobileServicesClient` through the `InvokeAPIAsync` method. A call to the POST verb on the earlier `Sample` API looks like this:

```
var client = App.WinRTByExampleBookClient;
var result = await client.InvokeApiAsync<Sample>("sample");
```

In this example, the `Sample` class includes a single `Int32` property called `Count`, which would be returned to the `result` object.

Integrated Push Notification Support

Chapter 6 introduced push notifications as a way an external system can issue requests through the Windows Notification Service (WNS) to communicate updates to Windows devices. Mobile Services provides integrated support for several push notification services:

- The Windows Notification Service (WNS), which supports Windows Store apps
- The Microsoft Push Notification Service (MPNS), which supports Windows Phone apps
- The Apple Push Notification Service (APNS), which supports iOS apps
- The Google Cloud Messaging service (GCM), which supports Android apps

To be able to use the WNS, APNS, and GCM services to send notifications, a Mobile Services instance must first be registered with each of these services. This registration process makes available authentication values that must be entered in the Mobile Services instance's Push page in the Windows Azure Management Portal. Mobile Services uses these values when sending notification requests. Each service requires different registration content; you can access instructions on how to gather the required information through the help link on the page. For WNS, the values come from the Dashboard section of the Windows Dev Center, where the app registering to receive notifications must be associated with an existing Windows Store App entry in this Dashboard for a particular Windows Developer account. Chapter 19, "Packaging and Deploying," details the process by which an app is associated with the Windows Store. Once registered, the configuration for WNS requires a Client Secret and Package SID value, which can be obtained from the app's Services tab in the Dev Center Dashboard. These values are used to authenticate the service issuing the push notification request, although after the settings have been provided, Mobile Services handles the details for doing so. Note that the Client Secret value is the same value that is used on the Identity page to support Microsoft Account authentication; it is shared between the two fields.

For a Mobile Services instance to be able to send a push notification to a particular device, that device must first supply its push notification channel, which the Mobile Services instance stores until it is needed.

Visual Studio 2013 includes integration with Mobile Services that provides a starting point for this process. From the **Project** menu, select **Add Push Notification**. This brings up the Add Push Notification Wizard. Log into your Windows Store account to select the app receiving the notification (when the Mobile Services instance sends a notification, it needs to authenticate with WNS, which requires values associated to an app's store record). After you select the app, you are prompted to select the Mobile Services instance that should be updated. Then you have a last chance to review your changes before applying them.

The wizard configures the WNS account settings for the current Mobile Services instance, and you can see the values entered on the Identity page in the Windows Azure Management Portal. Additionally, a channels table is created along with an Insert script that includes sample code for using the push object, as well as sample code for either inserting or updating an incoming channel value. The wizard also adds a services folder to the current Visual Studio project, which includes a new class whose name is derived from the Mobile Services instance's name contained in a push.register.cs file that is added to the project. In the case of the example project, the class is named `WinRTByExamplePush`. This class includes an `UploadChannel` method, and a call to this method is added to `OnLaunched` method of the project's App.xaml.cs file. This method contains code for obtaining the notification channel for the current app and then inserting the channel into the newly created channels table.

The notification channel upload code the wizard provides typically is updated, and the call to register the channel might be moved to a better location in code. In the example application, the `UploadChannel` call has been moved to the `CredentialsViewModel` class so that the channel information is not uploaded until after the user logs in. The data operations for the channels table have also been updated to require authentication, and the table's Insert script has been changed so that the incoming `item` value is modified to include an `ownerId` property whose value is set to the authenticated user's `userId` value. Listing 7.5 shows this updated script.

Listing 7.5 Updated Insert Script

```
function insert(item, user, request) {
    // Include the userId for the authenticated user
    item.ownerId = user.useId;

    var ct = tables.current;
    ct.where({ installationId: item.installationId }).read({
        success: function (results) {
            if (results.length > 0) {
                // we already have a record for this
                // user/installation id - if the
                // channel is different, update it
                // otherwise just respond
                var match = results[0];
                if (match.channelUri !== item.channelUri) {
                    match.channelUri = item.channelUri;
                    ct.update(match, {
                        success: function () {
                            request.respond(200, match);
                        }
                    });
                }
                else {
                    // no change necessary, just respond
                    request.respond(200, match);
                }
            }
            else {
                // no matching installation, insert the record
                request.execute();
            }
        }
    })
}
```

After the script in Listing 7.5 appends the `ownerId` value to the incoming channel item, the current table is examined to see if a channel has already been provided for an item with the matching installation id. The installation ID is obtained in the client through a call to `HardwareIdentification.GetPackageSpecificToken`. This method call returns an identifier that is unique to a specific device and app package. The identifier can be used to indicate the push notification channel that originated from a specific hardware device without having to be concerned about whether the device information can be correlated with similar device information that is sent on behalf of other apps. If the Mobile Services instance is already tracking a channel value for the current device, the value is replaced if the channel URI has been changed and a status code is returned indicating that the call was successful. Otherwise, the default action is simply executed, resulting in a new value inserted into the table.

At this point, all the necessary configuration has been performed. The sample app is providing the Mobile Services instance with the addresses to which push notifications should be sent, which is being stored in the channels table. The Mobile Services instance also has been configured with the values it requires to properly authenticate with the Windows Notification Service to send push notifications to the example app. The next step is to actually send a notification.

The Mobile Services instance for the sample app is configured to send push notifications to the user when one of the subscribers that user created has been updated by a different user. The logic for making this happen is contained in the Subscriber table's Update script (see Listing 7.6).

LISTING 7.6 Subscriber Table Update Script

```
function update(item, user, request) {
    // Validate the input
    if (!item.LastName || !item.FirstName) {
        console.error("Invalid user data was provided");
        request.respond(statusCodes.BAD_REQUEST,
                "First and Last Names are required");
    } else {
        var subscriberTable = tables.current;
        subscriberTable.where({
            id: item.id
        }).read({
            success: function(items) {
                if (items.length === 0) {
                    request.respond(statusCodes.NOT_FOUND,
                        { error: 'No matching item found to update.' });
                } else {
                    request.execute({
                        success: function() {
                            if (items[0].ownerId != user.userId) {
                                notifyOwner(items[0]);
                            }
                            request.respond();
                        }
                    });
```

```
                }
            }
        });
    }
}

function notifyOwner(changedItem) {
    var channelTable = tables.getTable("channels");
    channelTable.where({ userId: changedItem.ownerId }).read({
        success: function (results) {
            if (results.length > 0) {
                for (var i = 0; i < results.length; i++) {
                    var result = results[i];
                    sendNotifications(result.channelUri, changedItem);
                }
            }
        }
    });
}

function sendNotifications(uri, changedItem) {
    push.wns.sendToastText01(uri, {
        text1: 'One of your records - '
                + changedItem.FirstName + ' '
                + changedItem.LastName +
                ' - has been edited by another user.'
    });
}
```

As in the Insert script in Listing 7.2, the Update script starts by validating the incoming input values to ensure that first and last names are provided. Next, the current table is queried to find a record with an ID value that matches the ID of the item being updated. If no records are found, an error result code and message are returned. Otherwise, the default update action is executed. Upon its successful completion, the `ownerId` property of the updated item is compared with the authenticated user's `userId` value. If these values do not match, the `notifyOwner` function is called with the updated item.

The `notifyOwner` function queries the channels table to find any notification channels that have been configured for a user with an ID that matches the `ownerId` value. A user might have registered notification channels for several different machines, so the function iterates over the returned values, calling the `sendNotifications` function for each registration.

Finally, the `sendNotifications` function uses the `push` object to issue a push notification request to the wns service to send a toast message using the ToastText01 template. This message contains the text to inform the user that a specific subscriber has been updated by another user.

Scheduled Tasks

In addition to scripts that are executed as part of table operations or through custom API invocations, Mobile Services provides a scheduler service that is capable of running scripts at predefined time intervals. These scripts are useful for tasks such as archiving records; connecting with external services such as Twitter, Facebook, or RSS feeds to store periodic information; or perhaps performing some kind of delayed batch processing of data or images.

Scheduled jobs are managed through the Mobile Services instance's Scheduler page in the Windows Azure Management Portal. This page lists any existing scheduled jobs and provides functionality for creating new jobs, enabling or disabling existing jobs, performing one-time immediate execution of jobs, and opening jobs for editing and deleting jobs.

You create a new job by first clicking the **Create** button at the bottom of the page. This brings up the Create New Job dialog, in Figure 7.12. In this dialog, you must give the new job a name; optionally, you can define a schedule for the job. Jobs can currently be scheduled to run at intervals ranging from every 15 minutes to every 3 months. They can also be set to not run on a particular schedule and run only on demand, which can be useful for testing the script during development. Whatever value is chosen for the interval can be changed later. Upon completing the job definition, it is provisioned and opened for editing.

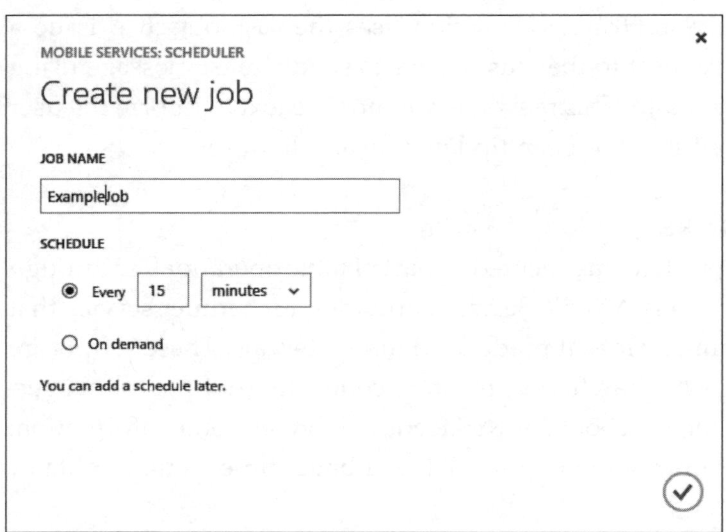

FIGURE 7.12 Creating a new scheduled job

Editing a job is handled through Configure and Script pages. The Configure page provides feedback on when the job was last run and when it is next configured to run, as well as the current scheduled interval for the job. The Script page defines the script that will execute at the given interval. These scripts follow the same syntax as the table operation scripts, except that the function is called without any parameters. Because the job is executing simply on a time interval, there is no data object to act on, no value to return, and no authenticated user for which credentials are provided. Otherwise, the script has access to the same ambient values in Table 7.2.

Mobile Services Deployment Tiers

Mobile Services instances can be deployed to one of three service tiers, labeled Free, Basic, and Standard. The tiers differ primarily in terms of cost and the amount of scalability each one provides.

> **NOTE**
>
> Things move especially quickly in the cloud. To meet market needs and stay competitive, Windows Azure is an environment in which change happens frequently. With that in mind, the features and constraints this chapter discusses could change by the time you read this, especially with the features and constraints that apply to each Mobile Services tier. Even the number and names of the available tiers could change. Please keep that in mind when considering the following details, and be sure to consult the Mobile Services documentation at www.windowsazure.com/en-us/services/mobile-services/ for the most up-to-date information.

The Free tier is meant for development and test scenarios; it is not really meant to support apps in production. Each Windows Azure account can create up to ten free services. The Free tier is the only one to include a throttled limit of 500 unique devices that can connect to a Mobile Services instance each day, with each device uniquely identified through an internal implementation within each of the Mobile Services client libraries. Services provisioned in the Free tier support a daily maximum number of API calls equivalent to 500,000 calls per month, prorated daily. No option exists for scaling Free tier Mobile Services instances to support more than one concurrent instance of the same service. Finally, Free tier services are limited to a single scheduled job definition that is limited to one execution per hour.

The Basic tier provides several enhancements over the features the Free tier offers and is meant to support apps in production scenarios. Services provisioned in the Basic tier support running between one and six concurrent instances, with billing based per instance. The Basic tier allows a maximum of 1,500,000 API calls per instance per month, prorated daily. For example, two instances in a 30-day month would support up to 1,500,000/30 * 2 = 100,000 API calls per day. Up to 10 scheduled jobs can be defined, and 50,000 job executions per month are allowed.

The Standard tier is also intended for use in production scenarios. Services provisioned in the Standard tier support running between one and ten concurrent instances, with billing based per instance. The Standard tier allows a maximum of 15,000,000 API calls per instance per month, prorated daily. Up to 10 scheduled jobs can be defined, and 500,000 job executions per month are allowed.

Both the Basic and Standard tiers support Autoscale functionality. When Autoscale is enabled, a Mobile Services service can be configured with lower and upper limits for the number of service instances to run. At the beginning of each day, the number of running instances is set based on the lower limit. Throughout the day, if the number of API calls begins to approach 90% of the allowed limit for the currently running number of instances and the total number of instances is below the upper limit, an additional instance automatically is provisioned until the upper limit is reached. At the end of the day, the daily API call count is reset, and the number of running instances is reset once again to match the lower limit value.

The tier selection and Autoscale values are defined in the Mobile Services instance's Scale page in the Windows Azure Management Portal (see Figure 7.13). Note that switching between tiers is possible. Thus, you can initially define a Mobile Services instance and work on it as a Free tier service, and then when the service and the corresponding apps that it serves are ready to be published, you can select the appropriate tier and number of running instances.

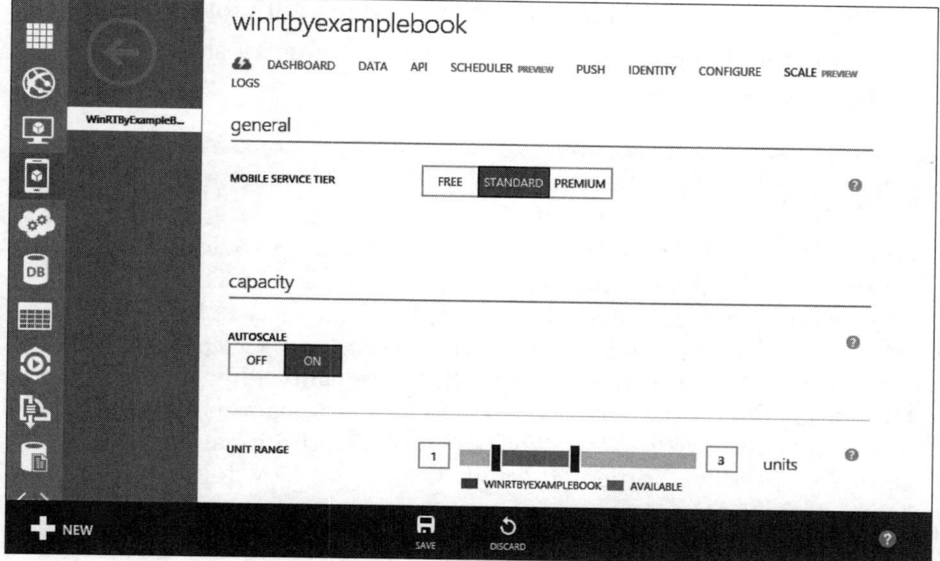

FIGURE 7.13 Selecting a Mobile Services deployment tier with Autoscale

Live Connect

Microsoft offers several important cloud-based services that millions of users interact with on a day-to-day basis, including the Microsoft Account service, OneDrive (previously SkyDrive), and Outlook.com. Live Connect is a collection of APIs that you can use to integrate functionality exposed by these services into applications. The Live Connect SDK provides client libraries that you can use along with the Windows Runtime to build connected apps for Windows 8.1. Live Connect includes this key functionality:

- Microsoft Account provides access to authentication and user profile information.
- Outlook.com provides tools for working with a user's contacts and calendars.

- OneDrive provides functionality for working with folders and files either stored in the user's personal cloud storage or shared with them by other users.

> **NOTE**
>
> Until recently, the Live Connect APIs and SDK provided tools for interacting with the Windows Live Messenger service. The Messenger service is being deprecated in favor of Microsoft's Skype Internet messaging and calling platform. As of this time, Live Connect does not include any APIs for interacting with Skype, and other than custom URI protocols used to invoke local Skype applications, no publicly available Skype API exists. You can obtain additional information about Skype development through the Skype Developer portal, at http://developer.skype.com/.

The functionality the Live Connect SDK provides is simply a wrapper around the Live Connect APIs, which themselves primarily use REST requests to exchange JSON data payloads. The Live Connect SDK also uses the OAuth 2.0 protocol for credential authentication, which supports authenticating users through the Live Connect services without having the app itself directly interact with the user's credentials.

Getting Started

You can find information about working with Live Connect and the SDK at the Live Connect Developer Center.[4] This portal includes documentation for the various APIs that are available, the capability to obtain a listing of apps that have been configured to work with the Live API, links to access the Live Connect developer support forum, and SDK download links for the various platforms for which API libraries are provided. It even includes an interactive SDK example that illustrates the use of a majority of the available API calls.

---

[4]Live Connect Developer Center, http://dev.live.com

You add a reference to the Live Connect SDK in your Windows app in two main ways. First, you can download and install the latest SDK from the Live Connect Developer Center. Then you can include the library reference by bringing up the Reference Manager dialog; selecting **Windows, Extensions**; and checking **Live SDK,** as in Figure 7.14. Alternatively, you can include the SDK by using the NuGet package manager and selecting the LiveSDK package.

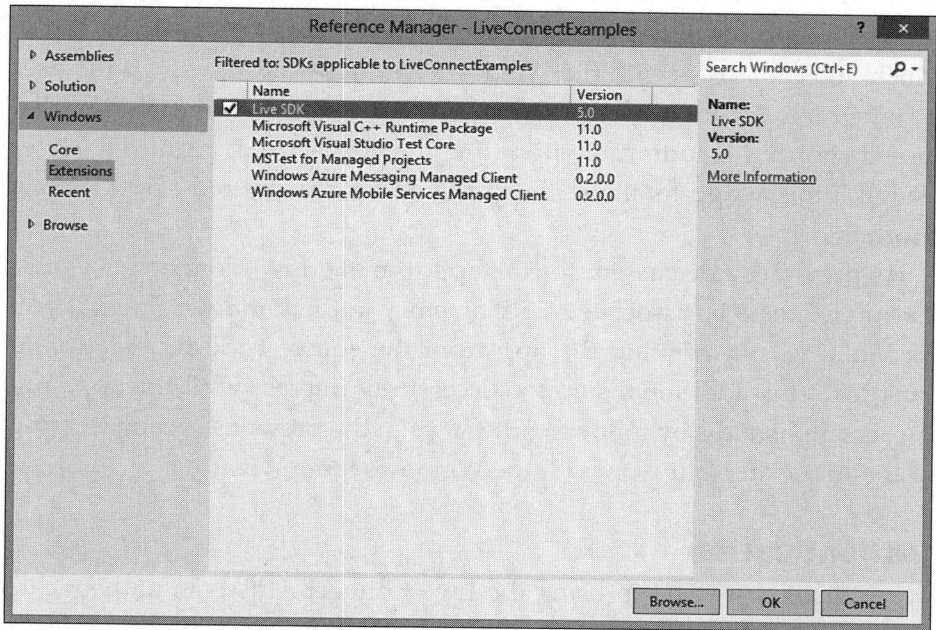

FIGURE 7.14 Adding the reference to the Live Connect SDK

Note that after the SDK Library assembly reference has been configured, to be able to successfully make calls to the Live Connect services from a Windows Store app, the app *must* be associated with a Windows Store entry. Failing to do so results in a nonobvious `NullReferenceException` being raised when attempting to call the API initialization or authentication methods. The "Push Notifications" section in Chapter 6 describes one of the processes available for associating an app with a store entry.

The Example App

The **LiveConnectExample** project in the source code for this chapter builds an app that illustrates how you can work with the Live Connect APIs. The app is basically a sampler-style app. For the user signed into the app, the app displays profile information and both displays and allows interaction with the user's related OneDrive, Contact, and Calendar information. If the user is signed into Windows with a Microsoft Account, the app attempts to use those credentials with its Live Connect API calls; otherwise, you can use a Sign In button in the Account tab in the app's Settings Panel, which you can access with the Windows Settings Charm. Even if the user is signed into Windows with a Microsoft Account, several scenarios discussed shortly (including the first time the app is used) require the user to sign into the app to allow the app to access the desired Live Connect information.

As previously discussed, for the app to make Live Connect API calls, the app needs to be associated with an entry in the Windows Store. If you are building and running the app from the source code provided, you must take this additional step to successfully interact with the app. You can accomplish this by following the steps in the previous section to bring up the Associate Your App with the Windows Store Wizard.

Authentication

The first step involved in using the Live Connect APIs is to authenticate with a Microsoft Account. If successful, the authentication process returns a `LiveConnectSession` object that you need to use for subsequent calls to get information from the Live Connect APIs.

Before discussing the mechanics of authenticating with Live Connect, it is important to discuss the concept of **scopes**. Scopes represent permission levels to the various Live Connect resources that the current login session can access. You can request only information that is contained within the scopes that were declared when the user logged in; calls to resources outside those scopes result in an error. Furthermore, the scopes determine what fields are returned during Live Connect API requests. For example, requesting profile information with only the `wl.basic` scope specified returns only the user values for the `id`, `name`, `first_name`, `last_name`, `link`, `locale`, and `updated_time` properties. Including an additional scope such as `wl.birthday` provides additional fields in the value that is returned for the same request, including `birth_day`, `birth_month`, and `birth_year`. The Live Connect API REST Reference[5] documentation includes a comprehensive list of the objects that are available through the API, what properties are included for those objects, and the specific scopes that must be specified for each property to be included in the returned values.

In the Live Connect SDK, instances of the `LiveAuthClient` class provide authentication support. For logging in, this class provides two key methods, `InitializeAsync` and `LoginAsync`. Both methods accept a list of the scopes being requested for the current client session. The key difference is that `InitializeAsync` attempts to sign into Live Connect silently, without showing any user interface. If the user has already signed into Live Connect from the app, or is running the app from an account that is logged into Windows with a Microsoft Account, and previously approved the app to have access to the indicated scope values, a valid session object returns, along with a status of `Connected`. This differs from `LoginAsync`, in that `LoginAsync` also tries to silently sign into Live Connect, but if it cannot connect because of a lack of valid credentials, it displays a Live Connect sign-in page prompting the user to enter Microsoft Account credentials. Even if the user has logged in previously or has logged into Windows with a Microsoft Account, if the client library code detects a difference between the scopes that were previously approved for the current app and the scopes being requested, it automatically displays a consent page informing the user which new permissions are being requested and asking for the user to accept the request. Figure 7.15 shows the initial consent request in the example application that appears the first time a user accesses the app.

[5]Live Connect API REST Reference, http://j.mp/LiveConnectRESTDocs

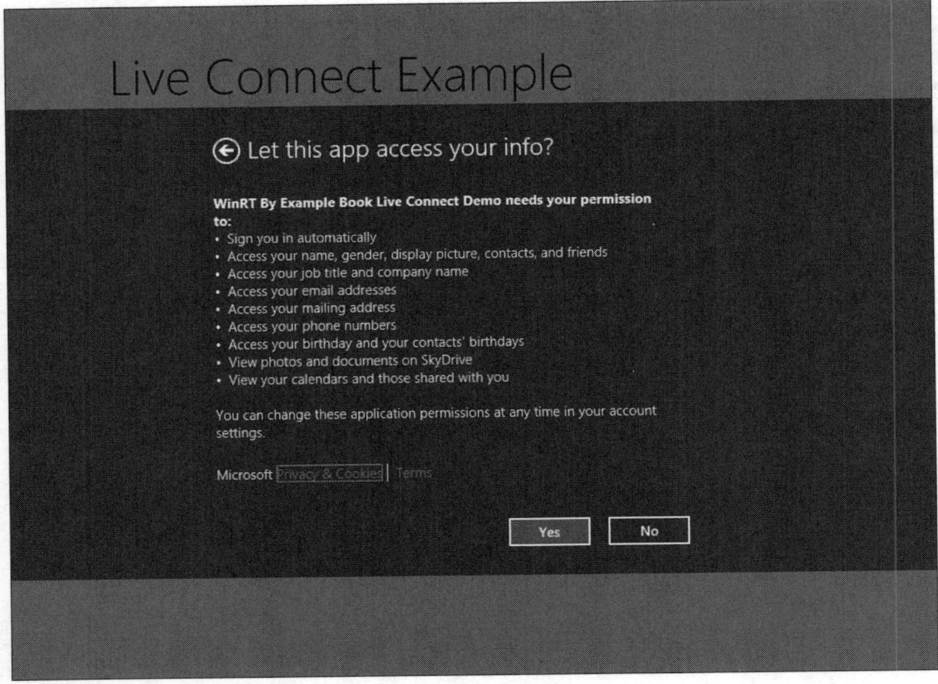

FIGURE 7.15 The Live Connect consent page

Because the user has to approve the requested functionality for Live Connect to access their information, it is important to keep the list of requested scope values to the absolute minimum that the app needs to function correctly. If users see an app requesting permissions to access data that makes no sense for that particular app to be accessing, they might understandably be reluctant to grant their consent. Then they will not be able to use the app for its intended purpose because this access consent is an all-or-nothing proposition.

> **NOTE**
>
> Users can see what apps they have approved by opening the Microsoft Account Management Portal at https://account.live.com. After they sign in, they can select **Permissions** and then **Apps and Services**. Selecting an app from the list provides a list of all the scopes that were requested and that the user approved, along with an option to remove the app. If the app is removed, the next time the user attempts to sign into the app, the app will be treated as if the user had never previously logged in and will need to re-approve the requested scopes.

In the example app, the main page attempts a silent sign-in with a call to `InitializeAsync` as part of the page's `OnNavigatedTo` method override. If the silent sign-in fails, a prompt displays instructing the user to open the app's settings and to sign in through the Account panel. When the Sign In button on this panel is clicked, it makes a call to `LoginAsync` to allow the user to provide the information needed to finish signing in. If either of these methods succeeds, the session value is stored for later use. Listing 7.7 details the code for showing the user login and consent page display.

LISTING 7.7 Logging in to Live Connect to Configure a Session

```
var authClient = new LiveAuthClient();
var sessionStatus = LiveConnectSessionStatus.Unknown;
LiveConnectSession session = null;
try
{
    var loginResult = await authClient.InitializeAsync(_scopes);
    sessionStatus = loginResult.Status;
    session = loginResult.Session;
}
catch (LiveAuthException ex)
{
    // TODO - handle notification/display of error information
}

// Set the current instance session based on the login
UpdateSession(session);
```

Working with Profile Information

To work with basic user profile information for the currently signed-in user, the `wl.basic` scope should be requested. This scope includes the properties listed previously and also provides access to the signed-in user's contacts and profile picture. Table 7.4 shows several additional scopes to obtain extended profile information.

TABLE 7.4 Extended Scopes for Obtaining User Profile Information

Scope	Description
`wl.birthday`	Read access to birthday, month, and year
`wl.emails`	Read access to the user's email addresses, including preferred, account, personal, and business addresses.
`wl.phone_numbers`	Read access to the user's phone numbers, including personal, business, and mobile.
`wl.postal_addresses`	Read access to the user's postal addresses, including personal and business. Values include street, city, state, postal code, and region information.
`wl.work_profile`	Read access to the user's employer information, including employer name and position.

The example application retrieves and displays the username, profile picture, and id, as well as a link to the user's profile management page. It also takes advantage of the fact that the profile values being returned are basically key-value pairs, so it iterates through the remaining list of the property values and displays any provided values as well.

When using the Live Connect SDK, requests for information are made with instances of the `LiveConnectClient` class. This class requires the current session value that was obtained from the authentication process as a constructor parameter. It mostly provides lightweight asynchronous wrapper methods around the REST actions used by the Live Connect API, including `GetAsync`, `PostAsync`, `PutAsync`, `DeleteAsync`, `MoveAsync`, and `CopyAsync`. To retrieve values, the `GetAsync` call is used along with a path value that identifies the value being requested. The results that are returned include the raw JSON response text, as well as a `Dictionary<String, Object>` value named

Result that contains the result properties and their corresponding values. To obtain user profile information, either the user's ID can be provided or the value me can be substituted for the actual user ID as a way to indicate that the request is for the currently logged-in user. The following code shows how the current user's profile information is obtained, using a session object obtained through one of the previous authentication requests:

```
var client = new LiveConnectClient(_session);
var operationResult = await client.GetAsync("me");
dynamic profileResult = operationResult.Result;
var userId = operationResult.id;
var userName = profileResult.name;
```

Note that this code is using the dynamic data type for the profileResult, which can be substituted for the Dictionary<String, Object> type that is actually returned. This allows the code that consumes the results to reference the profile properties as if they were properties on an actual class instance. The following code is functionally equivalent to the previous code, but it instead uses the Dictionary<String, Object> approach to working with the returned values:

```
var client = new LiveConnectClient(_session);
var operationResult = await client.GetAsync("me");
var profileResult = operationResult.Result;
var userId = operationResult["id"];
var userName = profileResult["name"];
```

In addition to listing the user profile information values, you also can request a URL to the location of the user's account profile picture. The Live Connect SDK can indicate the preferred size for the profile picture from the available small, medium, or large options. Small images are 96x96, medium images are 180x180, and large images are 360x360. To retrieve the URL, the GetAsync method is used with a path of <userId>/picture?type=<type-name>, remembering that the special value of me can be substituted for the user ID portion. The result that is returned includes a location property that contains the URL text. Therefore, a request for a large image takes this form:

```
var operationResult = await client.GetAsync("me/picture?type=large");
dynamic result = operationResult.Result;
var imageUrl = new Uri(result.location.ToString());
```

Working with Contacts

You can also return a list of contacts for a given user within the wl.basic scope by making the GetAsync request with the path of <userId>/contacts. To obtain the list of contacts for the currently logged-in user, the path for the GetAsync request is me/contacts, and the list of resulting values is returned in the data value within the results, as the following code illustrates:

```
var client = new LiveConnectClient(_session);
var operationResult = await client.GetAsync("me/contacts");
var contactsResult = operationResult.Result;
var contactsList = new List<dynamic>(contactsResult.data);
```

Detailed information for a specific contact is obtained the same way the user profile is, by simply substituting the contact ID value for the contacts path value in the GetAsync request. In the same way as for profile information, additional contact details are included for a contact if the wl.contacts_birthday, wl.contacts_calendars, wl.contacts_photos, or wl.contacts_skydrive scopes are requested. Specifying any one of these scopes also implicitly includes the corresponding wl.birthday, wl.calendars, wl.photos, and wl.skydrive scope.

In some cases, the contact also represents a user account. When this is the case, the contact information includes a user_id value. You can use this value to make the user profile information requests that were previously explained. In the example application, contacts that are also users are outlined in the contact listing. Bringing up the details page for one of these contacts takes the added step of retrieving and showing a user's account profile picture.

You also can use the Live Connect API to create new contacts, although no mechanism is provided to either update or delete existing contacts. To be able to create contacts, the wl.contacts_create scope must be requested. When creating a new contact, the PostAsync method is used with a parameter indicating <userId>/contacts and an IDictionary<String, Object> for the values to set for the new contact. The previously mentioned Live Connect REST Reference includes a list of the properties and value hierarchies that can be included in the request to add a new contact. Although you can omit values you do not want to set, at least one of the following values must be provided when defining a new contact: `first_name`, `last_name`, `preferred` (emails), `personal` (emails), `business` (emails), `other` (emails), or `name` (work – employer). If the contact is successfully added, the method returns the new contact, which includes the ID that is generated on the server, in case additional requests need to be made for this contact. The code in Listing 7.8 shows a new contact named Joe Smith being added for the currently logged-in user.

LISTING 7.8 Creating a New Contact

```
var newContact = new Dictionary<String, Object>
                {
                    {"first_name", "Joe"},
                    {"last_name", "Smith"},
                };
var client = new LiveConnectClient(_session);
var operationResult = await client.PostAsync("me/contacts", newContact);
dynamic result = operationResult.Result;
return result;
```

Working with Calendars and Events

You can use the Live Connect API to access a user's Outlook.com personal calendars, calendars that other users have shared to the user, and any online calendars the user has subscribed to. The API also can allow users to create new calendars, update calendar description properties, and delete calendars. Depending on the available permissions for each specific calendar, you also can use the API to read, create, update, or delete the events that the calendars contain.

To retrieve the list of available calendars, you need to have previously requested the `wl.calendars` scope. Then you can call the `GetAsync` method with a path value of `<userId>/calendars`. You retrieve details for an individual calendar with the `GetAsync` method and the ID value of the specific calendar to be obtained. The following code shows how you can retrieve the currently signed-in user's calendars:

```
var operationResult = await client.GetAsync("me/calendars");
dynamic result = operationResult.Result;
var resultList = new List<dynamic>(result.data);
return resultList;
```

Similarly, assuming that the wl.calendar_update scope has been requested, you can use PostAsync with the <userId>/calendars path and a dictionary containing a calendar name and an optional description value to create a new calendar. Or you can use a name and a subscription_location value that is set to the URL of an online iCal calendar to add a subscription to a public calendar. To update a calendar's name, description, or subscription_location (for subscribed calendars only), you can call the PutAsync method with the ID of the calendar to update and the new values. Note that you need to supply only a set of changed values, not the entire original object. Finally, you can delete a calendar with a call to DeleteAsync and the relevant calendar id.

You can also work with events in a calendar in a similar way. Retrieving events for a given calendar uses GetAsync and a path of <calendarId>/events. By default, this request returns events for the next 30 days. However, if you want to use a different date range, you can modify the path request to include start and end times. Listing 7.9 shows how to build and execute the request to get the events for a given timeframe.

LISTING 7.9 Getting Calendar Events for a Given Time Range

```
// First, convert the requested start and end values to
// the date/time format that the Live Connect API requires
const String DateTimeFormatString = "yyyy'-'MM'-'dd'T'HH':'mm':'sszzz";
var startTimeText = startTime.ToString(DateTimeFormatString);
var endTimeText = endTime.ToString(DateTimeFormatString);

// Build the path for the given calendar id and timeframe
var path = String.Format("{0}/events?start_time={1}&end_time={2}",
    calendarId, startTimeText, endTimeText);

// Make the request and return the results
var client = new LiveConnectClient(_session);
var operationResult = await client.GetAsync(path);
dynamic result = operationResult.Result;
var resultList = new List<dynamic>(result.data);
return resultList;
```

Note that a custom format was used when converting the supplied DateTimeOffset values to their String equivalents. The Live Connect API expects that the time values passed to it will line up with a variant of the ISO 8601 format, which produces values that look like 2014-01-01T12:00:00-05:00. Unfortunately, although the o standard `DateTime` format identifier available in .NET is available for converting values to the same standard, some small differences arise between what it produces and what the API expects, hence the explicitly defined custom format string. You can find more information about both standard and custom date and time format strings in the MSDN documentation.[6]

As you can imagine, you also can get details for a specific event, again using the `GetAsync` method with the desired specific event ID value for the path parameter.

When obtaining information about a calendar, a `permissions` property contains a value that indicates the kind of access the current user has for reading and modifying information in that calendar. Table 7.5 lists the available permission values and their implications.

TABLE 7.5 Extended Scopes for Obtaining Calendar Information

Permission Value	Description
`free_busy`	Events indicate only free or busy status information. Events cannot be added, modified, or deleted.
`limited_details`	Events contain only a subset of the complete details. Events cannot be added, modified, or deleted.
`read`	All event details are visible. Events cannot be added, modified, or deleted.
`read_write`	All event details are visible. Events can be added, modified, and deleted.
`co-owner`	All event details are visible. Events can be added, modified, and deleted.
`owner`	All event details are visible. Events can be added, modified, and deleted.

[6] Standard and Custom Date and Time Format Strings; http://j.mp/StandardDateTimeFormats, http://j.mp/CustomDateTimeFormats

To create a calendar event, the corresponding calendar's permissions structure must have a value of `owner`, `co-owner`, or `read-write`. Additionally, the `wl.events_create` scope must be requested. At a minimum, the `name`, `description`, and `start_time` values must be supplied. The same rules that were previously discussed for time values when requesting a date range apply to the values used for `start_time` and `end_time` when working with an event item. Calling the `PostAsync` method from an account that has the proper editing permissions with a path that has the syntax `<calendarId>/events` and the desired values adds the event to the specified calendar and returns the newly created event entry. Listing 7.10 shows an event being created.

LISTING 7.10 Creating a New Event

```
var newEvent = new Dictionary<String, Object>
                    {
                        {"name", eventName},
                        {"description", eventDescription},
                        {"start_time", startTimeDate},
                        {"end_time", endTimeDate},
                        {"location", locationText},
                        {"is_all_day_event", false},
                        {"availability", "busy"},
                        {"visibility", "public"}
                    };

var client = new LiveConnectClient(_session);
var path = String.Format("{0}/events", calendarId);
var operationResult = await client.PostAsync(path, newEvent);
dynamic result = operationResult.Result;
return result;
```

To update an existing calendar event, the `PutAsync` method is called with the ID of the event to be modified and the properties that have updated values. As with calendars, only modifications need to be included. Any properties in which values are not included in the update payload are left alone. To delete an event, you use the `DeleteAsync` method, also with the event id. Both updating and deleting events require the `wl.calendars_update` scope to be previously requested.

Working with OneDrive

> **NOTE**
>
> The SkyDrive service was recently renamed to OneDrive. However, as of this writing, the Live Connect API Scope values such as "wl.skydrive" have not been changed from their original values.

You can use the Live Connect APIs to allow an app to work with content stored in OneDrive. The OneDrive service provides file storage and management in the cloud. Every Microsoft Account is provisioned with some amount of OneDrive storage space, and you can purchase additional space or obtain space via various Microsoft promotions.

The example application initially shows the content of the root folder for the currently signed-in user. When an item is selected, a new page opens to display information about that item, including all its available properties and a thumbnail image if one is available. If the item is a folder, the item's contents are listed, and are also selectable, showing how you can navigate through a OneDrive folder hierarchy. The App Bar provides a special shortcut values Bar for directly navigating to one of the various special folders available in OneDrive. If the item that was selected is recognized as an audio or video file, a `MediaElement` control displays, with the item's URL set as its source so that you can play back the content. For photo files, the picture displays. Finally, if the item is just a regular file but is indicated as an embeddable item, a `WebView` control appears and the item's URL is set as the control's Source, allowing the item to be rendered directly in the sample application. This offers some interesting functionality for items such as PowerPoint documents: The Microsoft Office functionality that is integrated with OneDrive can be used with this embeddable functionality to actually display the document slideshow right in your app. In addition to navigating through the OneDrive hierarchy and displaying items and their properties, you can use the example app to create new folders and upload new content into folders. You can rename or delete selected items, and you can download individual items to the local file system.

Accessing content in OneDrive requires that at least one of several scopes be requested. The `wl.skydrive` scope grants access to a user's own OneDrive contents, and `wl.contacts_skydrive` both allows access to a user's contacts' OneDrive contents and also implicitly declares the `wl.skydrive` scope. The `wl.photos` scope allows access to a subset of the OneDrive contents, limiting access to photo, video, and audio content within albums. Albums are special types of folders in OneDrive that OneDrive has determined contain only media information. For the most part, they are functionally 100% identical to regular folders, except for three exceptions: They receive slightly different treatment in the OneDrive web user interface, their contents are included in aggregations of photos in the OneDrive web user interface, and user access in apps that use the Live Connect APIs can be limited to just their contents through the `wl.photos` scope just mentioned. A `wl.contacts_photos` scope is an analog to the `wl.contacts_skydrive` scope and also implicitly declares the `wl.photos` scope. To be able to make changes to content in OneDrive, you need to have approved the `wl.skydrive_update` scope. Declaring this scope also implicitly declares `wl.skydrive` scope.

As with most of the other requests to retrieve content through the Live Connect SDK, getting a list of a user's OneDrive content involves making a request through the `GetAsync` method with a path that indicates the desired content. For OneDrive content, you can use the following path values:

- `<userId>/skydrive/files` obtains the content in a user's OneDrive root directory. You can use the special value me for the user ID value to indicate the currently logged-in user.
- `<userId>/skydrive/<special folder name>/files` gets the contents of one of several special folders included in OneDrive by default. You can use `camera_roll` to access the OneDrive camera roll folder, `my_documents` to access the Documents folder, `my_photos` to access the Pictures folder, and `public_documents` to access the Public folder.
- `<folderId>/files` obtains the content of a given OneDrive folder (or album).

The items list is contained in the `data` value of the returned item's `Result` property, as the following code shows:

```
var client = new LiveConnectClient(_session);
var operationResult = await client.GetAsync("me/skydrive/files");
dynamic result = operationResult.Result;
return new List<dynamic>(result.data);
```

The returned values include the combination of files and folders that the requested parent item contains. Each item includes a type parameter in its properties that indicates whether the item is a folder, album, photo, audio, video, file, or notebook. We have already discussed folders and albums. Photo, audio, and video items are multimedia items, as their name suggests. Any other file types are returned as a file type, except for Microsoft OneNote notebooks, which are specially marked as a notebook. The Live Connect API REST Reference documentation has a complete set of properties returned for each item, previously discussed in the "Authentication" section.

To get information for an individual item, you can call `GetAsync` with the item's ID value as the path for the call. The returned item's `Result` property returns the item's properties, as the following code shows:

```
var client = new LiveConnectClient(_session);
var operationResult = await client.GetAsync(skyDriveItemId);
dynamic result = operationResult.Result;
return result;
```

You can also request a picture for an individual item stored in OneDrive. For folder items, this returns an image from within the folder that OneDrive has chosen, if one is available. For photo and video items, the photo is the image itself or a representative frame from the video. Pictures can be requested in several sizes, including Thumbnail, Small, Album, Normal, and Full. To request the picture for an item, use the `GetAsync` method and a path with the format `<itemId>/picture?type=<picture type>`.

To open an embeddable item in your app, first check its `is_embeddable` value. If this is set to true, you can embed the content in your app by getting a link from OneDrive for sharing the file with the app. You can obtain this link by calling `GetItemAsync` with a path value of either `<item-Id>/shared_read_link`, to allow read-only access, or `<item-Id>/shared_edit_link`, to give the app read/write access to the file. You can set this URL as the Source value for a `WebView` control to allow the control to render the item in your app.

OneDrive items include several updatable properties, depending on the item type. Regardless of the specific type, all the items include at least editable `name` and `description` properties. To update an item in OneDrive, use the `PutAsync` call with the ID of the item to be updated and a set of key/value pairs indicating the values to be updated. Listing 7.11 illustrates the process of renaming the identified item. As previously mentioned, making updates to OneDrive items requires the `wl.skydrive_update` scope.

LISTING 7.11 Renaming a OneDrive Item

```
var client = new LiveConnectClient(_session);
var updateData =
    new Dictionary<String, Object> { { "name", itemNewName } };
var operationResult =
    await client.PutAsync(skyDriveItemId, folderData);
dynamic result = operationResult.Result;
return result;
```

Deleting an item follows the same pattern, by using a call to `DeleteAsync` and providing the ID of the item to be deleted. Note that deleted items are not immediately disposed of: OneDrive includes a Recycle Bin where items are placed when they are initially deleted. No supported way exists for accessing or managing the Recycle Bin contents from the OneDrive API.

To create a new folder in OneDrive, you use the `PostAsync` method. This method takes the ID of the folder into which the new folder should be inserted and a list of key-value pairs for the parameters to set, the same as you provide to the update call. As you might expect, the `name` value is required when creating a new folder.

The last topic area to discuss regarding using the Live Connect SDK to work with OneDrive content is uploading and downloading files. Both the upload and download methods the Live Connect SDK provides internally use the Windows Runtime background transfer APIs,[7] allowing the background to continue outside the application's lifetime status and independent of network connection interruptions. Uploads and downloads both support cancellation, and both provide progress feedback.

[7]Transferring data in the background, http://j.mp/Win8BkgndTxfr

The Live Connect SDK provides the `BackgroundDownloadAsync` method for downloading files from OneDrive. Listing 7.12 shows this function. It first requires a path to the item to be downloaded, in the format `<itemId>/content`. It also needs an `IStorageFile` that indicates the file location where the item should be downloaded. This value can be a value in the app's local storage, or it can be a file reference obtained through the use of the Windows Runtime File Picker control discussed in Chapter 4, "Data and Content." The next item is a `CancellationToken`, which is part of the pattern to cancel asynchronous operations. When another part of the app (perhaps a Cancel button in the part of the user interface that shows download progress) signals the token by calling the `Cancel` method provided by the `CancellationTokenSource` from which the token was obtained, the background download service cancels the operation the next time it checks the token for cancellation. The final value that can be provided is an `IProgress<LiveOperationProgress>` instance, which is executed when the background download operation has progress to report to the app. When the call completes, it returns a `LiveDownloadOperationResult` value that includes file and stream references that your app can use to access the resulting downloaded file.

LISTING 7.12 Downloading from OneDrive

```
private async Task<LiveDownloadOperationResult> DownloadExample(
    String skyDriveItemId,
    IStorageFile downloadFile)
{
    var client = new LiveConnectClient(_session);
    var path = String.Format("{0}/content", skyDriveItemId);
    var progressHandler =
        new Progress<LiveOperationProgress>(ShowProgress);
    var result = await client.BackgroundDownloadAsync(
        path,
        downloadFile,
        _cancellationTokenSource.Token,
        progressHandler);
    return result;
}

private void ShowProgress(LiveOperationProgress liveOperationProgress)
{
    // Display some progress UI, making sure to check for thread access
    UpdateUserInterfaceProgress(
```

```
        liveOperationProgress.BytesTransferred,
        liveOperationProgress.TotalBytes,
        liveOperationProgress.ProgressPercentage);
}

private void CancelDownload(CancellationTokenSource tokenSource)
{
    // Respond to UI request to cancel the download
    tokenSource.Cancel();
}
```

To upload a file, you use the `BackgroundUploadAsync` method, which accepts basically the same parameters as its download counterpart, with a few differences. First, the ID that is supplied is the folder into which the item should be uploaded rather than a path to the download item content. It also expects the addition of a filename that the uploaded file will use in OneDrive in addition to the `IStorageFile` reference to the file to be uploaded. Finally, a value of the `OverwriteOption` enumeration specifies what should happen when a name collision occurs during upload.

Before uploading a file, you should check the user's OneDrive quota information to make sure enough space is available to accommodate the uploaded file. You can obtain a user's quota by calling the `GetAsync` method with a path to `<user id>/skydrive/quota`. The result includes a `quota` value that indicates the total space in the current OneDrive and an `available` value indicating the amount of remaining space available for the upload. Listing 7.13 shows the process of uploading a file to OneDrive.

LISTING 7.13 Uploading to OneDrive

```
private async void UploadExample(
    IStorageFile fileToUpload,
    String uploadFolderId)
{
    var fileInfo = await fileToUpload.GetBasicPropertiesAsync();

    var client = new LiveConnectClient(_session);
    var path = String.Format("{0}/skydrive/quota", Me);
    var quotaOperationResult = await client.GetAsync(path);
    dynamic quotaResult = quotaOperationResult.Result;
    if ((UInt64) quotaResult.available < fileInfo.Size)
    {
        // Handle quota error - not enough room available
    }
```

```
    var operationResult = await client.BackgroundUploadAsync(
        uploadFolderId,
        fileToUpload.Name,
        fileToUpload,
        OverwriteOption.Rename,
        cancellationToken,
        progressHandler);
    dynamic result = operationResult.Result;
    var uploadedItemId = result.id;
}
```

The value returned from the `BackgroundUploadAsync` function is the OneDrive item for the item that was uploaded. You can use it to obtain the newly added item's OneDrive ID or other properties. Note that to upload files to OneDrive, the `wl.skydrive.update` scope is required.

Summary

In this chapter, you learned about cloud services and how you can use them to enrich the experience you provide in Windows Store apps. You discovered how to use Windows Azure Mobile Services to quickly stand up cloud services with support for authentication, data storage, server-side business logic, integrated push notification support, and support for executing scheduled tasks. You also saw how the Live Connect SDK can enable an app to access user information through a Microsoft Account, access contact and calendar information in Outlook.com, and access and manage OneDrive cloud storage content.

In the next chapter, you learn how to secure your Windows Store apps. You see the WinRT APIs that enable you to encrypt data to hide it from prying eyes and sign data to prevent tampering. The chapter also covers web authentication and tells how to set up credentials and work with open authentication standards such as OAuth. Finally, you learn how to manage your credentials in Windows Store apps so you can securely save sensitive information such as usernames and passwords using WinRT APIs.

Summary

8
Security

SECURITY IS AN IMPORTANT COMPONENT OF WINDOWS STORE APPS, AND the Windows Runtime contains a full suite of APIs to implement security. Many scenarios involve security. When a user provides sensitive information to your app, you must ensure that the data is protected so that only individuals who have explicit approval can access the information. In some cases, you must take additional steps to ensure that the data has not been tampered with or manipulated. If a user claims to have access, you must be able to investigate the claim and verify that the user is indeed who he or she claims to be. All these concepts fall under the general umbrella of security.

Security involves multiple steps, the first of which is usually authentication (identifying who you are, as opposed to authorization that verifies what you can access). This step requires the app to verify a user's identity. The simplest way to do this is to require the user to enter a password, or a "secret" that only that user knows. Having multiple secrets can be tedious and often results in users using passwords that are easier to guess, enabling others to impersonate their identity. This is why many services offer a single sign-on (SSO) service that enables users to verify their identity in one place to gain access to multiple resources. Many SSO implementations are token based (a unique sequence of bytes called a token is generated and persists throughout the session to identify a user without using a password) and enable an application to verify the user's identity without having to take on the responsibility of storing passwords. Instead, you simply retrieve a unique token that can be used in place of a login to access information.

In earlier chapters, you learned how to locate the path to local storage for a Windows Store app and access the contents. On a system with multiple users, one user could potentially gain access to another user's data. Encryption scrambles the data so that it is unreadable unless you are able to decrypt it using a secret or group of secrets, referred to as keys. When a file is encrypted, another user might be able to access a file but won't be able to understand the contents. As an added security measure, you can sign documents to generate a unique value, referred to as a hash, which you can use to determine whether the data has changed since you last generated the hash.

In this chapter, you learn how to use WinRT APIs to secure your app. You learn to authenticate users (using single sign-on, if needed), determine what level of encryption your app needs, and encrypt data, along with how to use techniques for signing data. Finally, you learn how to store sensitive information such as passwords in a special vault that allows the information to roam securely among multiple Windows 8 devices.

Authentication

In Chapter 7, "Connecting to the Cloud," you learned how to use the Live Connect SDK to perform a single sign-on with a Microsoft Account. Behind the scenes, the SDK facilitates a web-based interaction with the servers to authenticate the user and gain access to resources. Your app can use many other authentication services or providers. Most of them implement some form of either OAuth[1] (versions 1.0 and 2.0) or OpenID.[2]

The goal of both protocols is to provide a safe, easy standard to use when logging onto websites. The functionality has been extended to include mobile clients that communicate with websites, such as Windows Store apps. Both protocols follow a similar format. In a nutshell, the app itself

---

[1]OAuth, http://oauth.net/; Version 2 is at http://oauth.net/2

[2]OpenID, http://openid.net/

does not acquire the user's credentials, thereby eliminating the need to secure them or the risk that the user identity can be compromised; instead, it sends the user to the provider's website. Users can verify that they are actually on a web page hosted by Facebook or Google, for example, by examining the URL they are taken to. The user enters the credentials, and the provider redirects the user to the app's web page. The redirect typically contains a special token that informs the app that the authentication was successful and can be used by the app for future calls. Figure 8.1 shows the general flow.

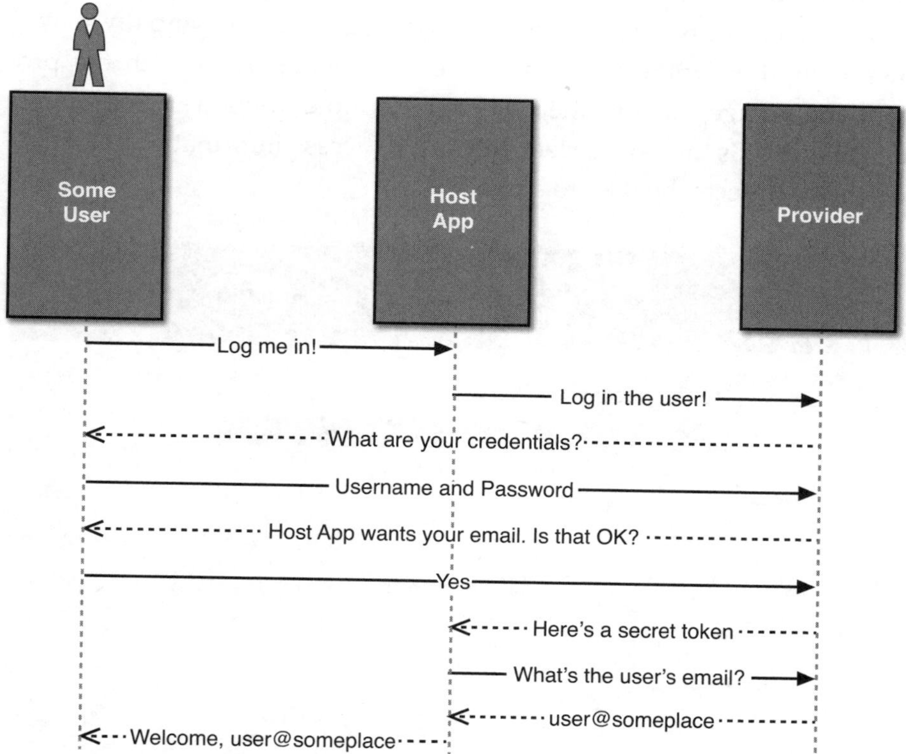

FIGURE 8.1 Typical sign-on flow

Various providers often supply documentation and even SDKs (such as the Live Connect SDK) that make it easier to connect with and authenticate to their service. The problem is, most scenarios assume a web-based application or specific mobile clients. How can you make a protocol modeled for the web work in an app that is running on a Windows 8 device? The answer is to use the `WebAuthenticationBroker` class.

The web authentication broker is designed to assist you with single sign-on scenarios by emulating a fully web-based experience. You provide the broker with a starting URL. This URL typically contains information such as special application codes and passwords used to verify your app's identity with the provider and a redirect URL where the provider should send users when they are authenticated. You also provide the broker with an ending URL. This is where the magic happens for the broker.

The broker starts by popping up a dialog that is essentially a web browser window without chrome. The user is presented with the provider's login page, such as the Facebook example in Figure 8.2. The user enters credentials and authorizes the app to access information. The provider then redirects the user to a final URL.

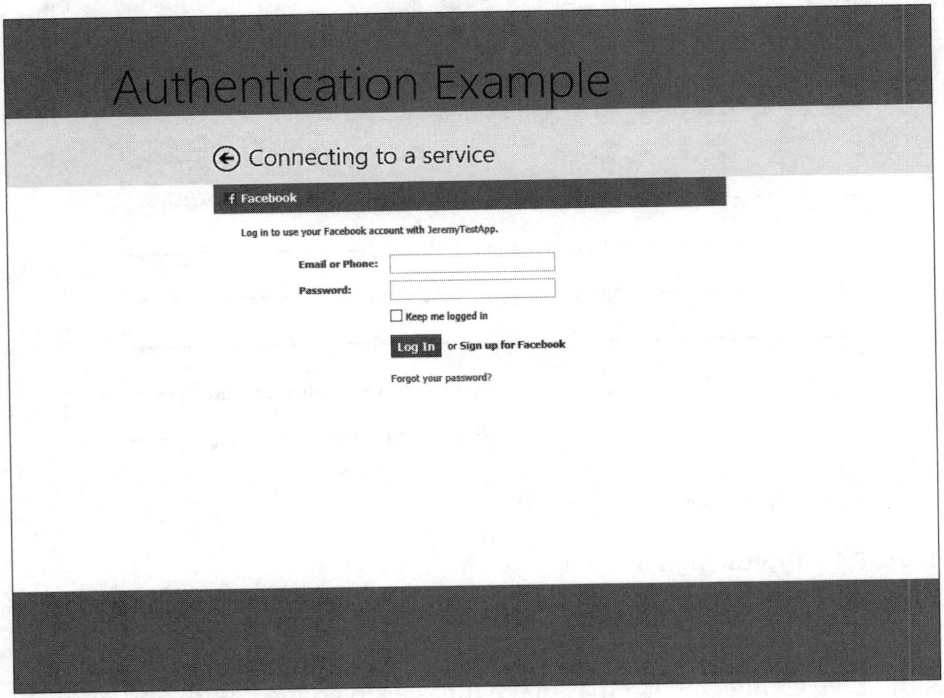

FIGURE 8.2 The Facebook single sign-on dialog

The web broker is configured to listen for this URL. Instead of serving the page, it intercepts the request and provides the details to your app. You can then parse the content of the redirect to obtain the access token that validates the user's identity and that can be used to make further requests from the provider.

The first example in the **AuthenticationExamples** project uses Facebook's OAuth process. Before you can use the Facebook API, you must register your app with Facebook on their developer website.[3] Simply follow the online prompts to register your application (for the purposes of this book, I created a test application named **JeremyTestApp**). After registration, you receive an app ID and an app secret. You use the app ID to access the API.

The `FacebookAuthenticator` class contains the logic to authenticate with Facebook and receive a token. Update the `FacebookAppId` constant with the app ID you registered. The class defines two URLs. The first is the URL used to authenticate with Facebook, named `FaceBookAuth`. The URL must be passed a client ID (your app ID), a redirect URL to send users to when they are authenticated, a scope to determine what information you will be requesting, and the type of response (we want a token).

The second URL is the redirect URL. Because the example is a client app, not a web page, Facebook's own confirmation URL serves as the redirect URL and is stored in the `FacebookRedirectUri` constant. After users authenticate, they are redirected to the Facebook page. The web authentication broker listens for the redirect and intercepts it.

The `AuthenticateAsync` method builds the start and end URLs and then calls the `AuthenticateAsync` method on the `WebAuthenticationBroker` in the `Windows.Security.Authentication.Web` namespace. It is passed a set of options, the URL to start with, and the URL to listen to.

```
WebAuthenticationResult result =
    await WebAuthenticationBroker.AuthenticateAsync(
        WebAuthenticationOptions.None,
        startUri,
        endUri);
```

---

[3]Facebook Apps, http://bit.ly/11Afx6I

The authentication options are provided by passing flags specified in the `WebAuthenticationOptions` enumeration. Possible values include the following:

- `None`—No options.
- `SilentMode`—Used for pure SSO that has no UI involved. If the provider displays a web page, the authentication fails.
- `UseTitle`—Instructs the web authentication broker to parse the title of the window for the web page and return it in the `ResponseData` property, to allow you to parse it as needed.
- `UseHttpPost`—Provides the contents of the POST in the `ResponseData` property when the provider performs a POST to the final website.
- `UseCorporateNetwork`—Renders the web page in a special container that supports enterprise authentication and private networks for intranet authentication and requires that similar capabilities are declared for the app.

The result returns a response status (to indicate success, an HTTP error, or user cancellation) and the contents of the final redirect. The Facebook redirect uses a hash to separate the URL from a set of response parameters sent in a query string format (name/value pairs). The first parameter is the token you can use for further access; the second tells when the token will expire. Use this to store the token; you can reuse it without having to request a new one each time.

```
var data = result.ResponseData.Substring(result.ResponseData
    .IndexOf('#'));
    var values = data.Split('&');
    var token = values[0].Split('=')[1];
    var expirationSeconds = values[1].Split('=')[1];
    var expiration = DateTime.UtcNow.AddSeconds(
        int.Parse(expirationSeconds));
```

After you receive the token, the main authentication step is complete. Now you can use the token to request information about the user. For example, you can obtain the user's preferred email address to use it as a default without asking or to identify the user internally to your app.

The `FacebookIdentity` class uses the token to retrieve the user's email address. Note that it expects an `Authorization` header to include the token retrieved in the previous step. The class then uses a simple `HttpClient` to fetch a URL with the access token and obtain a JSON result. The result is parsed and used to retrieve the email property. This is all done in a few lines of code.

```
var client = new HttpClient();
client.DefaultRequestHeaders.Authorization =
    new AuthenticationHeaderValue("OAuth", accessToken);
var result = await client.GetStringAsync(FacebookIdentityUrl);
var profileInformation = JsonObject.Parse(result);
var email = profileInformation["email"].GetString();
```

The sample app adds code to log the various steps so you can view the full process and review the raw data sent between the app and the provider as you run the examples. Figure 8.3 shows an example execution.

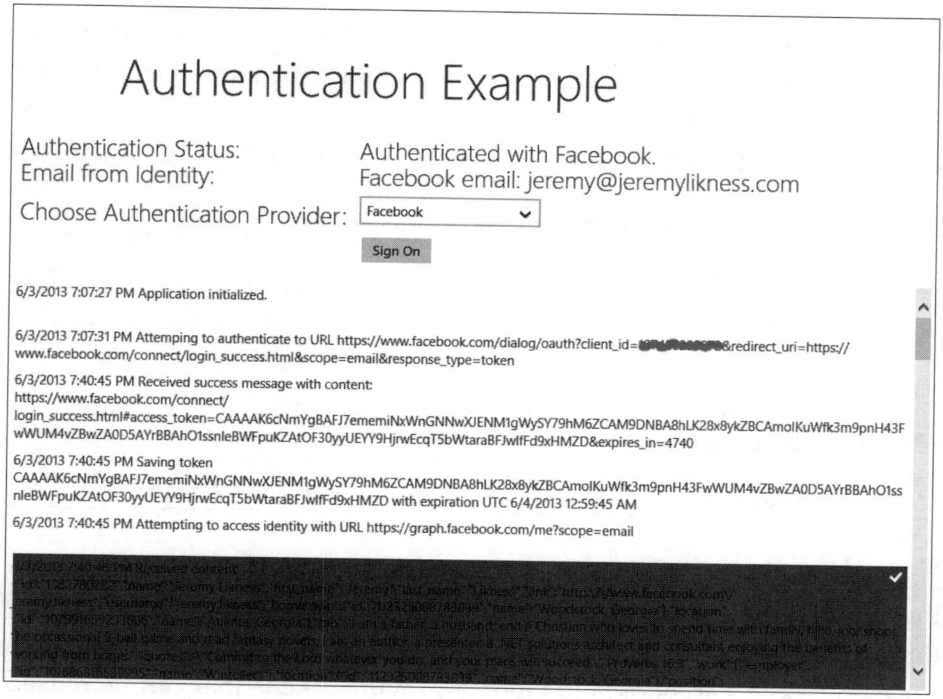

Authentication Example

Authentication Status: Authenticated with Facebook.
Email from Identity: Facebook email: jeremy@jeremylikness.com
Choose Authentication Provider: Facebook
Sign On

6/3/2013 7:07:27 PM Application initialized.

6/3/2013 7:07:31 PM Attemping to authenticate to URL https://www.facebook.com/dialog/oauth?client_id=[illegible]&redirect_uri=https://www.facebook.com/connect/login_success.html&scope=email&response_type=token

6/3/2013 7:40:45 PM Received success message with content:
https://www.facebook.com/connect/
login_success.html#access_token=CAAAAK6cNmYgBAFJ7ememiNxWnGNNwXJENM1gWySY79hM6ZCAM9DNBA8hLK28x8ykZBCAmolKuWfk3m9pnH43FwWUM4vZBwZA0D5AYrBBAhO1ssnleBWFpuKZAtOF30yyUEYY9HjrwEcqT5bWtaraBFJwlfFd9xHMZD&expires_in=4740

6/3/2013 7:40:45 PM Saving token
CAAAAK6cNmYgBAFJ7ememiNxWnGNNwXJENM1gWySY79hM6ZCAM9DNBA8hLK28x8ykZBCAmolKuWfk3m9pnH43FwWUM4vZBwZA0D5AYrBBAhO1ssnleBWFpuKZAtOF30yyUEYY9HjrwEcqT5bWtaraBFJwlfFd9xHMZD with expiration UTC 6/4/2013 12:59:45 AM

6/3/2013 7:40:45 PM Attempting to access identity with URL https://graph.facebook.com/me?scope=email

FIGURE 8.3 An authentication session with Facebook

Multistep Authentication (Google)

Some providers require multiple steps to authenticate. Google, for example, gives users a special code for your app when they authenticate and authorize your app. You must then use that code and send it back to Google with your client ID and secret password to obtain an authentication token. The `GoogleAuthenticator` class performs these steps. As with Facebook, you must first register with Google to obtain a client ID and secret. You can do this using the Google APIs console.[4]

The `GoogleUrl` constant contains the URL to the OAuth 2 provider that Google uses. The first step is similar to the first step in the Facebook scenario and involves redirecting the user to authenticate. This time, the result is a special code that you can use to request a token. It is parsed from the response after the authentication was successful.

```
var results = result.ResponseData.Split('=');
var code = results[1];
```

Another URL defined by the `OAuthUrl` constant is used to obtain the token. The client must POST to the URL and pass the parameters defined in the `OAuthPost` constant. No redirect occurs, so the web authentication broker isn't used. Instead, the POST is handled directly, as Listing 8.1 shows.

LISTING 8.1 Code to Obtain the Google Access Token

```
var client = new HttpClient();
var request = new HttpRequestMessage(HttpMethod.Post, OAuthUrl);
var content = string.Format(OAuthPost, code, ClientId, ClientSecret,
    RedirectUrl);
request.Content = new StreamContent(
    new MemoryStream(Encoding.UTF8.GetBytes(content)));
request.Content.Headers.Add("Content-Type",
    "application/x-www-form-urlencoded");
HttpResponseMessage response = await client.SendAsync(request);
```

After the response is received, the content is parsed as JSON to obtain the token and its expiration. You can inspect the `GoogleIdentity` class to see that the process for obtaining the email is similar to the method used with Facebook. Both Facebook and Google provide tokens that can be reused until they expire. Your app can save the tokens so users don't have to log

[4]The Google APIs Console, http://bit.ly/17jW7va

in every time they access your app, but the tokens represent sensitive information because they can provide access to the user's confidential information. How can you store them securely?

Unlocking the Password Vault

The Windows Runtime provides a special class for storing credentials, called `PasswordVault`. You can find this component in the `Windows.Security.Credentials` namespace. The class provides a special "credential locker" that your app can use to store credentials securely. The locker is scoped to the currently logged-in user and the Windows Store app. Use it to store usernames and passwords, to prevent the user from having to log in multiple times. The locker stores the credentials in a secure location on the device that is inaccessible to other accounts and other apps under the same account.

The locker is scoped to the currently logged-in Windows user. Under certain circumstances, the vault also automatically roams to other devices. The user must be logged in to the Windows device using a Microsoft Account, and the Microsoft Account must trust the device. To determine whether a device is trusted, you can log on to your Microsoft Account management page.[5] Navigate to **Security Info** to see the list of trusted devices under the **Trusted Devices** heading. If your device is not trusted, open the **Charms bar** using **Windows Key+C**, tap **Settings**, and then select **Change PC Settings**. Navigate to **Sync Your Settings**. Scroll down and tap the link titled **Trust This PC**. Follow the prompts to trust your device from your Microsoft account.

In the example app, the `AppCredentialStorage` class handles the credentials. A credential contains a resource identifier (in the case of our app, we use that to distinguish among various account types, such as Facebook or Google), a username, and a password. For single sign-on, we do not store the username or password, so the app hard codes the username to Current and instead stores the token in the password. To make it easier to prompt the user when the token expires, the token is saved with the expiration date.

---

[5]Microsoft Account, https://account.live.com/

Storing the password simply involves creating an instance of the `PasswordVault`, creating a `PasswordCredential`, and then adding the credential to the vault.

```
var vault = new PasswordVault();
var credential = new PasswordCredential(
    key,
    Username,
    string.Format("{0}|{1}", expiration, token));
vault.Add(credential);
```

To obtain the token, the `Retrieve` method on the vault is called with the resource and username. This throws a generic exception if the credential does not exist.

```
try
{
    credential = vault.Retrieve(key, Username);
}
catch (Exception)
{
    return false;
}
```

The `RetrievePassword` method populates the credential with the password so that it can be parsed. The password is split into the date part so that the expiration can be checked; if the token has not expired, it is set and returned. The API that the class implements makes it easy for any authentication protocol to store and retrieve tokens with expirations (if you have a token that always expires, just set the expiration to a date in the past).

Other methods on the vault enable you to retrieve all the credentials for a particular resource or iterate all the credentials in the vault. It is also good practice to destroy credentials when the user finishes with them. If the user chooses to sign out before the token expires, you can remove the credential from the vault.

```
vault.Remove(credential);
```

The credential vault helps secure usernames and passwords but is restricted to specific, granular pieces of information. This is great for tokens and access codes, but it is not suitable for larger amounts of data or other sensitive information. If your app must handle confidential or sensitive data, it should encrypt the data to keep it safe from unauthorized access and sign the data to guard against tampering.

Encryption and Signing

Your app can use encryption to secure data for local storage or transfer to third-party systems. In addition, you can sign data to ensure that it has not been tampered with. Encryption is a two-way operation that enables you to scramble and unscramble data. Signing is a one-way operation that uses a special secret to generate a value that can be checked against the data to ensure that it hasn't changed since the value was generated.

The Windows Runtime provides a built-in encryption API to use if you are not concerned with the type of encryption used or you will be using encryption solely to store data on the local system or to exchange with other Windows devices. The API plugs into the Windows Data Protection API (DPAPI) that uses the user's logon credentials to encrypt the data. It uses a symmetrical encryption algorithm, which means the same key or secret used to encode the data is used to decode the data. For this reason, the protected data can be decoded only on a Windows system using the same account it was encrypted with.

The Data Protection Provider

The data protection provider is useful for protecting locally stored data. The API exists in the `Windows.Security.Cryptography.DataProtection` namespace and is accessed via the `DataProtectionProvider` class. The four methods available enable you to protect (encrypt) a buffer or stream, and unprotect (decrypt) a buffer or stream. The constructor also takes a string value that indicates the scope of the protection.

The scope is a special string that indicates how you want to protect the data. Using `LOCAL=machine` uses the current machine to encrypt the data; any other user on the same machine can decode the data. `Local=user` uses the currently logged-in user's credentials; only that user can decode the data. You can also use a security descriptor (SID) or a security descriptor definition language (SDDL) to protect data at the enterprise level (for example, making it available to all users who are members of the same Active Directory group). This requires your app to have the enterprise authentication capability declared, and it can be deployed only in Windows Store apps built with company accounts. Microsoft's guidance is to avoid this capability unless absolutely necessary.

The **SafeNotes** project is an example project that enables you to enter notes with a title and description. The notes are secured to the current user. You can read them in the app and on the tiles in the Start screen, but they are protected when stored on disk so that someone with a different account cannot view them even if that person were able to gain access to the files. This is all done using the `DataProtectionProvider` class.

The main class to examine is the `DataSource` class under the `Data` folder. The class has an `InitializeAsync` method that simply ensures there is a `Notes` subfolder created in local storage. The `ProtectDataAsync` method takes a line of text and returns the encrypted text. It uses the `CryptographicBuffer` class (from the `Windows.Security.Cryptography` namespace) to transform the text into an instance of an `IBuffer` that you can use for encryption and decryption.

```
var dataProtection = new DataProtectionProvider(Scope);
IBuffer dataBuffer = CryptographicBuffer.ConvertStringToBinary(data,
    Encoding);
```

The `CryptographicBuffer` class contains a number of helper methods (see Table 8.1).

TABLE 8.1 Helper Methods of the `CryptographicBuffer` Class

Method	Description
`Compare`	Compares two instances of `IBuffer` and returns `true` if they are identical
`ConvertBinaryToString`	Converts an `IBuffer` to an encoded string instance
`ConvertStringToBinary`	Converts a string to an encoded `IBuffer` instance

Method	Description
`CopyToByteArray`	Copies the contents of an `IBuffer` instance to an array of bytes
`CreateFromByteArray`	Creates an `IBuffer` instance from an array of bytes
`DecodeFromBase64String`	Decodes a string from a base64-encoded string
`DecodeFromHexString`	Decodes a string from a hexadecimal-encoded string
`EncodeToBase64String`	Encodes a string to a base64-encoded string
`EncodeToHexString`	Encodes a string to a hexadecimal-encoded string
`GenerateRandom`	Creates an instance of an `IBuffer` of the specified length and fills it with random data
`GenerateRandomNumber`	Creates a random integer

After the `IBuffer` is created from the text that is passed in, the instance of the `DataProtectionProvider` class is used to encrypt the data. Finally, the encrypted data is encoded to a base64 string and returned to the caller. Base64 is used to encode binary data as ASCII text. The process makes the data longer but also makes it easier to work with because it can be passed around as plain text.

The `SaveNoteAsync` method encrypts and saves an individual note. First, a file is generated using the unique identifier of the note.

```
var fileName = note.Id;
var file = await this.notesFolder.CreateFileAsync(fileName,
    CreationCollisionOption.ReplaceExisting);
```

Next, the note itself is encrypted. This is done by protecting each part (title, text, and time stamp fields) individually and then writing them out to the file.

```
var data = new[]
    {
        await ProtectDataAsync(note.Title),
        await ProtectDataAsync(note.Description),
        await ProtectDataAsync(note.DateCreated.ToString()),
        await ProtectDataAsync(note.DateModified.ToString())
    };
await FileIO.WriteLinesAsync(file, data);
```

The first time you run the app, it creates a default note for you. After you see the note appear, you can navigate to local storage for the app, open the `Notes` directory, and view the contents of a note. Figure 8.4 shows an example of the encrypted result.

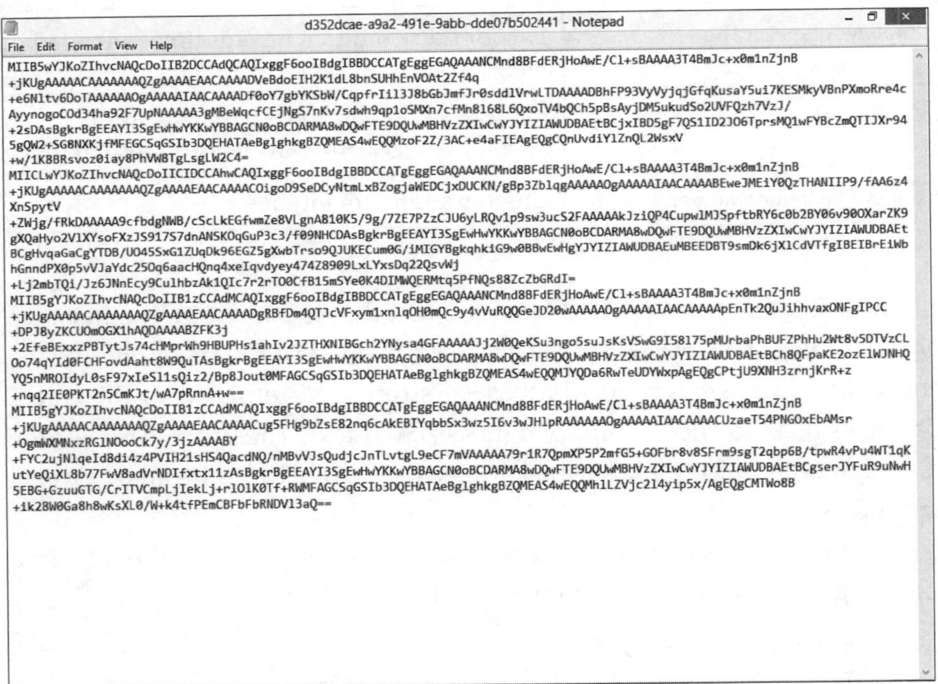

FIGURE 8.4 The protected data for an individual note

The Windows Runtime has plenty of support for other forms of encryption as well. If you are looking to secure data in a specific way or you require the use of a different algorithm, APIs exist to perform both symmetrical and asymmetrical encryption using a variety of algorithms.

Symmetrical Encryption

You already learned that symmetrical encryption involves using the same key, secret, or password to encode and decode the data. Dozens of ciphers exist for symmetrical encryption. A cipher refers to the algorithm the encryption and decryption routines use. Ciphers for symmetrical encryption are generally divided into two broad categories: block ciphers and stream ciphers.

Block Ciphers

A block cipher operates on a fixed-length block of bits. These algorithms are extremely fast but apply the same algorithm to each block of data. The data often must be padded so that its length is a multiple of the block size. For example, if the block is 4096 bits, or 512 bytes, and your data is only 500 bytes long, the data must be padded to fill 1024 bytes (the size of exactly two blocks) for the algorithm to work.

Block ciphers also have modes of operation to handle how they deal with subsequent blocks in large data sets. For example, the basic electronic codebook (ECB) mode applies the same operation to each block of text. The problem is that blocks with the same source data will have the same encrypted data. This makes it easy for hackers to compare similar blocks, make guesses about the source data, and use various forms of attacks to crack the encryption.

Cipher-block chaining (CBC) helps ensure that blocks containing the same source data don't generate the same output blocks. This mode takes each block and performs a logical exclusive or (XOR) operation against the previous block. The XOR operation operates at a bit level; it returns 0 when both bits are the same and 1 when either bit is different. If two blocks are the same, the XOR operation effectively flips the bits of the second block.

The first block has no predecessor, so an initialization vector (IV) is used for the first block. Using a different IV for each encryption ensures that the same source data produces a different set of decoded data.

In addition to the modes of operation, a cipher might conform to the Cryptographic Message Syntax Standard (PKCS #7). This standard simply defines a syntax for data that cryptography can be applied against, and for adding or extracting metadata from the message. This is the standard that most of the underlying Windows APIs conform to, but you have the flexibility to choose your own encryption algorithms.

WinRT supports the following symmetric algorithms:

- **DES**—Data Encryption Standard, a popular algorithm considered to be less secure than the other algorithms. (This standard has existed for several decades and has been demonstrably cracked in short time periods.)
- **3DES**—Triple Data Encryption Algorithm. This algorithm uses DES but makes it more secure by applying the algorithm three times to each block.
- **RC2**—Alternatively known as Ron's Code or Rivest Cipher because Ron Rivest designed it in 1987.
- **AES**—Advanced Encryption Standard, based on another cipher called Rijndael. The U.S. government has adopted it, and it also is used internationally.

The Windows Runtime contains support for various symmetric algorithms, as well as several different modes and implementations. The **EncryptionExample** project demonstrates the use of various encryption algorithms. Run the project, and type or paste some text you want to encrypt or verify. Enter a password to use to generate the key, and then click **Encrypt** to encrypt the text. The encrypted text is converted to base64 and displayed. You can then **Decrypt** that text (or paste other base64-encoded text to decrypt). Figure 8.5 shows the result. In the example, the source text was pasted back for illustration. The app blanks the text after it is encrypted so you can verify that the decryption is working.

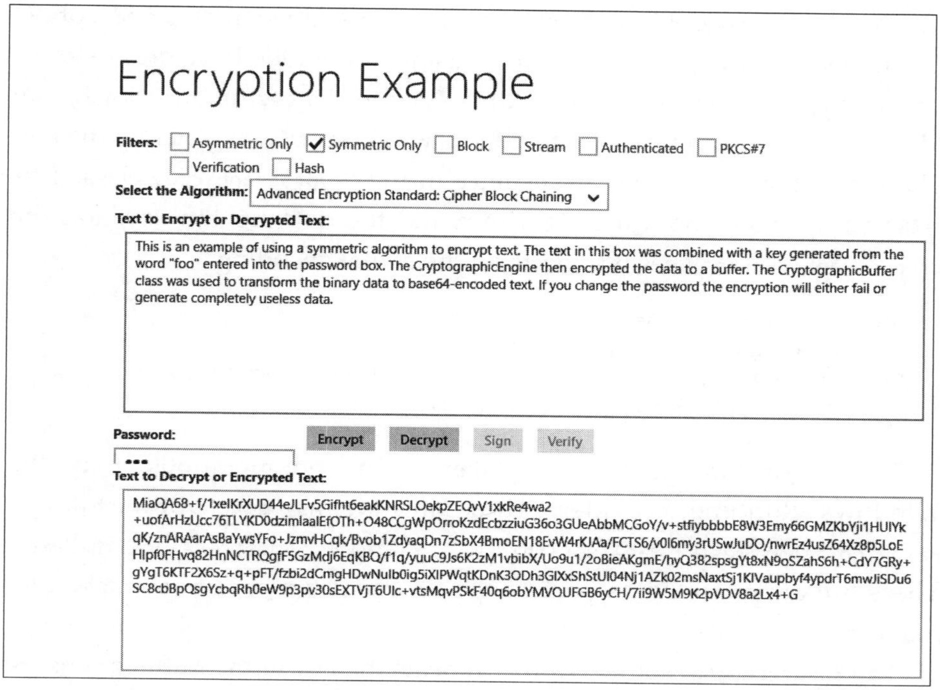

Encryption Example

Filters: Asymmetric Only ☑ Symmetric Only Block Stream Authenticated PKCS#7 Verification Hash

Select the Algorithm: Advanced Encryption Standard: Cipher Block Chaining

Text to Encrypt or Decrypted Text:

This is an example of using a symmetric algorithm to encrypt text. The text in this box was combined with a key generated from the word "foo" entered into the password box. The CryptographicEngine then encrypted the data to a buffer. The CryptographicBuffer class was used to transform the binary data to base64-encoded text. If you change the password the encryption will either fail or generate completely useless data.

Password: ••• Encrypt Decrypt Sign Verify

Text to Decrypt or Encrypted Text:

MiaQA68+f/1xeIKrXUD44eJLFv5Gifht6eakKNRSLOekpZEQvV1xkRe4wa2
+uofArHzUcc76TLYKD0dzimIaalEfOTh+O48CCgWpOrroKzdEcbzziuG36o3GUeAbbMCGoY/v+stfiybbbbE8W3Emy66GMZKbYji1HUIYk
qK/znARAarAsBaYwsYFo+JzmvHCqk/Bvob1ZdyaqDn7zSbX4BmoEN18EvW4rKJAa/FCTS6/v0l6my3rUSwJuDO/nwrEz4usZ64Xz8p5LoE
Hlpf0FHvq82HnNCTRQgfF5GzMdj6EqKBQ/f1q/yuuC9Js6K2zM1vbibX/Uo9u1/2oBieAKgmE/hyQ382spsgYt8xN9oSZahS6h+CdY7GRy+
gYgT6KTF2X6Sz+q+pFT/fzbi2dCmgHDwNuIb0ig5iXIPWqtKDnK3ODh3GlXxShStUI04Nj1AZk02msNaxtSj1KIVaupbyf4ypdrT6mwJiSDu6
SC8cbBpQsgYcbqRh0eW9p3pv30sEXTVjT6UIc+vtsMqvPSkF40q6obYMVOUFGB6yCH/7ii9W5M9K2pVDV8a2Lx4+G

FIGURE 8.5 The encryption example

The example uses the `BaseCrypto` class to encapsulate most of the work involved with encryption and decryption. The derived `Crypto` class is initialized with a flag indicating whether it supports a symmetric algorithm, a detailed name, and the algorithm name it represents. The `Encrypt` method converts the key and data to be encrypted into an instance of `IBuffer` using the `CryptographicBuffer` helper class.

```
IBuffer message = CryptographicBuffer.ConvertStringToBinary(data,
    Encoding);
if (this.IsSymmetric)
{
    IBuffer keyBuffer = CryptographicBuffer
        .ConvertStringToBinary(key, Encoding);
    return this.EncryptSymmetric(keyBuffer, message);
}
```

The EncryptSymmetric method performs the main steps for encryption. The first step is to open the algorithm using a provider. Providers exist for various types of algorithms, including symmetric, asymmetric, hash, and MAC-based algorithms. The provider is what you use to generate the key. The key is represented by an instance of the CryptographicKey class. This class encapsulates both the algorithm and the data for the key, and the CryptographicEngine uses it to perform the actual encoding.

```
var algorithm = SymmetricKeyAlgorithmProvider
    .OpenAlgorithm(this.AlgorithmName);
CryptographicKey keyMaterial = algorithm.CreateSymmetricKey(
    EnsureLength(keyBuffer, 32, true));
```

The algorithm names are taken from enumerations that the Windows Runtime provides. These include AsymmetricAlgorithmNames, HashAlgorithmNames, MacAlgorithmNames, and SymmetricAlgorithmNames. These are all provided as part of the Windows.Security.Cryptography.Core namespace.

The EnsureLength method simply repeats the key in the buffer to ensure that it is the desired length. The algorithms that follow the PKCS#7 standard automatically pad the blocks for a message of any length, but other block cipher algorithms require the message to be a multiple of the block length. For those algorithms, the required padding to reach a multiple of the block length is measured and used to pad the buffer.

```
var pad = message.Length % algorithm.BlockLength;
if (pad > 0)
{
    var desiredLength = message.Length + algorithm.BlockLength - pad;
    message = EnsureLength(message, (int)desiredLength, false);
}
```

For algorithms that require an initialization vector, some default text is converted to a buffer and used. This is done only to keep the examples consistent. A more common and secure method is to use the GenerateRandom method on the CryptographicBuffer class to create a unique IV, and then export the IV along with the encrypted data. Never use the same IV more than once, to protect the integrity of the encrypted data.

The actual encryption step takes in the key material, the buffer of data to encrypt, and the initialization vector (passed as null if it is not needed) and returns a buffer of encrypted data. In the sample app, this is then encoded to base64 for display.

```
var encryptedBuffer = CryptographicEngine.Encrypt(keyMaterial,
    message, initializationBuffer);
return CryptographicBuffer.EncodeToBase64String(encryptedBuffer);
```

The decryption works in reverse. First, the encrypted buffer is obtained by decoding the base64 text.

```
message = CryptographicBuffer.DecodeFromBase64String(data);
```

The key material and IV are generated, and then the `Decrypt` method is called on the `CryptographicEngine` to retrieve a buffer of decrypted data. The `ConvertBinaryToString` method on the `CryptographicBuffer` class displays the text back.

```
var decryptedBuffer = CryptographicEngine.Decrypt(
    keyMaterial, message, initializationBuffer);
return CryptographicBuffer.ConvertBinaryToString(Encoding,
    decryptedBuffer);
```

You can use the example app to see the various results of using different symmetric encryption algorithms and different keys.

Stream Ciphers

Stream ciphers encrypt 1 byte or bit at a time instead of operating against a fixed-length block. The key is used to create a stream of data that is applied to the buffer to be encrypted. As the algorithm moves through the data buffer, it also moves through the key stream. If the initial key is smaller than the data buffer to encrypt, it is typically either repeated, shifted, or otherwise modified in a consistent way to provide continuous material for the encryption process. The Windows Runtime supports the RC4 stream cipher. The "stream" refers to the mode of encryption; the same process is used to encrypt and decrypt information using this cipher as the other symmetric ciphers, except that the message does not have to be padded to meet a specific block length.

Authentication

You might notice that the encrypted data can be modified without interfering with the decryption step. Instead, it is possible to decrypt the text and receive corrupt information that might or might not have similarities to the actual source. To further protect data, some symmetric algorithms support authentication. This mode of encryption enables you to specify additional data to go with a message called *authentication data* that is used to generate a unique signature. The data is then both encrypted and signed to produce an encrypted buffer, and an authentication tag verifies the authenticity of the data. The Windows Runtime supports two authentication modes: Counter with CBC-MAC (CCM) and Galois Counter Mode (GCM).

The decryption process requires the key and the authentication tag in addition to the data. Instead of using a traditional initialization vector, the authenticated message uses a nonce, or a "number only used once." The number ensures that the message can be encrypted that way only once. If a recipient receives the same message with the same nonce, the message is discarded as invalid. The example app returns a single nonce to keep the encryption and decryption steps consistent; in real-world use, you typically increment the nonce or use a pseudo-random generator to ensure a new nonce for each message. Because the `EncryptAndAuthenticate` method returns two pieces of data (the encrypted data and the authentication tag), the example app encodes both as base64 and separates them with a pipe character.

```
EncryptedAndAuthenticatedData encryptedData = CryptographicEngine
    .EncryptAndAuthenticate(
    keyMaterial, message, GetNonce(), authenticationData);
return string.Format(
    "{0}|{1}",
    CryptographicBuffer.EncodeToBase64String(
        encryptedData.AuthenticationTag),
    CryptographicBuffer.EncodeToBase64String(
        encryptedData.EncryptedData));
```

The decryption step separates the authentication tag from the encrypted data and then calls the `DecryptAndAuthenticate` method to retrieve the result.

```
var decryptedData = CryptographicEngine.DecryptAndAuthenticate(

    keyMaterial, message, GetNonce(), authenticationTag,
    authenticationData);
return CryptographicBuffer.ConvertBinaryToString(Encoding,
    decryptedData);
```

Although the authenticated algorithms make it convenient to both encrypt and sign data in one step, the Windows Runtime supports several other methods for signing and verifying data.

Verification

Verifying data involves two steps: signing the data to generate a unique signature and verifying the data against the signature to ensure that it has not been changed or tampered with. Verification is often combined with encryption to ensure the secure transmission of messages. An encrypted message can be tampered with and can result in corrupt data received on the other end. Verification ensures that the data is intact and validates the integrity of the data to the recipient.

Hash Algorithms

A hash algorithm takes any length of data and maps it to another set of fixed-length data. The algorithm is designed so that inputting the same data results in the same output, but similar data results in a different output. This makes it harder to trace a hash value back to the original value or to tamper with the hash value to make it match corrupt data. Although hash algorithms are designed to have a low collision rate (when two different data inputs result in the same hash output), it is possible because of the fixed length of the hash.

The Windows Runtime supports Message Digest 5 (MD5) and multiple versions of the Secure Hash Algorithm (SHA). To generate a hash, you simply open the provider for the algorithm you want to use and call the `HashData` method with the data you are generating a hash for.

```
var algorithm = HashAlgorithmProvider
    .OpenAlgorithm(this.AlgorithmName);
IBuffer hash = algorithm.HashData(buffer);
return CryptographicBuffer.EncodeToBase64String(hash);
```

A common use for hash codes is to verify software. The publisher gives you the MD5 signature of the download. You can download the software from either the provider or a third party and then generate your own MD5. If they don't match, you know that either the download was corrupted or the software was tampered with, and you can avoid installing a potentially harmful app.

A weakness of the hash algorithm is that the same input always generates the same output, making it particularly susceptible to dictionary and plain-text attacks. Essentially, a hacker who gains access to a hash code can run various words or phrases through the hash algorithm and compare output until a match occurs. Fortunately, stronger algorithms can verify data integrity and authenticity.

Message Authentication Codes

A Message Authentication Code (MAC) is a special form of hash that also incorporates a secret key. This allows the generated MAC to validate both the integrity of the data and its authenticity. WinRT provides algorithms for Hash-based Message Authentication Codes based on MD5 and various flavors of SHA. The steps to generate a MAC are similar to the steps for encryption. The key is either generated or mapped to a buffer and then used to generate an instance of a `CryptographicKey`. The key and the message are passed to the `CryptographicEngine` via the `Sign` method, and the resulting MAC signature is returned.

```
var macAlgorithm = MacAlgorithmProvider.OpenAlgorithm(
   this.AlgorithmName);
IBuffer keyBuffer = CryptographicBuffer.ConvertStringToBinary(key,
    Encoding);
CryptographicKey keyMaterial = macAlgorithm.CreateKey(keyBuffer);
var signature = CryptographicEngine.Sign(keyMaterial, buffer);
return CryptographicBuffer.EncodeToBase64String(signature);
```

To verify the signature, you pass the key, the message, and the MAC into the `VerifySignature` method. It returns true if the data is valid and false if an issue with data integrity or authenticity arises.

```
var macAlgorithm = MacAlgorithmProvider.OpenAlgorithm(
    this.AlgorithmName);
IBuffer keyBuffer = CryptographicBuffer.ConvertStringToBinary(key,
    Encoding);
var keyMaterial = macAlgorithm.CreateKey(keyBuffer);
return CryptographicEngine.VerifySignature(keyMaterial, buffer,
    signatureBuffer);
```

One challenge with the symmetrical algorithms is that all of them (with the exception of the hash algorithms) require a secret key to be shared between the sender and recipients of messages. No algorithm is completely secure, and sometimes compromising security is as simple as intercepting the key. After you've shared the key, the other party can decrypt any messages that were encrypted with that key. Several asymmetrical encryption algorithms have been developed to address this issue.

Asymmetric Algorithms

Asymmetric algorithms, also referred to as public-key algorithms, are called asymmetric because the key used to encrypt the message is not the same as the key used to decrypt the message. Instead, two keys exist: a public key and a private key. The keys are mathematically related, but the algorithm is designed so that the public key is incapable of decrypting the message or generating the private key, and the private key cannot encrypt any message.

The advantage of this system is that you can generate a public and a private key (called a key pair) and share the public key while keeping the private key secret. For example, let's assume you want to trade secrets with Bob and Alice. With a symmetric key, if you used the same secret for Bob and Alice, Bob could easily grab a message from Alice and decrypt it. You could use a different secret, but then you'd have more keys to keep track of. Using an asymmetric key, you share the public key with both Bob and Alice. You're not concerned because they can only use the key to encrypt messages. Bob can't use it to decrypt Alice's messages, and vice versa. However, you can decrypt both Bob's and Alice's messages using your private key.

To ensure that the public and private keys are related, you cannot choose your own keys. Instead, you must generate them. In the example project, a key pair is generated the first time you encrypt a message. It is stored in the class and reused for subsequent sessions. This means that if you copy the decrypted text and then stop and restart the app, you cannot decrypt the message because you will generate a new key pair. If you want to persist the keys, you can add an input for the public and private keys and import them into the algorithm.

The provider for asymmetric algorithms enables you to generate a key pair by specifying the size of the key:

```
var algorithm = AsymmetricKeyAlgorithmProvider.OpenAlgorithm(
    this.AlgorithmName);
if (this.keyPair == null)
{
    this.keyPair = algorithm.CreateKeyPair(512);
}
```

You can then import the public key to encrypt the message. In the example app, the public key is imported immediately after being exported from the key pair, but you can also decode base64-encoded text to a buffer and use the buffer to import the key.

```
var publicKey = algorithm.ImportPublicKey(
    this.keyPair.ExportPublicKey());
var encryptedMessage = CryptographicEngine.Encrypt(publicKey,
    message, null);
return CryptographicBuffer.EncodeToBase64String(encryptedMessage);
```

To decrypt the message, you need the full key pair (the public key and your private key). In the example app, this is already saved to a property on the class, so it is simply passed in, but you can also import it from a buffer or decode it from text.

```
IBuffer messageData =
    CryptographicBuffer.DecodeFromBase64String(message);
var decryptedMessage = CryptographicEngine.Decrypt(this.keyPair,
    messageData, null);
return CryptographicBuffer.ConvertBinaryToString(Encoding,
    decryptedMessage);
```

The same tools used in this example also work with certificates. A certificate can contain a public key or a key pair along with information about the identity of the owner of the certificate and a signature to verify the authenticity of the certificate. Part of the certificate includes the actual key, which can be decoded (it is often base64 encoded) and then imported into the algorithms the Windows Runtime provides.

Summary

In this chapter, you learned how to secure your Windows Store apps. Authentication provides a means of verifying the identity of the user, as well as establishing trust to interact with third-party sites without having to learn or store the user's credentials. When you do need to store credentials, you can use the Windows password vault to securely store the information. The data protection provider can encrypt and decrypt information based on the logged-in user's credentials. WinRT also supplies various providers and utilities that enable you to take advantage of symmetric and asymmetric encryption algorithms, as well as well-known methods to verify the integrity and authenticity of information.

In the next chapter, you learn about the Model-View-ViewModel (MVVM) pattern. This pattern is used throughout this book to build Windows Store apps. You learn in that chapter why this pattern is so useful for Windows Runtime development because of XAML and data-binding, and you explore various MVVM-related patterns used to solve common problems.

9

Model-View-ViewModel (MVVM)

MODEL-VIEW-VIEWMODEL (MVVM) IS A PROVEN PATTERN USED IN applications that support data-binding. Introduced in 2005 to support Windows Presentation Foundation (WPF)[1] apps, it was popularized by Silverlight and has grown to encompass a variety of platforms, including XAML and JavaScript. MVVM was based on even older design patterns that date back to the late 1970s.[2] Windows Store apps written with C# and XAML are particularly suited to MVVM because of the data-binding support XAML provides. In fact, most of the store templates and examples support the concept of MVVM, to varying degrees. Therefore, you must understand MVVM when you are developing WinRT apps.

One challenge to MVVM adoption is the perception that it is overly complex and makes performing simple tasks difficult. Part of this misconception stems from the fact that multiple MVVM frameworks exist, and debates swirl about what MVVM really means. Some developers tend to be overly dogmatic in their application of MVVM (for example, making rules such as "You can never have code-behind in MVVM") and focus too much on the prescription instead of the problem it is designed to solve.

---

[1]Introduction to Model/View/ViewModel pattern for building WPF apps, http://bit.ly/14ebujM

[2]The original MVC reports (PDF), http://bit.ly/185QktD

I've purposefully used the ViewModel pattern throughout this book, to demonstrate various ways you can apply it to Windows Store apps. The previous chapters focused on the examples themselves and did not address much of the underlying pattern or methods for using MVVM. This chapter revisits some of the older projects to explain how and why the MVVM pattern was used.

In this chapter, you learn about UI design patterns and why they are important for application development. I cover a brief history of the MVVM pattern because it helps illustrate how and why it is used in applications that support data-binding. I share both the common misperceptions of MVVM and its advantages, and then break down MVVM into its various components. Finally, you learn how to solve common problems with the MVVM framework.

UI Design Patterns

Design patterns are solutions to common problems. Developers work with patterns every day, even if they are not aware of it. If you've written an interface to abstract access to your database, you've used the *adapter* pattern. Whenever you use a `for/each` loop in your code, you implement the *iterator* pattern. UI design patterns specifically address concerns related to the user interface or presentation layer of your application. Learning patterns is important because it helps you solve common problems that already have effective solutions that have been used and tested for decades.

UI design patterns have evolved to help decouple the presentation layer and presentation logic of applications from the business logic, services, and data. This is important for a variety of reasons. UI design patterns solve these problems:

- **Changing UX requirements**—The look, feel, and interaction of applications can change over time. UI design patterns help insulate such changes, minimize impact to other layers of the application, and reduce the overhead of refactoring.

- **Parallel workflows**—Most software projects have separate design and development teams that are not always working on the same schedule. Traditional projects can introduce dependencies on design (development cannot begin until design is complete). UI design patterns help facilitate parallel efforts by keeping the two activities separate.
- **Control independence**—Multiple controls solve similar problems, such as providing a list for the user to select from (this can be done with a type-ahead search box, a grid, a combo box, or a list view, for example). UI design patterns help decouple the requirement (present a list and obtain a selection) from the implementation (use a drop-down control). This makes it easier to change controls and test the selection logic independent of the control being used.
- **Presentation logic testing**—Some views have complex rules, such as showing only items that have not been selected or presenting cascading lists that filter based on other selections (such as selecting a state to be presented with a list of cities within that state). UI design patterns enable developers to test this logic without having to invoke the infrastructure required to stand up the full user interface.

The prevalent use of the Model-View-Controller (MVC) pattern illustrates just how effective UI design patterns can be. This pattern was first introduced in 1979 and is still popular today. Many frameworks for building web applications are based on the MVC concept. Microsoft released its own framework that supports the pattern and named it directly after the pattern: ASP.NET MVC.

Most UI design patterns address two specific areas of the application: the view and the model. They differ in how interactions between the view and the model are managed or supervised. This often requires an additional component referred to as the controller, the presenter, or, in the case of MVVM, the viewmodel.

The Model

Confusing the model with pure data is a common mistake. The model refers not to a specific data model, but to the application model in general.

Your application consists of services, logic, and data, and the model is a general term to reference those components. The term *model* dates back to the original patterns that talked about how the application models the real world. In some cases, the model is a simple data model and represents sets of properties; in other cases, it is a domain model that also encapsulates behavior and validation rules. It is easiest to think of the model as everything your app does to surface information for your user to consume.

To illustrate this, open the **SoapServiceExample** from Chapter 5, "Web Services and Syndication." The obvious "model" this app displays is the `WeatherForecast` class, which contains a collection of instances of `ForecastEntry`. Although these classes are an important part of the model, they are meaningless without a way to retrieve them. The `WeatherHelperService` class contains the logic to call a third-party web service to obtain the weather information. Therefore, this service is also part of the model because it must be invoked to obtain the necessary information. Note that the model classes have no dependency on the UI: The weather information can be fetched and loaded into the classes without ever showing it to the end user.

The View

The view is the UI portion of your application. It has two primary purposes. The first is to present data and information in a way that is meaningful to the user. The second is to receive input from the user to perform various actions. Input can be keystrokes, mouse clicks, screen taps, or gestures. In Windows Store apps built with C# and XAML, the view is typically defined through declarative XAML markup.

You must realize that the view represents all the components that support the user interface. It is not restricted to the XAML you instantiate to draw components or respond to input. Code-behind is also an important part of the view. For example, open the **SafeNotes** project from Chapter 8, "Security," and then open the `MainPage.xaml.cs` code-behind file. The `MainPageLoaded` method changes the visual state of the view as the initialization of the model progresses. The `MainGrid_OnItemClick` responds to a UI event (the `click` event) and passes information about that event to the view-model. It also performs a navigation that is part of the UI framework.

```
private void MainGrid_OnItemClick(object sender,
    ItemClickEventArgs e)
{
    var viewModel = ((App)Application.Current).CurrentViewModel;
    viewModel.CurrentNote = e.ClickedItem as SimpleNote;
    viewModel.SetEdit();
    this.Frame.Navigate(typeof(NotePage), viewModel.CurrentNote.Id);
}
```

Some MVVM "purists" argue that a view should have no code-behind. For example, you could create an attached dependency property that binds to the `click` event in XAML and marshals the information to the view-model. Although that approach eliminates code-behind, you have to ask whether it provides any advantage. Does it make it easier or harder to develop a page within your application? Does it make the logic for that page easier or harder to test? Is the resulting markup easy to understand and maintain, or does it add unnecessary indirection that is difficult to follow?

The view doesn't end at the code-behind. The `MainPage` class is based on the `LayoutAwarePage`. This class contains logic for managing the state of the view, handling journaling (navigation), saving, and restoring state. The Visual State Manager is a great example of a UI design pattern that separates the logic of changing states from how the view presents those states to the end user.

Model-View-Controller (MVC)

MVC is one of the oldest UI design patterns. It was first documented in a paper written in 1979. Figure 9.1 illustrates the MVC pattern.

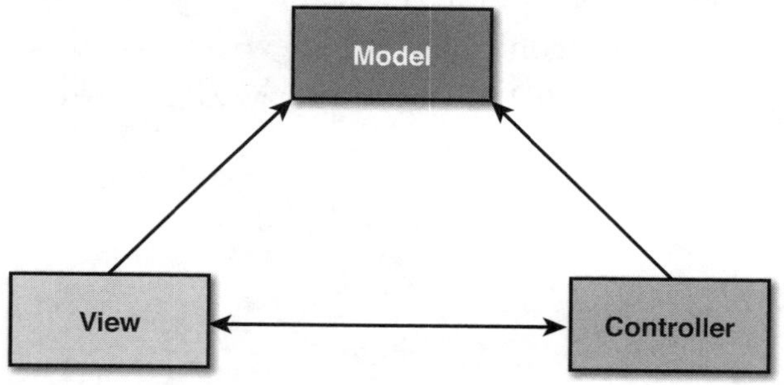

FIGURE 9.1 The Model-View-Controller (MVC) pattern

The arrows in Figure 9.1 indicate coupling rather than data flow. The view is aware of the model and can inspect the model to render the UI. It is also aware of the controller and receives commands to perform actions such as refreshing the display. Instead of responding to user input directly, the controller handles user inputs and issues commands to the view. The model is testable because it has no dependencies on the view or the controller, and the view is testable because it can be issued commands in the absence of user input.

This definition has evolved somewhat, and current implementations often have the view ignorant of the controller. The controller manipulates the view directly. Many modern web applications, including those built with ASP.NET MVC, follow this pattern. The server has a controller that renders the view. The view is a template for the data but does not react to input directly. Instead, the input is presented back to a controller on the server (via either a post or an AJAX callback), and the controller then maps this back to the model. An example of this is a post with query data that results in the controller executing a database command to perform a search.

Model-View-Presenter (MVP)

The MVP pattern evolved to further address separation of concerns. The coordination between the user, the model, and the view is delegated to a component called the *presenter*. Two flavors of the MVP pattern exist: *passive view* and *supervising controller*. In passive view, the view is completely ignorant of the model or the presenter. The presenter is responsible for updating the model, responding to changes in the model, and then refreshing the view. This is often done through an interface so that the view can be mocked for testing. In supervising controller, the view can use data-binding to work with the model. Figure 9.2 illustrates the MVP pattern.

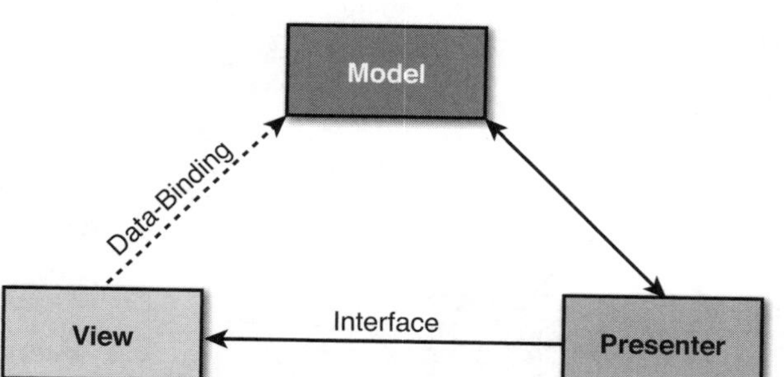

FIGURE 9.2 The Model-View-Presenter (MVP) pattern

Although the presenter is completely aware of the UI and the view, using a user interface means it is possible to mock the view and test the presentation logic without having to render a UI. Using the web example, a controller on the server can be tested by determining how it responds to input and what templates it chooses to render, even if the HTML pages aren't actually produced on a web server.

MVP allows for data-binding, but you can see from Figure 9.2 that this happens with the model. The presenter has coupling to the view (although different view implementations are possible when the coupling is through an interface) and is responsible for updating the view directly. This often leads to a one-to-one relationship between presenters and views, or a presenter that must work with multiple view interfaces.

Model-View-ViewModel (MVVM)

MVVM is similar to MVP, but it takes advantage of the advanced data-binding features of XAML. Figure 9.3 illustrates the MVVM pattern. In this pattern, a special component referred to as the viewmodel handles the interaction between the view and the model.

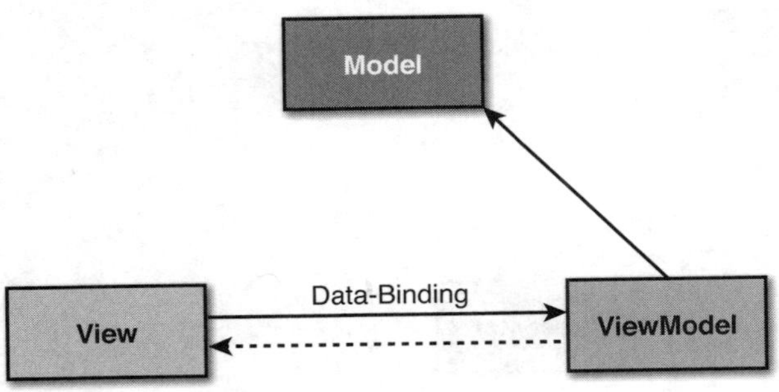

FIGURE 9.3 The Model-View-ViewModel (MVVM) pattern

The view does not have a direct dependency or awareness on the model in MVVM, except that the portion of the model that is exposed can view the viewmodel. Instead, the view uses data-binding to synchronize with the viewmodel directly. All changes to the view are handled either within the view itself (such as responding to gestures and user interactions) or through data-binding. The viewmodel is not directly aware of the view. Instead, the viewmodel manipulates properties that propagate changes to the view through data-binding. This makes the viewmodel testable because it does not depend on a specific view or view interface, nor does it depend directly on UI events.

This pattern also makes it easy for a single viewmodel to manage multiple views. A common scenario is a list of items with a separate view that enables you to view or edit the details of a particular item. MVVM makes it possible to manage the list, the selected item, and the logic for manipulating the selected item in the same viewmodel.

The ViewModel Decomposed

The viewmodel is the component that helps synchronize the state of the view and also interacts with the model. One of the most important characteristics of a viewmodel is that it should implement property change notification. This is required so that data-binding can both detect changes to the viewmodel and update the viewmodel in response to the UI. The `BindableBase` class provided with most of the examples for this book provides this functionality, and you can include it in projects as needed.

Open the ViewModel class in the **EncryptionExample** project from Chapter 8, and navigate to the EncryptionInput property. This pattern is common for a viewmodel to expose a property and then raise a property change notification when it is updated within the framework. The underlying method is decorated with a CallerMemberName attribute. This is a feature that enables the compiler to embed the name of the calling member as a parameter, which, in the case of the property, is the property's name. It is a convenient way to ensure that the property name is passed without using "magic strings."

```
public string EncryptionInput
{
    get { return this.encryptionInput; }
    set
    {
        this.encryptionInput = value;
        this.OnPropertyChanged();
    }
}
```

This approach is verbose because it always updates. You can also use the helper SetProperty method to trigger a property change notification only if the value changes (so if the setter is called with the same value, it does not raise the notification).

```
this.SetProperty(ref this.encryptionInput, value);
```

The viewmodel has dependencies on the model and is responsible for fetching data and executing business logic based on the user interaction. For example, the encryption project shows a message when the input is not valid. This is done through a dialog. To ensure that the viewmodel does not have a direct dependency on the UI, the dialog is exposed through an interface. This is implemented as part of the application model.

```
public interface IDialogService
{
    Task ShowDialog(string title, string message);
}
```

You can resolve the dependencies the viewmodel has on the model in several ways. In the example, the dialog is exposed as a public property. It is expected to be initialized once and not changed, so it does not implement property change notifications.

```
public IDialogService Dialog { get; set; }
```

The viewmodel does not control setting the property, so it must be set externally. This pattern is called *Inversion of Control* (IOC) because control is inverted from the component that has the dependency (the viewmodel) to some other provider. *Dependency Injection* (DI) is the solution to resolve the dependency: The implementation is injected to the viewmodel. In the example project, you can see that the `DialogService` implementation is injected into the XAML for the `MainPage` class.

```
<Grid.DataContext>
    <data:ViewModel>
        <data:ViewModel.Dialog>
            <data:DialogService/>
        </data:ViewModel.Dialog>
    </data:ViewModel>
</Grid.DataContext>
```

The technique used here is referred to as *property injection* because the implementation is resolved using a property. Another technique is to store the reference to the dialog service as a private property and pass it into the constructor. This is called *constructor injection.* I prefer property injection in Windows Store apps because you cannot pass parameters to the constructor in XAML. Exposing dependencies as properties allows them to be resolved by XAML declarations. This resolves them for the running application, but they can be set explicitly for tests.

If you open the **EncryptionExampleTests** project from this chapter, you can see a special `MockDialog` class is defined. Instead of showing an actual dialog, the class simply stores the latest title and message and keeps a history so you can count how many times the dialog service was called. The test version of the dialog service is injected into the viewmodel at the start of each test in the `ViewModelTests` class.

```
[TestInitialize]
public void TestInitialize()
{
    this.mockDialogService = new MockDialog();
    this.target = new ViewModel
                      {
                          Dialog = this.mockDialogService
                      };
}
```

The test "given no encryption input, when execute is called with an encrypt parameter, then the dialog should be shown and the method returns" explicitly sets an empty input, calls the execution method, and then uses the mocked dialog to verify that it was called.

```
[TestMethod]
public void GivenNoEncryptionInputWhenExecuteEncryptCalled
➥ThenShowsDialogAndReturns()
{
    this.target.EncryptionInput = string.Empty;
    this.target.Execute("encrypt");
    AssertIt.That(
        this.mockDialogService.DialogCount,
        Is.EqualTo(1),
        "Test failed: dialog should have been called exactly once.");
}
```

Many approaches exist for associating a viewmodel with a view. The example shown simply instantiates it directly in the data context through XAML. The **SafeNotes** project from Chapter 8 reuses the viewmodel for multiple views, so it cannot be instantiated directly in the data context, or multiple instances would exist. Instead, it creates the viewmodel as an application-wide resource in `App.xaml`.

```
<data:ViewModel x:Key="GlobalViewModel"/>
```

Then it is referenced as a static resource so that each view can reference the same copy.

```
DataContext="{Binding Source={StaticResource GlobalViewModel}}"
```

Frameworks called DI containers enable you to configure and resolve dependencies. If you use a DI container, the DI container must create the viewmodel so that all its dependencies can be resolved instead of instantiating the viewmodel directly. In those cases, the most common solution is to use a component called a viewmodel locator.

A viewmodel locator is simply a component that exposes a class or property to obtain a copy of the viewmodel. Inside the component, it resolves dependencies and serves a copy of the viewmodel. Although DI containers are powerful tools for large, modular applications, I do not believe they add nearly as much value for mobile client applications such as Windows Store apps. You can see from the examples for this book that the projects are modular and can be tested without relying on a DI container.

The **ViewModelLocator** example project from this chapter demonstrates this concept. The `IClockViewModel` interface defines the viewmodel. The `ViewModelLocator` class is instantiated in the `App.xaml` definition.

```
<local:ViewModelLocator x:Key="Locator"/>
```

Instead of referencing the viewmodel directly, the `MainPage.xaml` references a property on the locator.

```
DataContext="{Binding Source={StaticResource Locator},
➥Path=ClockViewModel}"
```

In this simple example, the locator is used to instantiate either a design-time view that loads the current time once or a runtime view that continuously updates the time. If you were using a DI container, you could create the container in the `ViewModelLocator` class and use that to wire up dependencies and expose your viewmodels.

In addition to properties and services, a viewmodel can expose commands. Commands implement the `ICommand` interface. Commands enable you to write components you can test independently of the UI and bind directly to buttons. The Portable Class Libraries examples from Chapter 2, "Windows Store Apps and WinRT Components," use a command that executes any action exactly once. The **SoapServiceExample** from Chapter 5 uses the `WeatherCommand` to obtain the forecast for a specific zip code. The command itself encapsulates the logic to validate the zip code but uses

DI to execute the action that actually retrieves the weather forecast. This makes the command testable, and it can be bound directly to the UI, as you can see in `MainPage.xaml`.

```
<Button Content="Get Forecast"
        Margin="20 0 0 0"
        Command="{Binding SubmitCommand}"
        CommandParameter="{Binding ZipCode}"/>
```

The **EncryptionExample** project from Chapter 8 demonstrates another way you can use commands. In this example, the commands are more tightly bound to the function of the viewmodel, so the viewmodel implements the `ICommand` interface directly. The command parameter designates which action to execute, so it is bound in the UI. This binds commands to the viewmodel directly but still allows the command execution to be tested, as shown in the testing example shown earlier.

```
Command="{Binding}" CommandParameter="encrypt"
```

Although the viewmodel preserves state for the view, keeping view logic as close to the view as possible makes testing, growing, and maintaining your application easier. For example, consider a viewmodel that exposes a date field. Exposing a text property that shows the date in a user-friendly format might be tempting. The problem with this approach is that a date has meaning and can be tested, whereas the string has less meaning and must be parsed for testing. Exposing the date as a string also restricts how the view can interpret the date because a date-time picker control might not know how to operate against a string.

The recommended approach is to expose data in its native format and then implement an `IValueConverter` to shape the data as needed. Instead of exposing a `Visibility` attribute, the viewmodel from the **EncryptionExample** project exposes Boolean properties that represent whether the currently selected algorithm requires a password. The `BooleanToVisibilityConverter` then hides the password dialog when the algorithm does not require a user-entered password.

```
Visibility="{Binding RequiresPassword, Converter={StaticResource
➥ BoolVisConverter}}"
```

You might see some examples in this book of a viewmodel that does expose formatted text, for convenience and to keep the example simple. As with all patterns, it's important to balance your needs with overhead. In some cases, the overhead of building a new converter class to support a format used in only one place might not justify any benefits it provides. Another pattern I've seen is to expose the property both ways, as a raw value and as a formatted value, so that views can bind to the version that's needed.

Common MVVM Misperceptions

I mentioned earlier that many misperceptions and a general lack of understanding circulate for the MVVM pattern. One common statement I hear is, "MVVM is extremely complex." Although I've seen implementations that certainly are complex, MVVM can be incredibly simple when implemented correctly. Hopefully the example projects from this book have demonstrated that.

"Code-behind isn't allowed."

This is a popular "rule" to apply to MVVM, but it fails to recognize the underlying XAML technology. XAML is simply a declarative method for instantiating classes and setting their properties, so the difference between setting a property in XAML and setting one in the code-behind is purely semantic. Adding business logic to code-behind reduces the testability and maintainability of the application, but there is no reason to not include UI logic in the code-behind. If you find yourself working hard to build special classes and properties just to avoid code-behind, you're probably doing it wrong.

"MVVM is hard to implement."

This goes along with the comment about complexity. Plenty of frameworks can stand up MVVM quickly. The built-in Windows Store app templates support a basic form of MVVM, and you can use the `BindableBase` class to get you started. The popular MVVM Light Toolkit[3] not only

[3]MVVM Light Toolkit, http://bit.ly/188NiEX

provides an MVVM framework, but also uses a consistent API across multiple platforms. It contains templates, snippets, and other out-of-the-box helpers that should accelerate your capability to develop and deliver applications, not hinder it.

> *"MVVM reduces the performance of the application."*

This is one I used to hear often when I worked on WPF and Silverlight projects. The bottom line is that the performance of your application reflects how you implement the code, not the pattern or framework you decide to use. MVVM can be implemented poorly just like any other pattern. MVVM by itself should have no impact on the performance of your app. In fact, most of the problems MVVM solves exist in the presentation layer. Most apps spend far more time waiting for information to travel across the network than they do rendering output for the user or handling user input.

> *"MVVM is good for only very large projects."*

Even small projects can benefit from MVVM. Many examples in this book are small projects and don't implement the full suite of capabilities required for a Windows Store app to be published, but they all were easier to write and test because of MVVM. In fact, I find that projects go far more quickly with MVVM because I can use design-time data to build my UI and navigation flow and begin writing tests before I ever wire up a live service or WinRT API call.

> *"MVVM is about commands and messaging systems such as the event aggregator."*

In its pure sense, MVVM is about the way concerns are separated by using a viewmodel with property change notification to synchronize the view. Many frameworks tackle issues such as generic command implementations and complex messaging systems (for example, the *event aggregator* pattern provides a way for components to communicate with each other without using direct references). Although all these components are helpful and useful in projects, they are part of a given framework and are not necessary for MVVM.

"MVVM is hard to understand and maintain."

This is one statement that has some truth to it. You will find MVVM easy to maintain when you understand it, but I have found that developers who are accustomed to other patterns sometimes have a hard time grasping the concept at first. This is why I like to take the approach of using the pattern in my examples while tackling other topics before I dive into the specifics of the pattern itself. The key to understanding MVVM is to shift into thinking about state rather than process.

To reuse the example of a cascading drop-down, a process-based way of thinking works like this: First, retrieve a list of items; next, expose the list of items and wait for an item selection. After an item is selected, use that item to expose another list of items. If the item selected is changed, go fetch a new list and expose that.

The state-based way of thinking is this: Expose a list that is synchronized to a selected item. Expose a second list that is filtered by the selected item. Whenever property notification indicates that the selected item has changed, refresh the filter. Both ways of thinking about the solution are valid, but the more you can shift to the idea of a synchronized state in your viewmodel, the easier it will be to grasp the concept and begin to build apps based on the pattern.

Benefits of MVVM

I've covered some of the implicit benefits of the MVVM pattern throughout this chapter, but it helps to look at an explicit list of advantages as well. These are the ways I've found MVVM can benefit projects after many years of applying the pattern to Silverlight, WPF, HTML5, and Windows Store projects.

MVVM provides a clean separation of concerns. When concerns are separated, it is possible to develop various areas of your application independently of each other. The development aspect is more important when larger teams are working on the application at the same time. The separation of concerns also helps isolate code so that you can maintain and test a specific section in isolation from the rest of the application. From a maintenance perspective, this makes it possible to work with a component by focusing on that area of the application without having to learn everything about the rest of the application. That often translates to focusing on a specific viewmodel and the services it depends on in MVVM.

MVVM promotes a parallel designer/developer workflow. This is a benefit I've experienced firsthand on several projects. I once worked on a major project that involved a third-party design team. The team members were revamping the entire UI and going through a full cycle of providing wireframes, mockups, and eventually full design comps of the new UI. Their process would take several months, but because the project could not afford that much of a delay, development began simultaneously with design. MVVM allowed us to define the "what" of a particular page or screen—in other words, a given page might have some information about a user, a list of items, or a set of values. This was enough to build the viewmodel and test it. After the design team worked out how it would be displayed, the final step was as simple as marrying the XAML to the viewmodel and applying the appropriate data-bindings and converters to make it work.

MVVM facilitates unit testing. Open the **EncryptionExampleTests** project in this chapter, and you can see how easy it is to test the viewmodel for the application. I included the **FluentTestHelper** project in the Common folder to show how to make Microsoft's built-in unit tests, such as `AssertIt.That(2, Is.GreaterThan(3))`, more readable. The tests themselves make explicit statements of the system. In an ideal world, you can identify requirements and write tests that match the requirements. It's then possible to verify the requirements through tests and ensure that your components map to the requirements. For example, consider the need to filter a list of encryption algorithms. The requirement is, "Given the filter for symmetric algorithms selected, the list of available algorithms should contain only symmetric algorithms." This is directly testable through the similarly named test method. After the viewmodel is verified as behaving correctly, it is a simple step to integrate the viewmodel with the view through data-binding.

MVVM directly supports the use of data-binding. In my opinion, a class that supports property change notification and is bound to the UI is a viewmodel because it synchronizes the state of the view. If you use a two-way binding and update a property of the class, it is reflected in the view.

The entire dependency property system in XAML supports data-binding, so MVVM is a natural pattern to use because it works directly with the data-binding system.

MVVM promotes improved code reuse. A well-designed viewmodel can be unit-tested without dependencies on any other part of the system. This design encourages the use of interfaces and isolated components, which other viewmodels in the system can reuse. A single viewmodel can also be reused, as evidenced in the **SafeNotes** app of Chapter 8. Code reuse is important because it isolates defects to one place and provides building blocks for developers to stand up other pieces of the application more rapidly. After the dialog service is written, anyone can reuse it in code.

MVVM helps contain refactoring. If you've been developing for any period of time, you've likely participated in refactoring an application. The signature of a third-party web service might have changed, or the new design team might have decided that all lists should be implemented as lists instead of drop-downs. The separation of concerns that MVVM promotes helps contain refactoring to a smaller footprint within your project. Imagine a system that calls a service directly in code-behind and binds the result directly to a grid. That system is extremely volatile because any change to the UI or the service will result in a change to all the code. An MVVM implementation, on the other hand, might require the service to be updated only if the signature changes (because the result is mapped to a local model, the only change is to map the new API to the existing model). If the control changes, it can be updated in XAML and bound to the existing properties on the viewmodel without requiring any other code modifications.

MVVM has extensive tooling support. Both Visual Studio and Blend support data-binding and, therefore, support MVVM. Using the MVVM pattern, you can set up design-time data that is visible while you are creating the application. Design-time extensions exist (`IsDesignTimeCreatable` in XAML and `Windows.ApplicationModel.DesignMode.DesignModeEnabled` in code-behind, as the next section discusses) that enable you to implement your runtime or design-time viewmodel, and the tools automatically instantiate a copy and use the properties that the viewmodel exposes in the designer.

Common MVVM Solutions

I mentioned earlier that there can be a learning curve for MVVM. In this section, I not only address common problems that MVVM solves, but I also share some solutions to scenarios that at first glance might not look like they are "MVVM compatible." MVVM handles most of these challenges in a way that is probably easier and more straightforward than expected.

Design-Time Data

One major benefit of data-binding is its built-in support for design-time data. This is data that you can wire into the designer so you can see how your controls will look when they are bound to real data. The **SoapServiceExample** project from Chapter 5 illustrates one approach to creating design-time data. In this example, the data class is `ForecastEntry`. A derived class called `DesignForecastEntry` populates the underlying class with sample data.

```
public DesignForecastEntry()
{
    this.Day = DateTime.Now;
    this.ForecastUri = new Uri(
        "http://ws.cdyne.com/WeatherWS/Images/mostlycloudy.gif",
        UriKind.Absolute);
    this.Description = "Sample day for weather";
    this.PrecipitationDay = "50";
    this.PrecipitationNight = "20";
    this.TemperatureLow = "25";
    this.TemperatureHigh = "49";
    this.TypeId = 1;
}
```

The same technique is used with the `WeatherForecast` and `DesignForecast` classes. `WeatherHelperService` detects the design-time mode and returns an instance of `DesignForecast` instead of calling the live web service.

Another way to handle design-time data is within the viewmodel itself. In the **AuthenticationExample** project from Chapter 8, the constructor for the main `ViewModel` class populates some sample log entries when the viewmodel is instantiated from the designer.

```
if (!Windows.ApplicationModel.DesignMode.DesignModeEnabled)
{
    return;
}
this.Log("This is just a test message.");
```

If you are concerned about the design-time data being compiled into your production app, you can always use a conditional compilation symbol. These symbols are set on the **Build** tab of the **Project Properties** dialog for the project. The symbols are stored based on the configuration you set for the build. For example, you can specify a new symbol called `DESIGN` for the **Debug** configuration. Create a private method to load the design-time data, and mark it with the `Conditional` attribute specifying the `DESIGN` compilation symbol. You can even make the class partial so you can place the design-time data code in a separate file. It would look something like this:

```
public partial class MainViewModel
{
    [Conditional("DESIGN")]
    private void WireDesignerData()
    {
        if (!Windows.ApplicationModel.DesignMode.DesignModeEnabled)
        {
            return;
        }
        Name = "This is a design-time name.";
    }
}
```

From the viewmodel constructor, you can call the method directly:

```
public MainViewModel()
{
    WireDesignerData();
}
```

When you are in the **Debug** configuration, the method compiles and the design-time data is wired into the viewmodel. If you switch to a different configuration such as **Release**, however, the conditional attribute prevents the method from being created. The compiler is smart enough to ignore the call to the conditional method from the constructor, and the code that is compiled has no references to design-time data whatsoever.

A final approach to design-time data is to expose the viewmodel as an interface and then wire it up using a viewmodel locator. This is how the **ViewModelLocatorExample** works.

```
public IClockViewModel ClockViewModel
{
    get
    {
        if (Windows.ApplicationModel.DesignMode.DesignModeEnabled)
        {
            return new DesignViewModel();
        }
        return this.viewModel = this.viewModel ??
            new ClockViewModel();
    }
}
```

In design time, it returns an instance of the `DesignViewModel`, but in run-time, it returns a `ClockViewModel` instance.

Accessing the UI Thread

In general, you should build your apps to take advantage of the `async` and `await` keywords and avoid spinning any unnecessary threads. It is not possible to update either properties of UI elements or properties of classes that are data-bound to UI elements from a non-UI thread. The **EncryptionExample** project from Chapter 8 illustrates several asynchronous methods that do not have to do anything special to update properties on the viewmodel because they use the `await` keyword. This automatically synchronizes with the current context and, therefore, returns the results to the UI thread. The `await` keyword basically allows another thread to run in the background without blocking the UI, but it returns to the UI thread when complete.

A similar example is shown in the **ViewModelLocatorExample** project because a `Task` is used to delay for a second to update the clock in an endless loop, but the delay does not block the main UI thread. The viewmodel is created on the UI thread, so the calls to await the delay allow the delay to happen without blocking the UI; then the time is updated and propagated to the UI on the correct thread.

Some circumstances require you to spawn a background thread from which you will update a property used in data-binding or display a dialog: You must marshal these calls back to the UI thread.

The **UIThreadExample** illustrates this. The command spawns a background task that waits for a half-second before refreshing the date. If you click the button that runs on the background thread, you get an exception in the debugger output, and the running app never updates. The button for the UI thread refreshes the time after a short delay. The first step to handling this is to define a `CoreDispatcher` property that will hold the instance of the dispatcher capable of marshalling work to the UI thread in the `ViewModel` class.

```
private readonly CoreDispatcher dispatcher;
```

The viewmodel is created on the UI thread, so you can capture the dispatcher in the constructor. Just make sure you aren't in design-time mode, or the call will fail.

```
if (Windows.ApplicationModel.DesignMode.DesignModeEnabled)
{
    return;
}
this.dispatcher = CoreWindow.GetForCurrentThread().Dispatcher;
```

Finally, when you need to update a property that fires a change notification, use the `RunAsync` method on the dispatcher to marshal it to the UI thread.

```
await this.dispatcher.RunAsync(
    CoreDispatcherPriority.Normal,
    () => this.Time = DateTime.Now);
```

Remember, unless you have a good reason to start background processing, you should double-check your code if you have to use this technique. Most of the time, using `async`/`await` from the existing thread will do what you intend.

Commands

Commands are a popular way to encapsulate logic triggered by actions in the UI, most often through a button tap. The example projects for this book show several techniques for using commands, whether to use a separate class that implements `ICommand` or to implement `ICommand` directly on the viewmodel itself. Regardless of the approach you use, it is possible to implement the command asynchronously to await other processes simply by decorating the appropriate method (`Execute` or `CanExecute`) with the `async` keyword, as shown in the **EncryptionExample** project.

Handling Dialogs

Viewmodels commonly trigger some sort of dialog, whether to confirm a request or to provide feedback to the user. To maintain the testability of the viewmodel, always consider removing any dependencies on UI namespaces. As explained in the section "The ViewModel Decomposed," earlier in this chapter, the **EncryptionExample** project defines a contract for dialogs and implements the contract with a service that calls a modal dialog during runtime, but provides a mocked dialog for testing.

Selection Lists

Viewmodels generally expose lists that are synchronized with a selected value. It is also common to have multiple lists that depend on each other, such as with cascading selections. If you are building a set of related selection lists, you can take advantage of data-binding as the trigger to synchronize and update the lists. The **CascadingListExample** project illustrates this technique. The app shows four columns, and each column depends on the previous column. It is used to build a number from 1 to 9999 by selecting the initial digits. When you select a digit in the first column, you get a range of numbers to select from in the second column, and so forth.

The lists are exposed as type `ObservableCollection` so that they participate in data-binding automatically. An observable collection raises events whenever the contents of the list change. The data-binding system listens for these events and uses them to refresh the list that displays. Notice that no logic is built into the lists themselves. Instead, the selection is synchronized with a set of selected properties. For example, the first digit is bound to the `SelectedOne` property in `MainPage.xaml`.

```
<ListView Grid.Row="1" ItemsSource="{Binding Digits}"
    SelectedItem="{Binding SelectedOne, Mode=TwoWay}"/>
```

The property definition handles property change notification and uses the selected value to build the list for the next column.

```
public int SelectedOne
{
    get { return this.selectedOne; }
    set
    {
        this.SetProperty(ref this.selectedOne, value);
        this.LoadTens();
    }
}
```

The `LoadTens` method invokes the `LoadService` method. This method checks to see if the appropriate list is already built. If it is, it simply returns.

```
var starter = selected * 10;
if (list.Contains(starter))
{
    return;
}
```

If it needs to build the list, it first clears the observable collection and then builds a list of ten numbers.

```
list.Clear();
foreach (var newNumber in this.GetList(starter))
{
    list.Add(newNumber);
}
```

Finally, if the currently selected item for that list is not in the list, it defaults to the first item in the list.

```
if (!list.Contains(selected))
{
    setter(list[0]);
}
```

Using this logic, you can select items from any column and immediately see the updates to all dependent columns. The logic is built based on the state of the viewmodel instead of a computation. Each selected item updates only its associated list; it doesn't try to synchronize all the remaining lists or selected items. However, this simple set of chained dependencies ensures that data-binding will cascade the changes so that all the lists are maintained. The example uses a `ListView` so you can see the full contents of the list. You could just as easily swap it out with a `ListBox` or a `ComboBox` control because the UI implementation is decoupled from the viewmodel.

Filtered Lists

The previous example used observable collections to synchronize multiple lists. Although this technique works well, it is also verbose. Each time the collection is cleared or a single item is added, the collection change notifications result in an update to the data-binding and the view. Filtering lists further complicate matters because you must retain a copy of the "pristine" list and then constantly rebuild the exposed list based on the filter criteria.

The **EncryptionExample** project demonstrates a different approach to managing filters. The filter logic consists of three parts. The first part is the list to filter. The second is the set of filters to apply to the list, and the third is a special list that is exposed for data-binding.

The list is maintained as a private field in the `ViewModel` class.

```
private readonly List<ICryptoAlgorithm> algorithms =
    new List<ICryptoAlgorithm>();
```

All the filters are exposed as properties, but when the properties are updated, they call a common method to indicate that the filter criteria has changed.

```
public bool Asymmetric
{
    get { return this.asymmetric; }
    set
    {
        this.asymmetric = value;
        this.OnPropertyChanged();
        this.OnFilterChanged();
    }
}
```

The `OnFilterChanged` method simply raises a property change notification for the third part of the filter pattern, the filtered list.

```
private void OnFilterChanged()
{
    this.OnPropertyChanged("Algorithms");
}
```

Listing 9.1 shows the code for the filtered list. It is simply a LINQ query that returns a filtered copy of the list. Note that, instead of an observable collection, the list is exposed as an `IEnumerable`. If you are filtering a long list, you can use this technique to return only the values you need for the UI.

LISTING 9.1 The Filtered List

```
public IEnumerable<ICryptoAlgorithm> Algorithms
{
    get
    {
        return this.algorithms
            .Where(a => !this.pkcs7 || a.IsPkcs7)
            .Where(a => !this.block || a.IsBlock)
            .Where(a => !this.stream || !a.IsBlock)
            .Where(a => !this.symmetric || a.IsSymmetric)
            .Where(a => !this.asymmetric || !a.IsSymmetric)
            .Where(a => !this.authenticated || a.HasAuthentication)
            .Where(a => !this.verification ||
                a.IsVerificationAlgorithm)
            .Where(a => !this.hash || a.IsHash)
            .OrderBy(a => a.Name)
            .ToList();
    }
}
```

The exposed list is not observable. Instead of notifying the data-binding system of changes to individual items, the entire property is refreshed whenever the filter changes. This causes the associated control to refresh the full list in one operation rather than have to apply multiple updates each time an item is removed or inserted.

Validation

Numerous approaches to validation exist. The .NET framework has built-in data annotations that can be applied, fluent validation libraries exist, and you can roll your own. Whatever method you choose to validate data, your viewmodel will likely be responsible for exposing the validation information to your view. The simplest way to do this is to expose a model with change notification that can surface validation issues.

The **SafeNotes** project from Chapter 8 demonstrates this. The `ValidationErrors` class contains a simple dictionary that maps a property name to a validation message.

```
private readonly Dictionary<string, string> validationErrors =
    new Dictionary<string, string>();
```

If you want to support more than one message per property, you can simply modify the implementation to support an array of values in the dictionary. The class exposes an indexer to access the messages. An indexer is simply a way to reference properties on a model using index notation such as `foo["bar"]`. You can use any value type for the parameter of the indexer; in this case, a string indexer is used to make referencing the property easy.

```
public string this[string fieldName]
```

The getter checks to see if any messages exist for the property and returns either the message or an empty string.

```
get
{
    return this.validationErrors.ContainsKey(fieldName) ?
        this.validationErrors[fieldName] : string.Empty;
}
```

The setter first checks to see if the property already exists. If it does, it either updates the property with the message or removes the property from the dictionary if the message is empty.

```
if (this.validationErrors.ContainsKey(fieldName))
{
    if (string.IsNullOrWhiteSpace(value))
    {
```

```
            this.validationErrors.Remove(fieldName);
        }
        else
        {
            this.validationErrors[fieldName] = value;
        }
    }
```

If the property does not exist, it is added only if there is a message.

```
    else
    {
        if (!string.IsNullOrWhiteSpace(value))
        {
            this.validationErrors.Add(fieldName, value);
        }
    }
```

The class then raises the property change notification to inform data-binding of the update. It exposes an `IsValid` property that is `false` when any validation messages exist. A `Clear` method removes all messages for the start of a new validation cycle.

The `ValidationBase` class exposes the errors class as a property.

```
public ValidationErrors ValidationErrors { get; set; }
```

It exposes a validation method that clears the errors, called a validation implementation that the derived class must implement, and then raises the property change notification for the `ValidationErrors` property. The `SimpleNote` class can then perform the appropriate validations.

```
protected override void ValidateSelf()
{
    if (string.IsNullOrWhiteSpace(this.title))
    {
        this.ValidationErrors["Title"] = "Title is required.";
    }
    if (string.IsNullOrWhiteSpace(this.description))
    {
        this.ValidationErrors["Description"] = "You must...";
    }
}
```

Any command that requires a valid model can check the status of the `IsValid` flag to determine whether it can execute. The helper class makes it easy to expose the results of validation in the UI. In this case, a `TextBlock` element binds to the indexer for the `Title` property to show an error message when the `Title` property doesn't pass validation.

```
<TextBlock Text="{Binding
 ➥CurrentEditableNote.ValidationErrors[Title]}" Foreground="Red"
 Grid.Row="2" Style="{StaticResource ItemTextStyle}"
 Margin="12 0 0 0"/>
```

This example shows a simple way to expose a validation message through data-binding. You can easily hook in a validation engine or fluent validation library that sets the validation messages based on results. Many third-party MVVM frameworks also provide built-in validation engines and ways to expose validation messages in the UI.

Summary

The app examples throughout this book have utilized the MVVM pattern. In this chapter, you learned about the history behind the pattern and why it is so well suited for XAML development. You learned about the design of the ViewModel component, debunked common misperceptions about MVVM, and explored the various benefits. Finally, you reviewed MVVM solutions to common problems you might encounter.

In the next chapter, you learn about the advanced APIs WinRT provides to check for network connectivity and determine the data plans available to the user. The chapter reviews APIs for HotSpot authentication, explores the Homegroup network share, and rounds out your knowledge of interaction with the web and HTTP. It also covers sockets for lower-level network communications and reveals how to use background transfers to download large files. In addition, you'll see an example of using Near Field Communications (NFC) to allow two devices to share data when they are close to each other.

10

Networking

NETWORK CONNECTIVITY IS A MAJOR FEATURE OF MOST WINDOWS STORE apps, as you learned in previous chapters. Although you have learned how to connect to services and keep your content fresh, Windows 8.1 devices are capable of connecting to the Internet and other devices in myriad ways. In this chapter, you learn some of these more advanced methods and how to integrate them into your own apps.

In addition to supporting the HTTP protocols, WinRT provides APIs that make it easy to enumerate resources on your HomeGroup network. You can enumerate network information and obtain the current data plan so that your app can modify its behavior to avoid downloading large amounts of data over a metered connection. The sockets APIs enable low-level communications using traditional UDP and TCP protocols, as well as the newer HTML5 WebSockets protocol. The proximity APIs enable communications between peer devices using Near Field Communications (NFC) and Wi-Fi Direct. Finally, the background transfer API allows your app to effectively manage long-running data transfers even when the app itself is not running.

Web and HTTP

In Chapter 5, "Web Services and Syndication," you learned how to use the `HttpClient` class to connect to an HTTP server and retrieve content using the REST architecture. The `Windows.Web.Http` namespace contains several classes that you can use to connect with HTTP-based services. The `HttpClient` class represents a simple and easy-to-use interface for sending HTTP-related requests and retrieving responses. Other classes provide more advanced features and fine-grained control over interactions.

To provide more control over HTTP requests, use the `HttpRequestMessage` class. For example, the following requests content from my blog:

```
var client = new HttpClient();
var httpResponse = await client.GetAsync(new Uri(
  "http://csharperimage.jeremylikness.com/", UriKind.Absolute));
```

If you want more control over the type of request and process the request immediately after the headers have been read (instead of having to wait for the entire body), you can issue the request like this instead:

```
var client = new HttpClient();
var request = new HttpRequestMessage(
    HttpMethod.Get, new Uri("http://csharperimage.jeremylikness.
                            com"));
var response = await client.SendRequestAsync(request,
    HttpCompletionOption.ResponseHeadersRead);
```

Using the latter method also gives you more control over the response. You can create a cancellation token and convert the response to a `Task` that uses the token:

```
this.cancellation = new CancellationTokenSource();
var response = await client.SendRequestAsync(
    request, HttpCompletionOption.ResponseHeadersRead)
    .AsTask(cancellation.Token);
```

When the page takes a significant time to load, from either a slow network or a large amount of information, you can cancel the load automatically or through user input by calling the cancel method on the cancellation token. You see an example of this in the `CancelUrl` method of the `ViewModel` class in the **AdvancedHttpExample** project:

```
cts.Cancel();
cts.Dispose();
```

The project enables you to enter a URL and then downloads and displays the content. The initial request ends when the headers are received so that you can stream the content with progress updates. You can cancel longer-running downloads and watch the progress. The content is exposed through the `Content` property of the `HttpResponseMessage` that is returned. The `LoadUrl` method demonstrates creating a progress handler that takes a type `ulong` and asynchronously downloads the content as a string.

```
this.progress = new Progress<ulong>(ProgressHandler);
var stringContent = await response.Content
   .ReadAsStringAsync().AsTask(cancellation.Token, this.progress);
```

The progress handler is passed the number of bytes received and uses the dispatcher to set them as a property on the viewmodel to show the progress to the user.

```
private void ProgressHandler(ulong progressArgs)
```

If you use the default URL of my blog, the content loads immediately and the progress method never gets called. Using a longer URL, such as the URL to a large book such as *Ulysses* in HTML format from the Gutenberg project, results in a longer download and progress updates. The URL, listed in the source of the viewmodel, to make it easy for you to copy, is www.gutenberg.org/files/4300/4300-h/4300-h.htm.

You can also use the request message to post content, including streams, to the server. The `Content` property of the `HttpRequestMessage` can be assigned any instance that implements `IHttpContent`. This includes the following content:

- `HttpBufferContent`—Content that uses an `IBuffer` instance
- `HttpFormUrlEncodedContent`—Content that uses name/value pairs for a form post
- `HttpJsonContent`—Content that is represented using the JSON format
- `HttpMultipartContent`—Content that uses the multipart MIME type for uploading multiple attachments

- `HttpMultipartFormDataContent`—A special format for forms encoded using the `multipart/form-data` MIME type
- `HttpStreamContent`—Content that uses a stream, such as when uploading files to the server
- `HttpStringContent`—Content that uses a string

The HTTP API also provides the `HttpProgress` class for tracking and handling the progress of long-running HTTP uploads. Simply create an instance of the progress handler and pass it to the extension method that converts the call to a `Task`:

```
var progress = new Progress<HttpProgress>(ProgressHandler);
HttpResponseMessage response = await httpClient.PostAsync(
    resourceAddress, streamContent).AsTask(cts.Token, progress);
```

The signature of the handler is a simple method that takes an instance of `HttpProgress` and can query items such as bytes sent versus total bytes sent, number of retries, and the stage of the process (for example, sending or receiving content).

HomeGroup

Microsoft provides a special service named HomeGroup that is designed to make it easier to share folders, files, and devices on home networks. If you are not familiar with HomeGroup, Microsoft provides an online tutorial to help you set one up "from start to finish."[1] The Windows shell handles the special network behind the scenes and exposes it as a file system in **Explorer**.

Figure 10.1 shows an example folder in the HomeGroup. Notice that the initial set of "folders" corresponds to users on the network, followed by the machines they are logged into. These, in turn, expose libraries based on the user's preferences for sharing pictures, documents, music, or other items. You can browse to the folders you have permissions for and access the items as you normally would.

---

[1]HomeGroup from start to finish, http://bit.ly/1ak28nC

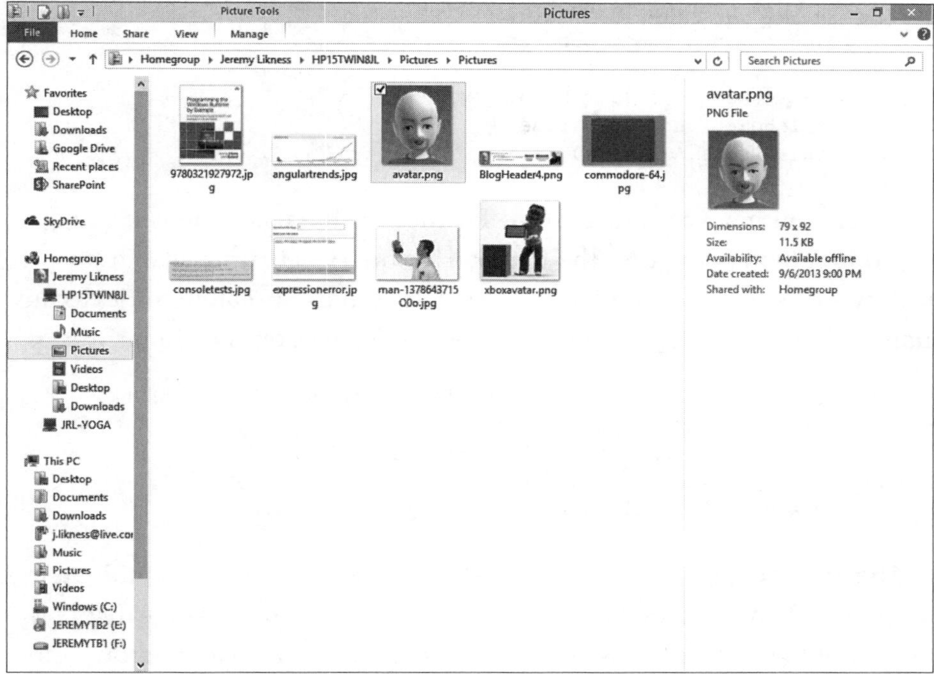

FIGURE 10.1 The HomeGroup network

The **HomeGroupExample** project for Chapter 10 demonstrates access to the HomeGroup. The first step is to declare your capabilities in the package manifest. You must have at least one of the available library capabilities (music, pictures, or videos) checked, or you will receive an access denied exception when you attempt to access the HomeGroup. Otherwise, you will have access only to the folder types that you specified capabilities for.

Use the `KnownFolders.HomeGroup` enumeration to access the HomeGroup network. The first set of folders you receive is mapped to the usernames of users currently participating in the HomeGroup. The following code in the `Initialize` method of the `ViewModel` class fetches the user-level folders:

```
var folders = await Windows.Storage.KnownFolders
    .HomeGroup.GetFoldersAsync();
```

The example project defines the `HomeGroupUser` class for user information and maps the `DisplayName` attribute of the folder to the username displayed.

```
foreach (var user in folders.Select(
    folder => new HomeGroupUser
{
        UserName = folder.DisplayName,
        IsHomeGroupUser = true
})) { this.Users.Add(user); }
```

When you have a StorageFolder instance for the user, you can use queries to iterate items within the folder. This query sets up a search for pictures with a known set of filename extensions and ultimately retrieves any shared photos that user is sharing across all devices on the HomeGroup.

```
var query = new QueryOptions(CommonFileQuery.OrderBySearchRank,
    new[] { ".jpg", ".png", ".bmp", ".gif" })
        { UserSearchFilter = "kind:picture" };
var files = await targetFolder
    .CreateFileQueryWithOptions(query).GetFilesAsync();
```

The app is designer-friendly and shows a sample image and title in the designer. When you run the app, you see either an error message displayed on a disabled button if the app cannot access a valid HomeGroup, or a list of buttons for each user on the HomeGroup. Tap the button to see the images that user is sharing. You can use similar functionality as covered in Chapter 4, "Data and Content," to access other folders and content types.

Connectivity and Data Plans

Windows Store apps can be connected in a number of ways. Although traditional wired connections (Ethernet LAN) and Wireless Fidelity (Wi-Fi) connections (also known as wireless local area connections, or WLAN) are still popular, many devices offer wireless wide area network (WWAN) connections over cellular technologies such as Global System for Mobile Communications (GSM) and Long Term Evolution (LTE). Many of these data plans have data limits and may charge for bandwidth usage. If users roam outside their regular coverage area, they could incur additional charges.

Windows Store apps should be aware of the type of connection they are using to access information over the Internet so they can implement specific behaviors that are suitable for the type of connection. An app might consider implementing this typical set of behaviors:

- **Offline**—The app cannot connect to the Internet and must rely on local cached data to function.
- **High Cost**—The app is connected to the Internet, but the data plan is either roaming, approaching a fixed data limit, or over the data limit and, therefore, might incur additional charges. The app should limit network activity to only extremely low bandwidth scenarios (such as loading a set of headers but deferring the details).
- **Conservative**—The app is connected to the Internet over a metered connection. Downloading data is fine but should be done only as needed and based on user-configurable preferences (the user must have a way to disable large downloads when the connection is metered). Lower-resolution images and lesser-bandwidth movies should be used when available.
- **Standard**—The app is connected to the Internet, and no charges appear to be associated with data usage; therefore, the application can download or upload data as needed.

The `Windows.Networking.Connectivity` namespace contains the APIs necessary to determine the types of connections that are available and examine data plans and usage. You interact with the `NetworkInformation` class to determine the available connections, the connection your app will use to access the Internet, and what type of connection is being used. The example app that demonstrates this API is called **NetworkInfoExample**; you can find it in the Chapter 10 solution folder.

Each network that your device either is currently connected to or has connected to in the past (as long as you did not ask Windows to forget the connection) has a `ConnectionProfile` instance associated with it. The `UpdateNetworkInformation` method in the `ViewModel` class in the `Data` folder demonstrates how to access this API. A simple call retrieves the full list of available profiles:

```
var profiles = NetworkInformation.GetConnectionProfiles();
```

You can iterate the various profiles and acquire information from each of them, but the most interesting profile is the one used to gain access to the Internet. You can use the `GetInternetConnectionProfile` call to get the profile associated with the active connection, if one exists. If the result is null, the user is not currently connected. In the example app, this call is used to get the identifier for the network adapter that is being used to connect and then select that connection from the list. If your connection is bridged for any reason (for example, you might be running Hyper-V virtual machines that use virtual adapters to connect to your wireless connection), the bridged connection might show up as the active connection instead of the connection you were expecting.

The `ConnectionProfile` has a name that matches what you see in the various network dialogs (either the list of available connections from the **Control Panel** or the list of networks in the **Networks** flyout accessed from the Charms bar). It indicates whether the network is a WLAN (wireless) or a WWAN (wide area network or cellular) connection. If it is neither, it is likely a wired Ethernet or Bluetooth connection.

You can quickly access information about the connected network adapter, as well as the security settings for the connection. For example, the wireless access point I run in my house uses RSNA-PSK authentication with CCMP encryption. You might have security settings available for both wired and wireless networks. The `FromConnectionProfile` method on the `ConnectionInfo` class demonstrates how these values are obtained.

```
if (profile.NetworkSecuritySettings != null)
{
    connectionInfo.AuthenticationType = profile
        .NetworkSecuritySettings.NetworkAuthenticationType.
➥ToString();
    connectionInfo.EncryptionType = profile
        .NetworkSecuritySettings.NetworkEncryptionType.ToString();
}
```

Other information is available through method calls. To get the signal strength from the connection (a value that ranges from 0 for no signal to 5 for maximum signal strength), you call the `GetSignalBars` method. The example app shows only four of five possible bars because it uses the built-in symbol library, and that provides only four bars.

```
connectionInfo.SignalBars = profile.GetSignalBars();
```

The main reason for examining the connection is likely to understand whether costs are associated with it. To find out, call the `GetConnectionCost` method. This returns a class that contains an enumeration and several flags. The enumeration provides you with details about how the connection is metered.

- **Unrestricted**—No costs are associated with data usage.
- **Fixed**—A data limit exists; until that limit is reached, usage is unrestricted.
- **Variable**—Data usage is charged on a per-byte basis.
- **Unknown**—No cost information is available for the connection.

Additional flags provide further insights into the current plan:

- **Roaming**—This flag is set when the user is outside the normal usage area. You can assume that additional charges will apply.
- **ApproachingDataLimit**—The plan has almost reached its limit; additional costs might be incurred.
- **OverDataLimit**—The plan has exceeded the data limit, and the user is likely being charged for any additional usage.

Use this information to strategize how you will access the Internet from your Windows Store app. When the type is fixed or variable, you should follow a conservative behavior. When the flags indicate that the connection is roaming or over the data limit, you should implement the high-cost behavior and allow the user to opt in to any data usage. Other scenarios can follow the standard or offline behavior, depending on the status of the connection.

If you need to find out more details about the plan, you can call the `GetDataPlanStatus` method, as shown in the `FromProfile` method on the `DataPlanInfo` class in the example app. The result gives you more details when available, including the data limit and how much has been used against the limit, the available speeds of the connection, and even when the next billing cycle begins so you know when the usage is reset.

You can also query for historical usage of any connection. The `GetNetworkUsageAsync` method enables you to specify a time range and a sample frequency (increments in minutes, hours, or days, or a total for the time period). Depending on how you call the method, you can get a list of `NetworkUsage` instances for each data sample. If you requested hourly samples, each instance represents a sample taken for a given hour. The instance contains the duration it represents, along with the bytes received and sent during that period. The `ConnectionInfo` class in the example app retrieves a total for the previous day:

```
var usage =
    await profile.GetNetworkUsageAsync(
        DateTimeOffset.Now.AddDays(-1),
        DateTimeOffset.Now,
        DataUsageGranularity.Total,
        new NetworkUsageStates { Roaming = TriStates.DoNotCare,
        Shared = TriStates.DoNotCare });
```

You might not sample data earlier than 60 days before the current date (about 2 months), and minute granularity is available for only the previous 2 hours. You can also specify what network states you want to sample. You can restrict the data to times when the connection was roaming or part of a shared connection, or indicate that you "do not care," as in the example code.

The advantage of many Windows 8.1 devices is that they are highly mobile. For this reason, it's common for the current active connection to change frequently. The user might be using a cellular connection and might come into range of a wireless connection that is lower cost, or the user might travel and switch to different connections. The `NetworkInformation` class raises an event when the current connection status changes. The `ViewModel` class in the example app registers for this event:

```
NetworkInformation.NetworkStatusChanged +=
    this.NetworkInformationNetworkStatusChanged;
```

The event itself does not provide other information. The typical practice is to query for the current Internet connection again to determine whether the app behavior should change. You can prompt the user or restrict data usage when you find that the user has roamed or moved from an unrestricted connection to a metered one. By default, Windows 8.1 prefers unrestricted networks over metered networks and automatically connects to the fastest available network in its category when multiple choices are available.

Sockets

Windows Store apps have the capability to communicate over lower-level networking protocols. The Windows Runtime provides built-in support for User Datagram Protocol (UDP),[2] Transmission Control Protocol (TCP),[3] Bluetooth RFCOMM,[4] and the recent HTML5 WebSocket Protocol.[5] Support for socket-based operations is provided through the types of the `Windows.Networking.Sockets` namespace. Sockets in general provide low-level network communications and enable real-time network notifications.

WebSockets

The WebSocket protocol was designed to be implemented in web browsers and web servers, and it is fully supported from Windows Store apps. Although it is part of the HTML5 group of specifications, it is an independent TCP protocol. Its main advantage is that it provides a way for the browser or Windows Store app to maintain a single connection with a server and send data both ways while keeping that connection open. The standard port for WebSockets is 80, the same one HTTP uses, which means it is less likely to be blocked by firewalls.

The **WebSocketsExamples** project for Chapter 10 demonstrates two APIs you can use from WinRT to take advantage of the WebSockets protocol. The example app leverages a server supplied by the WebSocket.org website that provides an "echo service." This service, when connected to,

---

[2]User Datagram Protocol, RFC 768, http://bit.ly/16TkVsS

[3]Transmission Control Protocol, RFC 793, http://bit.ly/HLcHtJ

[4]Bluetooth RFCOMM, http://bit.ly/1fu50ni

[5]WebSocket Protocol, RFC 6455

echoes back any data sent to it. WebSockets are accessed using a standard URI, as declared in `MainPage.xaml.cs`:

```
private readonly Uri echoService =
    new Uri("ws://echo.websocket.org", UriKind.Absolute);
```

The `MessageWebSocket` class is an abstraction of the protocol that focuses on sending simple messages. A message is either read or written in a single operation, instead of being streamed continuously. It is also the class you must use to support UTF8 messages; the stream-based API supports only binary (although you can encode and decode the binary to and from UTF8, the `MessageWebSocket` class provides native support for this). To use any socket type within a Windows Store app, you must enable a networking capability such as **Internet (Client)**.

The `ButtonBase_OnClick` method in the `MainPage.xaml.cs` file demonstrates how to use the `MessageWebSocket` class. After creating an instance of the class, set the type of the message (either binary or UTF8):

```
this.socket.Control.MessageType = SocketMessageType.Utf8;
```

You can also register for events that fire whenever a message is received and when the socket is closed. The socket uses underlying unmanaged resources, and you should dispose of it when you are done using it. The easiest way to do this is to call `Dispose` in the `Closed` event handler.

Initiate the connection by calling and waiting for `ConnectAsync` to complete:

```
await this.socket.ConnectAsync(echoService);
```

The example app accepts any message you type and sends it to the echo service. The message must be sent using the `OutputStream` property exposed by the socket. The easiest way to do this is to create an instance of a `DataWriter` to send the message. The `DataWriter` enables you to write various data types that it buffers until you call `StoreAsync`. This flushes the buffer to the underlying stream.

```
var writer = new DataWriter(this.socket.OutputStream);
writer.WriteString(this.Text.Text);
await writer.StoreAsync();
```

Not all error messages for the socket are mapped to .NET `Exception` class instances. Instead, you must inspect the `HResult` of the underlying exception to determine what went wrong. Fortunately, the `WebSocketError` class provides a static method that translates the result to the corresponding `WebErrorStatus` enumeration. The `ToErrorMessage` method returns a string with the original message and the enumeration value.

```
private static string ToErrorMessage(Exception ex)
{
    var status = WebSocketError.GetStatus(
        ex.GetBaseException().HResult);
    return string.Format("{0} ({1})", ex.Message, status);
}
```

The `MessageReceived` event is raised whenever a message is sent from the server to the client through the socket. In the example app, this should happen any time data is sent because the server echoes back the data. The event provides the socket that the information was received from with event arguments: You can inspect the message type (binary or UTF8) and open a reader or stream to access the message. In this example, the reader is set to use UFT8 encoding; then it obtains the message and displays it in the `SocketMessageReceived` event handler.

```
using (var reader = args.GetDataReader())
{
    reader.UnicodeEncoding = UnicodeEncoding.Utf8;
    var text = reader.ReadString(reader.UnconsumedBufferLength);
    this.Response.Text = text;
}
```

This is the simplest method for dealing with sockets that are designed to share messages. When you are using the socket to stream real-time information and you don't necessarily have simple messages, you might want to use the `StreamWebSocket` implementation instead. It provides a continuous two-way stream for sending and receiving information. The example app uses the same echo service to stream prime numbers and echo them back to the display when you click the **Start** button.

You create and connect to a `StreamWebSocket` the same way as with a `MessageWebSocket`. You can also register for the `Closed` event. Instead of sending and receiving messages, however, the stream version expects you to interface directly with the input and output streams provided by the socket. The app starts a long-running `Task` encapsulated in the `ComputePrimes` method. It is passed the `OutputStream` of the socket. It iterates through positive integers and writes out any that are computed to be primes; then it delays for 1 second:

```
if (IsPrime(x))
{
    var array = Encoding.UTF8.GetBytes(string.Format(" {0} ", x));
    await outputStream.WriteAsync(array.AsBuffer());
    await Task.Delay(TimeSpan.FromSeconds(1));
}
```

If the integer is not a prime, it delays for a millisecond just to prevent hogging the CPU. Another long-running task receives the echo. It allocates a buffer, waits for data to arrive in the stream, and then reads and decodes the data.

```
var bytesRead = await stream.ReadAsync(buffer, 0, buffer.Length);
if (bytesRead > 0)
{
    var text = Encoding.UTF8.GetString(buffer, 0, bytesRead);
    this.DispatchTextToPrimes(text);
}
```

This example also demonstrates that you can have multiple sockets open to the same server and port at once. You can run the example, click the button to start generating primes, and then use the message-based version to send and receive messages without interrupting the stream of prime numbers. Both methods for communicating with the socket simplify the amount of code you have to write by not worrying about the details of the underlying transport (TCP). When you need to manage a raw TCP connection, you can use the traditional sockets components.

UDP and TCP Sockets

UDP and TCP protocols have been around for decades. Many modern protocols, including HTTP, sit on top of these more low-level protocols (TCP is the transport used by both HTTP and the WebSocket protocol you learned to use in the previous section). Two main differences exist between UDP and TCP: UDP does not require a connection, and UDP does not require any special ordering of packets or chunks of data. As a result, TCP tends to be more reliable and useful for bidirectional communication, and UDP is used when faster transmission rates are required and the application understands how to deal with unordered data.

Examples of protocols that sit on top of UDP include Domain Name Service (DNS) and Simple Network Management Protocol (SNMP). Protocols that sit on top of TCP include HTTP and Simple Mail Transfer Protocol (SMTP). The UDP classes are all prefixed with `Datagram` and operate similarly to the TCP classes prefixed with `StreamSocket`. The API enables you to "connect" to either protocol and send or receive messages. This provides a consistent interface and approach to using each protocol. The main difference is that no specific "listener" service for the UDP implementation exists because a persistent connection is not needed. Instead, you simply create a socket, register for the event when a message is received, and then send data packets or process incoming data as needed.

The **SocketsGame** example provides a more comprehensive example of using a persistent TCP connection. Although the game starts a server to listen for incoming requests, it should be clear that you cannot use these types of connections for communication between Windows Store apps on the same machine. Network isolation prevents the loopback interface from allowing connections across processes. The only reason this works in the example project is that the client and server are hosted in the same process. The example should show how to spin up a server to listen when necessary (for example, the same type of connection can be used to host a service for a Bluetooth service that allows Bluetooth devices to connect), as well as act as a client for a server hosted on the Internet.

The game itself is a text-based adventure game. It creates a 10x10 matrix of rooms for 100 rooms total and randomly connects rooms and places trophies in the various rooms. The object of the game is to explore the rooms and collect trophies until all have been found. A rudimentary parser accepts commands such as "look," "get," "north," and "inventory." Instead of playing as a local game, however, the game is hosted on a socket; the app must connect as a client to issue commands and receive updates.

Two sockets are defined in `MainPage.xaml.cs`: a `StreamSocketListener`, which is the server that listens for and establishes connections to clients, and a StreamSocket, which emulates a client connecting to the server. The server provides several options to bind to a generic service and listen to all incoming connections, to bind to a specific address, or even to bind to a specific network adapter. The service name can be a local service name or a port, or it can remain empty to have a port assigned. If you are using the socket for Bluetooth (RFCOMM), use the Bluetooth service ID. In this example, the name is set to 21212 as a unique port for the game. Binding enables your app to use that specific port to listen for incoming requests. If another app has already bound to the specified service, an exception is thrown.

```
this.serverSocket = new StreamSocketListener();
this.serverSocket.ConnectionReceived +=
    this.ServerSocketConnectionReceived;
await this.serverSocket.BindServiceNameAsync(ServiceName);
```

As with Web Sockets, to understand errors thrown by the sockets API, use the GetStatus static method of the SocketError class, as shown in the GetErrorText method.

```
private static string GetErrorText(Exception ex)
{
    return string.Format("{0} ({1})", ex.Message,
        SocketError.GetStatus(ex.GetBaseException().HResult));
}
```

When a connection is received, the server creates a persistent writer and reader for the connection (note that this example uses exactly one client, so only one writer and reader are used—if you are building a server to manage multiple connections, you need to spin up a new reader and writer for each unique connection).

```
if (serverWriter == null)
{
    serverWriter = new DataWriter(args.Socket.OutputStream);
    serverReader = new DataReader(args.Socket.InputStream);
}
```

The listener for the socket goes into an infinite loop waiting for messages. As messages are received, they are passed to the parser to interact with the game world, and the result is written back to the client. To facilitate communication over the socket, the messages are written with a special format. The size of the string in bytes is sent ahead of the string itself so that the reader can allocate the appropriate buffer size to process the incoming message. The `SendString` method encodes the text and sends it over the socket.

```
writer.WriteUInt32(writer.MeasureString(text));
writer.WriteString(text);
await writer.StoreAsync();
```

Listing 10.1 shows the `GetStringFromReader` method that receives the incoming data. It loads enough data to constitute an unsigned integer, processes the integer, and finally loads enough data to create a string based on the size that was passed in.

LISTING 10.1 Reading a String from the TCP Socket

```
private static async Task<string> GetStringFromReader(
    IDataReader reader)
{

    var sizeFieldCount = await reader.LoadAsync(sizeof(uint));
    if (sizeFieldCount != sizeof(uint))
    {
        return string.Empty;
    }
    var stringLength = reader.ReadUInt32();
    var actualStringLength = await reader.LoadAsync(stringLength);
    if (stringLength != actualStringLength)
    {
        return string.Empty;
    }
    var data = reader.ReadString(actualStringLength);
    return data;
}
```

Just as the server goes into an infinite loop after a connection is received, waits for instructions, and then returns a response, the client also starts a long-running task. On the UI thread, the `Go_OnClick` method is called whenever the user clicks the button to send the next command. The click handler simply sends the command to the socket and then forgets about it. The long-running `ClientListener` method waits to get the data from the server and then writes it for the end user to see.

Figure 10.2 shows a game in progress. At the top, you can see the server messages that involve receiving the incoming connection, receiving commands, and sending responses. The bottom is the client console for game play; it shows all the responses from the server and provides an input box for the user to type and send commands.

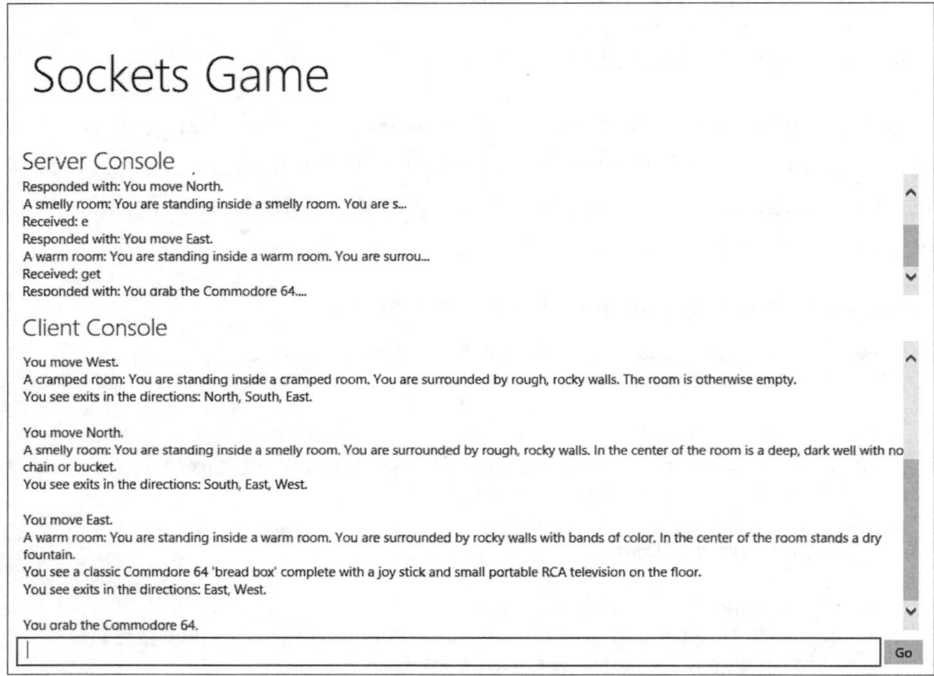

FIGURE 10.2 The example game played over a TCP socket

The provided example handles both client and server aspects for TCP connections. The RFCOMM for Bluetooth uses the same classes. Although UDP uses a different set of classes, the implementation is similar—the only difference is that you don't create a persistent listener for managing connections because the protocol is stateless.

Proximity (Near Field Communications)

Near Field Communications (NFC[6]) is a set of standards based on Radio-Frequency Identification (RFID) standards for smartphones, tablets, smart tags, and other devices to establish communications in extremely close situations (less than a few inches difference). Two main NFC scenarios exist. The first is a tap gesture for a short transmission of information, such as contact information, a URL, or a "smart poster." The second is a similar gesture used to create a handshake between two devices so they can establish a peer-to-peer connection over wireless to exchange large amounts of information.

NFC not only operates over extremely short distances, but it also has a fairly slow transfer rate, with theoretical speeds between 50 and 100 bytes per second. For this reason, it is useful for exchanging only a small amount of information, unless you use the NFC tap to establish a more persistent connection over a longer range and using faster technology, including Bluetooth, Wi-Fi, and Wi-Fi Direct. The WinRT API fully supports both of these scenarios.

NFC-Only Scenarios

When you exchange information via NFC, you must either send or receive a message encoded in the NFC Data Exchange Format (NDEF). This is a lightweight, platform-independent binary format for exchanging messages. The message allows one or more specific payloads (referred to as NDEF records) to be sent in a single package. Windows provides built-in support for a set of proprietary NDEF records that Windows 8.1 and Windows Phone devices can exchange. You can also format and exchange other types of records that target other platforms or are platform-independent by either building your own payload or using an open source library such as the NDEF Library for Proximity APIs that is available as a NuGet package.[7]

---

[6]Near Field Communication Technical Specifications, http://bit.ly/HQSnXA

[7]NuGet package for NDEF Library for Proximity APIs, http://bit.ly/1avcmFo

The **ProximityExample** project provides some examples of using the Proximity APIs defined in the `Windows.Networking.Proximity` namespace. The `ProximityDevice` class provides the simplest API to use and focuses specifically on short-range, short-duration NFC scenarios. To see whether the system has a proximity device available, simply call the `GetDefault` static method, shown in the constructor of the `ViewModel` class. Be sure to declare the **Proximity** capability in the application's manifest.

```
this.proximityDevice = ProximityDevice.GetDefault();
```

The call returns null when a device is not present. If this is the case on your machine, you will not be able to take advantage of NFC exchanges and gestures, but you may still be able to create peer-to-peer connections using Bluetooth, Wi-Fi, or Wi-Fi Direct. You learn more about that in a later section. The proximity device exposes properties for its unique identifier, the maximum number of bytes it can send in a single message, and the bits per second it is capable of transmitting or receiving. You can also register for events that fire when another proximity device comes within range:

```
this.proximityDevice.DeviceArrived +=
    this.ProximityDeviceDeviceArrived;
this.proximityDevice.DeviceDeparted +=
    this.ProximityDeviceDeviceDeparted;
```

The events are purely informational and do not provide any specific information. The `ProximityDevice` parameter of the handler is a reference back to the device that detected the event, which, in most cases, is the default device referenced in the constructor. Other classes exist for enumerating multiple proximity devices, in the rare case that the machine has multiple ones installed. This is a rare scenario because one NFC device is usually sufficient.

An easy way to share information with another NFC device is to use the `PublishMessage` method on the `ProximityDevice` class. This method is useful for sharing simple string data with other Windows or Windows Phone devices. It takes two parameters: the message type and the message itself. The message type is a unique identifier that enables other devices to determine how to handle the message. The message type always starts with a protocol, followed by a dot, followed by whatever custom identifier you prefer. In this case, the protocol must always be Windows. (The simple code for publishing and subscribing in this section is shared here for reference purposes but is not part of a specific example project.)

```
var publishedMessageId =
    proximityDevice.PublishMessage("Windows.WinRTByExampleMessage",
    "This is a simple message.");
```

The publication is not a transient event. The message will be available until you explicitly stop publishing, so multiple NFC devices over time can connect and subscribe for that message to receive it. To stop publishing, you call the `StopPublishingMethod` on the `ProximityDevice`.

```
proximityDevice.StopPublishingMessage(publishedMessageId);
```

If you want to know when the message has been transmitted, you can pass a `MessageTransmittedHandler` as a third parameter when you publish. The handler is called with the proximity device and the identifier for the message. You can use this to log that the message was transmitted, or even unsubscribe in the callback to ensure that the message is sent only once.

```
private void MessagePublished(ProximityDevice sender,
    long messageId)
{
    proximityDevice.StopPublishingMessage(messageId);
}
```

To receive a message, you use the `SubscribeForMessage` method on the `ProximityDevice` class. You do not have to wait for a device to arrive or depart before you subscribe, and the subscription is valid for any device that publishes that particular message type. The subscription includes a handler that is called whenever the message is received, and it is provided a unique identifier that you can use to unsubscribe when you want to stop receiving the message.

```
var subscribedMessageId =
    proximityDevice.SubscribeForMessage("Windows.
➥WinRTByExampleMessage",
    MessageReceived);
```

The method to receive the message is passed the `ProximityDevice` and a `ProximityMessage`. The message includes the data as a buffer, the data as a string, and the subscription ID, in case you want to use that to stop subscribing.

```
private void MessageReceived(ProximityDevice device,
    ProximityMessage message)
{
    var messageText = message.DataAsString;
    device.StopSubscribingForMessage(subscribedMessageId);
}
```

The subscription method enables you to subscribe to any type of message. For messages that use non-Windows protocols, you need to decode the message. For example, the message type `WindowsUri` provides a URI, but you must first decode it from UTF16LE:

```
void messageReceivedHandler(ProximityDevice device,
    ProximityMessage message)
{
    var buffer = message.Data.ToArray();
    var uri = Encoding.Unicode.GetString(buffer, 0, buffer.Length);
}
```

Note that some devices, such as the Windows Phone, handle URIs at the operating system level. In other words, you cannot override the default behavior. The OS itself intercepts the NFC tag and opens the corresponding program. The program depends on the protocol. HTTP launches the Internet Explorer browser and navigates to the encoded web page, and a `mailto` protocol results in the default mail program being launched.

You can use the NFC API to write to smart tags, or special tags that use induction to store and publish information. Smart tags have varying capacities, depending on the manufacturer. Publishing to a smart tag always overwrites the data, and most smart tags have a lifetime of several hundred thousand writes. To get the capacity of a smart tag, you can subscribe to the `WriteableTag` message. This transmits an `Int32` message that contains the capacity of the tag.

```
private void MessageReceived(ProximityDevice device,
    ProximityMessage message)
{
    var capacity = System.BitConvert.ToInt32(
        message.Data.ToArray(), 0);
}
```

Table 10.1 lists the various message types you can subscribe to.

TABLE 10.1 Common NFC Message Protocols

Protocol	Description
`Windows`	Consists of raw binary data.
`Windows.*`	Provides a custom string type proprietary to Windows, where * represents a custom type.
`WindowsUri`	Consists of a UTF-16LE encoded URI string. Note that the operating system shell intercepts these messages and marshals them to the appropriate protocol handler.
`WindowsMime`	Contains a specific MIME type–like image/jpeg for a bitmap image.
`WriteableTag`	Published by smart tags when they come within range of reading or writing. Contains the capacity of the smart tag in bytes.
`NDEF[:*]`	Consists of formatted NDEF records. Third-party libraries are available to easily encode and decode these record formats.

You also can publish messages for cross-platform compatibility or for the purpose of writing to smart tags. Instead of using the proprietary `PublishMessage` method, use the `PublishBinaryMessage` method. You can use this method to publish messages to other NFC devices, but it is also useful for writing messages to smart tags. The following code snippet encodes the URI to launch Skype and calls the echo service on a Windows or Windows Phone device.

```
var uri = new Uri("skype:echo123?call");
var buffer = Encoding.Unicode.GetBytes(uri.ToString());
var publishId = device.PublishBinaryMessage("WindowsUri:WriteTag",
    buffer.AsBuffer());
```

Table 10.2 lists various protocols you can use when writing messages to tags.

TABLE 10.2 Message Protocols for Writing to Smart Tags

Protocol	Description
`Windows:WriteTag`	Publish binary data to a static smart tag
`WindowsUri:WriteTag`	Write a URI to a static smart tag
`LaunchApp:WriteTag`	Write a tag that launches an app with specific launch parameters
`NDEF:WriteTag`	Write a cross-platform message using the NDEF format

To write a tag that launches an app, use the `LaunchApp:WriteTag` format; then provide a tab-delimited list that starts with the text to pass in as an argument and then includes pairs of platforms and application names. You can find the application name for a Windows 8.1 application in the application manifest. It is in the format of the **Package family name** (from the **Packaging** tab) and an exclamation mark. The following tag passes an argument named `id` with a value of `1` to both the Windows 8.1 **ProximityExample** app and a fictional app on Windows Phone 8 (the application name on Windows Phone is simply the GUID for the application ID).

```
var launchTag =
    "id=1\tWindows\tWinRTByExampleProximityExample_req6rhny9ggkj! " +
    "ProximityExample.App\tWindowsPhone\t{063e933a-fc8e-4f0c" +
    "-8395-ab0e84725f0f}";
```

If the app is present on the target device, it is launched with the arguments passed (the user is always prompted to opt in for the launch whenever this type of tag is encountered). If the app is not present, the device automatically takes the user to the app's entry in the Windows Store. This makes the tag extremely useful: If you pass out smart tags with the encoding, users can easily discover and install your app, as well as subsequently launch it.

In this section, you learned ways to publish small messages that can be sent to other devices or encoded in smart tags. You also learned how to subscribe to and receive these messages. I mentioned earlier a way to share much more information than permitted by the limited bandwidth and speed of the NFC protocol. In this next section, you explore the tap-to-connect scenario that uses NFC to establish a persistent peer-to-peer connection for exchanging information.

Tap-to-Connect Scenarios

The `PeerFinder` class enables you to find and interact with other devices capable of peer-to-peer communications. Although a common use case is through NFC, you can also use Bluetooth and Wi-Fi Direct to locate and communicate with peers. The WinRT API abstracts these decisions from you and enables you to focus on the actual process of locating a peer and establishing a socket so that you can stream data back and forth.

Even if you don't have a proximity device, chances are good that you can take advantage of the **ProximityExample** sample app to create a peer-to-peer connection. That's because the WinRT API supports a browse scenario using Wi-Fi Direct, a technology that enables peer-to-peer wireless connections between devices that exists in most modern radios. Using the browsing scenario, you can install the app on two different devices and use them to discover each other.

The proximity APIs support finding peers running the same application. The application is defined by the package family, a unique identifier for your app that is shared across target platforms. For this reason, your app on a machine running Windows 8.1 can easily connect to the same app on a machine running Windows RT. You can also extend the peer to find instances of your app on other platforms, such as Windows Phone and Android. The `PeerFinder` class contains a dictionary named `AlternateIdentities` that hosts a list of platforms and application identifiers. In the previous section, you learned how to create a tag that launches the application and can contain multiple platforms and identities. You can add the same identifier to recognize that app as a peer like this:

```
PeerFinder.AlternateIdentities.Add("WindowsPhone",
    "{063e933a-fc8e-4f0c-8395-ab0e84725f0f}");
```

You can discover and negotiate the peer connection either through an NFC tap gesture or by browsing Wi-Fi Direct. After the devices recognize each other and initiate the handshake, Windows tries to connect simultaneously using infrastructure (wireless or wired), Wi-Fi Direct, and Bluetooth. It uses whichever connection completes first (most likely, Bluetooth, when available) and passes the connection as an active socket to your app. You can restrict which connection types to allow by setting the static `AllowBluetooth`, `AllowInfrastructure`, and `AllowWiFiDirect` properties on the `PeerFinder` class.

The `PeerSocket` class in the example app provides a convenient way to manage a persistent socket connection. It takes a `StreamSocket` in the constructor and immediately creates a persistent reader and writer to interact with it.

```
public PeerSocket(StreamSocket socket)
{
    this.socket = socket;
    reader = new DataReader(socket.InputStream);
    writer = new DataWriter(socket.OutputStream);
}
```

It exposes a write method that uses the `DataWriter` to send a message to the socket and starts an infinite loop that runs on a background thread to listen for incoming messages. When it receives an incoming message, it raises an event so the app can register for the event, receive the message, and process it (in the case of the sample app, by marshalling it to the UI thread and showing it on the display). It also raises an error event whenever it encounters an error and disposes of both the reader and the writer when its own `Dispose` method is called.

To begin the process of connecting with a peer, you must first set your app to advertise. This broadcasts its identity over Wi-Fi Direct and makes it available for tap gestures if a proximity device is present. The Wi-Fi Direct mode is referred to as a browsed connect, and the NFC mode is referred to as a triggered connect. The `PeerFinder` class is instructed to begin advertising in the `StartPeerFinder` method on the `ViewModel` class.

First, the app registers to two events: the `TriggeredConnectionStateChanged` that is raised when an NFC tap gesture is received, and the `ConnectionRequested` event that is raised when another device browses your device and requests a connection.

```
PeerFinder.TriggeredConnectionStateChanged +=
    this.PeerFinderTriggeredConnectionStateChanged;
PeerFinder.ConnectionRequested +=
    this.PeerFinderConnectionRequested;
```

Next, the role is set. Three possible roles exist. In the `Peer` role (included in the example app), two apps can connect with each other and communicate as peers. In a client/server scenario, one app can serve as the host and must set the `Host` role; then up to four other apps can connect using the `Client` role. Note that only `Peer` roles can browse to each other. The `Host` role can browse only `Client` roles, and vice versa.

```
PeerFinder.Role = PeerRole.Peer;
```

Finally, some discovery text is set. This is additional text you can share, such as an application name, an invitation to connect, information about the host system, or any other data up to 240 bytes in length. This data is broadcast and can be displayed when browsing. After the data is set, the `PeerFinder` starts advertising when you call the `Start` method.

```
PeerFinder.Role = PeerRole.Peer;
PeerFinder.DiscoveryData = Encoding.UTF8.GetBytes(
    DiscoveryText).AsBuffer();
PeerFinder.Start();
```

When both peers have started advertising, one of two scenarios can take place. The first is the NFC tap-to-connect scenario. When the proximity devices are tapped together, the `TriggeredConnectionStateChanged` event is raised. This event fires multiple times as the devices come within range and negotiate a connection.

The event handler for the triggered connection receives a `State` property of the type `TriggeredConnectState` (an enumeration). The handler on the viewmodel is called `PeerFinderTriggeredConnectionStateChanged`. The `Listening` state indicates that the proximity device is waiting for a tap. When the state is `PeerFound` or `Connecting`, the connection is being established and the handler simply updates the status for the user. If the connection fails, a

`Failed` state is passed. The `Completed` state indicates success, and the arguments contain a `Socket` property with the active socket between the two devices:

```
case TriggeredConnectState.Completed:
    this.RouteToUiThread(() =>{this.IsConnecting = false;});
    this.InitializeSocket(args.Socket);
    break;
```

The `InitializeSocket` method sets up an instance of the `PeerSocket` to handle further communications. A state of `Canceled` means the connection was broken for some reason—for example, the devices moved out of range or a user intervention occurred.

The browse scenario starts when you request a list of available peers. The `BrowseCommand` method on the viewmodel calls the `FindAllPeersAsync` method and then loads the results to the list of available peers.

```
var peers = await PeerFinder.FindAllPeersAsync();
```

The user can then select a peer and request a connection. The connection is initiated in the `ConnectCommand` method.

```
var socket = await PeerFinder.ConnectAsync(
    this.SelectedPeer.Information);
this.InitializeSocket(socket);
```

Note that the end result is the same as the triggered connection scenario: A socket is obtained and initialized to establish communications. The mode of the connection is transparent to your app, and there is no way to determine whether the connection was made using Bluetooth, infrastructure, or Wi-Fi Direct (unless you have restricted the allowable connection types to a single mode).

If your device is running a version of the app and the connection is requested from another device, a `ConnectionRequested` event is raised. The viewmodel handles this in the `PeerFinderConnectionRequested` method. In this scenario, you typically prompt the user to confirm that he or she wants to accept the request, and then either ignore the request or connect. The sample app automatically initiates the connection. The method to connect is identical for the host, client, or peer; the only difference is that, instead of passing a peer from a list of selections, the peer requesting the connection is passed as arguments to the event.

```
var socket = await PeerFinder.ConnectAsync(args.PeerInformation);
this.InitializeSocket(socket);
```

If the call succeeds for both peers, a connection is established and duplex communication can be initiated. You can transmit anything over the binary socket—from images, to streaming videos, to text or documents. The sample app simplifies the connection by transmitting only text. The text you enter is sent to the peer via the output stream of the socket, and any text received raises an event that is marshalled to the UI.

To use the sample program, install it on two Windows 8.1 devices that support Wi-Fi Direct or have proximity devices. The easiest way is to build and deploy the source, but you can also use the **Store** option on the **Project Properties** menu to create a side load package. Copy the package to a thumb drive and execute the included PowerShell script to install it on the other device.

Run the app on both devices. You must start advertising on both devices to establish a connection. After you've started advertising, either tap the devices or tap **Browse** to use Wi-Fi Direct. If you browse, select another machine and tap **Connect**. When the connection is established, via either NFC tap or browsing, you can begin to send messages between the two peers (see Figure 10.3).

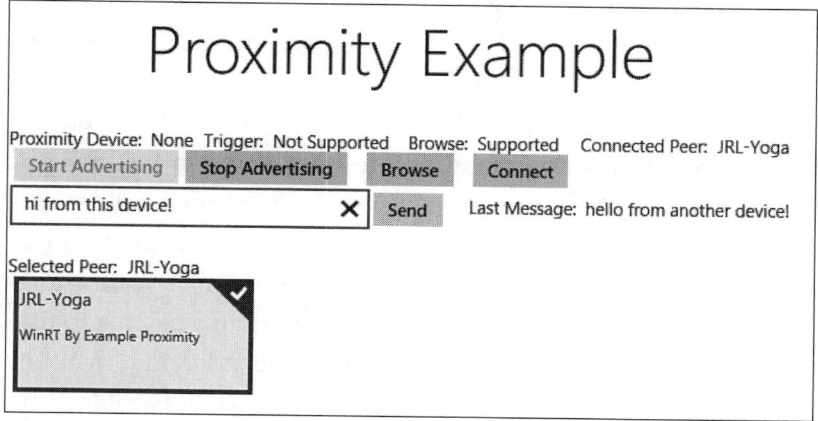

FIGURE 10.3 Example of communicating between peers using the Proximity API

Numerous possibilities exist for taking advantage of the peer connection. You can use it to share documents or pictures between devices, archive data, create a chat session, or even share game state in a multiplayer game. The API handles all the necessary low-level handshakes and connectivity so that you can focus on the implementation of your application without worrying about the underlying NFC protocol or even whether the devices connect over Bluetooth or Wi-Fi Direct. The Proximity API is nearly identical on the Windows Phone, making it possible to build apps that span devices and create a truly continuous user experience among Windows PCs, tablets, and phones.

Background Transfers

Many apps must download large amounts of information to present to the user. For example, an app focused on providing instructional videos might need to download new videos from the Internet. These files could be hundreds of megabytes or even gigabytes in size. Although the `HttpClient` class is capable of retrieving files of this size, you must also take into account the application lifecycle.

As you learned in Chapter 2, "Windows Store Apps and WinRT Components," whenever the user moves your app into the background, your app can be suspended or frozen, essentially stopping any downloads dead in their tracks. In some scenarios, the app might even be terminated, forcing you to create a new instance of the class in an attempt to start the download again. Fortunately, WinRT provides a way to handle this specific scenario using a background task.

You learn more about background tasks in Chapter 15. This chapter introduces a specific API for downloading files that exists in the `Windows.Networking.BackgroundTransfer` namespace. The API is defined for several reasons. The most obvious is to enable your app to download files without interruption. These download tasks should continue even if your app is swapped to the background or terminated. You should also be able to discover any existing downloads when your app is launched again, to either continue to download or cancel them as needed. The extra advantage this API provides is a power-friendly and cost-aware means of transferring files. The API is architected to handle the download in a way that maximizes battery life and can pause the transfer when the user switches to a metered network. These features combine to provide the best mobile experience possible for the device user.

The reference project **TapAndGoProximityNetworking** serves two purposes. As a follow-up to the previous section about the Proximity API, it downloads an excellent video presentation by my colleague Jeff Prosise from Microsoft's Channel 9 website. His talk, given at TechEd Europe in 2013, covers the Proximity API and provides working examples of encoding tags, reading tags, and tapping to share data between multiple devices. It is a great way to reinforce the information you learned in the previous section. The project downloads a high-fidelity version of the video that is almost 600MB in size. The second purpose is to demonstrate the background transfer capabilities.

To simplify the example, I placed all the code in the code-behind of the main page to simply download a file and then play it using the file launcher. The associated video player should pick up the file and begin playing the presentation after it is downloaded. The app first checks to see whether the movie already exists, based on a specific name in your video library. The **Video Library** capability must be enabled in the manifest for this to work. If the video exists, you are given the option to delete it to start over or launch it.

To start a background transfer, you need only two pieces of information: the URI of the resource to download and a file to download it to. The example app encodes the URI to the video download and creates a file with the name `TapAndGo_Prosise.mp4` in your video library in the `DownloadOnClick` method.

```
var source = new Uri(DownloadUri, UriKind.Absolute);
var destinationFile =
    await KnownFolders.VideosLibrary.CreateFileAsync(
        LocalName, CreationCollisionOption.ReplaceExisting);
```

An instance of the `BackgroundDownloader` class is created, and the `CreateDownload` method is called with the source and destination.

```
var downloader = new BackgroundDownloader();
download = downloader.CreateDownload(source, destinationFile);
```

You can provide a callback to receive updates as the download progresses. This is done by creating an instance of the `Progress` class of type `DownloadOperation` and passing the callback handler, as shown in the `DownloadProgressAsync` method.

```
var progress = new Progress<DownloadOperation>(UpdateProgress);
```

The download is then kicked off and cast to a `Task` with a cancellation token and the callback for progress.

```
await this.download.StartAsync().AsTask(cts.Token, progress);
```

The download is now kicked off and continues to execute even after your app terminates. If it encounters an error, it updates the error state for your app to query when the app is launched again. While the app is running, it provides progress updates, as shown in the `UpdateFromProgress` method.

```
BytesReceived.Text = download.Progress.BytesReceived.ToString();
TotalBytes.Text = download.Progress.TotalBytesToReceive.ToString();
```

Table 10.3 lists the possible statuses available via the `Progress.Status` enumeration. Use this to determine the state of the download and take appropriate action (in the example app, it is used to enable or disable the Pause and Resume buttons).

TABLE 10.3 `BackgroundTransferStatus` Enumeration

Status	Description
`Idle`	The application is idle (the download is still active).
`Running`	The transfer is in progress.
`PausedByApplication`	The app has paused the download by calling the `Pause` method on the `DownloadOperation`.
`PausedCostedNetwork`	The user transitioned to a metered network, and the download has been paused to avoid additional cost. It will resume when the user returns to a nonmetered network.

Status	Description
`PausedNoNetwork`	The user has lost network connectivity. The download will resume when Internet connectivity is restored.
`Completed`	The operation successfully completed.
`Canceled`	The operation was canceled.
`Error`	An error was encountered.

While the download is running, you can perform a number of actions. For example, you can call the `Pause` method on the `DownloadOperation` to temporarily pause the download. After it is paused, you can call `Resume` to continue the download. Calling `Pause` twice in a row or calling `Resume` before `Pause` results in an exception, so always keep track of or check the current status. If you passed a cancellation token to the task, you can also call `Cancel` on the token source to abort the download.

If the download completes while your app is still running, it returns control after `await` of the `StartAsync` call. The example app disposes of the cancellation token and then launches the video. If your app is terminated or exits before the download is finished, it will continue in the background. When the app is launched again, you can check for existing transfers, as the `CheckState` method shows.

```
var downloads = await BackgroundDownloader
    .GetCurrentDownloadsAsync();
```

An entry for the download exists whether it is still downloading or it completed when your app was not running. Either way, you can obtain the reference to the download, query the status, or attach to receive updates. The sample app always reattaches to update the status. If the download has completed, the call to `AttachAsync` returns immediately; otherwise, it continues the same way the call to `StartAsync` worked.

```
await this.download.AttachAsync().AsTask(cts.Token, progress);
```

To test the app, compile, deploy, and run it. Tap the Download button. You then see a status similar to Figure 10.4. You can pause, resume, or cancel the download. After the download has begun, close the app by stopping it if you are running through the debugger or by pressing **Alt+F4**. You can navigate to the video library and refresh the file list to verify that the download is still running. Start the app again; it should return to the progress display and begin showing you the current progress. If you let the download finish, the app automatically launches the video and closes itself.

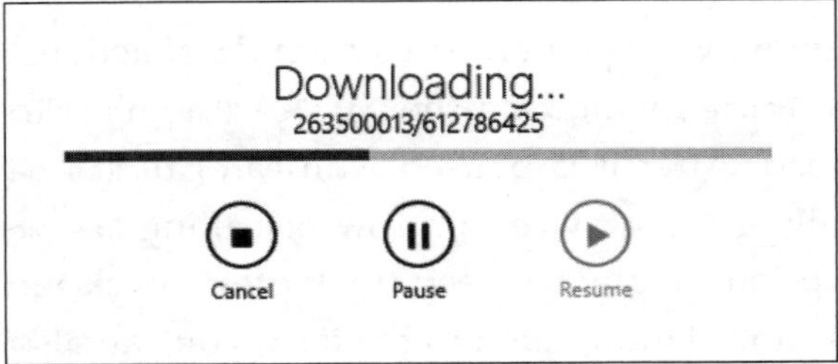

FIGURE 10.4 The download progress

The transfer API enables you to launch multiple downloads and keep track of each download individually. You can also group downloads and perform various tasks on the group. In addition, you can set a priority for the download and even request that the download run unconstrained so that it happens more quickly. This prompts the user and also can affect battery life and quality of the user experience. You learn more about the various background APIs in Chapter 15.

Summary

In this chapter, you learned how to use advanced features of the `HttpClient`. You used the Windows 8.1 seamless integration of HomeGroup technology to enumerate resources on your home network and then queried network information to determine what type of connection was active and see whether it was a metered plan. You leveraged the Sockets APIs to transfer messages and packets of data between a client and a server. You learned how to use NFC to transmit short, fast messages; subscribe to messages; and write data to smart tags. The APIs also enable a scenario to tap and create a persistent connection over your wired or wireless infrastructure, Bluetooth, or Wi-Fi Direct. Finally, the background transfer API enabled an app to download a large video resource even when it wasn't running.

In Chapter 11, "Windows Charms Integration," you learn more about the special icons that appear on the right side of your monitor when you swipe or hold down **Windows+C**. These icons, called charms, provide a special way for your app to integrate with the OS and communicate with other apps. Using charms enables scenarios such as streaming media to a projector, using one app to take notes and then sending those notes to another app to post them online, or accessing the specific settings of various apps in a consistent way.

11

Windows Charms Integration

THE WINDOWS RUNTIME PROVIDES THE OPPORTUNITY TO ENHANCE THE user experience an app running in Windows 8.1 offers, to include participation in several common Windows activities. Not only can this greatly enhance the overall usefulness of an app, but it also helps make common functionality more familiar and more discoverable for an app's users: Over time, they will expect to find certain features exposed by the same Windows interactions instead of seeing them implemented piecemeal in different ways across different applications.

One of the places you can find this kind of common functionality is the Windows Charms. The Windows Charms are a set of Windows-provided controls that appear along the right edge of the screen in response to user actions. These actions include a swipe gesture from the right edge of the screen into the screen area when the screen is touch-enabled, moving a connected mouse into the upper- or lower-right corners of the screen, or pressing the **Windows+C** hotkey combination on the keyboard. The buttons on the Windows Charm bar enable users to perform searches, share content, bring up the Start page, interact with devices connected to their machines, and update system or application settings. Apps can use the Windows Runtime APIs related to the Charms to define how content is shared either to or from other apps, to stream media to other devices on the network, to provide printing functionality, and to provide custom user interfaces where users can alter app settings. Through integration with the Charms, apps can expose several powerful features to their users.

The Settings Charm provides a common location where an app's settings must be located. Apps use the Windows Runtime APIs to indicate custom entries that should be listed in the Settings Charm Panel, alongside the entries that Windows itself provides for each app.

The functionality the Share Charm exposes can most conveniently be thought of as an enhanced version of the app-to-app data sharing that has previously been done through the Windows clipboard. Apps declare their intention and availability to integrate with the Share Charm. When the Charm is invoked, Windows works with APIs surfaced by the Windows Runtime to first broker the coordination of finding apps installed on the system that are available to receive the information that is being provided, and then actually manage the data exchange process after a receiving app has been selected.

With the Devices Charm, apps can use the Windows Runtime to indicate that they are able to stream image, audio, or video information to other available PCs or devices on the network that support Play To. Users can select the Play entry in the Devices Charm's panel, which then calls into the running app to coordinate the selected playback. Additionally, apps that support printing can use the Windows Runtime to declare their intent to do so, and users can use the Print entry displayed by the Devices Charm.[1]

> **NOTE**
>
> Windows 8.0 included the capability for apps to integrate with the Search Charm, to provide a centralized location for in-app search functionality. In addition to the default action of performing a system search, users could bring up the Search Charm and select an app to search for the words they entered, launching the app if necessary. Implementing search in this fashion was encouraged as a way to increase app visibility and extend an app's usefulness. Windows 8.1 changed this. The Search Charm functionality now focuses more

[1]Chapter 14, "Printers and Scanners," covers printing.

> on providing rich search results gathered from the system's apps and content, as well as integrated web search results from Bing. (In some select cases, a Microsoft-curated set of apps do still participate in the Search implementation.) As part of this change, the current guidance for implementing in-app search is to use on-canvas controls, including the new Search control that Chapter 2, "Windows Store Apps and WinRT Components," covered.

Displaying App Settings

The first Windows Charm integration point to discuss here is the Settings Charm. Nearly every app will likely include some kind of content for this Charm. The Settings Charm integration addresses a pervasive problem with Windows desktop applications: Settings are scattered throughout different user interface and menu locations. The Settings Charm provides a unique and consistent location for users to access any application settings. This use of a common location for app settings is actually reinforced in a couple ways. All apps are automatically provided with a Permissions entry in the Settings panel, which lists any capabilities that the app's manifest selections indicate. Any system-provided permissions that the user has opted into, such as use of the webcam and microphone, include entries in this panel that give users an opportunity to later retract their approval. Additionally, apps that are submitted and subsequently obtained through the Windows Store automatically include a Rate & Review entry that links to the Windows Store app and initiates the process of submitting a review for the chosen app. Also, to be published in the Windows Store, any app that is capable of transmitting data must provide access through the Settings Charm to a privacy policy explaining how that data will be used, stored, and shared. This content either can be included within a Settings panel itself or can be a link within the app to a website that contains the information. The same privacy policy must also be available through the app's Description content in the Windows Store.

The Settings Example

The **ShareTargetExample** project illustrates working with the Settings Charm. As the upcoming "Sharing" section explains in more detail, this app includes the capability to select between two different approaches to display data shared to the app. The Sharing Settings option in the Settings panel shows the setting that determines which panels display during sharing. The user interface also includes a `ListView` that enables a user to use drag and drop to indicate their preferred order for the relative priority of the data formats being shared. The order established in this list determines the priority for selecting the data format to display when the single-item Sharing panel is shown.

The same app also includes an About panel in the app settings. This entry displays an otherwise simple Settings panel that includes some information about the app itself, as well as a link to invoke the default web browser to open the app's Codeplex page.

Adding Settings Entries

When a user brings up the Settings Charm either from the Windows Charm bar or by pressing the **Windows+I** key combination, Windows tries to send a `CommandsRequested` event to the current app. Your app can opt to provide entries in the Settings panel that the Charm brings up by subscribing to this event and providing content in the `ApplicationCommands` collection in the event argument's `Request` parameter. The event subscription is usually handled in the `App` object itself, within the `OnWindowCreated` override; it involves retrieving the `SettingsPane` object for the current view and then setting a handler for that object's event, as the following code shows:

```
SettingsPane.GetForCurrentView().CommandsRequested
    += OnSettingsCommandsRequested;
```

When the event handler is invoked, entries for the Settings panel are provided by defining `SettingsCommand` objects, including an ID for the command, the label to display for it in the Settings Pane, and a callback to be invoked when the item is selected. These items are then added to the previously mentioned `ApplicationCommands` collection, which you can access through the provided event arguments. Listing 11.1 shows the process for including the Sharing Settings and About commands.

LISTING 11.1 Adding Sharing Pane Content

```
var settingsCommand = new SettingsCommand("sharingSettings",
    "Sharing Settings", ShowSettingsFlyoutHandler);
args.Request.ApplicationCommands.Add(settingsCommand);

var aboutCommand = new SettingsCommand("aboutSettings",
    "About", ShowAboutFlyoutHandler);
args.Request.ApplicationCommands.Add(aboutCommand);
```

The callbacks' responsibility is to display the settings user interface. Although in some rare cases displaying an entire page for settings information might be appropriate, usually the information is gathered within a control that is integrated into the Settings panel itself. Using the `SettingsFlyout` control greatly simplifies this process. To use this control, add a new Settings Flyout page to your project in Visual Studio by opening the **Project** menu and selecting **Add New Item**, or alternately right-clicking on your project in the **Solution Explorer** and selecting **Add** and then **New Item** from the context menus. In the Add New Item dialog, locate and select the **Settings Flyout** template. Give the flyout a name and press the Add button to add the new control to your project. After you have defined the contents and behavior for the control depending on your applications' needs, you can instruct the flyout to display as part of the Settings panel by calling its Show method:

```
var flyout = new SharingSettingsFlyout();
flyout.Show();
```

Settings panels in Windows 8.1 are expected to exhibit "soft-dismiss" behaviors, in which clicking outside the panel causes it to be dismissed without issuing a warning or providing some other opportunity for the user to intervene. With this in mind, the general approach with these panels is to immediately commit the settings changes the users make instead of requiring them to press some OK or Apply button before the changes are actually stored or applied.

You can see this behavior in action in the example app. One of the settings available in the ShareTargetExample app enables the user to select whether the app will either receive all the data formats that are being shared to it or whether it will choose only the highest designated format match from an ordered list. Focusing on the toggle switch control that determines which of these behaviors to respect, the switch is included in the XAML for the `SharingSettingsFlyout` as follows:

```
<ToggleSwitch x:Name="AcceptAllOrPreferredSwitch"
              OffContent="Accept All" OnContent="Preferred"
              Header="Accept All or Only Preferred"
              Toggled="HandleSwitchToggled" />
```

The `HandleSwitchToggled` event handler is called whenever the user changes the switch's value, and it simply updates an `AcceptAllSetting` property.

```
_appSettings.AcceptAllSetting = !AcceptAllOrPreferredSwitch.IsOn;
```

The value for the `AcceptAllSetting` is kept directly in Application Data storage, as Chapter 4, "Data and Content," explains. Listing 11.2 shows the implementation for this property. You could just as easily store the data in the Application Roaming Storage, to allow the setting value to roam across different PCs for the current user.

LISTING 11.2 Updating an App Setting in Application Data Storage

```
public Boolean AcceptAllSetting
{
    get
    {
        var result = false;
        var localSettings = ApplicationData.Current.LocalSettings;
        Object acceptAllObject;
        if (localSettings.Values.TryGetValue("AcceptAll",
            out acceptAllObject))
        {
            result = (Boolean) acceptAllObject;
        }
        return result;
    }
```

```
    set
    {
        var localSettings = ApplicationData.Current.LocalSettings;
        localSettings.Values["AcceptAll"] = value;
    }
}
```

Finally, when the share target app is activated in response to a share request, it examines this same property to decide which user interface to display:

```
var appSettings = new AppSettings();
var sharePage = appSettings.AcceptAllSetting
    ? new AllFormatsShareTargetPage() as IActivateForSharingPage
    : new PreferredFormatShareTargetPage() as IActivateForSharingPage;
sharePage.Activate(e);
```

Sharing

For many years, clipboard functionality has served as a way to exchange information between applications on Windows (and within other platforms as well). At its simplest, by using the Windows clipboard, users can deposit information from one app into another without the apps having to know anything about each other. The source app places data into the clipboard, and the target app retrieves it from the clipboard. In more sophisticated scenarios, the source app can choose to include different formats of the data in the clipboard, beyond simple text or images. This can include formatting, source information when the data is obtained from websites, or perhaps custom details. The target app can then choose what format it prefers to obtain at the time the data is being pasted, providing the richest possible experience for the user.

Apps built using the Windows Runtime can continue to use the Windows clipboard, but Windows 8.1 and the Windows Runtime also include support for integration with the Share Charm. The Share Charm continues the idea of allowing Windows to broker the exchange of information between applications without requiring the applications to have deep knowledge of each other's implementation, but it also allows apps to provide additional context and user-experience integration as part of the process.

Using the Share Charm is a straightforward process (see Figure 11.1). The sharing process is initiated when users want to share data from an app that they are currently using (known as the share source) and they bring up the Windows Charms and select Share, or alternatively invoke sharing by using the **Windows+H** keyboard shortcut. If the app has provided an event handler for the event that is raised when this data is requested, Windows asks the app to provide the formats and content of the data that it is intending to share. Windows then uses the information that the app provides to compile and display a list of apps that indicated at installation that they can receive one or more of the formats being supplied. These apps are known as share target apps. Note that Windows also attempts to obtain a screenshot of the current app as data to be shared, even if the app does not provide data of its own, although an app can specify that it does not want to allow this behavior.

When the user selects a share target app from the list, Windows activates that app, indicating that the activation is being requested as part of the share process and will include the data content that the share source app previously provided. The share target app then provides a user interface designed to support the app's approach to receiving shared data, which Windows displays within its Share panel. When the user has finished interacting with the sharing interface, the share target app can signal WinRT that the operation has completed successfully or otherwise.

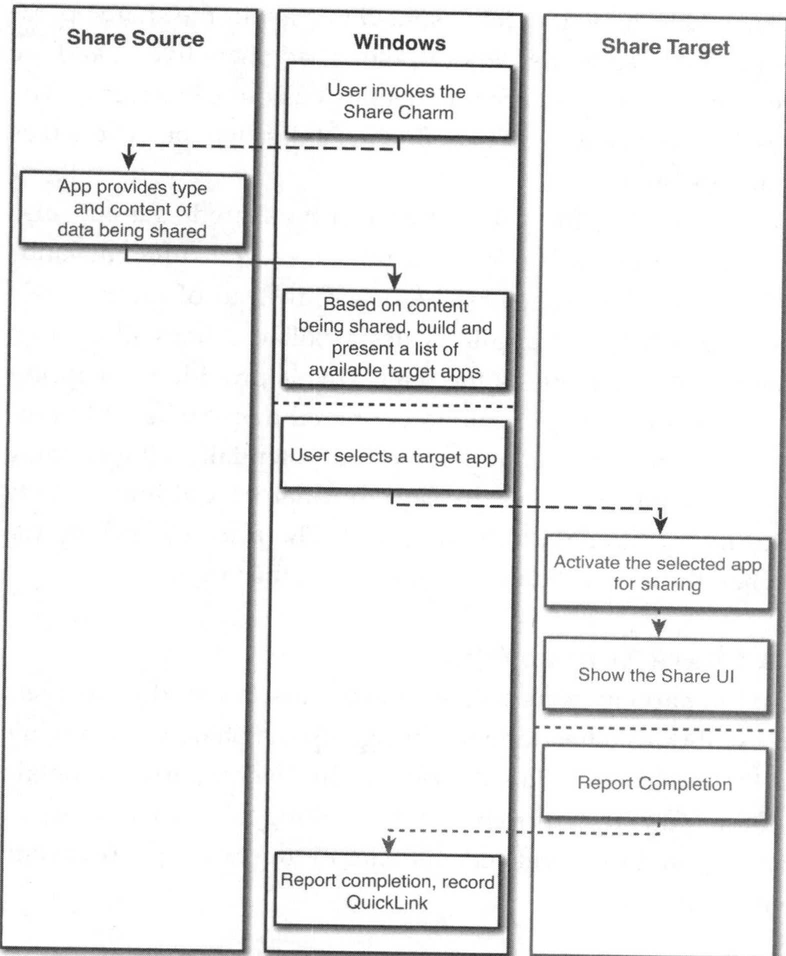

FIGURE 11.1 The share process

With this high-level view of the sharing process in place, we can now take a look at how apps that want to participate in this process use the Windows Runtime.

The Share Source Example

The Share Source example enables you to select and define what data will be exchanged when the user invokes the Share Charm. The interface is broken into two sections: Data Package Values and the Sharing Values.

The Data Package Values section defines metadata about the share operation. This metadata is used in the Windows-supplied Share flyout, and the share target application also can use it to display custom UI elements. The Sharing Values section enables you to define what data will be included as part of the Share operation.

In addition to selecting the values that can be shared, the app also includes the option to use a "delayed" send for several different kinds of content. When the delayed approach is used, instead of immediately providing the shared data, the app indicates a callback that will be used only when the target app requests the data. This is provided to support situations in which obtaining the data to be shared might take additional time, such as when network requests or other potentially long-running operations are involved. Windows displays the Share flyout immediately instead of waiting for the data to be retrieved. The price of fetching the data is paid when the user validates the transfer in the target app.

Creating a Share Source App

Apps that want to participate as a share source must respond to an event that Windows will raise when the user brings up the Share Charm while the app is in the foreground. To subscribe to this event, apps can obtain an instance of the `DataTransferManager` class by calling `DataTransferManager.GetForCurrentView()` and then register a handler for the `DataRequested` event, as the following code shows:

```
var transferManager = DataTransferManager.GetForCurrentView();
transferManager.DataRequested += OnShareDataRequested;
```

Whether an app registers to respond to this event might well depend on some application state or context. For example, if a user is looking at a page that shows grouped data or perhaps a menu-style page, there might not be anything to share, so the app might elect to not subscribe to the event. However, when the user navigates to a particular page in the app that shows detailed information, the app might choose to subscribe to the event and offer information for sharing. Therefore, it is not uncommon to subscribe to and unsubscribe from this event in an app page's `OnNavigatedTo` and `OnNavigatedFrom` methods.

> **NOTE**
>
> The DataTransferManager instance request is made for the "current view," which indicates that the value that is returned is scoped to an individual app window. If the app makes use of Windows Runtime APIs such as the ProjectionManager API that allow an app to have multiple windows (or views), each window needs to subscribe to its own DataRequested event for sharing and has the opportunity to provide its own set of data values to be shared, depending on which window is active when the user brings up the Share Charm.

The DataRequested event handler includes as its arguments an instance of the DataRequestEventArgs class. These arguments include a Request property that returns a DataRequest object. The app is responsible for providing the data for the share operation to the Data property of this DataRequest object, which is an instance of a DataPackage. However, the app can also signal a problem with the request by calling the FailWithDisplayText method, which cancels the request and displays the supplied text in the Share panel. Usually, this informs users that they need to take some additional action before the app is ready to share data, such as make a selection or provide some data on the current screen.

```
if (String.IsNullOrWhiteSpace(shareTitle))
{
    args.Request.FailWithDisplayText("A title must be supplied
➥ for sharing.");
    return;
}
```

Assuming that the app is in a state in which it has subscribed to the DataRequested event and the context is such that it determines it does not need to call the FailWithDisplayText method, the next step is to provide the data for the share operation. Two general kinds of data need to be provided. The first is the metadata that corresponds to the current share operation itself. The second is the actual data being shared. Keep in mind that Windows requires that an app respond to the DataRequested event within 200ms, so the information provided through the DataRequest object must not take a long time to get pulled together. For the data being shared, an option enables you to specify the intended data being shared and to have the actual data collected at a later point in the process.

The `Properties` dictionary property of the `DataPackage` object provides the sharing metadata. Windows sets several of these properties as part of the share operation, but the `Title` value must be supplied at the time the share data is provided; several others can optionally be supplied. Table 11.1 lists the properties that you can set.

TABLE 11.1 Predefined Metaproperties Available in the Share DataPackage

Property	Description
`Title`	(Required) This title is displayed for the share operation. This value is displayed at the top of the Share panel above the list of available share targets.
`Description`	An optional text description of the share operation. If included, it displays immediately below the title in the Share panel.
`Square30x30Logo`	An alternate logo value that can be displayed in the share target app. The app's small tile is used by default if this is not specified.
`LogoBackgroundColor`	A background color to accompany the optional `Square30x030Logo` value. The color specified as the Tile Background color is used by default if this is not specified.
`ContentSourceApplicationLink`	Optional custom URI to be used to launch the app that provided the share data, assuming that the protocol is registered as a protocol activation URI.
`ContentSourceWebLink`	Optional URI that points to a web page for the app that provided the share data.

As an example, setting the `Title`, `Description`, and `ContentSourceWebLink` properties is simply a matter of the following code:

```
var properties = args.Request.Data.Properties;
properties.Title = "Title Text";
properties.Description = "Description Text";
properties.ContentSourceWebLink =
    new Uri("http://winrtexamples.codeplex.com");
```

As previously mentioned, a share source app can provide a combination of one or more different data types in response to a share request. An app should supply only the data types that make sense for the data it is capable of supplying. However, the more data types an app is capable of providing, the more matching share target apps Windows selects. This gives end users more flexibility in how they can use the data in their apps.

Table 11.2 lists the available share data types.

TABLE 11.2 Available Share Data Types

Data Type	DataPackage Method	Description
Text	`SetText`	Exchanges plain text
Rich Text	`SetRtf`	Exchanges Rich Text Format content
HTML	`SetHtmlFormat`	Exchanges formatted HTML content
Bitmap	`SetBitmap`	Exchanges bitmap images
IStorageItem	`SetStorageItems`	Exchanges files and folders
Links	`SetApplicationLink` `SetWebLink`	Provides a link to launch either the share source application to a specific page/data item, or to navigate to a web page
Custom Types	`SetData`	Provides a stream of data that corresponds to a specified data format
Long-duration data load	`SetDataProvider`	For data items that might take more than 200ms to load into the DataPackage, provides a callback that can be executed to complete the load operation after the selected share target has been selected and has indicated a preference for the specified data format

Sharing simple text is the most straightforward operation—it is simply a matter of providing a value to the `SetText` function:

```
dataPackage.SetText("Some text to share");
```

Sharing HTML is a bit more complex. The HTML being shared needs to be formatted a certain way that includes several headers, and the fragments being shared must be properly enclosed in `HTML` and `BODY` tags. The `HtmlFormatHelper` class provides a `CreateHtmlFormat` method that takes care of this, both for sharing as well as for clipboard use. Furthermore, if the HTML content being shared contains images or other references, their `src` attributes must use absolute paths to their source locations, or a resource map must be provided and included in the `DataPackage`. The `ResourceMap` is basically a dictionary that the share source can use to provide stream reference content to the share target, indexed by a name, a URI, or another String key. The share target can then use this information to locate the named element in the HTML and replace the reference in whichever way is appropriate. An example is reading the image stream and substituting the original `img` tag with one that contains a Base-64 encoded version of the image. Listing 11.3 shows the process for sharing an HTML fragment.

LISTING 11.3 Sharing an HTML Fragment

```
var htmlFragment =
    "<h1>HTML Sharing Example</h1>" +
    "<p>This is an example of HTML sharing.<p>" +
    "<img src=file1>" +
    "<img src=file2>" +
    "<img src=file3>";

var uriForSample1 = new Uri("ms-appx:///Assets/SampleOne.png");
var uriForSample2 = new Uri("ms-appx:///Assets/SampleTwo.png");
var uriForSample3 = new Uri("ms-appx:///Assets/SampleThree.png");

dataPackage.ResourceMap["file1"] =
    RandomAccessStreamReference.CreateFromUri(uriForSample1);
dataPackage.ResourceMap["file2"] =
    RandomAccessStreamReference.CreateFromUri(uriForSample2);
dataPackage.ResourceMap["file3"] =
    RandomAccessStreamReference.CreateFromUri(uriForSample3);

var formattedHtmlFragment =
    HtmlFormatHelper.CreateHtmlFormat(htmlFragment);
dataPackage.SetHtmlFormat(formattedHtmlFragment);
```

Sharing a bitmap is considerably simpler than working with HTML, but you should be aware of some caveats. The `SetBitmap` function just requires a `RandomAccessStreamReference`, which itself provides several static methods that you can use to generate an instance from a file, a URI, or a random access stream. When sharing a file, however, it is generally good practice to also include a thumbnail, especially if the bitmap being shared is a high-resolution image. This allows share target applications to display the lightweight thumbnail image in the paired Share user interface if their implementation dictates that it is appropriate to do so. It is also considered good practice to include a Storage Item along with the bitmap, in case any source target apps are built to deal with general-purpose files instead of the specific case of images to be displayed or manipulated. Listing 11.4 shows this process for sharing a bitmap. Note that the use of an `async` operation requires using a deferral when responding to the `DataRequested` event.

LISTING 11.4 Sharing a Bitmap

```
var bitmapUri = new Uri("ms-appx:///Assets/Logo.png");
var streamRef =
    RandomAccessStreamReference.CreateFromUri(bitmapUri);
dataPackage.SetBitmap(streamRef);

var thumbnailUri = new Uri("ms-appx:///Assets/SmallLogo.png");
var thumbnailRef =
    RandomAccessStreamReference.CreateFromUri(thumbnailUri);
dataPackage.Properties.Thumbnail = thumbnailRef;

// NOTE - This will require obtaining a deferral!
var storageFile =
    await StorageFile.GetFileFromApplicationUriAsync(bitmapUri);
dataPackage.SetStorageItems(new[] { storageFile });
```

Be sure to understand the concept of deferrals when using asynchronous operations during the `DataRequested` event handler. Similar to what Chapter 2, "Windows Store Apps and WinRT Components," mentioned in its discussion of the application lifecycle, you need to take care in this scenario as well. Normally, Windows takes the return of the event handler as a signal that the share source app has completed its part of the work. If an asynchronous operation is present within this sequence, the event handler returns early, leaving the Share operation in a potentially confused state. To get around this problem, the `DataRequest` object provided as part of the `DataRequestEventArgs` that are supplied to the event handler includes a `GetDeferral` method. The `DataRequestDeferral` object that this method returns can then be used to signal Windows that the operation has truly completed, and the share operation can continue. The following code shows this:

```
var deferral = args.Request.GetDeferral();
// await asynchronous operation(s)
deferral.Complete();
```

Note that, just as in the case of application lifetime deferrals, these deferrals only prevent early completion of the share source portion of a share operation. They do not affect the maximum 200ms timeout that Windows enforces for the share source to complete its task.

Many of the concepts already discussed apply to directly sharing file or folder content. In this case, the `SetStorageItems` function expects an `IEnumerable<IStorageItem>`, allowing this data item to include multiple items in a single share call. Listing 11.5 shows the process for sharing files this way. As mentioned earlier, if async operations are used, a deferral is required. Again, see the "Using Deferrals When Sharing" section later in this chapter for more information about deferrals.

LISTING 11.5 Sharing Files

```
var uriForSample1 = new Uri("ms-appx:///Assets/SampleOne.png");
var uriForSample2 = new Uri("ms-appx:///Assets/SampleTwo.png");
var uriForSample3 = new Uri("ms-appx:///Assets/SampleThree.png");

// NOTE - The following async calls will require obtaining a deferral!
var file1 =
    await StorageFile.GetFileFromApplicationUriAsync(uriForSample1);
var file2 =
    await StorageFile.GetFileFromApplicationUriAsync(uriForSample2);
var file3 =
    await StorageFile.GetFileFromApplicationUriAsync(uriForSample3);
var items = new[] {file1, file2, file3};
dataPackage.SetStorageItems(items);
```

In many cases, it might be desirable to share a link that the share target app can display to its users to enable them to navigate to a web page that corresponds to the item being shared, or perhaps to even open the share source app directly to a representation of the item being shared. Much like the `ContentSourceApplicationLink` and `ContentSourceWebLink` properties that can be set, the `SetApplicationLink` and `SetWebLink` functions offer this functionality. The general guidance for an application link is for the URI to use a custom protocol that the application has registered for as an activation protocol and include information in the URI that the app can use to navigate to the specific record or data item being shared. See the "Protocol Activation" section in Chapter 12, "Additional Windows Integration," for more information about how to register for custom protocol activations. Listing 11.6 shows the addition of link content to the Share operation.

LISTING 11.6 Sharing Application and Web Links

```
var appUri = new Uri("winrt-by-example:contentlaunch");
dataPackage.SetApplicationLink(appUri);

var webUri = new Uri("http://winrtexamples.codeplex.com");
dataPackage.SetWebLink(webUri);
```

If one of the predefined data sharing formats doesn't meet your app's sharing needs, share source apps can also include custom data formats. These formats can offer a proprietary data exchange between two apps that are both aware of the details of the custom format, or they can exchange data that is defined using a well-known or standard format, such as those published at www.schema.org. Either way, the share source app calls the `SetData` function and provides a format identifier for the data, and then the data object itself. Share target apps register to be activated based on the format name, can look for the data in the data payload, and, if they find the data, can convert it to the appropriate object and make use of it. Note that multiple items can be added to a single share request with the `SetData` function, as long as they each use a different format identifier. The following code shows adding a custom data item based on the Person schema defined at schema.org, as well as adding a completely custom item.

```
dataPackage.SetData("http://schema.org/Person", personJson);
dataPackage.SetData("myCustomSchema", customSchemaObject);
```

The final option for sharing data is actually a specialization of the previous items, to be used when the process of pulling together the DataPackage information might exceed the system-imposed 200ms maximum time limit discussed previously. This might be the case when the content being shared needs to be processed in some way, such as adding watermarks to images, or when several large items need to be obtained from the file system or network locations. To support operations that require more time than Windows allows, you can provide a data type and callback method. Windows uses the data type to determine the available share target apps for the defined content the share source provides. The callback method is not invoked until the share target specifically requests the indicated data type. In this way, not only does a potentially expensive operation not conflict with the system-imposed time limit, but it also occurs only when the share target app is requesting that specific kind of data.

Supporting these delayed data requests involves two parts. The first is to use the SetDataProvider method on the DataPackage object to register the callback for the requested data type, as in the following code:

```
dataPackage.SetDataProvider(StandardDataFormats.Bitmap,
    DelayedBitmapRequestCallback);
```

In the preceding listing, the share source indicates that it will provide bitmap data as part of its sharing payload, as well as a callback method called DelayedBitmapRequestCallback to be used if the selected share target app selects bitmap.

The second part is the implementation of the callback method itself. The callback function accepts a DataProviderRequest value, which provides a SetData method that returns the requested data. It also includes a GetDeferral method, which can be used to support asynchronous operations in the same way as is required for DataRequest event handlers. The following code shows the content of the DelayedBitmapRequestCallback:

```
var defaultUri = new Uri("ms-appx:///Assets/Logo.png");
var bitmapFile =
    RandomAccessStreamReference.CreateFromUri(defaultUri);
request.SetData(bitmapFile);
```

Earlier you learned that Windows also provides a screenshot of the app as content to be shared, even if the app either does not register a handler for the `DataRequested` event or if it chooses to indicate in the event handler that there is nothing to be shared. Privacy or other concerns might make it a problem to have the capability to take or share screenshots of an app. In such a case, you can both instruct Windows to not provide an app's screenshot for sharing and ensure that screenshots taken using the functionality provided by either Windows or third-party applications results in a solid black image. You can accomplish this with the `IsScreenCaptureEnabled` property of the `ApplicationView` class, as the following code shows:

```
ApplicationView.GetForCurrentView().IsScreenCaptureEnabled = false;
```

The Share Target Example

Now that we've discussed how share source apps provide information, we can turn our attention to how the share target participates in the process of receiving that information. The **Share Target Example** project builds the counterpart to the share source example mentioned earlier.

This example app provides two different ways of looking at shared data. You can choose which to use by modifying settings through the Settings Charm. The previous "Displaying App Settings" section discusses how to include these settings in the Settings Charm. The first option that you can select for receiving shared data configures the example app to receive all the available sharing data types, to demonstrate how to go about handling receiving and making use of data that has been shared (in actuality, it can't be set up to receive every possible data type because you can specify a limitless number of custom types, but the **Share Target Example** app is configured to receive the custom data type that its counterpart **Share Source Example** project is sharing).

Most apps don't actually work this way with shared data. Instead, they are coded to have a preferred order in which they select the incoming data; when they find the "best" available data from the different kinds being shared, they use that one and ignore the rest. The second option for the **Share Target Example** app is more in line with this approach. In the same Settings panel, when Preferred sharing is selected, you can specify an order for the available data formats that determines the priority given to the different types of data that the app can receive. When data is shared to the app, it iterates through this preference list and stops as soon as it finds a matching data type in the shared data payload.

Creating a Share Target App

Share target apps implement what is known as the share target contract. Implementing this contract instructs Windows that your application can be discovered and activated as part of the sharing process that it brokers. In addition to building a dedicated Share user interface, this involves making configuration entries in the app manifest to provide information about which data types it supports. You can do this manually by opening the app manifest file, selecting the **Declarations** tab, selecting **Share Target** from the **Available Declarations** drop-down on the page, and pressing the **Add** button to include it in the Supported Declarations section. Alternatively, Visual Studio provides tooling that facilitates this process, as well as several other key steps involved in setting up a share target app.

To take advantage of the support that Visual Studio provides to enable an app to be a share target app, open the **Project** menu and select **Add New Item**, or right-click on your project in the **Solution Explorer** and select **Add** and then **New Item** from the context menus. In the **Add New Item** dialog, under the Installed | Visual C# | Windows Store section, locate and select the **Share Target Contract** template. Provide a name for the XAML page that will be added to your project to be invoked when the app is selected as a share target app, and press the **Add** button. At this point, Visual Studio makes several changes to your project. First, it updates the app's manifest file with the share target declaration that we just discussed and configures it to accept the text and uri data formats. Second, it adds the new XAML page whose name you provided in the dialog. Finally, the project's `App.xaml.cs` file is modified to include an override for the `OnShareTargetActivated` function, as follows:

```
protected override void OnShareTargetActivated
    (ShareTargetActivatedEventArgs e)
{
```

```
    var shareTargetPage = new ShareTargetPage();
    shareTargetPage.Activate(e);
}
```

This function is called as part of the app activation process when Windows invokes the app in response to it being selected as a share target. The default implementation Visual Studio provides creates an instance of the page you defined and calls a predefined `Activate` method that it includes. In addition to some basic viewmodel initialization, the `Activate` method handles the critical app initialization tasks of setting the app's current Window content and calling Activate after the content has been set (Chapter 2 covered this in the "Application Lifecycle" section).

Regardless of how the app manifest entry was created, the next step is to use it to specify at least one type of content for which this app can be invoked as a share target. You do this through either the Data Formats or Supported File Types sections in the Manifest Editor's Declarations tab. Each data format must be added individually; the Data Formats section lists the values to enter for the predefined data formats, or you can type a custom format into the Data Format textbox. In addition to the Data Formats, you can specify that the app supports receiving one or more specific file types by listing the file extensions of each desired file type in the Supported File Types section. A checkbox is also provided to indicate support for any file type. Note that if one or more file types are specified, it is not necessary to also include the `StorageItems` value in the Data Formats section because the `StorageItems` format is inferred by either including a file type or selecting to allow any file type.

One final sharing-related property to set in the app manifest is the Share Description. The text provided here appears with the app name in the share target listing that Windows provides. The intent of this text is to provide the end user with a brief description of how the share target app can use the shared data if it is invoked. Figure 11.2 shows an example of an app manifest for a share target app that has been configured to accept text and HTML data formats, as well as any file type, with a message to be displayed that reads "Sends data to the server."

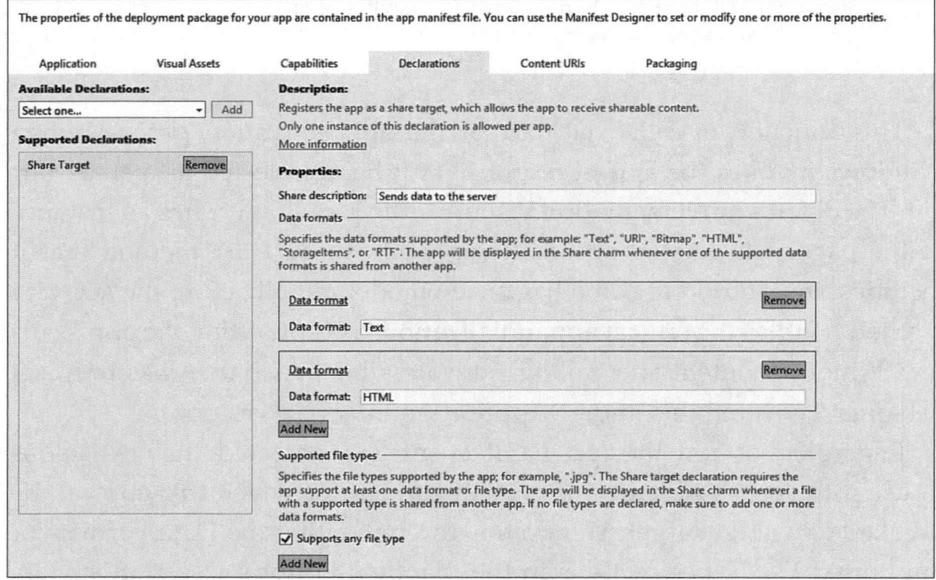

FIGURE 11.2 An app manifest configured for sharing

After you set up the app manifest entries that define when and how an app will appear in the share target listing, you can turn your attention to defining how the app identifies, selects, and processes the actual data being shared when the user selects it from the list of share targets.

When an app is activated as a share target, the activation arguments include an instance of the `ShareTargetActivatedEventArgs` class, whose `ShareOperation` property contains information about the content being shared and exposes the methods that the app will use to access the content. The main information here is provided through a `Data` property, which is an instance of the `DataPackageView` class. Table 11.3 summarizes the content of this value.

TABLE 11.3 Functionality Exposed by the `DataPackageView`

Member	Use
`Properties`	Provides access to the metadata properties for the share operation, including the title, description, and links set by the share source app, among others.

Member	Use
Contains	Method that returns whether the data type provided as its parameter is included in the set of shared data.
GetTextAsync GetRtfAsync GetHtmlFormatAsync GetBitmapAsync GetApplicationLinkAsync GetWebLinkAsync GetStorageItemsAsync GetDataAsync	Asynchronous methods that provide access to the indicated data format contained in the sharing payload.
GetResourceMapAsync	Provides access to the resource map provided by the share source app, which includes a string-keyed collection of RandomAccessStreamReference objects that can be used to map between a resource name and the file stream that exposes its contents. Used with HTML to retrieve content that is linked within the HTML document.

In addition to the metadata properties that the share source app sets, the Properties object includes several properties that Windows itself sets; they include information such as the share source application's name and a link to its entry in the Windows Store. Additionally, they include entries for the app logo and logo background color. If the share source app did not specify these values, they are populated with the Small Icon and Application Color values that it defined in its app manifest. The same applies to a thumbnail image and Web and App links, if these were provided.

Some share target apps use this metadata to provide context and information about the data being shared in the UI that the share target displays; others simply ignore it. Each app approaches the shared data a little differently because the app needs to select and use the data in a way that makes sense based on its own functionality.

To obtain the shared data, an app usually sets up a series of checks to see whether the incoming data contains a desired format, starting with the "best" or "most preferred" format and working down through the formats it supports, and then requesting and incorporating the data after it is located. For example, a mail-type app that has set HTML and Text as supported types in its manifest might start with HTML as a preferred format and, if that is not available, then fall back to using the Text data. Listing 11.7 illustrates this scenario.

LISTING 11.7 Choosing and Retrieving the Shared Data

```
_shareOperation.ReportStarted();

if (shareData.Contains(StandardDataFormats.Html))
{
    var formattedHtmlContent = await shareData.GetHtmlFormatAsync();
    UseFormattedHtmlContent(formattedHtmlContent);
}
else if (shareData.Contains(StandardDataFormats.Text))
{
    var textContent = await shareData.GetTextAsync();
    UseText(textContent);
}

_shareOperation.ReportDataRetrieved();
```

Notice that the methods that you can use to retrieve the shared data are all asynchronous methods. Recall from the previous discussion about preparing data to be shared that data of a given format can be specified by the share source through an immediate setter method, or the data format can be specified and a callback provided for later use. However, the methods available to the share target app do not make any distinction between how the data was provided. So the call to retrieve the shared data might be accessing data provided by the share source app through either approach, and the share target app cannot distinguish which approach is being taken. If the data was made immediately available, the retrieval method simply returns that data. Otherwise, Windows invokes the defined callback method in the share source app to get access to the data. As a result, the retrieval methods are asynchronous. Your share target app should be implemented with the assumption that the act of fetching the shared data could be time-consuming, possibly reflecting through the user interface that the data is being loaded. The calls to `ReportStarted` and `ReportDataRetrieved` in Listing 11.7 allow Windows to provide feedback in the Share panel as part of this process.

A share operation should conclude with the share target app notifying the share source app that it has completed the operation either successfully or not. This is accomplished by calling either the `ReportCompleted` or `ReportError` methods on the `ShareOperation` object. `ReportError` takes a text message that can provide information in the Share panel on what led the share operation to fail. Calling `ReportError` dismisses the share target UI; shortly after the error is reported, Windows pops up a toast message indicating the error, and information in the Share panel is updated to include the error message provided. The call to `ReportError` is shown here:

```
_shareOperation.ReportError(errorMessage);
```

The call to signal successful sharing is a little more interesting and also brings us to the topic of **QuickLinks**. The simplest way to indicate success is merely to call the `ReportCompleted` method without any parameters. This dismisses the share target UI. However, an overload for `ReportCompleted` also enables the share target app to supply a `QuickLink` object.

A QuickLink gives Windows a way to show a shortcut to a recent share activity for one or more given data formats. Windows shows any QuickLinks that it has supplied for the current data formats at the top of the share target selection panel. As an example, when an app shares content that includes data in a format that the built-in Mail app supports, Windows can include QuickLinks that include several recent mail recipients that the user has previously shared to (see Figure 11.3). If the user selects one of these links, the Share Target panel for the Mail app is displayed with that user's email address pre-entered in the To box.

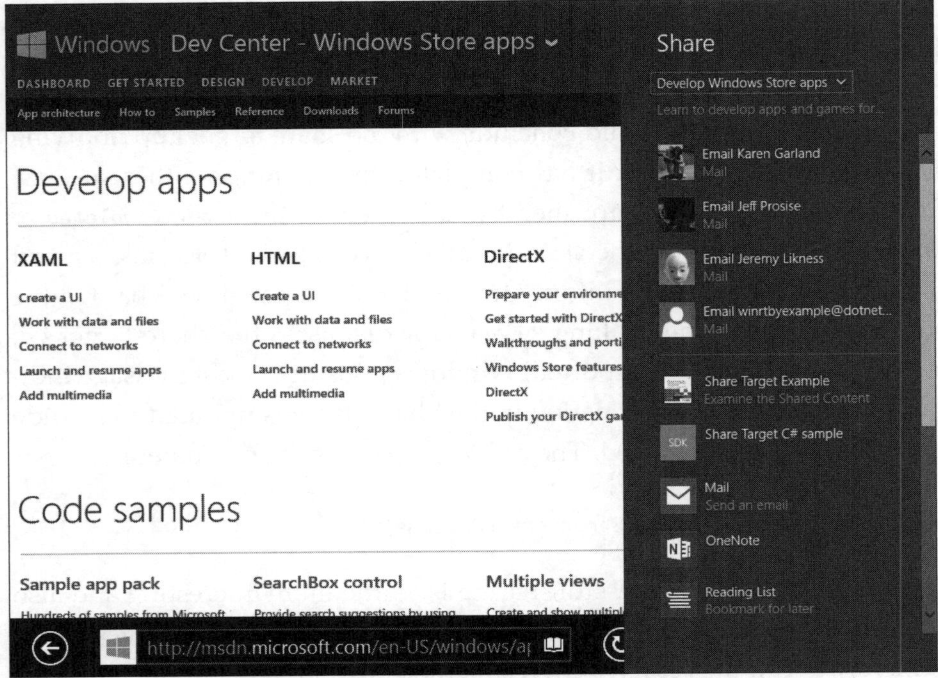

FIGURE 11.3 Email recipient QuickLinks

To set up a QuickLink, create an instance of the `QuickLink` class and provide it with a few important pieces of information, in some ways similar to the values used when setting up the app manifest of a share target app. The `SupportedDataFormats` property should be populated with a list of data formats for which the QuickLink is valid. Similarly, the `SupportedFileTypes` can include a list of file extensions, or a star (*) to denote any file. Additionally, you should supply the `Title` property with the text to display with the QuickLink in the Share panel, and you should set the `Thumbnail` property of the image to display. Finally, you must supply a value for the `Id` property. This value can be any nonempty `String` value, but it should be a value that has meaning to the share target app because it will be supplied to the app when it is activated, which you'll see shortly. When it is configured, you can set the QuickLink by calling `ReportCompleted` with the QuickLink as the argument to the call. Listing 11.8 shows a QuickLink configured to be available for HTML and Text content, as well as any file type.

LISTING 11.8 Configuring and Setting a QuickLink

```
var quickLink = new QuickLink
                {
                    SupportedDataFormats =
                    {
                        StandardDataFormats.Text,
                        StandardDataFormats.Html
                    },
                    SupportedFileTypes = {"*"},
                    Thumbnail = quickLinkThumbnail,
                    Title = "Quicklink Example",
                    Id = "XYZ_123",
                };
_shareOperation.ReportCompleted(quickLink);
```

All the properties mentioned must be set, with at least one data format or file type specified, or trying to set the QuickLink will result in WinRT throwing an exception.

When your share target app is invoked via a QuickLink, the `ShareOperation` object will include the value that was provided for the Quicklink's `Id` in a `QuickLinkId` property. The share target app can initially look for this value and, if it finds it, use it to prepopulate its user interface in whatever way is appropriate for your app. In some cases, the `Id` property includes all the data necessary to fill in the UI. In others, you might need to access the app's storage or other resources and use the `Id` value as a key to determine what content to display.

It is worth noting what successful sharing does and does not mean. In the context of a share target app that shares content via email, for example, a user cancelling the sending of a message typically constitutes a successful share. However, if the user presses send and the mail server is unavailable (assuming that the app is incapable of queuing messages until the issue is resolved), that could be cause to signal a sharing error.

Debugging Share Target Apps

Since Windows manages an app's activation in response to its selection in the Share Target panel, you might be wondering how to go about debugging a share target app. Fortunately, you can achieve this with Visual Studio in a couple ways.

First, you can use Visual Studio to launch the app as in a normal debugging context. Just start the app from Visual Studio as you do when normally debugging the app: For example, set the app's project as the StartUp Project in Visual Studio through either the **Project** menu or the Project's context menu, and select **Start Debugging (F5)** from the **Debug** menu. Switch to a share source app and select the data to be shared. Your share target app might no longer be in the foreground, but Visual Studio will still be in Debug mode, and if your app is selected as a share target, Visual Studio still catches the breakpoints you set, starting from the `OnShareTargetActivated` method.

If you do not want to launch the share target app before it is launched due to a share target activation and you want to examine methods that run earlier than the `OnShareTargetActivated` method (including the `App` class constructor), you have another option. To do this, open the project Properties in Visual Studio and select the Debug panel. In the **Start Action** section, check the **Do Not Launch, but Debug My Code When It Starts** checkbox. Then start to debug the app from Visual Studio as you normally do. The app won't actually launch in response to this sequence. However, if the app is now activated via a share target selection, through its Start Screen tile, or in any other way, Visual Studio still catches any breakpoints that have been set on the app. This technique is useful not only for share target activation, but also for any mechanism that activates the app, including several that you will learn about in Chapter 12.

Using Play To

Another Windows Charm that your app can interact with is the Devices Charm. This Charm provides a place where users can interact with some of the hardware devices that are attached to their systems, presenting them in three categories: Play, Print, and Project. The Play entry supports Play To, a feature that enables you to stream music, photos, and videos from apps to other systems and devices on a local network, such as an Xbox hooked up to your home TV, another PC on your home network that is running Windows Media Player, a Windows 8.1 app that is configured to be a Play To target app, or a Microsoft-certified DLNA consumer electronic device that supports Play To. The Print entry enables users to use a connected or otherwise available printer to print content from within an app. Finally, the Project entry enables users to control how content will be displayed on a system that is connected to multiple monitors or video projectors.

This section discusses the Play To functionality and shows both how you can create Play To source apps that can provide content and how you can create Play To target apps that can register themselves on the local network and display streamed content. As previously mentioned, Chapter 14 covers printing.

The Play To Example

The **PlayToExample** project included in the examples for Chapter 11 shows how to set up an app to stream video or images as a Play To source, as well as how to receive a stream of either video or images as a Play To target app. To work with Play To apps, the Play To source and target need to be distinct devices, so having access to a couple development systems is necessary to exercise both the Play To and Play Target code simultaneously. Otherwise, you can use a PC running Windows Media Player, an Xbox, or another DLNA-capable home electronic device connected to your home network that supports Play To as a Play To target. Additionally, you must configure the Play To source system's network connection to allow sharing and connections between devices.

To stream video or images, build and launch the app and select either the Video or Images button from the initial page. The Video option enables you to either capture a video from a connected webcam to be streamed, or to browse and select a pre-existing video file to use. The Images option enables you to browse for one or more images. The currently selected image from the list of available images is the one that is streamed, and changing the selected item updates the streamed content. With either option, after the content to stream has been selected, bringing up the Devices Charm and selecting Play lists available Play To targets that can be reached on the network, as well as provides an Add a Device link that you can use to access the **PC and devices** Windows configuration page, from which additional devices on the local network can be discovered. Selecting one of the listed devices from the Play panel begins streaming the content.

To receive streamed video or images, select the Receiver option from the initial page. On this page, you can use the Start Receiver and Stop Receiver buttons to toggle the app's network visibility as a Play To receiver. When content is streamed to the app, it is shown within the window; if the stream contains video, the onscreen transport controls allow interaction with the incoming video.

> **NOTE**
>
> In addition to configuring the Play To source to enable discovery of target devices and applications, the targets themselves might need some configuration. Windows Media Player must be configured to allow remote control via its Stream settings option, and Xbox 360 devices need Play To enabled through the Console Settings/ Connected Devices configuration. You can find streaming and Play To configuration instructions for Windows Media Player at http://j.mp/190h4tR and for Xbox at http://j.mp/16Yr35H.

Creating a Play To Source App

Creating an app that can stream content to a Play To target is a straightforward process. When a user brings up the Devices Charm from the Windows Charm bar or by pressing the **Windows+K** key combination and selects the **Play** entry, Windows tries to notify the current app to see if it is currently capable of providing streamed content via Play To. An app can handle this event by obtaining a reference to the current view's `PlayToManager` class and registering a handler to its `SourceRequested` event, as the following call shows:

```
var playToManager = PlayToManager.GetForCurrentView();
playToManager.SourceRequested += OnPlayToSourceRequested;
```

In the event handler, an app can use the provided event arguments to either return an error message, indicating that it currently cannot stream any content, or it can return a Play To source to use. Either way, much as when Windows is requesting share information, this request has a 200ms limit, by which time the handler must have completed or the results will simply be ignored. Furthermore, the only two sources for `PlayToSource` values currently are the `MediaElement` and `Image` controls. Because this request will occur on a non-UI thread, it must be marshalled to the UI thread to retrieve these values from these controls, which results in an asynchronous call being made. This implies making use of deferrals, similar to the previous "Creating a Share Source App" section discussion. Listing 11.9 shows a handler for the `SourceRequested` event from the example app that uses the `MediaElement` to retrieve the `PlayToSource` value to be returned.

LISTING 11.9 Responding to the SourceRequested Event

```
private void OnPlayToSourceRequested(PlayToManager sender,
    PlayToSourceRequestedEventArgs args)
{
    // This request will come in on a non-UI thread,
    // so it will need to be marshalled over.
    // Since doing that is an async operation,
    // a deferral will be required.
    var deferral = args.SourceRequest.GetDeferral();

    Dispatcher.RunAsync(CoreDispatcherPriority.Normal, () =>
    {
        if (MediaElement.PlayToSource == null)
        {
            var errorMessage =
                "There is no video selected to be streamed.";
            args.SourceRequest.DisplayErrorString(errorMessage);
        }
        else
        {
            args.SourceRequest.SetSource(MediaElement.PlayToSource);
        }

        deferral.Complete();
    });
}
```

After the `PlayToSource` is provided, the media is streamed to the Play To target device. Interaction with the `MediaElement` transport controls to play, pause, or seek through the media in the Source app is reflected in the video seen in the target.

Finally, if you want your Play To source app to receive some information about the Play To target app selected, you can optionally subscribe to the `SourceSelected` event on the `PlayToManager`. When this event is raised in your app, the arguments include the `FriendlyName` that is displayed for the selected target, its display icon, and values indicating whether the selected target supports audio, video, and image streams.

Creating a Play To Target App

Configuring a Play To target app is a little more involved than configuring a Play To source app, although much of the complexity occurs if the app is intending to support both video and image streams and will handle the necessary differences between the controls used to present the two.

For an app to receive a stream via Play To, it must use an instance of the `PlayToReceiver` class. Setting up the receiver involves providing it with the name it should show in the list of available devices, identifying the kinds of streams it can support, and then handling the events that can be raised before and during streaming. When the configuration is in place, calling the `StartAsync` method makes the receiver available on the local network. Listing 11.10 shows its sequence.

LISTING 11.10 Configuring a Play To Receiver

```
if (_receiver == null)
{
    _receiver = new PlayToReceiver();
}

// Set the Properties that describe this receiver device
_receiver.FriendlyName = "Example Play To Receiver";
_receiver.SupportsAudio = true;
_receiver.SupportsVideo = true;
_receiver.SupportsImage = true;

// Subscribe to Play To Receiver events
// Receive the request from the Play To source
// and map it to how it should be handled in this app
_receiver.SourceChangeRequested +=
    HandleReceiverSourceChangeRequested;

// Playback commands
_receiver.PlayRequested += HandleReceiverPlayRequested;
_receiver.PauseRequested += HandleReceiverPauseRequested;
_receiver.StopRequested += HandleReceiverStopRequested;
_receiver.PlaybackRateChangeRequested +=
    HandleReceiverPlaybackRateChangeRequested;
```

```
// Seek commands
_receiver.CurrentTimeChangeRequested +=
    HandleReceiverCurrentTimeChangeRequested;
_receiver.TimeUpdateRequested +=
    HandleReceiverTimeUpdateRequested;

// Volume commands
_receiver.VolumeChangeRequested +=
    HandleReceiverVolumeChangeRequested;
_receiver.MuteChangeRequested +=
    HandleReceiverMuteChangeRequested;

// Advertise the receiver on the local network
// and start receiving commands
await _receiver.StartAsync();

// Use the DisplayRequest to prevent power-save
// from interrupting the playback experience
if (_displayRequest == null)
{
    _displayRequest = new DisplayRequest();
    _displayRequest.RequestActive();
}
```

The `SourceChangeRequested` event is raised when the Play To source provides a new stream to the target. At this point, the target app examines the incoming stream and uses the information provided to set the UI content. For example, in the case of a video stream, the stream is passed for playback to an onscreen `MediaElement` control through a `SetSource` call:

```
VideoPlayer.SetSource(args.Stream, args.Stream.ContentType);
```

Additional event handlers are invoked for playback actions that originate in the Play To source app; the Play To target needs to map these to the appropriate UI action and then potentially report back to the receiver that the action has taken place. Note that the `PlayToReceiver` event handler invocations are not on the UI thread, so the `Dispatcher` must be used to prevent cross-thread access exceptions. In the example app, this code is mostly boilerplate code. For video playback, the event results in the corresponding video call being made to the `MediaElement` control, which, upon execution, fires an event so that the confirmation call is made back to the `PlayToReceiver` object. For image playback, most of the operations merely result in the corresponding PlayToReceiver callback because adjusting these values is meaningless for a static image. Listing 11.11 shows this pattern for the handler for the PlayRequested event; video playback results in the call being forwarded to the MediaElement, which then raises a CurrentStateChanged event that provides the proper notification. Image playback, on the other hand, simply updates the Image control and immediately issues the notification.

LISTING 11.11 Play Request Event Handling

```
private void HandleReceiverPlayRequested(PlayToReceiver sender,
    Object args)
{
    Dispatch(() =>
    {
        if (_currentPlaybackType == PlaybackType.Video)
        {
            VideoPlayer.Play();
            // Receiver notification occurs in the
            // HandleVideoPlayerCurrentStateChanged handler
        }
        else if (_currentPlaybackType == PlaybackType.Image)
        {
            ImagePlayer.Source = _imageSource;
            _receiver.NotifyPlaying();
        }
    });
}
```

Summary

In this chapter, you saw how to use the mechanisms exposed by the Windows Runtime to include integration with the Windows Charms in your apps. This included how an app can include content to be shown when the user invokes the Settings Charm, giving users one consistent place to go in their system to manipulate app settings. You also looked at how to set up an app to participate in sharing actions initiated by the Share Charm by sharing data to other apps, as well as receiving shared data. Finally, you saw how an app can respond to the Play entry in the Devices Charm to stream audio, video, and image data to other devices on the network via Play To, as well as how to add functionality to apps that enables them to function as Play To targets.

In the next chapter, "Additional Windows Integration," you look at other points of integration with Windows that you can access and configure with the Windows Runtime. You create custom content for the File Open Picker and the File Save Picker (see the "Pickers and Cached Files" section of Chapter 4), as well as the similar Contact Picker. You see how you can configure apps to be activated via requests for certain file types or certain URI protocols, and how you can set apps to run when certain storage or media devices are connected to the system. Finally, you see how an app can show system-provided user interface elements that support integration with the contact- and appointment-management tools that have been configured in Windows.

12

Additional Windows Integration

IN ADDITION TO INTERACTIONS WITH THE WINDOWS CHARMS, the Windows Runtime provides several other opportunities to integrate apps with the functionality that is available in Windows 8.1. Apps can be extended to provide content when the standard file save picker and file open picker dialogs display. Similar to the **Share** approach in Chapter 11, "Windows Charms Integration," this integration allows an app to give its users the capability to select and consume the content exposed as files and file hierarchies by other apps without the apps needing to have insight into each other's implementation. Also, similar to the file open picker dialog, apps can be extended to provide content as information about contacts through integration with the contact picker dialog.

Apps can also register themselves to be activated to handle requests for certain file types or communication protocols. Other apps can use the Windows Runtime to issue these requests and can indicate preferences for how Windows should position the apps' windows relative to each other when such requests are received. Apps that are registered as account picture providers are displayed in specific Windows settings screens and, if invoked, will receive a protocol activation request with a windows-defined protocol. In addition to apps being launched in response to requests from other apps, they can be registered with Windows to run when a user connects particular types of storage or media devices.

Finally, apps can tap into the Windows Runtime to show Windows-provided user interface elements that allow them to interact with the contact and appointment management tools that the user has configured in Windows. Windows brokers this interaction so that it displays user interface elements that are familiar to the user, and also so that the interaction takes place in a secure manner that doesn't allow an app to maliciously scan and scour places where personal information is being stored.

NOTE

The file open and file save pickers, the contact picker, file and protocol activation, the account picture provider, and AutoPlay all provide integrations that are capable of invoking an app that was not previously running. Debugging the process these apps go through as they are being started works the same as discussed for working with apps that are activated in response to a Share request (see the section "Debugging Share Target Apps," in Chapter 11).

Integrating with the File and Contact Pickers

In Chapter 4, "Data and Content," you saw how the WinRT API is used to invoke the file open and file save pickers to access or store information from within an app. At the core of these operations is the fact that these controls simply return instances of the `StorageFile` class that provides all the properties and methods that are necessary to access and manipulate the contents of the selected files.

The file open and file save pickers do not offer access to just the available portions of the Windows file system. Apps can be integrated with Windows so that they are included as available entries in one or both of these pickers. Apps such as **OneDrive** that provide custom access to what are essentially cloud-based virtual file systems are integrated in this way, so they serve as sources and destinations for file manipulation from within other apps. However, this functionality is not limited to just these file-storage-centric apps. Any app can be configured to integrate with Windows so that it is included as an entry in one or both of these pickers when it is invoked. This integration includes defining an app-specific user interface that is shown in the picker body. The contents of these user interfaces depend on how the app will expose access to whatever it is managing—in some cases, it might be simply an abstraction over the app's local storage, whereas in other cases, it might be either more elaborate or more abstract. When an app takes the set of steps necessary to participate in these kinds of integrations, the app is said to be implementing the File Save Picker contract or the File Open Picker contract.

In addition to the file open picker and file save picker, the Windows Runtime provides a contact picker for selecting one or more `Contact` objects. Not only does this picker provide much of the same functionality as its file-based brethren, but it also provides similar opportunities for integration with apps that track contact-type information.

The Example App

The **IntegrationExample** project in the source code for this chapter provides examples of several different kinds of integration, including integration with the file open, file save, and contact pickers. The app provides access to and management of a list of contacts, with information that includes names, email addresses, and phone numbers. Additionally, the app supports the idea of associating files with specific contacts, which the app manages by storing the files in a custom file hierarchy within the app's local storage. Viewing the details for an individual contact displays the list of files that have been associated with that contact. Also, other apps that support opening files via the file open picker can use the example app as a file source, with the picker providing a means for the user to select a contact and choose one of its associated files. For apps that allow users to select contacts, as the built-in Mail app does for selecting email recipient addresses, the example app is also integrated as a contact picker, letting users select the contacts it is managing.

File Open Picker

The file open picker has a more straightforward implementation than the file save picker, so it makes a good place to start. In addition, the concepts presented in the file open picker coverage provide a good foundation for the file save picker discussion.

Visual Studio provides a template for quickly getting started with integrating the file open picker into your app. To use this template, select **Add New Item** from the **Project** menu or select the corresponding **Add/New Item** entries from the context menu for the project's entry in the **Solution Explorer**. In the Add New Item dialog, select the **File Open Picker Contract** template item from the **Windows Store** group. Provide a meaningful name for the XAML page that will be added to the project, and click **Add**; the necessary changes then are made to your project's contents to present a file open picker.

Although you can have this Visual Studio template make these changes on your behalf, you can also make the changes directly yourself; the example app here uses the second approach.

The first change to make is to insert a **File Open Picker** entry in the **Declarations** section of the App Manifest file. This inclusion, along with its corresponding settings, is used when the app is installed to inform Windows that it can show content whenever a file open picker is displayed. Open the App Manifest file, select the **Declarations** section, and from the **Available Declarations** drop-down, choose the **File Open Picker** entry. Then click the **Add** button.

The **File Open Picker** entry enables you to either specify a certain combination of file extensions or use a default value of **Supports Any File Type**. When one or more file extensions are listed, an attempt is made to match the values indicated in the `FileTypeFilter` property of the `FileOpenPicker` instance to these values, to determine whether this particular app supports being invoked as a picker for the file types currently looked for. For example, assume that the following code is used to show a file open picker:

```
var fileOpenPicker = new FileOpenPicker
                     {
                         FileTypeFilter = {".jpg", ".png"}
                     };
var selectedFile = await fileOpenPicker.PickSingleFileAsync();
```

An app that specifies only a value of **.txt** as a file type will not be included in the available apps in the File Picker, whereas an app that includes a value of **.jpg** or one that has checked the **Supports Any File Type** value will be displayed. To add specific file types, deselect the Supports Any File Type check box and use the **Add New** button to create a new file type entry. You must provide one file type extension per entry, but you can add multiple entries.

Beyond the change to the App Manifest file, you also need to include a page in the project that provides the user interface the body of the File Picker dialog will show when your app is selected. This page is responsible for collecting and coordinating the user selections. In the example app, the `FileOpenPickerPage` class provides this functionality. The page's XAML markup is configured to display a `ComboBox` control with the list of the available contacts the app is managing, as well as the list of files that have been associated with the currently selected contact.

TIP

When you use the Visual Studio template to generate the file open picker page, you might notice that the XAML declaration includes a `d:ExtensionType` value set to `FileOpenPicker`. With this value present, the Visual Studio and Blend visual designers take on a layout that resembles that of a file open picker control. This gives you the capability to lay out your page as it will appear when it is actually used within an app. When creating file open picker pages directly instead of using the pages the Visual Studio template provides, you can also add this entry by hand. This same value is also useful for the layouts of file save and contact picker pages that Visual Studio does not provide a template for but that share the same basic layout as the file open picker.

The next step necessary to integrate with the file picker is to respond to the file open picker activation request in the `App` class. This is handled through an override of the `Application` class's `OnFileOpenPickerActivated` method. This method is responsible for creating an instance of the `FileOpenPickerPage`, setting it as the current window content for the app, and then providing this page with the instance of the `FileOpenPickerUI` that has been supplied as part of the application activation arguments so that the custom page can interact with the Windows-supplied user interface that will be displaying it. Listing 12.1 shows this process.

LISTING 12.1 Handling App Activation for the File Open Picker

```
protected override void OnFileOpenPickerActivated
    (FileOpenPickerActivatedEventArgs e)
{
    // Create the page to be displayed within the picker area
    var fileOpenPickerPage = new FileOpenPickerPage();

    // Activate the current Window
    Window.Current.Content = fileOpenPickerPage;
    Window.Current.Activate();

    // Initialize the window
    fileOpenPickerPage.Initialize(e.FileOpenPickerUI);
}
```

The implementation for the page includes an `Initialize` method that accepts the `FileOpenPickerUI` object that is included in the `FileOpenPickerActivatedEventArgs` parameter passed to the `OnFileOpenPickerActivated` override. This `FileOpenPickerUI` value is set aside in the `_fileOpenPickerUI` property and is used for communication between the user interface that the app supplies and the actual File Picker it appears within. When the user selects or deselects a file for the File Picker in the app user interface to return, the corresponding `_fileOpenPickerUI` `AddFile` or `RemoveFile` method is called and is provided with the `StorageFile` instance or instances that were involved in the action. Listing 12.2 shows this.

LISTING 12.2 Synchronizing the `FilePickerUI` with the User Selections

```
private void HandleSelectedFileChanged(Object sender,
    SelectionChangedEventArgs e)
{
    // Update the picker 'basket' with the newly selected items
    foreach (var addedFile in e.AddedItems.Cast<FileInfo>())
    {
        if (_fileOpenPickerUI.CanAddFile(addedFile.File))
        {
            _fileOpenPickerUI.AddFile(addedFile.Title, addedFile.File);
        }
```

```
    }

    // Update the picker 'basket' to remove any newly removed items
    foreach (var removedFile in e.RemovedItems.Cast<FileInfo>())
    {
        if (_fileOpenPickerUI.ContainsFile(removedFile.Title))
        {
            _fileOpenPickerUI.RemoveFile(removedFile.Title);
        }
    }
}
```

The `FileOpenPickerUI` instance includes a `SelectionMode` property that you can use to determine whether the picker is being displayed to select a single file or multiple files. If the file open picker is called with the option to allow multiple file selections, the UI that the File Picker supplies will include a "basket" of file selections in its bottom row, where the user can see what has been added and remove any items as needed. The `FilePickerUI` instance relays this act of removing items through a `FileRemoved` event that is subscribed to in the `Initialize` method. When the `FilePickerUI` instance fires the FileRemoved event, the corresponding file item is located and removed from the user interface's list of selected items. The event will actually occur off the UI thread, so the Dispatcher must execute the selection change on the proper thread. Listing 12.3 shows this.

Listing 12.3 Synchronizing the User Selections with the `FilePickerUI`

```
private async void HandleFilePickerUIFileRemoved(FileOpenPickerUI
sender,
    FileRemovedEventArgs e)
{
    await Dispatcher.RunAsync(CoreDispatcherPriority.Normal, () =>
    {
        // Synchronize the select items in the UI lists to remove
        // the item that was removed from the picker's 'basket'
        var removedSelectedGridItem =
            FileGridView.SelectedItems.Cast<FileInfo>()
            .FirstOrDefault(x => x.Title == e.Id);
        if (removedSelectedGridItem != null)
        {
            FileGridView.SelectedItems.Remove(removedSelectedGridItem);
        }
    });
}
```

The final step performed in the `Initialize` method is to initialize the viewmodel for the page and load the available contact information. At this point, the app is configured to participate in the integration with the file open picker and is included in the list of available apps for any file that uses the picker to select files.

File Save Picker

Integrating with the file save picker is similar to integrating with the file open picker. However, no Visual Studio template is provided for the File Save Picker contract to assist in the process. You need to either follow the steps by hand or start with the File Open Picker contract template and switch over.

Either way, the steps needed to implement the File Save Picker contract follow the same pattern as those for the file open picker, with just a few minor changes. These steps involve including the **File Save Picker** declaration in the App Manifest file, adding the user interface page and integrating it with the provided `FileSavePickerUI` object, and handling the file save picker application activation.

The App Manifest entry has the same set of options as the **File Open Picker** entry. You can select **Supports Any File Type** or indicate a set of specific file extensions to instruct Windows about the circumstances in which this app should be considered as part of the list of available apps that can appear in the file save picker drop-down.

Also as in the file open picker implementation, you must supply a user interface page that controls what content displays within the file picker and that coordinates user activities with a supplied `FileSavePickerUI` instance. In this case, the `FileSavePickerUI` element provides a `TargetFileRequested` event that is raised when the user clicks the Save button in the Picker. The custom user interface needs to handle this event to supply the `StorageFile` instance that the calling app will use as the destination for the file to be saved. Additionally, if the user selects a file within the user interface content, an attempt should be made to reset the filename for the save operation to the name of the file that was selected by calling the `TrySetFileName` method the `FileSavePickerUI` instance provided. If the selected file has an extension that matches the list of available extensions that were defined for the file save picker dialog in the app that invoked it, the name change should succeed; otherwise, it returns a value indicating that the operation is not currently allowed.

As in other cases in which Windows must wait for an event to complete before it can proceed with some action, the `TargetFileRequested` event that is raised when the user clicks Save includes the capability to request a deferral in case an asynchronous operation is performed during the handling of the event. Without the use of a deferral, the event handler would be allowed to complete before the asynchronous operation completes. Control then would return to the calling app that invoked the file save picker before the save target file was defined or properly configured.

The example app presents the file save picker contents much the same way as it does for the file open picker. Users can select a contact to associate with the file being saved. Selecting a contact from the displayed drop-down updates the user interface to list the files that have already been associated with that contact. If one of the displayed files is selected, an attempt is made to change the filename for the file being saved, as in Listing 12.4.

LISTING 12.4 Reacting to a File Item Selection

```
private void HandleSelectedFileChanged(Object sender,
    SelectionChangedEventArgs e)
{
    // The user selected a pre-existing file.
    // Use its name for overwriting.
    var selectedFile = ((ListViewBase)sender).SelectedItem as FileInfo;
    if (selectedFile != null)
    {
        _fileSavePickerUI.TrySetFileName(selectedFile.File.Name);
    }
}
```

The handler for the `TargetFileRequested` event uses the supplied `TargetFileRequestedEventArgs` to obtain a `Request` reference and then uses that to obtain a deferral. It then sets the request's `TargetFile` to the `StorageFile` that is obtained as a target for the requested file. Finally, it indicates that the deferral has completed. Listing 12.5 shows this.

LISTING 12.5 Handling the TargetFileRequested Event

```
private async void HandleTargetFileRequested(FileSavePickerUI sender,
    TargetFileRequestedEventArgs args)
{
    var currentContact =
        DefaultViewModel["SelectedContact"] as Contact;
    if (currentContact == null) return;

    // Requesting a deferral allows the app to call an
    // asynchronous method and complete the request.
    var deferral = args.Request.GetDeferral();

    // Get the target file based on the currently selected contact
    args.Request.TargetFile
        = await currentContact.SaveRelatedFile(sender.FileName);

    // Complete the deferral to let the Picker know
    // that the request processing has finished
    deferral.Complete();
}
```

Once again, the final change required is to handle the file save picker activation by including an override for the `Application` class's `OnFileSavePickerActivated` event that handles the app activation responsibilities. Much as with the file open picker, these responsibilities include creating an instance of the user interface element, setting it as the current window content, calling `Activate`, and then initializing the page by passing it a reference to the `FileSavePickerUI` that was provided in the `FileSavePickerActivatedEventArgs` arguments supplied in the activation event override.

Contact Picker

The contact picker is similar to the file open picker, except that it provides access to contact information instead of files. Invoking the contact picker to select one or more contacts follows the same process as for the file open and file save pickers, as the following code illustrates:

```
var contactPicker = new ContactPicker();
contactPicker.SelectionMode = ContactSelectionMode.Contacts;
var contacts = await contactPicker.PickContactsAsync();
```

Integrating your app with the contact picker follows the same sequence used in the file open and file save picker integration. This sequence includes modifying the App Manifest, providing the user interface page that integrates with the containing control, and providing handling for the application activation sequence. As with the file save picker, Visual Studio provides no template, so you must implement the steps directly.

The App Manifest simply needs the **Contact Picker** declaration included in the **Supported Declarations** section. Unlike with the file pickers, you cannot set any options after the **Contact Picker** declaration has been included.

As with the other picker pages, the user interface page needs to synchronize its content with the containing control; in this case, it is an instance of the `ContactPickerUI` class. The implementation for this is similar to the file open picker implementation. It includes subscribing to a `ContactRemoved` event to synchronize the local UI with changes made in the contact picker control itself, as well as making calls to `AddContact` and `RemoveContact` to respond to selections in the UI you are providing. The example app implementation for the interactions with these members is nearly line-for-line identical to that shown for the file open picker in Listings 12.2 and 12.3.

The final component to the integration is handling the activation request. In the case of the contact picker, the `Application` class does not provide a dedicated method, so you must override the general-purpose `OnActivated` method. In this method, the provided activation arguments implement the `IActivatedEventArgs` interface, which includes a `Kind` property that supplies a member of the `ActivationKind` enumeration. For activation in response to a contact picker request, the value should be set to `ContactPicker`. If this value is found, the app code should then cast the activation arguments to the `ContactPickerActivatedEventArgs` type, which can then be used to obtain the `ContactPickerUI` instance. Listing 12.6 shows the example app implementation of this activation override.

LISTING 12.6 Handling Activation for a Contact Picker

```
protected async override void OnActivated(IActivatedEventArgs args)
{
    if (args.Kind == ActivationKind.ContactPicker)
    {
        // Create the user interface element to be displayed
        // within the picker area
        var contactPickerPage = new ContactPickerPage();

        // Activate the current Window
        Window.Current.Content = contactPickerPage;
        Window.Current.Activate();

        var contactPickerArgs = (ContactPickerActivatedEventArgs)args;
        contactPickerPage.Initialize(contactPickerArgs.ContactPickerUI);
    }
    // Code for additional activation types omitted...
}
```

Application Activation Integration

You have seen several examples with sharing, the file save picker, the file open picker, and the contact picker in which an app can register to be activated in response to a user action. In response to these activations, a tailored user interface is shown inside a display that the Windows Runtime provides and manages during the lifetime of the request. In another set of scenarios, an application can register to be activated as a standalone app, effectively allowing the app to be activated in response to a request either by another app or as a reaction to some event ocurring in Windows 8.1 itself.

File activation supports registering an app to handle requests to open files that have a certain file extension. Protocol activation supports registering an app to handle requests for certain URL protocols. Registering as an account picture provider is a specialized form of a protocol activation in which a registered app is listed in the user's User Profile editing screen as one that can provide photos and/or a video to be used when profile information displays for the currently logged-in user. Finally, AutoPlay instructs Windows 8.1 to launch an app that has been registered in response to a certain device type connected to the computer, such as a camera or a storage device.

The Example App

The **IntegrationExample** project introduced in the previous section also provides the examples for the different activation integration types this section discusses. The example app includes support for activation via a request to handle files with a .wrtbe extension, which the app expects to include a JSON description of a contact to be added to the app. The protocol winrt-by-example-integration is associated with this example app as well, and the app can use the URL contents to view a specific contact's detail page. The example app is also registered as an account picture provider, supporting the capability to select an image file associated with one of the tracked contacts as the Account Picture for the user currently logged into Windows. Finally, the example app is configured to handle AutoPlay so that when a thumb drive is inserted that is configured to raise a particular custom insertion event, the app will scan the drive's root folder for .wrtbe files and merge the content of these files into the existing collection of contacts.

In addition to this app, a companion **IntegrationExampleLauncher** app is supplied. It provides user interface elements to issue some of the external activation requests discussed.

File Activation

As just mentioned, one function that the **IntegrationExampleLauncher** app provides is to allow the user to select a file with the .wrtbe extension and request that it be opened by one of the apps currently registered in Windows to handle that type of file. This launcher app even integrates itself with the file open picker, to provide access to sample files that have been distributed as part of the launcher example app package itself. It also enables the user to indicate a View Preference to use during the launch. The user can specify whether the launch should show a dialog that allows the user to select an app to handle the selected file type and indicate whether to set it as the default app. If the dialog is not displayed, Windows simply uses the default app. You can control this value by bringing up **PC**

Settings, selecting **Search and Apps**, choosing **Defaults**, and then clicking **Choose Default Apps by File Type**. When the user clicks the **Launch** button, the app calls the `LaunchFileAsync` method provided by the `Launcher` class with the selected file and the indicated preferences (see Listing 12.7).

LISTING 12.7 Calling a File Activation

```
var launcherOptions = new LauncherOptions
{
    DesiredRemainingView = selectedLauncherViewPreference,
    DisplayApplicationPicker = displayApplicationPicker,
};
await Launcher.LaunchFileAsync(_selectedLauncherFile, launcherOptions);
```

Registering an app to support being activated via file activation starts in the App Manifest file. In the Declarations panel, select **File Type Associations** and press the **Add** button to create a new File Type Association group entry in the manifest.

You can set several options for each file association group. The Display Name indicates the text that is displayed when information about this type is shown, such as in the Type column of the Windows File Explorer application. You can provide an image to display for this file type via the Logo property, or you can omit it (the app's Small Logo icon then is used by default). You can provide optional Info Tip text when additional information is displayed about the type. You must provide a Name value that specifies an ID given to the current group of file extensions. Note that Name and at least one Supported File Type are the only required values. The Edit Flags values are used when the file open request comes from an untrusted source, such as a website that hasn't otherwise been configured to be part of the Trusted Sites collection. Three possible combinations are available for specifying the Edit Flags values. Open Is Safe indicates that the option Windows provides to always directly open files of this type will be checked by default when the user is first presented with the security dialog box. Always Unsafe indicates that the option to always open files of this type will be disabled, and the user will not be able to select it.

With the description of the File Type Association Group set, the next step is to configure the actual file type information. Each group must specify at least one Supported File Type entry, but groups can support multiple entries if doing so makes sense. For example, when configuring the capability for an app to be associated with opening images, file types might include .jpg, .jpeg, .bmp, .png, and several others, all within the same File Type Association Group.

The final configuration item relates to how the app prefers to behave in response to a file activation. The Desired View option allows the app to inform Windows about its preference for how much screen real estate it should occupy when it is activated in response to a file activation. These values correspond to the `ViewSizePreference` enumeration. Table 12.1 lists the available values and their implications.

TABLE 12.1 Desired View Types

Desired View Value	Result
`(not set)` or `Default`	Default value. Indicates that the app has no inherent preference for how it will be positioned in response to an activation of this type. If neither the app making the request nor the app being activated has a preference, Windows assumes a value of `UseHalf`.
`Use More` or `Use Less`	Indicates that the app window should use either more or less than 50% of the available horizontal screen space.
`Use Half`	Takes exactly 50% of the available horizontal screen pixels.
`Use Minimum`	Uses the minimum width specified in the App Manifest file.

Keep in mind that this value is more a request than an actual demand of Windows. Several factors influence exactly how this setting is honored, including the fact that the launching app can also specify a preference indicating the amount of space it prefers to occupy following the launch operation. How these values are handled will be discussed later in this section.

After the app has been configured to register itself to activate in response to a file selection, you need to provide the code to actually handle the activation event and process the supplied file or files. This involves overriding the `OnFileActivated` method in the `App` class. This method accepts a FileActivatedEventArgs parameter that includes the files that are being passed to the app, the action verb associated with the activation action (examples include Open and Edit), and a StorageFile query object that can obtain information about nearby files. This latter property is often useful for apps such as photo viewer apps in which a user might want to see the other files in the same folder as the file that was passed in.

The example app is configured in its App Manifest to handle files that have the extension .wrtbe as part of the winrtbyexample File Type Association Group. For the purposes of these examples, it does not set a screen size preference, to allow the launching app to indicate the behavior of that preference. In the override for OnFileActivated, it simply uses the same user interface activation that is used when the app is launched, and then it iterates over the list of provided files and uses the data in the files to add new contacts to the list it is already managing. Listing 12.8 shows how this is handled. Note that the HandleBasicActivation method that is called is simply the application invocation logic that is normally called during the OnLaunched override and is responsible for setting up the application's navigation frame, setting the current windows content, and calling the Activate method (the "Application Lifecycle" section in Chapter 2, "Windows Store Apps and WinRT Components," covered this). It has been factored into its own method in the example app so that several of the different types of app activation being discussed can call the same code.

LISTING 12.8 Handling File Activation

```
protected async override void OnFileActivated
    (FileActivatedEventArgs args)
{
    await HandleBasicActivation(args);

    foreach (var storageFile in args.Files.OfType<IStorageFile>())
    {
        await SampleData.ProcessActivationFile(storageFile);
    }
}
```

Now that you have seen the basic approach to file activation, it makes sense to go back and discuss the role of the View Preference settings and how these are handled. Both the launching app and the app being activated have a voice in indicating what the window layout should be following this process, but Windows has the final say in determining how the requests that the apps are making will be respected. The apps are making requests, not demands, of Windows. Windows itself takes these requests into account and also considers the number of apps currently on the screen, the current screen orientation, the capabilities of the current display device, and whether the app being activated is already visible. After considering these factors, Windows ultimately makes the final decision about how the layout of the app windows should appear.

Protocol Activation

Protocol activations are similar to file activations. In this case, instead of being invoked by a request to open a file with a particular file extension, an app is activated in response to a request made to Windows to handle a URI with a given protocol designation. Beyond the http and https protocols you're probably familiar with for use in web browsers such as Internet Explorer, many other protocols are registered in Windows. For example, the mailto protocol is often associated with launching an email client application ready to compose an email to the specified addressee.

As you might expect, working with protocol activations is similar to working with file activations. You follow the same basic steps to prepare an app to accept protocol activations, including providing entries in the App Manifest file and handling the activation in the `Application` class.

To configure the App Manifest, open the **Declarations** panel, select the **Protocol** entry from the **Available Declarations** drop-down list, and press **Add**. Multiple protocol entries can be provided in a single app manifest, with each one supporting a separate protocol, in contrast to the File Type Activation groups used for file activation. Protocol activations require only that you define the name of the protocol, but they also allow several optional values. The Logo value supports defining a custom icon for this protocol and uses the app's Small Logo image by default. You can also provide a Display Name value. Finally, as with file activations, you can specify a Desired View value with the same options in Table 12.1.

Similar to the contact picker, no specific predefined method overrides handling the protocol activation. Instead, the general-purpose `OnActivated` method should be overridden, and the provided arguments should be examined to see if the `Kind` value matches `ActivationKind.Protocol`. If a match is found, the app can cast the provided arguments to an instance of the `ProtocolActivatedEventArgs` class, which provide the requested URI value in their `Uri` property. The URI generally includes some activation information in its body, such as its `Host` and `LocalPath` properties, which can direct the app to take some specific action.

The example app is configured in its App Manifest to respond to handle requests for URIs with the wrtbe-integration protocol. As in the file activation example, the protocol registration also omits setting a display size preference. In the `OnActivated` override, after checking for a `ContactPicker` activation, the code checks to see if this was a protocol activation. If so, it extracts the URI from the protocol activation event arguments and checks the `Scheme` property to determine how to handle the request. In this case, the `Host` value of the URI is retrieved and assumed to be the ID of a contact whose detailed information should be displayed. If the ID matches the ID of an existing entry, a request is made to navigate to that page. The code in Listing 12.9 shows this process.

LISTING 12.9 Handling Protocol Activation

```
protected async override void OnActivated(IActivatedEventArgs args)
{
    if (args.Kind == ActivationKind.ContactPicker)
    {
        // Additional code omitted
    }
    // Handle arrangements necessary if the app was launched via
    // a protocol request
    else if (args.Kind == ActivationKind.Protocol)
    {
        // Extract the arguments and do basic activation
        var protocolArgs = (ProtocolActivatedEventArgs)args;
        await HandleBasicActivation(protocolArgs);

        var providedUri = protocolArgs.Uri;
        if (providedUri.Scheme == "wrtbe-integration")
        {
            // If an Id is provided in the Uri, use it to try to locate
            // and navigate to the details page for a contact with the
            // matching Id
            var itemId = providedUri.Host;
```

```
            if (!String.IsNullOrWhiteSpace(itemId) &&
                SampleData.GetItem(itemId) != null)
            {
                var rootFrame = (Frame) Window.Current.Content;
                rootFrame.Navigate(typeof (ContactDetailPage), itemId);
            }
        }
        else
        {
            // Additional code omitted
        }
    }
    else
    {
        base.OnActivated(args);
    }
}
```

As it did for file activation, the Launcher App provides the capability to configure the content that will be used for the protocol activation, as well as the preferences to be used to make the request. The app allows a contact to be selected by issuing a contact picker request that can bring up the contact picker integration (provided by the Example App, as previously discussed). After a contact has been selected, the user can also select a View Preference and indicate whether the app selection dialog should appear. In this case, you can find the default apps that are registered as associated with protocols by bringing up **PC Settings**, selecting **Search and Apps**, choosing **Defaults**, and then clicking the link for **Choose Default Apps by Protocol**. When the user clicks the app's Launch button, the app builds a URI that corresponds to the indicated Contact selection and calls the `LaunchUriAsync` method provided by the Launcher class with the URI and the indicated preferences (see Listing 12.10).

Listing 12.10 Calling a Protocol Activation

```
// Build the URI to call
var uriBuilder = new UriBuilder
{
    Scheme = "wrtbe-integration",
    Host = _selectedContact.Id,
};

// Compose the options and make the call
var launcherOptions = new LauncherOptions
```

```
{
    DesiredRemainingView = selectedLauncherViewPreference,
    DisplayApplicationPicker = displayApplicationPicker,
};
await Launcher.LaunchUriAsync(uriBuilder.Uri, launcherOptions);
```

Account Picture Provider

In the **PC settings, Accounts, Your Account** page, users can set the account picture that will display when they are logged in to Windows. In addition to providing the capability to browse for files using a now-familiar file open picker, any installed apps that have been registered as account picture provider apps are listed under the heading Create an Account Picture. Apps that are capable of taking pictures then list themselves, and users can use familiar tools to set their profile image.

To register an app as an account picture provider, open the App Manifest file, select the **Declarations Panel**, choose **Account Picture Provider** from the **Available Declarations** drop-down list, and click **Add**. No additional options need to be provided.

After you supply this setting, when an app is activated from the Your Account page, the activation behaves the same as a protocol activation with the specific protocol value of `ms-accountpictureprovider`. As the earlier section "Protocol Activation" explained, you can retrieve this value in the `Application` instance's `OnActivated` method override. The app then can use it to navigate to the appropriate UI page, to allow the user to obtain and work with the account image. Listing 12.11 shows the general structure for this check in the overridden `OnActivated` method.

LISTING 12.11 Handling an Account Picture Provider Request

```
if (args.Kind == ActivationKind.Protocol)
{
    // Extract the arguments and do basic activation
    var protocolArgs = (ProtocolActivatedEventArgs)args;
    if (protocolArgs.Uri.Scheme == "ms-accountpictureprovider")
    {
        // The app was activated as an Account Picture Provider
        // Navigate to a page where the new picture can be obtained
    }
}
```

The example app does not do anything special in the activation method, but it does include the capability to set a selected image file that has been associated with a Contact as the currently logged-in user's account picture. When an image file is selected in the contact detail page, the Set Account Pic button in the App Bar is enabled. Clicking this button displays a prompt asking for confirmation on whether the current image should be applied as the User Account Picture; if confirmed, an attempt to reset the account picture is made using the `UserInformation.SetAccountPictureAsync` method.

AutoPlay

Apps can be registered to be activated in response to content or device events that occur when users connect devices to the computer the app is running on. Windows raises content events when a storage device such as a thumb drive is attached; device events are raised when devices such as photo cameras, video cameras, cellphones, or digital music players are connected.

To register an app to be activated in response to a content event, open the App Manifest file, select the **Declarations Panel**, then choose **AutoPlay Content** from the **Available Declarations** drop-down list, and click the **Add** button. You must complete several settings for the **AutoPlay Content** entry. The **Action display name** is the text to use for this particular entry in the AutoPlay UI that Windows displays when this type of content is first launched. It also is included in the list of options that appear for a matching device in the settings in **PC Settings, PC and devices, AutoPlay**.

The **Content event** text specifies the type of content event this entry is attempting to match. The **Verb** entry is a text value that is supplied to the app in the `Verb` property of the activation parameters it receives. Activations in response to AutoPlay content events appear as file activation events, but this verb parameter enables you to distinguish them from other file activations. Finally, for AutoPlay content events, your app must also have the **Removable Storage** capability set in the App Manifest file.

To register an app to be activated in response to a device event, open the App Manifest file, select the **Declarations Panel**, choose **AutoPlay Device** from the **Available Declarations** drop-down list, and click the **Add** button. As with the configuration for AutoPlay content, you must provide three settings. A device can be configured to raise a particular event when it is attached to a computer. The **Device event** value defines the event that this app will be configured to respond to. The **Action display name** and **Verb** settings serve the same purposes they do for **AutoPlay Content** configuration. App activation in response to AutoPlay device events occurs with the `Device` value for the activation `Kind`, and because no dedicated override is provided, they need to be handled in the generic `OnActivated` method override in the `Application` class. The event arguments are supplied as an instance of the `DeviceActivatedEventArgs` class, which provides a `DeviceInformationId` value that returns the device identifier for the device that invoked AutoPlay, as well as the `Verb` value specified in the configuration step.

The example app is configured to support AutoPlay content activation for devices that raise the custom `WindowsRuntimeByExampleAutoPlay` event. You can configure a regular thumb drive to raise this event by specifying it as a `CustomEvent` value in an `autorun.inf` file placed in the device's root folder. For convenience, the Launcher Example app includes a predefined `autorun.inf` file in its `AutoPlay` folder, which can be copied onto the root folder of a thumb drive for use with the example app. In addition to this file, one or more contact sample data files that contain contact information stored as JSON should be placed in the thumb drive root folder.

The example app's AutoPlay content entry responds to being selected as the handler for content devices that raise the `WindowsRuntimeByExampleAutoPlay` event with the `ScanWRTBEFiles` verb. The `OnFileActivated` method includes a check for this particular `Verb` value. If a match occurs, it retrieves the root folder of the thumb drive, which is the first entry in the list of files supplied as part of the event arguments for this activation type. It then locates any wrtbe files in the root folder and processes them to add their provided contact entries to the current list of managed contacts. Listing 12.12 shows this process.

LISTING 12.12 Handling AutoPlay Content Activation

```
if (args.Verb == "ScanWRTBEFiles")
{
    var rootFolder = args.Files.OfType<StorageFolder>().FirstOrDefault();
    if (rootFolder != null)
    {
        // Potentially recursively scan through all folders.
        // For now just use files at the root.
        var queryOptions = new QueryOptions(
            CommonFileQuery.DefaultQuery,
            new[] { ".wrtbe" });
        var query = rootFolder.CreateFileQueryWithOptions(queryOptions);
        var contactFiles = await query.GetFilesAsync();
        foreach (var contactFile in contactFiles)
        {
            await SampleData.ProcessActivationFile(contactFile);
        }
    }
}
```

Working with Contacts and Appointments

Most of the content you have seen so far relates to the idea of presenting your app in response to an interaction with Windows. Apps register to provide user interfaces and content in response to a user selecting the app from a file open, file save, or contact picker that Windows displays upon request. Apps provide custom activation behavior in response to file or protocol requests issued to Windows and so forth. This chapter discusses another category of integration as well. This category centers on Windows providing integrated behavior to an app in response to a request it makes to the Windows Runtime.

To some degree, you have seen this kind of integration in the previous discussions concerning the use of the Charms and the file open, file save, and contact pickers. An app calls the appropriate Windows Runtime method, and Windows shows the corresponding user interface that it manages in a way Windows can take steps to participate in ensuring the security and integrity of the operation. Despite the similarities, the integration elements this section discusses introduce some subtle differences.

This section focuses on the Contact and Appointment integration available through the Windows Runtime and Windows 8.1. In both cases, the Windows Runtime provides functionality that can show preconfigured pop-up dialogs that display information and provide interactive commands. In this way, apps can allow users to interact with these data sources, but with the actual data involved largely opaque to the calling app, thereby mitigating the associated security and privacy concerns.

The Example App

This section continues to use the **IntegrationExample** app from the previous sections. In the Contact Details page, clicking the image shown for the user information brings up a best-match Contact Card for that particular contact. Also on this same page, the App Bar includes commands to display Calendar information, as well as to create a new Appointment.

Contacts

Beyond obtaining references to contacts through user interaction with the contact picker, an app that displays information about people who might be contacts can use the Windows Runtime to display a Contact Card pop-up within the app. The pop-up includes a banner section that lists the contact's name and address, with a background color based on the app's tile color. It also shows some combination of several actions that can be performed from the card, depending on the information available for the contact. These actions include Email, Call, Send Message, Video Call, Map Address, and Post (to social media). Because the card has room for only three of the actions, a More Details link is shown that brings up the full profile for the contact in the People app. If the contact being shown cannot be located in the People app, an Add Contact link appears instead; when clicked, it activates the People app with the provided contact information ready to be added as a new entry. Figure 12.1 shows a sample Contact Card.

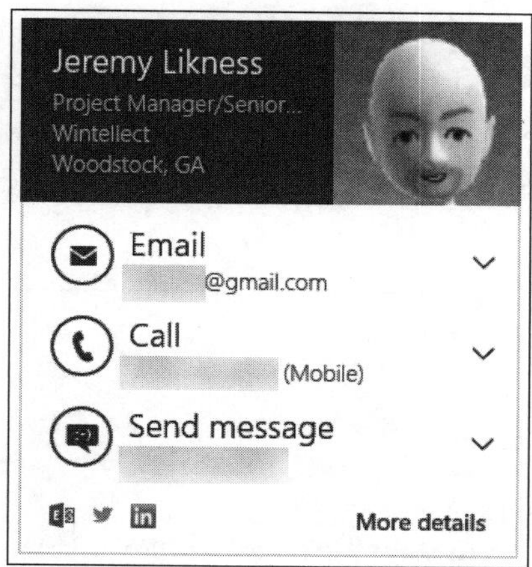

FIGURE 12.1 A Contact Card showing Email, Call, and Send Message actions

This functionality is accessed through the static `ContactManager` class, which provides the `ShowContactCard` method. The method accepts a `Contact` object, a rectangle value titled `Selection`, and an optional `PreferredPlacement` value. The Selection and Placement values inform the Windows Runtime about where to draw the pop-up. The `Selection` value defines a bounding rectangle within which you do not want the pop-up control to appear, if at all possible. Ideally, you want the pop-up to display in some way adjacent to the control used to invoke it. The `PreferredPlacement` value provides a value of the `Placement` enumeration that defines where the pop-up should be placed relative to the defined bounding rectangle; the default value instructs the Windows Runtime to determine the optimal placement.

The `Contact` value provided to the `ShowContactCard` method is used to find the contact in the People app that should be displayed in the Contact Card. This contact object must minimally include an ID, one or more email addresses, or a phone number; these are the values used to identify a match. The matching first attempts to find a match on the ID value and stops if it finds one. Email Addresses and Phone Numbers are matched first by exact value and then by a "best effort" that is defined within the Windows Runtime. If one or more matching values are found, the first match is returned and displayed in the Contact Card. If no match is found, a new custom Contact Card appears that shows the information provided in the input `Contact` parameter value.

In the example app, the current `Contact` object is used as the content to match. The bounding rectangle is computed from the control that was clicked and is the default placement of the card being used. Listing 12.13 shows the code to display the Contact Card in this way.

LISTING 12.13 Showing a Contact Card

```
private void HandleContactImageTapped(Object sender,
    TappedRoutedEventArgs e)
{
    var senderElement = (FrameworkElement)sender;
    var itemRect = senderElement.GetElementRect();
    var contact = (Contact)DefaultViewModel["Contact"];
    ContactManager.ShowContactCard(contact, itemRect, Placement.Default);
}
```

Appointments

Showing Calendar and Appointment information within an app is similar to showing Contact information, although a little more interactivity is available through this API. The information this API accesses is obtained from whichever app is currently registered to be the **Appointment Provider** app. This is usually the **Calendar** app, but the Windows Runtime offers some extensibility so that other apps can be selected to take its place. Whichever app is selected appears as the Calendar entry in the Choose Default Apps section within PC settings, Search and Apps.

Similar to the `ContactManager`, the Appointments API is provided by the static `AppointmentManager` class. This class provides several methods for interacting with Appointment information. These include `ShowTimeFrameAsync`, which activates the Calendar app to display the requested date and timeframe. It actually does not display a pop-up, but it activates the app externally as a file or protocol activation would.

The `AppointmentManager` class includes three additional methods for showing pop-ups that enable the user to interact with appointments. These methods all take the same `Selection` and `PreferredPlacement` values as the Contact Card display (see the previous section). The `ShowAddAppointmentAsync` method accepts an Appointment object that defines the desired values for an appointment that should be added to the calendar. The pop-up displays a preview of the appointment information and includes a button to confirm and accept the addition. If successful, this method returns an appointment identifier, which can be used in the calls to `ShowRemoveAppointmentAsync` and `ShowReplaceAppointmentAsync`. As their names imply, `ShowRemoveAppointmentsAsync` shows a pop-up to remove an appointment based on the ID that is supplied, and `ShowReplaceAppointmentAsync` requires an ID and a new appointment object; it replaces the contents of the appointment with the given ID with the new supplied value.

The example app includes an App Bar button to show the calendar for a given timeframe, configured to start at the current time and include seven days, as the following code shows:

```
await AppointmentManager.ShowTimeFrameAsync(
     DateTimeOffset.Now,
     TimeSpan.FromDays(7));
```

Another App Bar button is included to create a default 1-hour appointment set to start at the bottom of the next hour. Listing 12.14 shows this code.

LISTING 12.14 Adding a New Appointment

```
var senderElement = sender as FrameworkElement;
var itemRect = senderElement.GetElementRect();
var contact = (Contact)DefaultViewModel["Contact"];

var subject =
    String.Format("Sample appointment with {0}", contact.DisplayName);
var startTime =
    DateTimeOffset.Now
    - TimeSpan.FromMinutes(DateTimeOffset.Now.Minute)
    + TimeSpan.FromHours(1);

var details =
    "This is a sample appointment for the book WinRT by Example";

var appointment = new Appointment
{
    Subject = subject,
    StartTime = startTime,
    Duration = TimeSpan.FromHours(1),
    BusyStatus = AppointmentBusyStatus.Busy,
    AllDay = false,
    Details = details,
```

```
    Location = "Online",
};
var appointmentId =
    await AppointmentManager.ShowAddAppointmentAsync(
    appointment, itemRect, Placement.Default);
```

Summary

In this chapter, you learned about several different ways to use the Windows Runtime to integrate an app with Windows, above and beyond the integration available with the Windows Charms. You saw how an app can show a custom user experience within the file and contact pickers to allow users to select items that the app itself manages, without the calling app needing any insight into the implementation or storage approach used by the app supplying the information. You saw how to activate an app in response to requests to open a particular file or handle a certain protocol, or to provide the account picture for the user who is currently logged in to Windows. You also saw how an app can respond to new hardware being attached to the computer that the app is running on. Finally, you explored how the Windows Runtime provides the capability to bring Contact and Appointment user interface elements from Windows into an app.

In the next chapter, you see how the Windows Runtime enables you to integrate with a wide range of different devices connected to computers running Windows 8.1. This will include discussions about interacting with input devices as well as GPS and other sensors to further extend the interactivity that is offered by your computer.

13

Devices

IN EARLIER CHAPTERS, YOU SAW THAT ALTHOUGH THE BUILT-IN controls you can use in your Windows 8.1 apps include extensive support for touch-based interactions, input from mouse and keyboard input devices continues to be fully supported. The Windows Runtime also features extensive support for gathering information from other inputs, including sensors. The information these sensors provide includes details about a device's location, as well as knowledge about its position and motion within its immediate environment. Having the capability to incorporate this information into your apps means you can consider giving your users new kinds of interactivity and immersion.

In this chapter, you see how the WinRT APIs provide a common model for working with the various kinds of input pointer devices. This model provides a range of access, allowing you not only to obtain information about raw pointer events, but also to work with higher-level abstract gestures, depending on the needs of your app. You also see how you can access keyboard events from your code and obtain information about the user's key presses.

In addition, you learn about the WinRT APIs for working with location information, including the capability to set up geographic fences that can result in automatic notifications to your app when your device crosses a fence boundary. Furthermore, you learn how to work with the WinRT APIs that provide access to sensors that can give you information about your device's interactions with the physical world around it, including details about its orientation, its heading, the rate and direction of its motion, and even the amount of light currently shining on it.

Working with Input Devices

In Chapter 2, "Windows Store Apps and WinRT Components," you saw how the built-in controls that the Windows Runtime provides are designed to support first-class interactions through touch, as well as keyboard and mouse combinations. Although access to touch input is becoming more common in modern computers and devices, it is not yet available everywhere. Attached keyboards, mouse devices, and pens continue to be important tools for application interaction, not only when touch input is unavailable, but also in addition to touch input when certain interactions are simply easier and more natural using these other input mechanisms.

For touch, mouse, and pen inputs, the Windows Runtime API provides several different kinds of methods and events for working with these devices and responding to user interaction with them. In addition to the APIs for working with these devices, a set of methods and events are available for responding to user interactions with their keyboards.

The Example App

The **InputsExample** project illustrates several kinds of input device API integration that you can add to your apps. The app enables the user to add shapes to the application canvas, which are then animated to move around the canvas area. The app also detects what input devices are available and shows information about these connected devices, and it provides options for configuring what device types the app will listen to for input and which of the screen or keyboard events the app will respond to. Shapes can be added through buttons provided on the user interface or by pressing predefined keyboard buttons. The shapes themselves are configured to respond in several ways to interaction with pointer input devices. When a pointer intersects the edge of a shape, the shape is highlighted and stops moving. The shapes can also be manipulated to change position, degree of rotation, and size, with or without inertia. Finally, the shapes respond to gestures by changing color when tapped, changing direction when double-tapped, and resetting to their initial size, color, and rotation when they are held or right-clicked.

Identifying Connected Input Devices

You can determine which touch input devices are connected and what their capabilities are in a couple ways. One approach is to use the information that the `PointerDevice` class provides to obtain detailed information about available touch, mouse, or pen devices. Alternatively, higher-level classes can garner more general information about the current mouse and touch capabilities.

The `PointerDevice` class can obtain detailed information about one or more connected pointer devices. It provides a static `GetPointerDevices` method that returns a list of available devices as `PointerDevice` object instances, as well as a static `GetPointerDevice` method that can retrieve a specific device based on a pointer ID value (the "Pointer Events" section, later in this chapter, explains how to obtain a pointer ID). Properties of particular interest that the `PointerDevice` type exposes include the `PointerDeviceType`, which shows whether the device is a `Mouse`, `Touch`, or `Pen` device, and the `IsIntegrated` flag, to indicate whether the device is considered to be integrated into the current machine or has been connected externally. It also includes a `SupportedUsages` collection that lists Human Interface Device (HID) "usages" as `PointerDeviceUsage` objects. These usages are defined by Usage Page and Usage Id values that are part of the USB HID specification[1] and expose value ranges that the pointer device supports.

Listing 13.1 shows how the example application uses device information to determine whether touch, mouse, or pen devices are available. A list of available devices is obtained depending on whether the list should include only integrated devices. The resulting values are then queried to see if any of the desired device types are present.

---

[1]USB HID information, www.usb.org/developers/hidpage

LISTING 13.1 Determining Device Availability

```
var devices = PointerDevice.GetPointerDevices();
if (PointerIntegratedDevicesOnly)
{
    devices = devices.Where(x => x.IsIntegrated).ToList();
}
IsTouchAvailable
    = devices.Any(x => x.PointerDeviceType == PointerDeviceType.Touch);
IsMouseAvailable
    = devices.Any(x => x.PointerDeviceType == PointerDeviceType.Mouse);
IsPenAvailable
    = devices.Any(x => x.PointerDeviceType == PointerDeviceType.Pen);
```

The `MouseCapabilities` and `TouchCapabilities` classes obtain higher-level system-wide information about the available mouse and touch device support. When an instance of one of these types is created, its properties provide access to information about the respective device availability.

For `MouseCapabilities`:

- The `MousePresent` property is set to a value of `1` if one or more mouse devices are currently available.
- The `NumberOfButtons` value indicates the highest value available for any given device.
- The `VerticalWheelPresent` or `HorizontalWheelPresent` properties is set to a value of `1` to indicate whether a device is connected that has each respective feature.
- The `SwapButtons` property is set to `1` if the mouse buttons have been swapped in the system settings.

For `TouchCapabilities`:

- The `TouchPresent` property returns a value of `1` if a touch digitizer is present.
- The `Contacts` property indicates the highest number of concurrent contacts that are supported.

The example application uses these values to populate the message boxes that display when the user clicks the **Details** buttons next to the check boxes that it provides to enable or disable mouse and touch input (see Listings 13.2 and 13.3).

LISTING 13.2 Displaying Mouse Capabilities

```
var capabilities = new MouseCapabilities();
String message;
if (capabilities.MousePresent == 1)
{
    var rawMessage =
        "There is a mouse present. " +
        "The connected mice have a max of {0} buttons. " +
        "There {1} a vertical wheel present. " +
        "There {2} a horizontal wheel present. "  +
        "Mouse buttons {3} been swapped.";

    message = String.Format(rawMessage
        , capabilities.NumberOfButtons
        , capabilities.VerticalWheelPresent == 1 ? "is" : "is not"
        , capabilities.HorizontalWheelPresent == 1 ? "is" : "is not"
        , capabilities.SwapButtons == 1 ? "have" : "have not"
        );
}
else
{
    message = "There are no mice present.";
}
ShowMessage(message, "Mouse Properties");
```

LISTING 13.3 Displaying Touch Capabilities

```
var capabilities = new TouchCapabilities();
String message;
if (capabilities.TouchPresent == 1)
{
    var rawMessage =
        "Touch support is available. " +
        "Up to {0} touch points are supported.";

    message = String.Format(rawMessage, capabilities.Contacts);
}
else
{
    message = "Touch support is not available.";
}
ShowMessage(message, "Touch Properties");
```

Pointer, Manipulation, and Gesture Events

Instead of having a separate set of input events for touch, mouse, and pen inputs, the Windows Runtime API combines input from these devices and provides several distinct tiers of events that can be raised in response to input from any of these devices. At the lowest tier are the pointer events, which are raised for each press, move, release, or other simple interaction. Next are the manipulation events, which track and consolidate actions from one or more pointers into higher-level events related to motion, scale, rotation, and inertia. Finally, the gesture events consolidate pointer actions into even higher-level gesture abstractions, such as tapping, double-tapping, and holding.

In the example application, all the support for working with input device pointer, manipulation, and gesture events has been consolidated into a single `InputEventHandler` class. This class handles the subscriptions to the desired events and provides the event handler implementations for these subscriptions.

> **NOTE**
>
> Chapter 2 introduced you to the Visual Studio simulator for Windows Store Apps, which enables you to run and test your Windows 8.1 app within a simulated environment on your development system. Ultimately, testing touch support in an application is best done with a device that actually has touch support. However, if you happen to be using a development environment that does not provide this support, using the simulator's touch-emulation features is a good start toward exercising this kind of functionality in your app. Ultimately, however, it is a good idea to make sure your app is exercised for some amount of time in an actual touch environment.

Pointer Events

The Windows Runtime combines input from touch, mouse, or stylus devices into the abstract concept of a pointer. Each contact point from each device is represented by a unique pointer instance. For example, imagine an app running on a touch-enabled tablet that supports multiple touch points, and imagine that multiple fingers are pressing the screen simultaneously. In this case, each finger touching the screen is treated as a unique pointer. The same holds true if the touch actions include a combination of several fingers, as well as a click by a mouse or screen contact with a stylus. The mouse and/or stylus inputs are treated as additional unique pointers.

In Windows 8 XAML apps, the most common way to subscribe to pointer events is through events that individual `UIElement` objects expose. An alternative approach involves subscribing to similar events exposed by an `ICoreWindow` instance, which can be obtained through the `Window.Current.CoreWindow` property. This latter approach is primarily used by DirectX WinRT games when `UIElement` objects aren't readily available. Table 13.1 summarizes the pointer events that are available when a `UIElement` is used.

TABLE 13.1 Pointer Events

Event	Description
`PointerEntered`	A pointer has moved into the item's bounding area. For mouse and stylus input, this does not require a press. For touch input, because there is no "hover" support, an actual touch is required; it results in an immediate subsequent `PointerPressed` event, unless cancelled in this event's handler.
`PointerExited`	A pointer that was in an element's bounding area has left that area. For touch input, this event immediately follows a `PointerReleased` event.
`PointerPressed`	A pointer has been pressed while within the bounding area for an item. Note that a `PointerPressed` is not always terminated by a `PointerRelased` event, but it can instead be ended by `PointerCanceled` or `PointerCaptureLost` events.
`PointerMoved`	A pointer that has entered an item's bounding area is being moved within that area, or a pointer that has been captured by an item is moving, even if its position is beyond the item's bounding area.
`PointerReleased`	A pointer that was pressed has been released, usually within an item's bounding area. This occurs if the pointer was pressed while inside the item's bounding area; a corresponding `PointerPressed` event then has been raised, or if the pointer was already pressed when it moved into the item's bounding area, the `PointerPressed` event might have occurred elsewhere. If the pointer is currently captured by an item, this event can also be raised when the pointer is released outside the item's boundary.

Event	Description
PointerCanceled	A pointer has lost contact with an item in an unexpected way. This event can fire instead of the PointerReleased event. Potential reasons for unexpected contact loss include changes in an app's display size, the user logging off, or the depletion of available contact points. Note that this event is only part of the UIElement events, and the ICoreWindow interface does not provide or raise it.
PointerCapture-Lost	A pointer capture that the event source item obtained has been released either programmatically or because a corresponding PointerPressed has been released.

Several of the pointer events in Table 13.1 either are directly related to or have side effects that are related to the idea of a pointer being captured. When a pointer is captured, only the element that captured it receives any of the input events related to that pointer until the capture has been released. Typically, a pointer is captured within the handler for a `PointerPressed` event because a pointer must be pressed to be captured. To capture a pointer, the `UIElement` class includes a `CapturePointer` method that takes a `Pointer` class instance that identifies the pointer to capture. It just so happens that the `PointerRoutedEventArgs` that are passed to the `UIElement` pointer event handlers include this pointer object, as the following code illustrates:

```
private void HandlePointerPressed(Object sender,
    PointerRoutedEventArgs args)
{
    _eventSourceElement.CapturePointer(args.Pointer);
}
```

The `Pointer` object includes a `PointerId`, which is simply a unique integer that is assigned to the current pointer and identifies it throughout the various subsequent pointer events. It also includes a `PointerDeviceType` property that returns a value of the `PointerDeviceType` enumeration and indicates whether the current pointer is related to input from a touch device, a mouse device, or a pen device. In the example project, this value is used to ignore processing in the pointer events when a particular device type is deselected in the user interface.

```
if (!IsValidDevice(args.Pointer.PointerDeviceType)) return;
```

The Pointer object also includes a pair of flags to indicate the position of the pointer relative to the touch sensor. IsInContact indicates whether the device is actually contacting the sensor, such as whether a stylus is in direct contact with the screen when using a touchscreen tablet. In the case of a mouse device, this is true when one of its buttons is being pressed. IsInRange indicates whether the device is within detection range but not touching; it is primarily meant for pen devices because, unlike touch devices, they can usually be detected before they make physical contact. Generally, mouse devices always return True for this value, and touch devices return True only when a touch is actually occurring.

In addition to the Pointer object, the arguments passed to the pointer events include a KeyModifiers property that indicates whether one or more of the Control, Menu, Shift, or Windows special keyboard keys was pressed at the time of the event.

Finally, the event arguments include a pair of methods that obtain additional information about the input pointer associated with the current interaction. The GetCurrentPoint and GetIntermediatePoints methods both accept a UIElement to provide a frame of reference for any of the coordinate properties included in the method results. If this value is null, the coordinate values that are returned are relative to the app itself. Whereas GetCurrentPoint returns a single PointerPoint instance, the GetIntermediatePoints returns a collection of PointerPoint instances from the last pointer event through the current one. In addition to being able to obtain PointerPoint information from the pointer event arguments, the PointerPoint class itself includes static methods that accept a PointerId value and return the current or intermediate PointerPoint values, with coordinates relative to the app.

The PointerPoint class includes a lot of information about the current interaction. At the root, it includes the PointerId value, a Position value indicating the Point where the pointer event occurred, and a PointerDevice property that provides the same PointerDevice value discussed in the earlier section "Identifying Connected Input Devices." It also includes a

`Properties` value that provides access to significantly more detailed information. Among the properties provided, this value includes touch information, such as the contact rectangle value; mouse information, such as whether the left, middle, right, first extended, or second extended buttons are pressed; and pen information, including several values that describe the physical position of the pen, whether it is inverted, and the amount of pressure being applied to its tip. Furthermore, the `HasUsage` and `GetUsage` methods are useful in obtaining HID value information from the device for the current interaction. These are the same HID values that can be enumerated with the `SupportedUsages` method that `PointerDevice` class instances mentioned earlier provide. The following code shows how to request the amount of tip pressure (`usageId` value `0x30`) applied to a digitizer stylus device (`usagePage` value `0x0D`).

```
if (pointerDetails.Properties.HasUsage(0x0D, 0x30))
{
    pressure = pointerDetails.Properties.GetUsageValue(0x0D, 0x30);
}
```

Although the amount of detail provided by the pointer events can harness a lot of power, the information provided is at a very low level. For most application needs, this information needs to be synthesized into more abstract concepts. Examples might include recognizing a pair of `PointerPressed` and `PointerReleased` events potentially as either a single tap or a hold action, depending on how much time elapses between the two pointer actions, or perhaps tracking multiple pointer actions to determine whether pinch or rotation actions are occurring. Fortunately, you will most likely not need to write and maintain the state-tracking code required to achieve this level of abstraction; these kinds of events are already calculated and provided for you in the form of the manipulation events and gesture events.

Manipulation Events

Manipulation events are the result of grouping and translating several pointer events associated to an item that originate from either one or several pointers. During a manipulation, changes to translation (position), scale (size), and rotation are computed, tracked, and made available via the event argument parameters provided by these events. A manipulation also tracks the velocities with which these changes are occurring and includes the capability to optionally calculate and apply inertia based on these velocities when the pointer events complete.

In Windows 8.1 XAML apps, the most common way you subscribe to manipulation events is through the events that individual `UIElement` objects expose. For a `UIElement` to generate manipulation events, the element needs to have its `ManipulationMode` property set to a value of the `ManipulationModes` enumeration other than `None` or `System`. The default value for most controls is `System`, and it enables the `UIElement` to process manipulations internally, whereas a value of `None` suppresses all manipulations. Other significant values include `TranslateX` and `TranslateY` to track movement on the x- and y-axis, `Rotate` to track rotation, and `Scale` to track stretching or pinching. Values for `TranslateInertia`, `RotateInertia`, and `ScaleInertia` are also available to indicate that these manipulations should trigger inertia calculations. Table 13.2 summarizes the manipulation events exposed by the `UIElement` class.

TABLE 13.2 Manipulation Events

Event	Description
`ManipulationStarting`	A `PointerPressed` event has occurred, and manipulation processing starts looking for the pointer to move, to actually start tracking a manipulation.
`ManipulationStarted`	A pressed pointer has moved. This marks the beginning of the manipulation, which contains some number of `ManipulationDelta` events and is concluded with a `ManipulationCompleted` event.
`ManipulationDelta`	One or more of the pressed pointers have moved or inertia is being applied.
`ManipulationInertiaStarting`	The manipulation has been configured to support inertia, and the last pointer was released while the manipulation still had a velocity. `ManipulationDelta` events are raised until velocity falls below the inertia-defined threshold.
`ManipulationCompleted`	The last pointer is no longer pressed, and any inertia calculations have completed.

The first event received during a manipulation is the ManipulationStarting event. This event includes a Mode property that initially matches the ManipulationMode value set on the UIElement object. It allows the types of manipulations that will be tracked to be modified one last time before the manipulation tracking actually starts. If a pressed pointer is moved, the ManipulationStarted event is fired, followed by one or more ManipulationDelta events as the pointer continues to move.

The arguments provided to the ManipulationDelta event handler provide the information that can be used to react to the manipulation. The arguments contain some general-purpose informational properties that include the PointerDeviceType, which is the same as it was for the pointer events (note that this implies that a manipulation cannot span device types, such as a pinch occurring with both a finger and a mouse); a Container value that indicates the UIElement on which the manipulation is occurring; and an IsInertial flag that specifies whether the ManipulationDelta event is a result of inertia that occurs after pointers have been released. Of particular interest, however, are the Delta, Cumulative, and Velocity values.

The Delta property provides the changes in the values for Translation, Expansion, Scale, and Rotation that have occurred since the last ManipulationDelta event occurred. Translation indicates how much movement occurred on the x- and y-axis. Expansion specifies how far the distance grew or shrank between touch contacts. Scale is similar to Expansion, but it specifies the change in distance as a percentage. Finally, Rotation specifies the change in the rotation degrees. The Cumulative property returns the same items, except that the values returned are the overall changes that have occurred since the manipulation started instead of since the previous ManipulationDelta event. Finally, the Velocity provides a Linear property that contains the x and y velocities specified in pixels/milliseconds, an Expansion property that specifies the scaling change in pixels/ milliseconds, and an Angular property that specifies the rotational velocity in degrees/ milliseconds.

In the example application, the delta values are applied to the shape being manipulated to move it onscreen, resize it, or rotate it (rotation is better seen with the square shape than the circular one). Listing 13.4 shows the event handler in the `InputEventHandler` class for the `ManipulationDelta` event.

LISTING 13.4 Handling Manipulation Changes

```
private void HandleManipulationDelta
    (Object sender, ManipulationDeltaRoutedEventArgs args)
{
    // Check to see if this kind of device is being ignored
    if (!IsValidDevice(args.PointerDeviceType)) return;

    // Update the shape display based on the delta values
    var delta = args.Delta;
    _shapeModel.MoveShape(delta.Translation.X, delta.Translation.Y);
    _shapeModel.ResizeShape(delta.Scale);
    _shapeModel.RotateShape(delta.Rotation);
}
```

The processing in the `ShapeModel` class is fairly straightforward. The `MoveShape` method simply makes sure that adding the offset values to the current position doesn't move the shape beyond the current borders and adjusts the resulting position value accordingly. `ResizeShape` multiplies the current shape scale by the provided percentage and then makes sure the resulting shape size is within the minimum and maximum boundaries established for a shape. `RotateShape` simply adds the degree value to the current `Rotation` property. A `TranslateTransform` is bound to the shape position values. A `RotateTransform` has its `Angle` value bound to the rotation angle, as well as its `CenterX` and `CenterY` values bound to the position of the shape. Finally, a `ScaleTransform` has its `ScaleX` and `ScaleY` values bound to the scale of the shape, with the `CenterX` and `CenterY` values also bound to the shape position.

The final manipulation concept to be discussed is inertia. If one or more of the inertia `ManipulationMode` values is specified, the manipulation processing can include the application of inertia, depending on whether the last pointer involved in the manipulation was removed following an action that had a velocity. In the example app, this occurs when a shape is being dragged from one side of the screen to another and, halfway through, the finger/mouse/pen is suddenly released. In the physical world, the object would tend to continue to slide along until slowed by friction. With manipulation support for inertia, your app can include similar behavior without any extra work on your part.

When inertia starts, the `ManipulationInertiaStarting` event is raised. The arguments for this event include the arguments that were discussed for the `ManipulationDelta` event, as well as `TranslationBehavior`, `ExpansionBehavior`, and `RotationBehavior` arguments to control the behavior of the inertia effect. Each of these values includes a value called `DesiredDeceleration` that defines the deceleration rate, as well as a value to indicate the final desired value for each property, respectively named `DesiredDisplacement`, `DesiredExpansion`, and `DesiredRotation`. You can either leave the default values in place or replace them with your own value for more control over the inertia behavior. After the handler for this event has completed, the manipulation processor automatically raises `ManipulationDelta` events with values based on the application of inertia to the current state until either the desired value is reached (if specified) or deceleration results in a velocity of zero.

When the last pointer has been released, or when inertia has completed (when specified through the `ManipulationMode` setting), the `ManipulationCompleted` event is raised, signaling that the manipulation is now complete. The arguments to this event include the general-purpose informational properties that were discussed previously, as well as the `Cumulative` and `Velocities` information that was also provided to the `ManipulationDelta` event.

NOTE

Although the manipulation and gesture events the `UIElement` class provides will take care of most needs, more control or additional gesture types are required in some cases. The Windows Runtime provides the `Windows.UI.Input.GestureRecognizer` class, which can directly process pointer events to generate these high-level events.

Gesture Events

Gesture events are similar to manipulation events, in that they are the result of grouping and interpreting several pointer events. However, a few key differences set them apart. First, gesture events communicate more abstract and discrete concepts than manipulation events. Manipulation events communicate information about the beginning, middle, and end of a manipulation and include arguments that provide information about the different kind of changes that have occurred. Gesture events each relay information about the occurrence of a single, isolated event, such as a tap or a double-tap. Second, manipulation events provide information that synthesizes input from several pointers, whereas gesture events are concerned with the action of only one pointer at a given time.

As with manipulation events, the `UIElement` class provides the most commonly used access to gesture events and related configuration settings. Table 13.3 summarizes the gesture events made available by `UIElement` instances.

Table 13.3 Gesture Events Defined in `UIElement`

Event	Description
`Tapped`	A tap has occurred, defined by a quick pointer press and release (where a long press followed by a release results in `Holding` and `RightTapped` events). This is equivalent to a mouse `Click` event.
`DoubleTapped`	A second tap has occurred after a first tap event, within a system-setting defined time. This is equivalent to a mouse `DoubleClick` event.
`Holding`	A long-duration press is occurring or has completed. The event is raised when the long-press is initially detected, and once again when the long-press is either completed or cancelled. Mouse devices generally do not raise this event.
`RightTapped`	A right-tap has occurred, defined by either the completion of a holding gesture (for touch and pen devices) or a click with the right button (for mouse devices). This is equivalent to a mouse `RightClick` event.

All the gesture events include a PointerDeviceType property that indicates the type of device that generated the event, as well as a GetPosition method that returns the coordinates of the action that led to the event, relative to the UIElement argument in the method call. If a null value is provided to GetPosition, the coordinates returned are relative to the app itself. The Holding event also includes a HoldingState property that is discussed shortly. Note that the Tapped and Holding events are mutually exclusive. Also, when a double-tap occurs, a Tapped event is raised for the first interaction, but the second one generates only the DoubleTapped event.

The UIElement class also provides the IsTapEnabled, IsDoubleTapEnabled, IsHoldingEnabled, and IsRightTapEnabled properties. By default, they are all set to true; setting them to false prevents the corresponding event from being raised.

The Tapped, DoubleTapped, and RightTapped events are similar, but the Holding event behaves a little differently. As Table 13.3 mentioned, the Tapped event is usually generated only by interaction with touch and stylus devices, not by mouse devices. It is also the only event that is raised when the pointer involved in the event is in a pressed state. When a pointer is pressed and held steady, and after the initial hold time interval has passed, the Holding event is raised with its HoldingState property set to a value of Started. After the hold has begun, if the pointer is moved or the same element captures another pointer, the hold is considered to have been cancelled and the Holding event is raised once again, with the HoldingState property set to a value of Cancelled. Otherwise, when the pressed pointer is lifted, the Holding event is raised again with a HoldingState property set to a value of Completed. If the hold was successfully completed, the RightTapped event follows.

In the example application, the tap-related gesture events cause different actions to happen to the shapes they occur on. The Tapped event changes the shape color to a random value, the DoubleTapped event causes the shape to take a new randomly calculated direction, and the RightTapped event causes the shape to be reset to its original color, size, and rotation. The code in Listing 13.5 illustrates this interaction for a Tapped event.

LISTING 13.5 Processing a Gesture Event

```
private void HandleTapped(Object sender, TappedRoutedEventArgs args)
{
    // Check to see if this kind of device is being ignored
    if (!IsValidDevice(args.PointerDeviceType)) return;

    // Examine the current position
    var position = args.GetPosition(_eventSourceElement);
    Debug.WriteLine("Tapped at X={0}, Y={1}", position.X, position.Y);

    // Alter the shape based on the gesture performed
    _shapeModel.SetRandomColor();
}
```

Keyboard Input

In addition to the pointer-based input devices, the Windows Runtime includes support for working with input gathered from keyboards. To obtain information about the available keyboard support, you can use the `KeyboardCapabilities` class. Similar to the `MouseCapabilities` and `TouchCapabilities` counterparts, it includes a `KeyboardPresent` property that is set to a value of `1` if one or more keyboards are currently available. The example application uses this value to provide the text for a message box that displays when the user clicks the Details button next to the Keyboard header, as in Listing 13.6.

LISTING 13.6 Displaying Keyboard Capabilities

```
var keyboardCapabilities = new KeyboardCapabilities();
var message = keyboardCapabilities.KeyboardPresent == 1
    ? "There is a keyboard present."
    : "There is no keyboard present.";

ShowMessage(message, "Keyboard Properties");
```

The `UIElement` class provides two available keyboard events. The `KeyDown` event is raised when a key is pressed, and the `KeyUp` event is raised when a pressed key is released. These events are raised by a control only when the control has the input focus, either when the user taps inside the control or uses the Tab key to rotate focus to that control, or when the control's `Focus` method has been called programmatically.

As an alternative, the `CoreWindow` class provides three events related to keyboard interactions. Similar to the `UIElement`, it provides `KeyDown` and `KeyUp` events. However, these events are raised regardless of which control currently has input focus. The `CoreWindow` class also includes a `CharacterReceived` event, which is discussed in more detail shortly.

In the case of the `UIElement`, both the `KeyDown` and `KeyUp` events provide `KeyRoutedEventArgs` arguments; for the `CoreWindow` class, the `KeyDown` and `KeyUp` events provide `KeyEventArgs` arguments. The most significant difference between these argument types is the naming of the property used to identify the key involved in the action that led to the event being raised. `KeyRoutedEventArgs` provides a property named `Key` that returns a value of the `VirtualKey` enumeration indicating the specific key on the keyboard that was pressed or released. In the `KeyEventArgs` class, the corresponding property is named `VirtualKey`.

In either case, the `KeyStatus` property contains additional information about the key event. For `KeyDown` events, its `WasKeyDown` property is particularly interesting because it indicates whether the event is being raised in response to a key being held down. In this case, several `KeyDown` events usually are raised, followed by a single `KeyUp` event. The first `KeyDown` event has its `WasKeyDown` value set to `false`, with the subsequent `KeyDown` events setting the value to `true`.

The `CharacterReceived` event of the `CoreWindow` class was previously mentioned. This event is fired between the `KeyDown` and `KeyUp` events and provides access to the actual interpreted character resulting from the current key combination. This value is returned as an unsigned integer in the `CharacterReceivedEventArgs KeyCode` property. It can be converted to the corresponding `Char` character using the `Convert.ToChar` function:

```
var interpretedChar = Convert.ToChar(args.KeyCode);
```

To put this in perspective, with a standard U.S. keyboard, pressing the equals (=) key while the Shift key is also pressed is interpreted to result in the plus (+) character. The `KeyDown` and `KeyUp` events understand this key only as `VirtualKey` 187, regardless of whether the Shift key is pressed. However, the `KeyCode` value provided in the arguments to the `CharacterReceived` event provides either a value of `61` for the equals key or a value of `43` for the plus key.

To illustrate the use of the keyboard input events, the main page in the example application listens for `KeyUp` events via the `CoreWindow` class to add either a new ball or a square shape whenever the B or S keys are pressed, respectively. The following code illustrates this:

```
if (args.VirtualKey == VirtualKey.B)
    CreateShape(ShapeModel.ShapeType.Ball);
```

Note that if you are interested in key combinations in which a "modifier key," such as one or more of the Shift, Control, or Alt keys pressed in concert with another key, you have two options. First, you can track the individual key down and key up events to determine which keys are up or down at any given instant. Second, you can actively interrogate the state of a given key by using the `GetKeyState` method that the `CoreWindow` class provides. Because the result of `GetKeyState` returns a flag value, it is a best practice to mask the result value before comparing it with the desired value. Also note that the Alt key corresponds to the `Menu` member of the `VirtualKey` enumeration. Listing 13.7 shows this approach.

LISTING 13.7 Checking for Modifier Keys

```
// Check for shift, control, alt (AKA VirtualKey.Menu)
var currentWindow = CoreWindow.GetForCurrentThread();
var ctrlState = currentWindow.GetKeyState(VirtualKey.Control);
var shftState = currentWindow.GetKeyState(VirtualKey.Shift);
var altState = currentWindow.GetKeyState(VirtualKey.Menu);
var isControlKeyPressed =
  (ctrlState & CoreVirtualKeyStates.Down) == CoreVirtualKeyStates.Down;
var isShiftKeyPressed =
  (shftState & CoreVirtualKeyStates.Down) == CoreVirtualKeyStates.Down;
var isAltKeyPressed =
  (altState & CoreVirtualKeyStates.Down) == CoreVirtualKeyStates.Down;
```

Sensor Input

Devices such as touchscreens, mouse devices, styluses, and keyboards provide interactivity by allowing an app to respond to their interactions with components shown on their device displays. Users tap elements drawn to the screen or type characters that will appear inside onscreen text regions. However, a class of input devices known as sensors can give a running app information about the device's relationship to its physical environment. Examples of the information sensors gather include details about which way the device is facing, its velocity in any particular direction, its position on the globe, and how much light is shining on it at a given moment. Devices might or might not include one or more of these kinds of sensors.

The Windows Runtime API includes support for working with several different kinds of sensors and relaying the information they gather. These APIs not only enable an app to ask for sensor measurements, but they also provide events that can be subscribed to and, in most cases, the capability to throttle how often these events can be raised. Some of the environmental information that can be obtained through these APIs includes information about a device's physical location, its movement and orientation, and how bright of an environment it is in.

The Example App

The **SensorsExample** project highlights a few different ways sensors can be used from within an application. The app features an instance of the interactive Bing Maps control surrounded by boxes that show information from and allow interaction with each of the various sensors. The boxes along the left side also allow the app to coordinate the information it receives from the sensors with the display of the Bing Maps control. The Location section allows the map to be centered at the current geolocation coordinates and also offers support for working with geofencing (the upcoming sections explain geofencing). The Compass section enables the app to set the map's orientation to approximate the current compass heading (although the support offered for setting a specified heading in the Bing Maps control is currently somewhat limited). The Inclinometer section allows the map to be panned in concert with the direction in which the device itself is being tilted.

Working with the Bing Maps Control

The Bing Maps control in the example project is part of the Bing Maps platform, which includes the Windows control, controls for other platforms, and several related data services. You can access information about the Bing Maps control and the related services and the tools and resources you need to include in your project through the Bing Maps Platform Portal.[2] Although the control and the related services offer a tremendous amount of functionality, you need to be aware of some important license-related and technical considerations for this example application and in case you are considering their use in your own app.

From a licensing standpoint, some restrictions govern how this control can be used. The Bing Maps Platform Portal includes a Licensing Options page that explains how the restrictions apply to your app, under what circumstances the tools can be used for free, and when a fee needs to be paid to license the use of the control. As of this writing, you can access this page by clicking the Licensing link from the Bing Maps Platform Portal page. If you will use the Bing Maps control in your Windows Store App, be sure to look over the restrictions and conditions for use in the context of your application needs and ensure that you are abiding by the appropriate terms of use.

From a technical standpoint, before you can build the **SensorsExample** project, you need to download and install the Bing Maps SDK. You can get to the latest SDK installer by following links on the Bing Maps Platform Portal. Alternatively, you can use the Visual Studio Extension Manager to obtain the SDK.

To use the Extension Manager, launch Visual Studio and select **Extensions and Updates** from the **Tools** menu. In the **Extensions and Updates** dialog box, select the **Online** node and then select **Visual Studio Gallery**. Then type **Bing Maps SDK** into the search box in the upper-right corner (see Figure 13.1). In the search results, select the entry for **Bing Maps SDK for Windows 8.1 Store Apps** and click the **Download** button; then click the **Install** button in the ensuing dialog box after you have read and reviewed the included license agreement. After the installation has

---

[2]Bing Maps Platform Portal, www.microsoft.com/maps/

completed, you will most likely be instructed to restart Visual Studio so that you can use the installed SDK components.

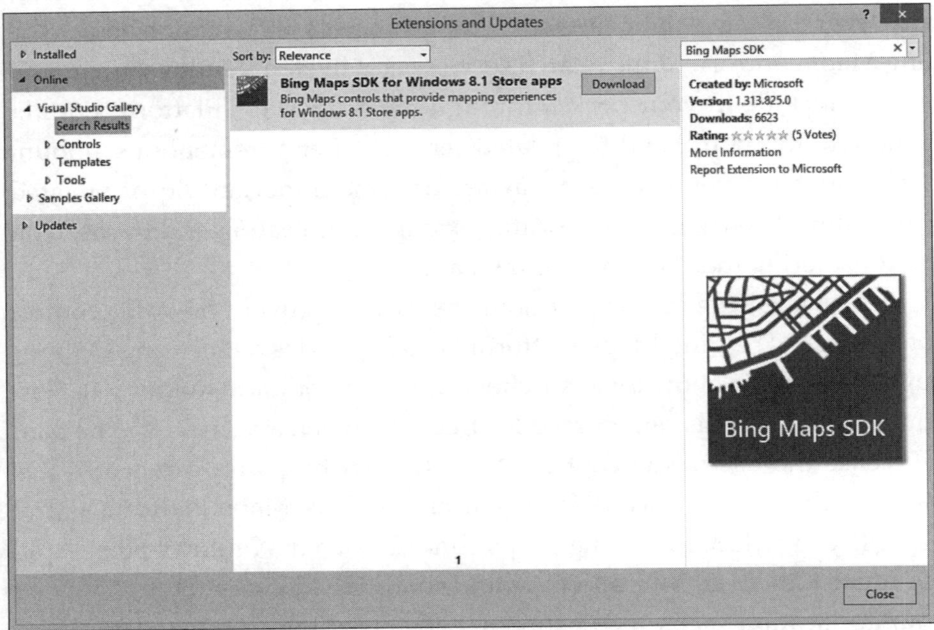

FIGURE 13.1 Locating the Bing Maps SDK Visual Studio extension

Because this additional download and installation is required to build the example project, the build configuration in the **WinRTByExample** solution has been configured to not include the **SensorsExample** project as part of the solution build by default. To build the project, you need to either select the project in the **Solution Explorer** and choose **Build** from the project file's context menu, or choose **Build SensorsExample** from the **Build** menu. Another option is to open the **Configuration Manager** entry from the **Build** menu and check the **Build** entry next to the **SensorsExample** project in the **Configuration Manager** dialog box that appears; the **SensorsExample** project then is built along with the other projects in the solution.

Another consideration when building a project that includes the Bing Maps control is the selection of a target platform. Most Windows Store apps are built with the target set to Any CPU. However, the Bing Maps control relies on the Visual C++ Runtime, which requires selecting a specific processor architecture to build a project that references it. You can set this value in the Configuration Manager dialog box. Select the appropriate Platform for your build either for the entire solution or for the **SensorsExample** project. For example, you need to select a value of **ARM** to create a version of the resulting app that will run on Windows RT devices. Note that in order to work with the XAML designer in Visual Studio, you need to select the value **x86**. If you prefer to have the interactive designer available, you can always set the value temporarily to x86 and then set it to your desired target platform when you have finished working in the XAML designer.

To deploy an app that includes the Bing Maps control, you need to specify a value for the map's `Credentials` property. If you do not specify a valid map key for the map `Credentials` property, the map control displays with a banner indicating that invalid credentials are being used, as you can see in the example app screen in Figure 13.2.

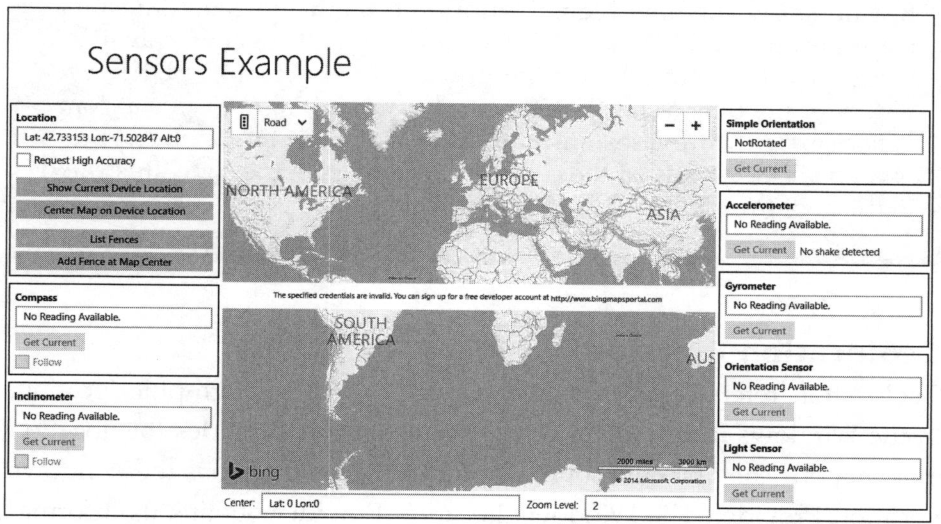

FIGURE 13.2 The Bing Maps control displayed without valid credentials

The following markup shows the credentials being set in the example project:

```
<maps:Map Credentials="{StaticResource MapKey}"/>
```

In this example, the credentials are located in the resource defined by the value `MapKey`, which is defined in the project's `App.xaml` file. The map key is a value you obtain from the Bing Maps Account Center.[3] Sign into the account center with your Microsoft Account credentials and select **Create or View Keys**. At this point, you can define a new key by specifying information about your application or retrieve a previously defined key. Place this key value into the `MapKey` resource in your project, and build and run your project to make sure that the warning message from Figure 13.2 no longer displays.

> **TIP**
>
> After you deal with the logistics related to licensing for the Bing Maps control and the mechanics related to installing the SDK, configuring the project build, and obtaining and configuring the map key, you will likely find that the Bing Maps control offers a tremendous amount of functionality. The Bing Maps Platform Portal includes both development guides and MSDN API documentation that covers the available functionality. Another helpful resource in the interactive SDK is provided for the Bing Maps AJAX control at www.bingmapsportal.com/isdk/ajaxv7: It provides an interactive map and the JavaScript and related HTML. Many of the concepts and much of the code illustrated in this tool translate readily to the corresponding .NET API.

Geolocation

Geolocation refers to information about an item's geographic location. In the Windows Runtime, one of two data sources provides this location information. The first data source for location information is the Windows Location Provider. The Windows Location Provider obtains its information from a couple different data sources. The first source it attempts to use is Wi-Fi triangulation, in which the proximity to different known Wi-Fi hotspots is used to determine a position. If Wi-Fi data is not available, IP

---

[3]Bing Maps Account Center, https://www.bingmapsportal.com/

address resolution is then used. The second data source that the Windows Runtime can use to obtain location information is available if the device optionally includes one or more Global Positioning System (GPS) sensors.

The network-based information that the Windows Location Provider gathers is limited in both accuracy and amount of available detail because only latitude, longitude, and accuracy information are made available. An installed GPS sensor most likely provides more accurate information (different sensors have different resolution capabilities) and also gives more location information than the Windows Location Service, potentially including details about direction, speed, and altitude. Note, however, that the additional detail afforded by GPS sensors tends to come with additional power use and, therefore, reduced battery life.

Getting Started

To start working with location information in a Windows 8.1 application, you first need to declare that the app will be accessing this information. Location information is considered to be personally identifiable information (PII), so any app that will access this information needs to explicitly declare its intent to do so. The App Store's certification process will refuse an app that includes use of the geolocation APIs if it does not provide such a declaration; if the app does provide the declaration, the app's entry in the store will indicate its intent to access this information. As an additional measure meant to protect users, Windows notifies users the first time an app accesses location information and prompts them to either allow or block access. Windows also provides several places where the user can choose to toggle this same permission on or off, as will be discussed shortly. To declare that an app will attempt to access location information, open the app manifest file, select the **Capabilities** panel, and check the **Location** entry under the **Capabilities** list (see Figure 13.3).

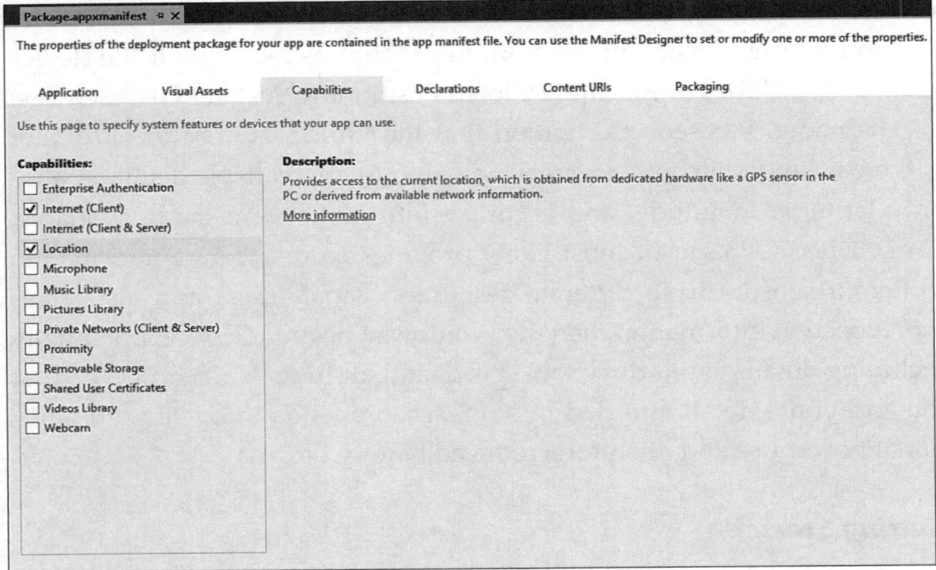

FIGURE 13.3 Setting the location capability in the app manifest

Using the Geolocator

The `Geolocator` class provides location information in the Windows Runtime. You can obtain the current position value from this class in two ways. The first option is to directly request the current position with the `GetGeopositionAsync` method. The second option is to provide a handler for the `PositionChanged` event that is called when a position change is detected, depending on the configuration of the `Geolocator` instance.

The first time an app calls the `GetGeopositionAsync` method or registers an event handler for the `PositionChanged` event, the user is prompted to grant permission for the app to access location information, as Figure 13.4 illustrates. Because this step might display a user interface element, it is important to make sure that this first call takes place on the UI thread; otherwise, an unexpected cross-thread exception might occur whose cause can be difficult to diagnose.

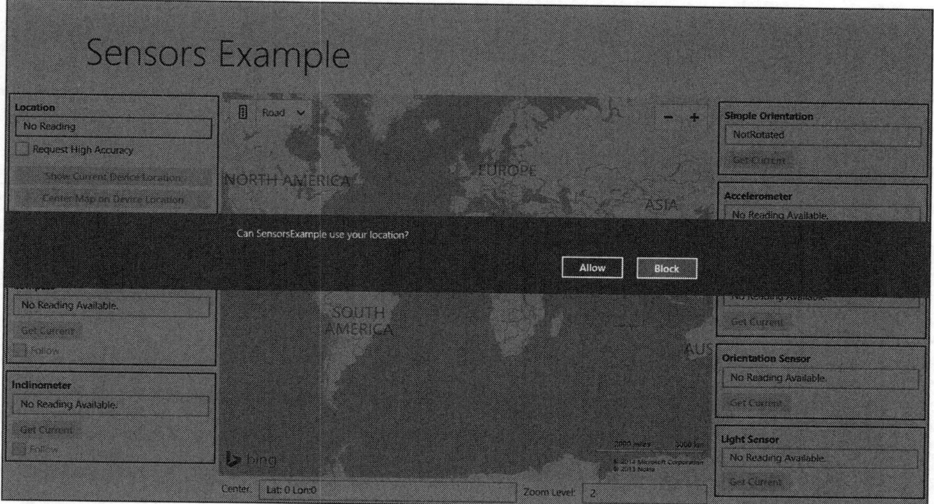

FIGURE 13.4 Windows prompting the user for location information permission

The value selected in the prompt is reflected in the **Permissions** panel that you can access through the app's **Settings Charm**, as well as within the **Location** panel in the **Privacy** section located in **PC Settings**. This system-wide location privacy screen lists all the applications that are registered to access position information and states whether access is currently blocked or enabled. It also includes a system-wide switch to disable access to location information for all apps that request it. However they access it, when users choose to block the app's access to location information, the `LocationStatus` property on the `Geolocator` instance returns a value of `PositionStatus.Disabled`. The potential consequences of this `LocationStatus` value and other values that can appear in this property are discussed shortly.

In the example app, interactions with the `Geolocator` are handled in the `GeolocationHelper` class. The code in Listing 13.8 shows the `Geolocator` initialization and subscription to the available events.

LISTING 13.8 Geolocator Initialization and Event Subscription

```
_geolocator = new Geolocator();

// Listen for status change events, but also immediately get the status.
// This is in case it is already at its end-state and therefore
// won't generate a change event.
_geolocator.StatusChanged +=
    (o, e) => SetGeoLocatorReady(e.Status == PositionStatus.Ready);
SetGeoLocatorReady(_geolocator.LocationStatus == PositionStatus.Ready);

// Set the desired accuracy. Alternatively, can use
// DesiredAccuracyInMeters, where < 100 meters ==> high accuracy
_geolocator.DesiredAccuracy = GetDesiredPositionAccuracy();

// Listen for position changed events.
// Set to not report more often than once every 10 seconds
// and only when movement exceeds 50 meters
_geolocator.ReportInterval = 10000; // Value in ms
_geolocator.MovementThreshold = 50; // Value in meters
_geolocator.PositionChanged += GeolocatorOnPositionChanged;
```

The first task in the code in Listing 13.8 is to work with the `LocationStatus` value. The `Disabled` status was previously mentioned, but it is important to note that an attempt to request the current position from a `Disabled` instance results in an `UnauthorizedAccessException`. If location access has not been blocked, the `LocationStatus` property has a value of `NoData` either before the first call to `GetGeopositionAsync` or before the first time an event handler is provided for `PositionChanged`. When either of these happens, the Windows Runtime might trigger a startup sequence that takes a little time to complete. During that time, the `LocationStatus` returns a value of `NotInitialized`. Additionally, if location data is coming from a GPS sensor, the sensor tries to retrieve information from some required minimum number of satellites. Until the device reaches this number, the `LocationStatus` has a value of `Initializing`. When the `Geolocator` instance is ready, the `LocationStatus` returns a value of `Ready`. With all that in mind, when including the `Geolocator` in your project, be sure to account for the fact that, even under ideal circumstances, a lag might occur before it is ready to be used; you need to check to ensure that it has reached the `Ready` status.

In the example code, the `SetGeoLocatorReady` function is called with a value of `true` only when the sensor is in a `Ready` state. It is used to set the

SensorSettings IsLocationAvailable property, which the application user interface uses to disable access to location retrieval functions. It also sets a local flag that prevents direct calls to get the current position through the GetCoordinate function from actually making the request through the Geolocator until it is in the Ready state.

The next step after working with initialization and status information involves establishing the desired accuracy for the Geolocator instance. The DesiredAccuracy property can be set to either PositionAccuracy.High or PositionAccuracy.Default. A value of High instructs WinRT to always try to use a GPS for its data if one is available, and to otherwise use the Windows Location Provider. A value of Default instructs WinRT to make use of only GPS sensors if it cannot obtain a value from the Windows Location Provider, such as when no Wi-Fi signals exist for triangulation (or the device is either not equipped or not configured to work with Wi-Fi) and when the device does not have an IP address that can be looked up for location information. Ultimately, setting either of these values does not guarantee how the WinRT will make use of GPS devices; it just indicates a preference for how it should behave.

NOTE

The Windows Runtime also includes a DesiredAccuracyInMeters property. When this property is set to a non-null value, it resets the DesiredAccuracy property value. A DesiredAccuracyInMeters value of less than 100 meters results in a DesiredAccuracy value of High; a value of 100 meters or higher sets DesiredAccuracy to Default.

The final task in Listing 13.8 is to configure how the Geolocator will go about raising PositionChanged events, which is controlled with the ReportInterval and MovementThreshold properties. Each of these properties limits how often the Geolocator instance can raise the PositionChanged events. Whereas the ReportInterval property specifies the minimum amount of time that must elapse between instances of the Windows Runtime attempting to obtain location information values, the MovementThreshold property indicates how much distance must pass before a subsequent event is raised. In the example code, the `ReportInterval` property is set to ensure that at least 10 seconds (10,000 milliseconds) pass between event updates. The `MovementThreshold` value is set to ensure that the position has changed by at least 50 meters. (The sensor is checked every 10 seconds, and the class instance raises an event only if the distance between checks exceeds 50 meters.) A value of `0` for `ReportInterval` generates events at whatever the maximum frequency is for the most accurate location source, and it should be used only for apps that require near-real-time position updates. Because it affects how often the location hardware is queried and, therefore, can impact battery life, it is important to set the `ReportInterval` to the maximum value possible for the needs of your app. Also note that not every scenario involving the `Geolocator` needs to subscribe to the `PositionChanged` event; some cases are served just fine by requesting the position directly only when it is needed. Each application has different needs in terms of how frequently to update position information and whether to individually request it with the `GetGeopositionAsync` method or use change events.

Working with Geocoordinate Values

An instance of the `Geoposition` class is returned both from a call to `GetGeopostionAsync` and within the `Position` member of the `PositionChangedEventArgs` event arguments that are provided to `PositionChanged` event handlers. Although the `Geoposition` class contains both `Coordinate` and `CivicAddress` properties, the `CivicAddress` values are not populated in Windows 8.1 (the only member that is set is the `Country` property, which is obtained from the country value set in the Windows region settings instead of the location information data sources that were previously mentioned). The `Coordinate` property is an instance of the `Geocoordinate` class and contains several different kinds of position information that are returned either from the Windows Location Provider or from GPS sensors (as you have seen, this depends on how the `Geolocator` is configured).

At its root, the `Geocoordinate` object provides a `PositionSource` property that either indicates how the location information was obtained or includes a value of `Unknown` if information about the source is not available. It also include an `Accuracy` property that indicates how accurate (in meters) the latitude and longitude position information are believed to be. If the location information is being obtained from a GPS sensor, values for the `Speed`, `Heading`, `AltitudeAccuracy`, and `SatelliteData` properties might also be included, depending on the sensor's capabilities.

The actual position information provided is a little buried in the object hierarchy. It is actually returned in the `Position` property within the `Point` property of the `Geocoordinate` instance. Regardless of whether the location information is obtained from a GPS sensor or the Windows Location Provider, values for `Latitude` and `Longitude` (measured in degrees) are provided in this `Point` property. If the information is obtained from a GPS sensor, the `Altitude` value might be provided as well.

To show how this information looks in practice, the example application includes the capability to display all the fields of the `Geocoordinate` object for the current location. Clicking the **ShowCurrent** button in the app's **Location** box displays a pop-up that contains these values, as provided by a call to the `GetGeoPositionAsync` method. The **Center Map on Current** button also makes a call to the `GetGeopositionAsync` method and sets a viewmodel property from the previously discussed `Point` property. The property in the ViewModel is data bound to the Bing Maps control so that when the value changes, the map centers itself at the `Latitude` and `Longitude` coordinates specified in the position value.

Using the Simulator Location Tools

Chapter 2 introduced you to the Visual Studio simulator for Windows Store Apps (the Simulator), which enables you to run and test your Windows 8.1 app within a simulated environment on your development system. In addition to being able to emulate various screen sizes and resolutions (along with the other functionality it provides), the simulator can be used to provide simulated geolocation values to a running app, which can help you test your location-aware app. To use the simulator's location functions, several requirements must be met, primarily related to Location Settings enabled on the local system. When you first try to use the location functions, you are prompted and instructed to take corrective action if your system does not meet the necessary requirements for the location simulator to run.

To use the location functions of the simulator with your location-aware app, start debugging in the simulator following the instructions in Chapter 2. When the app is running in the simulator, clicking the icon in the simulator toolbar that resembles a globe displays the location simulation dialog box (see Figure 13.5). When the Use Simulated Location check box is checked, it provides access to text boxes for setting location values such as Latitude, Longitude, and Altitude.

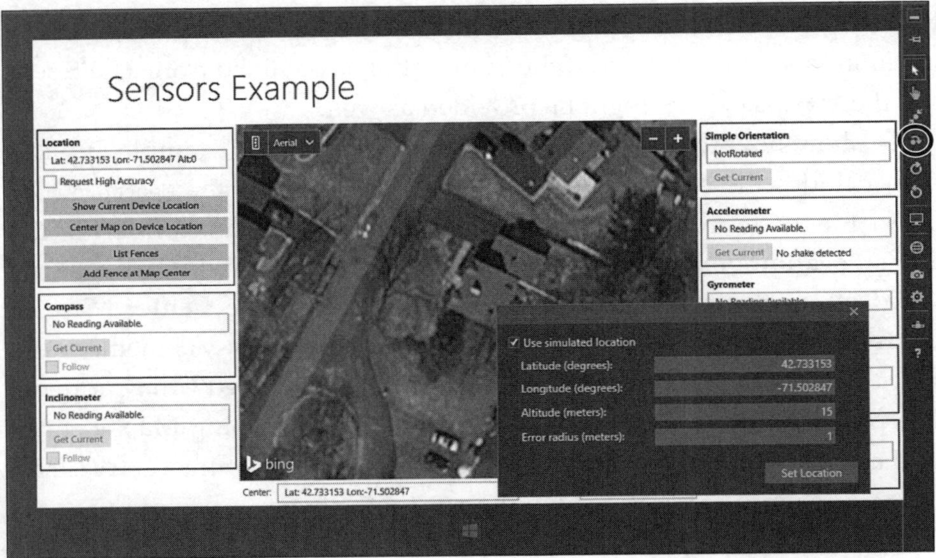

FIGURE 13.5 Using location tools in the Windows simulator

When the Set Location button is clicked, the `Geolocator` API methods and events that are used by the app running in the simulator use those values for their position information. Removing the check from the Use Simulated Location check box returns the simulator to using the host system values for its current position values.

Geofencing

Geofencing enables your Windows 8.1 app to define geographic boundaries (known as geofences) and monitor a device's position relative to those boundaries. Your app then produces notification events when the device enters or exits those boundaries. For applications that need to be alerted when a device has moved into or beyond one of these boundaries, this provides a much more efficient solution than polling the geolocation APIs and making the determinations programmatically. To support geofencing, the Windows Runtime includes APIs that allow registering and managing geofences, as well subscribing to and processing the related notifications.

Getting Started

The geofencing support the Windows Runtime provides is closely related to the geolocation support and includes several of the same restrictions and conditions related to working with personally identifiable information. To use geofencing, you must set the Location capability in the app manifest and set both the app-specific and system-wide permission settings to allow the app to access location information.

The `GeofenceMonitor` class provides geofencing support in the Windows Runtime. Unlike using the `Geolocator`, where you create a new instance of the class to access the functionality, a reference to the `GeofenceMonitor` is accessed through its static `Current` property:

```
var geofenceMonitor = GeofenceMonitor.Current;
```

The following sections discuss the functionality that the `GeofenceMonitor` exposes.

> **NOTE**
>
> Unlike with geolocation, accessing the geofencing properties and events does not automatically prompt the user to grant permission to location information. You might have to check to see if location functionality is currently disabled by checking the `GeofenceMonitor Status` property and instructing the user to access the permissions property in the Settings Charm. If your app also uses the `Geolocator` to potentially access the user's current location (perhaps to obtain the center point for a fence), that class access provides the necessary request for permissions.

Defining a Fence

The `GeofenceMonitor` works with a collection of `Geofence` instances. Each `Geofence` object describes the region the fence covers, the types of events to provide, and the conditions under which it indicates that an event has occurred. Table 13.4 describes the settings provided by the `Geofence` class. Be aware that these values must be set through one of the `Geofence` constructors and cannot be changed after the geofence has been defined.

TABLE 13.4 Geofence Settings

Setting	Description
`Id`	Specifies the ID for the fence. The ID is a `String` that must be unique within the scope of the current app, and it must be a maximum of 64 characters long. This value is required.
`Geoshape`	Specifies the geofence boundary. Currently supports being set to only a `Geocircle` instance, which defines the boundary via a center point and a radius. This value is required.
`MonitoredStates`	Specifies which events the `GeofenceMonitor` raises for this fence. Can be set to a combination of the `MonitoredGeofenceStates` enumeration values, which includes `Entered`, `Exited`, and `Removed`, but must minimally include either `Entered` or `Exited`. This value is optional and, by default, is set to the combination of `Entered` and `Exited`.
`SingleUse`	Specifies whether the fence is automatically removed. If set, when each of the `MonitoredStates` (with the exception of `Removed`) is reached at least once, the fence is automatically removed from the `GeofenceMonitor` collection. This value is optional and, by default, is set to false.
`DwellTime`	Specifies the time that must elapse when a geofence condition is met before an event is raised. This value is optional and, by default, is set to 10 seconds.
`StartTime`	Specifies the time at which the geofence monitoring begins. This value is optional and, by default, is set to a minimal value of `January 1, 1601` (which is the base value for the Windows `FILETIME` structure).

Setting	Description
`Duration`	Specifies the amount of time following `StartTime` during which the fence should be monitored. This value is optional and, by default, is set to `TimeSpan.Zero`, which indicates an indefinite duration.

After a `Geofence` instance has been defined, the `GeofenceMonitor` begins tracking it when it is added to its `Geofences` collection.

In the example app, the code for working with the `GeofenceMonitor` has been consolidated into the `GeofenceHelper` class. This class provides an `AddGeofence` method used to add new fences (see Listing 13.9). Clicking the Add Fence at Map Center button in the example application produces a flyout that enables the user to define a name for the geofence. The center point is retrieved from the map's current center point, and the radius is hardcoded to 20KM. Pressing the flyout's Add Fence button calls this method with the values in the flyout. This method then creates a `Geocircle` with the specified center and radius, which is provided to the `Geofence` constructor along with indications that the `GeofenceMonitor` should listen to `Entering`, `Exited`, and `Removed` events (the next section covers the events) and that the geofence is not configured to be single use. Default values are accepted for the remaining parameters. The resulting `Geofence` instance is then added to the `GeofenceMonitor` collection and returned so that it can be used to include a UI entry on the Bing Maps control.

LISTING 13.9 Adding a Geofence

```
public Geofence AddGeofence(
    String fenceId,
    BasicGeoposition fenceCenter,
    Double radiusInMeters)
{
    var fenceCircle = new Geocircle(fenceCenter, radiusInMeters);

    const MonitoredGeofenceStates states =
        MonitoredGeofenceStates.Entered |
        MonitoredGeofenceStates.Exited |
        MonitoredGeofenceStates.Removed;

    // Create the fence with the desired states and not single-use
```

```
    var fence = new Geofence(fenceId, fenceCircle, states, false);
    GeofenceMonitor.Current.Geofences.Add(fence);
    return fence;
}
```

When defining a geofence boundary, keep in mind the limitations of the accuracy of the various location providers available to the Windows Runtime. Depending on sensor capabilities and network connectivity, extremely small fences might not be all that useful.

Geofence Events

You can receive notifications that geofencing events have occurred in two ways. Foreground notifications are configured when an app registers an event handler for the `GeofenceStateChanged` event provided by the `GeofenceMonitor` class. Alternatively, you can set up a background task to process geofence notifications even when the app is not running in the foreground. To configure geofencing background task notifications, the `LocationTrigger` class needs to be provided to a `BackgroundTaskBuilder`, and that builder instance needs to be configured and then registered. Chapter 15, "Background Tasks," covers this in more detail.

As previously discussed, the `GeofenceMonitor` events can be triggered in response to the device entering or exiting a geofence, depending on the combination of the `Entered` or `Exited` `GeofenceState` enumeration values provided in the `MonitoredStates` value when the `Geofence` instance was defined. Additionally, the event can occur in response to the geofence being automatically removed from the list of monitored fences and depending on whether the `Removed` enumeration value was specified.

Automatic removal of a `Geofence` occurs in response to the values set in its `Duration` and `SingleUse` properties. `Duration` is the easiest to understand. When the time window indicated by the combination of the `StartTime` and `Duration` properties has expired, a geofence event is recorded indicating that this fence is no longer being monitored. In this case, the event includes a `RemovalReason` value that is set to `Expired`.

The other option for automatic removal relates to the `SingleUse` property. When this value is set to `true`, a geofence is removed after all its `MonitoredStates` have occurred. If a `Geofence` instance is defined with only

Entered or Exited specified, then as soon as the corresponding event takes place, the geofence is removed. If both Entered and Exited are specified, the geofence is removed only after both have occurred. In this case, the Removed state is accompanied by a RemovalReason value of Used.

When a geofence notification event is received, the app should call the ReadReports method of the GeofenceMonitor instance, which returns the collection of all notification reports that have accumulated since the last call to ReadReports was made. Each report is actually indicated in an individual GeoStateChangedEventReport, and a single GeofenceMonitor event can encompass multiple reports, especially in the case of background tasks, which run only periodically.

The example app subscribes to geofence notifications only in the foreground. To do so, the GeofenceHelper class registers its HandleGeofenceStateChanged method as a handler for the GeofenceStateChanged event (see Listing 13.10).

LISTING 13.10 Processing Geofence Events

```
private void HandleGeofenceStateChanged(GeofenceMonitor monitor,Object o)
{
    // Iterate over and process the accumulated reports
    var reports = monitor.ReadReports();
    foreach (var report in reports)
    {
        switch (report.NewState)
        {
            case GeofenceState.Entered:
            case GeofenceState.Exited:
                var updateArgs = new FenceUpdateEventArgs
                {
                    FenceId = report.Geofence.Id,
                    Reason = report.NewState.ToString(),
                    Timestamp = report.Geoposition.Coordinate.Timestamp,
                    Position =
                            report.Geoposition.Coordinate.Point.Position
                };
                OnFenceUpdated(updateArgs);
                break;
            case GeofenceState.Removed:
                var removedArgs = new FenceRemovedEventArgs
                {
                    FenceId = report.Geofence.Id,
                    WhyRemoved = report.RemovalReason.ToString()
                };
```

```
                OnFenceRemoved(removedArgs);

                break;
        }
    }
}
```

The event handler retrieves the reports from the provided GeofenceMonitor instance and then iterates over the individual report instances. In the case of Entered and Exited events, information is gathered about which fence caused the event, whether it was triggered on enter or exit, what position caused the event to be triggered, and when exactly the reported event occurred. This information is then used to relay an event out of the GeofenceHelper that displays the event's occurrence in the app UI. In the case of a Removed event, the event ID and Removal reason are obtained, and a similar event is raised to provide notification as well as remove the geofence entry from the Bing Maps control.

Be aware that because the GeofenceStateChanged events are raised from an external entity, the handler will not run on the UI thread. Any reaction to these events that affects the application UI needs to be marshalled to the proper thread using either the Dispatcher or a valid SynchronizationContext, as discussed in the section "Accessing the UI Thread" in Chapter 9, "Model-View-ViewModel."

Managing Geofences

You can manage geofences by working directly with the Geofences collection that the GeofenceMonitor instance provides. The example app enumerates these instances in two places. First, on app startup, the existing collection is obtained to put markers on the Bing Maps control for each geofence. Second, clicking the List Fences button shows a flyout that lists all the currently defined geofences. This flyout includes the option to remove the selected Geofence instance from the Geofences collection. Note that programmatically removing a fence from the collection in this way does not generate the previously discussed Removed events. Those occur only when the removal happens automatically in response to the conditions that the Geofence instance's settings identify.

> **TIP**
>
> Testing geofence functionality directly with a device can be perhaps more tricky than testing general geolocation functionality. An alternative to the potentially difficult, distraction-prone, and ultimately dangerous option of mounting a tablet in a car and driving around town (please do not do this) is to use the techniques discussed in the previous section "Using the Simulator Location Tools." From the simulator's location tools, you can set positions with coordinates that are inside or outside a particular geofence by setting the location to a particular latitude and longitude combination. The simulator then properly emulates the position changes along with the appropriate resulting geofence reactions.

Motion and Orientation Sensors

In addition to using the `Geolocator` and related APIs to obtain information about a device's physical location, the Windows Runtime provides APIs for interacting with a class of sensors related to the movement and positioning of the device itself. Table 13.5 lists the kinds of sensors these APIs can interact with and the kind of data they gather.

TABLE 13.5 Motion and Orientation Sensor Types

Sensor	Description
Simple Orientation	Reports the current orientation of the device based on values from the `SimpleOrientation` enumeration.
Compass	Provides information about the position of the device in relation to magnetic north. This is actually a composite sensor whose output is based on combined input from magnetometer and gyrometer sensors.
Inclinometer	Provides information about the pitch, yaw, and roll state of a device. This is a composite sensor whose output is based on combined input from accelerometer, gyrometer, and magnetometer sensors.
Accelerometer	Provides information about the G-forces affecting the device's x-, y-, and z-axes.
Gyrometer	Provides information about the angular velocity along the device's x-, y-, and z-axes.

Sensor	Description
Orientation Sensor	Provides detailed information about how a device is situated in space. This is a composite sensor whose output is based on combined input from accelerometer, gyrometer, and magnetometer sensors.
Light Sensor	Provides information about the amount of light currently striking the device display.

You might have noticed that several of these sensors' values are determined in part from a magnetometer, which is itself a sensor whose purpose is to measure the strength of magnetic fields. However, the Windows Runtime does not provide any APIs that allow direct access to output from magnetometers.

For the most part, the API for interacting with sensors is similar across all the different kinds. They all basically offer the capability to obtain a reference to a class instance that provides access to the sensor, as well as methods for obtaining the current sensor value. In addition, they provide events that you can subscribe to for notifications when the value changes. The majority of the sensor APIs define properties that specify the minimum interval with which the sensor can raise these change events, as well as properties that specify the requested interval for reporting value changes.

Most of the code for working with sensors in the example project resides in the `SensorHelper` class. You might be relieved to know that, unlike the location information, the information these sensors return is not considered to be personally identifiable information. As a result, you do not have to indicate entries in the application manifest, prompt the user for permission, or deal with users blocking access to the sensors if you include code to make use of them in your application.

Simple Orientation Sensor

The simple orientation sensor is the simplest of the available sensors. It does not work with the concept of a reporting interval for its change events, and the data values that it reports are simply members of the `SimpleOrientation` enumeration. When available, the purpose of this sensor is to describe which way the device is facing. The values it can return are `NotRotated`, for when the device is sitting in a "natural" landscape orientation; Rotated90, Rotated180, and Rotated270, to indicate that the device has been rotated to stand on one of its other edges; and FaceUp and FaceDown, to indicate that the device is lying flat.

The code in Listing 13.11 shows how the example project is configured to work with the simple orientation sensor, which is exposed via the SimpleOrientationSensor class. The GetDefault static method obtains a reference to the sensor, the value of which is null if the sensor is not available. After that, it simply provides a handler for the OrientationChanged event and then uses the GetCurrentOrientation method to obtain the current sensor value.

LISTING 13.11 Configuring the Simple Orientation Sensor

```
// Get the reference to the sensor and see if it is available
_simpleOrientation = SimpleOrientationSensor.GetDefault();
if (_simpleOrientation == null) return;

_sensorSettings.IsSimpleOrientationAvailable = true;

// NOTE - Simple Orientation does not offer a minimum interval setting
_simpleOrientation.OrientationChanged
    += SimpleOrientationOnOrientationChanged;

// Read the initial sensor value
_sensorSettings.LatestSimpleOrientationReading
    = _simpleOrientation.GetCurrentOrientation();
```

The Visual Studio simulator for Windows Store Apps, which the preceding section "Using the Simulator Location Tools" discussed, also includes support for simulating device rotation by providing buttons that rotate the simulator in 90-degree increments clockwise or counterclockwise.

Compass

The compass provides information about the current heading of the device relative to magnetic north. When available, this sensor returns readings as instances of the CompassReading type, which includes both HeadingMagneticNorth and HeadingTrueNorth properties, indicating degrees to magnetic north and degrees to true north, respectively. HeadingMagneticNorth always is provided; the availability of HeadingTrueNorth values depends on the individual capabilities of the actual sensor hardware. `HeadingTrueNorth` returns a value of `null` if it is not available.

Listing 13.12 shows how the example project is configured to work with the compass, which is exposed via the `Compass` class. The `GetDefault` static method obtains a reference to the sensor, the value of which is `null` if the sensor is not available. It next proceeds to set the sensor's reporting interval.

LISTING 13.12 Configuring the Compass

```
// Get the reference to the sensor and see if it is available
_compass = Compass.GetDefault();
if (_compass == null) return;

_sensorSettings.IsCompassAvailable = true;

// Set the minimum report interval. Care must be taken to ensure
// it is not set to a value smaller than the device minimum
var minInterval = _compass.MinimumReportInterval;
_compass.ReportInterval
    = Math.Max(_sensorSettings.SensorReportInterval, minInterval);
_compass.ReadingChanged += CompassOnReadingChanged;

// Read the initial sensor value
_sensorSettings.LatestCompassReading = _compass.GetCurrentReading();
```

The `ReportInterval` property is common to most of the available sensors. The purpose of the property is to provide access to the minimum time (in milliseconds) that must elapse between `ReadingChanged` events. Take care when setting this value; setting it to a value below the minimum value that the sensor can support can result in either an exception or unpredictable behavior, depending on the sensor. You can obtain the minimum allowable report interval value through the `MinimumReportInterval` property. Note that the `ReportInterval` setting has some of the characteristics of a request rather than a certain value. Several factors can influence how the actual sensor handles the `ReportInterval` setting. For example, when other apps on the system that make use of the same sensor set their own values for this property, the sensor might simply elect to use whichever is the smallest defined value. Also be aware that the `ReadingChanged` event is raised only when the reading actually changes, regardless of the `ReportInterval` setting. It is important to not confuse the `ReportInterval` value with a frequency value that somehow guarantees that the `ReadingChanged` event will be raised repeatedly in a steady cadence. After the `ReportInterval` is set, the code simply provides a handler for the `ReadingChanged` event and then uses the `GetCurrentReading` method to obtain the current sensor value.

Another important note is that the value the compass returns is relative to the device being in a regular landscape orientation, with the device base sitting at the bottom. (If the device is a tablet device built with Portrait as its primary orientation, this sensor landscape condition still applies; the "natural" landscape mode is the one where the hardware Windows button ends up on the right side of the display.) Figure 13.6 shows devices in natural landscape orientation.

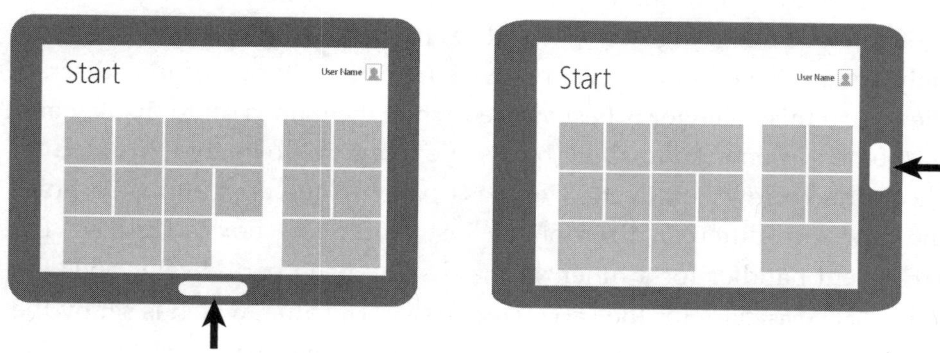

FIGURE 13.6 Devices in natural landscape orientation

If the device is in a different orientation, the value the sensor returns needs to be adjusted to account for this. The example project includes a `CompassOffset` extension method for the `DisplayOrientations` class that you can use to obtain the offset to apply to a compass direction based on a provided orientation value. This method simply returns a value of `0`, `90`, `180`, or `270`, depending on what is needed to correct the compass reading for the given orientation. You obtain the `DisplayOrientations` value to use from the `CurrentOrientation` property of the `DisplayInformation` class. After you determine the offset, you can add it to the `HeadingMagneticNorth` or `HeadingTrueNorth` values, using modular arithmetic to constrain the resulting value between `0` and `360` degrees, as follows:

```
(LatestCompassReading.HeadingMagneticNorth + offset)%360
```

The example project includes a Sensor Settings flyout that you can bring up using the Settings Charm. The panel includes a slider for updating the minimum reporting interval for the sensors. It also includes a check box that corresponds to a flag that the app uses to decide whether to compensate for orientation changes when using and displaying sensor values. By toggling these values and switching the orientation of the device on which the app is running from a landscape to an inverted landscape orientation, you can see the effect that changing an orientation has on sensor values, as well as how the compensation code will correct them to their expected state.

Another feature present in the example app is the capability for the Bing Maps control to "follow" the compass sensor value. Note that the current version of the Bing Maps control supports rotating its display contents only when viewed at high zoom levels (and to only one of four discrete views), so this behavior is best viewed when the map is set to display and is zoomed in enough to show bird's-eye imagery. To enable this feature, check the **Follow** box in the **Compass** panel in the app, and then point the device in different directions. When the Follow box is checked, the `Tick` event handler for a timer on the display page periodically polls the `SensorSettings` class for the `LatestCompassReading` value, which is set by the `ReadingChanged` handler for the compass. This value then is set to a view-model property that is data bound to the Bing Maps control. This approach of using a timer to check for the most recent value is used because the `ReadingChanged` event is fired only when a compass value actually changes, as previously discussed. Listing 13.13 shows the code in the timer event handler that obtains and applies the compass value.

LISTING 13.13 Applying the Compass Orientation to the Map Display

```
if (_sensorSettings.IsFollowingCompass)
{
    // Get the latest compass reading
    var compassReading = _sensorSettings.LatestCompassReading;

    // Adjust the reading based on the display orientation, if necessary
    var displayOffset = _sensorSettings.CompensateForDisplayOrientation
        ? _sensorSettings.DisplayOrientation.CompassOffset()
        : 0;
    var heading
        = (compassReading.HeadingMagneticNorth + displayOffset)%360;
```

```
    // Set the value used by data binding to update the map's heading
    DefaultViewModel["Heading"] = heading;
}
```

Inclinometer

The inclinometer provides information about the current pitch, yaw, and roll of the device. Pitch represents the degrees of rotation around the x-axis, yaw represents degrees of rotation around the z-axis, and roll represents degrees of rotation around the y-axis. Figure 13.7 illustrates how these values map to the physical position of a tablet device. When available, this sensor returns readings as instances of the `InclinometerReading` type, which provides its results in `PitchDegrees`, `RollDegrees`, and `YawDegrees` properties.

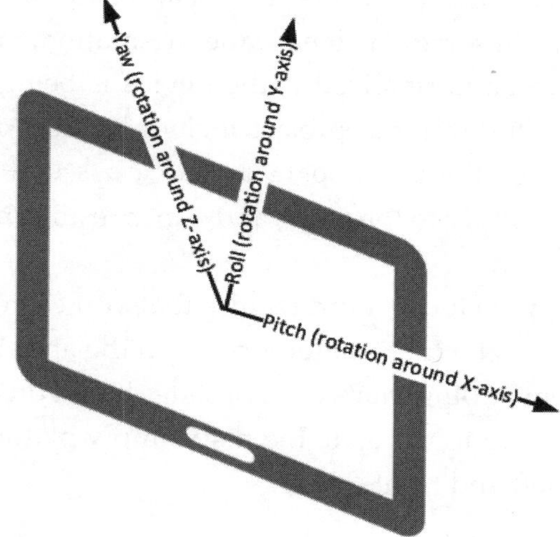

FIGURE 13.7 Pitch, roll, and yaw relative to a tablet device

Listing 13.14 shows how the example project is configured to work with the inclinometer, which is exposed via the `Inclinometer` class. The steps involved in configuring the inclinometer are basically identical to those shown in Listing 13.12 for configuring the compass.

LISTING 13.14 Configuring the Inclinometer

```
// Get the reference to the sensor and see if it is available
_inclinometer = Inclinometer.GetDefault();
if (_inclinometer == null) return;

_sensorSettings.IsInclinometerAvailable = true;

// Set the minimum report interval. Care must be taken to ensure
// it is not set to a value smaller than the device minimum
var minInterval = _inclinometer.MinimumReportInterval;
_inclinometer.ReportInterval
    = Math.Max(_sensorSettings.SensorReportInterval, minInterval);
_inclinometer.ReadingChanged += InclinometerOnReadingChanged;

// Read the initial sensor value
_sensorSettings.LatestInclinometerReading = GetInclinometerReading();
```

Much like the compass, the values the inclinometer returns are relative to the device being in a regular landscape orientation, and the resulting values also need to be normalized if the device is being used from any other orientation. The example project includes an `AxisAdjustmentFactor` extension method for the `DisplayOrientations` class that you can use to obtain the factors to apply to the x-, y-, and z-axis results, based on the current device orientation.

The example app includes a fun feature that you can enable by checking the **Follow** box in the **Inclinometer** panel in the app. When this box is checked, the content of Bing Maps control slides based on the Inclinometer readings, allowing you to navigate the map simply by tilting your device back and forth or left and right.

NOTE

If you find that tilting your device is causing your screen orientation to be toggled, you can disable the automatic screen rotation feature that Windows provides by bringing up the Settings Charm, selecting Screen, and tapping the rectangular icon above the brightness adjustment slider. If that icon has a pair of arrows next to it, automatic rotation is enabled. If it has a small padlock next to it, the current screen orientation is locked and will not automatically adjust as you tilt your device.

As with the Follow feature discussed previously for the compass sensor, implementation for this feature simply polls the `SensorSettings` class in response to the same timer `Tick` event. In this case, the value used to obtain the current device orientation is the `LatestInclinometerReading` value, which the inclinometer's `ReadingChanged` handler sets. The `displayAdjustment` value used to compensate for device orientation changes returns per-axis values of +1 or –1 that are multiplied to the sensor result to normalize the value.

Listing 13.15 shows the calculations that move the map. First, the inclinometer reading is obtained and normalized, depending on the value of the compensation setting and the device orientation. Next, a rate of one full screen per timer tick was found to be a good maximum rate of traversal, so the number of x- and y-axis pixels to move are obtained from the map control. Then trigonometric functions convert the adjusted pitch and roll values to percentage values so that the traversal is nearly nothing when the device is lying flat and is full-value when it is held vertically. This percentage determines the actual number of x and y pixels to move in the current tick, which is applied to the center point to determine the equivalent destination point. From here, the Bing Maps `TryPixelToLocation` utility function converts a pixel onscreen to equivalent latitude and longitude values, which then set the new map position.

LISTING 13.15 Applying the Inclinometer Reading to the Map Display

```
if (_sensorSettings.FollowInclinometer)
{
    var inclinometerReading = _sensorSettings.LatestInclinometerReading;

    // Optionally normalize the sensor reading values
    var displayAdjustment
        = _sensorSettings.CompensateForDisplayOrientation
            ? _sensorSettings.DisplayOrientation.AxisAdjustmentFactor()
            : SensorExtensions.AxisOffset.Default;
    var adjustedPitchDegrees
        = inclinometerReading.PitchDegrees * displayAdjustment.X;
    var adjustedRollDegrees
        = inclinometerReading.RollDegrees * displayAdjustment.Y;

    // At full speed/inclination, move 100% map size per tick
    const Double maxScreensPerTick = 1.00;
    var mapWidth = ExampleMap.ActualWidth;
    var xFullRateTraversalPerTick = mapWidth * maxScreensPerTick;
    var mapHeight = ExampleMap.ActualHeight;
    var yFullRateTraversalPerTick = mapHeight * maxScreensPerTick;
```

```
    // Turn rotation angles into percentages
    var xTraversalPercentage
        = Math.Sin(adjustedRollDegrees*Math.PI/180);
    var yTraversalPercentage
        = Math.Sin(adjustedPitchDegrees*Math.PI/180);

    // Compute the final traversal amounts based on the percentages
    // and compute the new destination center point
    var xTraversalAmount
        = xTraversalPercentage*xFullRateTraversalPerTick;
    var yTraversalAmount
        = yTraversalPercentage*yFullRateTraversalPerTick;
    var destinationPoint = new Point(
        mapWidth/2 + xTraversalAmount,
        mapHeight/2 + yTraversalAmount);

    // Use the Bing Maps methods to convert pixel pos to Lat/Lon
    // rather than trying to figure out Mercator map math
    Location location;
    if (ExampleMap.TryPixelToLocation(destinationPoint, out location))
    {
        // Obtain the current map position (for altitude)
        var position = (BasicGeoposition)DefaultViewModel["Position"];

        var newPosition = new BasicGeoposition
        {
            Altitude = position.Altitude,
            Latitude = location.Latitude,
            Longitude = location.Longitude
        };

        DefaultViewModel["Position"] = newPosition;
    }
}
```

Accelerometer

The accelerometer provides information about the current G-forces acting on the device in the x, y, and z directions. At rest, the most significant G-force affecting a device is the force of gravity, which pulls down along whichever axis corresponds to the bottom edge of the device with a value of –1.0. For example, if a device is standing up on its bottom edge in a landscape profile, the y value has a value of approximately –1.0. When available, this sensor returns readings as instances of the `AccelerometerReading` type, which provides its results in `AccelerationX`, `AcclerationY`, and `AccelerationZ` properties.

Listing 13.16 shows how the example project is configured to work with the accelerometer, which is exposed via the `Accelerometer` class. The steps involved in configuring the accelerometer are otherwise identical to those shown previously for configuring the other sensors, with one notable exception. The accelerometer sensor includes an additional `Shaken` event that is raised when the sensor detects that the device is being subjected to several quick back-and-forth motions.

LISTING 13.16 Configuring the Accelerometer

```
// Get the reference to the sensor and see if it is available
_accelerometer = Accelerometer.GetDefault();
if (_accelerometer == null) return;

_sensorSettings.IsAccelerometerAvailable = true;

// Set the minimum report interval. Care must be taken to ensure
// it is not set to a value smaller than the device minimum
var minInterval = _accelerometer.MinimumReportInterval;
_accelerometer.ReportInterval
    = Math.Max(_sensorSettings.SensorReportInterval, minInterval);
_accelerometer.ReadingChanged += AccelerometerOnReadingChanged;
_accelerometer.Shaken += AccelerometerOnShaken;

// Read the initial sensor value
_sensorSettings.LatestAccelerometerReading = GetAccelerometerReading();
```

Gyrometer

The gyrometer provides information about the device's current rate of rotation around the x-, y-, and z-axes, measured in degrees per second. When available, this sensor returns readings as instances of the `GyrometerReading` type, which provides its results in `AngularVelocityX`, `AngularVelocityY`, and `AngularVelocityZ` properties.

Listing 13.17 shows how the example project is configured to work with the gyrometer, which is exposed via the `Gyrometer` class. The steps involved in configuring the gyrometer are otherwise identical to those shown previously for configuring the other sensors.

LISTING 13.17 Configuring the Gyrometer

```
// Get the reference to the sensor and see if it is available
_gyrometer = Gyrometer.GetDefault();
if (_gyrometer == null) return;

_sensorSettings.IsGyrometerAvailable = true;

// Set the minimum report interval. Care must be taken to ensure
// it is not set to a value smaller than the device minimum
var minInterval = _gyrometer.MinimumReportInterval;
_gyrometer.ReportInterval
    = Math.Max(_sensorSettings.SensorReportInterval, minInterval);
_gyrometer.ReadingChanged += GyrometerOnReadingChanged;

// Read the initial sensor value
_sensorSettings.LatestGyrometerReading = GetGyrometerReading();
```

Orientation Sensor

The last sensor directly related to motion and/or orientation to be discussed is the orientation sensor. As Table 13.4 described, the orientation sensor is a composite sensor whose output consists of information gathered from accelerometer, gyrometer, and magnetometer data. As you can see in Listing 13.18, the orientation sensor is configured using the `OrientationSensor` class in the same way the rest of the sensors have been in this section. Its results are returned in an instance of the `OrientationSensorReading` class, which contains properties for `Quaternion` and `RotationMatrix` values, structures that 3D and gaming apps often use.

LISTING 13.18 Configuring the Orientation Sensor

```
// Get the reference to the sensor and see if it is available
_orientationSensor = OrientationSensor.GetDefault();
if (_orientationSensor == null) return;

_sensorSettings.IsOrientationSensorAvailable = true;

// Set the minimum report interval. Care must be taken to ensure
// it is not set to a value smaller than the device minimum
var minInterval = _orientationSensor.MinimumReportInterval;
_orientationSensor.ReportInterval
    = Math.Max(_sensorSettings.SensorReportInterval, minInterval);
_orientationSensor.ReadingChanged += OrientationSensorOnReadingChanged;
```

```
// Read the initial sensor value
_sensorSettings.LatestOrientationSensorReading
    = GetOrientationSensorReading();
```

Light Sensor

The light sensor isn't actually a motion-/orientation-related sensor, but it is included as an honorable mention with these sensors because the APIs for working with this sensor are closely related to the rest of the APIs in this section. The light sensor reports the intensity of the light shining on the current device display in units of lux, is accessed through the `LightSensor` class, and returns its values in a `LightSensorReading` instance (which contains the property `IlluminanceInLux`). Listing 13.19 shows how the example project is configured to work with the light sensor.

Listing 13.19 Configuring the Light Sensor

```
// Get the reference to the sensor and see if it is available
_lightSensor = LightSensor.GetDefault();
if (_lightSensor == null) return;

_sensorSettings.IsLightSensorAvailable = true;

// Set the minimum report interval. Care must be taken to ensure
// it is not set to a value smaller than the device minimum
var minInterval = _lightSensor.MinimumReportInterval;
_lightSensor.ReportInterval
    = Math.Max(_sensorSettings.SensorReportInterval, minInterval);
_lightSensor.ReadingChanged += LightSensorOnReadingChanged;

// Read the initial sensor value
_sensorSettings.LatestLightSensorReading = GetLightSensorReading();
```

Summary

In this chapter, you learned how to work with several different user input devices, including pointer-based devices such as touch inputs, mouse devices, stylus devices, and keyboards. You saw how the Windows Runtime provides the capability to determine which devices are connected, as well as how adding the capability to interact with the various different kinds of pointer devices has coalesced into a set of APIs that are differentiated more by the level of abstraction than the characteristics of a specific device type.

You also saw how the Windows Runtime provides the capability to work with sensors that supply information about how the device is interacting with its physical environment. This includes working with the geolocation APIs to obtain device position information. It also includes the related geofencing APIs for defining geographic boundaries that can result in app notifications when a device either enters or exits those boundaries. You also worked with the motion and orientation sensor APIs that provide insight into the device's physical position and movement.

In the next chapter, you learn about the support the Windows Runtime offers for working with these peripheral devices. This includes a discussion about how you can add the capability to scan from your Windows Store apps. You also see how you can print from your app, including how to generate content and layouts specifically for printing, as well as how to customize and interact with the Print Settings and Print Preview experiences.

14

Printers and Scanners

DESPITE LONGSTANDING PREDICTIONS ABOUT THE INEVITABILITY OF A "paperless world," users continue to rely on printing as an important feature of many of the apps that they use on a day-to-day basis. Conversely, users also continue to interact with a variety of paper documents and hard-copy pictures that they want to be able to scan into their computers to then manipulate and store digitally. Not surprisingly, multifunction printers that offer both printing and scanning capabilities continue to be a popular item for consumer electronic and office supply retailers.

This chapter shows you how you can use the WinRT printing APIs to control the printing process from your app. You will see how to respond to user requests for printing that are initiated both in Windows and from within your own application. Other topics include providing customized content to be both previewed and sent to the printer, modifying the standard print options, and providing app-specific custom options to the user in the Windows print preview panel.

This chapter also covers how to use the WinRT scanning APIs to obtain images from an attached digital scanner. This includes how to go about identifying the currently connected scanners, running a low-res scan preview, and scanning content to files. It concludes with a discussion of how to modify the settings that determine how a scan job obtains, processes, and stores images for your application.

Working with Printers

Adding the capability to print content from your app using the Windows Runtime is a fairly straightforward process. This process starts with registering an event handler to configure your app to respond when a user opens the **Print** panel within the **Devices** charm. In response to this event, you need to define an object that encapsulates the interactions that occur during the lifetime of a single printing request, including reacting to requests for providing preview content, determining which of the standard print options to display, possibly providing a set of custom print options that are specific to your application, and handling requests for the actual content to be sent to the printer itself. You also need to define another separate object that manages the content being either previewed or printed. Finally, you need to respond to events that occur throughout the lifetime of the printing request, to coordinate the interaction between the preview or print requests and the content to be displayed or printed, respectively.

The Example App

The **PrintersAndScannersExample** project that is included in the source code for this chapter illustrates the printing process just described. The app enables users to select one or more pictures and then displays both a file-system-provided thumbnail and the actual image for each one. Each picture display also includes a text area where users can provide a caption for the image. After some pictures have been selected, the user can print the pictures along with the provided captions, selecting an app-defined print layout in the process.

When the user chooses to print the selected pictures, the app defines which standard settings to display to the user by default, along with several custom settings. These custom settings include the capability to select which predefined picture layout to use, a title to display on each printed page, and whether the previewed content should use thumbnail images or the full-resolution image. Based on the value of these settings, the app supplies the content to be shown in the print preview display, as well as the final content that is sent to the printer when the user chooses to actually print that content.

Note that, in the example app's source code, access to the Windows Runtime printing APIs is encapsulated within the `PrintHelper` class.

Getting Started

A user can invoke the Windows print functionality by bringing up the Devices charm from the Windows Charm bar (or by pressing the **Windows+K** key combination) and then selecting the **Print** entry. When the printing functionality is initiated, Windows attempts to notify the current app to see if it is currently capable of providing content to be printed. An app can handle this notification by obtaining a reference to the current view's `PrintManager` instance and registering a handler to its `PrintTaskRequested` event, as the following code shows:

```
var printManager = PrintManager.GetForCurrentView();
printManager.PrintTaskRequested += HandlePrintTaskRequested;
```

It is important to make sure that only one handler is registered for this event for the current app view at any one time. An attempt to register an additional handler before unsubscribing the first one will result in an `InvalidOperationException`. In apps where printing is handled on a page-by-page basis, it might be appropriate to register a handler for this event in each page's `OnNavigatedTo` method and then, likewise, to unregister the event handler in each page's `OnNavigatedFrom` method.

In the `PrintTaskRequested` event handler, your app can indicate that it is ready to print by using methods exposed by the `Request` property that the event arguments provide to create a `PrintTask` instance. The upcoming section "Configuring a Print Task" discusses this process. Creating a `PrintTask` results in Windows displaying the list of currently configured printers that are available for the user to select. Alternatively, if a `PrintTask` is not defined, Windows simply displays a message saying, "This app can't print right now."

In addition to obtaining an instance of the `PrintManager` for the current view, the `PrintManager` type provides the static `ShowPrintUIAsync` method. Calling this method from your app is equivalent to initiating the Windows printing functionality by selecting the Print entry from the Devices charm. This is useful if you want to provide a more explicit reference to your app's printing capabilities by supplying a dedicated print button in the screen canvas or on the app bar.

Configuring a Print Task

Earlier, you learned that, to support printing, a `PrintTask` needs to be defined in response to the `PrintTaskRequested` event. Listing 14.1 shows the example app's `PrintTaskRequested` event handler.

LISTING 14.1 Handler for the `PrintTaskRequested` Event

```
private void HandlePrintTaskRequested
    (PrintManager sender, PrintTaskRequestedEventArgs args)
{

    // Make sure there actually are some pictures to be printed.
    var picturesToBePrinted = _pictureProvider();
    if (!picturesToBePrinted.Any()) return;

    // Create the task
    var printTask = args.Request.CreatePrintTask(
        "WinRT Printing Example",
        HandlePrintTaskSourceRequested);

    // Subscribe to lifecycle events for the current task/job
    // Note - Unsubscribe in "completed", which will always be called
    printTask.Previewing += HandlePrintTaskPreviewing;
    printTask.Submitting += HandlePrintTaskSubmitting;
    printTask.Progressing += HandlePrintTaskProgressing;
    printTask.Completed += HandlePrintTaskCompleted;

    // Define the list of print options to be shown
    var printOptions = printTask.Options.DisplayedOptions;
    printOptions.Clear();
    printOptions.Add(StandardPrintTaskOptions.Copies);
    printOptions.Add(StandardPrintTaskOptions.Orientation);

    // Change the default orientation to Landscape
    printTask.Options.Orientation = PrintOrientation.Landscape;

    // Add/incorporate the app's custom print
    ConfigureCustomOptions(printTask.Options);
}
```

The implementation first checks to see if there are any pictures to be printed. If not, the method simply returns without defining a `PrintTask` instance; the user then is informed that the app is not ready for printing. If pictures are available, the `PrintTask` is defined using the `CreatePrintTask` method that is defined in the `Request` property of the provided `PrintTaskRequestedEventArgs`. The `CreatePrintTask` method requires a title for the print job and a `PrintTaskSourceRequestedHandler` callback that will be invoked when the user selects a printer. The upcoming section "The `PrintTaskSourceRequestedHandler` Callback," discusses this callback method. The specified title will be used as the document name that accompanies the job when it is sent to a printer, which appears in the various print status displays available in Windows (see Figure 14.1).

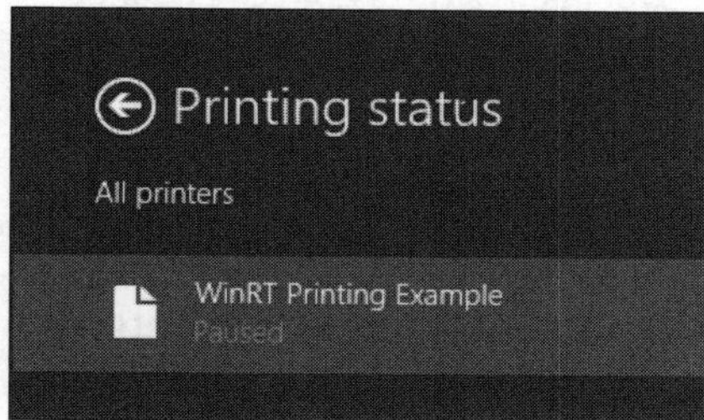

FIGURE 14.1 The print job title in a print status display

Next, event handlers are registered for the lifecycle events exposed by the `PrintTask` instance that is returned. Table 14.1 lists these lifecycle events and when they occur in the printing lifecycle.

TABLE 14.1 Print Task Lifecycle Events

Event	Description
`Previewing`	Called before pages are requested for the print preview panel.
`Submitting`	Called when the user presses Print.
`Progressing`	Called once for each page that is printed. Provides the current page number in the event arguments' `DocumentPageCount` property.

Event	Description
`Completed`	Called after the printing task has completed. Includes a `Completion` property that indicates the status of the job when it was considered complete. `Submitted` indicates that the job was successfully sent to the Windows print manager. `Failed` indicates that some error occurred when submitting the job. `Abandoned` indicates that the user dismissed the print dialog box before selecting a printer. `Canceled` indicates that the user dismissed the print dialog box after selecting a printer, but without pressing the Print button.

If the actions performed in these event handlers will result in updates to the app user interface, you must explicitly switch the actions back to the UI thread using either a `Dispatcher` or a `SynchronizationContext` object to prevent a cross-thread access exception from being thrown.

The final steps performed in the method in Listing 14.1 involve configuring the printing options to display to the user. First, the set of standard options to be displayed is specified, followed by the addition of some custom application-specific options. The section "Customizing Print Options" explains this process further.

Because Windows normally reacts to the changes made in the `PrintTaskRequested` event handler when the handler completes its execution, special care must be taken when performing asynchronous actions within the handler method. In the case of asynchronous operations, control is returned to the Windows Runtime before the asynchronous action's completion. To handle this, the `Request` property of the event arguments to the `PrintTaskRequested` event includes a `GetDeferral` method. Chapter 2, "Windows Store Apps and WinRT Components," first explained deferrals, and you saw them again in both Chapter 11, "Windows Charms Integration," and Chapter 12, "Additional Windows Integration." Basically, deferrals provide a mechanism that you can use when something outside your app is waiting on the completion of an asynchronous method call that is occurring within your app. When a deferral is requested, the external process waits for the `Complete` method of the provided `Deferral` instance to be called as a signal that processing may proceed instead of simply relying on the method's completion.

> **NOTE**
>
> With or without the use of a Deferral, the PrintTaskRequested event expects its handlers to complete their work in a relatively small amount of time so that the initial print dialog box can be shown to the user in a timely fashion. However, the PrintTaskSourceRequestedHandler callback has a longer delay (several seconds versus a few hundred milliseconds). Take care to ensure that longer async operations that provide content for printing occur either in the PrintTaskSourceRequestedHandler callback or elsewhere in the print job lifecycle.

The PrintTaskSourceRequestedHandler Callback

When the user selects a printer from the list that is presented in response to the creation of a PrintTask, the Windows Runtime invokes the PrintTaskSourceRequestedHandler that was provided in the CreatePrintTask method. The code in this callback method is responsible for setting the document source that will be used for the current print job by calling the SetSource method provided in the callback arguments. This document source is typically obtained from the DocumentSource property provided by an instance of the PrintDocument class. Whereas the PrintTask class largely relates to the print job itself, the PrintDocument class is responsible for managing requests related to the content that is to be both previewed and printed. The upcoming section "Providing Content" discusses the functionality that the PrintDocument class provides. Listing 14.2 shows the example app's implementation of the PrintTaskSourceRequestHandler callback.

LISTING 14.2 Defining the Print Job Document Source

```
private void HandlePrintTaskSourceRequested
    (PrintTaskSourceRequestedArgs args)
{
    // Request a deferral to accommodate the async operation
    var deferral = args.GetDeferral();

    // Set the document source for the current print job.
    // This MUST happen on the UI thread.
    _dispatcher.RunAsync(CoreDispatcherPriority.Normal, () =>
    {
        args.SetSource(_printDocument.DocumentSource);
```

```
        // Complete the deferral to indicate completion
        deferral.Complete();
    });
}
```

Note that a worker thread of the runtime initiates the PrintTaskSourceRequestHandler callback. Because the call to SetSource must occur on the UI thread, the call to SetSource is marshalled asynchronously using RunAsync call provided by the CoreDispatcher instance. In much the same way that the arguments provided to the handler for the PrintTaskRequested event supplied the capability to request a deferral that could be used to notify the event source of the completion of asynchronous operations, the arguments provided to the PrintTaskSourceRequestHandler also provide a GetDeferral method. The GetDeferral method is called at the beginning of the callback method to obtain a Deferral instance, and the deferral's Complete method is called within the code that the dispatcher executes asynchronously.

Customizing Print Options

The last few steps you saw in the PrintTaskRequested event handler in Listing 14.1 involve customizing the print options that will be displayed to the user. Print options can be customized in two ways. First, you can change the list of standard print options that display. Second, you can define and display custom print options that are specific to the needs of your app.

The print options are accessed through the Options property of the PrintTask object. The Options value includes properties to both access and set the current value of each one of the standard properties. It also includes the MinCopies and MaxCopies read-only values that specify the minimum and maximum number of copies for a given print job, respectively, as well as a DisplayedOptions property that contains the list of the options that appear to the user on the print preview panel. You can alter both the content and order of the items that display to the user by changing the contents of the DisplayedOptions list. In Listing 14.1, the list is first cleared; then the Copies and Orientation properties are added back to the list of values to be displayed, in that order. Additionally, the Orientation property is changed to

`Landscape` to set the default value that displays to the user when the print preview panel first appears.

Note that, no matter which values the `DisplayedOptions` list includes, if the printer that has been selected doesn't support a particular option, the indicated value simply is omitted from the display. Furthermore, excluding items from the `DisplayedOptions` list doesn't completely hide the value. The print preview panel includes a **More Settings** link that switches the print preview panel to display all the standard properties that the current printer supports.

You also can add custom print options to the `DisplayedOptions` list, but you must first define them. The example app defines three custom options. The first one enables the user to choose a page layout template to use for the selected pictures. The second one allows the user to indicate whether the images used in the print preview display should use the thumbnail image or the full-resolution image. The final option allows the user to specify title text to display on each printed page. Listing 14.3 shows how these options are configured.

LISTING 14.3 Configuring Custom Print Options

```
private void ConfigureCustomOptions(PrintTaskOptions printTaskOptions)
{
    if (printTaskOptions == null)
        throw new ArgumentNullException("printTaskOptions");

    var detailedOptions =
        PrintTaskOptionDetails.GetFromPrintTaskOptions(printTaskOptions);

    // Create the list of options for choosing a layout
    var selectedLayoutOption = detailedOptions.CreateItemListOption(
        LayoutOptionId, "Layout");
    selectedLayoutOption.AddItem(
        PrintLayoutId.LayoutOneByOne.ToString(),
        PrintLayout.Layouts[PrintLayoutId.LayoutOneByOne].LayoutName);

    selectedLayoutOption.AddItem(
        PrintLayoutId.LayoutTwoByTwo.ToString(),
        PrintLayout.Layouts[PrintLayoutId.LayoutTwoByTwo].LayoutName);

    selectedLayoutOption.TrySetValue(DefaultPrintLayoutId.ToString());
    detailedOptions.DisplayedOptions.Add(LayoutOptionId);
```

```
    // Create the list of options for choosing whether the preview
    // should use thumbnails or full-res images
    var previewTypeOption = detailedOptions.CreateItemListOption(
        PreviewTypeOptionId, "Preview Type");
    previewTypeOption.AddItem(
        PreviewTypeOption.Thumbnails.ToString(),
        "Thumbnails");
    previewTypeOption.AddItem(
        PreviewTypeOption.FullRes.ToString(),
        "Full Res");

    previewTypeOption.TrySetValue(DefaultPreviewTypeOption.ToString());
    detailedOptions.DisplayedOptions.Add(PreviewTypeOptionId);

    // Create the option that allows users to provide a page title
    // for the printout
    var pageTitleOption = detailedOptions.CreateTextOption(
        PageTitleOptionId, "Page Title");
    pageTitleOption.TrySetValue(DefaultPageTitle);
    detailedOptions.DisplayedOptions.Add(PageTitleOptionId);

    detailedOptions.OptionChanged += HandleCustomOptionsOptionChanged;
}
```

The first step is to obtain a reference to the `PrintTaskOptionDetails` collection for the current options using its static `GetFromPrintTaskOptions` method. This class provides more advanced insight into the print option values than what the `PrintTaskOptions` value provides. The `PrintTaskOptionDetails` class provides methods for creating two different kinds of custom options. `CreateItemListOption` creates a setting whose values appear in a drop-down list, whereas `CreateTextOption` creates a setting that allows text to be entered in a textbox.

The layout setting is created by using the `CreateItemListOption` method and providing it with both a unique ID and a value to use as the label for the setting in the print preview panel. Possible values for this setting are then added with the `AddItem` method, with both ID and display labels, and then the option's default value is set by calling `TrySetValue` with the desired value. Finally, the option is added to the print preview page by adding its unique ID to the `DisplayedOptions` collection in the same way that the standard options were added. The preview type option is created in the same way. The page title option is created with the `CreateTextOption` method. Because this is just a text field, no options need to be set, so the code simply sets the default initial value for the text and also adds the option to the `DisplayedOptions` collection.

Next, an event handler is registered for the `PrintTaskOptionDetails` `OptionChanged` event (see Listing 14.4). In the handler function, the `OptionId` property on the event arguments indicates the property whose value change has caused the event to be raised. If this value corresponds to one of the custom option IDs, the `InvalidatePreview` method is called on the underlying `PrintDocument`, which tells it that it needs to recalculate the content that it has been asked to provide for display.

LISTING 14.4 Handling Custom Print Option Value Changes

```
private void HandleCustomOptionsOptionChanged
    (PrintTaskOptionDetails sender, PrintTaskOptionChangedEventArgs
➥args)
{
    // Called in response to a setting being changed.
    // Determine if it was a custom setting and react accordingly
    var optionId = args.OptionId as String;

    if (LayoutOptionId.Equals(optionId)
        || PreviewTypeOptionId.Equals(optionId)
        || PageTitleOptionId.Equals(optionId))
    {
        // Invalidate the preview content to force it to refresh.
        // This has to happen on the UI thread.
        _dispatcher.RunAsync(CoreDispatcherPriority.Normal,
            () => _printDocument.InvalidatePreview());
    }
}
```

Figure 14.2 shows the effect of these changes to the print options. You can see that the standard options have been set to include only the Copies and Orientation standard options, with Landscape being the selected value for the Orientation option. Additionally, the custom Layout, Preview Type, and Page Title options have been integrated into the print preview panel.

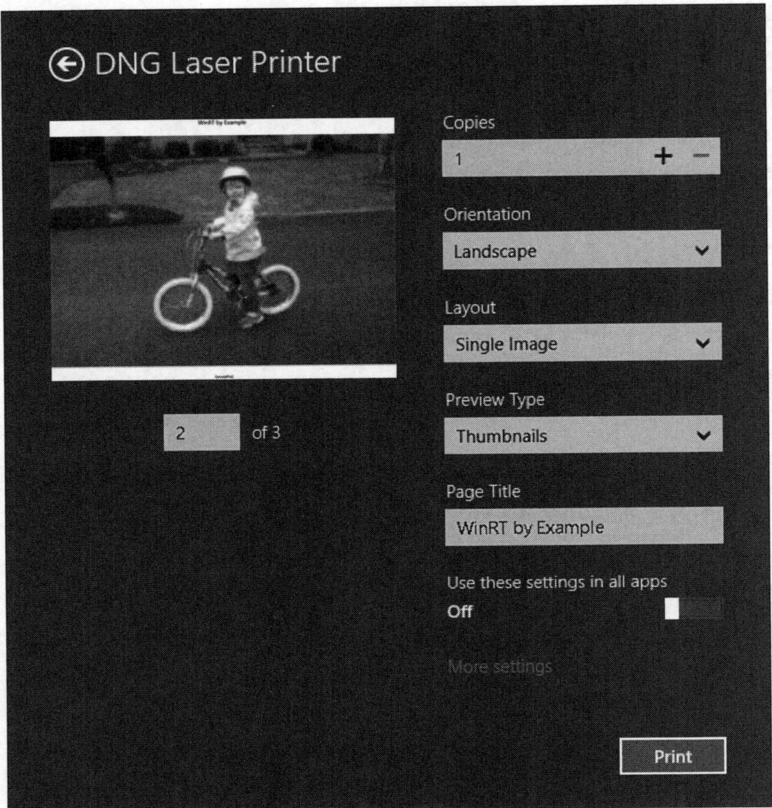

FIGURE 14.2 Customized settings in the print preview panel

The example app also includes methods to retrieve the custom option values. To do so, it is again necessary to obtain the `PrintTaskOptionDetails` based on the value of the regular print options. The `PrintTaskOptionDetails` class provides all the option values within a dictionary that is accessed through its `Options` property. The dictionary is keyed by each option's ID and returns the setting value as a `String`, which can then be converted to the appropriate data type, if necessary.

Providing Printing Content

So far, the discussion has focused on the display and configuration of the print preview panel, primarily through interactions with the `PrintManager` and `PrintTask` classes. This section is primarily concerned with using and interacting with the PrintDocument object, which, as discussed earlier, brokers requests to obtain the content to be displayed in the print preview panel or to be submitted for printing. The PrintDocument instance communicates these requests through its Paginate, GetPreviewPage, and AddPages events. In response to these events, your app needs to call PrintDocument methods with information about the content being previewed or printed.

You obtain the information to provide to these PrintDocument methods by using the print options defined for the current PrintTask and applying these to the content to be printed, to determine how this content should be presented on one or more printable pages. One of the key concepts related to printing is the fact that the content to be printed is usually laid out or formatted differently than what is displayed onscreen. When printing using the Windows Runtime, you can programmatically define the visual elements to be used for previewing printable pages and to be sent to the printer, or you can create them using custom controls that you define using XAML. The latter approach has the added benefit of using the same design-time data and visual layout concepts and tools that you use for defining onscreen layout, to help approximate how the printed content will appear.

Printing generally involves two phases. The first is generating content for preview, and the second is generating the final content to send to the printer. The PrintDocument Paginate and GetPreviewPage events are raised to support the preview phase, and the AddPages event is raised to collect the final content to send to the printer.

Generating Print Preview Content

The first content-related event that the PrintDocument raises is the Paginate event. This event is raised when preview content is initially presented, such as when the print preview panel is first displayed or in response to a call to the PrintDocument InvalidatePreview method. During this event handler, you need to determine the total number of preview pages that will be displayed for your app. If the currently selected print options are affecting your page calculation, you can access them through the PrintTaskOptions parameter provided by the event arguments. This page calculation is given to the PrintDocument instance by calling its SetPreviewPageCount method.

The code in Listing 14.5 shows how the `Paginate` event is handled in the example app. The code first retrieves the custom option values for the page title, selected layout, and preview type and stores them for later use. Additionally, the selected layout information indicates how many pictures per page are in the current layout selection. The total count of the pictures to be printed is also obtained. These values determine the total number of pages that will be printed, and then that value is returned to the `PrintDocument` through a call to the `SetPreviewPageCount` method.

LISTING 14.5 Handling the Paginate Event

```
private void HandlePagination(Object sender, PaginateEventArgs args)
{
    var printDocument = (PrintDocument)sender;
    var options = args.PrintTaskOptions;
    options.DebugPrintTaskOptionDetails(args.CurrentPreviewPageNumber);

    // Record the options driving the current pagination calculations
    _previewOptions.PageTitle = GetPageTitle(options);
    _previewOptions.Layout = GetSelectedPrintLayout(options);
    _previewOptions.PreviewType = GetSelectedPreviewType(options);

    var picturesPerPage = _previewOptions.Layout.PicturesPerPage;
    var picturesToPrint = _pictureProvider().Count();

    // Calculate the total page count based on number of pictures
    // per page and total number of selected pictures
    var totalPageCount =
        (Int32)Math.Ceiling(picturesToPrint / (Double)picturesPerPage);

    // Set the page count to be intermediate if the number of pages
    // is not 100% known at this point, Final if it is certain.
    printDocument.SetPreviewPageCount(
        totalPageCount,
        PreviewPageCountType.Final);
}
```

As each preview page is displayed, the `PrintDocument GetPreviewPage` event is raised. In this event handler, you need to provide the actual content to display in the preview region on the print preview panel. This content is returned to the `PrintDocument` instance by calling its `SetPreviewPage` method with the page number and the visual element to display. Note that the event arguments provided to the handler for this event include only the page number, not the print options. As a result, during the `Paginate` event, the relevant print options should be cached. Another approach is to build and cache the print preview UI elements themselves. In either case, it might be important to cache information in the `Paginate` event handler for later access in the `GetPreviewPage` event handler.

Listing 14.6 shows how the example app handles the `GetPreviewPage` event. The event handler uses both the preview options that were cached in the `Paginate` event handler and the page number to call the `BuildPicturePage` helper function. The `BuildPicturePage` function is responsible for returning an instance of the appropriate custom layout template control and marrying it to a viewmodel that is built with the pictures and other settings to display on the current page. The result of the `BuildPicturePage` function is then returned to the `PrintDocument` by calling its `SetPreviewPage` method along with the indicated page number.

LISTING 14.6 Handling the `GetPreviewPage` Event

```
private void HandleGetPreviewPage
    (Object sender, GetPreviewPageEventArgs args)
{
    var printDocument = (PrintDocument)sender;
    var currentPageNumber = args.PageNumber;

    // Get the visual to be displayed for the currently requested page
    var pageVisual = BuildPicturePage(
        currentPageNumber,
        _previewOptions.Layout,
        _previewOptions.PreviewType == PreviewTypeOption.Thumbnails,
        _previewOptions.PageTitle);
    printDocument.SetPreviewPage(currentPageNumber, pageVisual);
}
```

An interesting consequence of the fact that printing is split into separate preview and printing phases is that you can supply different page renderings in each phase. In the preview phase, the print preview window is relatively small. As such, going through the full effort involved in producing a full-fidelity print layout might not make sense if the goal is just to provide the user with a rough idea of how the final document will appear. This then defers the potentially time-consuming task of calculating the actual print layout until the user has provided all the necessary settings and has submitted the job to the printer.

Generating Content to Send to a Printer

When the user presses the **Print** button in the print preview panel, the Windows Runtime submits the print job for processing. At this point, the `PrintDocument` needs to obtain the final rendered versions of the pages to send to the printer. To give your code a chance to provide this content, the `PrintDocument` raises the `AddPages` event.

As with the `Paginate` event, the `AddPages` event provides the current print options in the event argument's `PrintTaskOptions` property. During the `AddPages` event handler, you need to use the option information to calculate the individual pages and provide them to the `PrintDocument` through its `AddPage` method, followed by a final call to the `AddPagesComplete` method to signal that all the pages for the current job have been provided.

Listing 14.7 shows how the example app handles the `AddPages` event. First, the custom options are retrieved. Then the number of pages to print is calculated, based on the `PicturesPerPage` value obtained from the selected layout option and the total number of pictures to be printed. A loop then iterates through each page, using the `BuildPicturePage` function to construct the page visual and passing that to a call to the `PrintDocument AddPage` method. Note that the page numbers used during printing are one-based. When all the pages have been added, `AddPagesComplete` is called, the job is sent to the printer, and the print preview panel is dismissed.

LISTING 14.7 Handling the AddPages Event

```
private void HandleAddPages(Object sender, AddPagesEventArgs args)
{
    var printDocument = (PrintDocument)sender;
    var options = args.PrintTaskOptions;

    // Get the page title selection
    var pageTitle = GetPageTitle(args.PrintTaskOptions);

    // Determine the value of the layout template setting
    var selectedLayout = GetSelectedPrintLayout(options);

    // Determine how many pages total will be printed
    var picturesPerPage = selectedLayout.PicturesPerPage;
    var picturesToPrint = _pictureProvider().Count();
    var pageCount =
        Math.Ceiling(picturesToPrint / (Double)picturesPerPage);
```

```
    // Calculate the pages (being sure to use high resolution images)
    for (var i = 1; i <= pageCount; i++)
    {
        var pageVisual
            = BuildPicturePage(i, selectedLayout, false, pageTitle);
        printDocument.AddPage(pageVisual);
    }

    // Indicate that the page calculation has completed.
    printDocument.AddPagesComplete();
}
```

Working with Scanners

Now that you have seen how to go about integrating printing functionality into your app, it seems appropriate to discuss scanning, especially because many users own a multifunction printer/scanner combination. Microsoft recently shared that around 66 percent of the printers that are connected to Windows are also scanners.[1] Fortunately, the Windows Runtime includes an easy-to-use API for interacting with any scanners currently connected to Windows that support the Windows Imagine Acquisition (WIA) platform.

The Example App

This section references the same example app presented in the previous "Working with Printers" section. The app not only enables users to select pictures on disk to be printed, but it also provides the capability to scan images to be printed. When the user brings up the scanner flyout by pressing the **Scan** button on the app bar, the app lists the scanners that are currently available and, for the selected scanner, the different scan sources it supports.

If the scanner supports previewing, the user can perform a preview scan by pressing the **Preview** button. After previewing the scan, the user can manipulate sliders to configure the actual area to include in the final scan. Pressing the **Scan and Open** button prompts the user for a folder

[1] Build 2013 session 3-025, "Building Windows Apps That Use Scanners," Slide 7.

location in which to store the scanned image; then the image is scanned and loaded into the app so that it can be captioned and printed.

As with printing, access to the Windows Runtime scanner APIs in the example app's source code is encapsulated within the `ScanHelper` class.

Determining Scanner Availability

The `ImageScanner` class enables you to interact with scanners. To access an instance of the `ImageScanner` class, you first need to retrieve an ID for the scanner that you want to communicate with. You can obtain this ID by querying for the currently connected scanners with the `DeviceInformation` class. This class includes the capability to directly query for specific device types with its `FindAllAsync` method, as well as the capability to use its `CreateWatcher` method to configure a `DeviceWatcher` instance that raises events as devices are added, removed, or updated.

One option that you can provide to either of these `DeviceInformation` methods is a selection string that instructs the queries to only look for devices that meet certain criteria. The `ImageScanner` class includes a static `GetDeviceSelector` method that returns a selection string that can be used with the `DeviceInformation` class to focus the query to just return connected scanners.

The example app uses the `GetScannersAsync` method in Listing 14.8 to obtain the list of scanners presented to the end users. Using the selection string obtained from the call to `GetDeviceSelector`, the `DeviceInformation` `FindAllAsync` method is called. The relevant properties from the items in the resulting list of scanners are then projected into a collection of `ScannerModel` objects, which are then returned to its caller. These properties include the `Id` value, which is used by the `ImageScanner` methods that you see used throughout the remainder of this topic.

LISTING 14.8 Enumerating the Available Scanners

```
public async Task<IEnumerable<ScannerModel>> GetScannersAsync()
{
    // String to be used to enumerate scanners
    var deviceSelector = ImageScanner.GetDeviceSelector();
    var scanners = await DeviceInformation.FindAllAsync(deviceSelector);
    var result = scanners
        .Select(x => new ScannerModel
        {
```

```
            Id = x.Id,
            Name = x.Name,
            IsDefault = x.IsDefault,
            IsEnabled = x.IsEnabled,
        });
    return result;
}
```

Working with Scan Sources

A **scan source** refers to the mechanism a scanner uses to obtain its image information. The Windows Runtime scanner API supports three types of scan sources. Flatbed sources are probably the most common; they refer to models in which the image is typically placed flat on a piece of glass and the scan sensor moves under the glass to capture the image. Feeder sources allow one or more images (typically pages) to be put into a feeder mechanism that either moves the paper into position to be scanned or controls the movement of the image past a stationary sensor. Both flatbed and feeder scan sources can provide a variety of configurable settings to adjust the scanned image quality and the surface area to be scanned. The final supported scan source is the autoconfigured scan source. Autoconfigured sources automatically detect the optimal scan settings instead of allowing them to be configured. Some scanners that support autoconfiguration include both a flatbed and a document feeder, along with functionality to detect whether documents are loaded into the feeder or whether one is already positioned on the flatbed, and automatically choose the appropriate source.

When a scanner is selected in the example app, the `ImageScanner` methods obtain information about the selected scanner. They check what scan sources the scanner supports and determine if each of these scan sources supports previewing. Listing 14.9 shows the `GetSupportedScanSources` method that the example app uses to determine what scan sources a scanner supports, based on the given device ID. First, an `ImageScanner` instance for a scanner with the given ID is located with the `ImageScanner FromIdAsync` method. Next, a LINQ query is used to find the sources that the `ImageScanner` instance supports; the results are projected into a list of `ScanSourceDetailsItem` instances, which provides access to the supported sources and indicates the current scanner's default scan source, which the `ImageScanner DefaultScanSource` property supplies.

LISTING 14.9 Determining Supported Scan Sources for a Scanner

```
public async Task<ScanSourceDetails> GetSupportedScanSources
    (String deviceId)
{
    // Check whether each of the known scan sources is available
    // for the scanner with the provided ID
    var scanSources = new[]
                      {
                          ImageScannerScanSource.Flatbed,
                          ImageScannerScanSource.Feeder,
                          ImageScannerScanSource.AutoConfigured
                      };

    var scanner = await ImageScanner.FromIdAsync(deviceId);

    var supportedSources = scanSources
        .Where(x => scanner.IsScanSourceSupported(x))
        .Select(x => new ScanSourceDetailsItem
                    {
                        SourceType = x,
                        SupportsPreview = scanner.IsPreviewSupported(x)
                    })
        .ToList();

    var results = new ScanSourceDetails
                  {
                      SupportedScanSources = supportedSources,
                      DefaultScanSource = scanner.DefaultScanSource
                  };
    return results;
}
```

Previewing

For scanner and scan source combinations that support it, capturing a preview image is relatively trivial. The `ImageScanner` class provides a `ScanPreviewToStreamAsync` method that, as its name suggests, performs a preview scan of the indicated scan source and returns the results in an `IRandomAccessStream` instance. Listing 14.10 uses an `InMemoryRandomAccessStream` for the scan and then uses the resulting stream to populate a `BitmapImage` instance.

LISTING 14.10 Obtaining a Preview Scan

```
public async Task<BitmapImage> ScanPicturePreviewAsync
    (String scannerDeviceId, ImageScannerScanSource scanSource)
{
    var scanner = await ImageScanner.FromIdAsync(scannerDeviceId);
    if (scanner.IsPreviewSupported(scanSource))
    {
        var stream = new InMemoryRandomAccessStream();
        var result =
            await scanner.ScanPreviewToStreamAsync(scanSource, stream);
        if (result.Succeeded)
        {
            var thumbnail = new BitmapImage();
            thumbnail.SetSource(stream);
            return thumbnail;
        }
    }
    return null;
}
```

Scanning

The process for actually scanning an image to disk is similar to the process you saw for previewing an image, but the `ImageScannerScanFilesToFolderAsync` method is used instead. Like the `ScanPreviewToStreamAsync` method, this method also expects the desired scan source to be identified, but it takes a `StorageFolder` reference that specifies where the scanned items should be written instead of a reference to an `IRandomAccessStream`.

In the example app, the `ScanPicturesAsync` method performs the scan (see Listing 14.11). Note a few key differences between this method and the `ScanPicturePreviewAsync` method that we previously discussed. First, the method expects a `StorageFolder` to specify where the scanned artifacts should be placed. In the example app, this folder was obtained using the WinRT `FolderPicker` control before this method was called. Next, before actually scanning the image, a `ConfigureScanner` method is called and is given information about the scanner, along with horizontal and vertical percentage values. The upcoming section "Scanner Settings" discusses scanner configuration. Finally, the resulting scanned files are returned as a collection of `StorageFile` instances. Note, however, that enumerating this collection with a `foreach` statement results in a `COMException` being thrown, so each item must instead be referenced by index. In the example code, this merely builds a new list that is returned to the calling function.

LISTING 14.11 Scanning Images to Files

```
public async Task<IEnumerable<StorageFile>> ScanPicturesAsync(
    String scannerDeviceId, ImageScannerScanSource source,
    StorageFolder destinationFolder,
    Double hScanPercent, Double vScanPercent)
{
    var scanner = await ImageScanner.FromIdAsync(scannerDeviceId);
    if (scanner.IsScanSourceSupported(source))
    {
        ConfigureScanner(scanner, source, hScanPercent, vScanPercent);

        var scanResult = await scanner
            .ScanFilesToFolderAsync(source, destinationFolder);

        var results = new List<StorageFile>();
        // Caution - enumerating this list (foreach) will result in a
        // COM exception. Instead, just walk the collection by index
        // and build a new list.
        for (var i = 0; i < scanResult.ScannedFiles.Count; i++)
        {
            results.Add(scanResult.ScannedFiles[i]);
        }
        return results;
    }
    return null;
}
```

Scanner Settings

Depending on the scan source that is selected, as well as the capabilities of any particular scanner, several options can be set to affect how the image is captured and stored. These configuration options fall into three categories. Source configuration refers to the actual image information that the scanner sensor obtains. Format configuration refers to the file format used to store images on disk. Finally, feeder configuration refers to options that can affect the behavior of the document feeder mechanism.

Examples of source configuration options include setting the area to be scanned with the `SelectedScanRegion` property, indicating a value for the `DesiredResolution`, and adjusting image quality values with the `Brightness` and `Contrast` settings. You can also set whether an image should be scanned in color, grayscale, or monochrome with the `ColorMode` setting.

Format configuration is limited to specifying a `Format` value from the `ImageScannerFormat` enumeration, which determines the file type of the images saved to disk. Options include the PNG, JPG, BMP, and TIF image formats, as well as XPS, Open XPS, and PDF document formats. Before setting a format option, use the supplied `IsFormatSupported` method to see if the current scanner supports a desired format. Instructing a scanner to output a format that it cannot handle results in an exception.

Examples of feeder configurations include determining whether duplex scanning (referring to two-sided documents) is available and instructing the scanner on whether to use it, setting the document page size and dimensions, determining whether automatic document feeding is available and indicating whether to use it, and specifying other information and settings related to the document page size and orientation.

Feeder scan sources support all three kinds of configuration options. Flatbed scan sources support the source and format configuration options. Autoconfigured scan sources support only setting the format configuration; the scanner device itself automatically determines all the other values.

The example app includes a pair of sliders that can be set relative to the preview image to indicate how much of the scan surface to include in the final scan. The sliders provide percentage values that are then passed through the `ScanPictureAsync` method and, ultimately, are included in the call to `ConfigureScanner` (see Listing 14.11). These sliders are visible in the scanner flyout in Figure 14.3.

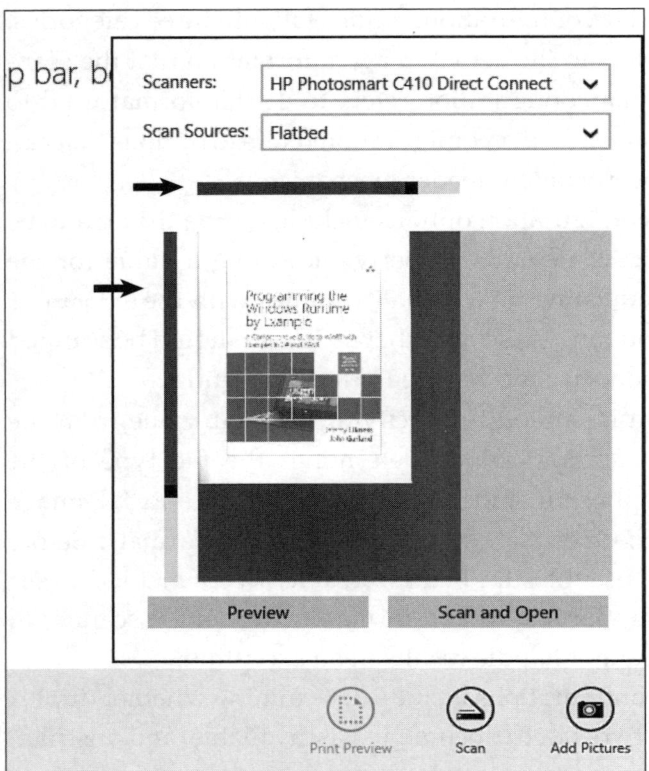

FIGURE 14.3 Setting the area to be scanned based on the preview image

Listing 14.12 shows the `ConfigureScanner` method that the example app uses to set the final scan area and the preferred file format. First, the available configuration options are obtained based on the current scan source selection. The `ImageScanner` instance's `FlatbedConfiguration` or `FeederConfiguration` values retrieve both source and format configuration options, depending on whether the scan source is a flatbed or feeder source. If the scan source is set to an autoconfiguration source, the `AutoConfiguration` property provides the format configuration value.

If a source configuration is available, the provided width and height percentages are applied to the scanner's maximum scanning area to set the current scan region using the source configuration instance's `SelectedScanRegion` property.

Finally, the desired image format is set from a collection of preferred formats. Each format is checked to see whether the scanner supports the particular format. Checking stops as soon as the first compatible format is found and the `Format` property is set.

LISTING 14.12 Configuring Scanner Settings

```
private static void ConfigureScanner(
    ImageScanner scanner, ImageScannerScanSource source,
    Double hScanPercent, Double vScanPercent)
{
    if (scanner == null) throw new ArgumentNullException("scanner");

    IImageScannerSourceConfiguration sourceConfig = null;
    IImageScannerFormatConfiguration formatConfig = null;

    switch (source)
    {
        case ImageScannerScanSource.Flatbed:
            sourceConfig = scanner.FlatbedConfiguration;
            formatConfig = scanner.FlatbedConfiguration;
            break;
        case ImageScannerScanSource.Feeder:
            sourceConfig = scanner.FeederConfiguration;
            formatConfig = scanner.FeederConfiguration;
            break;
        case ImageScannerScanSource.AutoConfigured:
            formatConfig = scanner.AutoConfiguration;
            break;
    }

    // Potentially update the scanner configuration
    if (sourceConfig != null)
    {
        var maxScanArea = sourceConfig.MaxScanArea;
        sourceConfig.SelectedScanRegion = new Rect(
            0,
            0,
            maxScanArea.Width * hScanPercent,
            maxScanArea.Height * vScanPercent);
    }

    // Potentially update the format that the end product is saved to
    if (formatConfig != null)
    {
        // NOTE: If your desired format isn't natively supported, it may
        // be possible to generate the desired format post-process
        // using image conversion, etc. libraries.
```

```
        var desiredFormats = new[]
        {
            ImageScannerFormat.Png,
            ImageScannerFormat.Jpeg,
            ImageScannerFormat.DeviceIndependentBitmap,
            //ImageScannerFormat.Tiff,
            //ImageScannerFormat.Xps,
            //ImageScannerFormat.OpenXps,
            //ImageScannerFormat.Pdf
        };

        foreach (var format in desiredFormats)
        {
            if (formatConfig.IsFormatSupported(format))
            {
                formatConfig.Format = format;
                break;
            }
        }
    }
}
```

Summary

This chapter showed how the Windows Runtime provides APIs that you can use to add both printing and scanning functionality to your apps. You saw that the printing APIs enable you to provide a custom print configuration experience, including selecting which standard options the user sees, as well as to define custom options that are specific to your app. You also saw how you can create custom content that displays in the print preview panel, as well as custom content submitted for printing.

The chapter also included a discussion of the scanning APIs and how you can use them to integrate scanning into your app. You can obtain a list of currently connected scanners, along with information about the different scan sources each one supports. You saw how to instruct a scanner to capture both a preview image and a final collection of images on disk. The chapter concluded with coverage of how to set scanner settings, depending on the selected scan source and the features the scanner itself offers.

In the next chapter, "Background Tasks," you see how to provide functionality for Windows Store apps even when they are not running in the foreground. You learn how to include support for transferring files in the background, how to play audio in the background, how to provide at-a-glance status information to the Windows lock screen, and how to respond to system events to trigger the execution of background tasks related to your app.

15

Background Tasks

WINDOWS STORE APPS OFTEN MUST PERFORM A VARIETY OF TASKS EVEN when they are not running in the foreground. Your app might need to fetch data from a remote server, scan directories for changes, or communicate with a web service to retrieve updates. Chapter 2, "Windows Store Apps and WinRT Components," covers the application lifecycle and explains how apps are suspended and sometimes even terminated when they are not in the foreground. Chapter 10, "Networking," demonstrated a special background task that can run to download large files even when the app is suspended or terminated.

Your app can use several more types of background tasks. Some of these tasks can drive updates that display for the user on the lock screen, such as incoming messages or special alerts your app might raise. Other tasks can be configured to listen for incoming messages or to fire only when the device is connected to power. Background tasks enable your app to play audio in the background with a special set of system-provided controls and even open a persistent network connection to send and receive data through connected standby.

In this chapter, you learn about background tasks and what makes them special compared to other facilities available to Windows Store apps. You learn how to check for existing background tasks and configure new ones. You learn how to give your app access to the lock screen and display badges and detailed status messages, and how to update this information in the background when your app is not running. First, I explore how to take advantage of background threads to run short-lived tasks that can perform parallel work when your app is running.

The Thread Pool

Sometimes you want to perform work in the background without blocking your app's user interface. Although these types of tasks do run in the background, they are referred to as parallel threads. Parallel threads share resources with your app. The work executes on a different thread from the main UI thread, but it also is suspended and/or terminated when your app is.

You might already be familiar with the thread pool, even though you haven't directly interacted with it. This is because the `Task` class uses the thread pool. Whenever you wrap a long-running job in a `Task`, you are using the thread pool behind the scenes. `Task` is a convenient wrapper and a way to manage jobs that run in the thread pool.

The best way to accomplish asynchronous work is to use the thread pool. Threads are operating system resources that take up memory and impact performance when they are being created and destroyed. The thread pool is a special feature of WinRT that runs at the operating system level and is capable of optimizing threads based on the multiple cores your CPU might have. It can balance the number of threads for apps in the foreground and, most importantly, can reuse existing threads to reduce the overhead of spawning new threads.

The thread pool is capable of submitting work items, managing their priority, and cancelling items that are running (provided the jobs check for cancellation). It can schedule work using timers or by responding to system events. It is best when used for short-lived processing. The one caveat to working in the background is that you must be prepared to marshal results back to the UI thread using the dispatcher.

The **ThreadPoolExample** project demonstrates two possible uses of the thread pool. The first is a long-running task that estimates the value of pi in the `CalculatePi` method of `MainPage.xaml.cs`. One method for estimating envisions throwing random darts at a board that contains a target that is a perfect circle. The radius of the circle is the same as the half length of a side of the board. The ratio of hits to misses represents a guess at pi. In the example, darts are thrown and the number of hits is tracked compared to the number of tries (iterations).

The method takes an `IAsyncAction` that represents the asynchronous work. The method iterates until either the maximum allowed range for an integer is reached or the work is canceled. It checks to see whether it is canceled by querying the `Status` property on the `IAsyncAction` instance. It immediately breaks out of the loop when it detects a cancellation.

```
while (iterations < int.MaxValue &&
    action.Status != AsyncStatus.Canceled)
```

The work is submitted to the thread pool by calling the static `RunAsync` method. This schedules the given method to run on an available thread (or spins up a new one, if needed) and returns an instance of `IAsyncAction`.

```
piAsyncAction = ThreadPool.RunAsync(this.CalculatePi);
piAsyncAction.Completed = this.CalculationComplete;
```

Using the `Completed` property, you can set a method that is called when the work is completed or cancelled. The example app uses this to update the estimate and tag it as the final guess. You can also use the thread pool to configure work that runs after a specified period of time or on a regular interval. The example app sets up a timer that runs twice every second to update the UI with the results of the long-running background task.

```
iterationTimer = ThreadPoolTimer.CreatePeriodicTimer(
    this.Iterate, TimeSpan.FromMilliseconds(500));
```

The iterate method uses the dispatcher to update the UI with the total iterations and latest guess.

```
this.Dispatcher.RunAsync(CoreDispatcherPriority.Normal,
    () =>
        {
            Iterations.Text = iterations.ToString();
            Pi.Text = PiEstimate.ToString();
        });
```

You can cancel the periodic work by calling its `Cancel` method. Run the example outside the debugger and open the task manager. You can verify that the app is not taking up CPU cycles when you suspend the app. But note that all threads are terminated when you suspend and shut down the app. For this reason, you should not assume that long-running tasks scheduled to the thread pool will complete. If the work has important results, you should save them periodically to local storage. If special clean-up is involved, register to the `Suspending` event on `Application.Current` and use that to perform your clean-up.

The thread pool is useful for short work items that run in parallel without blocking the UI, but you often have longer-running tasks that must be more resilient. Chapter 10 explained how to use background tasks to download large files even when the app itself is shut down. You can use the same mechanism for other types of work as well.

Uploads and Downloads

A common activity is downloading large amounts of data in a Windows Store app (for example, an eBook app might need to download a large file representing a book in your local library). Chapter 10 demonstrated this. You also can perform uploads in the background. For example, imagine an accounting app that enables you to scan or take photos of documents to upload to the server. For this scenario, you use the `BackgroundUploader` class.

As with the `BackgroundDownloader`, you can query for existing uploads and take appropriate action based on the current status.

```
var uploads = await BackgroundUploader.GetCurrentUploadsAsync();
```

To schedule an ordinary upload, simply pass the file, filename, and URL of the server that is prepared to receive the upload.

```
StorageFile file = await picker.PickSingleFileAsync();
var uploader = new BackgroundUploader();
uploader.SetRequestHeader("Filename", file.name);
var uploadOperation = uploader.CreateUpload(url, file);
```

If you want to upload multiple files at once (called a multipart upload), you can set up a list of content parts.

```
var parts = new List<BackgroundTransferContentPart>();
var part = new BackgroundTransferContentPart("part 1", file.Name);
part.SetFile(file);
parts.Add(part);
var uploadOperation = await uploader.CreateUploadAsync(uri, parts);
```

When you have the operation set, you can either call `StartAsync` to kick off the upload or call `AttachAsync` to attach to an existing operation that is already in progress. As with the download tasks, you can provide a callback to receive progress updates while your app is running in the foreground.

Audio

Windows 8.1 makes it extremely easy to develop an app that plays audio in the background using low power. The Windows Runtime provides a standard set of minimal system controls that provide a consistent experience to the user when streaming audio. These controls appear briefly when the user manipulates an audio control (such as adjusting the volume), take up a small portion of the screen, and provide relevant data and a simple way to navigate through playlists.

Setting up your app to handle background audio has additional advantages. Windows 8.1 supports hardware offloading of audio streams. This enables Windows to route audio streams directly to the hardware and bypass the software audio engine. The main processing tasks for audio then can be performed in the audio hardware instead of the main CPU and can both improve performance and increase battery life.

The **AudioBackgroundExample** project demonstrates how to set up your app for background audio. The main elements of the app are no different than an app that supports only foreground audio. Listing 15.1 shows an instance of a `MediaElement` and some supporting buttons you'll find in `MainPage.xaml`.

Listing 15.1 UI for Playing Audio

```
<MediaElement x:Name="MediaPlayer" Grid.Row="1"/>
<TextBlock Text="Initializing..." x:Name="Status"
    Grid.Row="1" Style="{StaticResource SubheaderTextBlockStyle}"/>
<StackPanel Orientation="Horizontal" Grid.Row="2">
    <AppBarButton x:Name="PlayButton" Icon="Play"
```

```
    Label="Play" Click="PlayOnClick"/>
    <AppBarButton x:Name="PauseButton" Icon="Pause"
    Label="Pause" Click="PauseOnClick"/>
    <AppBarButton x:Name="StopButton" Icon="Stop"
    Label="Stop" Click="StopOnClick"></AppBarButton>
</StackPanel>
```

If you want to use the system-provided controls for playing audio, simply set the AreTransportControlsEnabled property to true. The MainPage instance fires a Loaded event that initializes some settings. This includes preventing the system controls from displaying and preventing the audio from playing automatically after it is loaded, as well as registering for the event that signals when the state of the audio changes. I wait to cover the code related to the transport controls until later in this section because that code is specifically for background audio.

```
MediaPlayer.AudioCategory = AudioCategory.BackgroundCapableMedia;
MediaPlayer.AreTransportControlsEnabled = false;
MediaPlayer.AutoPlay = false;
```

Table 15.1 lists the available settings for the AudioCategory. The only setting that enables background playback is the BackgroundCapableMedia category. ForegroundOnlyMedia is not intended for background playing, but is eligible to be offloaded to the audio hardware.

TABLE 15.1 Available Settings for AudioCategory

Value	Description
Alerts	System or app notifications, such as ring tones
BackgroundCapableMedia	General media, including streaming audio and video audio that can be played in the background
Communications	Peer-to-peer audio for chat applications
ForegroundOnlyMedia	General media, including streaming audio and video audio that cannot be played in the background (the system fades out this audio when the app is no longer in the foreground)
GameEffects	Sound effects for games

Value	Description
`GameMedia`	Background and ambient audio for games
`Other`	Any stream not covered by the other settings
`SoundEffects`	Sound effects for any app, including nongames

After the page is loaded, and whenever the state of the media player changes, the `SetButtonStates` method is called. This method sets up the status of the player and enables or disables the onscreen buttons, depending on the media state. For example, the Pause button is enabled only if the stream supports the pause operation and the stream is currently playing.

```
PauseButton.IsEnabled = MediaPlayer.CanPause &&
    MediaPlayer.CurrentState == MediaElementState.Playing;
```

Before you can manipulate the audio, you must select an audio file to play. This is handled in the `SelectFileOnClick` method. A `FileOpenPicker` is used to select files that end in either `.mp3` or `.wav`, using the Music Library as the default start location. The file is used to set the source on the `MediaElement` instance and the filename is stored to display subsequent messages in the UI.

```
this.MediaPlayer.SetSource(await file.OpenAsync(FileAccessMode.Read),
    file.ContentType);
this.fileName = file.DisplayName;
```

If the file is a valid audio file, the `MediaElement` fires a change event when the audio is ready to play. This triggers the code that enables the Play button. When the user presses the button, the `Play` method on the `MediaElement` is called. The various playback methods to start, stop, and pause playback all call methods on the element.

The steps detailed so far are all you need to provide an app capable of playing audio in the foreground. Figure 15.1 shows the controls for the running app.

FIGURE 15.1 The app UI for media playback

The rest of the code you noticed is additional code required to support the background playback. The first step in enabling this is declaring the audio background task. Figure 15.2 shows how this is done on the **Declarations** tab of the manifest UI. Add the **Background Tasks** declaration, check the **Audio** option, and copy the entry point field from the **Application** tab (the fully qualified name of your `App` class).

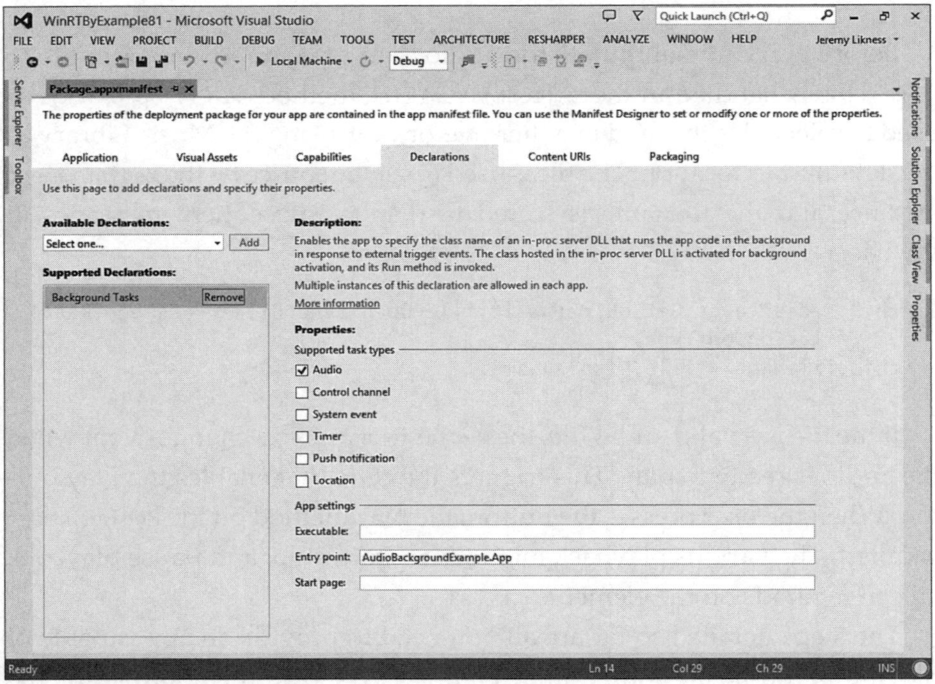

FIGURE 15.2 The declaration for background audio

Your app must keep track of the `SystemMediaTransportControls` instance that the Windows Runtime provides. You can see two important steps in the `MainPageLoaded` event handler. The first captures the instance of the control, and the second registers for the `ButtonPressed` event. Only one event is fired for the control, and the type of event is provided in the arguments passed to the event handler.

```
this.transportControls = SystemMediaTransportControls
    .GetForCurrentView();
this.transportControls.ButtonPressed +=
    this.TransportControlsButtonPressed;
```

I also added a method called `SetTransportControlStates` to synchronize the state of the system controls with the main window media element. The method determines whether it is even valid to show the control and enables the entire transport. If the music is valid, it enables various buttons based on the capabilities of the stream.

```
this.transportControls.IsEnabled = validMusic;
this.transportControls.IsPlayEnabled = validMusic;
this.transportControls.IsPauseEnabled = MediaPlayer.CanPause;
this.transportControls.IsStopEnabled = validMusic;
```

Note that enabling play, pause, or stop doesn't change the status of the actual button on the transport controls; it affects only the availability of the button. If you don't enable pause, it will never be available to the user. Whether it shows as enabled or disabled depends on whether the audio is currently playing.

The system transport controls are capable of displaying information about the currently playing track and an associated thumbnail. Although you can set these explicitly, the easiest way is to use the metadata associated with the file. If the file was downloaded from Xbox Music, for example, it automatically has metadata, including the artist name, the song title, and a thumbnail of the album provided. The following code is called when the user picks a new file. It copies the metadata to the system controls and informs the controls of the update.

```
await this.transportControls.DisplayUpdater
    .CopyFromFileAsync(MediaPlaybackType.Music, file);
this.transportControls.DisplayUpdater.Update();
```

The result of the call to copy the data is a Boolean. If the call returns `false`, it means the copy failed, and you should supply other information to the control. You can also call the `ClearAll` method on the `DisplayUpdater` to clear any previous titles or thumbnails that are present. Figure 15.3 shows the default transport overlay. The file has no metadata, so the player defaults to the app display name and the app thumbnail. The volume control on the left is typically the only control the user sees when adjusting volume; the more comprehensive control on the right displays when the system transport controls are enabled. Notice that the Fast Forward and Rewind buttons are disabled because the app did not enable them. In apps that provide a playlist, you would have a series of files and enable these controls.

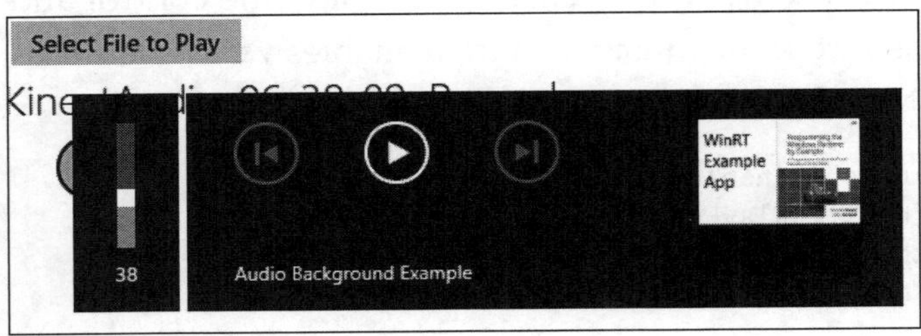

FIGURE 15.3 The transport controls

Whenever the user presses a button on the transport control, the registered `TransportControlsButtonPressed` handler is called. The button press is initiated from the Windows shell and does not arrive on the UI thread. Therefore, any updates must be marshalled using the `Dispatcher`. The handler calls the same methods used by the buttons in the app's own UI.

```
if (args.Button.Equals(SystemMediaTransportControlsButton.Play))
{
    await RunOnUiThread(this.Play);
    return;
}
```

Whether the action was initiated from the app UI or the transport controls, the handling methods all call `SetTransportControlStates` to inform the system controls of the action. For the transport controls to show the correct state, the playback status of the media must be set. The enumeration for this is different from what the `MediaElement` uses, so the app sets up a map between the `MediaElementState` enumeration and the corresponding `MediaPlaybackStatus` enumeration.

```
this.transportControls.PlaybackStatus =
    this.map[MediaPlayer.CurrentState];
```

The transport controls are capable of more advanced functionality. For example, you can set up a playlist and enable the Fast Forward and Rewind controls. When the user presses these buttons, you can use the event to update the media source to a new file. The audio background capability keeps your app running in the background without rendering the UI (except for the transport overlay) until the user stops the stream. At that time, the system can suspend your app and resume it when playback starts again, to preserve battery life and performance.

In summary, you follow these steps to enable background audio in your app:

1. Set the audio category on your `MediaElement` to `BackgroundCapableMedia`.
2. Add a **Background Tasks** declaration to your manifest and check the **Audio** task type.
3. Capture the instance of the `SystemMediaTransportControls` for the current view.
4. Enable the transport controls and the appropriate buttons.
5. Register for button press events from the system transport controls, and inform the transport controls of the current playback status.

Don't forget to update the thumbnail and text accordingly, preferably using the feature to copy metadata from the file itself.

Lock Screen Tasks

Some background tasks are not available to your app unless you use the lock screen. These apps take advantage of the lock screen capabilities to provide real-time information to the user. This section explains the lock screen, tells how to register your app to use the lock screen, and details the tasks you are required to declare to have lock screen access (conversely, you cannot use these background task types unless your app uses the lock screen).

Lock Screen Capabilities

The Windows 8.1 lock screen provides "at a glance" information to users. Apps can present their own information on the lock screen. If your app has summary information that changes in real time, it might be a candidate for the lock screen. Example lock screen information includes upcoming appointments, current weather conditions, recent emails, and message alerts.

The lock screen information mirrors the app's tile and badge content. In fact, the same API for updating tiles and badges is used for the lock screen. The only difference is that your app manifest indicates that it has a presence on the lock screen, and a special lock screen badge is presented. Depending on whether you configure the app for badge or badge and tile access, tile updates and badge notifications automatically propagate to the lock screen for your app.

You can opt to display either badge or badge and tile text on the lock screen. When you choose the badge option, the badge (whether it is a glyph or number) displays on the lock screen next to a badge logo. The badge logo is a 24x24-pixel monochrome (white) .PNG. The tile option displays the text portion of a wide 310x150 logo, so you must define a wide logo for your app. Failure to provide a wide logo when you specify badge and tile text prevents the app from building. When you trigger a live tile update, choose a wide tile template that has only text; image-based tiles do not display on the lock screen.

The **LockScreenExample** app from Chapter 15 illustrates the proper way to set up an app to display on the lock screen. The first step is to configure lock screen notifications on the **Application** tab of the manifest. Figure 15.4 shows the available settings when you activate the lock screen: either **Badge** or **Badge and Tile Text**. When you select either option, you must specify at least a 24x24-pixel monochrome icon to represent your app on the lock screen.

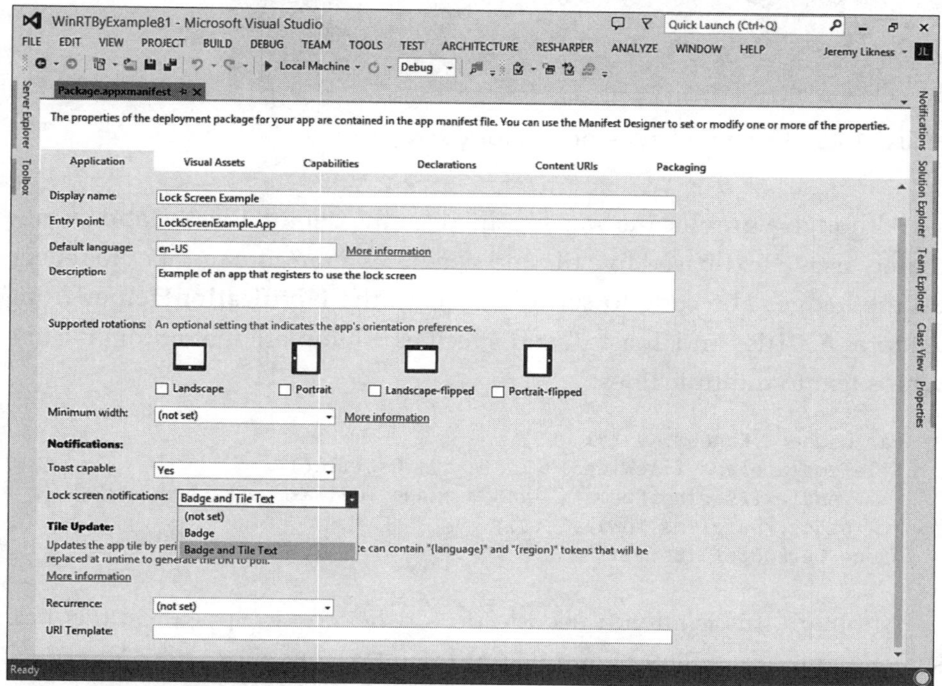

FIGURE 15.4 Lock screen options

The example app uses a simple black-and-white logo, as in Figure 15.5. The rightmost indicator is the badge logo, followed by an actual badge. If you choose a glyph badge, the glyph renders in place of the number 95. The text above the date is the text portion of the wide tile template. This is required when you choose the **Badge and Tile Text** option.

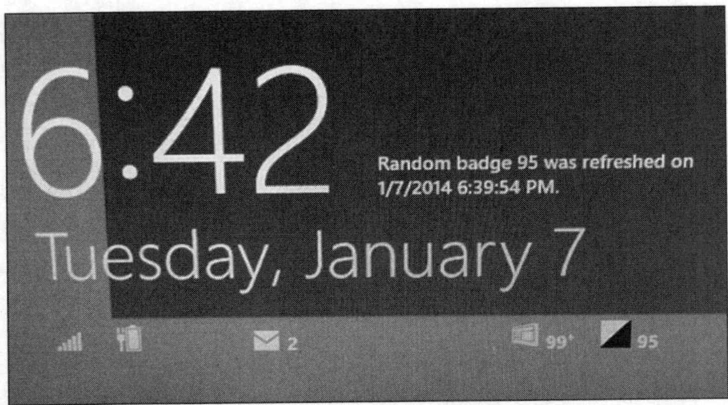

FIGURE 15.5 Example badge on the lock screen

Although a graphic tile was specified for the default tile, the app immediately uses a text-based live tile and generates a random number to reflect on the badge. The code to set this up uses the **NotificationHelper** from Chapter 6, "Tiles and Toasts," and specifies a template that automatically wraps text to multiple lines:

```
var badge = Random.Next(1, 99);
TileTemplateType.TileWide310x150Text04.GetTile()
    .AddText(string.Format("Random badge {0} was refreshed on {1}.",
    badge, DateTime.Now)).Set();
badge.GetBadge().Set();
```

Although this is all you need to do for the icon to appear on the lock screen, your app will not compile until you take one more step. You must specify a background task that is a Windows Runtime component implementing the `IBackgroundTask` interface. Lock screen apps require that you declare either a control channel, a timer, or a push notification background task. You only have to declare the tasks for the app to compile; the app will run if you never implement the task, but it won't be very functional for the user.

To declare the background task, add **Background Tasks** from the **Declarations** tab in the manifest. Figure 15.6 shows the declaration from the sample app. Note that the entry point references the fully qualified name for a class (namespace and class name) that is used to run the task.

You learn how to build the class later in this section. The **Timer** task type is checked.

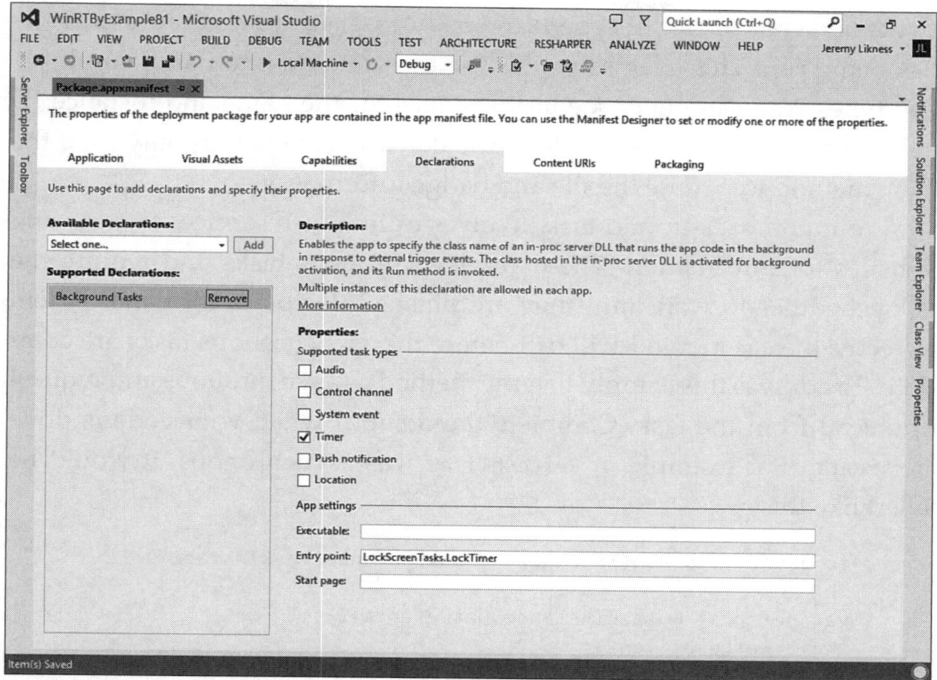

FIGURE 15.6 Declaring the background task

The Background Task

To build your background task, create a new Windows Runtime project that will be referenced from the application project. This is necessary because of the way the system activates and executes the background task. The **LockScreenExample** app references the **LockScreenTasks** project. The project should contain a class that implements the `IBackgroundTask` interface. This is the class you have specified as the entry point for the background task in the application manifest: the `LockTimer` class.

The class exposes the `RefreshTiles` static method that generates a random badge and sets the badge and tile text. This is the same code you saw in the previous "Lock Screen Capabilities" section. The main app is reusing this method to configure the initial badge and tile status (you can verify that the `OnLaunched` method in the `App.xaml.cs` file for **LockScreenExample** calls `LockTimer.RefreshTiles`).

The `Run` method is required to implement the `IBackgroundTask` interface. It takes one parameter of type `IBackgroundTaskInstance` that represents the task being run. This enables you to use the same class to handle multiple task types. You can query the task instance for the name and instance ID and to fire various events. This particular implementation only calls the static method to update the tile and badge information.

A common background task involves calling web services or querying websites for information. These are asynchronous tasks and require the task scheduler to wait until they are finished. If you don't handle them correctly, the `Run` method will exit before the asynchronous tasks are complete. To address this, simply flag the method as asynchronous and request a deferral from the task. Complete the deferral when your code is done processing. For example, if `RefreshTiles` was asynchronous, it would be called like this:

```
public async void Run(IBackgroundTaskInstance taskInstance)
{
    var deferral = taskInstance.GetDeferral();
    await RefreshTiles();
    deferral.Complete();
}
```

The capability to run background tasks is useful especially when you don't have a server set up to send push notifications. Your app might need to poll other websites periodically or even create a persistent connection that controls the apps. Now that you have the task written, you must set up the trigger that makes the task run and registers it. The **LockScreenExample** project sets up the background task in `MainPage.xaml.cs`. The first step is to request access to the lock screen.

```
await BackgroundExecutionManager.RequestAccessAsync();
```

Your app may request access only once. The example app requests this each time the app is run because, according to the Windows documentation, subsequent calls are ignored. The request prompts the user as in Figure 15.7.

Registered.
Last Run Unknown.
Let Lock Screen Example run in the background?
This app can also show quick status and notifications on the lock screen. (You can change this later in PC settings.)
Allow
Don't allow

FIGURE 15.7 Requesting access to the lock screen

The call returns one of several values represented by the `BackgroundAccessStatus` enumeration. `Denied` means the user chose not to opt in, and your app will not appear on the lock screen. This does not prevent you from running background tasks; it only limits access to the lock screen. If the user accepts, you receive either `AllowedWithAlwaysOnRealTimeConnectivity` or the alternative "accepted" value of `AllowedMayUseActiveRealTimeConnectivity`. You learn more about real-time connectivity in the "Control Channel" section later in this chapter.

Although the user can opt in for your app to appear on the app screen, an additional step is required to show the detailed status if you are using tile text. The only way your app will automatically show detailed status is if it is the first app to register for the lock screen. With built-in apps such as **Mail** and **Calendar**, this is rarely the case. To see your detailed status (not just the badge) on the lock screen, the user must activate the Charms bar and choose **Settings**, followed by **Change PC Settings**, **PC and Devices**, and then **Lock Screen**. The user then must click the icon below **Choose an App to Display Detailed Status** and select your app from the list. See Figure 15.8.

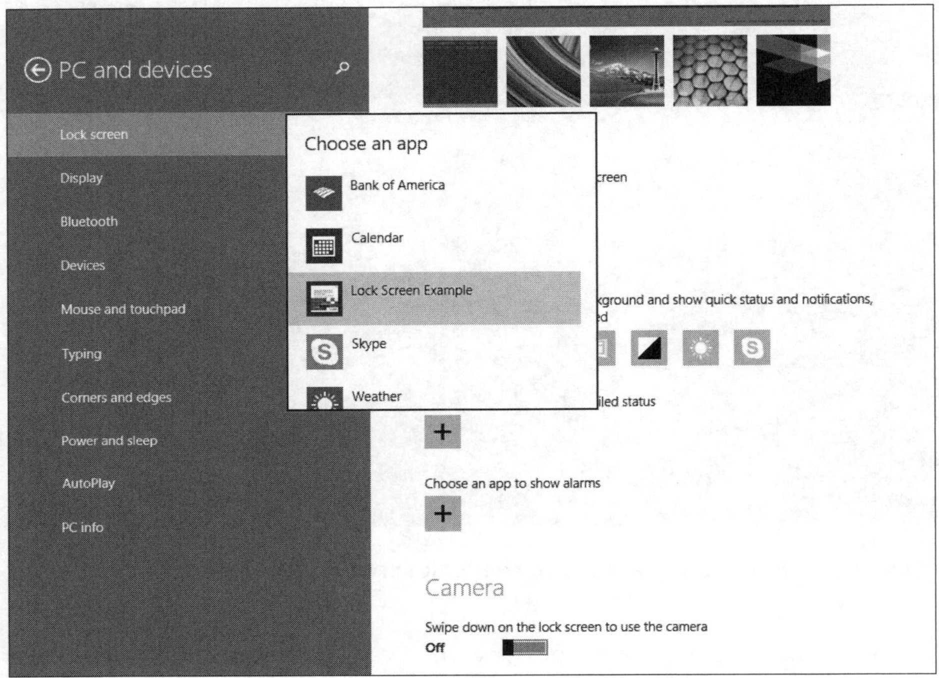

FIGURE 15.8 Configuring detailed status on the lock screen

Assuming you are allowed access, the app then determines whether the background task needs to be configured. It should be configured only once; multiple instances negatively impact performance. This is done by requesting a list of background tasks and checking the task names.

Listing Background Tasks

Inspect the `AllTasks` collection on the static `BackgroundTaskRegistration` class to query what tasks have been configured for the current app. The reference app declares a task name and searches for the existence of that name in the task list in the `OnNavigatedTo` method of the main page.

```
private const string TimerTask = "Lock Timer Task";
if (BackgroundTaskRegistration.AllTasks.Any(t => t.Value.Name ==
    TimerTask))
```

If the task already exists, the method notifies the user with a status update and then registers a handler for the `Completed` event on the task. This event fires each time the background task has finished running (its `Run` method returns or the given deferral is completed), enabling your app to update the UI. The event fires from a non-UI thread, so the handler must be marshalled using the `Dispatcher`, as shown in the `TaskRunCompleted` handler.

```
await Dispatcher.RunAsync(
    CoreDispatcherPriority.Normal,
    () => LastRun.Text = string.Format("Last Run: {0}",
        DateTime.Now));
```

If the task doesn't exist, the app creates it. You create a background task using the `BackgroundTaskBuilder`. Create an instance of this class, and set the `Name` property as well as the entry point for the task. The entry point is the fully qualified name of the class that implements the `IBackgroundTask` interface.

```
var builder = new BackgroundTaskBuilder
    {
        Name = TimerTask,
        TaskEntryPoint = "LockScreenTasks.LockTimer"
    };
```

The builder exposes a `Register` method to register the task that returns the instance of the task itself.

```
var registration = builder.Register();
registration.Completed += this.TaskRunCompleted;
```

You can use this to subscribe to the `Completed` event when the task is first registered.

Timer

The task by itself cannot fire without a trigger. You can use numerous types of triggers. This example uses a `TimeTrigger`. The `TimeTrigger` fires at a specified interval, to enable your app to perform some work. In the example app, that work is simply generating a random number to update the badge and the tile. Create an instance of the trigger, and pass the appropriate parameters to its constructor:

```
var trigger = new TimeTrigger(15, false);
```

The first value is the time, in minutes, to wait before running the task. This value cannot be less than 15 minutes. If you attempt to specify a shorter interval, an exception is thrown when you register the related task. The second value determines whether the trigger is intended to be fired only once or whether it is a recurring trigger. A value of `true` indicates that it should be called only once; a value of `false` indicates that it is recurring and should be called repeatedly.

After you've created the trigger, you must update the background task with the trigger. You do this by calling the `SetTrigger` method. You may have only one trigger per background task.

```
builder.SetTrigger(trigger);
```

Triggers ordinarily fire immediately, so a time-based trigger runs every 15 minutes. Some tasks might not make sense to run even when the trigger is ready. For example, a task that fetches data from the Internet doesn't need to run when the Internet is not available. A task that fetches large volumes of data should run only when the user is on a free network. You can control when your tasks run using a set of system-provided conditions.

Conditions

A task can have multiple conditions. You specify a condition by creating an instance of the `SystemCondition` class and passing a `SystemConditionType` to the constructor. You then add the condition to the task using the `AddCondition` method.

```
var condition = new
    SystemCondition(SystemConditionType.InternetAvailable);
builder.AddCondition(condition);
```

The task in the example app runs only if the Internet connection is available. Although it obviously doesn't require an Internet connection, this illustrates how the conditions work. Table 15.2 lists the available conditions your app can specify.

TABLE 15.2 Background Task Conditions

SystemConditionType Value	Description
BackgroundWorkCostNotHigh	Run the task only when the cost for performing the background work is low.
FreeNetworkAvailable	Run the task only when a nonmetered network connection exists.
InternetAvailable	Run the task only when an Internet connection is available.
InternetNotAvailable	Run the task only when the Internet is not available.
Invalid	—
SessionConnected	Run the task only when a user session is connected (that is, the user is logged in).
SessionDisconnected	Run the task only when the user is logged out.
UserNotPresent	Run the task only when the user is away (the device is locked and/or idle).
UserPresent	Run the task only when the user is present (the device is not locked or idle).

You can test the `InternetAvailable` condition the sample app uses by putting your device in airplane mode and waiting. You should notice that the tiles and lock screen no longer update for the app. When you turn off airplane mode, if you've waited longer than 15 minutes, you should see the tiles update immediately. This is because of the way triggers work.

A trigger is latched and then fired. The latch happens after the specified interval. If the trigger is a timer set to 15 minutes, it will latch after 15 minutes. A latched trigger is ready to run your background task, and if no conditions are set, it executes the task immediately. However, when conditions exist, the latched trigger waits for the conditions to be met before it calls your task. In the case of the example app, if the Internet is not available, it latches and then waits for the condition to become true. When the Internet is available, the latched trigger fires and runs the background task, and then schedules the next recurrence.

Debugging Background Tasks

As with any other code you write, you must debug your background tasks. At first, a few problems might be associated with this. The tasks run in the background, so how can you find and attach to the correct process? Furthermore, some tasks might be configured based on a timer or might be conditioned to fire only once every few hours. You certainly don't want to have to wait for a task to run before you can troubleshoot it.

Fortunately, debugging background tasks is incredibly easy and is supported right inside Visual Studio. Simply launch the app from Visual Studio in debug mode. When your tasks are successfully registered and you are in the debugger, a new option appears in the debug menu. A list of task names that you've registered should appear underneath the normal debugging operations, as in Figure 15.9.

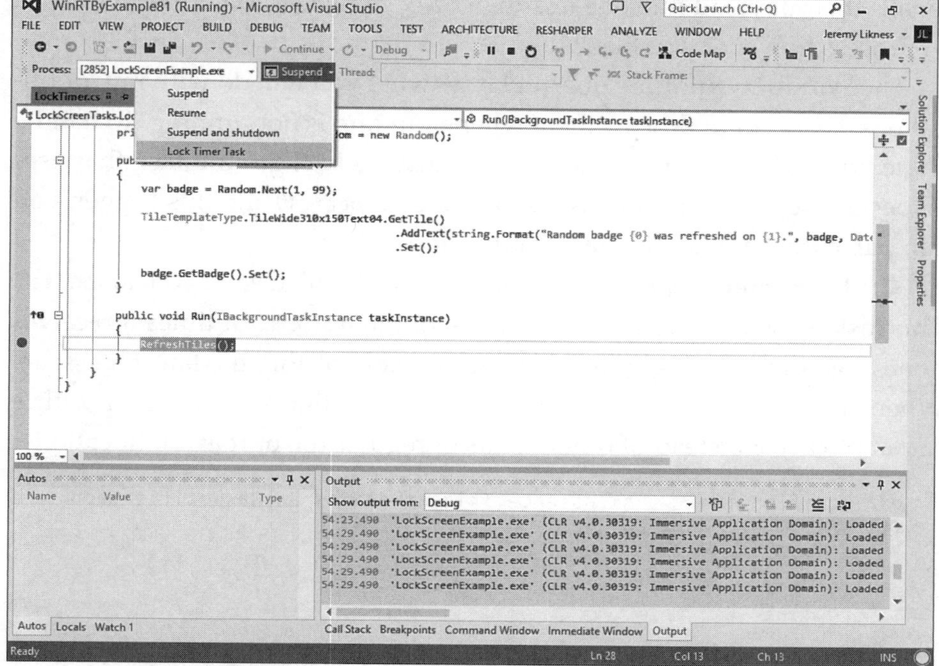

FIGURE 15.9 Debugging background tasks

All you need to do is set the breakpoint in your code and select the task you want to fire. Regardless of the triggers or conditions, the task runs immediately. This gives you the opportunity to troubleshoot "on demand," no matter how infrequently the task runs.

Raw Push Notifications

You learned about push notifications in Chapter 6. Several types of push notifications exist. The Windows Runtime automatically handles the badge, tile, and toast types. Even if your app is not running in the foreground, Windows updates your tile or sets the badge for the app when it receives one of these notification types.

A fourth type of notification is a raw notification. You must format the badge, tile, and toast forms as XML. Raw notifications can be any string format—XML, JSON, or even plain text. They are designed for sending small (their payload must be less than 5KB) messages to your app for you to process however you like.

The Windows Runtime doesn't know what you will do with raw notifications, so it cannot process them when your app is not running. To handle these types of notifications, you must register a background task that uses a special trigger called the `PushNotificationTrigger`. Using this trigger, you can parse the payload of a raw notification offline.

The **LockScreenTasks** project contains a task called `RawNotificationTask`. This task exposes one key to keep track of the number of times it receives a message in the background and another key to store the latest message. When the task is run, it first checks to ensure that it is invoked with a `RawNotification` instead of other forms of regular tile or toast notifications.

```
var notification = taskInstance.TriggerDetails as RawNotification;
if (notification == null)
{
    return;
}
```

It then grabs the content from the message and stores it. It sends a toast to the user (this enables the user to tap on the toast to launch the app and view the latest message). It increments the message count and sets the badge to the count. This way, the lock screen always shows how many message the app has received since it was last run.

```
var content = string.Format("{0}: {1}", DateTime.Now,
   notification.Content);
ApplicationData.Current.LocalSettings.Values[MessageKey] = content;
ToastTemplateType.ToastText01.GetToast().AddText(content).Send();
var count = MessageCount + 1;
(count > 99 ? 99 : count).GetBadge().Set();
MessageCount = count;
```

The **RawNotificationExample** project is set up to expose a channel for push notifications and to receive and process the raw notifications. The main work is performed in the `OnNavigatedTo` method of `MainPage.xaml.cs`. First, the badge is cleared and the message count is reset because the app is running (those counts represent messages sent while the app is not running).

```
BadgeHelper.ClearBadge().Set();
ApplicationData.Current.LocalSettings.Values[
    RawNotificationTask.GetCountKey()] = 0;
```

Next, it configures the channel and ensures that a valid channel was set up (this is handled in the `App` class). It latches to the channel's `PushNotificationReceived` event and uses this event to handle messages sent while the app is running. In the `ChannelPushNotificationReceived` method, it dispatches the message to the UI and indicates that the message was received locally. When a notification is received, it is passed to an active app first before the background task picks it up. Because the message is handled in the app, it sets the `Cancel` flag on the event arguments to `true` to prevent the background task from being notified. Otherwise, the same notification will be sent to the `RawNotificationTask` instance.

The last message sent from the background is loaded from storage and displayed in the "remote" section of the UI. The app then calls the `ConfigureBackgroundTask` method to set up the task, as shown previously in the earlier section "The Background Task" of this chapter. Instead of using a `TimeTrigger`, a `PushNotificationTrigger` is used.

```
builder.SetTrigger(new PushNotificationTrigger());
```

The solution folder also contains a WPF project named **RawNotificationSender** for testing the functionality of the app. To run the example, you must associate the app to the Windows Store as Chapter 6 described. Retrieve the app secret and identifier, as Chapter 7, "Connecting to the Cloud," explained. Paste these into the `Secret` and `Sid` constants defined at the beginning of `MainWindow.xaml.cs`. First, run the **RawNotificationExample** app and copy the channel from the Channel URI (see the top of Figure 15.10).

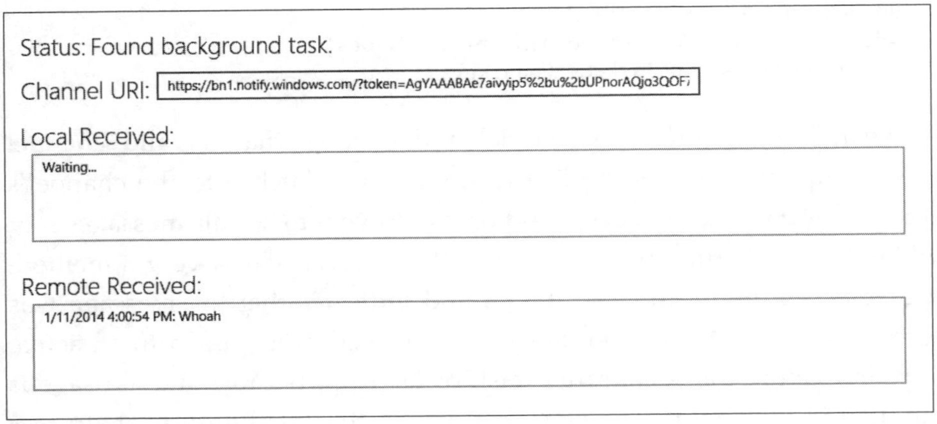

FIGURE 15.10 The example app for raw notifications

You can keep the app running or close it, depending on your preference. After updating the secret and store identifier in the **RawNotificationSender** app, compile and run it. Paste the channel URI in the first field, enter some text into the second field, and click the large **Send** button (see Figure 15.11).

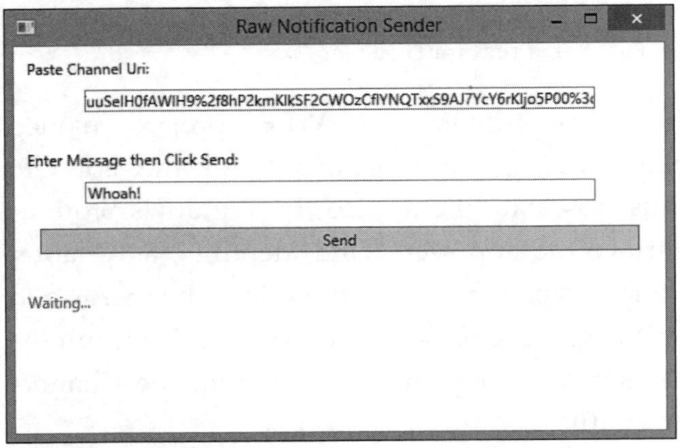

FIGURE 15.11 Notification sender app

If the example app is running, it updates with the message. If it is not running, you should see a toast notification appear. If you ignore the notification, the badge on the app and lock screen updates with a message count. Tap the notification or run the app to clear the badge and view the most recent message you sent. The WPF app uses a PCL library named **PushNotificationHelper**. You can reference this library from your own .NET or Windows Store apps to facilitate sending notifications of any type.

Control Channel

Two possible "success" responses prompt a request to appear on the lock screen. Both are related to real-time connectivity (RTC) and notify the app whether connectivity is allowed in low-power mode. Although the triggers already covered should suffice for most apps, some applications require a more persistent channel for communication. An example is an email app that must load message headers and even retrieve full message bodies for the user when the device is in standby mode so they are readily available when powered on. Fortunately, Windows 8.1 enables this capability with the `ControlChannelTrigger`.

The `ControlChannelTrigger` enables real-time network status and triggers for communication using a `MessageWebSocket`, a `StreamWebSocket`, or a `StreamSocket` (Chapter 10 covered this). The network trigger is designed to minimize network and system resource usage. The device can drop into low-power mode for periods of time while maintaining the network connection. The app can supply an interval for the system to wake up the app and can also set a trigger to wake the app when network data is received.

The steps involved include setting up the socket for communication, creating the trigger, and then setting up another task to keep the connection alive. Yet another task can be configured to run when network data is received over the connection. The main trigger is constructed with a unique channel identifier you provide, an interval to keep the network alive (in minutes), and a request type (software or hardware). The hardware request is required when you want to have the channel operate even when the device is on connected standby.

```
var channel = new ControlChannelTrigger("Hope", 30,
    ControlChannelTriggerResourceType.RequestHardwareSlot);
```

The request fails if your app has not been successfully added to the lock screen. The channel trigger itself exposes a trigger you can use to set up the task to keep the connection alive. The Windows Runtime provides a built-in task to keep WebSockets alive. The task is named `WebSocketKeepAlive` and exists in the `Windows.Networking.Sockets` namespace. The following code illustrates using the channel's trigger to run this task.

```
var builder = new BackgroundTaskBuilder();
builder.Name = "Keep Hope Alive";
builder.TaskEntryPoint =
    "Windows.Networking.Sockets.WebSocketKeepAlive";
builder.SetTrigger(channel.KeepAliveTrigger);
builder.Register();
```

The next step is to associate the socket you've created with the channel. This is done through the `UsingTransport` method:

```
var socket = new StreamWebSocket();
channel.UsingTransport(socket);
await socket.ConnectAsync(uri);
```

Finally, you must wait for push functionality to be enabled to ensure you obtained a slot from the system.

```
var status = channel.WaitForPushEnabled();
```

The status enumeration indicates whether the slot was allocated or whether an error occurred. Using this type of trigger requires you to keep track of the trigger itself because it is disposable and tied to the underlying connections. The way you handle messages is highly dependent on the architecture of your app. The MSDN Library provides examples of using a `StreamSocket`[1] and `WebSocket`,[2] as well as using the existing persistent socket to attach an HTTP client.[3]

---

[1]ControlChannelTrigger StreamSocket sample http://bit.ly/1gxHYw9

[2]ControlChannelTrigger StreamWebSocket sample http://bit.ly/1eNBKqz

[3]ControlChannelTrigger HTTP client sample http://bit.ly/1dfU2Cj

System Events

The SystemTrigger enables you to run your background task when a certain event occurs. This differs from a trigger that latches and waits for a condition because the SystemTrigger latches immediately when the event specified in the SystemTriggerType is generated by the system. Certain events require the app to be added to the lock screen. These apps must request lock screen access to use the trigger type. Other events can be used by apps without being placed on the lock screen. Table 15.3 lists the events and tells whether they require lock screen access.

TABLE 15.3 Common HTTP Content Type Header Values

SystemTriggerType	Description	Lock Screen
BackgroundWorkCostChange	The cost to perform background work has changed.	Required
ControlChannelReset	The control channel being used has been reset.	Required
InternetAvailable	The Internet has become available.	Not required
Invalid	—	—
LockScreenApplicationAdded	The user has added the app to the lock screen.	Required
LockScreenApplicationRemoved	The user has removed the app from the lock screen.	Required
NetworkStateChange	A network change has occurred (for example, moving to a metered connection or losing connectivity).	Not required
ServicingComplete	The system is finished updating the app (used when the app is upgraded or updated).	Not required

SystemTriggerType	Description	Lock Screen
SessionConnected	The user has logged in.	Required
SmsReceived	The system has received an SMS message.	Not required
TimeZoneChange	The device has detected a change in the local time zone that results in updating the system time.	Not required
UserAway	The user has gone away from the device.	Required
UserPresent	The user has returned to the device.	Required

Note that the events are fired based on state changes, not time intervals. For example, the `InternetAvailable` event is triggered when the system first can reach the Internet. This event does not trigger again unless the Internet is no longer available. After the Internet connection is lost, the trigger fires again when connectivity is restored.

Summary

In this chapter, you learned how to use the thread pool to manage short parallel works that can run in the background without blocking your app's UI. You explored the process for uploading files in the background and looked at an example app that can play audio in the background and give the user control over playback using a system-supplied control. You then learned about lock screen capabilities and how to display both text and badges on the lock screen, and you saw what background tasks require a lock screen presence. Finally, you learned about system events that you can use to trigger various tasks that run in the background to service your app.

In the next chapter, you explore Windows 8.1's multimedia capabilities.

16

Multimedia

THE WINDOWS RUNTIME INCLUDES A RANGE OF OPTIONS FOR working with audio and video multimedia content within your Windows Store apps. Several available components provide out-of-the-box experiences for both playback and capture, and they require only a few lines of code to get running. Additionally, the Windows Runtime provides mechanisms to offer highly customized experiences and deep integration into your apps, depending on your specific needs.

You have already seen some examples of the Windows Runtime multimedia functionality in action throughout other chapters in this book. Chapter 7, "Connecting to the Cloud," showed how to play back multimedia files stored in OneDrive. Chapter 11, "Windows Charms Integration," showed how you can either use a webcam to capture video or select a preexisting file to play as a Play To source file, or create a Play To target page that is capable of playing back video shared over the network. Finally, Chapter 15, "Background Tasks," showed how you can play audio in the background, even when the app isn't displayed on the screen.

In this chapter, you see how to use the `MediaElement` control to play multimedia content in your Windows Store apps with both built-in transport controls and custom controls that you provide yourself. You also learn how various settings control the appearance and behavior of the `MediaElement` control, how to work with audio playback settings, and how to place metadata marker elements that trigger events when the app encounters them during playback.

This chapter also presents information about how to capture your own media assets using the black-box functionality of the `CameraCaptureUI` class. You see how you can exercise finer control over the capture process by leveraging the more flexible and, hence, more complex `MediaCapture` class.

The chapter concludes with a discussion of the text-to-speech functionality of the Windows Runtime. You see how you can use either plain text or special text markup to create a stream of audio that can be played back with the `MediaElement` control.

Playing Multimedia Content

Similar to their WPF and Silverlight predecessors, Windows Store apps use the `MediaElement` control to play back audio and video content. The `MediaElement` control can play a variety of popular audio and video formats[1] and provides several options and extensibility points for presenting content within an application. As mentioned in the chapter introduction, you have already seen the `MediaElement` object used to play back different media types. In this section, you see more on how you can use `MediaElement` instances to provide audio and video playback in your app.

The Example App

The **MultimediaExample** project included in the source code for this chapter provides examples for the various multimedia interactions that this chapter discusses. The app that this code creates enables users to select or create video files that can play one after the other in sequence, to explore the multimedia playback functionality the Windows Runtime exposes.

The app illustrates how you can use the `MediaElement` control for video playback. The behaviors shown include these:

- Working with the option to enable or disable the display of the built-in media transport controls

[1] Supported audio and video formats for Windows Store Apps, http://msdn.microsoft.com/en-us/library/windows/apps/hh986969.aspx

- Toggling full-screen playback, automatic playback, and playback that loops over a single file (meaning that when it reaches the end of the file, it starts again at the beginning)
- Using custom controls and `MediaElement` methods to control playback
- Switching between slow motion and regular playback rate
- Skipping to a specific position in the file
- Setting audio volume and balance adjustments
- Displaying information about the current media displayed

The app also provides access to the media marker functionality exposed by the `MediaElement` control. Users can define markers within a selected video file. When a marker is hit during normal video playback, the app stops playing video and uses the text-to-speech functionality the Windows Runtime provides to "speak" a message to them. The later section "Text-to-Speech Support" discusses this text-to-speech functionality more.

Getting Started

To play multimedia content with the `MediaElement` control, you first need an instance of the control. This is typically provided by including a `MediaElement` in the XAML for a page or user control. Note that you can create the `MediaElement` instance in code and not include it in the page's visual tree if you are interested only in audio playback. You'll see this technique in use in the upcoming "Text-to-Speech Support" section.

After you have defined an instance of a `MediaElement` control, you provide content to be played back to the control by setting the current media source value. You can set the current source in three ways. The first one involves setting the `Source` property of the `MediaElement` to a `Uri` that references the content to be played. The following code shows how you set the current source to a media file titled `Sample.wmv` contained within your project's `Assets` folder, using the **ms-appx** syntax introduced in Chapter 4, "Data and Content."

```
_mediaElement.Source = new Uri("ms-appx:///Assets/Sample.wmv");
```

Another option is to use the `SetSource` method, which takes an `IRandomAccessStream` reference and text that indicates the MIME content type of the media to play. This approach typically is used to play back a file from the local file system, perhaps using an `IStorageFile` reference that you can obtain using the `FileOpenPicker`. In such a case, you can easily obtain the MIME type information from the `IStorageFile` `ContentType` property. The example app uses this technique to play back selected files, as the following code shows:

```
var stream = await fileToPlay.OpenReadAsync();
_mediaElement.SetSource(stream, fileToPlay.ContentType);
```

The final possibility for setting the `MediaElement` source that you can use is the `SetMediaStreamSource` method. This is a more advanced scenario in which you provide an instance of a `MediaStreamSource` object that is responsible for handling lower-level requests for the media content to be played. In this case, your app code is responsible for fulfilling requests for `MediaSample` instance buffers that include samples from your audio or video, depending on each particular request. You can thus provide custom audio and video sources, including custom playlist implementations with seamless transitions from one file to the next, since you're just providing a continuous set of samples.

Regardless of the technique, setting the source prompts the `MediaElement` control to raise either a `MediaOpened` event if the source is successfully accessed or a `MediaFailed` event if a problem occurs.

Controlling Playback

With the playback source set, you can turn your attention to working with the actual media playback. If the transport controls are enabled, basic playback functionality is provided out of the box (the upcoming "Appearance" section discusses controlling the appearance of the transport controls). However, if you want to create custom controls or exercise more fine-grained control over the playback experience, the `MediaElement` control provides properties and methods that enable this.

The `MediaElement` control provides three fundamental playback methods: `Play`, `Pause`, and `Stop`. `Play` initiates or resumes playback. `Pause` suspends playback at the current point. `Stop` is similar to `Pause`, except that it also resets the playback point to the beginning of the current source. Not all media sources support pausing, so it is often appropriate to see if you can enable pause functionality by first using the `MediaElement` `CanPause` property:

```
if (_mediaElement.CanPause) _mediaElement.Pause();
```

Seeking to a particular place in the media is accomplished with the `Position` property, which accepts a `TimeSpan` value to specify the new location from which playback should proceed. Listing 16.1 shows the `SetPosition` method that the example app uses to set this property in response to either a `Seek` or an `Offset` request.

LISTING 16.1 Setting the Current Playback Position

```
private void SetPosition(TimeSpan position)
{
    // Make sure that seek is an option
    if (!_mediaElement.CanSeek) return;

    // Make sure the new position is "in bounds"
    if (position < TimeSpan.FromMilliseconds(0))
    {
        position = TimeSpan.FromMilliseconds(0);
    }

    // Note that NaturalDuration returns "Automatic" until after
    // the MediaOpened event has been raised
    var duration = _mediaElement.NaturalDuration;
    if (duration.HasTimeSpan)
    {
        if (position > duration.TimeSpan) position = duration.TimeSpan;
    }

    _mediaElement.Position = position;
}
```

In the case of an offset, the current `Position` value is obtained and the offset time is added to it to get the corresponding seek position to pass to the `SetPosition` method. As with `Pause`, not all media sources can accommodate seek requests, and a `CanSeek` property is available to check with the `MediaElement` control to determine whether the current media source supports seeking. Next, checks are performed to ensure that the position that has been specified is within the bounds of the current media being played. A check is made to ensure that the new position being requested is later than the source start, indicated by a `TimeSpan` value of zero. Then the `NaturalDuration` property determines whether the selected position is less than the overall source duration. In either case, the desired position is adjusted to keep the request in bounds. Finally, the new position is set using the `Position` property. If the seek operation will take a while (for example, if the media is being streamed over a network connection and some latency is involved in requesting the media at the new position), the `SeekCompleted` event can trigger an action when the `MediaElement` control is ready to resume playback.

The `MediaElement` control also supports setting different playback rates. A playback rate value of 1.0 indicates regular, forward playback; values less than zero indicate reverse playback. The two properties you can use when adjusting the playback rate are `PlaybackRate` and `DefaultPlaybackRate`. When the `Play` method is called or the Play button on the transport controls is clicked, the `PlaybackRate` will be set to the `DefaultPlaybackRate` value. From there, you can change the `PlaybackRate` value, but `DefaultPlaybackRate` overwrites it if the media pauses or stops and must be restarted. The example app toggles "slow-motion" playback by setting the `DefaultPlaybackRate` to either `0.5` or `1.0`, as the following code shows:

```
var playbackRate = isSlowMotion ? 0.5 : 1.0;
_mediaElement.DefaultPlaybackRate = playbackRate;
```

The `MediaElement` control raises a `RateChanged` event when one of these properties' values is changed, regardless of which one is actually set.

The `MediaElement` control updates its `CurrentState` property in response to the various actions of setting sources, or playing, pausing, and stopping and the related processing actions that the control needs to take in response to them. When the `MediaElement` control is initially rendered and a valid source has not been set, the `CurrentState` property returns a value of `MediaElementState.Closed`. When a source is set, this state changes to `MediaElementState.Opening`. Both before and during playback, if the `MediaElement` needs to retrieve media for playback, its `CurrentState` property reports a value of `MediaElementState.Buffering`; during that time, any displayed video frames appear as if the media was paused. While media buffering is occurring, you can use the BufferingProgress property to determine how close the MediaElement control is to completing the operation, with values between 0 and 1.0 representing the degree of completion. Finally, the CurrentState property returns values of MediaElementState.Playing, MediaElementState.Paused, or MediaElementState.Stopped in response to the corresponding playback methods or transport controls, or if the media enters a paused state as a result of reaching the end of its current source. When the CurrentState property changes, the MediaElement control raises a CurrentStateChanged event.

When the playback in a MediaElement control reaches the end of the current source, the MediaElement control raises a MediaEnded event. In the example project, the event handler for the MediaEnded event determines whether another source should be played following the current source; if so, that source is made current for playback to start on the new source.

Two more playback properties are relevant here. When set to true, the AutoPlay property instructs the MediaElement control to begin playback as soon as a source is set instead of waiting for the Play method to be called or the Play button on the transport controls to be clicked. Finally, the IsLooping property can instruct the MediaElement control to restart playback of the current source when it reaches the source's end.

Appearance

Several properties alter the basic appearance of the MediaElement control. First, the PosterSource property provides a background image that displays when the MediaElement source content is not displayed. This occurs before setting a valid source, during the time a source is being loaded, and when the current display is being sent to a **PlayTo** target. To use the PosterSource property to display an image, you simply set the property to an ImageSource value, much as when working with an Image control. The example project sets this value in the MultimediaPage XAML content's MediaElement declaration to use the **SplashScreen.png** image from the project's **Assets** folder, as follows:

```
PosterSource="Assets/SplashScreen.png"
```

Another property that you can set to control the appearance of the `MediaElement` control is the `AreTransportControlsEnabled` property. When set to `true`, the `MediaElement` control is shown with a default set of controls for the current playback. The transport controls provide UI elements that can play or pause, skip forward or back by 30 seconds, show a seek bar that displays the current playback position or seek to a specific location, mute audio or display a volume slider, toggle video zooming, and toggle full-screen display. Although the controls that the `MediaElement` displays when the `AreTransportControlsEnabled` property are predefined, you can disable these controls and provide your own custom controls, or you can provide your own controls in addition to these out-of-the-box controls. The **Playback Behavior** section of the example app illustrates this kind of customization.

The final property related to the appearance of the `MediaElement` that the example application shows is the `IsFullWindow` property. This property toggles the same full-screen playback that you can set with the transport controls. When set, the `MediaElement` display area is resized to take up the entire app display area. If the app is running and takes up your entire monitor, setting this property accomplishes full-screen playback. Note that instead of simply scaling pixels to fit in the entire playback region, the `MediaElement` control optimizes the video display when in full screen mode to provide a more efficient playback experience for the media on the current hardware.

Audio Settings

In addition to the properties discussed so far that apply to playback of both audio and video media with the `MediaElement` control, the Windows Runtime provides some properties you can manipulate specifically for playing audio content, regardless of whether this content is a standalone audio file or a video file that contains one or more audio tracks.

The most common audio-specific property is the `Volume` property. You can set this property to a value between `0` and `1` to adjust the loudness of the audio playback. In addition to the `Volume` property, the `MediaElement` control provides an `IsMuted` property to override the `Volume` property and set its effective value to zero. Muting does not actually modify the `Volume` property, so the property retains its value if your app is muted and then later unmuted.

The final audio-related property that you can set is the `Balance` property, which adjusts the volume ratio across your system's left and right stereo speakers, assuming that you have an available stereo output. The `Balance` property can accept values between `-1` and `1`, with 0 indicating an equal amount of sound directed to the left- and right-side speakers.

Note that these values are relative to the system volume settings that you can adjust either through your device's dedicated volume hardware buttons or via the volume entry in the Settings charm (or by using several other tools Windows provides). You can think of the `MediaElement Volume` setting as a percentage of the current system volume value. For example, if you set system audio to 50 percent, then setting the `MediaElement Volume` to a value of .5 would result in the app playing at half the loudness of the system's 50 percent volume.

Media Information

You also can use the properties and methods that the `MediaElement` control provides to obtain information about the current media source. You have already seen how the `NaturalDuration` value obtains the length of a given media source. For video sources, the `AspectRatioWidth` and `AspectRatioHeight` describe the relationship between the width and height of the video frame. Additionally, the `NaturalVideoWidth` and `NaturalVideoHeight` properties provide the native pixel height and width of the current video frame, respectively. Audio information is also provided; it includes the `IsAudioOnly` property, which indicates that the current source contains only audio information. The **Information** section in the example app shows several of these properties.

Markers

The final concept to discuss related to the `MediaElement` control is media markers. Media markers allow arbitrary metadata to be associated with a particular point in time within a media source. Media markers are exposed as `TimelineMarker` objects that you can access and manage through the `MediaElement Markers` collection.

A media marker contains a `Time` property, which represents the marker's position within the current source. It also contains two text properties, `Text` and `Type`, which you can set to contain some arbitrary text.

When the `MediaElement` is playing back media at the regular playback rate and it reaches a time that is indicated in one of the items in its `Markers` collection, the `MediaElement` raises a `MarkerReached` event. You then can call some application-specific logic related to that particular marker value:

```
PlaybackWindow.MarkerReached += HandlePlaybackWindowMarkerReached;
```

When the example app encounters a marker, the code in its event handler pauses playback, uses the marker's `Time` property to locate a corresponding entry in the current playback file's `FileMarkers` collection, and then uses the text-to-speech support to "speak" some associated text (see Listing 16.2). The later section "Text-to-Speech Support" explains this text-to-speech functionality in more detail.

LISTING 16.2 Responding to Reaching a Media Marker

```
private void HandlePlaybackWindowMarkerReached
    (Object sender, TimelineMarkerRoutedEventArgs e)
{
    PlaybackWindow.Pause();

    var markerItemTime = e.Marker.Time;
    var matchingFileMarker = ViewModel.CurrentPlaybackFile.FileMarkers.
        FirstOrDefault(x => x.Time == markerItemTime);
    if (matchingFileMarker == null) return;

    ViewModel.CurrentFileMarker = matchingFileMarker;
    TextToSpeechHelper.SpeakContentAsync(
        matchingFileMarker.TextToSpeechContent,
        matchingFileMarker.IsSsml,
        matchingFileMarker.SelectedVoiceId);
}
```

Acquiring Audio and Video

You've just seen how you can go about playing back media content. Now is a good time to look into how you can capture some of your own content. The Windows Runtime APIs supply two basic tools to capture media. The `CameraCaptureUI` class provides a predefined full-screen user interface that can capture pictures or videos from an attached webcam with minimal custom application code. If you need more control over the capture process, you can use the `MediaCapture` class instead, with the caveat that the additional control comes at the expense of additional implementation effort.

The Example App

The same **MultimediaExample** project that you saw in the previous section provides examples of using the `CameraCaptureUI` and `MediaCapture` classes to capture video files. Instead of selecting **Choose Files** from the app bar, instead select the **CameraCaptureUI** or **MediaCapture** buttons to use these different capture APIs.

Declaring Application Capabilities

Because cameras and microphones provide access to private or otherwise sensitive user information, extra steps are taken to ensure that a user is aware of and in control over which applications can access these devices and when the apps can do so. Before you can try to access the video feed from an attached webcam or the audio from an attached microphone, you need to declare your app's intent to interact with these devices in the app manifest, as in Figure 16.1.

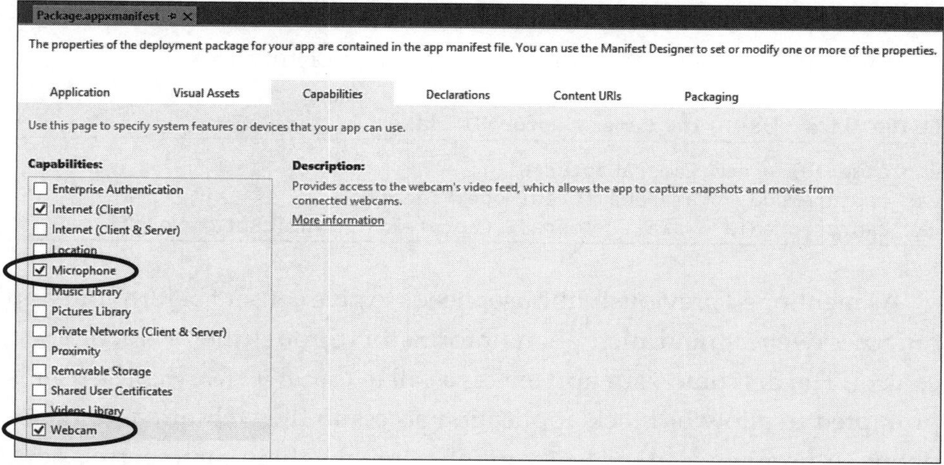

FIGURE 16.1 App manifest capability declarations for webcam and microphone access

When these entries are added, the app's listing in the application store indicates that the app intends to use both your webcam and your microphone. The Permissions panel in your application settings also includes both webcam and microphone entries that the user can use to enable or disable the application's access to these devices. The first time your app attempts to access these devices, Windows prompts the user, requesting permission for the app to access the webcam and microphone. Your app must be built to handle the case in which the user chooses not to allow access to these devices, or it will be rejected by the app store certification process.

If you plan to publish your app to the Windows Store, be sure to consider your intended age rating when you are thinking about including webcam and/or microphone functionality. Apps with age ratings of less than 12+ are not permitted to include access to webcams, microphones, or other sources of personal information. Chapter 19, "Packaging and Deploying" discusses application age ratings and other considerations related to submitting your app to the Windows Store.

Using `CameraCaptureUI`

Using the `CameraCaptureUI` class to capture videos or photos is fairly straightforward. You create an instance of the `CameraCaptureUI` class and then call `CatptureFileAsync`, passing in a value of the `CameraCaptureUIMode` enumeration that specifies whether the `CameraCaptureUI` interface should be configured for capturing videos, photos, or either. See Listing 16.3.

LISTING 16.3 Using the `CameraCaptureUI` Class

```
var cameraUI = new CameraCaptureUI();
var captureMode = CameraCaptureUIMode.Video;
var capturedMedia = await cameraUI.CaptureFileAsync(captureMode);
```

As mentioned previously, the user needs to give consent before your app can access webcam and microphone information through the `CameraCaptureUI` control. The first time your app makes a call to `CaptureFileAsync`, the user is prompted to allow or block application access to the webcam and microphone. A user can also explicitly grant or revoke these same permissions through the Permissions panel in the application settings. If the user elects to not grant access or has revoked permissions for either the webcam or the microphone, and your app calls CaptureFileAsync, the CameraCaptureUI user interface displays but just shows a black background instead of passing through video from your webcam. This screen also contains text indicating that the app needs permission to use the camera and that the user can grant this permission through the app settings.

Before showing the CameraCaptureUI, you should consider several settings that can be configured to define the tool's behavior. These values are set through the VideoSettings and PhotoSettings properties of the CameraCaptureUI instance; Table 16.1 and Table 16.2 describe them.

TABLE 16.1 CameraCaptureUI VideoSettings Properties

Property	Value
AllowTrimming	Determines whether trimming controls are displayed following a video capture. It defaults to true.
Format	Determines the video file format to use for the captured file. It is expressed as a member of the CameraCaptureUIVideoFormat enumeration and can be either Mp4 or Wmv (defaults to Mp4).
MaxDurationInSeconds	Determines the maximum length of the captured content. Note that a capture does not stop when this value is reached. Instead, the user is required to trim your video to meet this duration. As a result, AllowTrimming must be set to true if this value is set to anything other than zero (default), or an exception will be thrown.
MaxResolution	Determines the largest resolution value that will be shown to the user in the Camera Options flyout's Video Resolution drop-down within the CameraCaptureUI interface. It is expressed as a member of the CameraCaptureUIMaxVideoResolution enumeration. The default value is HighestAvailable.

TABLE 16.2 CameraCaptureUI PhotoSettings Properties

Property	Value
AllowCropping	Determines whether cropping controls are displayed following a photo capture. It defaults to true.
CroppedAspectRatio	Determines the aspect ratio that the captured photo must have. The user is required to crop the photo to the indicated aspect ratio if a nonzero value is supplied. As a result, AllowCropping must be set to true if this value is set to anything other than zero-by-zero (default), or an exception will be thrown.
CroppedSizeInPixels	Determines a fixed size in pixels that the captured photo must be cropped to. If the size is larger than the highest available camera resolution, the photo is scaled up to accommodate. As a result, if a nonzero size is specified, the MaxResolution property must be set to HighestAvailable, or an exception will be thrown. AllowCropping must also be set to true when this value is nonzero, or an exception will be thrown.
Format	Determines the image file format for the captured file. It is expressed as a member of the CameraCaptureUIPhotoFormat enumeration and can be either Jpeg (default), Png, or JpegXR.
MaxResolution	Determines the largest resolution value shown to the user in the Camera Options flyout's Photo Resolution drop-down within the CameraCaptureUI interface. It is expressed as a member of the CameraCaptureUIMaxPhotoResolution enumeration. The default value is HighestAvailable.

When the user has finished working with the capture interface that the CameraCaptureUI instance displays, the call to CaptureFileAsync returns a StorageFile object that provides access to the file that was captured, or null if nothing was captured or the captured content was rejected. Content captured by the CameraCaptureUI class is stored in the app's temporary storage folder, so the amount of data that can be captured is limited by the amount of space on the drive where the user settings folder is stored.

In the example application, the `CaptureAsync` method of the `CameraCaptureUIHelper` class contains the work done to use the `CameraCaptureUI` to capture and save a video file (see Listing 16.4).

LISTING 16.4 Capturing and Saving a Media File with the CameraCaptureUI

```
public static async Task<IStorageFile> CaptureAsync
    (CameraCaptureUIMode captureMode)
{
    var cameraUI = new CameraCaptureUI();
    var capturedMedia = await cameraUI.CaptureFileAsync(captureMode);
    if (capturedMedia == null) return null;

    // Set the default save to location based on the content MIME type
    var contentType = capturedMedia.ContentType;
    var defaultLocation = contentType.StartsWith("image")
            ? PickerLocationId.PicturesLibrary
            : PickerLocationId.VideosLibrary;

    // Save type options
    var fileSaveType = new KeyValuePair<String, IList<String>>(
        capturedMedia.DisplayType,
        new List<String> {capturedMedia.FileType});

    // Get the file to save the content to
    var savePicker = new FileSavePicker
                     {
                         SuggestedStartLocation = defaultLocation,
                         SuggestedFileName = capturedMedia.Name
                     };
    savePicker.FileTypeChoices.Add(fileSaveType);
    var fileToSaveTo = await savePicker.PickSaveFileAsync();
    if (fileToSaveTo == null) return null;

    // Move the file return the new file
    await capturedMedia.MoveAndReplaceAsync(fileToSaveTo);
    return fileToSaveTo;
}
```

The code creates an instance of the `CameraCaptureUI` class and calls `CaptureFileAsync`. The user is then shown a `FilePicker` that defaults to either the Windows video or the picture library, depending on the type of file captured. If the user chooses to save the captured file and specifies a valid location, the file is moved from the app temporary storage folder into the new location and a reference to the new file is returned to the calling function, which adds it to the list of chosen files to be played.

Using `MediaCapture`

If your app requires finer control over the media capture process than the "black box" approach of the `CameraCaptureUI`, you will want to look to the `MediaCapture` class for your capture needs. Whereas the `CameraCaptureUI` provides its own user interface elements for selecting capture device settings and showing the video stream coming from your webcam, when working with the `MediaCapture` class, you are responsible for defining the user interface elements and the related interactions.

Getting Started and Previewing

To start using the `MediaCapture` class, you create an instance of the class and call the `InitializeAsync` method provided by that instance. `InitializeAsync` provides two overrides. The first you can call without any arguments, resulting in the `MediaCapture` instance being initialized with default values. The second override takes an instance of the `MediaCaptureInitializationSettings` class, which enables you to set several key properties related to the media acquisition process.

The first few media capture initialization settings to discuss are the `CaptureMode`, `VideoDeviceId`, and `AudioDeviceId` values. Capturing with `MediaCapture` enables you to specify whether you want to capture only audio, only video, or both streams. You specify this by setting the `CaptureMode` property to the corresponding value of the `StreamingCaptureMode` enumeration. Additionally, you can specify which devices to use to supply audio and video samples to the `MediaCapture` instance during initialization. If you do not set this value, the first available device is used for each media type, depending on the `CaptureMode` setting.

As the `AudioDeviceId` and `VideoDeviceId` property names indicate, you define which devices to use by providing the appropriate device IDs. You obtain the device IDs from the `DeviceInformation` class, which provides an `Id` property (as well as a more human-readable `Name` property, among others) and also a static `FindAllAsync` method that you can use to find all the available devices that match a given criteria. To find audio and video capture devices, you specify device class values of `DeviceClass.AudioCapture` and `DeviceClass.VideoCapture`. The following code demonstrates how to find the available video capture devices:

```
var devices =
    await DeviceInformation.FindAllAsync(DeviceClass.VideoCapture);
```

In the example app, the `ApplyDeviceSettings` method handles the call to the `MediaCapture` `InitializeAsync` method (see Listing 16.5). This method is called whenever the currently selected `AudioDeviceToUse` and `VideoDeviceToUse` values change from the `MediaCapturePage` user interface page that illustrates the `MediaCapture` functionality.

LISTING 16.5 Creating and Initializing the `MediaCapture` Object

```
private async void ApplyDeviceSettings()
{
    // Determine the current capture mode, based on device selections
    var captureMode = StreamingCaptureMode.AudioAndVideo;
    if (VideoDeviceToUse == null && AudioDeviceToUse == null) return;
    if (VideoDeviceToUse != null && AudioDeviceToUse == null)
        captureMode = StreamingCaptureMode.Video;
    if (VideoDeviceToUse == null && AudioDeviceToUse != null)
        captureMode = StreamingCaptureMode.Audio;

    // Set up the initialization settings
    var settings = new MediaCaptureInitializationSettings
    {
        StreamingCaptureMode = captureMode,
        VideoDeviceId = VideoDeviceToUse == null
                                ? String.Empty
                                : VideoDeviceToUse.Id,
        AudioDeviceId = AudioDeviceToUse == null
                                ? String.Empty
                                : AudioDeviceToUse.Id,
    };

    // Create and initialize a new MediaCapture instance
    var captureManager = new MediaCapture();
    try
    {
        await captureManager.InitializeAsync(settings);
    }
    catch (UnauthorizedAccessException)
    {
        // The user has declined/blocked access to the camera/microphone
        // Prompt the user properly to enable access
        return;
    }
    _captureManager = captureManager;
```

```
    // Raise the CaptureSettingsReset event
    OnCaptureSettingsReset();
}
```

In this method, the StreamingCaptureMode, VideoDeviceId, and AudioDeviceId values of MediaCaptureInitializationSettings are set depending on the presence or absence of values in the VideoDeviceToUse and AudioDeviceToUse properties. A new MediaCapture instance is then created and initialized with the settings that were defined. This instance is stored for future use in the corresponding MediaCaptureHelper instance variable. Finally, the CaptureSettingsReset event is raised.

Note that, as a consequence of this arrangement, whenever the audio or video device selection changes, the app must create a new MediaCapture element instead of reusing the existing instance. This is because you can call the InitializeAsync method only once for each instance of the MediaCapture class; subsequent calls result in an exception. Thus, when changing values that are set through the InitializeAsync method, you must throw away the existing instance and start again.

Also be aware that the first call your app makes to InitializeAsync prompts the user for permission to access the webcam or microphone (if permission hasn't already been granted elsewhere in the application). If the user declines the request, the InitializeAsync method throws an UnauthorizedAccessException. Likewise, if the user later goes back through the Permissions panel in the application settings and revokes the app's permission to access the webcam or microphone, subsequent calls to InitializeAsync will throw an UnauthorizedAccessException.

To render a video stream from your capture device to your application's user interface, the MediaCapture class is most often used in tandem with a CaptureElement placed on your app's UI. The CaptureElement control is paired to the MediaCapture instance by setting the Source property of the CaptureElement instance to the related MediaCapture instance whose video stream should be displayed.

In the example app, the MediaCapturePage includes a handler for the CaptureSettingsReset event that calls the StartCapturePreview method in the MediaCaptureHelper instance with the current CaptureElement. In this method, the new MediaCapture instance is associated to the CaptureElement to preview the content from the selected video device. After the `MediaCapture` instance has been initialized and set as a source for a `CaptureElement`, you can start previewing the video by calling the `MediaCapture` instance's `StartPreviewAsync` method. Listing 16.6 shows the `StartCapturePreview` method.

LISTING 16.6 Starting Capture Preview

```
public async void StartCapturePreview(CaptureElement captureUIElement)
{
    // Associate the MediaCapture instance with the CaptureElement
    // and start video preview
    captureUIElement.Source = _captureManager;
    await _captureManager.StartPreviewAsync();
}
```

Working with Camera Settings

The `MediaCapture` class includes `VideoDeviceController` and `AudioDeviceController` properties. These properties provide access to various settings that might or might not be available, depending on the currently selected device's capabilities.

Some example properties that the `VideoDeviceController` property exposes include `Brightness`, `Contrast`, `Exposure`, `Focus`, `Tilt`, and `Zoom` settings. These properties are each exposed as a `MediaDeviceControl` instance. To work with these `MediaDeviceControl` properties, you can use their `Capabilities` property. This value has properties of its own that determine whether the current hardware supports the property and, if so, specify the minimum, maximum, step (increment), and default value, as well as whether the camera can automatically set the value. After determining the capabilities of the device for a given property, you can use the `TryGetValue` and `TrySetValue` methods to retrieve and set the property values, or use the `TryGetAuto` and `TrySetAuto` methods to see or set whether the setting is configured to let the device automatically determine its value.

The `AudioDeviceController` simply exposes `VolumePercent` and `Muted` properties, which you can set directly instead of checking whether they are supported.

In addition to setting these properties programmatically, you can show a predefined user interface for the camera settings. The software that is installed for the selected device determines which elements are shown in this interface. To display these settings for the current `MediaCapture` instance, you call the `CameraOptionsUI` class's static `Show` method:

```
CameraOptionsUI.Show(_captureManager);
```

Capturing Video and Audio

To capture media using the `MediaCapture` class, you use one of the `StartRecordTo[Target]Async` methods, along with the `StopRecordAsync` method to stop recording. The `StartRecord` methods have three target types: `StartRecordToStorageFileAsync`, `StartRecordToStreamAsync`, and `StartRecordToCustomSinkAsync`. Each method accepts a `MediaEncodingProfile` value that specifies the way the media should be encoded when it is captured, as well as a method-specific parameter that identifies the target for the current capture operation. `StartRecordToStorageFileAsync` expects an `IStorageFile` instance that identifies the file where the capture should be saved. `StartRecordToStreamAsync` expects an `IRandomAccessStream` instance that identifies a stream to which the captured data should be written. `StartRecordToCustomSinkAsync` expects an `IMediaExtension` that specifies a custom **Media Foundation** element, which enables the `MediaCapture` instance to participate in advanced media capture scenarios. (Media Foundation is a lower-level platform that you can use to develop digital media applications and components on Windows-based operating systems.) The `StartRecordToCustomSinkAsync` method also includes an override that enables some additional properties related to the capture target.

The `MediaEncodingProfile` parameter provides information about how the audio and video will be encoded (if present), along with information about the media's container, which specifies how the multimedia data is actually packaged and arranged, typically within a file on disk. The `MediaEncodingProfile` provides several static methods that create common profiles, given a desired encoding quality value. When you create them this way, you can adjust the profile properties to match the specific encoding profile your app requires.

When the user initiates a capture operation in the example app, the static `CreateCaptureToFileJobAsync` method of the `MediaCaptureJob` class is called to present the user with a `FileSavePicker` that prompts him or her to select a target file for the capture operation. If a valid file is selected, a new `MediaCaptureJob` instance is returned, configured to capture media to the selected file. The app then calls the `StartCaptureAsync` method that the `MediaCaptureJob` instance provides (see Listing 16.7).

LISTING 16.7 The `StartCaptureAsync` Method

```
public async void StartCaptureAsync(VideoEncodingQuality captureQuality)
{
    // Build the media encoding profile from the selected file type and
    MediaEncodingProfile profile;
    switch (_fileBeingCaptured.FileType)
    {
        case WindowsMediaExtension:
            profile = MediaEncodingProfile.CreateWmv(captureQuality);
            break;
        case Mp4Extension:
            profile = MediaEncodingProfile.CreateMp4(captureQuality);
            break;
        default:
            throw new InvalidOperationException("Unknown file type");
    }

    await _captureManager.StartRecordToStorageFileAsync
        (profile, _fileBeingCaptured);
}
```

The call to the `StartCaptureAsync` method accepts a member of the `VideoEncodingQuality` enumeration. This enumeration provides values representing several common video resolutions, each of which is included in the **Video Quality** drop-down in the example app for the user to select. Based on the file type that the user selects for the capture operation, an appropriate `MediaEncodingProfile` static method is called to generate the desired media encoding profile settings. These settings can be further modified after they've been created, with one key exception. Using the `VideoEncodingQuality` enumeration value of `Auto` tells the encoder to use the properties defined by the current camera. As a result, any changes made to the resulting `MediaEncodingProfile` instance are ignored.

After the encoding profile has been defined, the capture is started with a call to the `StartRecordToStorageFileAsync` method, with parameters that specify the desired encoding profile and the file that the media should be captured into. To end the capture, a call is made to the `StopRecordAsync` method.

Capturing Images

You also can capture images using the `MediaCapture` class. As with capturing audio and video, `CapturePhotoToStorageFileAsync` and `CapturePhotoToStreamAsync` expect an `ImageEncodingProperties` instance that describes the settings for the new image, as well as an `IStorageFile` or `IRandomAccessStream` instance to which the image data should be written. The `ImageEncodingProperties` class provides several static methods that create predefined encoding settings:

```
var encoding = ImageEncodingProperties.CreateJpeg();
await _captureManager.CapturePhotoToStorageFileAsync
   (encoding, imageFile);
```

Text-to-Speech Support

The final multimedia-related item to discuss is the functionality the Windows Runtime provides to convert text to an audio stream for playback. This essentially allows your apps to "speak" to their users. The text-to-speech functionality in the Windows Runtime is capable of speaking in several languages, using different voices based on gender and region. This speech synthesis support is capable of interpreting both raw text and customized Speech Synthesis Markup Language[2] (SSML) content. Using SSML provides the capability to use a variety of options to tailor precisely how text should be spoken, including altering the spoken pitch throughout a word or phrase, specifying how to interpret numbers, inserting pauses, or indicating specific phonetic pronunciations.

[2]Speech Synthesis Markup Language Specification, www.w3.org/TR/speech-synthesis/

The Example App

Once again, the **MultimediaExample** project showcases the functionality discussed in this section. When a user presses the Add Marker button to play back a given media file, that user has the opportunity to specify some text that the app will speak when that marker is hit during normal video playback. The user can specify whether the text is simply to be spoken as raw text or, alternatively, can specify whether he or she is providing SSML text. Users can also choose which of the available voices will be used to speak the provided text and can click the **Speak** button to quickly sample how the text will sound.

As with the other areas this chapter covers, the text-to-speech functionality has been encapsulated within a helper class: the `TextToSpeechHelper` class.

Using the `SpeechSynthesizer`

The primary class you use to add text-to-speech functionality to your app is the `SpeechSynthesizer` class. To use the `SpeechSynthesizer` class to convert text to an audio stream that can be played back, you create an instance and then call either the `SynthesizeTextToStreamAsync` or `SynthesizeSsmlToStreamAsync` methods, passing in the text to be converted. You then pass the resulting stream to a `MediaElement` instance to hear the text being spoken.

You can choose which voice the `SpeechSynthesizer` instance uses to read back the text by setting its `Voice` property to a member of the `VoiceInformation` class. You can obtain the list of voices that are installed and available for the current system language by using the static `AllVoices` property that the `SpeechSynthesizer` class provides. You can also obtain the default voice used through the `DefaultVoice` static property, also provided by the `SpeechSynthesizer` class.

In the example app, the list of voices the `AllVoices` property returns appears to users in a combo box, where they can select a voice to use to play back their text. When they click the **Speak** button, or when a marker is hit during normal video playback, the text they entered is played using the `SpeakContentAsync` method that the `TextToSpeechHelper` class provides (see Listing 16.8).

LISTING 16.8 Speaking Text Content

```
public static async void SpeakContentAsync
    (String content, Boolean isSsml, String voiceId)
{
    if (String.IsNullOrWhiteSpace(content)) return;

    // Find the voice with the matching Id or just use the default
    var voice = Voices.FirstOrDefault(x => x.Id == voiceId) ??
                        DefaultVoice;

    using (var synthesizer = new SpeechSynthesizer {Voice = voice})
    {
        // Get the voice stream for the given text
        var voiceStream = isSsml
          ? await synthesizer.SynthesizeSsmlToStreamAsync(content)
          : await synthesizer.SynthesizeTextToStreamAsync(content);

        // Create a new MediaElement and use it to play the voice stream
        var mediaElement = new MediaElement();
        mediaElement.SetSource(voiceStream, voiceStream.ContentType);
        mediaElement.Play();
    }
}
```

This method is called with the content to be spoken, an indication of whether this content is SSML, and the ID of the voice to use, based on the user's selection. First, an attempt is made to find a voice based on the provided voice ID. If no voice is located, the default voice is used.

When a voice is determined, a new instance of the `SpeechSynthesizer` class is created and its voice property is set based on the previously obtained value. Next, the voice stream is obtained using either the `SynthesizeTextToStreamAsync` or `SynthesizeSsmlToStreamAsync` methods, depending on the indicated SSML preference. Finally, a new `MediaElement` instance is created to be used for playback of the audio stream. Note that this `MediaElement` is not added to the app's visual tree, but instead provides audio playback without any user interface. To actually play back the stream, the `MediaElement` source is set to the provided stream, and the `Play` method is then called to start playing the corresponding audio.

Summary

In this chapter, you saw how you can use the `MediaElement` control to add media playback functionality to your app, and you looked at several ways to customize both the look and behavior of the `MediaElement` control. You also saw that you can capture your own media files using either the black-box functionality of the `CameraCaptureUI` class or the more customizable `MediaCapture` class. Finally, you saw how you can use the `SpeechSynthesizer` class along with a `MediaElement` to take advantage of the text-to-speech functionality the Windows Runtime offers. Chapter 17, "Accessibility," shows how you can increase the reach of your Windows Store app by adding features that allow the app to work with screen readers, high-contrast themes, and other functionality of Windows and the Windows Runtime.

17 Accessibility

Windows Store apps go beyond tailoring their experience to the end user's device by facilitating unique user preferences. Building your app to support those preferences is important, especially when the user requires assistive technology. Your app should expose the appropriate information to support screen reading, including when it generates dynamic content. Many users prefer to use the keyboard as their primary means of interaction, so your app should support keyboard navigation, activation of controls, and the capability to execute commands using keyboard shortcuts.

Visually impaired users rely on high-contrast content to make it easier to read. When users configure Windows to make everything display bigger, your app should scale content accordingly. Users who are colorblind need alternative cues on the screen to distinguish content. All these scenarios are supported by Windows Store apps, although some require extra effort by the developer to implement.

In this chapter, you learn how to build an accessible app. The example app for the chapter, named **AccessibilityExample**, illustrates the correct XAML and programmatic elements to support accessibility. You also learn how to use several applications, including the built-in **Narrator**, to test for accessibility.

Requested Theme

Windows Store apps support two built-in themes called `Light` and `Dark`. The default built-in theme is the `Dark` theme. Many of the examples in this book request the `Light` theme to make the screenshots easier to read. You can set the requested theme in several ways, but you can set it only once. Subsequent attempts to change the application-wide theme result in a `NotSupportedException` being thrown. A high-contrast mode also is an option, as the next section explains. When the user has selected `HighContrast`, Windows ignores the requested theme.

The easiest way to set the requested theme is in the `Application.xaml` file. This is an example of what it look likes in the **AccessibilityExample**:

```
<Application x:Class="AccessibilityExample.App"
    xmlns="http://schemas.microsoft.com/winfx/2006/xaml/presentation"
    xmlns:x="http://schemas.microsoft.com/winfx/2006/xaml"
    xmlns:local="using:AccessibilityExample" RequestedTheme="Light">
</Application>
```

You can achieve the same result programmatically as shown in the code-behind file `App.xaml.cs`.

```
RequestedTheme = ApplicationTheme.Light;
```

The example app uses the programmatic approach because it saves the user's preference. The app features a button to toggle the theme, and when the theme is toggled, it is saved it to the application's roaming settings. This enables the app to set the preference upon startup.

Changes to the theme do not immediately reflect in design view. Fortunately, you can use the special **Device** tab in design view to manipulate the display. Figure 17.1 shows how to use the **Device** tab to set the simulated theme in design view. You can use this to flip between the `Light` and `Dark` themes to see how your app behaves.

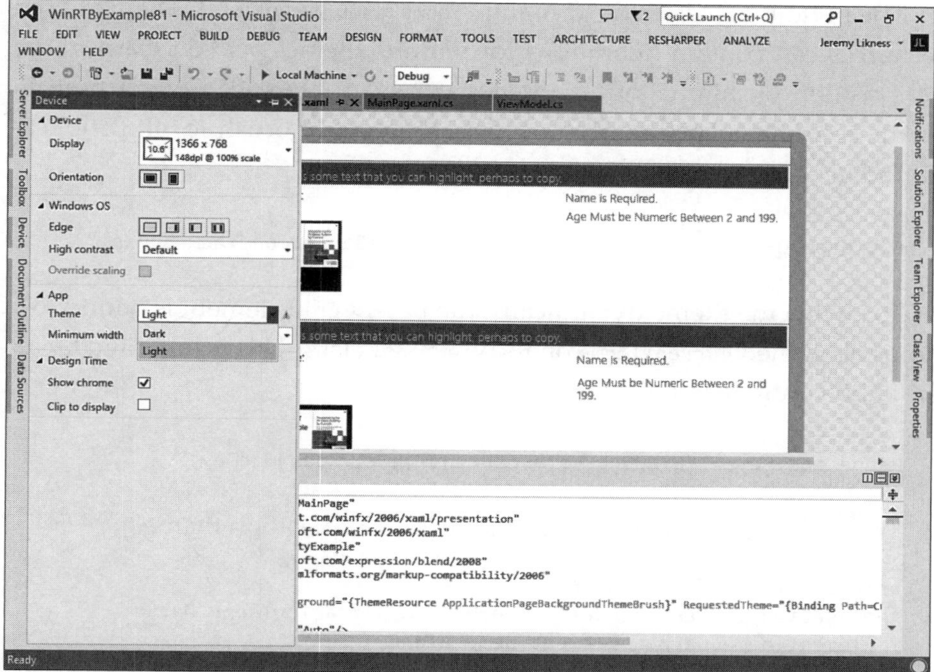

FIGURE 17.1 Changing the requested theme in design view

Although you can set the requested theme for the application only once, the example application supports changing the theme at runtime. How is this possible? All framework elements have a `RequestedTheme` property that can be changed at runtime. By default, the property inherits from the application theme. The property is inherited by child elements, so it is possible to change it at a parent level and propagate the change throughout the UI.

The **AccessibilityExample** app has two sections: an upper portion that does not explicitly support accessibility and a bottom portion that does. When you switch to the dark theme, the upper portion does not go dark and the labels disappear. This is because the `Background` property of the upper grid is set to a `StaticResource`. The `Grid` control cannot adapt to a new setting because it has a static setting:

```
Background="{StaticResource GridBackgroundStyle}"
```

The bottom `Grid` uses the dynamic `ThemeResource` instead. Theme-based resources can contain definitions for various themes, as you learn in the next section on high-contrast themes. You can reference several built-in theme resources. The bottom `Grid` uses the default brush for the application's background.

```
Background="{ThemeResource ApplicationPageBackgroundThemeBrush}"
```

To switch the theme dynamically, the parent `Grid` element is bound to a property named `CurrentTheme` on the `ViewModel` class. This is inherited by all the child controls on the page.

```
RequestedTheme="{Binding Path=CurrentTheme, Mode=OneWay}"
```

The `ViewModel` class defaults to the current application theme.

```
private ElementTheme currentTheme =
Application.Current.RequestedTheme == ApplicationTheme.Dark
? ElementTheme.Dark : ElementTheme.Light;
```

Note that element-based themes have a different enumeration, compared to the requested application-level theme. When the user toggles the theme, the property is toggled. Through data-binding, the elements are then updated to the new theme. The `ViewModel` class saves the value to set the application-level theme on future application launches. This demonstrates a full cycle of support for requested themes.

High Contrast

In addition to the requested theme, a user can specify a high-contrast setting. To set up high contrast, press **Windows key+U** and choose **Set Up High Contrast**. Ensure that **Turn On or Off High Contrast When Left Alt+Left Shift+Print Screen Is Pressed** is checked.

Compile and run the **AccessibilityExample** app. Hold down **left Alt+left Shift+Print Screen** and confirm your desire to switch to high contrast when the dialog box appears. Note that the bottom half of the screen changes to high contrast, but some of the elements in the top half do not. This is because the bottom half was designed to support high contrast.

In addition to using the ThemeResource markup extension instead of StaticResource:

```
Style="{ThemeResource GreenStackPanelAccessibleStyle}"
```

a difference arises in how the style is implemented. The top half hard-codes a single style:

```
<Style x:Name="GreenStackPanelStyle" TargetType="StackPanel">
    <Setter Property="Background" Value="Green"/>
</Style>
```

The bottom half appropriately encodes the style inside a theme dictionary:

```
<ResourceDictionary.ThemeDictionaries>
    <ResourceDictionary x:Key="Default">
        <Style x:Key="GreenStackPanelAccessibleStyle"
            TargetType="StackPanel">
            <Setter Property="Background" Value="Green"/>
        </Style>
        ...
```

The resources include styles for the specific contrast settings. In this example, the style is declared without any setters, so it falls through to the default system-supplied style:

```
<ResourceDictionary x:Key="HighContrastWhite">
    <Style x:Key="GreenStackPanelAccessibleStyle"
        TargetType="StackPanel"/>
</ResourceDictionary>
```

Although you can provide your own custom high-contrast styles, all controls have a default implementation that works best across various accessibility settings. A common practice is to define custom styles for the Default key and allow the system to handle the other styles. You can augment your own custom styles by basing them on the system-provided styles that all feature contrast support. Using the ThemeResource tag has the added benefit of enabling the app to update themes dynamically when the user switches modes. StaticResource supports the correct theme, but the user must relaunch the app after switching modes to see the changes.

Keyboard Support

Many screen readers rely on using the keyboard for navigation and to access various features. Users might also prefer the keyboard to interact over touch, pointers, or a mouse. To provide full keyboard support, ensure that the app can be appropriately navigated using **Tab** and arrow keys and that you can activate elements using **Space** or **Enter**. The built-in controls, such as `Button`, implement this automatically. When you provide special commands, consider making the commands accessible via keyboard shortcuts.

The key to enabling keyboard navigation is to ensure that you configure your controls correctly. For example, even though the image in the nonaccessible grid can be pressed or clicked, by default, an image is not considered a control that you can activate. You cannot tab to the image in that grid. Furthermore, although the default action is to submit the form, tabbing out of the box for age will land you on the **Reset** button. That means typing an age, clicking **Tab**, and then clicking **Enter** will not have the desired effect of submitting the form.

In the bottom accessible portion of the sample app, the image is made into a navigable element by wrapping it inside a `Button` element. The button automatically handles navigation as well as activation through a variety of events, including tapping, clicking, and pressing **Space** or **Enter**. When you use **Tab** in the bottom form, the default is to tab onto the **Submit** button before the **Reset** button. This is done by setting the `TabIndex` property on the buttons:

```
<Button TabIndex="4000"
    Content="Reset" Click="AccessibleResetOnClick"></Button>
<Button TabIndex="3000"
    Content="Submit" Click="AccessibleSubmitOnClick"></Button>
```

The default order for navigating controls is left to right and top to bottom. If your form is laid out differently (for example, you want the user to navigate the form elements in vertical order by column), you can set this up using the `TabIndex`. It is common practice to use larger numbers so that inserting new controls is easier if they are added later (for example, the `Button` that wraps the image was inserted between the `TextBox` for age and the `Button` to submit by giving it a `TabIndex` of 2500).

Providing shortcut keys for various commands is also a good idea. In the accessible `Grid`, you can submit the form by pressing **Ctrl+S** and reset it using **Ctrl+R**. These keys can be pressed from anywhere within the `Grid` because the events are wired up on the `Grid` itself and, therefore, pick up child events that bubble up.

```
<Grid Grid.Row="2" Margin="5" HorizontalAlignment="Stretch"
    KeyUp="AccessibleGridOnKeyUp"
    KeyDown="AccessibleGridOnKeyDown" ...>
```

The page keeps track of whether the **Ctrl** key is pressed using a private field. The `KeyDown` event handler sets the variable:

```
private void AccessibleGridOnKeyDown(object sender,
    KeyRoutedEventArgs e)
    {
        if (e.Key == VirtualKey.Control)
        {
            isCtrlPressed = true;
        }
    }
```

A similar method handles clearing the field when the **Ctrl** key is released. If the **Ctrl** key is being pressed, the `KeyDown` handler then checks to see if the **S** or **R** keys are also pressed. If so, the appropriate method is called.

```
switch (e.Key)
{
    case VirtualKey.S:
        this.AccessibleSubmitOnClick(this, e);
        break;
    case VirtualKey.R:
        this.AccessibleResetOnClick(this, e);
        break;
}
```

All the processing for the special keys is done within the code-behind, so it's not clear on the form what is possible. You could decorate the buttons with a ToolTip, but screen readers have a special way to indicate keyboard shortcuts. Use the `AutomationProperties` attached property to set either the `AccessKey` property (for commands that are used in conjunction with the

Alt key) or the AcceleratorKey (for commands that are used in conjunction with the **Ctrl** key). For example, the **Submit** Button is declared like this:

```
<Button TabIndex="3000"
    Content="Submit" Click="AccessibleSubmitOnClick"
    AutomationProperties.AcceleratorKey="Control S"></Button>
```

This informs the screen reader about the shortcut key so it can be read to the user. The AutomationProperties attached property is important for providing additional information about controls.

Automation Properties

Using the AutomationProperties attached property, you can annotate controls to provide more information for a screen reader. Controls such as a TextBlock are automatically read based on their contents, such as the Text property. When a control doesn't have an obvious property that contains the description for the control, such as an input TextBox or a bitmapped image, you can set the Name property:

```
AutomationProperties.Name="Special Description"
```

This enables the screen reader to access the additional information and provide this to the user. Each item that participates in automation should have its own unique identifier. This is separate from the XAML name because, in some cases, there may be multiple items with either the same name or no name at all. You set the unique identifier using the AutomationProperties.Id property.

If you need more detailed information, you can use the HelpText property. A common way to annotate controls is to base them on labels. In most forms, you provide a TextBlock or similar control to describe the input, followed by the input control itself. In those cases, you can create a binding between the input control and its label. This correlates the two controls and automatically updates the description if and when it changes. In the MainPage.xaml, you can see that the AccessibleNameBox control specifies its label by binding to the TextBlock named NameLabel:

```
AutomationProperties.LabeledBy="{Binding ElementName=NameLabel}"
```

This causes the screen reader to reference the bound element and use the active text for that element to describe the input. The easiest way to test that your controls are properly annotated is to use the built-in **Narrator** in Windows.

Testing with Narrator

Narrator is a screen reader that ships with Windows 8.1.[1] Its purpose is to read text on the screen to enable using your PC without a display. The easiest way to turn on **Narrator** is to press **Windows key+Enter**. If you are using a tablet, you can press **Windows key+Volume Up**. Use the same combination to turn off **Narrator**. Run the **AccessibilityExample** app, and place your cursor in the first input box in the top half of the display.

Notice that **Narrator** simply reads "editing" because it has no context for the input box. Type some text. **Narrator** attempts to read the text. **Tab** to the next input box, and you will hear "editing" read again. The **Reset** and **Submit** buttons are read only because the default "hint" for buttons is the **Content** property.

Now click the first input box in the lower "accessible" portion of the screen. The first thing you should notice is that **Narrator** now understands the association between the input box and its label, so it will read "name, editing." When you **Tab** to the input box for age, you will hear "age, editing." **Narrator** also reads the image button. It is able to describe the button because the `LabeledBy` is bound to the caption. Finally, when you **Tab** to the buttons, you will hear not only the button's name, but also the shortcut key. This is because **Narrator** knows how to read the `AccessKey` and `AcceleratorKey` properties.

If you submit the form with an error, you might wonder how **Narrator** will read the error text. It is not something you can **Tab** to. **Narrator** provides you with a special navigation command you can use to iterate over elements on the page. With an error showing on the accessible form, hold down **Caps Lock** and press the **Right Arrow** key. The error message should highlight and be read back to you. You can use the **Left Arrow** and **Right Arrow** keys to navigate over various elements on the page.

---

[1]Hear text read aloud with Narrator at http://bit.ly/1cw5CJX

Automation and Lists

Lists require special attention for automation because of the potentially dynamic nature of their content. Because list items can be generated from list templates, screen readers must be informed of how to interpret the description for a list item. To see this in action, run the **AccessibilityExample** project and turn on **Narrator**. Navigate to the ComboBox control in the top, nonaccessible portion of the app.

The screen reader can name the control only as "combo box" and cannot read the selected items. Instead, you hear only the namespace for the item. The list is bound to a collection of item types, so the reader describes the item as "accessibility example dot item." This is not very informative to the user.

Now navigate to the bottom portion of the screen and **Tab** to the ComboBox control there. First, the screen reader can describe it as "selection of items" because the AutomationProperties.Name is set on the ComboBox. When you select an item, the reader can read the description of the item. Making this happen is a little more complicated for lists than other controls. You cannot simply set up the properties in your DataTemplate because the reader is expecting them to be on the actual container for each item in the list. To address this, I created a converter named AccessibleItemConverter that converts an item to an identifier or a name.

```
if (parameter != null && parameter.ToString().Equals("id",
    StringComparison.CurrentCultureIgnoreCase))
{
    return string.Format("ListItemId{0}", item.Id);
}
return item.Description;
```

Notice that if the parameter passed to the converter is for an identifier, it returns something like ListItemId2. Otherwise, it returns the contents of the Description property. To use the converter, I created a custom ComboBox called AccessibleItemComboBox. It inherits from the base ComboBox control but overrides the PrepareContainerForItemOverride method. This enables me to add the attached AutomationProperties to the container and specify a binding that uses my custom converter:

```
source.SetBinding(AutomationProperties.AutomationIdProperty,
    new Binding
{
    Converter = converter,
    ConverterParameter = "id"
});
```

This is like setting a `Binding` without a path so that it defaults to the current item (which is the current `Item` in the list). Then it is passed a converter so that the property actually receives the ID or name that the converter generates. This is a little extra effort, but it is necessary to make the app fully accessible.

Live Settings

Letting screen readers know when there is dynamic content on the screen that might change is important. This can include text that changes, lists that update with new items, and regions that contain dynamically loaded content such as web browsers. To inform the reader that content has changed, set the `LiveSetting` property to either `Assertive` or `Polite`, depending on how important the change is (for example, `Polite` indicates that it is fine for the reader to wait for a current task to finish).

```
AutomationProperties.LiveSetting="Assertive"
```

Next, whenever the content changes, inform the reader by raising an event. Two steps are involved in this. The first step is to obtain a helper for the control, known as an `AutomationPeer`. The next is to raise the event on the peer. For example, when the user changes the selected item in the `ComboBox` control, the text of that item is displayed in a `TextBlock`:

```
var peer =
    FrameworkElementAutomationPeer.FromElement(DynamicTextBlock);
peer.RaiseAutomationEvent(AutomationEvents.LiveRegionChanged);
```

This informs the reader that a change has occurred. Every control in the Windows Runtime has a corresponding `AutomationPeer`.

Automation Peers

The WinRT namespace `Windows.UI.Xaml.Automation.Peers` contains several classes and methods that assist with automation and accessibility. Automation peers work in conjunction with controls to expose a standard interface for interacting with the control. All peers derive from `FrameworkElementAutomationPeer` (itself based on `AutomationPeer`). Each instance implements various methods that describe the current state of the control and provide a means to interact with the control.

Chapter 17, "Accessibility," contains an example coded UI test project named **AccessibilityTestProject**. It provides an example of interacting with automation peers for test automation. The example test is in `CodedUITestMethod1`. The first step is to launch the app using the package identifier:

```
var myapp = XamlWindow.Launch(
    "WinRTByExampleAccessibilityExample_req6rhny9ggkj!App");
```

This actually launches an instance of the **AccessibilityExample** app. A map of the UI was constructed using the Coded UI Test Builder. This is accessed by going into the Visual Studio **Test** menu, selecting **Generate Code for Coded UI Test**, and then selecting **Use Coded UI Test Builder** from within a Coded UI Test Project. I identified the textboxes for name and age and the error text for the name validation, and this was generated as part of the UI map. You can place the crosshairs on a control, add an assertion, and then generate code to capture the map.

The `TextBox` control has an automation peer that is capable of responding to the tap gesture. This allows me to set focus to the input for age.

```
Gesture.Tap(this.UIMap.UIAccessibilityExampleWindow.UIAgeEdit);
```

Before I do anything, I want to make sure that the name validation error isn't showing because I haven't tried to submit the form yet. I do that by calling the `TryGetClickablePoint` method.

```
Assert.IsFalse(this.UIMap.UIAccessibilityExampleWindow
    .UINameisRequiredText.TryGetClickablePoint(out pt));
```

Next, I enter some text into the age input and emulate clicking **Control+S** to submit the form.

```
this.UIMap.UIAccessibilityExampleWindow.UIAgeEdit.Text = "32";
Keyboard.SendKeys("s", ModifierKeys.Control);
```

When I test the error text, it should now be visible; therefore, my attempt to get a clickable should succeed.

```
Assert.IsTrue(this.UIMap.UIAccessibilityExampleWindow
    .UINameisRequiredText.TryGetClickablePoint(out pt));
```

The test then continues by entering a name into the box (it uses keyboard input for this, but the property could also be set directly), submitting the form, and then verifying that the error message goes away. All these steps are made possible by the automation peers. If you create your own custom controls, you should consider either inheriting from an existing peer or creating a custom one.[2] By properly setting up automation properties, you ensure that screen readers that also use the automation peers are able to interface with your app and provide an accessible experience. Coded UI tests are one way to test that your app is readily accessible through the automation interfaces.

Accessibility Checker

Visual Studio ships with software to help you validate the accessibility of your app. You can find it under this path:

```
C:\Program Files (x86)\Windows Kits\8.1\bin\x64\AccChecker
```

If you are on a 32-bit system, remove the `(x86)` and change `x64` to `x86` in the path. Run the `acccheckui.exe` program. Next, launch the **AccessibilityExample** app. Select the title of the app (Accessibility Example) from the list and check all the verification routines in the right panel, as Figure 17.2 shows.

[2]Custom automation peers, http://bit.ly/1fx6xtY

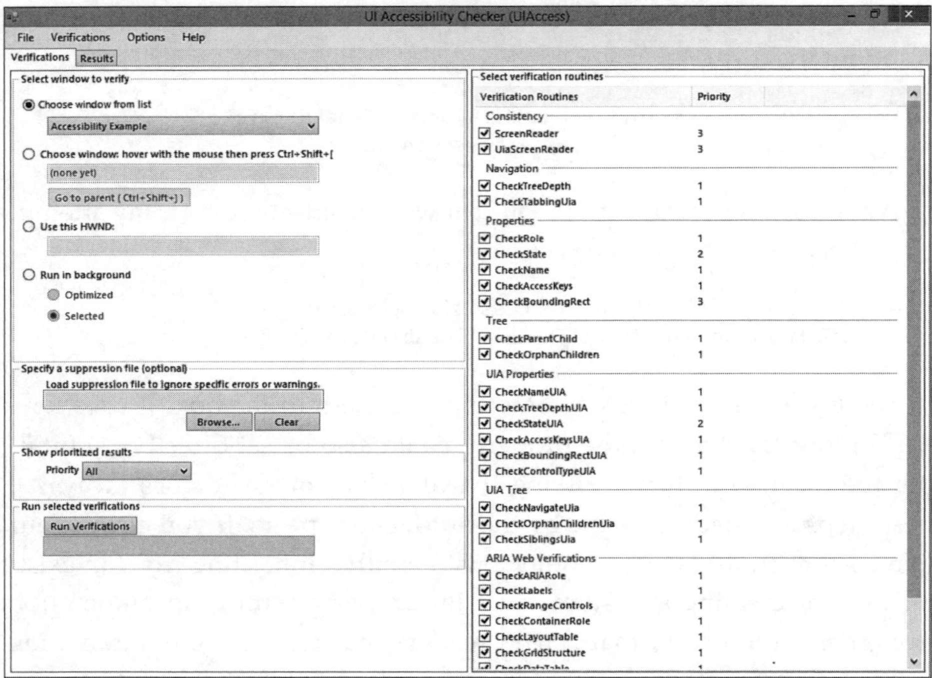

FIGURE 17.2 The accessibility checker main screen

As an alternative, if you have multiple windows, you can hover your mouse pointer over the running **AccessibilityExample** app and then press **Control+Shift+[**. This also accesses the window. Tap **Run Verifications** to begin testing accessibility. You should notice activity in the app, followed by a report. Several warnings about "duplicate siblings" are related to the fact that the form is repeated to demonstrate how it was made accessible. The list of legitimate errors indicates the input elements in the nonaccessible portion that don't have valid names.

After you run the verifications, several additional tabs appear. These tabs enable you to browse the app from the perspective of various screen readers. You can see how the readers interpret the layout of the page and how the various labels and inputs appear. You can quickly determine what controls have not been given the appropriate accessibility treatment so that you can update your app to be more accessible.

Summary

In this chapter, you learned about the various accessibility features available to Windows Store apps and how to update your content to support screen readers and user preferences. You learned how to support requested themes, the correct way to set up resources for high-contrast themes, and how to integrate keyboard support into your pages. Narrator can be used to read the screen for you on any Windows 8.1 device. Live settings inform readers about dynamic content, and automation peers work with controls to provide a common interface that can be used for accessibility and coded UI testing.

Accessibility features help you reach a broader audience and make your app easier to use. In the next chapter, "Globalization and Localization," you learn how to integrate language and culture support, to make your app accessible to foreign markets and further broaden its reach.

18

Globalization and Localization

GLOBALIZATION REFERS TO THE PROCESS OF BUILDING YOUR APP to support multiple cultures and locales. It involves understanding what target cultures and locales you want to support, designing your app (and creating assets) to support those targets, and writing your code so that it operates correctly. Localization is the more specific process of adapting your app to a target culture or locale. For example, you might author your globalized app in English and then localize it for Spanish and French.

Globalization involves more than just translating text and displaying a different set of characters on the page. Certain language texts are rendered right to left and require the app to render complex interconnected glyphs. Date and time are handled differently within various cultures, as is the formatting and display of numbers, currency, and measurements. Rules for sorting text can also vary between cultures and languages.

The Windows Runtime addresses localization through a combination of conventions and tags. Naming conventions identify localized resources to the compiler and are automatically cataloged and packaged for you. Tags map to string-based localizable content, including text, colors, and even dimensions for controls that can change based on locale. The tags are stored in a special **Resources File** with the `.resw` extension.

This differs from desktop applications built for the .NET Framework. Desktop applications embed a default language in the main assembly. Satellite assemblies provide localization support. When a resource is requested in the .NET Framework, the `ResourceManager` class scans those assemblies to find the appropriate translation. Applications that run on the desktop expose a `CultureInfo.CurrentCulture` property that can be changed at runtime.

The Windows Runtime does not use satellite assemblies. Instead, it uses the concept of a *resource package*. You can compile multiple localized resources into the main app package and then distribute separate, optional resource packages for additional cultures. This enables you to optimize the size of your main package while providing the flexibility of servicing multiple locales. You learn more about packaging in Chapter 19, "Packaging and Deploying."

Windows users can configure language preferences that can include multiple languages and are independent of location. For example, a Windows user might be located in the United States but have a language preference for French. Even if the Windows OS is installed with one language version, such as English, users can run apps using a different language preference. You learn how to set these preferences in the section "Configuring Preferred Languages."

Design Considerations

Approaching the design of your app with globalization in mind is important. Fortunately, both HTML and XAML provide flexible, responsive layout controls that can accommodate changes in the size of text. You want to design in a way that allows the localized text to flow into the containers instead of relying on specifying fixed container dimensions in resource files. This requires you to leave extra space for text when it becomes translated; in some cases, the translation is half again as long as the original text. Extra vertical padding is also important to accommodate accents and tildes.

In general, you want to avoid images that contain text. To support localized images, you must provide a copy of the image for every target translation. In many cases, you can use the layout engine to overlay images with text where needed, and you can take advantage of text translation rather than image substitution. Keep in mind that icons might have different meanings in different cultures and might need to be localized as well.

Default Language

The default language of your app is important because it is the language the app presents when it doesn't support any of the user's language preferences. The default language is set on the **Application** tab of the app's manifest, as in Figure 18.1. The setting requires you to enter a valid BCP-47 language tag.[1]

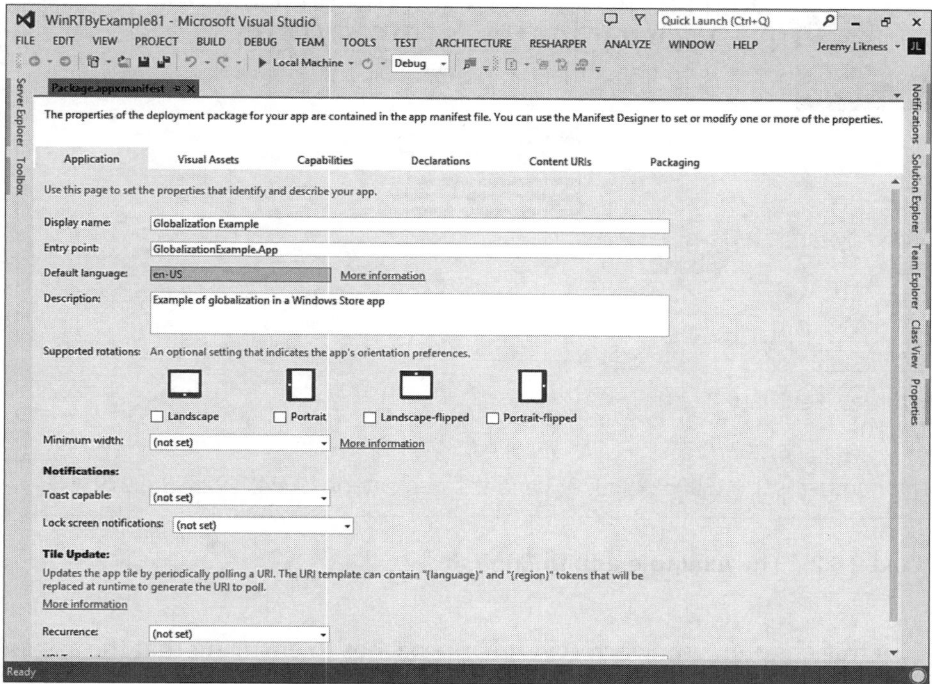

FIGURE 18.1 Setting the default language

[1]BCP-47, http://bit.ly/1ljtxhH

Although you can choose any valid language, you must choose one of a specific group of languages to meet Windows Store app certification requirements. The Windows Store groups languages into *certification languages* (you must support at least one of these to meet certification requirements) and *allowable languages* (which Windows supports but are not part of the certification process). A list of these languages is available online.[2]

The example project **GlobalizationExample** demonstrates an app that defaults to English and has been localized to Spanish. Compile, deploy, and run the app; you should see something similar to Figure 18.2. Notice the image assets, including the book cover and flag, various text elements, dates, and currency. You can localize all these assets.

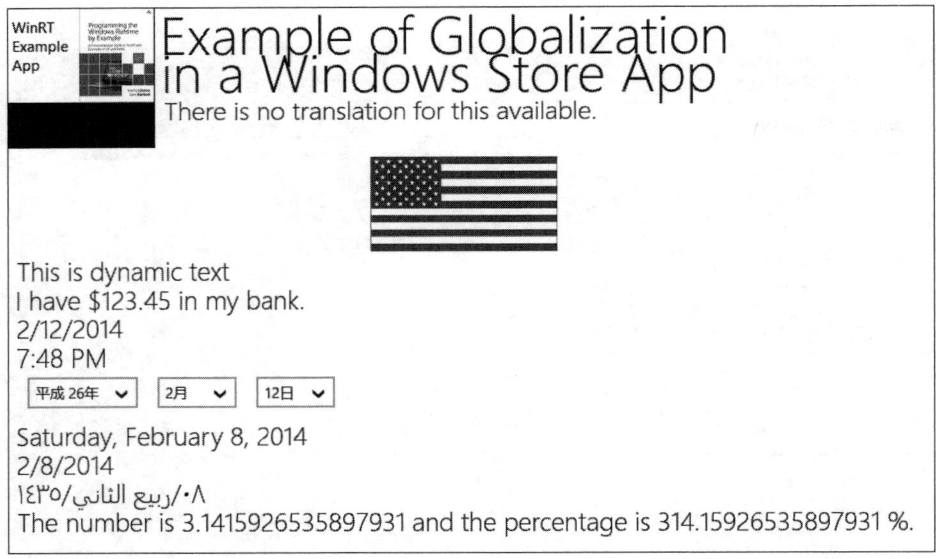

FIGURE 18.2 The example app in English

In this chapter, you learn several approaches to ensuring that the assets are correctly reflected in the target language.

---

[2]Choosing your languages (Windows), http://bit.ly/X29FBg

Configuring Preferred Languages

In Windows 8.1, you can set a list of preferred languages and list them in order of precedence. Windows Store apps then can find your most preferred language supported by the app. To access language preferences, tap the **Windows key** to bring up the **Start Screen** and then type **control** to begin searching. The **Control Panel** appears as an option in the list. Select the **Control Panel**, choose **Clock, Language, and Region**, and then select **Language**.

The result looks similar to Figure 18.3. You might have only one language listed. To add a new language, choose **Add a Language**.

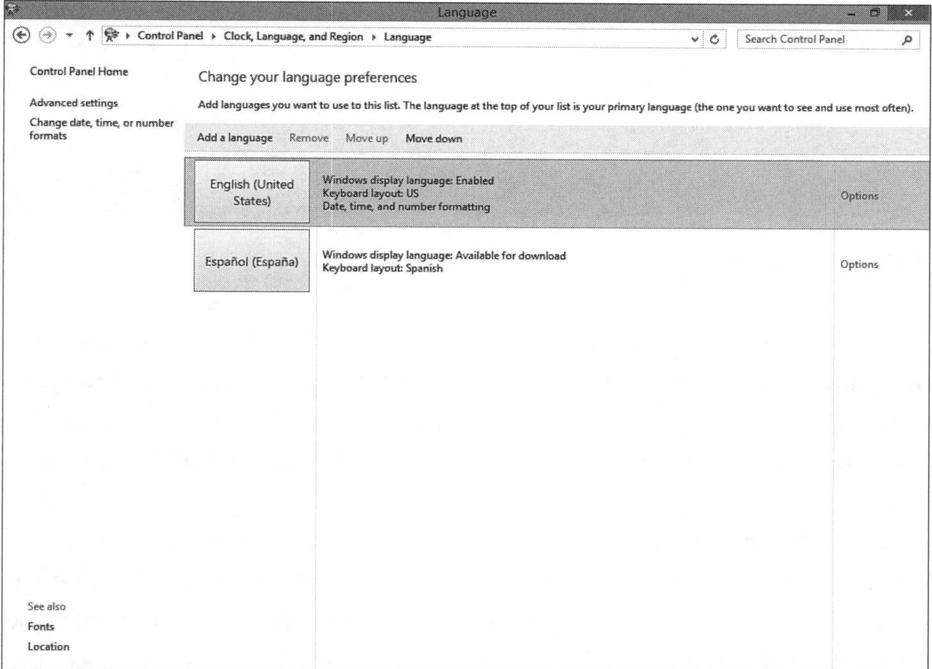

FIGURE 18.3 Languages

The **Add a Language** dialog box lists languages alphabetically or by their corresponding writing system, depending on your preference. For the example provided with the book to work, you need to choose Spanish, as in Figure 18.4.

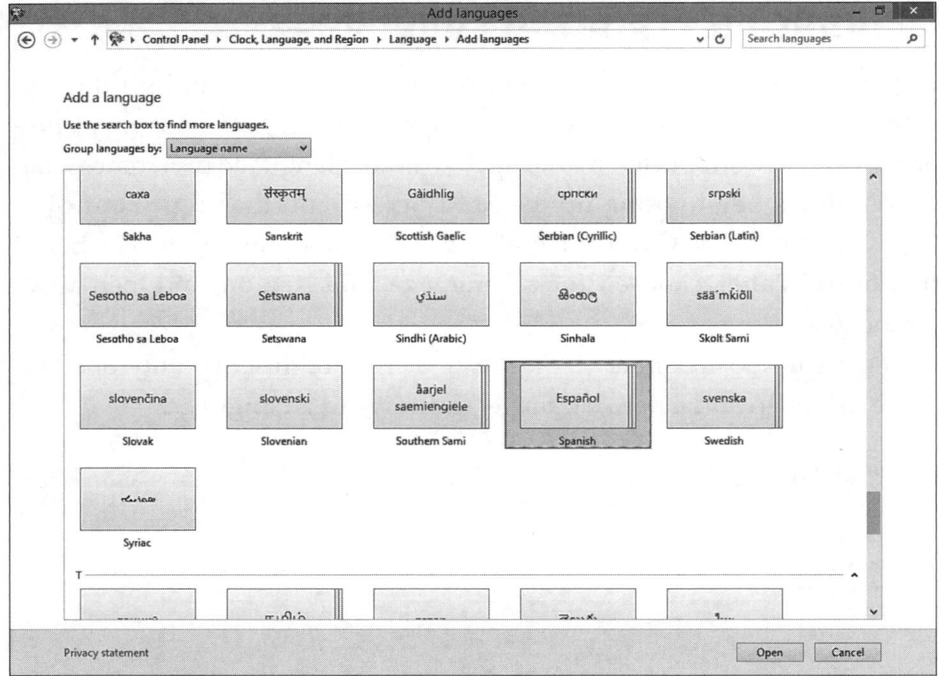

FIGURE 18.4 Selecting a new language to add

Choosing the language enables the **Open** button. Notice that the icon for Spanish shows multiple squares stacked on each other. This indicates multiple dialects to choose from. Tap **Open** to see the list of dialects. For this example, choose **Spanish (Spain)** and select **Add**; this adds the option to your list of preferences.

To see the app in Spanish, you must make it your preferred language. In the dialog box in Figure 18.3, simply select Spanish and choose **Move Up** to move it to the top of the list. If you are running the example app, close it. Run the app again to see it rendered with Spanish as the preference (see Figure 18.5).

Notice that some of the controls (including the `DatePicker` and one of the date displays) stayed in the same language, and one of the texts remains in English. The rest of the information is rendered based on the Spanish language and preferences. You can examine the example project to see how this was achieved.

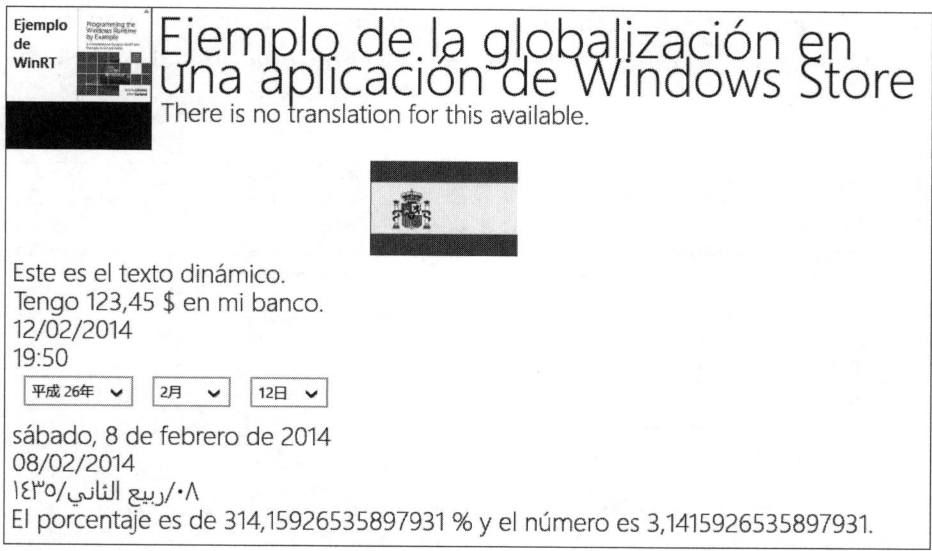

FIGURE 18.5 The app with Spanish set as the preferred language

Resource Qualification and Matching

The first step in localizing your app is to understand the localization conventions that Windows Store apps use. The convention is simple. You can organize assets by locale in two ways. The first is to create a set of subfolders at the same level that are given a language code. The second is to include the language code in the filenames. The example app demonstrates both of these options.

Notice that, instead of including the assets directly under the `Assets` folder as in other examples, a new set of subfolders has been created. These are named `en-US` and `es-ES`, respectively. The assets are dropped inside these folders. When you compile the app, Visual Studio automatically recognizes these locale-specific folders and adds the languages to the generated package. You don't have to do this manually because the convention automatically instructs Visual Studio to do so.

You can also use the filename itself to specify locale. Under the `Images` folder are two files, named `flag.lang-en.jpg` and `flag.lang-es.jpg`. Windows picks up the appropriate version the same way it finds the correct scale setting for an image. In both cases (using folders or filename), you reference the asset without the locale. Figure 18.6 shows the **Visual Assets** tab of the manifest.

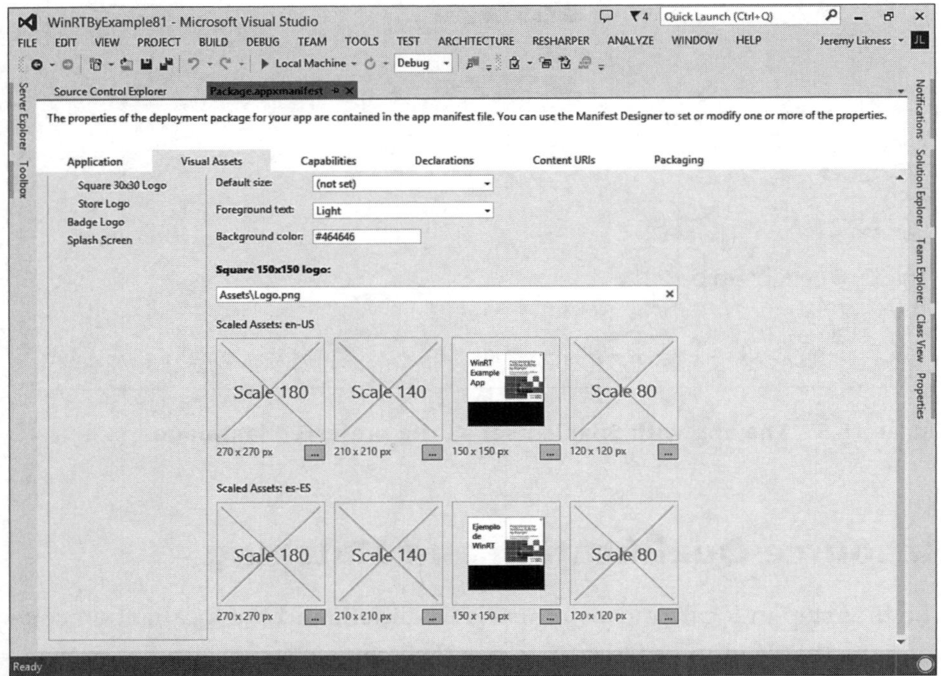

FIGURE 18.6 Visual assets for a localized app

Notice that the asset for the 150x150 logo is referred to by a path without the locale (`Assets\Logo.png`), but the correct scale and language version are picked up based on the folder convention. A filename can contain an extension for both scale and language. Notice the two rows, one for each locale that was detected. Likewise, the image for the flag is referenced like this in `Main.xaml`:

```
<Image Source="Images/flag.jpg" Width="300" Height="100"/>
```

It is typical to name folders using the language tag itself (as in `en-US`), but you can also prefix it with `lang-` or `language-` (as in `lang-en-US` or `language-es`). For filenames, you must prefix the language code. This means that `images.en.png`, for example, will *not* resolve; it must be named `images.lang-en.png` or `images.language-en.png`.

The locale is added at runtime and is based on the user's preferences. If the user's preferred languages are not found in the path or the filename, the default language is used instead. Windows uses sophisticated language-matching algorithms to find the appropriate language. For example, it can detect regional variations (such as United States English compared to British English) and match a regional variation over a completely different language. So although you can mark resources with the less specific `en` or `es` tag, it's not necessary to "catch all." If you localize to United States English and the user's preference is British English, Windows will still find the correct assets for the closet match. A full list of language subtags is available online.[3]

Localizing XAML Elements

Only two steps are necessary to localize your XAML elements. The first is to provide them with an app-wide unique identifier known as a `UID`. This identifier is separate from the `Name` property that can be used to refer to instances of XAML elements in code-behind. The `Name` property may be duplicated between different pages, but the `UID` should not. Consider an example from the `Main.xaml` file:

```
<TextBlock x:Uid="Header" Text="Placeholder"
    Style="{StaticResource HeaderTextBlockStyle}"/>
```

Notice that the `TextBlock` element doesn't have a name. It doesn't need one if it isn't going to be referenced by code-behind or by an `ElementName` binding. Although the `Text` property is set, this shows only in the designer. The value is replaced by the actual localized text during the runtime. Where does the localized text come from?

The answer is a special **Resources** file. Figure 18.7 shows an example of adding the file to the project. Although the name does not matter because

[3]Language subtag registry, http://bit.ly/1gbhste

Visual Studio automatically scans for resources when the app is compiled, typical practice is to keep the default name and place it within a folder by locale. In the example project, the locale folders for resources are placed under a top-level `Culture` folder. Another common name for this folder is `Strings`, to indicate that it contains the translated text.

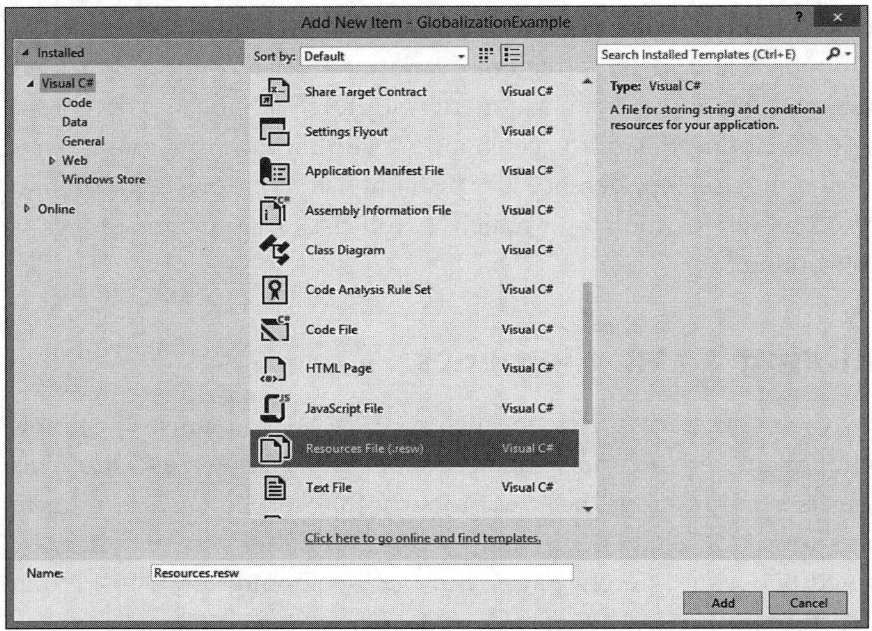

FIGURE 18.7 Adding a Resources file

Double-click one of the files to edit it. You should see something similar to Figure 18.8, the English version of the resources. Notice that several conventions are used in the **Name** column. For XAML elements, you specify the UID followed by the property. A feature of localization in Windows Store apps is that you can set various properties on controls by locale. Although it is recommended that you build a UI that scales naturally, you can specify properties such as `Length` and `Width` in your Resources file. In this example, the `Header` control is given a `Text` property with a value of `Example of Globalization in a Windows Store App`, and the `Width` is set to 600. If you run the app with Spanish set as your preferred language, the `Width` property is set to 800 and allows more text before wrapping the heading.

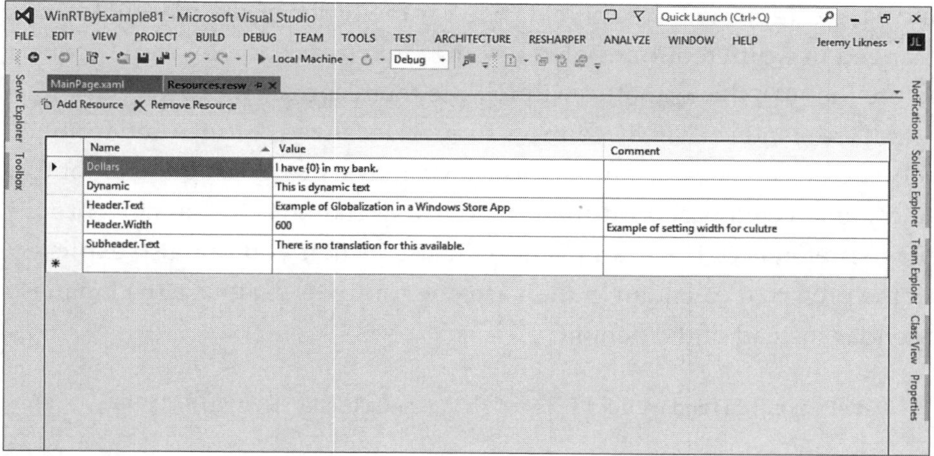

FIGURE 18.8 The resources editor

Windows handles all the mapping for you. When a control is encountered with a `UID`, the resource files included in the project are scanned for the preferred language. Entries that map the resource name and property are referred to as *scopes*. For example, `Header.Text` is a scope because it specifies a property on a control with the `UID` of `Header`. An entry without a property is referred to simply as a resource. `Dollars` and `Dynamic` are both examples of resources.

Resources can be programmatically referenced using the `ResourceLoader`. In the `OnNavigatedTo` method of the `Main.Xaml.cs` code-behind file, you can see an example of retrieving the current `ResourceLoader` instance and retrieving an entry. The call automatically resolves to the most qualified value based on the user's language preferences. If you don't pass a string, it defaults to a file named `resources`. If you name your resource file something different, pass the name as a string.

```
var loader = ResourceLoader.GetForCurrentView();
DynamicText.Text = loader.GetString("Dynamic");
```

Programmatic access is especially useful when you need to prepare dynamic text. `String.Format` is useful for applying parameters to portions of the localized text that can change. Although different translations might reorder verbs and nouns, you use the same placeholders, such as `{0}` and `{1}`, to represent the content. Even if the order of the placeholders is changed in a different translated resource text (for example, the `{1}` comes before the `{0}`), the formatter will replace them correctly.

All the standard XAML controls support localized cultures and formats. The `DatePicker` control automatically displays the appropriate months, dates, and years based on the calendar associated with the current language preference. The example app illustrates that you can also explicitly set the preferred calendar. In this case, the control is set to use the Japanese calendar instead of the default.

```
<DatePicker CalendarIdentifier="JapaneseCalendar" Margin="10"/>
```

If you want to support a different flow direction based on language preference (such as right to left), you should set up a `UID` at the `Page` level. This enables you to specify the `FlowDirection` scope in the resources file for the appropriate language. For example, if your page has a `UID` of `MainPage`, you can set `MainPage.FlowDirection` to `RightToLeft` for languages that flow in the reverse direction from English. This is inherited by child controls on the same page.

Formatting Dates, Numbers, and Currencies for Locale

The `Windows.Globalization` namespace provides special classes for formatting currencies and dates. In the example app, you see the use of the `NumberFormatting.CurrencyFormatter` to format a number as local currency.

```
var currencyFormatter = new CurrencyFormatter(
Windows.System.UserProfile.GlobalizationPreferences.Currencies[0]);
Currency.Text = string.Format(currencyText,
    currencyFormatter.Format(CurrencyValue));
```

The user's preferences are scanned to get the most preferred currency, and then the formatter obtains a string value that represents the currency in that locale. The text is then injected into a dynamic string that was loaded previously from the `ResourceLoader` to display to the end user.

You can also enumerate currencies and pass your own currency to the formatter if you want to format and display currencies for a specific locale. To format either decimals or percentages, use the `DecimalFormatter` and `PercentFormatter` classes, respectively (see the upcoming section "MVVM and Localization").

To format the date and time to the current locale, use the `DateTimeFormatter`:

```
var dateFormatter = new Windows.Globalization
    .DateTimeFormatting.DateTimeFormatter("shortdate");
Date.Text = dateFormatter.Format(DateTime.Now);
```

The example app outputs a sample date and time using the short formats. Some common templates include the short and long formats for date and time, respectively. You can also combine a specialized "template grammar" to create your own format. The syntax and rules for the grammar are available in the remarks section of the `DateTimeFormatter` documentation.[4]

MVVM and Localization

Although most of the example app is loaded through the code-behind for the main page, there is also a `ViewModel` class. This demonstrates how you can globalize your viewmodels. In most cases, the best practice is to use implementations of `IValueConverter` to convert raw values for display. Sometimes you need to dynamically load and format text, and you want to do this in the viewmodel. Fortunately, a viewmodel has access to the same globalization tools as the rest of your app.

The example app defines a few properties to capture the `ResourceLoader` class, the user's language preferences, and the user's home geographic region:

```
private readonly ResourceLoader resourceLoader;
private readonly string geographicRegion;
private readonly IReadOnlyList<string> languages;
```

During design time (when `DesignMode.DesignModeEnabled` is true), you can set these to predefined values in the constructor:

---

[4]DateTimeFormatter class, http://bit.ly/1nuYI95

```
this.resourceLoader = new ResourceLoader("Resources");
this.geographicRegion = "US";
this.languages = new[] { "en-US" };
```

During runtime, the user's preferences are queried and stored:

```
this.resourceLoader = ResourceLoader.GetForCurrentView();
this.geographicRegion = Windows.System.UserProfile
    .GlobalizationPreferences.HomeGeographicRegion;
this.languages = Windows.System.UserProfile
    .GlobalizationPreferences.Languages;
```

With these values, the exposed `FormattedNumber` property can create the formatters for decimal and percentage:

```
var decimalFormatter = new DecimalFormatter(
    this.languages, this.geographicRegion);
var percentageFormatter = new PercentFormatter(
    this.languages, this.geographicRegion);
```

When the formatters are initialized, the viewmodel can retrieve the text from the resource, use `String.Format` to replace the formatted values, and return the result for data-binding to the UI.

```
return string.Format(
    this.resourceLoader.GetString("FormattedNumber"),
    decimalFormatter.FormatDouble(Number),
    percentageFormatter.FormatDouble(Number));
```

Note that this example works because the `ViewModel` class is created as part of the visual tree in the XAML markup. If you create the `ViewModel` class outside of a view, you need to expose a property for the `ResourceLoader` and set it from within the view's code-behind. If you are not on the UI thread, the call to `GetCurrentForView` will fail.

Multilingual Toolkit

You can use the Multilingual App Toolkit[5] to help streamline localization of your apps. It integrates directly with Visual Studio. Using the toolkit, you can manage translation files for your app, as well as generate a

[5]Multilingual App Toolkit, http://bit.ly/1g8WUSF

"pseudolanguage" that helps identify issues with localization and translation. The toolkit manages the languages used in your app and also provides a workflow to translate resources. It even offers machine translation for a "rough guess" on a starting point for translators to review.

The following walkthrough demonstrates basic use of the multilingual toolkit and assumes that you have already downloaded and installed it. For more advanced scenarios, you can follow the documentation online. The solution has no example project because all steps are outlined. To begin, create a new project using the **Blank App (XAML)** template. Add a `StackPanel` and two `TextBlock` elements inside the grid in `MainPage.xaml`:

```
<StackPanel Orientation="Vertical" Margin="10">
    <TextBlock Text="Placeholder for Heading" x:Uid="Heading"
            Style="{StaticResource HeaderTextBlockStyle}"/>
    <TextBlock Text="Placeholder for Subheading" x:Uid="Subheading"
            Style="{StaticResource SubheaderTextBlockStyle}"/>
</StackPanel>
```

Don't forget the `Uid` attributes! Next, create a folder at the root level for English resources, and name it `en-US`. Add a `Resources.resw` file to the folder and create two resources, as in Table 18.1. Run the app to confirm that your resources are being used. You might want to comment out the diagnostics code in `App.xaml.cs` to avoid seeing the performance counters.

Table 18.1 Resources

Name	Value
`Heading.Text`	`This is a multilingual application.`
`Subheading.Text`	`It was very easy to localize this software.`

Now you are ready to use the toolkit. Make sure that your project is selected in the **Solution Explorer** and that you are no longer in debug mode. Choose **Tools** and then **Enable Multilingual App Toolkit**. This creates a folder named `MultilingualResources` that hosts the industry-standard XML Localization Interchange File Format[6] (`.xlf`) files. These are files

[6]XLIFF 1.2 Specification, http://bit.ly/1mhqTx5

you can use to send to translation teams to help localize your content. By default, a file with the `qps-ploc` suffix is added for pseudocode.

Build the project. Any time you add new resources, you should build your solution so they are added to the translation files. When the app is done building, right-click the file under `MultilingualResources` and choose **Generate Machine Translations**. This automatically creates some values for testing. The pseudovalues use strange characters and pad the text to accommodate larger translation sizes; they are ideal for testing how the content will flow after translation. To test it, go into your **Languages** and add the pseudolanguage. The easiest way is to search for `qps-ploc` and add **English (qps-ploc)**. Be sure you move it to the top of your preferences; then build, deploy, and run the app. You should see something similar to Figure 18.9.

FIGURE 18.9 The pseudolanguage

Now you can add a real language to the app. Stop debugging, and choose **Project** and then **Add Translation Languages**. A dialog box opens with all the available languages (see Figure 18.10). Scroll down and check the top-level item listed as **Spanish [es]**. Click OK. This creates a new file in the `MultilingualResources` folder. By default, it copies over the English resources as a starting point for translation.

Double-click or tap on the new file. A new dialog box opens. It looks similar to the tool used to edit resources, but it includes several more options. For example, a status is associated with the resource so you can track its progress through a translation services workflow. For now, ensure that you are connected to the Internet, and click **Translate** in the ribbon bar and then **Translate All**. Microsoft's machine translation services translate all your resources. You will see the source English and the translated Spanish in the next column, as shown in Figure 18.11. The status changes to **Needs Review** so that you can verify the text with someone fluent in the target language.

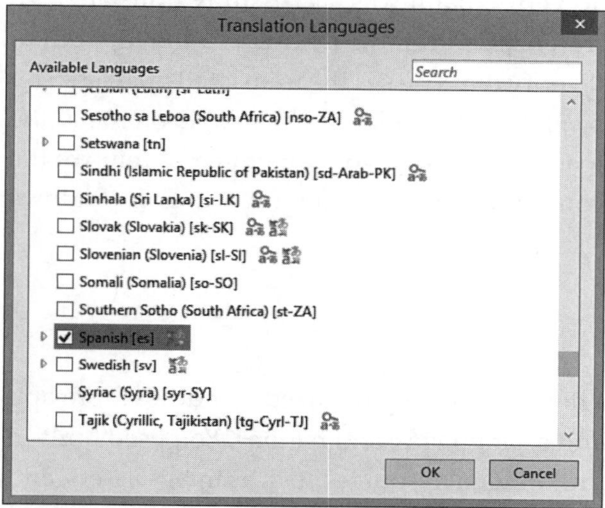

FIGURE 18.10 The Translation Languages dialog box

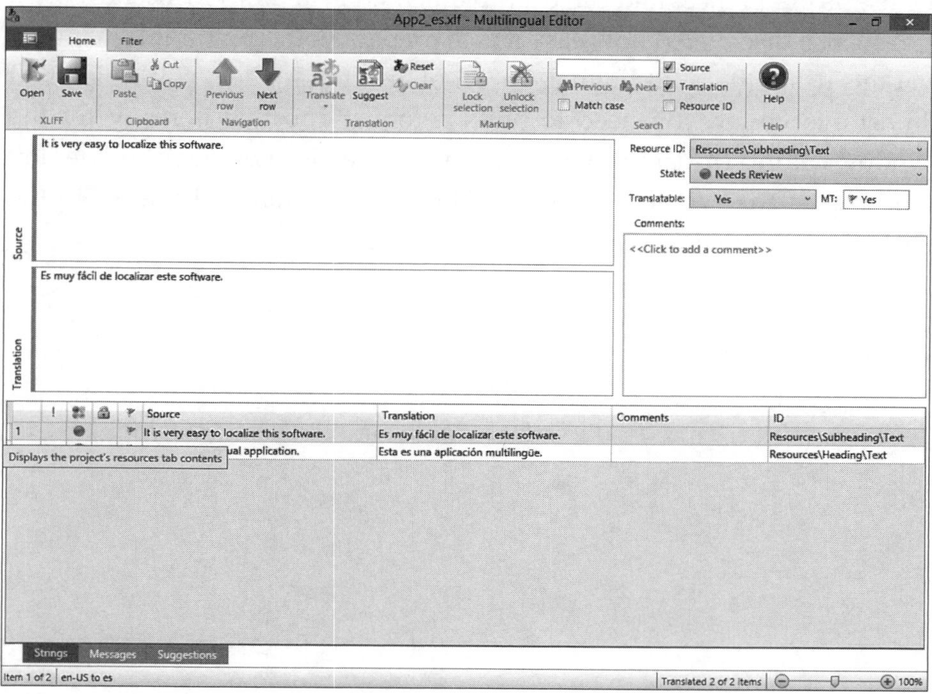

FIGURE 18.11 The Multilingual Editor after Spanish translation

That's all it takes to not only enable a new language for your app, but also take an initial pass at translation. Tap the **Save** icon in the ribbon bar to save the translated text. To verify that it was successfully translated, go back to your **Language Preferences** and move **Spanish** to the top. Build, deploy, and run the app, and verify that you see the translated Spanish. You can do a lot more with the toolkit, and tutorials are available online at the same site where you downloaded it. Be sure you remember to remove the pseudolanguage file from your app before you submit it to the Windows Store.

Summary

In this chapter, you learned how to build a globalized Windows Store app and localize it for target cultures, languages, and regions. You used built-in naming conventions to tag multilingual resources such as image assets, and you used the special resources files to include translations. Currency, time, and numeric formatters enable your app to display those values based on the user's preferences and can be implemented in an MVVM-friendly way.

You also discovered how easy it is to prepare your app for international markets using the Multilingual App Toolkit. At this stage, you've learned almost everything you need to build a robust app that is ready for the Windows Store. The last and most important step is to package and deploy your app to the Windows Store for final certification and release to the market; you learn how to do this in Chapter 19.

19
Packaging and Deploying

IN THE PREVIOUS CHAPTERS, YOU SAW THAT YOU HAVE MANY DIFFERENT OPTIONS at your disposal for including functionality in your app. You saw how to use different controls and layouts to build up your app's user interface, how to access data for the app to use, ways to integrate with built-in Windows features and installed devices, and how to include features related to accessibility, globalization, and localization to make your app available to the widest possible audience. However, regardless of how much of this functionality actually gets included in your app, at the end of the day, you need to be able to put your app into the hands of its intended users. This chapter discusses how to make that happen.

The first order of business is to address how your app is packaged for deployment. You will see how to go about generating an app deployment package, what is included in such a package, and the options that affect how the app deployment package creation process takes place.

This chapter then discusses how to deploy your app, focusing initially on the process for publishing your app package to the Windows Store. Several previous chapters have discussed functionality that depends on your app being associated with an entry in the Windows Store. In Chapter 6, "Tiles and Toasts," such an association was necessary to work with push notifications provided by the Windows Notification Service. In Chapter 7, "Connecting to the Cloud," integration with Windows Azure Mobile

Services and the Live Connect APIs also required the app to be associated with an entry in the Windows Store. You will learn how you can create this kind of entry for your app, along with other steps you must accomplish for your app to be published and made available through the Windows Store. Additionally, this chapter discusses other options for deploying your app via a process known as sideloading.

The chapter concludes with a discussion of some techniques for making money from your app. This includes options for adding trial modes to your app and supporting in-app purchases, as well as including in-app advertising.

Packaging Your App

Windows Store apps (whether or not they are deployed through the Windows Store itself) are deployed using a single file that contains all the components of the application. This file is known as the **app package**, and the file itself is basically a signed ZIP file with an `.appx` file extension. You can examine the contents of your app package files by renaming their file extensions to `.zip` and extracting their contents. App package files are digitally signed, and the digital signature is used along with a couple other security measures to ensure that neither the package nor its contents have been tampered with from the time they were built until the user runs them on their own machines. This contrasts with older deployment approaches that sometimes involved users copying files of dubious origin onto their disk drive, running these files, and hoping they weren't some kind of disguised malware.

Creating an App Package

Visual Studio provides the Create App Packages Wizard that walks you through the steps to collect the information it needs to generate the appropriate package for your app. To display this wizard, click the **Project** menu and then click **Store, Create App Packages** (alternatively, you can right-click your project in the **Solution Explorer** and select **Store, Create App**

Packages from the project's context menu). Figure 19.1 shows the Create App Packages Wizard.

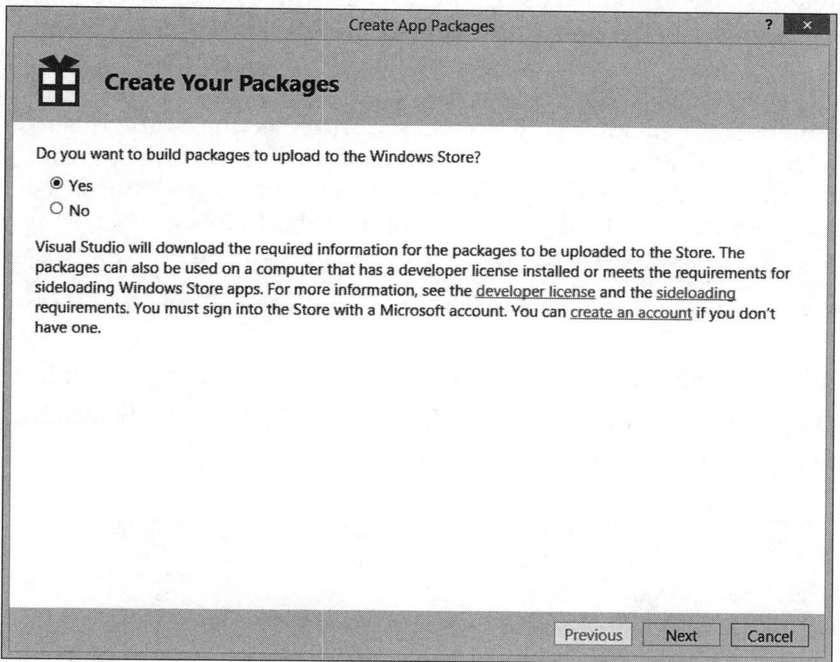

FIGURE 19.1 The Create App Packages Wizard

The first page in the Create App Packages Wizard determines whether the wizard should include steps related to publishing the app to the Windows Store. If you select Yes in this dialog box, the wizard shows a sign-in page where you can enter your Windows Store developer account credentials, followed by a page where you can choose whether to link your app with a previously reserved entry for an app in the Windows Store or to create a brand-new entry for the app to be linked to. As part of creating your app package, if the app has not yet been associated with the selected store entry, the app's manifest will be updated to reflect the association. The next section discusses in more detail this process and the options available.

NOTE

The same steps you follow using the Create App Packages Wizard are also provided in the Associate Your App with the Windows Store Wizard. You invoke this wizard by opening the **Project** menu in Visual Studio and then clicking **Store, Associate App with the Store** (or, alternatively, right-clicking your project file and selecting **Store, Associate App with the Store**). This wizard is useful for performing the store associations that are necessary for features such as push notifications or integration with Mobile Services and the Live Connect API when you're not ready to actually generate an app package.

Regardless of whether you choose to prepare your app for deployment to the Windows Store, the final page in the wizard is the Select and Configure Packages page (see Figure 19.2).

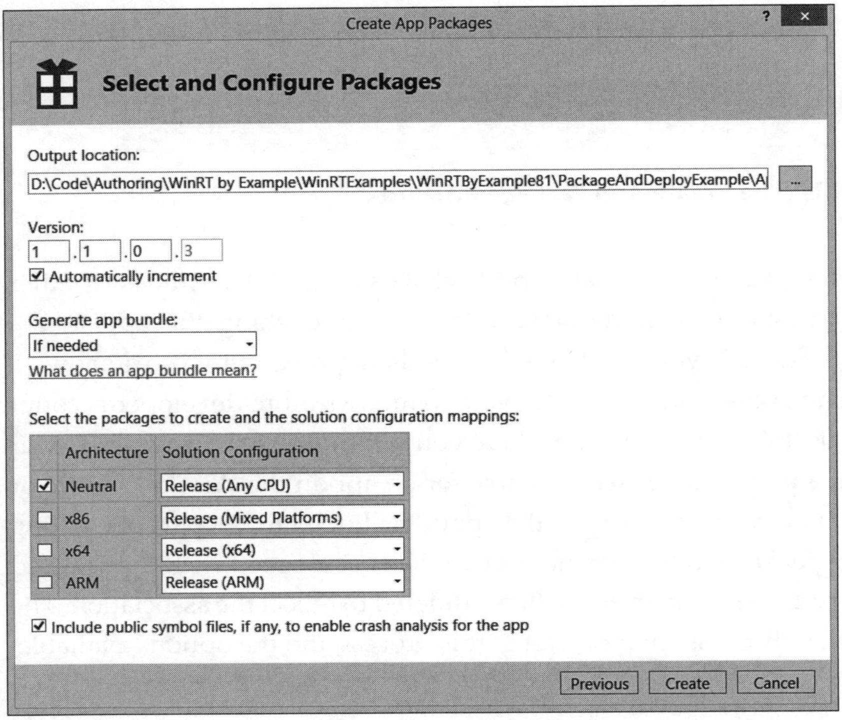

FIGURE 19.2 The Select and Configure Packages Wizard page

This page first includes an entry for the location on disk where the package will be created. It then provides you with several options that are initially based on settings specified in the app manifest's Packaging tab. These settings include the following:

- **The version number for the app package.** Note the option to automatically increment the value every time an app package is generated. If you have a version of your app that targets Windows 8.0, its version number must always be lower than the version number for the 8.1 edition. As a result, you need to be sure to leave enough space between version numbers to allow patches or revisions to the 8.0 edition if you will be continuing to support it.
- **Whether to generate an app bundle.** Options include Never, Always, and If Needed. The If Needed option generates a bundle if it detects any language-specific resources, image-scale options, or DirectX version-specific resources for which an optimized download experience might result if a bundle is created. The upcoming section "App Package and App Bundle Contents" discusses app bundles.
- **The specific processor architecture and build configuration to build with.** You can select Neutral for a package that is platform-agnostic for the app (as long as your app does not have any platform-specific dependencies). You can also create platform-specific packages that target the x86, x64, or ARM processor architectures. Note that you cannot create an app bundle that simultaneously targets a neutral architecture and other additional processor architectures.

The final option on this page involves whether to include debug symbol files in your package's upload file. Including these symbols in your app package makes it possible for the Windows Store to provide telemetry information about crashes that might occur in your app.

After you have set your desired package configuration options, you can click the **Create** button to have Visual Studio generate the package or packages based on your settings. When package creation completes, you see a link to the location where the package was created. You also have the option to run your app through the Windows Application Certification Kit to see if it complies with Windows Store submission requirements. The next section details this process as part of the larger discussion of the available app deployment options.

App Package and App Bundle Contents

The app package for your application includes your app's compiled executable and related assemblies, any content resources, the app manifest, and several files to validate that the app package contents have not been tampered with between the app's source and the system it is being deployed on. These latter files include the app package block map file (AppXBlockMap.xml), which includes cryptographic hash values for every file in your app, and the digital signature file, which ensures that neither the package nor its contents have been modified since they were signed.

In addition to using a basic app package to deploy your application, you can use an **app bundle** as an enhanced mechanism for delivering only the parts of an app that a given system requires. In a way, you can think of the app bundle as an optimized app package of app packages: It is basically a signed ZIP file with an appxbundle file extension and it contains one or more app package (.appx) files. Of these included package files, several application appx packages might include your app's compiled payload, as long as each one is targeting a unique processor architecture. The bundle might also include additional resource appx packages that contain information specific to a particular language, scale, or DirectX feature set but that do not contain any executable code themselves. Chapter 18, "Globalization and Localization," discussed the capability to include localized resources.

App bundles also include an app bundle manifest file (AppxBundleManifest.xml) that describes each package included in the bundle. Each package descriptor includes an indication of the type of package (application or resource), the target architecture (if it is an application package), and the information about the criteria that indicates the applicability of a given resource package, based on the language, resolution, or DirectX level it is intended to support. As with basic app packages, app bundle packages include a block map file and a digital signature file to verify the integrity of the bundle package and its contents.

The key advantage of app bundles is that only a subset of their contents is downloaded and installed on a target machine, based on matching the corresponding packages to the target machine's capabilities and settings. This results in deployments that require less space on end users' hard drives, as well as reduced download times for app installations, particularly when a lot of localized resources are to be included in the app deployment.

Package Identifier

Every app package includes a set of attributes that together define a unique identifier for the package, known as the **package identity**. Table 19.1 lists the attributes that make up the package identity. You can see the current values for these fields for your app by examining the Packaging tab in your app's manifest file.

TABLE 19.1 Components of the Package Identity

Attribute	Description
Name	The app package name. Typically not displayed to the end users. When Visual Studio creates an app, this is set to a GUID, although it can be overwritten with a string. When an app is associated with the Windows Store, this is changed to a concatenation of your publisher ID and the name with which the app was reserved in the store, truncated to 50 characters (minimum 3 characters).
Publisher	The publisher of the app, using the `Publisher` value from the certificate that signs the app package.
Version	The four-part version descriptor for the app package, using the standard format `major.minor.build.revision`. All four parts are required.

Attribute	Description
ProcessorArchitecture	The processor architecture that this package targets. Acceptable values include `x86`, `x64`, `arm`, and `neutral`. The `neutral` value indicates that the package can target all the other processor architectures. This value is present (and is required) only if the package contains executable code.
ResourceID	The type of UI resources contained in the package. This value is optional.

Generating a package for the `GlobalizationExample` example shown in Chapter 18 generates an app bundle that contains two packages. The first package contains the app payload itself, and the second package contains the specific resources to be used when the app is localized for the Spanish language. The XML declarations of the identifiers for each of these packages have been extracted from the `AppxManifest.xml` files contained in these packages; Listing 19.1 shows them.

LISTING 19.1 Package Identifiers in the GlobalizationExample Bundle

```
<!-- App Payload Package Identifier -->
<Identity
    Name="WinRTByExampleGlobalizationExample"
    Publisher="CN=Jeremy"
    Version="1.0.0.0"
    ProcessorArchitecture="neutral"/>

<!-- Spanish Resource Package Identifier -->
<Identity
    Name="WinRTByExampleGlobalizationExample"
    Publisher="CN=Jeremy"
    Version="1.0.0.0"
    ResourceId="split.language-es"/>
```

Note that the identifier for the app payload package includes values for `Name`, `Publisher`, `Version`, and `ProcessorArchitecture`. The Spanish resource package also contains `Name`, `Publisher`, and `Version`. However, instead of `ProcessorArchitecture` (because it does not contain any executable code), it includes a `ResourceId` value.

Deploying Your App

Two mechanisms exist for deploying Windows Store apps. As the "Windows Store app" name implies, you can deploy an app by publishing it to the Windows Store, where users can go to find the apps they are interested in and have them installed onto their systems. This is the normal and most common way to deploy these applications. The second option is known as **sideloading;** it refers to applications obtained outside the Windows Store process.

Publishing Your App in the Windows Store

Getting your app published in the Windows Store involves a few steps. First, you need to obtain a developer account to identify you as the author of the app. Next, you must provide the necessary information to the Windows Store about the app you intend to publish. Finally, you need to ensure that your app passes the Windows Store certification process before it is made available to end users. This section examines each of these steps.

Developer Accounts

To publish your app to the Windows Store, you first need to purchase a developer account. These accounts are associated with a Microsoft Account and are used to associate applications with publishers. They also coordinate app payouts for apps that are sold through the Windows Store or for apps that provide additional features that users can purchase at an extra cost (known as in-app purchases) and the app developer has elected to use the Windows Store to broker the process. Developer accounts must be renewed annually. You can sign up for a developer account at http://j.mp/WindowsStoreSignUp or by opening the **Project** menu from Visual Studio and selecting **Store, Open Developer Account**.

Two kinds of developer accounts exist: individual accounts and company accounts. In most cases, you obtain an individual account. Company accounts have increased access to app capabilities, including the `enterpriseAuthentication` capability, which enables apps to programmatically access remote servers and other corporate intranet resources by logging in with the current user's Windows credentials; the `sharedUserCertificates` capability, which allows apps to access hardware and software certificates; and the `documentsLibrary` capability, which gives an app programmatic access to the user's Documents folder without requiring the use of a file picker. (Note that additional guidelines beyond just the use of a company account restrict the approval of apps that intend to use these capabilities.[1]) Company accounts are also eligible to publish "traditional" desktop apps in the Windows Store. However, company accounts are also more expensive, and obtaining one requires additional verification steps to ensure that you are actually authorized to represent the company the account is issued for.

When you have a developer account, you can access your Windows Store dashboard at https://appdev.microsoft.com/storeportals/. The dashboard enables you to manage the apps you have published, as well as any app names that you have reserved but for which you have not yet published an app package. You can also reserve new app names from the dashboard (the next section discusses reserving an app name).

Before you publish apps to the Windows Store, make sure you look over the Windows Store App Developer Agreement, published at http://j.mp/WindowsStoreDeveloperAgreement. This document outlines the relationship that you, as a developer, have with Microsoft and the Windows Store as the publishers of your content.

Preparing Your App to Be Published

When you have a developer account set up, you are ready to go through the steps involved in publishing an app to the Windows Store. The Windows Store dashboard is set up to guide you through these steps, outlined in Table 19.2.

[1]App capability declarations (MSDN), http://j.mp/AppCapabilities

TABLE 19.2 Steps Involved in Publishing an App to the Windows Store

Step	Description
Reserve the app name	Indicate the name for the app in the store. This must be unique throughout the entire Windows Store catalog. An app can have additional names for different languages.
Specify selling details	Specify the information related to how the app is sold: • The cost of the app. • Whether the app supports trial modes. • Whether the app uses a third-party commerce system for in-app purchases or uses the Windows Store system (if at all). • The markets in which the app should be made available. • The earliest release date for the app. • The Windows Store listing category and subcategory information. • Hardware requirements for the app, such as minimum DirectX level and minimum system RAM. • Whether the app has been designed for accessibility.
Identify external service usage	Tie into Windows Azure Mobile Services and define any in-app purchase offers that your app will provide through the Windows Store purchase management system.
Set the app age rating	Set the minimum age rating for the app and upload any game rating information or certificates (this step is required for game deployment to some countries). Note that apps available for ages 3 to 12 *cannot* access online services, collect personal information, or access microphones or webcams.
Describe uses of cryptography	Indicate whether your app uses cryptography or encryption, to ensure that the app complies with appropriate laws about exporting those kind of technologies.
Upload app packages	Upload the packages you have prepared that contain your app content. Packages uploaded to the store must include content built in Release mode, or they will fail the technical certification portion of the app publication process.

Step	Description
Set the app description information	Provide the information that the Windows Store uses to display your app: • A text description of the application's functionality. (Required) • A listing of the key features the app includes. (Optional) • Screenshots of the app in action and related captions. At least one screenshot is required. Note that the app simulator includes a Copy Screenshot button that is ideally suited to the task of capturing screenshots for your app. • Additional notes about the app (often used to include information about features included or issues addressed in the most recent update). (Optional) • Listing of recommended hardware configurations. (Optional) • Keywords to use when searching for the app (not shown to customers). (Optional) • Copyright text to display to users. (Required) • Images to use when the app is featured in Windows Store promotions. (Optional) • URL of the web page that describes the app. (Optional) • Email address or URL where customers can obtain support for the app. (Required) • URL to your app's privacy policy text that describes how customer information will be used and protected. If your app supports more than one language, be sure to provide description information for each one supported, and make sure links point to properly localized content.
Provide notes to app testers	Provide any notes to be read by the testers who review the app to approve its inclusion in the Windows Store. You might want to include test username and password information for them to use if the app requires login information to access functionality or any special operating instructions.

As you work through the steps in the dashboard for your app, the dashboard interface indicates which steps are complete and which ones are incomplete, providing you with a checklist of the steps you must complete before publishing your application. Figure 19.3 shows this display of completed and in-progress tasks for the example app related to this chapter.

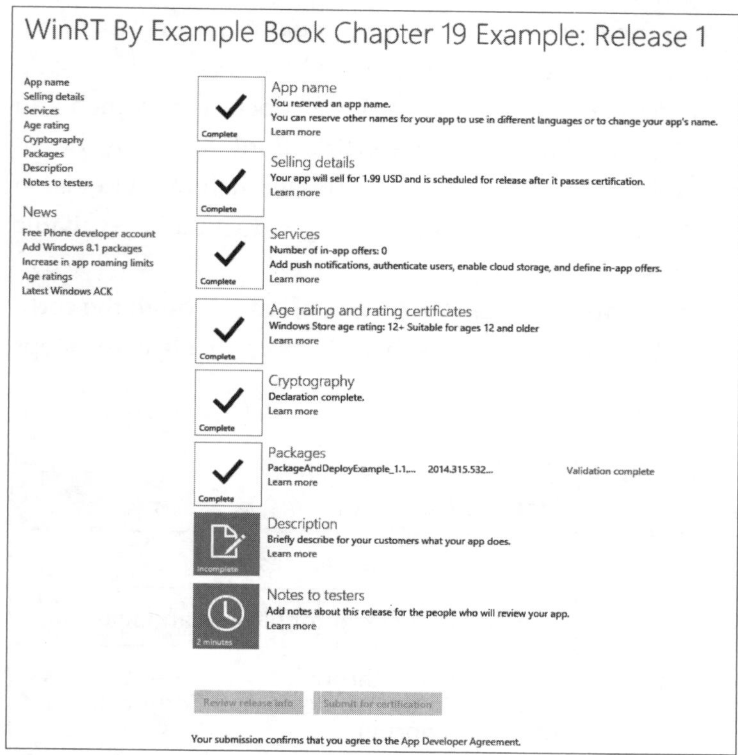

FIGURE 19.3 The Windows Store dashboard checklist

When you have completed all the steps, the **Review Release Info** and **Submit for Certification** buttons are enabled. The first button allows you to examine the values you have entered throughout the preparation process before submitting the app. The second button immediately submits the app for certification and approval.

Application Certification

Every app that is published to the Windows Store goes through a certification review process to ensure that the app is functional, does something useful, behaves in a predictable fashion, ensures that customers are in control of their private data, complies with the local restrictions for the markets it targets, and clearly states its intended functionality and target audience when the app package is submitted. This process is partly automated and partly manual; the manual testers have access to a set of notes that you can supply as the final step in the app preparation process.

The app certification requirements are published in the "App Certification Requirements for the Windows Store" document, which you can access at http://j.mp/WindowsStoreCertificationReqs. This document's contents change periodically, but the document includes a Revision History section and makes older versions of the document available through the document's archive link.

After you submit your app, you can track its progress through the certification process in the Windows Store dashboard. Table 19.3 lists the steps in the process.

TABLE 19.3 Application Certification Steps

Step	Description
Preprocessing	The app is queued for testing.
Security tests	The app is checked for viruses and malware.
Technical compliance tests	The app is run through the automated tests included in the Windows App Certification Kit (detailed shortly).
Content compliance	The app is manually tested to ensure that the content complies with the Windows Store policies.
Signing and Publishing	The app has passed testing, and its packages are digitally signed. At this point, the submission cannot be cancelled and the release date cannot be changed.

If the app fails to be certified, you receive a report indicating the reason for the failure so that you can take corrective actions and then resubmit the app.

Before you submit your app for certification testing, you can check for technical compliance by running it through the **Windows App Certification**

Kit (a.k.a. the WACK). You previously saw the WACK mentioned when you finished using the Create App Packages Wizard in Visual Studio and the Package Creation Completed dialog box appeared (see Figure 19.4). When the wizard completes, you are prompted to run your newly created package through the WACK to determine whether it is ready to be submitted to the Windows Store.

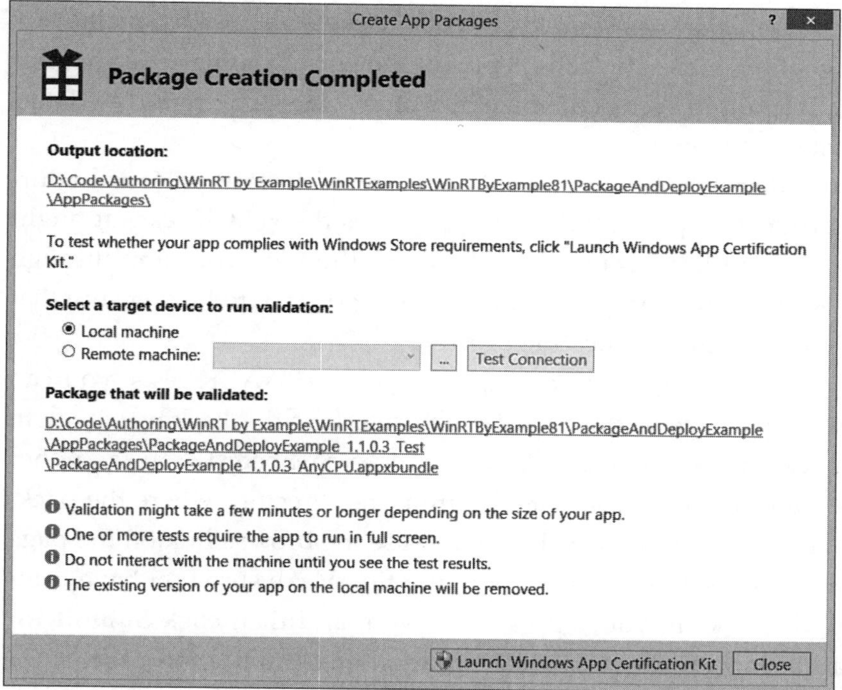

FIGURE 19.4 The Package Creation Completed dialog box, with the option to run the WACK

Note that simply passing the WACK tests does not guarantee that your app will be certified for publication to the Windows Store. Table 19.3 shows that technical compliance is only one of several compliance steps to pass.

You can also choose to run the WACK from the Windows Start menu by searching for the Windows App Cert Kit. You can download versions of the WACK onto other machines as well, including Windows RT systems, to test the app running on different hardware combinations.

If you run the WACK directly from the file system, you must select the app that it should analyze, whereas launching it from Visual Studio automatically selects the app you are building. In either case, you then have the opportunity to select which tests to run. After you select either all the tests or a subset of them, you click the **Next** button to start running the analysis. This can take several minutes, and the app might appear on your monitor multiple times throughout the process.

When the analysis has completed, you are presented with a dialog box indicating either successful completion of the tests or some error that has occurred. If a failure occurred, you can examine the result report to determine what went wrong.

Be aware that WACK testing is only one facet of the tests performed during the certification process; if your app passes the WACK tests, it might still fail store certification in some situations. Running your app through the WACK yourself is simply an important good start, to help ensure that it is ready to pass the certification process.

After you have adjusted your app to pass the WACK tests, you can upload your package to the app store by selecting the **Packages** page in your application's entry in the Windows Store dashboard. You can either drag the appropriate `.appxupload` files from the directory where the package was generated onto the web page, or use the browse link on the page to search for and select the corresponding file. Make sure you have completed all the tasks in your app's dashboard, and then click **Submit for Certification** to start the official certification and publication process for your app. You can return to the dashboard page to see your app's certification status. If your app fails certification, you can see the reason why, remedy the situation, and then repackage, reupload, and resubmit the corrected app.

When your app passes certification, the Windows Store checks to see whether an earliest publication date has been set. If it has, the app remains on hold until that date is met. If no earliest publication date was set or the date has passed, the app moves to the signing and release process. During this process, the app is signed with a Windows Store certificate that is chained to a root certificate included in the Trusted Root Certification

Authorities certificate store for Windows 8 deployments. At the conclusion of this step, the entry for your app is included (or updated) in the Windows Store.

Other Deployment Options

For many line-of-business (LOB) scenarios, publishing your app to a public store is neither desirable nor permissible. In these cases, a mechanism is needed for privately distributing these apps. Windows Store apps support this deployment model through a technique known as sideloading. However, to preserve some of the assurances related to the security and trustworthiness of these new Windows Store apps that use the Windows Runtime, this process has some restrictions; it is not as simple as old-fashioned XCopy-based deployment.

The primary restriction related to sideloading Windows Store apps involves the configuration of the operating system on which it is running. To deploy an app to a system via sideloading, one of the following conditions must be met:

- The machine must have Windows 8.1 and a developer license installed. You generally won't want to purchase and install developer licenses throughout your entire enterprise, so this mainly is useful for developers to be able to run and test sideloaded applications on different machines. Note that developer licenses applied to a machine require periodic renewal, making them even less worthwhile for consideration as a deployment tool other than for development and testing scenarios.
- The machine must be running Windows 8.1 and be joined to a domain that has the Group Policy value Allow All Trusted Applications to Install set.
- The machine must be running Windows 8.1 and, if it is not domain-joined, it must have a Sideload Activation Key applied. You can purchase a Sideload Activation Key for $100 and apply it to any number of machines. For Microsoft customers who are members of certain Volume Licensing programs, these keys are provided free of charge.

Additionally, the machine on which the app is being sideloaded must trust the certificate used to sign the app. The temporary certificate that Visual Studio generates by default when the project is created won't likely be adequate for this task. Furthermore, because the app is not being published to the Windows Store, the store-generated certificate trusted by Windows 8 installations is not an option. Instead, you should use a certificate specific to the enterprise to sign the app by clicking the **Choose Certificate** button in the Packaging tab of your app's manifest file and selecting the appropriate certificate. The enterprise IT team/process should ensure that machines that will be running apps signed with this certificate are configured to trust it by ensuring that the certificate is chained to a trusted root certificate.

Finally, the app can be deployed to the end-user machines using one of three available mechanisms. First, you can deploy sideloaded apps using the Microsoft System Center[2] configuration management tool. Second, you can use the Windows Intune[3] device-management service to deploy sideloaded applications. Finally, you can sideload applications using a PowerShell cmdlet.

Only the Microsoft System Center and Windows Intune options provide the capability to continue to manage an app after it has been deployed, performing actions such as automatically applying app updates or automatically uninstalling apps from one or more machines for either security or support reasons. Microsoft System Center and Windows Intune are elaborate device-management tools, and a more thorough discussion is beyond the scope of this book. Table 19.4 includes links to resources that detail the steps required to sideload Windows Store apps using these tools.

TABLE 19.4 Tools Available for Publishing an App to the Windows Store

Tool	Link
Microsoft System Center Configuration Manager	http://j.mp/SideloadingWithSystemCenter
Windows Intune	http://j.mp/SideloadingWithWindowsIntune

[2]http://technet.microsoft.com/systemcenter

[3]http://technet.microsoft.com/intune

In addition to using these device and configuration management tools, you can deploy Windows Store apps directly to a machine by using the PowerShell `Import-Module` cmdlet, which is part of the `appx` module. To deploy an app with this cmdlet, open PowerShell, navigate to the folder that contains the application package (`.appx` file) to be deployed, and run the following commands:

```
Import-Module appx
Add-AppxPackage "file name of appx package file to be deployed"
```

> **NOTE**
>
> When you use Visual Studio to create an app package, the resulting folder includes a PowerShell script titled `<app-name>.ps1` (where `app-name` is the name of your app). This script is not meant to deploy the app to end-user machines; it is provided to let developers easily deploy the app on different machines for development and testing purposes. Among other issues, this script file prompts users to acquire a developer license and can also notify them that they need to install the app's certificate. Feel free to examine the contents of this file when preparing your own deployment script, but be aware that this file involves steps that you will most likely not want to include as part of your own deployment process.

Making Money with Your App in the Windows Store

Many different business models surrounding apps are being made available to consumers through app stores such as the Windows Store. In some cases, making the app freely available to end users might be ideal. In other cases, you might be interested in trying to make some money from the app's publication or use. This section focuses on some of the tools available for apps that are being published to create some kind of revenue stream for the publisher.

The Windows Store and Microsoft's pubCenter advertising portal offer three primary ways to make money from an app published in the Windows

Store. The first is by selling the app itself so that the end user must pay for use of the app. This includes apps that are initially offered in some kind of trial mode but that then must be upgraded to full status within a particular time window or in order to access the app's full feature set. The second option for making money from a Windows Store app is through the use of in-app purchases. Users can opt to pay for additional pieces of app functionality throughout the lifetime of the application. The final technique is to use in-app advertisements. Ads are placed within the viewing area of the app, and a payout to the publisher is determined based on the number of times ads are viewed and the number of times users click on the ads to learn more about their content.

Note that publishers can combine elements of these three techniques within a single application. In fact, it is not uncommon to find apps that include trial modes that display advertisements until users buy the full-featured version of the app.

Be aware that these three tools discussed in this chapter are not the only techniques at your disposal for making money from an app published through the Windows Store. Additional examples include content subscription services, third-party in-app purchase tools, and third-party ad providers, among many others.

The Example App

The **PackageAndDeployExample** project included in the source code for this chapter provides examples for the different kinds of revenue-generating approaches you can include in your Windows Store apps. The app supports being configured simulate the app's inclusion in the Windows Store with two distinct profiles. The first profile is an app that provides a non-expiring trial mode that can be upgraded to full functionality. The second profile is an app that does not include a trial mode but does include support for in-app purchases. The app includes buttons for switching between these profiles.

The main body of the app displays information about the app's store listing as indicated by the currently selected profile, as well as the app's current license status. (Note that toggling profiles resets the app's licensing status.) When the app is configured with the trial-mode profile and is in trial mode, the app indicates the trial expiration date (if there is one) and includes a button to upgrade the app to the fully functional mode.

When the app is configured with the full-mode profile, it displays a list of products that are available for in-app purchase. A combo box allows one of these items to be selected for a simulated purchase. Any in-app purchased items display alongside the rest of the license information in the app.

Finally, the app is set up to display two differently sized advertisements when it is running in trial mode. When the app is no longer in a trial mode, either after upgrading the trial to the full version of the app or by starting with the full profile, the advertisements no longer appear.

Pricing Your App in the Windows Store

Apps published in the Windows Store are available in more than 200 countries and regions throughout the world. Apps can be made available for free or can be sold at one of various fixed pricing tiers, ranging from $1.49 through $999.99 (U.S. dollars), including these:

- $1.49–$4.99 at $.50 intervals
- $4.99–$49.99 at $1.00 intervals
- $49.99–$99.99 at $5.00 intervals
- $99.99–$249.99 at $10.00 intervals
- $249.99–$999.99 at $50.00 intervals

The Windows Store App Developer Agreement spells out the split agreement between app publishers and Microsoft for transactions brokered by the Windows Store, including both app purchases and in-app purchases. The current agreement states that 70 percent of the revenue returns to the publisher until the app earns its first $25,000 in revenue. Above this value, the app publisher earns 80 percent of the revenue.

The earlier section "Preparing Your App to Be Published" discussed the steps involved in publishing your app to the Windows Store. One of those steps, specifying the selling details, mentioned several actions related to pricing your app and setting it up for trial modes and in-app purchases. In this step, you can select the price tier for your app (or specify that the app should be distributed free of charge).

Trial Mode Apps

In addition to specifying a price tier in the app's selling details step, you can establish a trial period for the app. Paid apps that include trial periods give your customers the opportunity to try before they buy, which might lead to your app seeing increased downloads and, subsequently, increased purchases. Although good descriptions, a wide assortment of screenshots, and a study of the existing customer reviews can help potential customers decide whether they want to buy an app, the capability to try it out themselves—either for a brief period of time or with a limited subset of the overall functionality—can go a long way toward helping them decide to spend their money. Therefore, it is strongly recommended that paid apps include some sort of trial mode functionality.

Options for specifying a trial mode in the Windows Store include choosing not to offer a trial; offering a trial that expires after 1 day, 7 days, 15 days, or 30 days from the date when the app is installed; and offering a trial that never expires. If an expiration time limit is chosen, the Windows Runtime enforces it; after an app's trial period has passed, the app will not launch until it is upgraded to a full version. For apps running in trial mode without expirations or ones whose trial period has not yet passed, the publishers decide and implement how their apps should reflect that trial experience to the end users and whether to alter or limit an app's functionality in some way based on the value of the `LicenseInformation` object (discussed shortly).

Inside your app, you use the static `CurrentApp` class provided by the Windows Runtime to obtain information about your app's listing in the Windows Store and to interact with the current licensing state of the app and any features that are eligible for in-app purchase. To access details about the app's listing in the Windows Store, the `CurrentApp` class provides `AppId` and `LinkUri` properties that provide the Windows Store–generated GUID for the app's entry in the catalog, as well as the URI to the app's listing page in the web version of the catalog. It also provides a

LoadListingInformationAsync method that obtains information about the app's listing in the store, including the app's Name, Description, AgeRating, CurrentMarket (which specifies the country code for the current user's location), and FormattedPrice (the app purchase price in the current market and its currency). Also included is a ProductListings value that contains a list of the available in-app purchasable content. The next section discusses product listings and in-app purchases further.

The CurrentApp class also provides a LicenseInformation property that returns an instance of the LicenseInformation class. This LicenseInformation instance includes the information about the current app license as it relates to the app being in a trial mode, as well as any in-app purchases. Your app will use the information the LicenseInformation instance provides to display the appropriate user experience based on whether your app is currently in a trial or full-feature mode. For example, when the example application is running in a trial mode, it features a dedicated button that allows the user to upgrade the app to full functionality simply by binding the IsEnabled property of the button to the value of the LicenseInformation IsTrial property:

```
<Button Content="Upgrade to Full"
        IsEnabled="{Binding LicenseInformation.IsTrial}"
        Command="{Binding UpgradeTrialCommand}"/>
```

The information the LicenseInformation class provides includes the IsActive property, which indicates whether the app license is active, meaning either that the app is running a full version or that a trial has not yet expired. This property is often used along with the IsTrial property, which indicates whether the app is currently running in trial mode. Finally, the ExpirationDate property is used for time-limited trials to indicate when the trial mode is set to expire for the app. The LicenseInformation class also includes a LicenseChanged event to notify the app when its license status has changed. The ExpirationDate value can also be checked in response to a LicenseChanged event to see if the app has expired while running; if so, application logic can react in a manner that makes sense depending on the nature of the app. You don't need to check the ExpirationDate value when launching an app; the Windows Runtime handles that for you.

By now, you might be wondering how it is possible to test this functionality in your app without actually waiting until you have submitted the app to the Windows Store. To accomplish this, the `CurrentApp` class is paired with the nearly identical `CurrentAppSimulator` class. From an API point of view, the two classes are identical, except that the `CurrentAppSimulator` class includes the `LoadListingInformationAsync` method, whose functionality is discussed shortly. The `CurrentAppSimulator` class works by using an XML proxy file to indicate the values it should return in response to the corresponding calls to the `CurrentApp` class. This XML file can be preinstalled to a specific storage location for the app to find, or you can use the `LoadListingInformationAsync` method to put a file of your choosing in the correct place on your behalf.

Turning to the example app, the code for working with the `CurrentApp` and `CurrentAppSimulator` has been put into the `DeploymentHelper` class for convenience. In this class, the app loads an XML proxy file based on the trial or full mode configuration specified in the app's user interface and then provides access to the listing and license information for the current app based on that information.

To accomplish this, the app first aliases the `CurrentAppSimulator` class to the `CurrentApp` name in a `using` statement wrapped in a `#if` precompilation directive (see Listing 19.2).

LISTING 19.2 Switching to Use the `CurrentAppSimulator` Class

```
#if DEBUG
using CurrentApp = Windows.ApplicationModel.Store.CurrentAppSimulator;
#endif
```

With that in place, calls that normally would be directed to the `CurrentApp` class are instead rerouted to the `CurrentAppSimulator` equivalents.

The example project includes several proxy XML files to simulate various application licensing states in the `WindowsStoreProxy` folder. For example, the `WindowsStoreProxy_Trial.xml` file indicates that the file is in a trial mode without an expiration date, whereas the `WindowsStoreProxy_Purchased.xml` file indicates that the file is running in full mode as if the user had purchased the app from the Windows Store. These Windows Store proxy files are used in the `DeploymentHelper` class's `LoadStoreProxyFile` method by locating the file within the current app package contents, creating a `StorageFile` reference to the file, and calling the `CurrentAppSimulator ReloadSimulatorAsync` method. With the desired XML file in place, a subsequent call to the `CurrentApp LoadListingInformationAsync` method returns the current app's Windows Store listing information.

The Windows Store proxy XML files are broken down into three sections. The first is the `ListingInformation` section. This section provides information about the app that proxies the app's entry in the Windows Store, including the app ID, link, current market, age rating, and market sales information, as well as any products that are configured to be available for in-app purchase. The `LicenseInformation` section provides the values for the app's current licensing status, such as whether the license is currently active, whether it is a trial mode, and when the trial is set to expire.

The final section details how the app simulation behaves. The simulation behavior is configured by setting the `SimulationMode` attribute of the `Simulation` element. When `Interactive` mode is indicated, the app displays a dialog box for requests to the `CurrentApp RequestAppPurchaseAsync` and `RequestProductPurchaseAsync` methods. In the dialog box, you can select whether each function call should complete successfully or you can indicate an error code that the function call should simulate. Figure 19.5 shows the dialog box and the available error codes for a call to `RequestAppPurchaseAsync`.

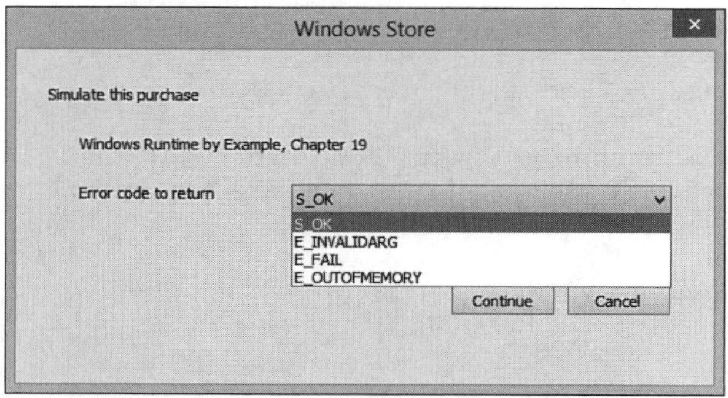

FIGURE 19.5 The simulated trial-mode upgrade dialog box

As an alternative to the behavior of the `Interactive` mode, `Automatic` mode can be indicated in the XML file. When `Automatic` mode is selected, no dialog boxes appear in response to `CurrentApp` requests. Instead, you can predefine `DefaultResponse` elements within the `Simulation` element that describe how to handle method calls. Supported methods for which `DefaultResponse` values can be provided include `LoadListingInformationAsync`, `RequestAppPurchaseAsync`, and `RequestProductPurchaseAsync`. For each method in which a `DefaultResponse` element is provided, the `HResult` value must be included to specify whether the method should complete successfully (by indicating an `HResult` of `S_OK`) or whether it should fail by returning the desired error code (for example, `E_FAIL`).

Listing 19.3 shows the Windows Store proxy XML file that is configured for trial mode support, similar to the one included in the example project. This file has been altered to set the Simulation mode to Automatic, and various `DefaultResponse` elements are provided.

LISTING 19.3 A `WindowsStoreProxy.xml` File for Automatic Simulations

```
<?xml version="1.0" encoding="utf-16"?>
<CurrentApp>
  <ListingInformation>
    <App>
      <AppId>CC6E9774-794C-44B4-9D31-15580C8258BF</AppId>
      <LinkUri>
        http://apps.windows.microsoft.com/app/
➥CC6E9774-794C-44B4-9D31-15580C8258BF
      </LinkUri>
      <CurrentMarket>en-US</CurrentMarket>
      <AgeRating>12</AgeRating>
      <MarketData xml:lang="en-us">
        <Name>Windows Runtime by Example, Chapter 19</Name>
        <Description>
          This example application demonstrates how to work with the
          Windows Store for trial mode and in-app purchase scenarios.
        </Description>
        <Price>1.99</Price>
        <CurrencySymbol>$</CurrencySymbol>
      </MarketData>
    </App>
  </ListingInformation>
  <LicenseInformation>
    <App>
      <IsActive>true</IsActive>
      <IsTrial>true</IsTrial>
```

```
    <!-- Uncomment the next line to simulate a time-limited trial -->
    <!--<ExpirationDate>2014-11-10T00:00:00.00Z</ExpirationDate>-->
  </App>
 </LicenseInformation>
 <Simulation SimulationMode="Automatic">
  <DefaultResponse MethodName="LoadListingInformationAsync_GetResult"
                   HResult="S_OK"/>
  <DefaultResponse MethodName="RequestAppPurchaseAsync_GetResult"
                   HResult="E_FAIL"/>
  <DefaultResponse MethodName="RequestProductPurchaseAsync_GetResult"
                   HResult="E_INVALIDARG"/>
 </Simulation>
</CurrentApp>
```

TIP

Although the provided Windows Store Proxy XML files include a reference to the `WindowsStoreProxy.xsd` schema file included in the project, the value is currently commented out. Including this schema declaration in the `CurrentApp` element provides design-time Visual Studio IntelliSense for editing the XML file. However, including the schema declaration when the file is used programmatically currently causes a runtime exception. In the interim, you can use the schema to help in making changes to these files by toggling the comments on the provided `CurrentApp` declarations when editing the file, then reverting to the original state when you are ready to run the app.

In-App Purchases

For some apps, it might make sense to allow users to enhance the app by purchasing additional content or functionality as they consume the app. Examples might include purchasing additional levels in a game or perhaps purchasing additional book or magazine content for a reader-style app. The Windows Store includes support for adding these kinds of in-app purchases, and they can be included with both free and paid apps. In addition to the Windows Store's own mechanisms, several third-party e-commerce services can add in-app purchases to your app. This section focuses only on the tools the Windows Store provides in concert with the Windows Runtime APIs.

Individual pieces of functionality that can be added to a Windows Store app via an in-app purchase are referred to as **products**. The set of available products your app can offer to its users is initially defined through the Services page in your app's Windows Store dashboard content. When you configure a product, you provide it with an ID value, which you can use to track the item for selection and purchase. You also select a price tier, which mirrors the values that were previously discussed for app pricing (including free). You indicate the lifetime for the purchase; you can choose to have it not expire by selecting the value Forever, or you can select an expiration lifetime ranging from one day through one year. Finally, you can optionally indicate a content type that describes the kinds of content included in this in-app purchase option. Be aware that after an app or an update that includes new products has been published for certification, those product IDs can neither be changed nor deleted. In addition to specifying these values when you define a product, you must provide a language-specific description for each product entry for each language that you intend to support within the Description page in the app's Windows Store dashboard entry.

You can retrieve the list of products available for your app by calling the `LoadListingInformationAsync` method provided by the `CurrentApp` or `CurrentAppSimulator` classes. The list is provided in the `ProductListings` property of the returned `ListingInformation` object, which makes the information available as a dictionary that is keyed by each product's ID. The `Name` value in each object returns the description you provided, localized to the current market that the app is running in, and the `FormattedPrice` value returns a textual representation of the price of the product, formatted and adjusted for the current market's currency and its value. You can use this value to let your users know how much the in-app purchase of the product costs.

Simulated product definitions for use by the `CurrentAppSimulator` are included as `Product` elements within the `ListingInformation` element in the XML file. Each `Product` element must include one or more `MarketData` elements that specify the product information for a specific language, including the name, price, currency symbol, and optional currency code for that language. Listing 19.4 shows an excerpt of the `ListingInformation` element that includes the configuration for the product definitions that will be displayed in the example app when the Full profile is chosen. In this case, the app will show two products available for in-app purchase, titled First Sample Product and Second Sample Product, each with a price of USD $5.99 and with ID values of `ID0` and `ID1`, respectively.

LISTING 19.4 Simulated In-App Purchase Product Listings

```
<ListingInformation>
  <App>
    <!-- Omitted for brevity -->
  </App>
  <Product ProductId="ID0" LicenseDuration="0">
    <MarketData xml:lang="en-us">
      <Name>First Sample Product</Name>
      <Price>5.99</Price>
      <CurrencySymbol>$</CurrencySymbol>
    </MarketData>
  </Product>
  <Product ProductId="ID1" LicenseDuration="0">
    <MarketData xml:lang="en-us">
      <Name>Second Sample Product</Name>
      <Price>5.99</Price>
      <CurrencySymbol>$</CurrencySymbol>
    </MarketData>
  </Product>
</ListingInformation>
```

To trigger the in-app purchase of a selected product, you must call the `RequestProductPurchaseAsync` method provided by the `CurrentApp` and `CurrentAppSimulator` classes with the ID of the product to be purchased. If the purchase is successful, the method returns an instance of the `PurchaseResults` class with a status value of `ProductPurchaseStatus.Success`.

The `ProductLicenses` property of the `CurrentApp` or `CurrentAppSimulator` `LicenseInformation` class provides details about the license status for complete in-app purchases. Similar to the `ProductListings` property, `ProductLicenses` is a dictionary that contains `ProductLicense` values indexed by the product ID. This makes it easy to check the license status for a particular product from your app. To do so, you simply see if the `ProductLicenses` value contains a key with the desired product ID value; if so, you can examine the `ProductLicense` value to determine the license's expiration date and see whether the license is currently active or expired.

You also can simulate pre-existing license purchases in the Windows Store proxy XML file. To do so, you can include `Product` elements within the `LicenseInformation` element. The `Product` element should specify the desired ID in its `ProductId` attribute, state whether the license is active, and give the expiration date for the license. Listing 19.5 shows an excerpt of the `LicenseInformation` element that is displayed in the example app when the Full profile is chosen. The included `Product` element indicates that the product with ID `ID0` has been purchased and that its license status is active.

LISTING 19.5 Simulating Purchased In-App Purchase Products

```
<LicenseInformation>
  <App>
    <IsActive>true</IsActive>
    <IsTrial>false</IsTrial>
  </App>
  <Product ProductId="ID0">
    <IsActive>true</IsActive>
  </Product>
</LicenseInformation>
```

In addition to simulating pre-existing in-app purchases, the `CurrentAppSimulator` includes support for the `SimulationMode` setting. As in the call to `RequestAppPurchaseAsync`, the call to `RequestProductPurchaseAsync` respects the indicated mode value. When the mode is set to `Interactive`, calling this method displays a dialog box that enables you to indicate the success or error code to be returned. When the mode is set to `Automatic`, it returns the `HResult` value contained in the `DefaultResponse` element with the `MethodName` of `RequestProductPurchaseAsync_GetResult`.

Including Advertisements

In addition to monetizing apps through purchases, trial mode upgrades, and in-app purchasing, another common way to earn money from an app is to include advertisements inside the app. You can include ads in your application by making use of the **Microsoft Advertising SDK for Windows 8.1,**[4] which works with Microsoft's **pubCenter**[5] advertising platform. These

[4]Ads in Apps for Windows 8, http://adsinapps.microsoft.com

[5]Microsoft pubCenter, http://pubcenter.microsoft.com

tools work together to determine which specific ads should be shown in your app and to track ad viewing and click-throughs.

> **TIP**
>
> The terms specified in the Windows Store App Developer Agreement do not mandate that you use the Microsoft Advertising SDK and pubCenter tools to display ads in your app. In fact, you can use any ad display tool of your choice. For example, one popular alternative ad provider that has published an SDK for Windows Store apps is AdDuplex (www.adduplex.com); creating a custom ad system also is certainly possible. However, regardless of the tool you use, you still must ensure that your app meets the certification and privacy requirements for apps to be sold through the Windows Store. This chapter focuses exclusively on using the Microsoft Advertising SDK because it is normally included in Visual Studio 2013.

pubCenter Configuration

The first step in putting ads from pubCenter into your app is to set up the ads in pubCenter. Open your web browser to the pubCenter website, at http://pubcenter.microsoft.com, and either sign up for an account or sign in with an existing account if you have already signed up. Ads are configured in the site's Setup panel. From the Setup page, choose **Applications** to see the list of registered applications, and then click the **Register Application** button to create an application entry for your app. Provide a unique name for the app, indicate that it is a Windows 8 app in the Device Type drop-down list, and click the **Save** button to complete your app entry. This displays your app details page.

Now that you have your app configured, you need to configure ad units for your app. Ad units are associated with your app entry and specify information about the types of advertisements to display in your app. This includes the size of the advertisement, as well as metadata about your app and its intended audience that help pubCenter choose the ads to display in your app. Because ad revenue is computed based on a combination of the number of ads viewed and the number of ads users have clicked on, the better an app connects with your end users, the more likely they are to click on it, and the more revenue you can expect to receive from the ads placed in your apps.

In pubCenter, select the **Ad Units** entry from the Setup panel and choose the **Windows 8** application tab. Click the **Create Application Ad Unit** button to define a new ad unit for your application. On the Create a Windows 8 Application Ad Unit page, specify a name for the ad unit. The name is used only for reference within pubCenter and is not displayed to end users. Select the application, and then choose the size of ad to present for this ad unit. Available sizes include 728x90 (for banner-style ads), 300x600, 300x250, 250x250 (which is ideal for including in a layout that uses the default `GridView` template), and 160x600. You also need to specify the App Store category information that you will be using when you publish your app, which helps determine which advertisers supply ads to your app. Click the **Save** button to complete your ad unit entry. This displays a detailed summary for your new ad unit, including the application ID for your app and the ad unit ID for your ad unit. Copy these values from the page and put them somewhere you can find them later; you will need them in your application (you can always retrieve them later from the ad unit listing or the ad unit details pages).

Another option that you can set in pubCenter is a list of ad exclusion URLs. This enables you to define specific URLs for which your app should not show advertisements. You might use this feature, for example, to prevent pubCenter from using competitors' ads in your app. Including a URL on this page prevents ads that link to web pages that start with that URL value from appearing in applications that you define.

Including the Ad Control in Your App

To display ads in your app, you need to place and configure the `AdControl` component in your app's user interface. To access the `AdControl`, you need to add a reference to the **Microsoft Advertising SDK for Windows 8.1** assembly that is included in the **Windows Extensions** node in the **Reference Manager** in Visual Studio (see Figure 19.6). Alternatively, the `AdControl` should be included by default in an Advertising panel in the Toolbox pane when you have the XAML designer open in Visual Studio. If it is available, you can simply drag and drop the `AdControl` from the Toolbox either to your design surface or into your XAML markup content, and the appropriate reference is added for you. This drag-and-drop approach has the added benefit of including the appropriate XAML namespace declaration for you.

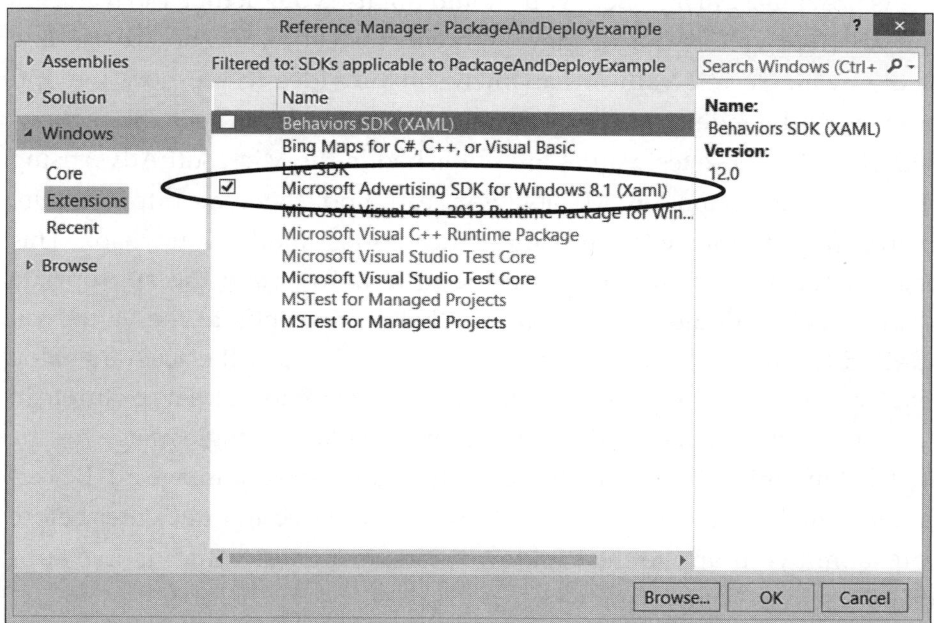

FIGURE 19.6 Including a reference to the Microsoft Advertising SDK

When you include this control in your app, you need to take two actions. First, you need to configure the `AdControl` with `ApplicationId` and `AdUnitId` values to specify what ad to display. For production, use the values that you obtained earlier from pubCenter. During development and testing, you want to use some well-known values instead; these values are discussed shortly. Second, you need to specify the `Width` and `Height` of the `AdControl` to match the values for the ad unit that you intend to use. Listing 19.6 shows the `AdControl` included in the example application.

LISTING 19.6 Including an AdControl in the Application User Interface

```
<ui:AdControl ApplicationId="d25517cb-12d4-4699-8bdc-52040c712cab"
              AdUnitId="10043055"
              Width="300" Height="250"/>
```

As previously mentioned, you should not use your actual ApplicationId and AdUnitId values during development. Instead, you should use one of the available test values that Microsoft provides to see how the app receives and renders advertisements and responds to user interactions with the ads. These test values are published in the Microsoft Advertising SDK documentation on MSDN; you can find them at http://msdn.microsoft.com/library/advertising-windows-test-mode-values.aspx. This page includes the ApplicationId value to use. To obtain the appropriate AdUnitId value, locate the ad unit size that corresponds to the value you selected for your ad unit in pubCenter and then select the AdUnitId value that corresponds with the user experience you want to test. The example in Listing 19.5 shows the 300x250 ad unit that displays a single image for the ad. Clicking this ad expands the ad to show a full-screen image ad. Be certain to switch these values back to the ones provided in pubCenter before you submit your app to the Windows Store; using test values in live apps keeps ads from being displayed.

To suppress the display of the advertisements for apps not running in Trial mode, you can simply toggle the Visibility property for the AdControl itself, or do the same for one of the container controls that includes the ads. In the example app, the StackPanel that houses the AdControl instances and the Advertisement titles is data-bound to the IsTrial property of the LicenseInformation value in the current viewmodel. A value converter converts between the Boolean IsTrial value and the corresponding value of the Visibility enumeration (the "Data-Binding" section of Chapter 3, "Layouts and Controls," covered value converters). When an update to the LicenseInformation value sets the IsTrial value to false, the advertisements are removed from the page. Listing 19.7 shows the markup for the StackPanel that contains a 300x250 ad unit.

LISTING 19.7 Controlling the Display of an Ad Based on the Current IsTrial Property Value

```
<StackPanel Grid.Row="99" Grid.Column="0" Grid.ColumnSpan="2"
            Margin="10"
            Visibility="{Binding LicenseInformation.IsTrial,
➥Converter={StaticResource IfTrueThenVisible}}">
    <TextBlock Text="Advertisement:" FontWeight="Bold"/>
    <ui:AdControl ApplicationId="d25517cb-12d4-4699-8bdc-52040c712cab"
                  AdUnitId="10043055"
                  Width="300" Height="250"/>
 </StackPanel>
```

You should be aware of a couple important restrictions when publishing an app that uses pubCenter and the Microsoft Advertising SDK. First, a section in the license agreement indicates specific text that you must provide in your app's privacy policy. Second, because the advertising control obtains information from the Internet, it is necessary to declare the Internet (client) capability in the app manifest for applications that include this functionality. This restricts the available age ratings for apps that include this advertisement technology to apps that have an age rating of at least 12+. Apps targeted to younger age groups may not include this capability (this network access restriction is called out in the Windows Store dashboard on the Age Rating page). You can find information about these requirements online in the Advertising SDK documentation.[6]

Summary

In this chapter, you learned about the options available to you for packaging your app for deployment. You saw the process involved in submitting your application for publication and distribution in the Windows Store, from obtaining a developer account through completing the final certification process for your app to be listed in the store. You also saw how you can deploy the app without using the Windows Store, through the process known as sideloading.

---

6 Microsoft Advertising SDK restrictions and requirements, http://msdn.microsoft.com/library/advertising-windows-eula.aspx

Additionally, you looked at three different approaches available for monetizing Windows Store apps, including offering upgradable trial modes, providing support for in-app purchases, and including advertisements using pubCenter and the Microsoft Advertising SDK.

In the next chapter, you explore several techniques to make your application as successful as possible. This includes exploring tools and techniques for tracking down defects in your applications and approaches you can take to minimize issues that need this kind of attention in the first place. You also explore several tools that help you better understand your application's performance characteristics, in an effort to identify and eliminate issues that impede your app's capability to delight its end users.

20 Debugging and Performance Optimization

ALTHOUGH MOST DEVELOPERS SHARE THE SAME GOAL OF PRODUCING perfect, fast, scalable code that is entirely free of defects, the reality is that bugs exist. The best time to find a defect is when you're writing the related code. It is far more difficult to triage a defect that you discover later in the development lifecycle or, even worse, that a customer discovers when the app is in production. Fortunately, Microsoft provides a powerful set of tools that enable you to both proactively improve the quality of your code and retroactively triage issues with a production application to track down the problem and provide a fix.

Many of the examples in this book began with the debugger, and you've already learned several ways to launch Visual Studio in debug mode to analyze your application. Now that you've learned about the various components that can go into an app and how to package and deploy your app to the Windows Store, it's time to cover more advanced techniques. In addition to exploring the tools you use to track down defects, this chapter shares how to use built-in utilities that help prevent defects from appearing in the first place. You also learn how to use Visual Studio to profile your app early and often to quickly identify potential performance bottlenecks and address them before they become an issue in production.

Understanding the Debugger

The Visual Studio debugger involves a lot more than pressing F5. In fact, Visual Studio uses several types of debuggers, depending on the type of project you are debugging. The default is usually fine, but in some cases, you need to debug a different type of code. For example, you might need to debug a native component in your app.

Native, Managed, and Script Debuggers

Open the **PrimeCheckerExample** project for this chapter. Navigate to `MainPage.xaml.cs` and place a breakpoint on line 39:

```
if (!checker.IsPrime(x))
```

You can either click the left margin or press **F9** while the cursor is on the line to set it. This statement uses a native WinRT component to determine whether the number passed in is a prime number. Press **F5** to start debugging. Click the **Compute Primes** button; the debugger should break on the statement, as in Figure 20.1.

Normally, pressing **F11** or the corresponding icon to step into the method takes you inside the `IsPrime` method. If you try it with this project, however, it simply steps over the statement. This is because the default debugger is for managed code only and the component is native.

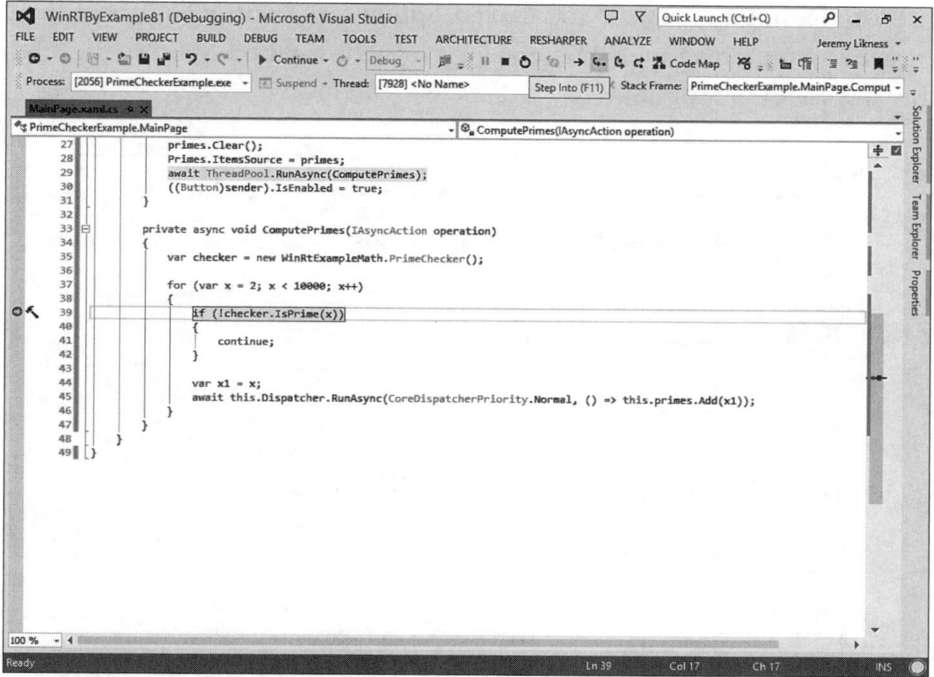

FIGURE 20.1 Breakpoint

To fix this, right-click the project in **Solution Explorer** and choose **Properties** (or press **Alt+Enter**) and then navigate to the **Debug** tab. Notice the section titled **Enable Debuggers** that provides the following options:

- **Managed Only**—Managed (.NET) code running in the current app
- **Native Only**—Native (typically C++) code running in the current app
- **Mixed (Managed and Native)**—Both managed and native code
- **Script Only**—JavaScript (for Windows Store apps built with the JavaScript option)

Stop debugging, choose the **Mixed** option (see Figure 20.2), and then press **F5** again. This time when you step into the method, you should find yourself viewing C++ source.

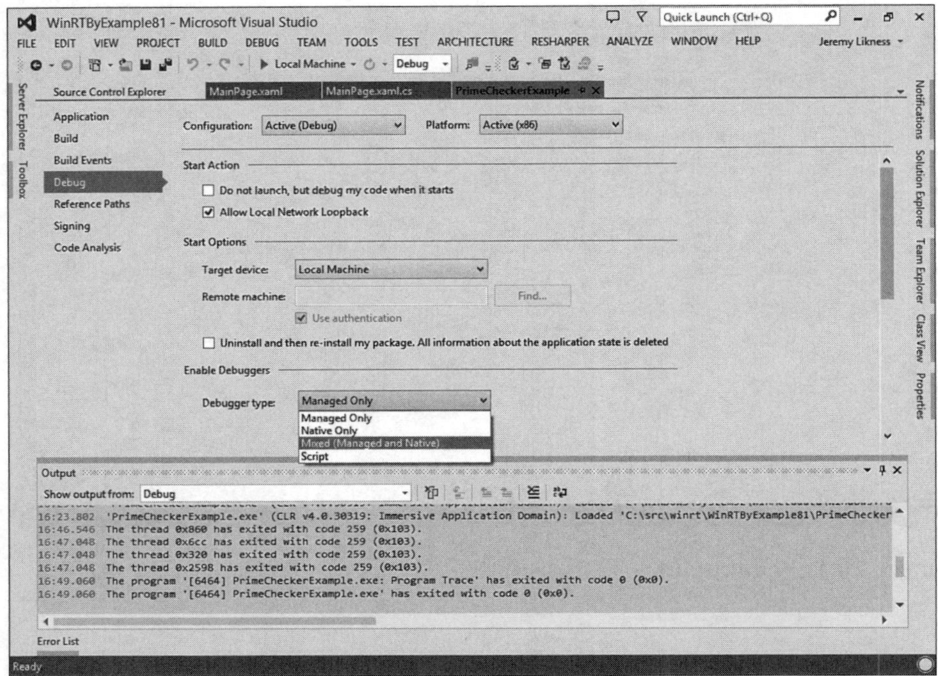

FIGURE 20.2 Debugger options

Be sure to set the appropriate debugger for the task. If your app does not include any native components, the default Managed Only setting is fine.

Just My Code

Visual Studio provides a setting called Just My Code to make it easier to troubleshoot apps by focusing on the code you wrote. Code that is built from an open Visual Studio project is considered "yours" unless the code is optimized. The standard setting is for debug mode to compile non-optimized code and release mode to compile optimized code. This is an important distinction to keep in mind. In general, if you are running the app in debug mode, Just My Code works fine.

To see the difference this setting makes, navigate to **Debug** and then **Options and Settings**. Under **General**, ensure that **Enable Just My Code** is checked. Keep or add back the breakpoint on line 39 in `MainPage.xaml.cs` for the **PrimeCheckerExample** project, and press **F5** to start debugging. Click the button and hit the breakpoint. Press **F5** again to hit the breakpoint a second time. Ensure that the **Call Stack** window is open by pressing **Ctrl+Alt+C**. You should see something similar to the top of Figure 20.3. Now go back into the options and uncheck **Enable Just My Code** (you can do this while the app is running). The **Call Stack** window refreshes, with the extra code similar to what appears at the bottom of Figure 20.3.

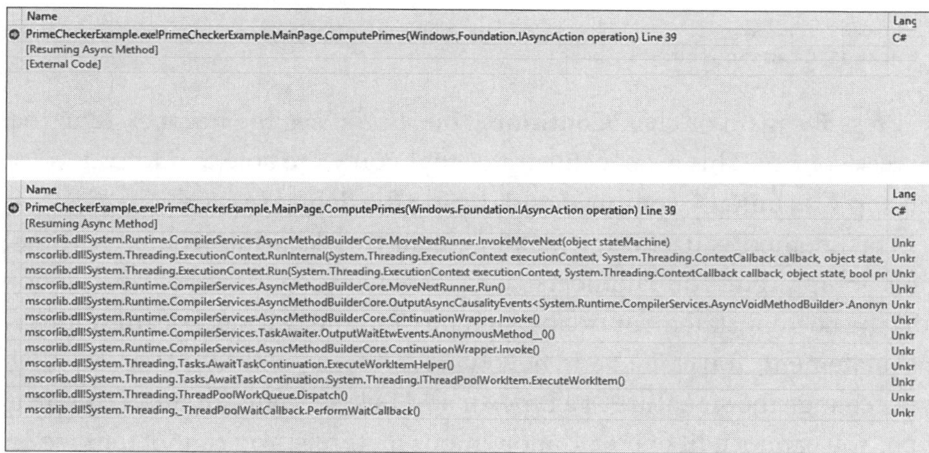

FIGURE 20.3 Just My Code differences

Notice that the call stack provides far more detail when Just My Code is not enabled. This is because it looks at debug symbols and assemblies for system-provided components and includes those in the call stack. When the option is enabled, the call stack is collapsed so that you can focus only on the code you wrote.

Edit and Continue

Visual Studio provides a feature called Edit and Continue that allows you to make changes to code while you are debugging it. You must enable Edit and Continue by navigating to **Debug**, then **Options and Settings**, and finally check **Enable Edit and Continue** on the **Edit and Continue** section. To see Edit and Continue in action, ensure that it is turned on and then place a breakpoint on line 21 in `MainPage.xaml.cs` of the **PrimeCheckerExample** project:

```
this.InitializeComponent();
```

Press **F5** to launch the app in the debugger. When the breakpoint is hit, add two lines of code after the statement:

```
primes.Add(42);
Primes.ItemsSource = primes;
```

Press **F5** again or click **Continue**. You should see the number 42 in the `ListBox` control. This clearly illustrates that you were able to add code *after* the app was initially compiled and during the debug session.

This method is useful for making small tweaks while you are debugging an app, but you should be aware of many restrictions. You cannot edit the current statement or any statement in the call stack leading up to that statement. You cannot add new types, add new methods to an existing type, change the signature of a type, or add fields, events, or properties to a type. You cannot edit or create anonymous methods. You cannot remove or change local variables, although you can add new ones. You cannot change the context of the current statement (for example, place it within a `foreach`, `using`, or `lock` block). You cannot modify an iterator method (a method that contains a `yield` statement).

Despite the many restrictions, this feature is useful when you need to make only small changes "on the fly." It's especially useful for fixing typos you find during your debug session. Note that Edit and Continue is not available when you are debugging using the Mixed (Managed and Native) debugging option.

Just in Time Debugging

You might be familiar with a feature named Just in Time debugging. This feature enables you to launch the Visual Studio debugger automatically when an application running outside Visual Studio throws an exception. This feature is not available for Windows Store apps. Exceptions thrown in Windows Store apps either are swallowed or cause the app to be closed or terminated so that the user returns to the Start Screen.

How to Launch the Debugger

You launch and attach the debugger to Windows Store apps in several ways. The most common is to do so from Visual Studio itself by pressing **F5**. The **Debug** tab in **Project Properties** also provides the option for **Do Not Launch, but Debug My Code When It Starts**. This is useful for debugging scenarios such as activating an app as a share target.

You also can configure an installed app package for debugging when you are not in the associated project. Close the solution and all open windows so that you have no projects loaded in Visual Studio. Choose **Debug** and then **Debug Installed App Package**. You see a list of available app packages installed on your machine. Navigate to the **Prime Checker Example** and choose **Managed Only**, **Do Not Launch**, and **Stop at First Statement** (see Figure 20.4).

Click the **Start** button to begin running Visual Studio in an empty solution. Navigate to the app in the **Start Screen** and launch it. Visual Studio immediately loads the source and breaks on the initial statement that sets up the `App` class.

If you attempt to debug a package you've installed from the Windows Store, you receive an exception that the `app.pdb` file could not be loaded. The `.pdb` extension stands for *program database* and is a special file that holds debugging symbols and state information about your app. This file is necessary for debugging apps; for security reasons, apps that you purchase or install from third parties typically do not include this information.

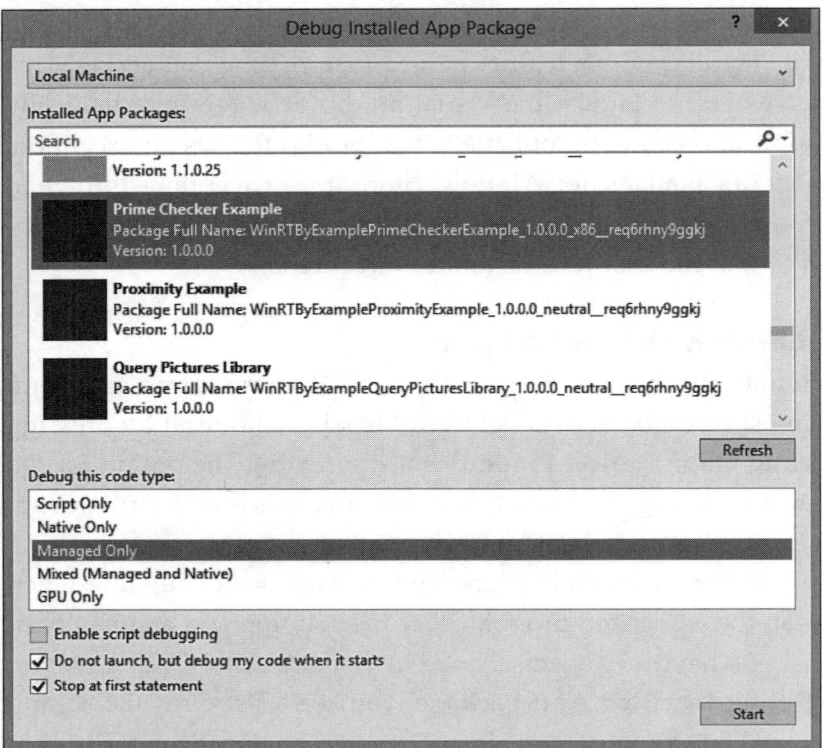

FIGURE 20.4 Debugging an installed app package

Program Databases

Whenever you build an app, a PDB file is generated by default. The file is even generated in release mode. The database contains public symbols (such as functions and variables), name and type information for local variables, and source file and line number information. When you debug a crashed application, the debugger attempts to provide a call stack and requires the PDB to provide function names, parameters, and local variables. For .NET applications, the PDB file only needs to store source filenames and their line numbers for reference because the debugger extracts the rest of the information from .NET metadata.

The PDB files are generated under the `bin` directory for your app. For example, if you right-click the **PrimeCheckerExample** project in the **Solution Explorer** and choose **Open Folder in File Explorer**, you can navigate to `bin/x86/Debug` to find `PrimeCheckerExample.pdb`. These files are not included in the package that is deployed to the Windows Store to prevent third parties from reverse-engineering your code. You can, however, share or copy the files to other machines if you need the information to debug (likewise, if the author of an app you downloaded from the Windows Store provides you with the corresponding PDB file, you can debug that app on your machine). Functionality is still limited without the corresponding source code.

The debugger checks for a PDB file with the same name as the executable used to launch your Windows Store app. Each time you build the app, a unique GUID is generated. This GUID is embedded in the executable and the PDB file. Even when the filenames match, if the GUIDs do not match, the debugger cannot use the PDB file. This is why it is important to track PDB files to your most recent build.

Whenever you build your app on your development machine, the build is considered a *private build*. A build performed on a build machine or configured for release is referred to as a *public build*. If you are building using a build machine, it's important to have a symbol server[1] set up. This is a server that stores the PDBs and binaries for all your public builds. You can set up a symbol server locally as a place to store PDB files for troubleshooting apps.

Debug Windows

Several debug windows are available when you are debugging your app. You can access them through **Debug**, **Windows** in Visual Studio. The Autos window provides information about the current context, including the names of local variables in the current and previous statements, values contained in those variables, and the data types for those variables. An important item in the Autos window is `this`, which provides the current instance for a nonstatic executing statement (for example, if you break on code in `MainPage.xaml.cs`, `this` references the `MainPage` class). The Locals window provides variables, arrays, objects, and their members visible in a given program and method. As with Autos, the name, value, and type all display.

---

[1]Symbol server and symbol stores, http://bit.ly/1hetKkQ

The Immediate window[2] enables you to debug and evaluate expressions or statements, including printing or setting variable values. The shortcut to access this window is **Ctrl+Alt+I**. If you break inside a loop that is using the `x` variable, you can print the current value by typing `?x` and change the value to something new, such as the number `9`, by typing `x=9`. This is useful for breaking out of large loops or testing unexpected inputs. You can perform these actions using the Auto, Local, or Watch windows, but the Immediate window enables more complicated statements and interactions.

Several Watch windows are available to help keep track of variables and expressions. To start a watch, simply right-click the variable in the IDE, and choose **Add Watch** or drag and drop it to the window. This adds the variable to a convenient window that displays the most recent value of the variable. Use this to watch values change as you are stepping through code without having to highlight them explicitly in the source. It really helps in detecting changes because updated values appear red on the screen.

The Call Stack window gives you information about how the program got to the current statement. It displays the name of each function and programming language that was called to reach the current statement. When a method calls another method that then calls a third method containing the statement you are debugging, the entire stack of method calls displays. This helps you work your way backward to the source of the problem. For example, the failed attempt to parse an integer might throw an exception in the framework class, but the root cause can be traced to a method in your code that called the `Parse` method. The call stack reveals where the statement that threw the exception was called.

Managing Exceptions

By default, the debugger does not automatically break when an exception is thrown. Any unhandled exception causes the debugger to break. Many

---

[2]The Immediate Window http://bit.ly/1bZa4Ta

times, third-party components throw exceptions or your own app throws exceptions that are subsequently captured and handled. Although this ensures that your app can continue running, sometimes you want to break when those exceptions occur, to troubleshoot why they are happening and prevent them in the future.

The **PrimeCheckerExample** app explicitly throws an exception in the `App` constructor. The code in `App.xaml.cs` looks like this:

```
try
{
    throw new ActionNotSupportedException(
        "This is for demonstration purposes only.");
}
catch { }
```

As the code indicates, this is solely to demonstrate how to configure exception handling. When you run the app in debug mode, the Output window includes the following text:

```
A first chance exception of type
'System.ServiceModel.ActionNotSupportedException' occurred in
PrimeCheckerExample.exe
```

Because the exception was handled, it does not halt app execution. You might see exceptions similar to this in the Output window and want to debug the app when they occur. To trigger this, open the **Debug** menu in Visual Studio and choose **Exceptions**, or press **Ctrl+Alt+E**. This opens the **Exceptions** dialog box. Now click **Find** and enter the name of the exception, `ActionNotSupportedException`, to open the exception in the dialog box. Check the box under the **Thrown** column (see Figure 20.5) and choose **OK**. Debug the app again; this time, it automatically breaks when the exception is thrown.

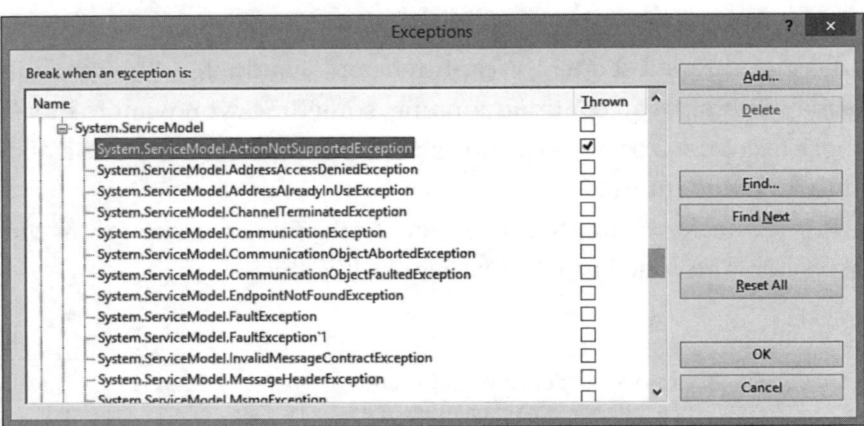

FIGURE 20.5 Configuring how exceptions are handled

Using this technique, you can specify whatever exceptions you want to always break on to troubleshoot. If you find that certain exceptions should be ignored but are causing the debugger to break anyway, this is the dialog box to use. To stop from breaking automatically, simply uncheck the corresponding exception. As mentioned earlier, any exception that is unhandled causes the debugger to break, regardless of the configuration.

Logging and Tracing

Logging is a generic term for recording information about your application. *Tracing* specifically refers to diagnostic information you can use to debug your app in post-mortem analysis. In the .NET Framework, the `System.Diagnostics` namespace provides types that enable you to interact with event logs. Because WinRT does not provide its own tracing APIs, a common solution is to use the .NET types to interface with Event Tracing for Windows (ETW).

Windows 2000 introduced ETW. It provides logging for components through a tracing mechanism. Programs (and even kernel-level device drivers) can raise events. The ETW system picks up these events, and then you can enable or disable the logging dynamically to troubleshoot apps in production environments without changing the configuration or redeploying the app.

ETW is based on an event provider that writes out the events. ETW then adds information about time, process, and the thread the event was written from. Event consumers pick up this information and read and process the logs or real-time events.

Receiving bug reports from the field is not uncommon, and unless you have specific information about the user's environment, troubleshooting the problem after the fact can be difficult. Tracing enables you to record the diagnostic information you need to determine the state of the app before the crash or unintentional behavior occurred. Although most apps record information only when serious problems occur, you can provide a setting that enables the user to save more verbose information when necessary.

Be careful about the level of tracing you use in your app; it can reveal proprietary information about the inner working of your application. You also want to avoid revealing personal information about your customers. You don't want to make it easier for a hacker to understand your app if you are securing sensitive information such as financial records or health information. One approach is to wrap your sensitive trace statements in compiler directives so they are generated only for debug builds and are not packaged as part of your production app. It's up to you to decide how much tracing you will provide and whether including information such as a call stack in the trace logs is risky. Also be conscious of disk space, and have code in place to purge old trace data, to keep it from taking up too much space.

The alternative to tracing is simply logging enough information to enable you to diagnose problems without compromising the security of the application. One approach is to capture the latest error by encrypting and Base64-encoding the error details and call stack, and then providing the user with the option to mail the crash report. Other approaches include logging only minimal information or embedding codes in the log files that you can match to the source but won't reveal to third parties.

The **LoggingHelper** project is included for you to use in your projects when you want to incorporate tracing using .NET classes. Feel free to use and modify the code as needed for your apps. The `LogEventSource` class inherits from `EventSource`, the base class for ETW. Use this class to provide an API to your app for writing trace information. The implementation here is simple and takes in a message, but you can extend the signature to include the method name or other diagnostic information as well. Each method is tagged with the `Event` attribute, to notify ETW what type of event the method logs. It uses the `CallerMemberName` attribute to automatically show where it was called from. This is an example of the method to process a warning:

```
 [Event(WarningLevel, Level = EventLevel.Warning)]
public void Warn(string message, [CallerMemberName]string member =
    UnknownMember)
{
    this.WriteEvent(WarningLevel, Format(message, member));
}
```

Notice that it calls the base `WriteEvent` method. The first parameter in that call is a number indicating the warning level. This is captured in several constants, from warning to critical, defined at the top of the class, to make it easier to read and understand. The class also exposes a singleton instance to make it easy to access from anywhere within the application. The `Format` method combines the message with the member name.

An `EventSource` is simply a place to send trace information. The `EventSource` does not really do anything with the information; that responsibility is delegated to the `EventListener`. The listener is responsible for actually recording the information. A listener can be configured to a particular level and will ignore information below that level. You might have multiple listeners that use the same source so that you can track various information or save it in different ways. For example, you might want to record only events that are errors or that are critical to your application. In that case, you would configure the listener to the `EventLevel.Error` level and ignore anything below that level (such as `Verbose`, `Informational`, or `Warning`).

The `EventListener` is responsible for recording, displaying, and otherwise processing the information sent to it. You might write a listener that sends information to a web service. The `LogEventListener` class provided in the **LoggingHelper** project uses local app storage to record traced events. It inherits from the base `EventListener` class and implements the

OnEventWritten override. The override is called only if the event source is enabled for the event level of incoming event.

The LogEventListener class has three constructors. By default, it uses the package name for the log file and uses the supplied date and time formatter to time-stamp the events. The other constructors enable you to pass in your own filename and also provide your own format for the date and time.

The listener sets up an instance of SemaphoreSlim to ensure that it does not attempt to write to the same file from multiple threads. It is initialized with the number of concurrent requests (in this case, one). To ensure that no concurrent access is offered, the Write method calls WaitAsync on the SemaphoreSlim instance. This call returns only when no other threads are accessing the semaphore and immediately takes up a new "slot." This slot is now taken, and all other threads trying to access the semaphore are blocked until the owning thread calling the Release method releases that slot.

The OnEventWritten method parses the event information into a comma-separated list, to make it easy to open in a program such as Excel.

```
var eventInfo = String.Format("{0},{1},{2}",
    string.Format(this.timeFormat, DateTime.Now),
    eventData.Level,
    eventData.Payload[0]);
```

This line is then written to the log file:

```
await FileIO.AppendLinesAsync(this.logFile, new[] { info });
```

The **LoggingExample** project demonstrates the use of the tracing in a Windows Store app. When the app is launched, the OnLaunched method in App.xaml.cs configures two event listeners. One is set to maximum verbosity and uses the default log name, which is the package name. The other is set to log only errors and is set to the name Errors.

```
appListener = new LogEventListener();
appListener.EnableEvents(LogEventSource.Log, EventLevel.Verbose);
errorListener = new LogEventListener("Errors");
errorListener.EnableEvents(LogEventSource.Log, EventLevel.Error);
```

Various methods in the app write to the trace log. An informational message notes that the app has been initialized:

```
LogEventSource.Log.Info("App initialized.");
```

When the `OnNavigationFailed` method is called, a critical message is logged before throwing an exception that aborts the app:

```
LogEventSource.Log.Critical(string.Format(
    "Failed to navigate to page: {0}", e.SourcePageType.FullName));
```

The `ItemPage` class has been modified to randomly throw an exception 20% of the time. If you run the app in debug mode, this breaks into the debugger. When you access the app without debugging, the navigation error is swallowed. You might notice that every few times you try to navigate to an item by clicking on it in the Section 3 portion of the hub, it does nothing. Although no feedback is visible to the app, the error is logged in the trace files.

Run the app and click through it. Use the debugger to suspend and resume the app. Make sure you click on items enough times to throw an exception. Next, navigate to the location of the local storage for your package. It is most often in this path:

```
C:\Users\<username>\AppData\Local\Packages
```

You can sort the list of packages by date modified to find the logging example and then navigate to its `LocalState` subdirectory. You might see a file named `_sessionState.xml`. In addition, you should see two files named `Errors_log.csv` and `WinRTByExampleLoggingExample_log.csv`. The first should contain only a few entries that relate to the navigation error; the second should contain these errors plus many more diagnostic messages, such as page construction, loading, and unloading.

The app also includes an example using Windows Runtime tracing APIs that Windows 8.1 introduced. These APIs also wrap the ETW functionality. The difference is that messages are generated in a fixed format and are designed to be flushed periodically so that your app can upload them to a back end for processing. Similar to the .NET class approach, the

WinRT APIs that exist in `Windows.Foundation.Diagnostics` provide multiple "channel listeners" for single "session sources." Creating a channel is as simple as creating a new instance and passing the name of the listener to the constructor:

```
channel = new LoggingChannel("WinRTChannel");
```

You can configure the channel with a logging level, but it is not enabled until you add it to a session. You can listen for that event and capture information about the channel through the `LoggingEnabled` event:

```
channel.LoggingEnabled += (o, args) =>
{
    this.winRtLoggingEnabled = o.Enabled;
    this.winRtLogLevel = o.Level;
};
```

To start using the information the channel generates, create a session and add the channel to the session:

```
session = new LoggingSession("WinRTSession");
session.AddLoggingChannel(channel);
```

You have two options for sessions. The `LoggingSession` provides a circular, in-memory buffer. It is up to you to flush it when something important, such as a crash, occurs so that you can retrieve the information. The typical pattern is to save the session that contains the most recent information and then transmit the file to your back end:

```
var file = await session.SaveToFileAsync(
    ApplicationData.Current.TemporaryFolder, "log_" +
        DateTime.Now.Ticks);
// send file
```

In the sample app, a critical error such as the page navigation failure results in the file being flushed. You can view the file by navigating the app package's temporary file location. The file is generated in a special trace format that is viewable using the Windows Performance Toolkit (WPT)[3] or `tracerpt.exe`.

---

[3]Windows Performance Toolkit, http://bit.ly/1gKT6Jr

You can also use a `FileLoggingSession`. This saves all activity to disk. It stores events in memory and periodically flushes them to disk. The log file grows to a predetermined size (the documentation does not specify this), and then a `LogFileGenerated` event is raised. You should attach a handler to this event and immediately process the file because the `FileLoggingSession` will create a new file and possibly overwrite the existing information. The typical pattern is to move the file to a different folder and then upload it to the back end and delete it from local storage.

Profiling and Performance Analysis

Evaluating how well your application performs should be a continual part of the development process. Identifying bottlenecks early on and addressing them proactively is much easier than responding to issues in the field. Visual Studio provides tools that help you analyze your application to determine where you might have performance bottlenecks so that you can troubleshoot and fix them before your app goes to production or so that you can respond to issues that customers note after your app is live.

Performance is important because people won't use apps that take a long time to start or that respond poorly to input. An app that exhibits choppy transitions between pages is less likely to be used than one that is smooth and fluid. It is also important to understand the impact your app has on battery life because users will likely uninstall an app that rapidly drains their laptop or tablet battery.

You can think of performance as almost a competition with other apps as well. When the user's system stops responding well, savvy users might open the task manager and kill the process that is taking up the most CPU cycles. You don't want your app to appear on the top of that stack any more than you want the Windows Process Lifetime Manager to shut it down to release resources for other apps. In this section, you learn how to profile your app to maximize responsiveness and minimize bottlenecks that impact performance or increase energy usage.

The first and easiest way to profile your app is to determine how many CPU cycles it is using and check its relative frame rate. The built-in Visual Studio project templates automatically include code in `App.xaml.cs` to enable a set of frame rate counters for you when the app is compiled in debug mode. You can see this in the **PrimeCheckerExample** project.

```
#if DEBUG
    if (System.Diagnostics.Debugger.IsAttached)
    {
        this.DebugSettings.EnableFrameRateCounter = true;
    }
#endif
```

When you run the app, you see four numbers across the top of the display. The two at the left show statistics for the UI thread for your app, and the two on the right show statistics for the system in general. My system typically shows `16 01` on the left and `60 01` on the right. The numbers on the right are generally more important because they represent the frame rate and CPU usage (in milliseconds) of the composition thread. This is the thread that is responsible for rendering the graphics to the display. It should run at the optimal 60 frames per second (fps); if it drops below this, your app will appear jittery or unresponsive.

The numbers on the left represent the frame rate and CPU usage of the UI thread. This thread is responsible for parsing XAML elements, computing the display layout, handling data-binding, and processing user input. It does the heavy lifting and turns over the results to the composition thread for rendering. You should expect this frame rate to be lower because of everything that is happening. Whenever the UI thread's CPU usage spikes (indicating that more CPU time is being spent on the UI thread) or frame rate drops significantly, the app can become unresponsive to input and touch interactions can become choppy.

Run the app locally on your machine and note the counters. If you watch carefully, you should see the composition frame rate drop slightly and see the CPU cycles increase when the app first starts up, then settle at about 60 fps. Click the button to compute the prime numbers, and you should see the frame rate and CPU change on the left. The frame rate might actually go higher, indicating more work. One nuance is that when the UI thread is idle, the frame rate drops because it is not being updated due to inactivity. You will also notice these numbers change when you scroll through the populated list box or select items.

Although the frame rate counters are useful to provide an at-a-glance dashboard of your app's performance, they don't give you any information about what could be causing issues when the frame rate is low or the CPU time is high. Fortunately, Visual Studio ships with the built-in capability to profile your application. You can use several built-in profilers to generate data that you can then analyze to determine the areas your app needs to improve. Next, you get some tips on performance to help optimize your app before you have to run it through a profiler.

Performance Tips

As you learned in the previous section, the UI thread is responsible for doing the heavy lifting for your app. The **PrimeCheckerExample** demonstrates how to keep the UI thread responsive by taking advantage of asynchronous APIs to run non-UI work on a separate thread. In the example, the thread pool spawns an asynchronous task that does the heavy computations in the background and only marshals results to the UI thread.

XAML parsing takes a heavy toll on the UI thread. The fewer the XAML elements, the better your performance will be. One point to keep in mind is that resource dictionaries are parsed when they are encountered, not when the resources are used. If you have resources that are specific to a single page, you should place them in that page and not default to loading them into a resource dictionary that `App.xaml` references. This ensures that the resources are created and referenced only when they are needed, such as when the page is loaded. On the other hand, if you have a common resource that several pages use, you should place it in `App.xaml` so that it does not have to be re-created multiple times. Avoid declaring the same resource (such as a reused brush) in multiple places.

To reduce elements, consider your strategy for creating the UI. For example, you might be tempted to create a background by using a `Rectangle` element. However, this increases your element count; you likely could do the same thing by setting the `Background` property on a parent element. If foreground elements have the same color as the background, don't explicitly set their color. Instead, inherit from the background by not setting an explicit color. When an element is not displayed for any reason, set its `Visibility` property to `Collapsed` instead of trying to hide it from being another element or setting it to transparent.

Plenty of best practices for performance[4] aren't specific to Windows Store apps or the Windows Runtime. For example, if you have to manipulate strings or build complex strings, consider using the .NET `StringBuilder` class. Minimize boxing and unboxing (casting value types to reference types and back) by providing explicit method signatures and using generics where possible. When you need to create transient objects, consider using `struct` instead of `class` to minimize overhead from garbage collection.

Even if you follow these tips, you want to be sure you understand how your app is performing. Some issues might not be evident on your development machine, so it's important to deploy to slower models with less memory to test performance on devices similar to what end users might be using. Finally, you can profile your app using Visual Studio's Performance and Diagnostics. (*Note:* the following features are provided with the Pro level of Visual Studio and higher; they are not packaged as part of Express.)

You can access the Performance and Diagnostics dialog box by navigating to **Debug** and then choosing **Performance and Diagnostics** or by pressing **Alt** + **F2**. You are presented with options similar to Figure 20.6.

By default, the profiler launches the project you are currently working in. You can also target an app that is running or another package that is installed. Before profiling, ensure that your app is built and deployed in release mode. This introduces optimizations that are not part of the debug build.

---

[4]Performance Best Practices at a Glance, http://bit.ly/1mz51wo

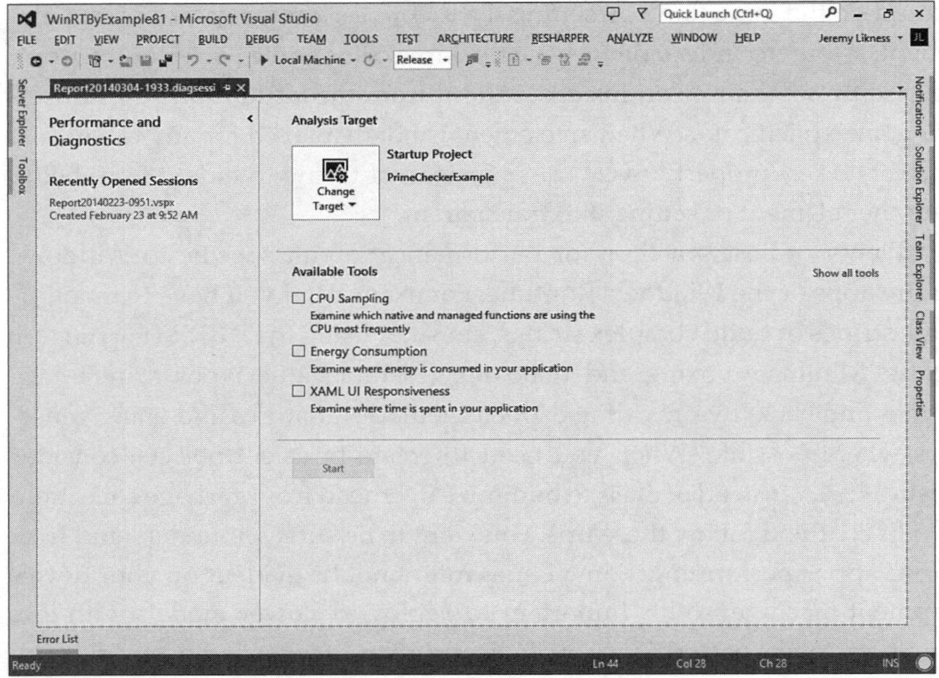

FIGURE 20.6 Profiling and Diagnostics

CPU Sampling

The first option for profiling is CPU sampling. Profiling is always a catch-22 because the act of profiling itself can impact performance. CPU sampling attempts to minimize the overhead of sampling by observing the code without adding overhead to the app itself. Instead, the profile takes periodic snapshots of the call stack from the running threads in the application and uses this to determine where the code is spending the majority of its time.

Check the box to select **CPU Sampling** and click the **Start** button to launch your app (you might get a confirmation dialog box for security). If you have multiple windows, you will see a spinner appear in the Visual Studio window with a notice that samples are being collected. Navigate through the app and perform the functions you are most interested in analyzing. For the **PrimeCheckerExample** app, tap the button to generate primes; then select a number in the `ListBox` control and scroll through the list. The easiest way to terminate the session is to close the app.

After you stop the session, the profiler might spin for a little longer as it writes information into a special report format. It writes a file with the profile data that has the `.vspx` extension. You can open this later to continue your analysis. The summary page appears with a graph showing the CPU usage over time. In Figure 20.7, you can see the spike when the primes were generated, followed by a shorter set of spikes from scrolling the list.

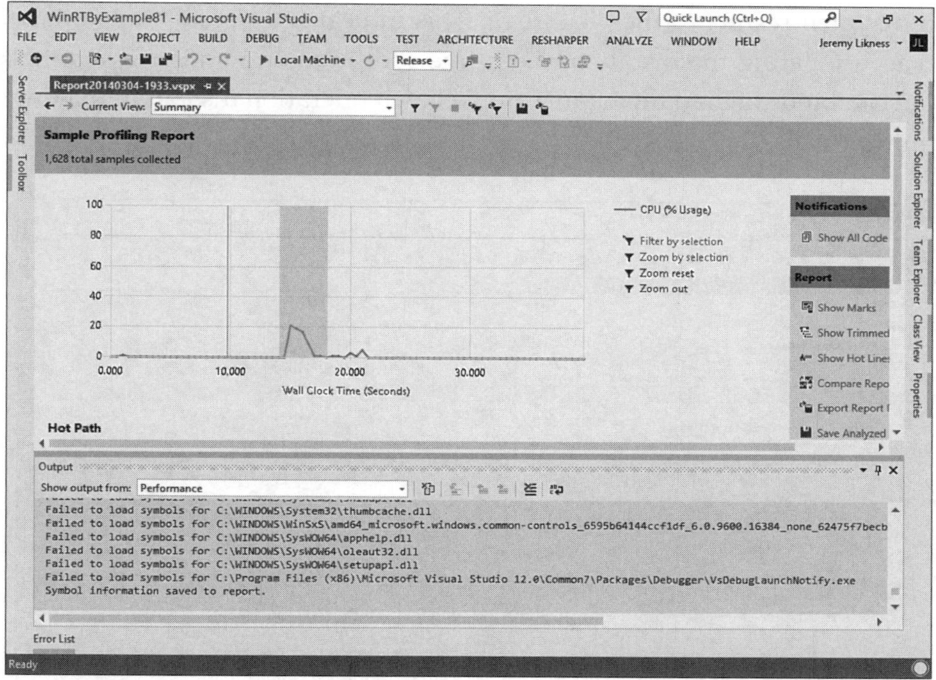

FIGURE 20.7 The profiler Summary view

For a more interesting view, select **Modules** in the **Current View** drop-down list to see a list of libraries that you can sort by samples. Exclusive samples refer to samples directly in the module or function in question. Inclusive samples include samples taken from a module or function and its children. The most samples were taken from `PrimeCheckerExample.exe`, but the next-most-accessed module within was `WinRtExampleMath.dll`, which contains the WinRT component to compute the prime. The library is written in C++.

If you expand the module, you can drill down to the functions within that module and sort those by samples (the exclusive sample focuses on your app and is more useful in general than inclusive samples). You'll find that an iterator (the method name that ends in `MoveNext`) is the most sampled function, followed by an anonymous method. Expanding the method should reveal line number 45 from the `Main.xaml.cs` page (see Figure 20.8). If you navigate to the line in the source, you will see that this is the call to dispatch results to the UI thread. This indicates a possible advantage to accumulating the results of the prime computation in an array so that you can bind them to the UI in a single batch operation instead of making multiple calls.

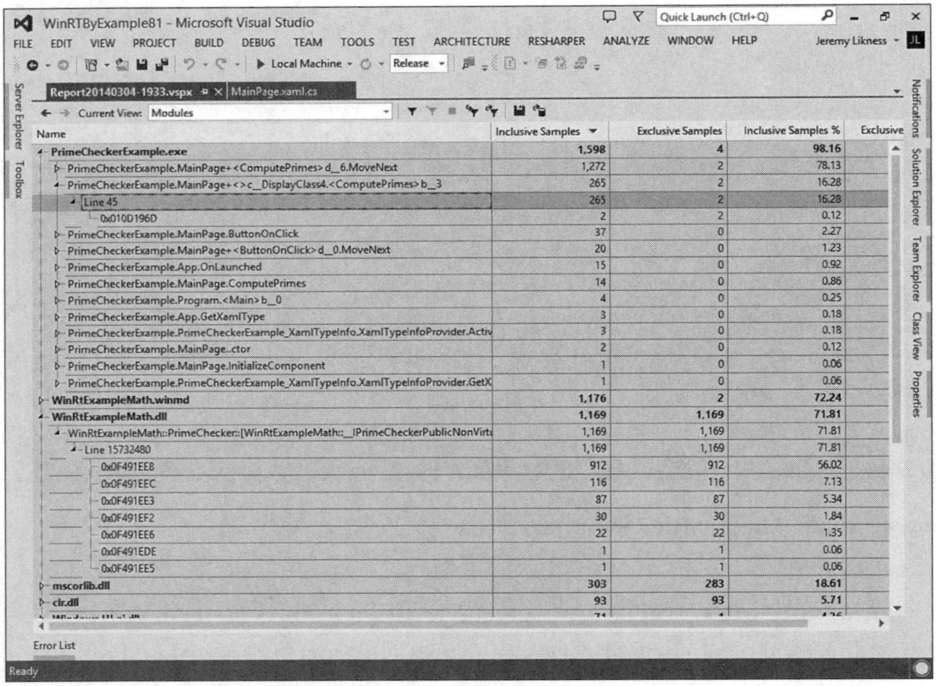

FIGURE 20.8 The Modules Tree view

The other views give you insights into the samples at various levels. You can use the Functions view to determine that the most samples were taken inside the `IsPrime` method of the `PrimeChecker` component. The Lines view enables you to sort by function and show the source code lines that contain the function. Function Details enables you to drill into the samples via a visual interface.

XAML UI Responsiveness

To analyze and optimize the XAML in your app, check the **XAML UI Responsiveness** option on the **Performance and Diagnostics** panel and start the app. Run the app for a short period of time and perform typical functions such as tapping buttons and navigating between pages. For this example, set the **LoggingExample** project as the startup project. After the app launches, swipe the hub control back and forth, navigate into sections, and click into individual items. Navigate using the Back button. Terminate the app and stop the data collection.

When the profiler stops collecting information, it presents a chart similar to Figure 20.8. The chart is specifically designed to provide information about the XAML engine in your app and enable you to determine what areas to focus on to improve responsiveness.

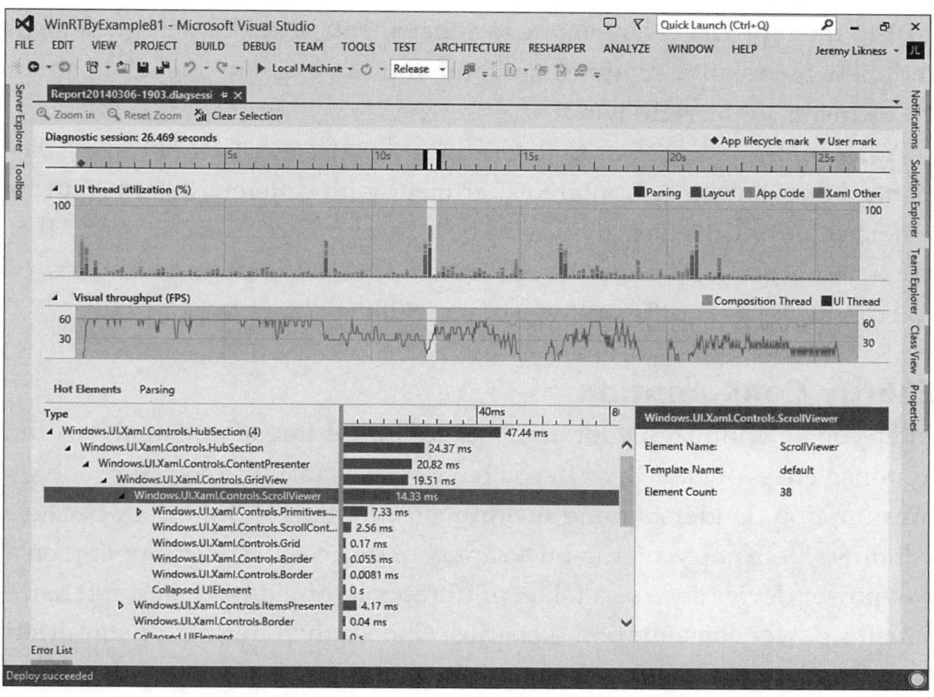

FIGURE 20.9 The XAML UI Responsiveness profiler

The top of the chart shows a timeline ruler for your app. You can click on various tick marks on the timeline to focus on that period of time. Clicking on an area highlights that area and gives you a set of bands that you can drag to adjust the interval of time you want to analyze. In the previous example, the interval is focused on a 500-millisecond slice of time.

The UI thread utilization portion breaks down the work the UI thread performs. It shows you overall work as a stacked graph. Portions of the graph include parsing XAML, laying out the display, and executing code from your app that runs on the UI thread. The XAML Other category is for XAML operations that submit the final layout for final rendering to the screen. You can hover over any part of the graph to see the percentage contribution of the individual category to the overall workload for that time slice.

The visual throughput graph reports the fps for the composition and UI threads. You can choose to drill down based on the effort the UI spent parsing the XAML, or you can select hot elements to view which elements required the most time during the layout pass. The most expensive items float to the top. You can navigate to subelements within a parent element and view the relative render times, and you can examine metadata about the elements in the right window.

You can use this profiler to determine your strategy for optimizing elements. For example, you might experiment with different layout controls to determine which one provides the best performance. You might find that a `ListBox` outperforms a `ListView` because it is easier to lay out elements, or you might choose a different type of panel that is more responsive.

Energy Consumption

After you've optimized your app's use of the UI thread and analyzed the responsiveness of your XAML, you have one last factor to consider: energy consumption. Understanding energy consumption is important because Windows Store apps can run on a variety of devices. Testing your app on a low-power device such as a tablet or ultrabook provides the best reference data for power consumption scenarios. Choose the **Energy Consumption** option and start the app. The example in Figure 20.10 shows the results from profiling the **RestServiceExample** project from Chapter 5, "Web Services and Syndication."

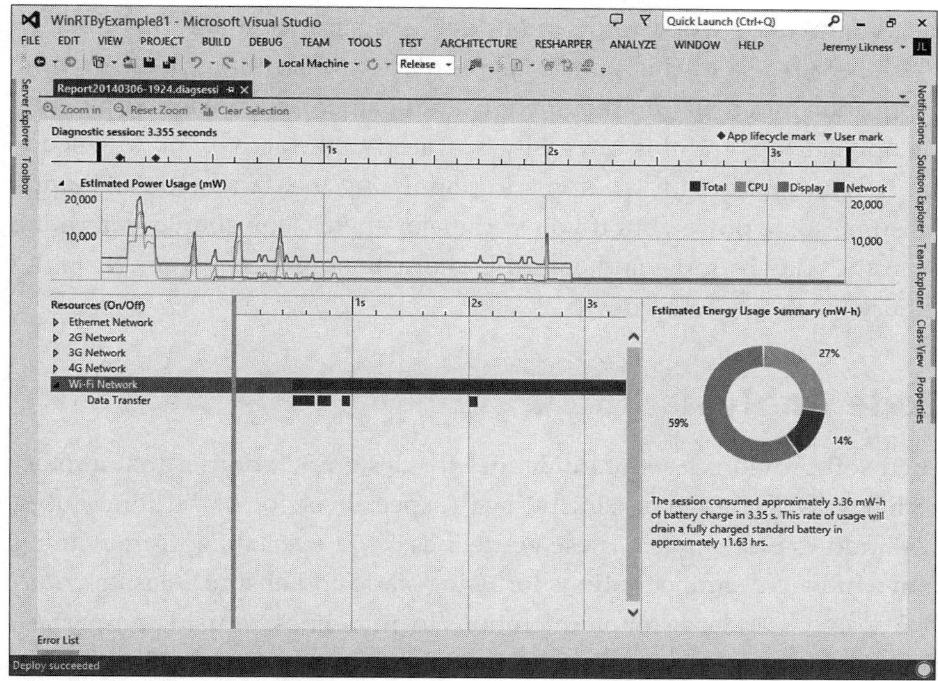

FIGURE 20.10 Energy consumption

The familiar timeline ruler at the top enables you to zoom into various time segments. The red marks indicate application lifecycle events. In the example, it is notable that the application start-up takes significant time and incurs an energy cost. This is because the data source for the app is initialized during startup and the Wi-Fi network has been used to connect to a web service and download information. You can see the history of Wi-Fi usage in the Resources section of the bottom-left panel. Directly below the timeline ruler is the estimated power usage graph that breaks down usage by CPU, display, and network.

The donut graph illustrates how much energy was consumed overall for each of these categories. In the snapshot, 59% of the power consumption was to drive the display, 27% represented CPU cycles, and 14% was for the network. The estimated energy usage summary gives you an idea where most of the power for your app is coming from. If the majority of power is from networking activity, you might want to consider reducing the amount of network traffic and possibly caching more information.

The main use of this particular profiler is to identify spikes in your application and drill into them. For example, there is a notable spike during app startup, and this can easily be traced to the activity of downloading the information for the app and populating the data model. All apps consume some power, but if you find major spikes, you should determine what the code is doing and consider alternate approaches to increase the battery life of the user's device.

Code Analysis

Microsoft provides a set of guidelines for designing libraries that interact with the .NET Framework, including the special version of the library used in Windows Store apps.[5] These guidelines cover everything from naming conventions, recommendations for using static and abstract classes, interface design, standards for enumerations to guidelines for using properties, methods, constructors, events, and other constructs. The guidelines also recommend common patterns for implementing dependency properties and implementing `IDisposable`.

Visual Studio encapsulates the guidelines in a set of rules. Using code analysis, you can scan your assemblies to obtain reports about violations of the various rules. Code analysis is fully configurable. You can choose which sets of rules to use and whether violations generate errors or warnings. You can set up code analysis to run on a build and even integrate it with your build system to prevent check-ins of noncompliant code. Using code analysis can help standardize your code across large teams, reduce errors by avoiding common pitfalls, and, above all, serve as a tool to learn solid programming techniques.

Code analysis can be configured at the solution and project level. You can navigate to the **Code Analysis Settings** tab of the solution **Property**

[5]Framework Design Guidelines, http://bit.ly/1i1vPRR

Pages to see an overview of code analysis by project. This view enables you to set up the rules for code analysis. More settings are available at the project level. Using different rule sets by project is not uncommon. For example, you might want to have less strict rules for a test project than production code because you don't care about localizing string literals used by tests, or you might invoke functions in a nonstandard way to test edge cases.

Right-click the **SocketsGame** project from Chapter 10, "Networking," set it as the startup project, and then choose **Properties** or highlight the project in the **Solution Explorer** and press **Alt+Enter**. Navigate to the **Code Analysis** tab. The dialog box enables you to configure analysis by configuration and platform. You can choose to enable code analysis on build. If you choose this option, the build will fail if any code analysis violations generate an error. You can also choose the rule set you want to use. Select a rule set to see a detailed description of what it entails (see Figure 20.11).

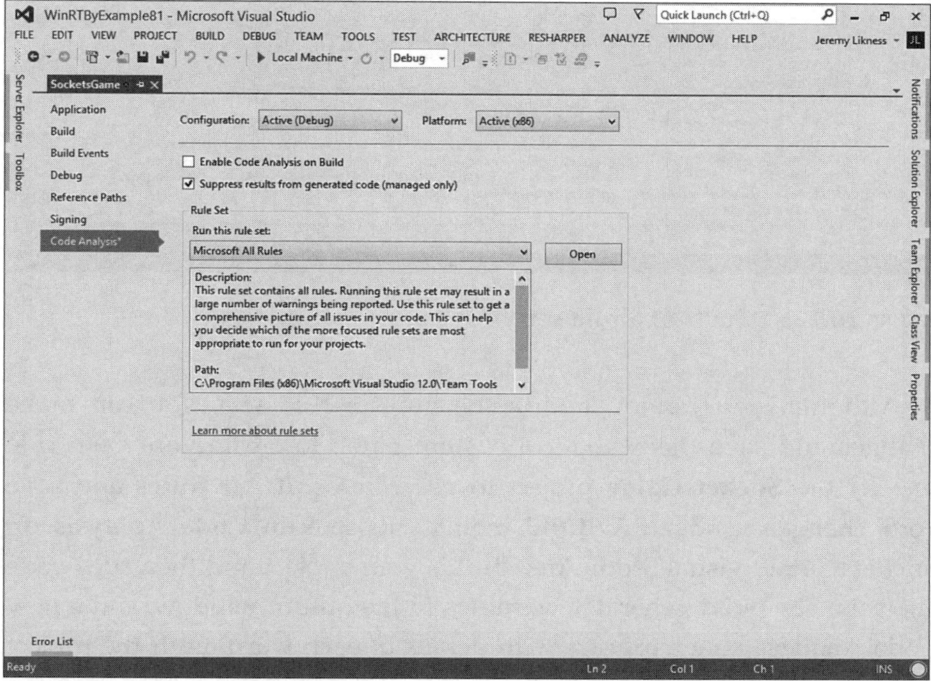

FIGURE 20.11 Code analysis settings

Figure 20.12 shows the result of selecting Open after you choose a rule set. A detailed list of the included rules is shown. You can choose which rules to apply by checking them, and you can select the action to take when a rule is violated (such as ignoring the rule or generating an error). Selecting a rule also shows details about that rule.

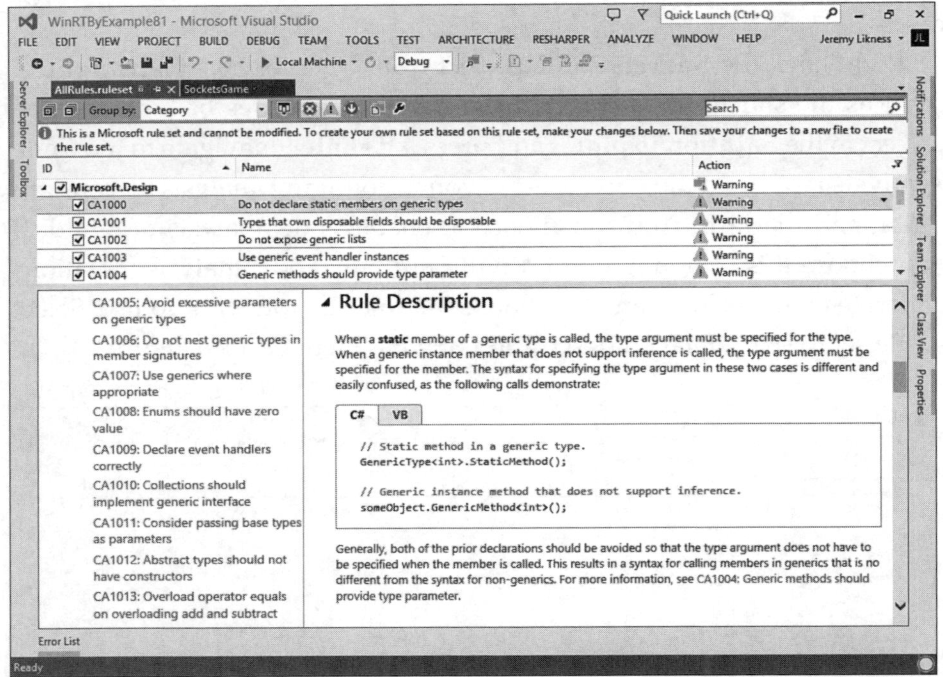

FIGURE 20.12 Details of a rule set

Although you cannot modify the built-in rule sets, you can make changes and save them under a custom name to create your own rule set. Set the **SocketsGame** project to use **Microsoft All Rules** and save your changes. Under the **Build** menu, choose **Run Code Analysis on SocketsGame**. Visual Studio first builds your project and then runs code analysis. The build generates warnings in the output window, and a new Code Analysis panel appears with details of each warning. If the project had any errors, the build would fail and list the violations that generated an error. Figure 20.13 shows the result of running code analysis against the example project.

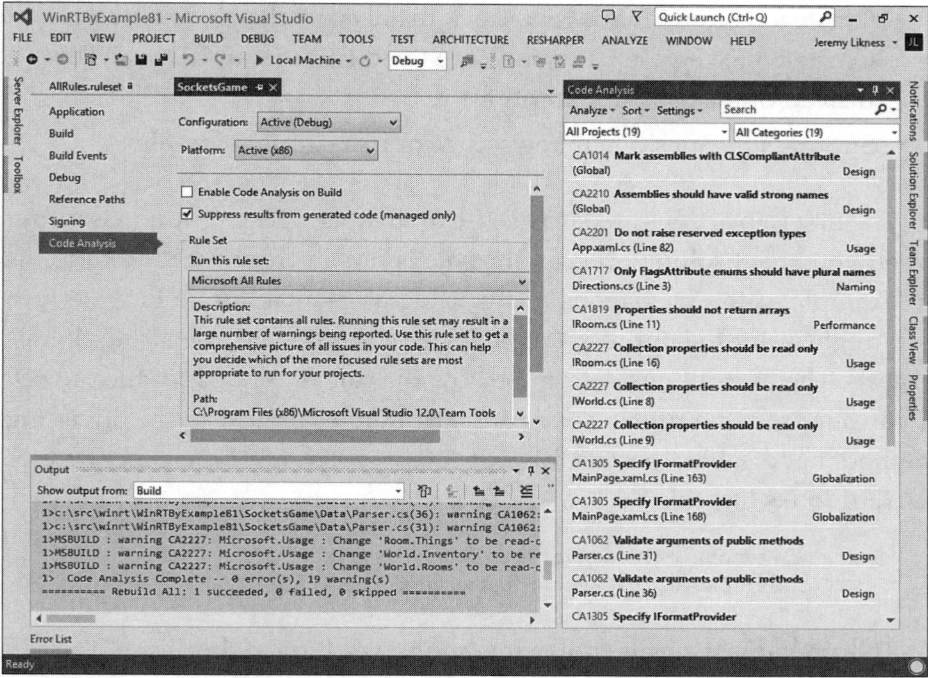

FIGURE 20.13 Code Analysis results

To address a rule, select it in the Code Analysis window. You can see details about the warning. If applicable, this also opens the related source file and highlights the offending line of code. For example, select the violation CA2201, Do Not Raise Reserved Exception Types. This highlights line 82 in the `App.xaml.cs` file. The description explains that generic exception types should never be used. Instead, you want to create a custom exception type that is more descriptive. In the example, you might create a `PageLoadException` class with a `PageName` property that is far more descriptive than the generic `Exception` type.

For each violation, you can perform some actions directly from the Code Analysis panel. For CA2201, these options are available:

- Copy the message to the clipboard so you can paste it into a report or email to deal with later

- Create a work item in TFS to track the needed change (such as Create an Exception Class for Page Load Failures and Throw This Instead of the System Exception)
- Suppress the message in the source or in a suppression file

The first two actions are fairly self-explanatory. The last option is useful when you are absolutely certain the rule is not a concern for the code. As an example, if the message is about using a resource file to localize text, you might want to suppress that message for tests and use string literals instead. The two options determine how the rule is applied for the project. If you suppress the rule in source, an attribute is applied to the offending method that disables the rule for code analysis. The attribute generated for CA2201 looks like this:

```
[System.Diagnostics.CodeAnalysis.SuppressMessage("Microsoft.Usage",
    "CA2201:DoNotRaiseReservedExceptionTypes")]
```

This prevents that rule from generating a warning in the future. You can add a parameter that explains why, like this:

```
Justification="My boss says this exception is fine. "
```

Sometimes you want to suppress the rule for the entire project. You might have a special project that violates the rule on purpose, or you might decide that the rule is simply not important enough to enforce. If that is the case, choose to suppress the rule in a suppression file. This adds a `GlobalSuppressions.cs` file to your project that includes the suppression. The default is to generate a rule that is scoped to the type. You can edit the scope to the member, type, resource, namespace, or module level and change the target (such as the fully qualified type name or namespace) in the source.

Summary

In this chapter, you learned about the debugger and its various features. You implemented a custom trace source and listener to implement logging in your app to help troubleshoot it when the debugger is not available. To create apps that are responsive and perform well without impacting battery life, you utilized the built-in profilers that Visual Studio provides to sample CPU, monitor energy consumption, and analyze XAML responsiveness. Finally, you saw how code analysis can perform an automated "code review" to ensure that you are following Microsoft's design guidelines.

We hope you found detailed, comprehensive coverage of building apps with the Windows Runtime using C# and the .NET Framework in this book. In addition to detailed descriptions of the hundreds of Windows APIs, we included more than 80 example projects with full source code for you to reference and use in your own WinRT programs. The source is shared under the MIT license, which can be summarized as, "Take it—it's yours!" The goal was to provide you with deep insights, valuable tricks, and helpful techniques to build quality code and overcome hurdles as you develop your own software for Windows 8.1 devices. Please take a moment to share your appreciation by leaving a review on Amazon.com at http://bit.ly/winrtxmpl. Don't hesitate to reach out to us if you have any questions or just want to say hi. You can also follow us on Twitter: Jeremy Likness as @JeremyLikness, and John Garland as @dotnetgator.

A

Under the Covers

Fundamental WinRT Concepts

WinRT uses Partition II of the ECMA 335 standard[1] ("Metadata Definitions and Semantics") to describe types. This is the same standard the .NET Framework uses to encode assembly metadata. Therefore, you can use many of the same tools you use to inspect .NET assemblies to also explore WinRT types. Visual Studio 2013 ships with the Microsoft Intermediate Language (MSIL) disassembler, also known as `ildasm.exe`. In the same way assemblies are encoded in files that end with a **DLL** extension (for Dynamic Link Library), WinRT encodes type data in files that end with the `winmd` extension (Windows Metadata). Types must follow a set of specific standards for WinRT.

WinRT components can be implemented in several different languages. Only publicly exposed APIs must conform to the WinRT type system. Internal code can use types and constructs that are not part of the WinRT type system. Anything that is flagged as internal or private is not exposed in the metadata for that WinRT component. The following sections describe the WinRT type system at the language-agnostic level.

[1] Standard ECMA-335, http://bit.ly/WrEekW

Namespaces

WinRT supports the concept of namespaces. In fact, all Windows Runtime types must be declared within a namespace. The name of the `winmd` metadata file that describes the types must exactly match the root namespace of those types. Unlike .NET, which allows types within the same namespace to be distributed across multiple assemblies, you may describe only types that belong to a namespace in the single metadata file that is provided for that namespace. For example, a metadata file named `JeremyLikness.winmd` could contain a type in the `JeremyLikness.Utility` namespace but would not be allowed to describe a type that exists in the `System.Utility` namespace.

The WinRT component and the Windows file system share the convention used to match the namespace to the component definition. Even though types in WinRT are case sensitive, the underlying file system is not. You are not allowed to have two files with the same name that differ only in case; therefore, you cannot have two different namespaces that differ only in case. The same applies to class names.

Base Types

The WinRT type system has no equivalent `System.Object` class. All types in WinRT derive from the primitive data types. The most basic type is described by the interface `IInspectable`.

Primitives

WinRT contains support for various primitives that correlate to different value types (with the exception of string) in the .NET Framework. Support is included for Boolean, character, integer (8-bit, 32-bit, and 64-bit signed and unsigned), floating point (both single and double precision), string, and void types. Table A.1 lists the Windows Runtime primitives.

TABLE A.1 Windows Runtime Primitives

Type	Description
`Boolean`	`true` or `false` value
`Char16`	16-bit character
`Double`	Double precision floating-point number
`Int16`	Signed 16-bit integer
`Int32`	Signed 32-bit integer
`Int64`	Signed 64-bit integer
`Single`	Single precision floating-point number
`String`	Text (immutable sequence of 16-bit UNICODE characters)
`UInt8`	Unsigned 8-bit integer
`UInt16`	Unsigned 16-bit integer
`UInt32`	Unsigned 32-bit integer
`UInt64`	Unsigned 64-bit integer
`Void`	Empty type

WinRT does not support null strings; it supports only empty strings. All WinRT types consist of these primitives. With the exception of XAML, all new classes are sealed because they are not usable in JavaScript. As with COM, there is no true concept of inheritance, and all components are based on interfaces.

Classes and Class Methods

WinRT supports the definition of classes. A class is a template for an entity that can be used to create multiple instances and that can contain data (fields) and logic (functions and methods). WinRT has support for object-oriented features such as inheritance and polymorphism; however, inheritance is used only in XAML, and polymorphism is achieved via interfaces.

JavaScript, for example, does not support inheritance. For this reason, most WinRT classes are defined in a way that restricts these features (for example, public WinRT classes created with C# must be marked as `sealed`). This also affects how you design class methods, because you may overload `methods` based only on the number of parameters, not the type of individual parameters. The runtime also supports only explicit *in* and *out* parameters; no parameters can exist as two-way parameters.

Classes in the Windows Runtime may contain constructors, methods, properties, and events. They may not contain nested enumerations, classes, and structures. Classes also may inherit from a base class (only inheritance from XAML classes is supported) and may implement any number of interfaces. Public classes that will be used from JavaScript must be sealed to prevent derivation.

Structures

Structures in the Windows Runtime resemble value types in .NET. WinRT structures may contain only public fields defined as primitive types or other structures. No support exists for properties, methods, or constructors in WinRT structures.

Generics

The Windows Runtime supports generics but does not allow custom generics. When you create a custom WinRT component, you cannot expose a public class or interface that is generic. Classes *can* expose methods that use generics in the return type, but the type argument must be a WinRT type. For the most part, think of generics in WinRT as something you can use or consume from the runtime (for example, asynchronous operations are exposed using generics), but not something you typically expose or produce from your custom components. Languages such as JavaScript do not support generics because of the built-in support for dynamic types.

Null

The Windows Runtime supports null values for primitives through the `IReference<T>` interface.[2] This interface allows the system to "box" Windows Runtime types in order to handle null values. The implementation returns null if there is no value. When a value exists, it returns an implementation of the interface, and the value is available through the `Value` property.

Enumerations

Enumerations are fully supported in WinRT and map to either signed 32-bit integers or unsigned 32-bit integers. Signed enumerations are considered mutually exclusive values; unsigned enumerations should be defined with a value that is a power of 2 so they can be combined with a logical OR operation.

Interfaces

Interfaces are declared in a namespace the same way classes are. Interfaces describe the signature of properties, methods, and events for other interfaces to extend or classes to implement. All interface declarations are implicitly public. As with the CLR, you cannot declare fields or static methods in WinRT interfaces. All properties, method parameters, and return values declared in WinRT interfaces must be valid WinRT types.

Properties

The Windows Runtime supports properties defined with "getters and setters," or methods that retrieve and set the value. By convention, you simply inspect the value of a property or assign a value to it, and the underlying access method is called. You can then add code to implement the property, such as validation and/or triggers.

---

[2]IReference<T> Interface, http://bit.ly/10qfe3w

Properties often use a private field (known as a *backing store*) to hold the actual value. Properties that provide only a getter are read-only; properties that provide only a setter are write-only; all other properties are read/write. WinRT does not support write-only properties. If no additional code is implemented for the getter or setter of a property, the compiler can automatically implement the access methods and backing store. This type of property is known as a *trivial property*.

Delegates

A delegate in the Windows Runtime is a type that encapsulates executable code and can be thought of as a type-safe function pointer. The return type and parameter types for the delegate are defined and can be filled by a named or anonymous function. Delegates are often used in conjunction with events to specify a handler for the event.

Events

WinRT classes can publish events. Event signatures are defined by delegates, and client code can subscribe to an event by providing a delegate that handles the event when it is raised. Only the type that owns the event can raise the event. Events can be declared in interfaces or classes. They must be declared in the interface, but C# handles this automatically when you're building a WinRT component.

Events in the Windows Runtime use a token-based registration mechanism. When a delegate is registered with an event, a token of type `EventRegistrationToken` is returned from the event's `add` method. To unsubscribe from an event, the token is passed to the event's `remove` method. The C# compiler performs some special actions to transparently manage this pattern, as you see later in this chapter.

Arrays

Array support in the Windows Runtime is limited to one-dimensional arrays of a specific type. Multidimensional arrays of any type are not supported. It is also important to note how arrays are passed by WinRT. Arrays are handled in only three valid ways in a method:

1. **Passed array:** Use this type of parameter to pass an existing array into a method. The contents of the array are copied from the calling method to the called one, so any modifications are not be visible to the calling method.
2. **Filled array:** Use this type of parameter when the calling method will allocate the array but expects the called method to fill it. Note that the called method is guaranteed to receive a buffer based only on the allocated array and might not have access to the contents of the array.
3. **Received array:** Use this type as the return parameter for a method that will both allocate and fill the array.

Choosing the right type of array is important, to avoid unexpected side effects. For example, modifying the contents of a passed array is not recommended because they will not necessarily be visible to the calling method. When a filled array is passed to a method, the called method should not try to inspect or depend on the contents of the array and should only add content to the array.

WinRT Internals

The Windows Runtime is built on top of the Component Object Model (COM) to manage components and expose APIs. COM refers to a set of technologies that were introduced in 1993. The idea behind COM is to provide a standard way for binaries created by multiple languages to communicate with each other and dynamically instantiate components. COM can describe a variety of technologies, including ActiveX and OLE, but the version of COM that the Windows Runtime uses is far more advanced and virtually transparent to the developer.

In COM, every component is identified by a globally unique identifier (GUID) known as a class ID (CLSID). Components provide a set of interfaces, and each interface is also identified by a GUID known as an interface ID (IID). The interfaces are declared in a language-agnostic fashion but provide a set of bindings specific to the language being used. This is a true application binary interface (ABI) because the underlying implementation is executable binary code. All the identifiers are stored in the Registry under the top-level `HKEY_CLASSES_ROOT` key.

The "magic" of the Windows Runtime is the language projection and implicit mapping between type metadata and the underlying COM interface. If you open a developer command prompt and navigate to the following folder, you will find a list of files ending in the `.winmd` extension that indicates a Windows metadata file:

```
C:\windows\system32\winmetadata
```

This file is compliant with partition II of the ECMA 335 specification that contains type metadata. The file is in binary format, but because it follows the same standard used for .NET assemblies, you can read the contents using the `ildasm.exe` tool. For example, navigate to the metadata directory from a developer command prompt and type the following:

```
ildasm Windows.Data.winmd
```

Figure A.1 shows the result. With the tool, you can inspect the available namespaces, interfaces, and type definitions for various WinRT components within that namespace.

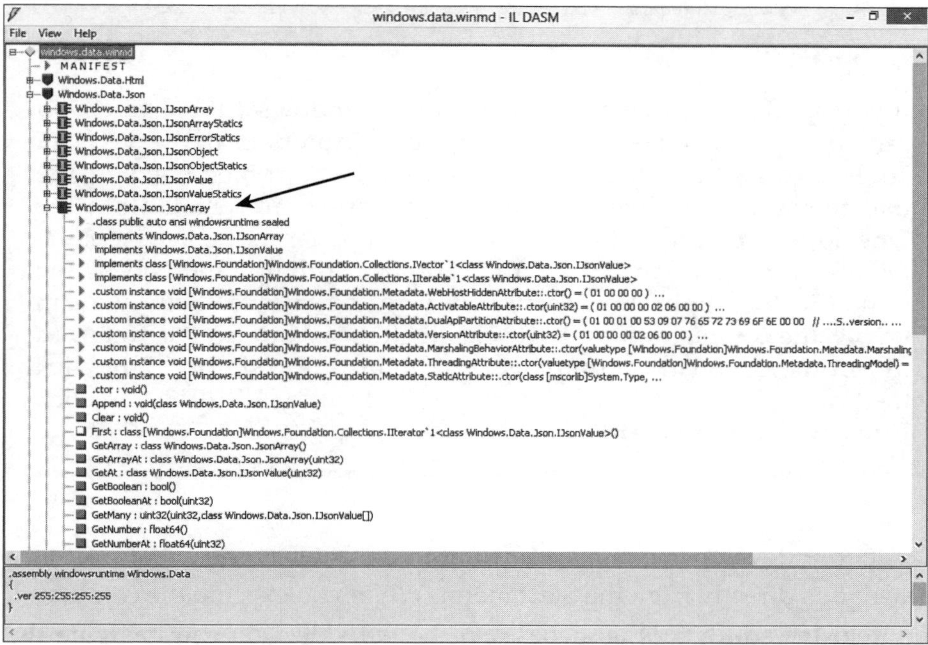

FIGURE A.1 The metadata information for WinRT components

If you try to expand any of the methods, you'll find there is no implementation in the file. Only metadata information is stored. Of course, to use the component, your software needs to call actual code. How does WinRT determine what code to call to execute the implementation of the type the metadata describes? The answer lies in the Registry.

The Registry is a hierarchical database that has existed in Windows since version 3.1 (that was in 1992, more than two decades ago). It was introduced to store information about COM components, but over time, it was extended to include other configuration information. To query and edit the Registry, you use a tool named `regedit.exe`.

TIP

If you are doing heavy development on a Windows 8.1 machine, you can quickly access the developer command prompt from the desktop. To do this, start typing the word `cmd` from the Start menu and ensure that the search type is set to the **Apps** option. You should see the **Developer Command Prompt** executable appear in the list of search results in the left pane. Select the command prompt and choose the option in the application bar to pin it to the taskbar. You then can launch the command prompt by clicking the taskbar icon. If you need to run the command prompt as an administrator, simply right-click the taskbar icon, right-click **Developer Prompt for VS 2013**, and click **Run as an Administrator**.

Open a developer command prompt and enter `regedit`. You can also launch this directly from the Start menu. When you execute the command, the Registry editor tool launches. On the left side, you can navigate the Registry to view nodes and values. Expand the path:

```
HKEY_LOCAL_MACHINE → Software → Microsoft → WindowsRuntime →
ActivatableClassId
```

There you find the full list of available WinRT components. One node exists for `Windows.Data.Json.JsonArray`. When you select the node, you see a list of keys and values in the right pane. In addition to the unique class identifier (CLSID) for the component is a path to the DLL that contains the code for the component and an activation type.

In COM, the code that calls a component is referred to as the COM client; the component itself is referred to as the COM server. The activation type indicates the type of COM server to create. Options include 0 for In-Proc (or "in process") and 1 for Out-Proc (or "out of process"). A process is simply a running program and contains one or more threads and resources. An "in process" COM server runs in the current process, and an "out of process" COM server causes a new process to spin up.

Most WinRT components are "in process" so your applications can use them. Windows Store apps, on the other hand, are full applications and, therefore, are set to run out of process. You can trace the execution of a Windows Store app through the registry as well. The Chapter 1 sample code online at http://winrtexamples.codeplex.com contains a Windows Store app called **HelloWorldGridApp**. If you haven't already, build and deploy the application so that it is available on your system. From the **Solution Explorer**, double-click **Package.appxmanifest** to open the manifest dialog box. You will learn more about this dialog box in Chapter 2, "Windows Store Apps and WinRT Components." For now, navigate to the **Packaging** tab and note the **Package Name**. It should look something like what Figure A.2 shows.

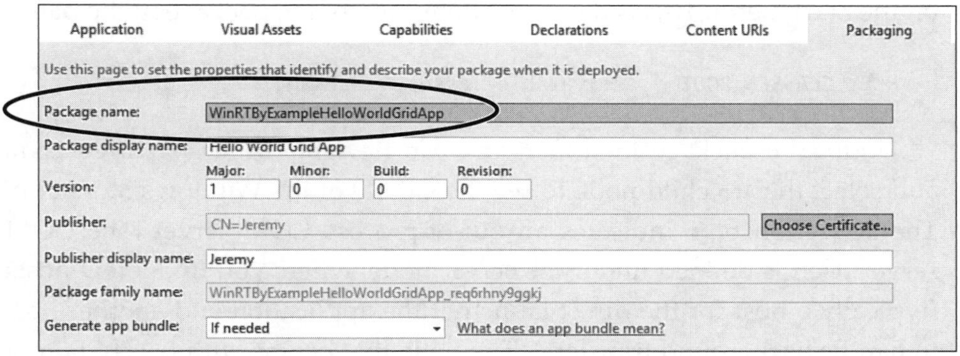

FIGURE A.2 The package information for a Windows Store app

Now open the **Registry Editor** and navigate to the following node:

```
HKEY_CLASSES_ROOT → Extensions → ContractId → Windows.Launch →
PackageId
```

Beneath that node, you find a list of nodes that correspond to packages. Figure A.3 shows the node expanded for the sample application.

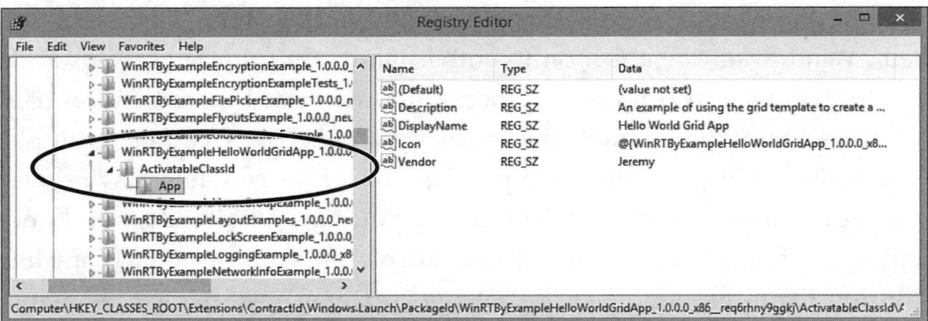

FIGURE A.3 The Registry entry for a package that is available to the Launch contract

One contract, the Launch contract, is invoked when you tap on a tile on the Start menu. This is the actual definition of the package in the path:

```
HKEY_CLASSES_ROOT → ActivatableClasses → Package
```

Under the package identifier, you can navigate to `ActivatableClassId` and select the `App` child node to see the CLSID of the Windows Store app. The activation type indicates an out-of-process COM server. The COM server itself is defined under the `Server` node, where you find a few hosts (typically a host for the direct launch of the application and another host to handle background transfers). The node that begins with `App` contains a path to the compiled executable produced when you build the application.

Although C++, VB.NET, and C# programs produce a WinRT path to an executable, JavaScript programs always point here:

```
C:\windows\system32\wwahost.exe
```

This is the HTML and JavaScript host that is capable of taking a JavaScript application and rendering the UI within the modern Windows 8.1 interface. It contains a version of the Chakra JavaScript interpreter that is extended with a special library to interface with WinRT components. Because of a feature of the runtime known as language projection, the components appear as native JavaScript entities to the developer.

Language projections are how the CLR interacts with WinRT components. If you want to understand how the Windows Runtime type system enables language projection, you don't have to look any further than COM. The technology requires all components to implement a special binary interface called `IUnknown`.[3] This interface contains three specific methods: `QueryInterface`, `AddRef`, and `Release`.

Clients call `QueryInterface` to obtain a specific interface. If the client is going to invoke the server, `AddRef` is called to indicate that the COM server is being referenced. This prevents the server from being disposed before the client is done using it. Clients use `Release` when they are done with the object so that the host can safely dispose of it.

The Windows Runtime introduces an additional interface that all WinRT classes are required to implement, called `IInspectable`.[4] The interface inherits `IUnknown` and adds several useful methods:

- `GetIIds`, to list the interfaces implemented by the WinRT class
- `GetRuntimeClassName`, to get the fully qualified name of a WinRT instance
- `GetTrustLevel`, to get the trust level of the WinRT instance (base, partial, or full trust)

You can call `RoResolveNamespace`[5] to iterate the children of a namespace. When you find the component you want to activate, you call `RoGetActivationFactory`.[6] This looks up the corresponding CLSID, figures out the activation context, and launches the appropriate host. If this sounds like a lot of work, it is. Here's the good news: You really don't have to understand any of the details "under the hood" because .NET handles all these actions for you.

---

[3]IUnknown Interface (COM), http://bit.ly/109AuWq

[4]IInspectable Interface (Windows), http://bit.ly/W6M2Lw

[5]RoResolveNamespace Function (Windows), http://bit.ly/11GQWTd

[6]RoGetActivationFactory Function (Windows), http://bit.ly/Xn55xZ

B Glossary

ABI: Application binary interface; a low-level interface between computer programs that allows for direct access at the binary level.

Accelerometer: Sensor used to provide information about the G-forces affecting a device along its x-, y-, and z-axes.

ActiveX: Software framework developed to deliver *COM* over networks, most often the Internet.

Adapter: Software pattern to translate one interface to an API to another, to solve the problem of connecting incompatible APIs.

Animation: In Windows Store apps, an animation refers to transitions between elements and other components of the page; similar to transitions between slides in a PowerPoint presentation.

API: Application program interface; a reference to an interface used for software components to communicate with each other.

APM: Asynchronous programming model; a design pattern using `IAsyncResult` that allows asynchronous calls.

App Bundle: Single file containing multiple app packages, used to optimize delivery of app packages during Windows Store app deployment. App bundles typically have the `.appxbundle` file extension.

App Package: Single file used to deploy Windows Store applications. App packages conform to the Open Packing Conventions (OPC) standard and typically have the `.appx` file extension.

ARM: Advanced RISC machine; an architecture based on the *RISC* instruction set that supports lower-voltage *SoC* processors and is popular in smaller devices, including smartphones and tablets.

Assembly: In the *.NET Framework*, an assembly is a compiled library of code and/or localized resources that contains multiple *modules*, along with a version and security information.

Asymmetric Encryption: *Encryption* that uses one key (the *public key*) to encode data and a different key (the *private key*) to decode the data; typically is far slower than *symmetric encryption*.

Atom (Chip): Intel's low-voltage *SoC* microprocessors that support the x86 and x64 architectures.

Atom (Syndication Format): An *XML*-based web content and metadata syndication format.

AtomPub: Atom Publishing Protocol; an *HTTP*-based protocol for updating web resources.

Authentication: Verification of the identity of a resource or user.

Authorization: Validating the rights or permissions a resource has to access or manipulate other resources.

Backing Store: A private field used to hold the value for a property used by the get and/or set access methods for that property.

Badge: A small overlay (typically over a *tile*) that displays either an informational icon or a numeric value that indicates some level of action can be taken with the associated app (for example, a number of unread mail messages, prompting the user to read the mail).

Binding Source: The data object that provides values for a data-binding operation.

Binding Target: The dependency property on a XAML element that renders values from *binding source* data in a data-binding operation.

Block Cipher: An encryption algorithm that works on a fixed length of bytes, called a block.

Bluetooth: Wireless technology standard for exchanging data over short distances.

Buffer: An in-memory sequence of bytes.

C++: A statically typed, object-oriented programming language.

C++/CXC++: with Component Extensions; an extension of C++ that allows developers to create components for *WinRT*.

CCW: COM Callable Wrapper; an internal object that the CLR uses as an interface between *COM* clients and an instance of a managed type. It keeps track of COM interfaces and reference counts.

Chakra: Codename for Microsoft's JavaScript engine used in Internet Explorer 9.0 and later.

Charms: Set of controls provided by Windows that appear along the right edge of the screen in response to either a particular user gesture, a mouse movement, or a keyboard combination and allow access to several common Windows tasks, including Searching, Sharing, Devices, and Settings.

CIL: Common Intermediate Language; a stack-based programming language that the .NET Framework uses to represent compiled managed languages such as C# and VB.NET.

Cipher: Specific algorithm used for encryption and/or decryption.

CLR: Common Language Runtime; a part of the *.NET Framework* that runs code and provides services for the development process.

CLSID: Class ID; globally unique identifier (*GUID*) for *COM* classes.

Code Analysis: Feature of Visual Studio that uses rule sets to apply framework design guidelines to an assembly and generate warnings and errors based on violations.

COM: Component Object Model; a Microsoft technology designed in the early 1990s to enable software components to communicate with each other. See www.microsoft.com/com/default.mspx.

Compass: Sensor that provides information about the position of a device in relation to magnetic north.

Controller: Connects the *view* to the *model* in an app by interpreting user input and updating the view and model as needed.

CPU: Central processing unit; a hardware component (typically a microchip) responsible for interpreting and executing instructions.

CPU Sampling: A noninvasive form of profiling that periodically captures the call stack of running threads to determine where a program spends the most time.

Data-Binding: A declarative approach to connecting the *view* with the underlying *model*.

Dependency Object: An instance that derives from `DependencyObject` to participate in the dependency property system.

Dependency Property System: Special framework that provides property change notification, can configure defaults, and can obtain property values from multiple sources. It also provides property inheritance and the capability to attach properties to types that do not otherwise have those properties defined.

Design-Time Data: Data that is configured to display only when an app is in the context of an interactive development environment such as Visual Studio 2013; used to render a realistic layout using data representative of the running app, to make it easier to design the user experience.

Desktop Application: Application that targets non-WinRT APIs, such as the .NET Framework or Win32 with non-Modern UI experience.

DI: Dependency injection; technique to remove coupling at development and compile time and instead inject them at runtime using a provider, service locator, or other specialized component.

Direct2D: Two-dimensional vector graphics *API* with support for hardware acceleration that is part of *DirectX*.

Direct3D: Set of *APIs* that are part of *DirectX* and provide the capability to develop animated three-dimensional graphics with support for hardware acceleration.

DirectX: A group of technologies that enable using Windows as a development platform for rich multimedia, including graphics, video, 3D animation, and audio, through a set of common APIs.

DLL: Dynamic Link Library; a library that contains both code and/or data that multiple applications can use.

DOM: Document Object Model; a cross-platform, language-independent convention for interacting with objects in HTML- and XML-derived documents.

DPAPI: Data Protection API; a simple API that Windows uses to enable *symmetric encryption* of data.

ECMA: Formerly European Computer Manufacturer's Association; an international industry association focused on the standardization of computer technology and electronics; no longer restricted to just Europe.

Edit-And-Continue: Feature that enables you to make modifications to code while you are debugging it.

Encryption: Converting data into a form that resources not authorized to access the data cannot recognize.

Extension SDK: Optional component that extends a platform.

Geofencing: The process of monitoring a device or person's position relative to predefined geographic regions of interest (geofences).

Geolocation: Information about the real-world geographic location of an object.

Globalization: The process of building an app to support multiple languages, cultures, and locales.

GSM: Global System for Mobile Communications; standard for protocols used in cellular networks by mobile phones.

GUID: Globally unique identifier; most often a unique 128-bit number generated by a complex algorithm designed to reduce the probability of duplicate identifiers being generated to almost nothing.

Gyrometer: Sensor used to provide information about the angular velocity of a device along its X-, Y-, and Z-axes.

Hash: The result of applying an algorithm to data of any length to generate a fixed-length value.

HomeGroup: Specialized network provided by Windows 7 and later that allows sharing and access to libraries across computers in a small (home) network.

HTTP: Hypertext Transfer Protocol; application protocol used for delivering Hypertext documents and web-based apps; traditionally hosted on TCP port 80.

IaaS: Infrastructure as a Service; the capability to provision equipment through a hosting provider so that the physical hardware and components are completely outsourced.

IEEE: Institute of Electrical and Electronics Engineers; professional association that develops many technical standards.

IID: Interface ID; globally unique identifier (*GUID*) for *COM* interfaces.

ildasm.exe: MSIL Disassembler; tool used to identify *MSIL* contained within *portable executable* files, as well as associated type metadata.

Inclinometer: Sensor used to determine information about the pitch, yaw, and roll state of a device.

Initialization Vector: *Block ciphers* use the initialization vector to obfuscate the first block in the series of blocks to be encrypted.

IoC: Inversion of control; programming technique to late-bind dependencies at runtime so that the implementation is not generally known at development or compile time.

Iterator: Software pattern to provide an entity that is used to solve the problem of traversing elements in a container or list.

JavaScript: A prototype-based scripting language that is object based (not object oriented) and weakly typed, and is most commonly implemented within web browsers.

JSON: *JavaScript* Object Notation; a text-based format for storing structured data that JavaScript can easily consume.

Just My Code: A debugger feature that eliminates extraneous code from system frameworks and third-party libraries to provide a more streamlined call stack when debugging.

Layout Root: The topmost rendered element in a XAML control that defines the overall layout for the child controls it contains.

Light Sensor: Sensor used to determine information about the amount of light shining on a device.

LINQ: Language Integrated Query; a set of features that enables a consistent query syntax to be used across multiple types of data stores from various languages, including C#.

Live Connect: A collection of APIs used to access functionality provided by the Microsoft Account service, Outlook.com, and OneDrive. The Live Connect SDK provides client libraries for several popular client frameworks, including Windows 8.1, to build apps that interact with these APIs.

Live Tile: A special form of *tile* that updates with relevant and timely information about the app it launches.

Localization: The process of updating an app to target a specific language, region, and/or culture (locale).

Logging: Generating information from an app that is typically either written to disk or surfaced through event logs.

LTE: Long Term Evolution; a standard for high-speed wireless communication.

MAC (Message Authentication Code): A *hash* that combines authentication information to verify both data integrity and authenticity of the message.

Media Foundation: Microsoft's COM-based platform for multimedia development. Media Foundation is the successor to the DirectShow API and Windows Media SDK, along with several other multimedia APIs.

Microsoft Account: Microsoft's public authentication service, formerly known as Windows Live ID. Microsoft Accounts can be used to access many popular Microsoft Services, including Outlook.com and Office 365, and are used extensively in Windows 8.

Microsoft Azure: Microsoft's cloud computing and services platform.

Microsoft System Center Configuration Manager: Tool used by enterprise IT to manage software deployment, compliance management, and asset management throughout an enterprise. Includes support for devices running Windows 8.1 and can be used to deploy and manage sideloaded apps.

Mobile Services: Windows Azure Mobile Services; a Windows Azure feature that enables you to create a cloud-based back-end service for mobile apps, including *Windows Store* apps.

Model: The way an app represents the solution to a real-world problem through data, persistence, services, and business logic.

MSIL: Microsoft Intermediate Language; former name of *Common Intermediate Language* (CIL).

MVC: Model-View-Controller; UI pattern that solves the problem of separating the presentation of information (view) from the internal application model by using a controller to connect them.

MVP: Model-View-Presenter; variation of *MVC* that replaces the controller with a presenter responsible for presentation logic.

MVVM: Model-View-ViewModel; a specialized pattern to take advantage of data binding, to create a separation of concerns between the presentation layer (the view) and the application (the model) using a specialized supervisor (the view model).

Namespace: A scope used to organize code and ensure that types are unique by containing them within that scope.

.NET Framework: A framework that exists primarily on Windows-based machines that offers language interoperability and provides an application framework for software to run in a virtual environment known as the Common Language Runtime (CLR). See www.microsoft.com/net.

NFC: Near Field Communications; communication standard for devices in very close proximity (either touching or within a few centimeters of each other).

Nonce: Number used only once; used in cryptography to ensure that old messages cannot be reused in attacks and ensure that the current version of the message is used only once. If a message is received with the same nonce, it is discarded as invalid.

NuGet: Open-source package manager used by the Microsoft development platform, most commonly to simplify the process of obtaining and updating project assembly references for .NET projects. NuGet also provides the NuGet Gallery as a public repository for publishing and consuming packages.

OAuth: An authentication protocol used to allow a website or an application to access data on a user's behalf without the users having to share their username and password directly with that application.

OData: Open Data Protocol; standardized protocol for creating and consuming data built on top of Atom and JSON.

Orientation Sensor: Sensor used to obtain detailed information about how a device is situated in space.

ORM: Object Relational Mapper; a tool that is designed to automatically generate a map between database objects and application objects to facilitate data access.

PaaS: Platform as a Service; a provision model in which the host provides a specific technology stack and the consumer uses that setup to configure and deploy software.

Package Identity: A collection of attributes that uniquely identify a Windows Store app package.

Pattern: Solution to a common problem.

PCL: Portable Class Library; special type of assembly that can be referenced from multiple platforms and frameworks without recompiling.

PDB: Program database; a file generated during the build process that contains public and/or private symbols, including functions and variables, name and type information, and source file and line numbers.

PE: Portable Executable; binary file format used to store code and resources used by Windows operating systems.

PII: Personally identifiable information; refers to data that can be used to identify or locate someone. Windows Store apps require users to be informed of and give consent to activities that access and make use of their PII.

Platform SDK: Development kit that is required to develop apps for a platform.

Play To: Protocol that enables users to stream music, photos, and videos from their computers to other PCs and devices in their home network.

PLM: Process Lifetime Management; refers to the Windows Store app execution model that allows apps to be suspended, terminated, and resumed based on system resources.

POCO: Plain old CLR object; simple object in the .NET Framework that is not derived from or dependent on a third-party library, such as an *ORM*.

Private Key: In *asymmetric encryption* or *symmetric encryption*, the private key is the secret key used to decode data (symmetric encryption uses the same key to encode the data as well).

Profiling: Gathering information from a running application to analyze where the CPU spends the most time, what routines consume the most energy, how memory is allocated, or where potential bottlenecks exist.

pubCenter: Microsoft's ad serving and in-app advertisement management service.

Public Key: In *asymmetric encryption*, the public key is used to encode data and can be shared with third parties because it cannot be used to decode the same data.

Push Notification: A notification sent from an external resource (such as a web server in the cloud) to a Windows Store app to update the *tile* or *badge* or to raise a *toast*.

RCW: Runtime Callable Wrapper; an internal object that the *CLR* uses to expose a *COM* object as a managed instance to managed code. It keeps track of COM interfaces and reference counts behind the scenes to ensure that its lifetime is consistent with the garbage collector processing.

Recycle Bin: Temporary storage for files that have been deleted, to allow for recovery in case they were deleted by accident.

Registry: Hierarchical database of configuration options and settings for the Windows operating system.

Resource Dictionary: A special dictionary that contains reusable resources for an application, such as styles.

REST: Representational State Transfer; a web *API* design model for sharing messages using *HTTP*.

RISC: Reduced Instruction Set Computing; design strategy for *CPUs* that focuses on a simplified instruction set to enable faster execution.

RSS: Really Simple Syndication (formerly Rich Site Summary); an XML-based web content syndication format.

SAK: Sideload Activation Key; a special license sold through Microsoft Volume Licensing to allow a specific device running Windows 8.1 or Windows RT to run sideloaded apps.

Secondary Tile: A special form of *tile* that deep-links to a particular page or resource within the target app.

Sensor: Input devices that provide information about a device's relationship to its physical environment. Examples include a GPS receiver, a compass, and various orientation sensors.

Sharing: A mechanism in Windows 8.1 for providing user-initiated exchange of information between applications in such a way that the apps do not need to have prior knowledge of each other. A share source app initiates the share action and provides data, and a share target app receives the data.

Sideloading: For enterprises that typically manage the installation of applications, sideloading refers to a method of installing the software that circumvents the Windows Store.

Signing (code): Process of applying a cryptographic hash to executable code, to verify the identity of the publisher and ensure that the code has not been altered or corrupted.

Simple Orientation Sensor: Sensor used to obtain the current orientation of a device in 90-degree intervals and determine whether it is in a face-up or face-down position.

SOAP: Simple Object Access Protocol; no longer an acronym, this is a protocol used to exchange information that defines an envelope with *XML* that contains the header and body for a message used by web services.

SoC: System on a Chip; architecture that supports multiple components and circuits on a single chip.

Socket: An endpoint for communication between processes across a network.

Solution Explorer: Component of *Visual Studio* that provides a tree structure used to browse solutions, projects, and files.

SSML: Speech Synthesis Markup Language; a standard specification for XML-based description of text-to-speech instructions.

Stream: Abstraction of byte sequences; allows operations for writing, reading, and randomly accessing bytes independent of their source (memory, disk, or other storage).

Stream Cipher: An encryption algorithm that encrypts the stream 1 byte (or bit) at a time, as compared to a block cipher that operates against a fixed length of bytes.

Strong Name: *Assembly's* identity (text name, version number, and culture information), along with a public key and digital signature.

SVG: Scalable Vector Graphics; an XML-based vector graphics format used in modern browsers.

Symmetric Encryption: *Encryption* that uses the same key to encode and decode data.

TCP: Transmission Control Protocol; a core protocol for communication over the Internet for streams that is ordered and reliable.

Tile: A dynamic app shortcut that can display images, messages, badges, and other information and that either activates the app or deep-links to an area in the app.

Toast: A small information window that might fade after a period of time, can be dismissed by the user, and can be invoked to activate content in a Windows Store app.

TPL: Task Parallel Library; a set of types and APIs that make it easier to handle parallelism in .NET code.

Tracing: Generating detailed debug information from a running app.

Trident: Code name for the layout engine used in Microsoft Internet Explorer.

Trivial Property: A property that simply returns or sets the backing store and does not have additional code in its access methods.

UDP: User Datagram Protocol; an Internet-based protocol for sending short messages that do not require guaranteed delivery or order of delivery.

UI: User interface; the part of the application that interacts with end users by producing output for the user to consume and processing input that the user provides.

UTC: Coordinated Universal Time; standard international time zone used to calculate all other time zones using offsets.

UX: User experience; broad term that encompasses all aspects of a user's interaction with a system, including not only look and feel, but also navigation, information density, and other elements that contribute to the overall experience.

VB.NET: Visual Basic for the .NET Framework; a managed language used to create code that runs in the .NET Framework.

View: The presentation layer of an app; represents the interface (both input and output) to the user.

Viewmodel: A special entity used to synchronize the state of the view without depending on the view implementation; typically implements some type of property and collection change notification.

Visual Studio 2013: Interactive development environment from Microsoft, used to build both native and managed code for a variety of Windows platforms.

Visual Tree: The hierarchy of visual controls in the *UI*.

VSM: Visual State Manager; controller that uses animations to impact the appearance of controls based on predefined states.

WACK: Windows App Certification Kit; a tool that provides automated testing of Windows Store apps to ensure that they meet a subset of the app certification requirements.

WebGL: Web Graphics Library; a *JavaScript* API for rendering graphics in the browser without plug-ins.

WebSocket: Protocol for bidirectional communication using a single *TCP* connection.

WiFi: Wireless Fidelity; technology that enables wireless connections to networks based on the IEEE 802.11 standards.

Wi-Fi Direct: Standard based on *Wi-Fi* that enables a direct connection between Wi-Fi devices without using an access point (essentially a peer-to-peer connection that is not transmitted over the rest of the network).

Windows 8: Version of the Windows operating system based on *WinRT* that runs on *x86* and *x64* machines.

Windows Intune: Cloud service provided by Microsoft that allows for the central management of PCs through a web-based console. As in Microsoft System Center Configuration Manager, it includes support for devices running Windows 8.1 and can be used to deploy and manage sideloaded apps.

Windows Location Provider: A service built into Windows 8.1 that supplies apps with location data based on Wi-Fi triangulation and IP address data.

Windows Store: Software distribution platform used by Windows 8.1 and Windows RT.

Windows Store App: Special application that runs on Windows 8.1 and Windows RT devices to provide Modern UI.

winmd: Windows metadata; extension of metadata files that describes WinRT types using Partition II of the ECMA 335 specification also used by the .NET Framework.

WinRT: Windows Runtime; a set of object-oriented and language-independent Windows operating system *APIs*.

WLAN: Wireless local area network; a private network that is configured and enabled using wireless networking products.

WNS: Windows Notification Services; set of services that enables communication with Windows Store apps from behind corporate firewalls and on roaming networks. Other popular notification services include MPNS (Windows Phone), APNS (Apple iOS), and GCM (Android apps).

WSS: Windows Search Service; optimized service provided by the Windows platform that creates a catalog of indexes of file system properties to facilitate fast file system queries.

WWAN: Wireless wide area network; a type of wireless network that spans larger distances than typical private networks using cellular and other technologies.

XAML: Extensible Application Markup Language; an *XML*-based declarative language used for creating instances of classes and initializing properties with values.

XML: Extensible Markup Language; a markup language that defines special documents that can be processed programmatically but that users also can read and edit.

x64: Short for x86-64; an extension of the *x86* instruction set that can address 64-bit memory addresses and operate on 64-bit registers.

x86: CPU architectures based on the Intel 80386 CPU that are capable of addressing 32-bit memory addresses.

Index

Numbers

A

B

C

D

H

I

J

K

L

M

O

P

Q

R

S

V

W

X

Z

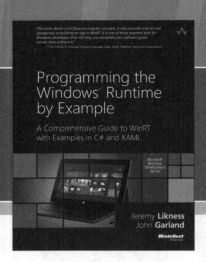